PSYCHOTHERAPY RELATIONSHIPS THAT WORK

Steering Committee of the APA Division of Psychotherapy Task Force on Empirically Supported Therapy Relationships

Steven J. Ackerman, student member

Lorna Smith Benjamin, Department of Psychology, University of Utah

Larry E. Beutler, Counseling/Clinical/School Psychology, University of California, Santa Barbara

Charles J. Gelso, Department of Psychology, University of Maryland

Marvin R. Goldfried, Department of Psychology, State University of New York, Stony Brook

Clara E. Hill, Department of Psychology, University of Maryland

Michael J. Lambert, Department of Psychology, Brigham Young University

John C. Norcross, Department of Psychology, University of Scranton (Chair)

David Orlinsky, Committee on Human Development, University of Chicago

Jackson P. Rainer, liaison to Division 29 Publication Board

Psychotherapy Relationships That Work

*Therapist Contributions and
Responsiveness to Patients*

EDITED BY
John C. Norcross

UNIVERSITY PRESS

2002

OXFORD
UNIVERSITY PRESS

Oxford   New York
Auckland   Bangkok   Buenos Aires   Cape Town   Chennai
Dar es Salaam   Delhi   Hong Kong   Istanbul   Karachi   Kolkata
Kuala Lumpur   Madrid   Melbourne   Mexico City   Mumbai   Nairobi
São Paulo   Shanghai   Singapore   Taipei   Tokyo   Toronto
and an associated company in Berlin

Copyright © 2002 by Oxford University Press, Inc.

Published by Oxford University Press, Inc.
198 Madison Avenue, New York, New York 10016

www.oup.com

Oxford is a registered trademark of Oxford University Press

Library of Congress Cataloging-in-Publication Data
Psychotherapy relationships that work : therapist contributions and responsiveness
to patients / edited by John C. Norcross.
p. cm.
Includes bibliographical references and index.
ISBN 0-19-514346-9
1. Psychotherapist and patient.   I. Norcross, John C., 1957–
RC480.8 .P78   2002
616.89'14—dc21   2001055959

1 3 5 7 9 8 6 4 2

Printed in the United States of America
on acid-free paper

Preface

The purpose of this volume is to extend and counterbalance extant efforts to promulgate treatment guidelines based solely upon lists of empirically supported treatments. Specifically, the dual aims are to identify elements of effective therapy relationships and determine efficacious methods of customizing psychotherapy to the individual patient. That is, we endeavor to disseminate relationship guidelines rather than technique guidelines, to advance empirically supported relationships (ESRs) rather than empirically supported treatments (ESTs).

Clinicians and researchers alike have found recent efforts to codify evidence-based treatments seriously incomplete. While laudable in their goals, these efforts have largely ignored the therapy relationship and the persons of the therapist and patient. If one were to read previous efforts literally, disembodied therapists apply manualized interventions to discrete Axis I disorders. Not only is the language offensive to some practitioners on clinical grounds, but the research evidence is weak for validating treatment interventions in isolation from the therapy relationship and the individual patient. Both clinical experience and research findings underscore that the therapeutic relationship accounts for as much of the outcome variance as particular treatments.

Suppose we asked a neutral scientific panel from outside the field to review the corpus of psychotherapy research to determine what is the most powerful phenomenon we should be studying, practicing, and teaching. Henry (1998, p. 128) concludes that the panel "would find the answer obvious, and *empirically validated*. As a general trend across studies, the largest chunk of outcome variance not attributable to preexisting patient characteristics involves individual thera-

pist differences and the emergent therapeutic relationship between patient and therapist, regardless of technique or school of therapy. This is the main thrust of three decades of empirical research."

Within this context, in 1999 I commissioned an APA Division of Psychotherapy Task Force to identify, operationalize, and disseminate information on empirically supported therapy relationships. The Division 29 Task Force on Empirically Supported Therapy Relationships, as it was called, focused on relationship qualities and therapist stances as opposed to treatment techniques, and it adopted broader decision rules concerning what qualifies as evidence for inclusion, including both effectiveness and efficacy studies. In addition, we systematically addressed the crucial research on matching therapeutic relationships to client features beyond discrete Axis I diagnoses. *Psychotherapy Relationships That Work* represents the culmination of the Division 29 Task Force's three-year work.

POTENTIAL AUDIENCES

One of our earliest considerations in planning the book was the intended audience. All of psychotherapy's stakeholders—patients, practitioners, researchers, trainers, students, organizations, insurance companies, and policymakers, among them—expressed different preferences for the content, organization, and length of the volume.

We prepared and structured the book for multiple audiences but followed a definite order of priority. The first priority was for clinical practitioners and trainees representing diverse theoretical orientations and professional disciplines. Their immediate need is to address the urgent questions: What do we know from the empirical research about the therapy relationship? What are the evidence-based practices for cultivating and customizing that relationship? Our second priority was accorded to the mental health disciplines themselves, specifically those organizations, committees, and task forces that are promulgating lists of empirically supported practices or treatments. We hope our work will inform and balance any efforts to focus exclusively on techniques or treatments to the neglect of the humans involved in the enterprise.

Our third priority was insurance carriers, many of whom devalue the person of the therapist and the central, curative role of the therapist-patient relationship by virtue of their reimbursement decisions. Although we support the recent thrust toward science informing practice, we must remind all parties to the therapy relationship that healing cannot be replaced with treating, caring cannot be supplanted by managing. Finally, our book is intended for psychotherapy researchers seeking a central resource on the empirical status of the multiple, interdependent qualities of the therapy relationship.

ORGANIZATION OF THE BOOK

Part I introduces the content and scope of the book. The opening chapter outlines the rationale and history of the Division 29 Task Force, its relation to previous efforts to identify empirically supported treatments, the process of defining empirically supported therapy relationships, and the limitations of our work. The second chapter presents a general research summary of the centrality of the therapeutic relationship to psychotherapy outcome.

The heart of the book is composed of practice-friendly research reviews on the therapist's relational contributions, those in general (parts IIA and IIIA) as well as those on tailoring the therapy relationship to individual patients (parts IIB and IIIB). Our goal is to identify both relationship elements applied generally in psychotherapy and therapist stances applied to specific circumstances and clients.

The middle sections of the book are divided along two axes or considerations. One is whether the relationship quality or element applies to most patients (IIA and IIIA) or is used primarily to customize the relationship to individual patients (IIB and IIIB). The other consideration is the strength of the research evidence—whether the relationship quality is considered, in the Steering Committee's judgment, to be demonstrably effective with extensively replicated research results (part II) or promising with initially favorable research results (part III). An independent rater, the editor, and the chapter's author jointly determined the strength of the empirical evidence. The criteria encompassed the number of supportive studies, the consistency and magnitude of the positive relationship, the directness to outcome, the experimental rigor of the studies, and the external validity of the research base. The criteria and the mean ratings for individual relationship elements and patient qualities are presented in the appendix.

Part IV of the book consists of a single chapter. It presents the Task Force conclusions, including a list of empirically supported relationship elements, and our practical recommendations, divided into general, practice, training, research, and policy recommendations. The chapter was coauthored by members of the Task Force's Steering Committee.

CHAPTER GUIDELINES

In parts II and III, authors followed guidelines provided by the editor in order to facilitate comprehensiveness, comparison, and ease of reader use. Each chapter defines the relationship or patient quality, provides clinical examples, reviews the empirical research, and highlights therapeutic practices ensuing from the research results. The guidelines in abbreviated form follow:

- Chapter title (the name of the relationship quality or the patient characteristic)
- Definitions (defining in theoretically neutral language the relationship behavior/patient quality being reviewed and identifying highly similar constructs from different theoretical traditions)
- Clinical examples (several concrete examples of the relationship behavior or patient quality)

- Research review
- Patient contribution (description of the patient's contribution to the therapy relationship and the distinctive perspective he/she brings to the interaction)
- Mediators and moderators of the research
- Limitations of the research reviewed
- Therapeutic practices
- References

The guidelines for the Research Review and Therapeutic Practices sections deserve additional comment. Authors compiled and systematically summarized the body of research pertaining to the relationship quality, restricting themselves to empirical studies that linked the relationship behavior, therapy interaction, or patient quality specifically to treatment outcome. Outcome was broadly and inclusively defined.

The authors also indicated whether the therapist contributions in the research studies were assessed by the therapist, by the patient, or by external raters; when possible, they noted the relation of each separately to measures of outcome. The observational perspective has been found to be a fundamental consideration; it is not just a question of how much the patient contributes and how much the therapist contributes, but a matter of determining who is best positioned to perceive which aspects of the therapeutic process. Therapists can discriminate some aspects (especially the patient's contribution), while patients can discriminate other aspects (especially the therapist's contribution), to a greater extent. Analyzing the research findings by observational perspective moves the discourse beyond the naive realism that anyone should be able to perceive whatever is objectively happening. In this respect, it is not just a methodological question, but also one of offering an adequate conception of the relationship and helping therapists transcend the inherent limitations in what they can perceive of therapeutic processes.

In the Therapeutic Practices section of each chapter, authors highlighted the practice implications of their research review, primarily in terms of the therapist's contribution and secondarily in terms of the patient's contribution and perspective. These, then, represent evidence-based relational contributions or empirically supported relationships (ESRs).

ACKNOWLEDGMENTS

This book has been, in the words of a classic 1960s tune, "a long time coming." It has been years, if not decades, since the cumulative empirical research on the therapy relationship has been drawn together in a single book. The book probably represents the first time that the research evidence on clinical attempts to individualize the therapy relationship has been aggregated in a single source. At the same time, *Psychotherapy Relationships That Work* itself has taken several years to reach fruition.

On the organizational front, I would like to publicly express appreciation to the Board of Directors of the American Psychological Association's Division of Psychotherapy for approving and promoting the Task Force on Empirically Supported Therapy Relationships. Two individuals in particular merit acknowledgment: Wade Silverman, the 1999 president, and Diane Willis, the 2001 president, who served as supportive pillars around my 2000 presidential term.

The Task Force's Steering Committee endured two lengthy meetings and endless e-mails in our deliberations. With grace and good will, they assisted in canvassing the literature, defining the parameters of the project, organizing the book contents, selecting the contributors, and reviewing early drafts of the chapters. The Steering Committee consisted of myself and:

Steven J. Ackerman (student member)
Lorna Smith Benjamin (University of Utah)
Larry E. Beutler (University of California, Santa Barbara)
Charles J. Gelso (University of Maryland)
Marvin R. Goldfried (State University of New York, Stony Brook)
Clara E. Hill (University of Maryland)
Michael J. Lambert (Brigham Young University)
David Orlinsky (University of Chicago)
Jackson P. Rainer (liaison to Division 29 Publication Board)

The contributors freely provided their expertise in the interest of science and in the advancement of psychotherapy. Later in the process, they simultaneously served as members of the Task Force and assisted in shaping the final product.

Last but not least, several people modeled and manifested the ideal therapeutic relationship throughout the course of the project. Joan Bossert, executive editor at Oxford University Press, shepherded the book from its initial planning stage and perceived early that this book would complement Oxford's landmark *A Guide to Treatments That Work* (Nathan & Gorman, 1998). My immediate family—Nancy, Jonathon, and Rebecca—tolerated my absences, preoccupations, and irritabilities associated with editing this book with a combination of empathy and patience that would do any seasoned psychotherapist proud.

When I invited authors to contribute to *Psychotherapy Relationships That Work* three years ago, they were asked to join the Division 29 Task Force on Empirically Supported Therapy Relationships and Oxford University Press in "producing a clinically sensitive, empirically grounded, and practice-responsive book." I enthused at that time that this important project was the most exciting of my career and potentially the most significant. My enthusiasm and pride in the work of the Task Force have only been strengthened in the interim.

John C. Norcross, Ph.D.
Clarks Summit, Pennsylvania

Contents

Contributors

Shabia Alimohamed Counseling/Clinical/School Psychology, University of California, Santa Barbara

Diane B. Arnkoff Department of Psychology, Catholic University of America

Dean E. Barley Comprehensive Clinic, Brigham Young University

Robinder P. Bedi Department of Educational and Counseling Psychology, University of British Columbia

Lorna Smith Benjamin Department of Psychology, University of Utah

Larry E. Beutler Counseling/Clinical/School Psychology, University of California, Santa Barbara

Sidney J. Blatt Departments of Psychiatry and Psychology, Yale University School of Medicine

Arthur C. Bohart Department of Psychology, California State University at Dominguez Hills

Gary M. Burlingame Department of Psychology, Brigham Young University

Sarah Chisholm-Stockard Department of Psychiatry, University of Wisconsin

Charles D. Claiborn Division of Psychology in Education, Arizona State University

Paul Crits-Christoph Department of Psychiatry, University of Pennsylvania School of Medicine

Robert Elliott Department of Psychology, University of Toledo

Barry A. Farber Program in Clinical Psychology, Teachers College, Columbia University

Addie Fuhriman Department of Psychology, Brigham Young University

Charles J. Gelso Department of Psychology, University of Maryland

Mary Beth Connolly Gibbons Department of Psychiatry, University of Pennsylvania School of Medicine

Carol R. Glass Department of Psychology, Catholic University of America

Rodney K. Goodyear Counseling Psychology Program, University of Southern California

Leslie S. Greenberg Department of Psychology, York University

T. Mark Harwood Counseling/Clinical/School Psychology, University of California, Santa Barbara

Jeffrey A. Hayes Department of Counselor Education and Counseling Psychology, Pennsylvania State University

Clara E. Hill Department of Psychology, University of Maryland

Pamela A. Horner Department of Counseling Psychology, Arizona State University

Adam O. Horvath Graduate Program in Counseling Psychology, Simon Fraser University

Jennifer E. Johnson Program in Clinical Psychology, Brigham Young University

Christie P. Karpiak Department of Psychology, University of Scranton

Marjorie H. Klein Department of Psychiatry, University of Wisconsin

Sarah Knox Department of Counseling and Educational Psychology, Marquette University

Gregory G. Kolden Departments of Psychiatry and Psychology, University of Wisconsin

Amy G. Lam Department of Psychology, University of California, Davis

Michael J. Lambert Department of Psychology, Brigham Young University

Jodie S. Lane Program in Clinical Psychology, Teachers College, Columbia University

Mary Malik Counseling/Clinical/School Psychology, University of California, Santa Barbara

Björn Meyer Department of Psychology, Louisiana State University

Jennifer L. Michels Department of Psychiatry, University of Wisconsin

Carla M. Moleiro Graduate School of Education, University of California, Santa Barbara

J. Christopher Muran Department of Psychiatry, Albert Einstein College of Medicine

John C. Norcross Department of Psychology, University of Scranton

Paul A. Pilkonis Department of Psychiatry, University of Pittsburgh School of Medicine

James O. Prochaska Cancer Prevention Research Center, University of Rhode Island

Jeremy D. Safran Department of Psychology, New School University

Lisa Wallner Samstag Department of Psychology, Long Island University

Steven J. Sandage Department of Marriage and Family Therapy, Bethel Theological Seminary

Golan Shahar Departments of Psychiatry and Psychology, Yale University

Stephanie J. Shapiro Department of Psychology, Catholic University of America

Christopher Stevens Department of Psychology, New School for Social Research

William B. Stiles Department of Psychology, Miami University

Stanley Sue Department of Psychology, University of California, Davis

Hani Talebi Graduate School of Education, University of California, Santa Barbara

Georgiana Shick Tryon Educational Psychology, City University of New York

Jeanne C. Watson Department of Counseling Psychology, University of Toronto

Greta Winograd Educational Psychology, City University of New York

Everett L. Worthington, Jr. Department of Psychology, Virginia Commonwealth University

David C. Zuroff Department of Psychology, McGill University

Part I

INTRODUCTION

1

Empirically Supported Therapy Relationships

John C. Norcross

Recent years have witnessed the controversial promulgation of practice guidelines and evidence-based treatments in mental health. In the United States and other countries, the introduction of such guidelines has provoked practice modifications, training refinements, organizational conflicts, and strident rebuttals. For better or worse, insurance carriers and government policymakers are increasingly turning to such guidelines and compilations to determine which psychotherapies to approve and fund. Indeed, alongside the negative influence of managed care, there is probably no issue more central to clinicians than the evolution of evidence-based practice in psychotherapy (Barlow, 2000).

Foremost among these initiatives in psychology has been the American Psychological Association's Society of Clinical Psychology's Task Force efforts to identify empirically supported treatments (ESTs) for adults and to publicize these treatments to fellow psychologists and training programs. Since 1993 a succession of APA Division 12 Task Forces (now a standing committee) has constructed and elaborated a list of empirically supported, manualized psychological interventions for specific disorders based on randomized controlled studies that pass for methodological rigor (Chambless et al., 1996, 1998; Chambless & Hollon, 1998; Task Force on Promotion and Dissemination of Psychological Procedures, 1995). Oxford University Press published the influential *A Guide to Treatments That*

Work (Nathan & Gorman, 1998), a volume that emanated from the work of a related Division 12 Task Force. Subsequently, ESTs have been identified for both older adults and children (e.g., Gatz et al., 1998; Lonigan, Elbert, & Johnson, 1998).

The APA's Society of Clinical Psychology has not been alone in developing and promoting such guidelines. The APA Division of Counseling Psychology has issued their own principles of empirically supported interventions (Wampold, Lichtenberg, & Waehler, 2002), and the APA Division of Humanistic Psychology (Task Force for the Development of Guidelines for the Provision of Humanistic Psychosocial Services, 1997) published guidelines for the provision of humanistic psychosocial services. The Practice Guidelines Coalition, a developing organization sponsored by the Association for Advancement of Behavior Therapy and the American Association of Applied and Preventive Psychology, is creating clinical practice guidelines that are brief, evidence-based, multidisciplinary, and disorder-specific. In Great Britain, a Guidelines Development Committee of the British Psychological Society authored a Department of Health (2001) document entitled *Treatment Choice in Psychological Therapies and Counseling: Evidence-Based Practice Guidelines.*

Foremost among the evidence-based initiatives in psychiatry has been the American Psychiatric Association's practice guidelines. The organization has published at least ten practice guidelines on disorders ranging from schizophrenia and anorexia to nicotine dependence.

All of the efforts to promulgate evidence-based psychotherapies have been noble in intent and timely in distribution. They are praiseworthy efforts to distill scientific research into clinical applications and to guide practice and training. They wisely demonstrate that, in a climate of accountability, psychotherapy stands up to empirical scrutiny with the best of health-care interventions. Within psychology, these efforts have attempted to proactively counterbalance those documents that accord primacy to biomedical treatments for mental disorders and largely ignore the outcome data for psychological therapies (such as the Depression Guideline Panel, 1993). On many accounts, then, the extant efforts have addressed the realpolitik of the socioeconomic situation (Messer, 2001; Nathan, 1998).

WHAT'S MISSING?

The ethical and professional commitment to evidence-based psychotherapy is widely, if not universally, accepted among mental health practitioners. It is similar to publicly prizing Mother and apple pie (Norcross, 1999). In principle, we are all committed to identifying, practicing, and promulgating those psychosocial treatments that "work." In principle, that is.

In application, the controversies reside in the definitions and details of identifying evidence-based or empirically supported therapies. The internecine conflicts occur around what material is validated and what qualifies as evidence, a process described as decision rules.

Many researchers and practitioners find the decision rules in these early efforts to be seriously incomplete or inapplicable. Examination of the Society of Clinical Psychology Task Force's initial decision rules is illuminating and representative. Those treatments designated as "empirically validated"—or the more recent, accurate, and felicitous phrase "empirically supported"—were restricted to manualized therapies for a fixed number of sessions. The treatments were brand name or pure-form. (For scholarly reviews of the contributions and criticisms of ESTs, refer to several special issues of journals, e.g., Elliott, 1998;

Glass & Arnkoff, 1996; Kazdin, 1996; Kendall, 1998). Three decision points are particularly applicable here, beginning with the EST lists as oddly personless.

The Person of the Therapist

The first point is that the EST lists and most other practice guidelines depict disembodied therapists performing procedures on Axis I disorders. This stands in marked contrast to the clinician's experience of psychotherapy as an intensely interpersonal and deeply emotional experience. Although efficacy research has gone to considerable lengths to eliminate the individual therapist as a variable that might account for patient improvement, the inescapable fact is that the therapist as a person is a central agent of change (Lambert & Okiishi, 1997). The curative contribution of the therapist is, arguably, as empirically validated as manualized treatments or psychotherapy methods (Hubble, Duncan, & Miller, 1999).

Multiple and converging sources of evidence indicate that the *person* of the psychotherapist is inextricably intertwined with the outcome of psychotherapy. Luborsky and colleagues (1986) reanalyzed the results of four major studies of psychotherapy outcome to determine the variance accounted for by therapist effects. They found that therapist effects generally overshadowed the variance attributed to treatment differences. A subsequent meta-analysis of therapist effects in psychotherapy outcome studies showed consistent and robust effects—5% to 9% in one of the best estimates (Crits-Christoph et al., 1991). In reviewing the research, Wampold (2001, p. 200) concluded, "A preponderance of evidence indicates that there are large therapist effects . . . and that the effects greatly exceed treatment effects." "The inescapable fact of the matter," observed Orlinsky and Howard (1977, p. 567), "is that the therapist is a person, however much he may strive to make himself an instrument of his patient's treatment."

Two recent articles examining therapist variables in the outcomes of cognitive-behavioral therapy are instructive (Huppert et al., 2001; Project MATCH Research Group, 1998). In the Multicenter Collaborative Study for the Treatment of Panic Disorder, considerable care was taken to standardize the treatment, the therapist, and the patients in order to increase the experimental rigor of the study and minimize therapist effects. The treatment was manualized and structured, the therapists were identically trained and monitored for adherence, and the patients rigorously evaluated and relatively uniform. Nonetheless, the therapists significantly differed in the magnitude of change among caseloads. Effect sizes for therapist impact on outcome measures ranged from 0% to 18%. In the similarly controlled multisite study on alcohol abuse conducted by Project MATCH, the therapists were carefully selected, trained, supervised, and monitored in their respective treatment approaches. Although there were few outcome differences among the treatments, over 6% of the outcome variance (1%–12% range) was due to therapists. Despite impressive attempts to experimentally render individual practitioners as controlled variables, it is simply not possible to mask the person and the contribution of the therapist.

The Therapy Relationship

Second, and most relevant for our purposes, have been the decisions to validate the efficacy of treatments or technical interventions, as opposed to the therapy relationship or therapist interpersonal skills. This decision both reflects and reinforces the ongoing movement toward high-quality comparative outcome studies on techniques or brand-name therapies. "This trend of putting all of the eggs in the 'technique' basket began in the late 1970s and is now reaching the peak of influence" (Bergin, 1997, p. 83).

But both clinical experience and research findings underscore that the therapy relationship accounts for as much of the outcome variance as particular treatments. Quantitative reviews and meta-analyses of psychotherapy outcome literature consistently reveal that specific techniques account for only 5% to 15% of the outcome variance (e.g., Beutler, 1989; Lambert, 1992; Shapiro & Shapiro, 1982; Wampold, 2001), and much of that is attributable to the investigator's therapy allegiance (Luborsky et al., 1999). An early and influential review by Bergin and Lambert (1978, p. 180) anticipated the contemporary

research consensus: "The largest variation in therapy outcome is accounted for by pre-existing client factors, such as motivation for change, and the like. Therapist personal factors account for the second largest proportion of change, with technique variables coming in a distant third." In my more strident moments, I have adapted Bill Clinton's unofficial campaign slogan: "It's the relationship, stupid!"

Even those practice guidelines enjoining practitioners to attend to the therapy relationship do not provide specific, evidence-based means of doing so. The APA *Template for Developing Guidelines* (Task Force on Psychological Intervention Guidelines, 1995, pp. 5–6), for example, sagely recognizes that factors common to all therapies, "such as the clinician's ability to form a therapeutic alliance or to generate a mutual framework for change, are powerful determinants of success across interventions." However, the template only vaguely addresses how research protocols or individual practitioners should do so. For another example, the scholarly and comprehensive review on treatment choice from Great Britain (Department of Health, 2001) devotes a single paragraph to the therapeutic relationship. Its recommended principle is that "Effectiveness of all types of therapy depends on the patient and the therapist forming a good working relationship" (p. 35), but no evidence-based guidance is offered on which therapist behaviors contribute to or cultivate that relationship.

Likewise, although most treatment manuals mention the importance of the therapy relationship, few specify what therapist qualities or in-session behaviors lead to a curative relationship. As practice guidelines and treatment manuals are increasingly required in training, research, and practice, there is a real and imminent danger that the therapy relationship, therapist interpersonal skills, and patient matches will be overlooked.

The Patient's (Nondiagnostic) Characteristics

Third, most practice guidelines and evidence-based compilations unintentionally reduce our clients to a static diagnosis or problem. The impressive, 90-chapter *Treatments of Psychiatric Disorders* (Gabbard, 2000), to take one prominent example, is hailed as the "cumulative knowledge base of psychiatric treatment," yet the entire two volumes are organized exclusively around diagnoses. Virtually all practice guidelines are directed toward single categorical disorders. *DSM* diagnoses have ruled the evidence-based roost to date.

This choice flies in the face of clinical practice and research findings that a categorical, nonpsychotic Axis I diagnosis exercises only a modest impact on treatment outcome (Beutler, 2000). While the research indicates that certain psychotherapies make better marriages for certain disorders, psychological therapies will be increasingly matched to people, not simply diagnoses. In the behavioral medicine vernacular, it is frequently more important to know what kind of patient has the disorder than what kind of disorder the patient has.

As every clinician knows, different types of patients respond better to different types of treatments and relationships. Different folks do require different strokes. A clinician will strive to offer or select a therapy that fits the patient's personal characteristics, proclivities, and worldviews—in addition to suiting the diagnosis. The differential effectiveness of different therapies may well prove to be a function of cross-diagnostic patient characteristics, such as treatment goals, coping styles, stages of change, personality dimensions, and reactance level.

Research studies problematically collapse numerous patients under a single diagnosis. It is a false and, at times, misleading presupposition in randomized clinical trials that the patient sample is homogeneous. Perhaps the patients are diagnostically homogeneous, but nondiagnostic variability is the rule, as every clinician also knows. It is precisely the unique individual and the singular context that many psychotherapists attempt to treat (Lazarus, Beutler, & Norcross, 1992).

Moreover, practice guidelines and EST lists do little for those psychotherapists whose patients and theoretical conceptualizations do not fall into discrete disorders (Messer, 2001). Consider the patient who seeks more joy in his or her life, but who does not meet diagnostic criteria for any disorder, whose psychotherapy stretches beyond 12 sessions, and whose treatment objectives are not easily specified in measurable, symptom-based outcomes. Current evidence-based compilations

have little to contribute to his or her therapist and treatment (see O'Donohue, Buchanan, & Fisher, 2000, for general characteristics of ESTs). Not all psychotherapies or practitioners embrace an action-oriented model in which treatment is rendered to a patient.

All of this is to say that extant lists of empirically supported treatments and practice guidelines give short shrift—some would say lip service—to the person of the therapist, the individual patient's characteristics, and their emergent relationship. Current attempts are thus seriously incomplete and potentially misleading, both on clinical and empirical grounds.

TASK FORCE ON ESRs

An APA Division of Psychotherapy Task Force was commissioned to identify, operationalize, and disseminate information on evidence-based therapy relationships. Our objective was to identify empirically supported (therapy) relationships rather than empirically supported treatments—or ESRs rather than ESTs.

The dual aims of the Division 29 Task Force were to:

- Identify elements of effective therapy relationships
- Determine efficacious methods of customizing or tailoring therapy to the individual patient on the basis of his/her (nondiagnostic) characteristics

These dual objectives attempt, at once, to address the generality and the particularity of the therapy relationship. The general elements are those that the therapist provides (or tries to provide) to most patients; the particular matching elements are those used to individualize or tailor the relationship to certain patients. That is, practitioners require evidence-based guidance on what to do in general in the therapy relationship as well as how to tailor that relationship to the particulars of the specific patient.

Compared to extant efforts, the Division 29 Task Force focused on relationship qualities and therapist stances, as opposed to treatment techniques, and adopted broader decision rules as to what qualifies as evidence for inclusion, including both effectiveness and efficacy studies. In addition, we addressed research on matching therapy relationships to client features beyond discrete Axis I diagnoses. Table 1.1 summarizes the salient differences in decision rules between our APA Division 29 Task Force and previous efforts, notably the Division 12 Task Forces.

The remainder of this chapter sets the context for *Psychotherapy Relationships That Work* by explicating the purposes, summarizing the processes, and introducing the products of the Task Force on Empirically Supported Therapy Relationships. The latter part of the chapter features the limitations of the Task Force's work and responds to frequently asked questions.

TASK FORCE PROCESSES

Definitions

One of our first process challenges was to define the psychotherapy relationship. We adopted Gelso and Carter's (1985, 1994) operational definition: "The relationship is the feelings and attitudes that therapist and client have toward one another, and the manner in which these are expressed." This definition is quite general, and the phrase "the manner in which these are expressed" potentially opens the relationship to include everything under the therapeutic sun (see Gelso & Hayes, 1998, for an extended discussion). Nonetheless, it was concise, consensual, theoretically neutral, and sufficiently precise for our use.

A second definitional quandary was to find a term that encompasses what the therapist contributes to the relationship—qualities, conditions, stances, aspects, components, elements, or behaviors. We tried to identify an accurate, brief, and theoretically neutral term. None of the proposed terms was universally appealing, but *elements* won out after an extended discussion and three rounds of e-mails among the Steering Committee. The term denotes components, parts, or aspects—implying that it is not the entire story. However, we understand that relationship *elements* can sound mechanistic, like attending a chemistry class.

A related challenge was to establish the inclusion and exclusion criteria for the elements of the therapy relationship. We readily agreed that the traditional features of the therapy relationship, such as the alliance in individual therapy and cohesion in group therapy, and the Rogerian facilitative conditions, such as empathy, positive regard, and genuineness/congruence, would constitute core elements. We further agreed that dis-

Table 1.1. Decision Rules of the Division 29 Task Force in Comparison to Previous Efforts

Decisions	Previous Efforts	Division 29
Change mechanism	Treatments/technical interventions	Therapy relationships Therapist interpersonal behaviors Therapist responsiveness to patient characteristics
Treatment type	Manualized Pure-form	Manualized and natural Pure-form and integrative/eclectic
Client feature	Primary diagnosis/problem	Single, multiple, or no diagnoses Cross-diagnosis dynamics and personality
Treatment length	Typically brief Typically fixed	Brief, intermediate, or lengthy Fixed or variable
Research design	Two randomized clinical trials (RCT) in which the EST demonstrated superiority *or* 9+ single-case design experiments (Division 12 Task Force)	RCT and naturalistic studies Process-outcome studies, correlational studies

crete, relatively nonrelational techniques were not part of our purview, but that a few relational methods would be included. Therapy methods were considered for inclusion if their content, goal, and context were inextricably interwoven into the emergent therapy relationship. We settled on therapist self-disclosure and relational interpretations because these methods are deeply embedded in the interpersonal character of the relationship itself. But which relational techniques to include and which to exclude under the rubric of the therapy relationship bedeviled us, as it has the field.

We unanimously acknowledged the deep synergy between techniques and the relationship. They constantly shape and inform each other. Both clinical experience and research evidence (e.g., Rector, Zuroff, & Segal, 1999; Rounsaville et al., 1987) point to a complex, reciprocal interaction between the interpersonal relationship and the instrumental techniques. The relationship does not exist apart from what the therapist does in terms of technique, and we cannot imagine any techniques that would not have some relational impact. Put differently, techniques and interventions are relational acts (Safran & Muran, 2000).

The research reviews were based on the results of empirical research linking the relationship element to psychotherapy outcome. This definition deliberately included both quantitative and rigorous qualitative studies. Outcome was broadly and inclusively defined, encompassing proximal in-session outcomes as well as distal treatment outcomes. Authors were asked to specify the outcome criteria if a particular study did not employ a typical end-of-treatment measure of symptoms or functioning.

Decision-Making

The Steering Committee's early deliberations were not easy or unanimous. Democracy is messy and inefficient; science is even slower and painstaking. We debated and, in most instances, voted on terminology, on the division of the therapy relationship into manageable elements, and on the minimal criteria for empirical evidence linking a relationship quality to psychotherapy outcome.

How does one divide the indivisible relationship? For example, is support similar enough to positive regard to be combined or is it conceptually and technically distinct enough to deserve a separate chapter and research review? We struggled on how finely to slice the therapy relationship. As David Orlinsky opined in one of his e-mails, "It's okay to slice bologna that thin, but I doubt that it can be meaningfully done to the relationship." We agreed, as a group, to place the research on support in the positive regard chapter, but we understand that psychodynamic practitioners may understandably take exception to collapsing these relationship elements. More generally, we opted to divide the research reviews into smaller chunks so that the research conclusions were more specific and the practice implications more concrete.

In our deliberations, several members of the Steering Committee advanced a favorite analogy: the therapy relationship is like a diamond, a diamond composed of multiple, interconnected facets. The diamond is a complex, reciprocal, and multidimensional entity. The Task Force endeavored to separate and examine many of these facets in the therapy relationship.

What sort of evidence is sufficient to declare that a relationship element is, in fact, associated to treatment outcome? Some on the Steering Committee wanted to see some true experimental evidence or persuasive, unconfounded lagged correlational evidence that elements of the therapy relationship contribute to treatment outcome. Other members of the Steering Committee scoffed at the value or possibility of such methodological rigor in the area of the therapy relationship where the "variables" cannot be readily controlled or manipulated.

Upon review of the quantity and quality of the empirical research, the Steering Committee characterized the strength of the research on the relationship element as either *demonstrably effective, promising and probably effective,* or *insufficient research to judge.* This tripartite categorization emerged from our review of the research; fewer categories would have resulted in crude and incomplete characterizations, and more categories would have accorded more precision than warranted by the findings. Some elements were clearly established as effective on the basis of the size and regularity of supportive studies. Other elements were considered promising—few studies or lots of conflicting studies or supportive but flawed studies. Still other elements were just tantalizing or preliminary. Accordingly, we christened these as having insufficient research to judge. (Of course, these categorizations refer solely to the empirical evidence linking relationship elements and outcome, and not to the "treatability" of patients with specific characteristics.)

In the end, we employed a systematic and stepwise approach to identifying and interpreting the evidence. First, the Steering Committee identified potential relational and matching elements with sufficient empirical research and practical importance. Second, we consulted extant reviews and gathered expert opinions before commissioning chapters on those elements. Third, at least three scholars independently reviewed the evidence as compiled by the chapter authors and provided numerical ratings on six evaluative criteria (appendix). Fourth, the Steering Committee reviewed the ratings, deliberated by e-mail, and voted using an expert consensus method. The decisions were made both empirically and consensually—the Steering Committee examined the empirical research and then followed consensus.

When no overwhelming majority emerged, we consulted with other experts in the field, including the authors of the research review. In all four cases when members of the Steering Committee were divided on the strength of the empirical evidence linking a relational or matching element to outcome, the authors of the respective chapter opined for the conservative option. That is, they characterized the element as "promising and probably effective" rather than "demonstrably effective" or as "insufficient research to judge" rather than "promising and probably effective."

These and other decisions were arrived at by expert opinion, professional consensus, and review of the empirical evidence. But these were all human choices—open to cavil, contention, and future revision.

TASK FORCE PRODUCTS

The Task Force on Empirically Supported Therapy Relationships has generated three products. First, we prepared and published a synopsis of our work in a 2001 special issue of *Psychotherapy* (Norcross, 2001), which contains a summary of our findings and conclusions. Second, the entire research reviews, detailed therapeutic practices, and Task Force recommendations are published in this book, *Psychotherapy Relationships That Work*. Third, members of the Task Force are presenting a series of addresses, workshops, and symposia on its conclusions and recommendations. Presentations to date have been made at conferences of the APA, the Society for Psychotherapy Research, the Society for the Exploration of Psychotherapy Integration, and the International Society for Clinical Psychology.

The goals of these products are identical: to disseminate evidence-based means of improving the therapy relationship and effective means of customizing that relationship to the individual patient. A frequent lament of mental health researchers is that their best research results often remain unused by practitioner and policymakers alike. The dissemination and uptake problem is a genuine concern for us as well. We plan to reach stakeholders by distributing the results in their preferred communication formats: for researchers, a scholarly book and academic presentations; for practitioners, a professional journal and clinical workshops. Our fervent hope is that the Task Force's multiple products and communication formats will increase awareness and use of effective elements of the therapy relationship.

LIMITATIONS OF THE TASK FORCE WORK

A single book can cover only so much content area and research material. As such, *Psychotherapy Relationships That Work* possesses a number of necessary omissions and unfortunate truncations that we wish to publicly acknowledge at the outset.

The products of the Task Force suffer, first, from a series of omissions. We have not systematically reviewed the research evidence pertaining to the therapy relationship in couples and family therapy. Nor have we specifically provided research reviews on the therapy relationship with children or older adults. Research findings from studies with children and older adults have, however, been incorporated into the reviews of the respective therapist behaviors and client characteristics. In addition, we have not and could not canvas every possible therapist relationship behavior. In our decisions we relied on the best available reviews, but invariably we have missed a few that other reviewers would find salient. Three therapist contributions to the relationship not covered are confrontation, credibility, and the provision of a rationale or explanation. One element of relational matchmaking neglected is limits on the number of therapy sessions, which clinically seems to impact the therapy relationship. We could not locate sufficient empirical research on this crucial topic to include it in the book.

A converse concern with the Task Force's work is content overlap. We may have cut the "diamond" of the therapy relationship too thin at times, leading to a profusion of highly related and possibly redundant constructs. Therapist empathy, for example, correlates highly with parts of the therapeutic alliance, but these are reviewed in separate chapters. Collaboration and goal consensus, reviewed in another chapter, are part of the alliance as it is typically operationalized and measured. The stages of change and assimilation of problematic experiences both track the patient's change over the course of therapy; in fact, they were originally planned to appear in the same coauthored chapter, but it did not functionally come to pass. Thus, to some the book's content may appear swollen; to others, the book may fail to make necessary distinctions.

Another lacuna in the Task Force work is that we may have neglected, relatively speaking, the productive contribution of the client to the therapy relationship. We decided not to commission a separate chapter on the client's contributions; instead, we asked each author in the chapter guidelines to address client contributions to that relationship element. We encouraged authors to pay attention to the chain of events among the therapist's contributions, the patient processes, and eventual outcomes. This, we hoped, would maintain the focus on what is effective in patient change. Further, one half of the chapters examine patient contributions directly in terms of specific patient characteristics. Nonetheless, by omitting separate chapters, we may be understandably accused of an omission akin to the previous error of leaving the relationship out at the expense of

technique. This book tends to be "therapist-centric" in minimizing the client's relational contribution and self-healing processes.

A prominent limitation across the Task Force research reviews is the modest causal connection between the relationship element and treatment outcome. Causal inferences are always difficult to make concerning process variables such as the therapy relationship. Does the relationship cause improvement or simply reflect it? Is the relationship produced by something the therapist does or is it a quality brought to therapy by patients? The interpretation problems of correlational studies (third variables, reverse causation) render such studies less convincing then experiments. It is methodologically difficult to meet the three conditions to make a causal claim: nonspuriousness, covariation between the process variable and the outcome measure, and temporal precedence of the process variable (Feeley, DeRubeis, & Gelfand, 1999). A central limitation of our research base is the failure to convincingly demonstrate causal, as opposed to correlational, linkages between relationship elements and treatment outcomes.

However, more recent studies and methodologies are showing the way. Barber and colleagues (2000), for example, demonstrated that alliance at all sessions significantly predicted subsequent change in depression when prior change in depression was partialled out. The alliance remained a potent and causal predictor of further improvement. Structural equation modeling, lagged correlational, and aptitude-by-treatment interaction studies are also demonstrating the cause-effect nature of selected relationship elements.

Several researchers have taken us to task for the relative exclusion of process approaches to psychotherapy and the concomitant emphasis on a fairly static view of change. Although the research reviews of Stiles, Safran, Prochaska, and colleagues in this book cover some of the landscape, we may have overlooked some of the research on how the therapy relationship evolves over time (e.g., Tracey, 2002). In this book, we have not adequately specified how the client and therapist move into each state or how an outcome is reached.

Finally, an interesting drawback to the present work—and psychotherapy research as a whole— is the paucity of attention paid to the disorder-specific and therapy-specific nature of the therapy relationship. It is too early to aggregate the research on how the patient's primary disorder or the type of treatment impacts the therapy relationship. But there are early links, and these have not been consistently represented in the book. For example, in the National Institute on Drug Abuse Collaborative Cocaine Treatment Study, higher levels of the working alliance were associated with increased retention in supportive-expressive therapy, but in cognitive therapy, higher levels of the alliance were associated with decreased retention (Barber et al., 2001). In the treatment of anxiety disorders (GAD and OCD), the specific treatments seem to exhibit many times the effect size than the therapy relationship. In treating depression, however, the relationship appears more powerful. The therapeutic alliance in the NIMH Treatment of Depression Collaborative Research Program, in both psychotherapy and pharmacotherapy, emerged as the leading force in reducing a patient's depression (Krupnick et al., 1996). The therapy relationship probably exhibits more causal impact in some disorders and in some therapies than others. As with research on specific treatments, it may no longer suffice to ask "Does the relationship work?" but "How does the relationship work for this disorder and this therapy?"

FREQUENTLY ASKED QUESTIONS

The Division of Psychotherapy's Task Force on Empirically Supported Therapy Relationships has provoked considerable interest and enthusiasm in the professional community. At the same time, it has led to misunderstandings and reservations. I will conclude by addressing frequently asked questions about the Task Force's objectives and results.

What is the relation between the APA Division 29 Task Force and the Division 12 Task Force (now the standing Committee on Science and Practice)?

Questions abound regarding the connection of the Division of Psychotherapy (29) and the Society of Clinical Psychology (12) Task Forces, probably because they are both divisions of the APA. Organizationally, the Task Forces are separate creatures, reporting to different divisions. Their respective foci obviously diverge: one looks at therapist contributions to the relationship and patient responsiveness, the other looks at treatment methods for specific disorders. However, they do have several task force members (Paul Crits-Christoph and Larry Beutler), a publisher (Oxford University Press), and goals (to identify and promulgate evidence-based practices) in common.

The aims of the Division of Psychotherapy Task Force and the aims of previous evidence-based initiatives can be conceptualized in three ways. First, the work of the Division of Psychotherapy Task Force represents a *continuation* of previous efforts in that all attempt to apply psychological science to the identification and promulgation of effective psychotherapy. It is a complementary continuation of the elusive search for evidence-based psychotherapy. Second, the Division of Psychotherapy Task Force constitutes an *expansion* of extant work in that we enlarge the focus to empirically supported therapist behaviors and emergent therapy relationships. And third, the Division 29 Task Force represents, in several ways, a *reaction against* previous decision rules that tend to represent psychotherapy as the disembodied, manualized treatment of Axis I disorders.

Are you saying that techniques or methods are immaterial to psychotherapy outcome?

Absolutely not. The empirical research shows that both the therapy relationship and the treatment method make consistent contributions to treatment outcome. It remains a matter of judgment and methodology on how much each contributes, but there is virtual unanimity that both the relationship and the method (insofar as we can separate them) "work." Looking at either treatment interventions or therapy relationships alone is incomplete. We encourage practitioners and researchers to look at multiple determinants of outcome, particularly client contributions.

But are you not exaggerating the effects of relationship factors and/or minimizing the effects of treatments in order to set up the importance of your work?

This may be true, but we think not and hope not. With the guidance of Task Force members and external consultants, we have tried to avoid dichotomies and polarizations. Focusing on one area—the psychotherapy relationship—in this volume may unfortunately convey the impression that it is the only area of importance. This is certainly not our intention.

Relationship factors are important, and we need to review the scientific literature and provide clinical recommendations based on that literature. This can be done without trivializing or degrading the effects of specific treatments.

What, then, is the association between techniques and therapy relationship?

We conceive the association broadly and atheoretically. We find any hard-and-fast distinctions between them untenable. Further, we do not desire to impose any singular theoretical vision of their association upon our colleagues.

For historical and research convenience, we have made distinctions between relationships and techniques. Words like "relating" and "interpersonal behavior" are generally used to describe *how* therapists and patients behave toward each other. By contrast, terms like "technique" or "intervention" are used to describe *what* is done in therapy, especially what is done by the therapist. In research and theory, we often treat the how and the what—the relationships and the interventions, the interpersonal and the instrumental—as separate categories.

In reality, of course, what therapists do and how they do it are complementary and inseparable. To separate the interpersonal dimension of behavior from the instrumental may be acceptable in research, as done in this book, but disregarding the connection may be a fatal flaw when the aim is to extrapolate from research results to clinical practice. Thus, while we focus here on important associations between treatment outcome and qualities of the therapist-patient relationship, we never forget that what the therapist does is also influential and inseparable (Orlinsky, 2000).

Isn't your report just warmed-over Carl Rogers?

No. While Rogers's (1957) facilitative conditions are represented prominently in the research base, they comprise less then 25% of the research we critically review. More fundamentally, we have moved past simplified notions of a limited and invariant set of necessary relationship conditions. Monolithic theories of change and one-size-fits-all therapy relationships are out; tailoring the therapy to the unique patient is in.

How did the Task Force handle the responsiveness problem?

Much of the research on the effectiveness of psychotherapy processes and relationships is constrained by the responsiveness problem. Responsiveness refers to behavior that is affected by emerging context; it occurs on many levels, including choice of an overall treatment approach, case formulation, strategic use of particular techniques, and adjustments within interventions (Stiles, Honos-Webb, & Surko, 1998). Experienced therapists tend to be responsive to the different needs of their clients, providing varying levels of relationship elements in different cases. When this occurs, highly effective relational ingredients may have null or even negative correlations with outcome variables in the cumulative research. Successful responsiveness can confound attempts to find naturalistically observed linear relations of outcome with therapist behaviors (such as interpretations, self-disclosures, and feedback). Because of such problems, the statistical relations between relationship variables and outcome variables cannot always be trusted.

In the work of the Task Force, chapter authors were aware of the responsiveness problem (and other limitations of the empirical research on process-outcome linkages). The majority of authors addressed this issue in the chapter sections on the mediating effects of client qualities and as a limitation of the research reviewed. Moreover, the responsiveness premise—that seasoned therapists have learned to respond flexibly to patient qualities and alter their relational stance on a patient-by-patient or moment-to-moment basis—is built into half of the book.

An interpersonal view of psychotherapy seems at odds with what managed care and bean counters ask of me in my clinical practice. How do you reconcile these?

It is true that the dominant image of psychotherapy today, among both researchers and reimbursers, is of a mental health treatment. This "treatment" or "medical" model inclines people to define process in terms of technique, therapists as providers trained in the application of techniques, treatment in terms of number of contact hours, patients as embodiments of psychiatric disorders, and outcome as the end result of a treatment episode (Orlinsky, 1989).

It is also true that the Task Force members believe this model to be restricted and inaccurate. The psychotherapy enterprise is far more complex and interactive than the linear equation, "Treatment operates on patients to produce effects" (Bohart & Tallman, 1999). We would prefer a broader, integrative model that incorporates the relational and educational features of psychotherapy: one that recognizes both the interpersonal and instrumental components of psychotherapy, one that appreciates the bidirectional process of therapy, and one in which the therapist and patient co-create an optimal process and outcome.

Finally, it is incontestably and sadly true that psychotherapy research to date has exerted a negligible effect on reimbursement decisions.

Won't these results contribute further to deprofessionalizing psychotherapy? Aren't you unwittingly supporting efforts to have any warm, empathic person perform psychotherapy?

Perhaps some will misuse our conclusions in the way you fear, but that is neither our intent nor commensurate with the research. It trivializes psychotherapy to characterize it as simply "a good relationship with a caring person." The research shows an effective psychotherapist is one who employs specific methods, who offers strong relationships, and who customizes both discrete methods and relationship stances to the individual person and condition. That requires considerable training and experience—the antithesis of "anyone can do psychotherapy."

Are psychotherapists really able to adapt their relational style to fit the proclivities and personalities of their patients? Where is the evidence we can do this?

Relational flexibility conjures up many concerns, but two are of particular import for this question: the limits of human capacity and the possibility of capricious posturing (Norcross & Beutler, 1997). Although the psychotherapist can, with training and experience, learn to relate in a number of different ways, there are limits to our human capacity to modify relationship stances. It may be difficult to change interaction styles from client to client and session to session, assuming the therapist is both aware and in control of his or her styles of relating (Lazarus, 1993).

Can therapists authentically differ from their preferred or habitual style of relating? There is meager research on this question. What does exist suggests that experienced therapists are capable of more malleability and "mood transcendence" than might be expected. In Gurman's (1973) research, for example, expert therapists appeared to be less handicapped by their own "bad moods" than were their less skilled peers. From the literature on the cognitive psychology of expertise, Schacht (1991) affirms that experienced psychotherapists are disciplined improvisationalists who have stronger self-regulating skills and more flexible repertoires than novices. The research on the therapist's level of experience suggests that experience begets heightened attention to the client (less self-preoccupation), an innovative perspective, and in general, more endorsement of an "eclectic" orientation predicated on client need (Auerbach & Johnson, 1977). Indeed, several research studies (see Beutler, Machado, & Neufeldt, 1994) have demonstrated that therapists can consistently use different treatment models in a discriminative fashion.

The question of whether they can shift back and forth among different relationship styles for a given case is still unanswered. We expect, however, that this is possible. When doing so, we caution therapists to be careful that the blending of stances and strategies does not deteriorate into play-acting or capricious posturing.

What should we do if we are unable or unwilling to adapt our therapy to the patient in the manner that research indicates is likely to enhance psychotherapy outcome?

Four possible avenues spring to mind. First, address the matter forthrightly with the patient as part of the evolving therapeutic contract and the creation of respective tasks, in much the same way you would with patients requesting a form of therapy or a type of medication that research has indicated would fit particularly well in their case but that is not in your repertoire. Second, treatment decisions are the result of multiple, interacting, and recursive considerations on the part of the patient and the therapist. A single evidence-based guideline should be seriously considered, but only as one of many determinants of treatment itself. Third, an alternative to the one-therapist-fits-most-patients perspective is practice limits. Without a willingness and ability to engage in a range of interpersonal stances, the therapist may limit his or her practice to clients who fit the specific range of behaviors he or she has to offer. And fourth, consider a judicious referral to a colleague who can offer the relationship stance (or treatment method or medication) indicated in a particular case.

Are these intended as practice standards?

No. These are research-based conclusions that can lead, inform, and guide practitioners toward evidence-based therapy relationships and responsiveness to patient needs. They are not intended as legal, ethical, or professional mandates. As we state in Part IV: "The preceding conclusions do *not* by themselves constitute a set of practice standards, but represent current scientific knowledge to be understood and applied in the context of all the clinical data available in each case."

Well, aren't these the official positions of the Division of Psychotherapy or the American Psychological Association?

No. This is not the case for either.

Isn't it premature to launch a set of research-based conclusions on the therapy relationship and patient matching?

Science is not a set of answers. Science is a series of processes and steps by which we arrive closer and closer to elusive answers. Considerable research over the past three decades has been conducted on both the general elements of the therapy relationship and the particular means of adapting it to individual patients. It is premature to proffer the last word or the definitive conclusion; however, it is time to codify and disseminate what we do know. We look forward to regular updates on our conclusions.

So, are you saying that the therapy relationship (in addition to discrete method) is crucial to outcome, that it can be improved by certain therapist contributions, and that it can be effectively tailored to the individual patient?

Precisely. And this book shows specifically how to do so on the basis of the empirical research.

REFERENCES

Auerbach, A. H., & Johnson, M. (1977). In A. S. Gurman & A. M. Razin (Eds.), *Effective psychotherapy: A handbook of research.* New York: Pergamon.

Barber, J. P., Connolly, M. B., Crits-Christoph, P., Gladis, L., & Siqueland, L. (2000). Alliance predicts patients' outcomes beyond in-treatment change in symptoms. *Journal of Consulting and Clinical Psychology, 68,* 1027–1032.

Barber, J. P., Luborsky, L., Gallop, R., Crits-Christoph, P., Frank, A., Weiss, R. D., Thase, M. E., Connolly, M. B., Gladis, M., Foltz, C., & Siqueland, L. (2001). Therapeutic alliance as a predictor of outcome and retention in the National Institute on Drug Abuse Collaborative Cocaine Treatment Study. *Journal of Consulting and Clinical Psychology, 69,* 119–124.

Barlow, D. H. (2000). Evidence-based practice: A world view. *Clinical Psychology: Science and Practice, 7,* 241–242.

Bergin, A. E. (1997). Neglect of the therapist and the human dimensions of change: A commentary. *Clinical Psychology: Science and Practice, 4,* 83–89.

Bergin, A. E., & Lambert, M. J. (1978). The evaluation of outcomes in psychotherapy. In S. L. Garfield & A. E. Bergin (Eds.), *Handbook of psychotherapy and behavior change* (pp. 139–189). New York: Wiley.

Beutler, L. E. (1989). Differential treatment selection: The role of diagnosis in psychotherapy. *Psychotherapy, 26,* 271–281.

Beutler, L. E. (2000). David and Goliath: When empirical and clinical standards of practice meet. *American Psychologist, 55,* 997–1007.

Beutler, L. E., Machado, P. P. P., & Neufeldt, S. A. (1994). Therapist variables. In A. E. Bergin & S. L. Garfield (Eds.), *Handbook of psychotherapy and behavior change* (4th ed., pp. 229–269). New York: Wiley.

Bohart, A. C., & Tallman, K. (1999). *How clients make therapy work: The process of active self-healing.* Washington, DC: American Psychological Association.

Chambless, D. L., et al. (1996). An update on empirically validated therapies. *The Clinical Psychologist, 49*(2), 5–14.

Chambless, D. L., et al. (1998). Update on empirically validated therapies, II. *The Clinical Psychologist, 51,* 3–16.

Chambless, D. L., & Hollon, S. D. (1998). Defining empirically supported therapies. *Journal of Consulting and Clinical Psychology, 64,* 497–504.

Crits-Christoph, P., Baranackie, K., Kurcias, J. S., Beck, A. T., Carroll, K., Perry, K., Luborsky, L., McLellan, A. T., Woody, G. E., Thompson, L., Gallagher, D., & Zitrin, C. (1991). Meta-analysis of therapist effects in psychotherapy outcome studies. *Psychotherapy Research, 2,* 81–91.

Department of Health. (2001). *Treatment choice in psychological therapies and counseling: Evidence-based practice guidelines*. London: Department of Health Publications.

Depression Guideline Panel. (1993). *Depression in primary care: Vol. 2. Treatment of major depression*. Rockville, MD: U.S. Department of Health and Human Services.

Elliott, R. (1998). Editor's introduction: A guide to the empirically supported treatments controversy. *Psychotherapy Research, 8*, 115–125.

Feeley, M., DeRubeis, R. J., & Gelfand, L. A. (1999). The temporal relation of adherence and alliance to symptom change in cognitive therapy for depression. *Journal of Consulting and Clinical Psychology, 67*, 578–582.

Gabbard, G. O. (Ed.). (2000). *Treatments of psychiatric disorders* (3rd ed.). Washington, DC: American Psychiatric Publishing.

Gatz, M., Fiske, A., Fox, L. S., Kaskie, B., Kasl-Godley, J. E., McCallum, T. J., & Wethereall, J. L. (1998). Empirically validated psychological treatments for older adults. *Journal of Mental Health and Aging, 4*, 9–46.

Gelso, C. J., & Carter, J. A. (1985). The relationship in counseling and psychotherapy: Components, consequences, and theoretical antecedents. *The Counseling Psychologist, 13*, 155–243.

Gelso, C. J., & Carter, J. A. (1994). Components of the psychotherapy relationship: Their interaction and unfolding during treatment. *Journal of Counseling Psychology, 41*, 296–306.

Gelso, C. J., & Hayes, J. A. (1998). *The psychotherapy research: Theory, research, and practice*. New York: Wiley.

Glass, C. R., & Arnkoff, D. B. (Eds.). (1996). Psychotherapy integration and empirically validated treatments. *Journal of Psychotherapy Integration, 6*, 183–226.

Gurman, A. S. (1973). Effects of therapist and patient mood on the therapeutic functioning of high- and low-facilitative therapists. *Journal of Consulting and Clinical Psychology, 40*, 48–58.

Henry, W. P. (1998). Science, politics, and the politics of science: The use and misuse of empirically validated treatment research. *Psychotherapy Research, 8*, 126–140.

Hubble, M. A., Duncan, B. L., & Miller, S. D. (Eds.). (1999). *The heart and soul of change*. Washington, DC: American Psychological Association.

Huppert, J. D., Bufka, L. F., Barlow, D. H., Gorman, J. M., Shear, M. K., & Woods, S. W. (2001). Therapists, therapist variables, and cognitive-behavioral therapy outcome in a multicenter trial for panic disorder. *Journal of Consulting and Clinical Psychology, 69*, 747–755.

Kazdin, A. E. (1996). Validated treatments: Multiple perspectives and issues—Introduction to the series. *Clinical Psychology: Science and Practice, 3*, 216–217.

Kendall, P. C. (1998). Empirically supported psychological therapies. *Journal of Consulting and Clinical Psychology, 66*, 3–6.

Krupnick, J. L., Sotsky, S. M., Simmens, S., Moyer, J., Elkin, I., Watkins, J., & Pilkonis, P. A. (1996). The role of the therapeutic alliance in psychotherapy and pharmacotherapy. *Journal of Consulting and Clinical Psychology, 64*, 532–539.

Lambert, M. J. (1992). Psychotherapy outcome research: Implications for integrative and eclectic theories. In J. C. Norcross & M. R. Goldfried (Eds.), *Handbook of psychotherapy integration*. New York: Basic.

Lambert, M. J., & Okiishi, J. C. (1997). The effects of the individual psychotherapist and implications for future research. *Clinical Psychology: Science and Practice, 4*, 66–75.

Lazarus, A. A. (1993). Tailoring the therapeutic relationship, or being an authentic chameleon. *Psychotherapy, 30*, 404–407.

Lazarus, A. A., Beutler, L. E., & Norcross, J. C. (1992). The future of technical eclecticism. *Psychotherapy, 29*, 11–20.

Lonigan, C. J., Elbert, J. C., & Johnson, S. B. (1998). Empirically supported psychosocial interventions for children: An overview. *Journal of Clinical Child Psychology, 27*, 138–142.

Luborsky, L., Crits-Christoph, P., McLellan, T., Woody, G., Piper, W., Liberman, B., Imber, S., & Pilkonis, P. (1986). Do therapists vary much in their success? Findings from four outcome studies. *American Journal of Orthopsychiatry, 51*, 501–512.

Luborsky, L., Diguer, L., Seligman, D. A., Rosenthal, R., Krause, E. D., Johnson, S., Halperin, G., Bishop, M., Brennan, J. S., & Schweitzer, E. (1999). The researcher's own therapy allegiances: A "wild card" in comparisons of treatment efficacy. *Clinical Psychology: Science and Practice, 6*, 95–106.

Messer, S. B. (2001). Empirically supported treatments: What's a nonbehaviorist to do? In B. D. Slife, R. N. Williams, & S. H. Barlow (Eds.), *Critical issues in psychotherapy*. Thousand Oaks, CA: Sage.

Nathan, P. E. (1998). Practice guidelines: Not yet ideal. *American Psychologist, 53,* 290–299.

Nathan, P. E., & Gorman, J. M. (Eds.). (1998). *A guide to treatments that work.* New York: Oxford University Press.

Norcross, J. C. (1999). Collegially validated limitations of empirically validated treatments. *Clinical Psychology: Science and Practice, 6,* 472–476.

Norcross, J. C. (Ed.). (2001). Empirically supported therapy relationships: Summary report of the Division 29 Task Force. *Psychotherapy, 38*(4).

Norcross, J. C., & Beutler, L. E. (1997). Determining the therapeutic relationship of choice in brief therapy. In J. N. Butcher (Ed.), *Personality assessment in managed health care: A practitioner's guide* (pp. 42–60). New York: Oxford University Press.

O'Donohue, W., Buchanan, J. A., & Fisher, J. E. (2000). Characteristics of empirically supported treatments. *Journal of Psychotherapy Practice and Research, 9,* 69–74.

Orlinsky, D. E. (1989). Researchers' images of psychotherapy: Their origins and influence on research. *Clinical Psychology Review, 9,* 413–441.

Orlinsky, D. E. (2000, August). *Therapist interpersonal behaviors that have consistently shown positive correlations with outcome.* Paper presented at the 108th annual convention of the American Psychological Association, Washington, DC.

Orlinsky, D., & Howard, K. E. (1977). The therapist's experience of psychotherapy. In A. S. Gurman & A. M. Razin (Eds.), *Effective psychotherapy: A handbook of research* (pp. 566–589). New York: Pergamon.

Project MATCH Research Group. (1998). Therapist effects in three treatments for alcohol problems. *Psychotherapy Research, 8,* 455–474.

Rector, N. A., Zuroff, D. C., & Segal, Z. V. (1999). Cognitive change and the therapeutic alliance: The role of technical and nontechnical factors in cognitive therapy. *Psychotherapy, 36,* 320–328.

Rogers, C. R. (1957). The necessary and sufficient conditions of therapeutic personality change. *Journal of Consulting Psychology, 22,* 95–103.

Rounsaville, B. J., Chevron, E. S., Prusoff, B. A., Elkin, I., Imber, S., Sotsky, S., & Watkins, J. (1987). The relation between specific and general dimensions of the psychotherapy process in interpersonal psychotherapy of depression. *Journal of Consulting and Clinical Psychology, 55,* 379–384.

Safran, J. D., & Muran, J. C. (2000). *Negotiating the therapeutic alliance.* New York: Guilford.

Schacht, T. E. (1991). Can psychotherapy education advance psychotherapy integration? A view from the cognitive psychology of expertise. *Journal of Psychotherapy Integration, 1,* 305–320.

Shapiro, D. A., & Shapiro, D. (1982). Meta-analysis of comparative therapy outcome studies: A replication and refinement. *Psychological Bulletin, 92,* 581–604.

Stiles, W. B., Honos-Webb, L., & Surko, M. (1998). Responsiveness in psychotherapy. *Clinical Psychology: Science and Practice, 5,* 439–458.

Task Force for the Development of Guidelines for the Provision of Humanistic Psychosocial Services. (1997). Guidelines for the provision of humanistic psychosocial services. *Humanistic Psychologist, 25,* 65–107.

Task Force on Promotion and Dissemination of Psychological Procedures. (1995). Training in and dissemination of empirically validated psychological treatments: Report and recommendations. *The Clinical Psychologist, 48*(1), 3–23.

Task Force on Psychological Intervention Guidelines. (1995). *Template for developing guidelines: Interventions for mental disorders and psychosocial aspects of physical disorders.* Washington, DC: American Psychological Association.

Tracey, T. J. G. (2002). Stages of counseling and therapy: An examination of complementarity and the working alliance. In G. S. Tryon (Ed.), *Counseling based on process research* (pp. 265–297). Boston: Allyn & Bacon.

Wampold, B. E. (2001). *The great psychotherapy debate: Models, methods, and findings.* Mahwah, NJ: Erlbaum.

Wampold, B. E., Lichtenberg, J. W., & Waehler, C. A. (in press). Principles of empirically-supported interventions in counseling psychology. *The Counseling Psychologist.*

2

Research Summary on the Therapeutic Relationship and Psychotherapy Outcome

Michael J. Lambert
Dean E. Barley

The identification of effective psychotherapy has been a hotly debated topic for decades. Recent publications by the APA's Division of Clinical Psychology, for example, proposed criteria for what constitutes empirical validation of specific psychotherapy techniques for the purpose of "educating" clinical psychologists, third-party payers, and the public, thereby attempting to set standards of practice (Task Force on Promotion and Dissemination of Psychological Procedures, 1995). This resulted in controversial lists of techniques that met criteria as empirically supported treatments, as well as an attendant landslide of criticism from practitioners and researchers who found the project to be scientifically questionable as well as overzealous in its assertions (e.g., Garfield, 1996; Silverman, 1996; see review by Norcross, chapter 1 in this volume).

To many of those familiar with the findings of psychotherapy outcome research, the standards of practice advocated by the Division 12 Task Forces may not have placed appropriate emphasis on relationship factors, while overemphasizing therapy techniques. Psychotherapy outcome research, as will be summarized in this chapter, has not supported the notion that specific therapy techniques are a major contributor to client progress when compared with the contributions attributable to the therapeutic relationship. We

share the view of many—that the advocacy of specific forms of treatment for specific disorders can lead to an overemphasis on the least curative aspects of the therapeutic endeavor. The promotion of empirically supported treatments may lead us to inadvertently overlook some consistent findings of psychotherapy outcome research, that the therapeutic relationship is vital in contributing to client progress. Consequently, this summary highlights empirical research that strongly and consistently supports the centrality of the therapeutic relationship as a primary factor contributing to psychotherapy outcome.

Research on psychotherapy outcome has examined the relationship between a host of variables and client progress. Such variables include: extratherapeutic factors (spontaneous remission, fortuitous events, social support); expectancy (placebo effects, the client's knowledge that he/she is being treated, or the client's belief in the treatment techniques and rationale); techniques (factors specific to the prescribed therapy such as biofeedback, hypnosis, or systematic desensitization); and common factors (variables found in most therapies regardless of the therapist's theoretical orientation such as empathy, warmth, acceptance, encouragement of risk taking, client and therapist characteristics, confidentiality of the client-therapist relationship, the therapeutic alliance, or process factors). The relative importance of these various factors in producing client change has been vigorously debated on theoretical and empirical grounds for over six decades.

This debate has been documented through many extensive reviews of the outcome research literature (e.g., Bergin, 1971; Bergin & Lambert, 1978; Gurman & Razin, 1977; Lambert, 1982; Lambert & Bergin, 1994; Lambert, Shapiro, & Bergin, 1986; Luborsky, Singer, & Luborsky, 1975; Meltzoff & Kornreich, 1970) along with meta-analytic summaries of this same literature (e.g., Andrews & Harvey, 1981; Lipsey & Wilson, 1993; Shapiro & Shapiro, 1982; Smith, Glass, & Miller, 1980; Wampold et al., 1997). Based on these reviews and related literature, we have drawn several conclusions about the relative impact of the above variables on patient outcome. The comparative importance of each of these factors is summarized in figure 2.1. The percentages presented in figure 2.1 are based on decades of research and years of reviewing research studies. The estimates presented, while not formally derived from meta-analytic techniques, characterize the research findings of a wide range of treatments, patient disorders, dependent variables representing multiple perspectives of patient change, and ways of measuring patient and therapist characteristics as applied over the years. These percentages are based on research findings that span extremes in research designs, and are especially representative of studies that allow the greatest

divergence in the variables that determine outcome. The percentages were derived by taking a subset of more than 100 studies that provided statistical analyses of the predictors of outcome and averaging the size of the contribution each predictor made to final outcome. Figure 2.1 is offered as a painstakingly derived albeit crude estimate of the relative contribution of a variety of variables that impact outcome. Later in this chapter we provide evidence that supports the data presented in figure 2.1. It is readily apparent from this diagram that of the factors most closely associated with the therapist, the therapeutic relationship is central in contributing to positive therapy outcome. In what follows, we first summarize some of the research concerning the contribution of extratherapeutic factors and techniques to client outcome. This may help place into perspective the above factors as they relate to client progress. We then turn to a more extensive summary of the role of the therapeutic relationship as it impacts psychotherapy outcome.

SUMMARY OF RESEARCH

Extratherapeutic Factors

Many people suffering from mental/emotional disorders improve without formal professional treatment (Bergin & Lambert, 1978; Lambert, 1976). The median rate of patient improvement

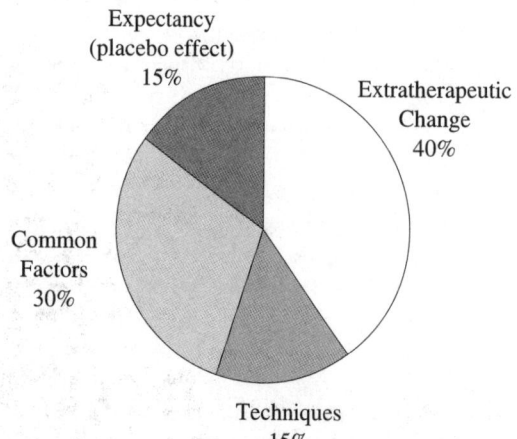

Figure 2.1. Percent of Improvement in Psychotherapy Patients as a Function of Therapeutic Factors

is approximately 43%, with a range of 18 to 67% depending on study methods, definitions of improvement, diagnosis, and the like. Factors that impact the rate of spontaneous remission include the number of organ systems involved in a disorder (severity and complexity of the condition); the length of time the disorder has persisted (chronicity); the presence of an underlying personality disorder and other comorbid Axis I disorders; the nature, strength, and quality of social supports (especially the marital relationship); and diagnosis (Andrews & Tennant, 1978; Mann, Jenkins, & Belsey, 1981; Schapira, Roth, Kerr, & Gurney, 1972). Such research lends support to the conclusion that patient outcome is highly influenced by individual patient characteristics and circumstances outside of therapy.

Those suffering from emotional conditions frequently seek and engage in many self-help remedies. A closer look at factors and relationships that help "untreated" people recover yields useful information about the change process. To a large extent, people with psychological disorders list a variety of people they see as being essential to their improvement. Friends, family, clergy members, self-help literature, and self-help groups help significant numbers of people. In addition, many of those who find help outside of professional interventions and who are viewed as "untreated" actually receive psychological interventions from their natural environment or through indirect means such as self-study or participation in groups led by people with some training (Finch, Lambert, & Brown, 2000; Lewinsohn, Antonuccio, Breckenridge, & Teri, 1984; Ogles, Lambert, & Craig, 1991). It is important to note that most informal helping systems (such as religious organizations and Alcoholics Anonymous) rely heavily on supportive relationships as well as the techniques found in many formal therapeutic interventions.

Specific Therapeutic Techniques

As many as 250 different therapies (Herink, 1980) have been identified, most of which have not been empirically tested. Major schools of therapy (psychodynamic, cognitive-behavioral, behavioral, or humanistic) have expended tremendous energy in attempts to support their approaches.

The available research has led to one basic conclusion: psychotherapy, in general, has been shown to be effective (Lambert & Bergin, 1994). The average treated client is better off than 80% of untreated comparison control subjects. This finding alone, though helpful, does not clearly isolate or identify the healing components of psychotherapy or specify which of the various therapeutic approaches contributes most meaningfully to client improvement.

Conventional reviewing procedures of the comparative studies of different psychotherapies have not consistently demonstrated the preeminence of any particular school of therapy in treating clients across the broad categories of anxiety, depression, and interpersonal problems (Bergin & Lambert, 1978; Luborsky, Singer, & Luborsky, 1975; Meltzoff & Kornreich, 1970). Several early meta-analytical reviews (Dobson, 1989; Dush, Hirt, & Schroeder, 1983; Nicholson & Berman, 1983; Quality Assurance Project, 1983; Robinson, Berman, & Neimeyer, 1990; Shapiro & Shapiro, 1982; Smith, Glass, & Miller, 1980) have shown a small but consistent advantage for cognitive and behavioral methods over traditional dynamic and humanistic therapies. Some reviewers, however, have cast doubt on the slightly larger effect sizes obtained by cognitive-behavioral therapies, saying that they result from strong biases in the behavioral and cognitive literature toward analog studies, mild cases, and highly reactive criteria. It has also been proposed that the treatments and cases used in these studies were not representative of typical clinical practice (Shapiro & Shapiro, 1982; Smith, Glass, & Miller, 1980).

More recent meta-analytic reviews have not strengthened the case for the superior effectiveness of specific techniques with disorders (Wampold et al., 1997). A number of studies found almost no evidence for differences between major schools (Gloaguen, Cottraux, Cuchert, & Blackburn, 1998; Lipsey & Wilson, 1993; Shadish, Navarro, Matt, & Phillips, 2000). Lambert and Ogles (in press) reviewed more than 50 meta-analytic reviews of outcome research. They concluded that while statistically significant differences can sometimes be found favoring the superiority of one treatment over another, these differences are not so large that their practical effects are noteworthy. Furthermore, approximately two-thirds of the observed small differences between psychotherapies in outcomes can be attributed to investigator allegiance (Luborsky et al., 1999). The presentation of an illustrative study that is representative of comparative outcome studies, both in terms of design and findings, will help the reader grasp the nature of evidence in this domain.

The National Institute of Mental Health (NIMH) multisite collaborative study of depression (Elkin et al., 1989) addressed the degree to which specific manualized school-based techniques contribute to client outcome. This extensive study compared a standard reference treatment (imipramine plus clinical management) with two psychotherapies (cognitive-behavior therapy and interpersonal psychotherapy). The two psychotherapy treatments were carefully defined, and the participating therapists followed training manuals that clarified the theoretical issues, general strategies, major techniques, and methods of managing typical problems. All treatments were compared to a drug placebo plus clinical management control group. This condition was intended to control for the effects of regular contact with an experienced and supportive therapist, the general support of the research setting, and the effects of receiving a drug that was thought to be helpful. One of the most thought-provoking findings resulted from the comparison of the two client groups who received one of the psychotherapy-based interventions with clients who received the medication placebo plus clinical management (PLA-CM). Conclusions showed limited evidence for superiority of the interpersonal psychotherapy (IPT) approach and no evidence for superiority of cognitive-behavioral therapy (CBT) above this placebo condition. The two therapies were effective, but the patients who received the placebo "treatment" also similarly improved. Interpersonal psychotherapy, however, did show some advantage with the more severely disturbed patients when compared with outcome in the placebo condition. In comparisons between IPT and CBT, no significant differences appeared in any of the major analyses or in comparisons with the more and less severely disturbed patients. The authors concluded, "The general lack of differences between the two psychotherapies, together

with the good results for the PLA-CM condition, suggests once again the importance of common factors in different types of psychologically mediated treatment" (Elkin et al., 1989, p. 979).

Such research emphasizing manualized treatment protocols are efforts to mimic the designs of clinical drug trials to establish empirically supported treatments. This research is designed to uncover direct relationships between specific treatments, diagnoses, and outcome. This type of research requires that the effects of the other factors in the figure 2.1 pie chart (extratherapeutic, common, and placebo factors) be removed or "controlled" by the research design in order to isolate the specific effects of treatment techniques. When this is attempted, the usual result is that such specific factors exert little effect on client outcome when compared to the effect of relationship or common factors.

Research with "early responders" also questions the relative importance of specific techniques in promoting client improvement. Early responders are clients who show improvement more quickly than what might usually be expected. Haas, Hill, Lambert, and Morrell (in press) note that early responders evidence their rapid improvement usually *before* specific therapeutic techniques have been fully applied. This being the case, it is difficult to attribute improvement in outcome to a specialized treatment protocol with this group of clients because they are not in therapy long enough to be exposed to such procedures.

The positive outcomes of this group cannot be easily dismissed because early responders maintain their gains for as long as two years after termination. They do not resemble premature dropouts who do not show improvement. Neither does their improvement resemble the placebo effect, which usually has a short duration with a characteristic return of symptoms (Lambert & Anderson, 1996; Renaud et al., 1998).

Rapid response has been noted across different treatment approaches (e.g., CBT, nondirective supportive treatment, and behavioral family therapy; Renaud et al., 1998). This could lend support to the idea that the contribution of specific techniques may not be as important to client outcome as other factors common to all therapies

(Ilardi & Craighead, 1999), at least with early responders. Other factors of importance with this group could possibly include client variables such as readiness for therapy, motivation, and the ability to maintain focus and accomplish the early tasks of therapy (Agras et al., 2000; Fennel & Teasdale, 1987; Lambert & Anderson, 1996; Tang & DeRubeis, 1999) as well as the relationship factors (such as the therapeutic alliance) that are the focus of this volume (Orlinsky, Grave, & Parks, 1994; see also Rachman, 1999, and Wilson, 1999, for commentaries on early response).

It should be noted that a few specialized techniques have shown superiority with some specific diagnostic categories. These include, for example, exposure treatments with specific phobic disorders, gradual practice with some sexual disorders, cognitive restructuring and exposure with agoraphobia, and response prevention for obsessive-compulsive disorders (Lambert, 1992). Also reported in the literature are other specific techniques, such as using a more supportive versus a more aggressive approach in interpretation in short-term dynamic therapy depending on the severity of the client's symptoms (Jones, Cumming, & Horowitz, 1988). These matching studies hold some promise of helping clinicians modify their interpersonal approaches according to what is most likely to lead to better client outcome. However, it must be remembered that the accumulative psychotherapy research shows that specific techniques contribute much less to outcome than do important interpersonal factors common to all therapies.

Relationship Factors

As we summarize some of the research on the association between client outcome and the therapeutic relationship, it is difficult to conceptually differentiate between therapist variables (interpersonal style, attributes), facilitative conditions (empathy, warmth, positive regard), and the client-therapist relationship (therapeutic alliance, working endeavor). The imposed structure of this summary does not imply that these concepts are mutually exclusive or distinct; rather we acknowledge from the start their interdependent, overlapping, and interrelated nature.

Therapist Attributes and Facilitative Conditions

We know from both research and experience that certain therapists are better than others at promoting positive client outcome, and that some therapists do better with some types of clients than others. For example, Orlinsky and Howard (1980) reported the outcome ratings of 143 female cases treated by 23 therapists who offered a range of traditional verbal psychotherapy. As would be expected, some therapists' clients experienced better outcome than others. Few factors predicted better outcome, although having a therapist with experience beyond six years was associated with better results in this study. A review of the data showed that some therapists did well with difficult cases, while others did not. Those with poor average outcomes did not perform poorly across all cases, but did well with some clients.

Some have attempted in research designs to minimize the effects that individual therapists have on therapy outcome. Shapiro and Firth (1987) conducted a comparative study designed to maximize sensitivity to technique effects while minimizing variance from therapist variables. The purpose of this design was to examine the comparative contribution of the therapeutic techniques to client progress. They used a crossover design in which 40 outpatients received eight sessions of cognitive-behavioral therapy and eight sessions of humanistic-dynamic psychotherapy. The same four therapists provided therapy, but the order of exposing patients to treatments was varied. Results of the analysis showed few differences between the two treatments with only a slight superiority for the cognitive-behavioral treatment. Shapiro, Firth-Cozens, and Stiles (1989) then examined the effects of specific therapists on the outcome of therapy in this study. In spite of research design efforts to control for therapist effects, differences between therapists were found. Although the project used manuals and supervision to minimize the effect of individual therapists on treatment outcome, the authors discovered that one of the therapists had significantly better results than the other therapists when using cognitive-behavioral therapy. This finding concurs with Luborsky, McClellan, Woody, O'Brien, and Auerbach's (1985) observation that despite concerted efforts to suppress unique therapist effects (training, manuals, supervision) a considerable portion of the variance in outcome between patients is likely due to the particular therapist who provides treatment.

Clients often attribute their positive therapy outcome to the personal attributes of their therapist (Sloane, Staples, Cristol, Yorkston, & Whipple, 1975). Lazarus (1971) noted in an uncontrolled study of 112 clients that they chose adjectives such as "sensitive," "gentle," and "honest" to describe the therapist. Clients appeared to believe that the personal qualities of the therapist were more important than specific technical factors of treatment. Similarly, Strupp, Fox, and Lessler (1969) reported that patients who felt that their therapy was successful described their therapist as "warm, attentive, interested, understanding, and respectful" (p. 116).

Ricks (1974) published an in-depth naturalistic case study of two therapists working with a group of equally disturbed adolescent boys to identify what better therapists do. Marked divergence was found in the outcomes for the most severe cases of the two therapists. Differences in outcome were attributed to the differences in the two therapists' styles of interaction with the clients. The therapist whose patients had the better outcome spent more time with the difficult cases, made use of resources outside of the immediate therapy circumstances, was firm and direct with parents, encouraged autonomy, implemented problem-solving skills, and had a strong therapeutic relationship with the clients. The less successful therapist seemed frightened by the boys' pathology and withdrew from them.

In their comprehensive review of more than 2,000 process-outcome studies since 1950, Orlinsky, Grave, and Parks (1994) identified several therapist variables that have consistently been shown to have a positive impact on treatment outcome. Therapist credibility, skill, empathic understanding, and affirmation of the patient, along with the ability to engage with the patient, to focus on the patient's problems, and to direct the patient's attention to the patient's affective experience, were highly related to successful treatment. Most of these therapist contributions

to outcome are subjects of subsequent chapters in this book.

Perhaps the relationship factors most frequently studied have been the facilitative conditions proposed by the person-centered school: (1) empathic understanding (the degree to which the therapist is successful in communicating awareness and understanding of the client's current experience in language that is attuned to that client); (2) nonpossessive warmth and positive regard (the extent to which the therapist communicates nonevaluative caring and respect for the client as a person); and (3) congruence (the extent to which the therapist is nondefensive, real, and "non-phony" in interactions with the client). These conditions have been thoroughly investigated in psychotherapy research and in the preparation of future therapists in essential relationship skills (Carkhuff, 1972; Gurman, 1977; Lambert, De-Julio, & Stein, 1978; Parloff, Waskow, & Wolfe, 1978; Truax, 1971; Truax & Carkhuff, 1967).

Although the empirical research linking these facilitative conditions to therapy outcome is reviewed in the following three chapters, let us illustrate some typical findings. Lambert, DeJulio, and Stein (1978) reviewed 17 well-designed and executed studies of facilitative conditions and outcome. They concluded that these studies presented "only modest evidence in favor of the hypothesis that such factors as accurate empathy, warmth and genuineness relate to measures of outcome" (p. 472). Further, there was little direct evidence showing a cause-effect relationship between the facilitative conditions and outcome. Other reviewers (Gurman, 1977; Mitchell, Bozarth, & Krauft, 1977; Levant & Shlien, 1984; Patterson, 1984) suggest that the relationship between therapist attitudes and interpersonal skills and outcome is more ambiguous than originally postulated. Much of this ambiguity results from the way the proposed relationship factors have been measured. As will be seen below, research findings have shown that client-perceived relationship factors, rather than objective raters' perceptions of the relationship, obtain consistently more positive results. The larger correlations of relationship measures with client outcome are often between client ratings of the relationship and client self-report of outcome.

In an effort to clarify the impact of these factors on client improvement, Greenberg, Elliott, and Lietaer (1994) conducted a meta-analysis of four studies that examined the correlations between therapist facilitativeness (provision of the facilitative conditions) and client outcome. The overall correlation between facilitativeness and client outcome was .43. Measures of client improvement correlated with therapist warmth, concreteness, and activeness (mean $r = .34$; Stuhr & Meyer, 1991), with facilitative interventions ($r = .25$; Horton & Elliott, 1991), with at least two of the three person-centered facilitative conditions ($r = .31$; Rudolph, Langer, & Tausch, 1980), and with therapist "self-relatedness" or genuineness ($r = .61$; Grawe, Caspar, & Ambuhl, 1990). This review would lend some support to the person-centered concepts of facilitative conditions and their proposed influence on client progress.

Miller, Taylor, and West (1980) investigated the comparative effectiveness of various behavioral approaches aimed at helping problem drinkers control their alcohol consumption. The authors also collected data on the contribution of therapist empathy to patient outcome. At the 6- to 8-month follow-up interviews, client ratings of therapist empathy correlated significantly ($r = .82$) with client outcome, thus accounting for 67% of the variance on the criteria. These results argue for the importance of therapist empathy, even within behavioral and other technique-centered interventions.

Murphy, Cramer, and Lillie (1984) had outpatients list curative factors that they believed to be associated with their successful cognitive-behavioral therapy. The factors endorsed by a significant portion of patients were advice (79%), talking to someone interested in my problems (75%), encouragement and reassurance (67%), talking to someone who understands (58%), and instillation of hope (58%). The two factors that correlated most highly with outcome, as assessed by both therapist and client, were "talking to someone who understands" and "receiving advice." The clients in this study were mainly from a low socioeconomic class, and past research has demonstrated that such patients expect advice in therapy (Goin, Yamamoto, & Silverman, 1965).

In another illustrative study, Lafferty, Beutler, and Crago (1991) examined differences between more and less effective trainee psychotherapists. Outcome was determined by client self-ratings on the Symptom Checklist 90–Revised. The less effective therapists were shown to have low levels of empathic understanding. As stated by the authors, "The present study supports the significance of therapist empathy in effective psychotherapy. Clients of less effective therapists felt less understood by their therapists than did clients of more effective therapists" (p. 79).

Lorr (1965) requested that 523 psychotherapy patients describe their therapists with 65 different statements. A factor analysis identified five factors: understanding, accepting, authoritarian (directive), independence-encouraging, and critical-hostile. Clients' ratings on the understanding and accepting factors correlated most highly in a positive direction with client and therapist-rated improvement. Likewise, Elliott, Clark, and Kemeny (1991) analyzed the content of clients' and therapists' post-session descriptions of the most helpful events in process-experiential therapy. The highest ratings by clients and therapists were given to feeling understood, self-awareness, and feeling close to or being supported by the therapist.

In a similar fashion, Cooley and LaJoy (1980) examined the relationship between therapist self-ratings on facilitative attributes and therapist ratings of client outcome. They also examined discrepancies between client ratings and therapist ratings of therapist attributes and client outcome. In this study, 56 adult community mental-health outpatients were treated by one of eight therapists. Client ratings of therapist understanding and acceptance correlated most highly with client-rated outcomes. However, when self-ratings of therapists' attributes were compared to therapist-rated client outcomes, the correlations were insignificant, suggesting that therapists' self-perceptions of personal attributes did not predict therapist-rated therapeutic outcome. What appears to be of importance is that the *client* feel understood and accepted.

This relates to Bachelor's (1988) observation that different clients perceive empathy in different ways. For example, some clients considered empathy to be when the therapist "said what I felt," while other clients thought an affective response was most meaningful ("I felt that she felt what I was telling her"). Other clients believed that empathy was reflected in a nurturing response or the therapist sharing personal information. The correlation of measures of empathy with client outcome will most likely be higher as we understand more about what constitutes an empathic response for the client.

In an investigation by Najavits and Strupp (1994), 16 therapists (8 psychologists and 8 psychiatrists), who were recommended by previous supervisors as "caring empathic clinicians," were each assigned five clients with similar difficulty levels. After 25 sessions, therapists were evaluated according to outcome, client length of stay, and therapist in-session behavior. Therapists whose clients evidenced better outcome employed more positive behaviors and fewer negative behaviors than the less effective therapists. Warmth, understanding, and affirmation were considered positive, while subtle forms of belittling, blaming, ignoring, neglecting, attacking, and rejecting were considered negative behaviors. Although the better therapists showed much less negative behavior than the lowest-rated therapists, even the best therapists showed some negative behaviors. The largest differences among therapists were found on nonspecific relationship variables rather than specific technical ones. From these results, the authors concluded, "Thus, basic capacities of human relating—warmth, affirmation, and a minimum of attack and blame—may be at the center of effective psychotherapeutic intervention. Theoretically based technical interventions were not nearly as often significant in this study" (Najavits & Strupp, 1994, p. 121).

Greenberg and Watson (1998) compared the effectiveness of person-centered psychotherapy and process-experiential psychotherapy in treating adults suffering from major depression. Person-centered therapy was defined as therapist provision of empathy, positive regard, and congruence. Process-experiential treatment provided an empathic relationship along with three techniques designed to help clients deal with cognitive-affective problems (for example, gestalt empty-chair dialogues, gestalt two-chair dialogues, and systematic evocative unfolding). Both treatments produced typical treatment effect sizes for depression, and there was no difference between treatments on ratings of depression at six-month follow-up. This study initiated an important step

in demonstrating the general effectiveness of therapist relational behaviors (empathy, positive regard, and congruence) in facilitating change in depressed adults within the experimental framework. However, it is important to note that the process-experiential treatment produced greater improvement in clients' self-esteem and interpersonal functioning, reduced clients' overall level of distress at termination, and produced quicker changes by midtreatment. The authors suggested that person-centered therapists should consider using active experiential interventions at appropriate times to promote quicker and more pervasive changes in clients.

Ablon and Jones (1999) rated transcripts from the NIMH Treatment of Depression Collaborative Research Program, described earlier, using the psychotherapy process Q-sort. Findings revealed that both interpersonal psychotherapy (IPT) and cognitive-behavioral therapy (CBT) were equally effective and that both included, in session, facilitative factors. The IPT therapists were observed to frequently clarify, rephrase, or restate the client's communication and encouraged self-reflection about interpersonal relationships. CBT therapists offered strong support, encouragement, and approval to control negative affect. The authors concluded that IPT represents a kind of "common factor" treatment where empathy, support, and nonjudgmental acceptance from the therapist are present.

The Therapeutic Alliance

The therapeutic alliance (also referred to as *alliance* or *working alliance*) has a broader definition than the facilitative conditions (see Horvath & Bedi, chap. 3 in this volume). The therapist's contribution to the alliance includes the provision of the facilitative conditions, the therapist's ability to effectively deal with ruptures in the alliance, and the ability to come to a mutual agreement with the client on the goals of treatment and how those goals will be accomplished (Hatcher & Barends, 1996).

This tripartite characterization concurs with Bordin's (1976, 1989) conceptualization of the therapeutic alliance as having three components: tasks, bonds, and goals. Tasks are the behaviors and processes within the therapy session that constitute the actual work of therapy. Both the therapist and the client must view these tasks as important and relevant for a strong therapeutic alliance to exist. The goals of therapy are the objectives of the therapy process that both parties endorse and value. Bonds include the positive interpersonal attachment between therapist and client of mutual trust, confidence, and acceptance.

The therapeutic alliance, like the person-centered facilitative conditions, has been measured by client ratings, therapist ratings, and judges' ratings. There are now several popular methods for measuring this construct. Gaston (1990) reports that some of the following aspects of the alliance are measured by some but not all of the current scales: (1) the client's affective relationship with the therapist, (2) the client's capacity to work purposefully in therapy, (3) the therapist's empathic understanding and involvement, and (4) the patient-therapist agreement on the goals and tasks of therapy. While measurements of the facilitative conditions typically focus only on the therapist's behaviors, conceptualizations and measures of the therapeutic alliance contain an additional emphasis on patient variables, mainly his or her ability to participate in therapy. As such, these measures would be expected to correlate more highly with client outcome than the measures of facilitative conditions.

Investigators who espouse psychodynamic theories have produced most of the research on the therapeutic alliance (Gaston, 1990; Horvath & Greenberg, 1994; Horvath & Luborsky, 1993; Horvath & Symonds, 1991; Luborsky, 1994; Luborsky & Auerbach, 1985). However, the therapeutic alliance is also receiving more emphasis in investigations of behavioral therapy (DeRubeis & Feeley, 1991), cognitive therapy (Castonguay, Goldfried, Wiser, Raue, & Hayes, 1996; Krupnick et al., 1996), gestalt therapy (Horvath & Greenberg, 1989), and person-centered therapy (Grawe, Caspar, & Ambuhl, 1990). Reviews of the research (Gaston, 1990; Horvarth & Bedi, chap. 3 in this volume; Horvath & Greenberg, 1994; Horvath & Luborsky, 1993; Horvath & Symonds, 1991; Martin, Garske, & Davis, 2000) have consistently reported a positive relationship between the therapeutic alliance and outcome across studies, even though there are instances where it fails to predict outcome, or where associations are nonsignificant. In Horvath and Symonds's (1991) meta-analysis of 24 studies, the average effect size reflected that 26% of the difference in the rate of therapeutic success was accounted for by the quality of the alliance.

A brief discussion of a few studies will give examples of typical conclusions concerning the relationship between the therapeutic alliance and client outcome. Safran and Wallner (1991) studied a sample of 22 outpatients who received time-limited cognitive therapy. Outcome was assessed using a variety of client and therapist measures. The therapeutic alliance was measured using the Working Alliance Inventory (WAI) and the California Psychotherapy Alliance Scale (CALPAS). Results indicated that both alliance measures were predictive of outcome when administered after the third session of treatment. These findings underscore the importance of the alliance in cognitive therapy and are consistent with research indicating that therapy outcome can be predicted by ratings of the therapeutic alliance in the early stages of treatment (Horvath & Luborsky, 1993).

In another study, Gaston, Marmar, Thompson, and Gallagher (in press) used hierarchical regression analysis to examine the therapeutic alliance in elderly depressed patients who participated in dynamic, cognitive, or behavioral therapy. Symptomatic improvement up to time of alliance measurement and patient and therapist CALPAS scores were used to predict symptoms at termination of treatment. The alliance assessed near termination accounted for 36 to 57% of outcome variance in this study.

Castonguay and colleagues (1996) compared the impact of the treatment variable unique to cognitive therapy (the therapist's focus on distorted cognition and depressive symptoms) and two variables common with other forms of treatment (the therapeutic alliance and client emotional involvement) on treatment outcome. The subjects were 30 clients suffering from major depressive disorder who received either cognitive therapy alone or cognitive therapy with medication over a 12-week period. Clients were treated by experienced clinicians who conducted cognitive therapy according to manualized guidelines. Outcome was assessed through client ratings and independent evaluators. Results revealed that the two common variables, the therapeutic alliance and the clients' emotional involvement, were both found to be positively related to client improvement. To the contrary, the variable deemed to be distinctive to cognitive therapy, connecting distorted thoughts to unwanted emotion, was positively correlated to depressive symptoms following therapy. The authors proposed that this finding could have been due to the therapists' efforts to mend the therapeutic alliance through trying to convince the client to accept the legitimacy of the cognitive therapy approach or by viewing alliance difficulties as evidence of the client's distorted cognitions that required disputation.

In the NIMH Treatment of Depression Collaborative Research Program that has been discussed previously, Krupnick and colleagues (1996) examined the impact of the therapeutic alliance in the treatment of depressed individuals. As mentioned earlier, the 250 clients suffering from major depressive disorder were randomly assigned to one of four treatment modalities: interpersonal psychotherapy, cognitive-behavioral therapy, imipramine with clinical management, or placebo with clinical management. The therapeutic alliance was measured using a modified version of the Vanderbilt Therapeutic Alliance Scale. In this study, the therapeutic alliance had a significant impact on client outcome for both of the psychotherapy procedures and for the active and placebo pharmacotherapy. However, the therapist contribution to the therapeutic alliance in this analysis was not significantly related to outcome measures. One possible reason for this finding is the relative lack of variability between the therapists. In summarizing the results of this study, the authors stated, "These results are most consistent with the view that the therapeutic alliance is a common factor across modalities of treatment for depression that is distinguishable from specific technical or pharmacological factors within the treatments" (p. 538).

CONCLUSIONS

The cumulative empirical research on psychotherapy outcome now numbers hundreds of studies across 60 years. We can reliably conclude the following about the therapeutic relationship:

1. Psychotherapy is successful in general, and the average treated client is better off than 80% of untreated subjects.
2. Comparative studies of psychotherapy techniques consistently report the relative equivalence of therapies in promoting client change.
3. Measures of therapeutic relationship variables consistently correlate more highly with client outcome than specialized therapy techniques. Associations between the therapeutic relationship and client outcome are strongest when measured by client ratings of both constructs.
4. Some therapists are better than others at contributing to positive client outcome. Clients characterize such therapists as more understanding and accepting, empathic, warm, and supportive. They engage in fewer negative behaviors such as blaming, ignoring, or rejecting.

PRACTICE IMPLICATIONS

In managed-care environments accountability is emphasized, and empirically supported psychotherapies (Task Force on Promotion and Dissemination of Psychological Procedures, 1995), treatment guidelines, and manual-based interventions (Wilson, 1998) are often advocated. Therapists must indeed make every effort to stay current with new developments in the field; however, there are serious concerns with empirically supported treatments (Silverman, 1996) and treatment manuals (Strupp & Anderson, 1997). These approaches may overemphasize technical procedures and adherence to specific treatment guidelines and de-emphasize the necessity to develop and sustain an effective therapeutic relationship (Henry, Strupp, Butler, Schacht, & Binder, 1993). Clinicians would do well to keep a balanced perspective when using empirically supported treatments and treatment manuals. While these may be helpful in structuring treatment, psychotherapy is, at a fundamental level, an interpersonal process characterized by the therapist's and the client's ability to engage in a therapeutic relationship.

In addition to providing the facilitative conditions and a positive alliance, therapists must avoid the negative communication patterns that detract from outcome, especially in treating more difficult clients. These styles would include comments or behaviors that are critical, attacking, rejecting, blaming, or neglectful (Najavits & Strupp, 1994). Special care would need to be taken with clients who are more negative, hostile, and blaming of the therapist and who are more likely to provoke critical, defensive attacking or even abusive behavior from the therapist (also see Gelso & Hayes, chap. 14 in this volume).

Despite a therapist's best efforts to cultivate a positive alliance, strains in the therapeutic relationship naturally occur and are a part of the evolving therapeutic process (Safran, Muran, & Samstag, 1994). It is imperative that therapists carefully observe client behaviors for any indication of difficulties with the alliance (see Safran, Muran, Samstag, & Stevens, chapter 12 in this volume). Since most clients are reluctant to initiate discussion of dissatisfaction or negative feelings about the therapist, especially in the early stages of treatment (Hill, Nutt-Williams, Heaton, Thompson, & Rhodes, 1996), it is essential for therapists to inform clients that dialogue about the therapy relationship is a vital part of therapy and that expressions of negative feelings are allowed and appreciated.

Empirical research suggesting that some therapists are more effective than others, at least with some kinds of clients, has implications for the referral process. Individual clinicians would be well advised to track client outcomes and client satisfaction to maximize client-therapist matching. Insightful and aware clinicians could improve client outcome by actively choosing the kinds of clients they accept for treatment. Moreover, therapists may well learn to customize their relational presence to different clients based on client desires, personality, stage of change, motivational level, attachment style, and the like. Not every therapist can treat every patient; however, relational matchmaking may hold considerable promise.

Given the importance of the facilitative conditions and the therapeutic alliance for successful treatment, training in relationship skills is crucial for the beginning therapist. This could include didactic instruction, supervision, modeling, role-playing, and personal participation as a client in group or individual therapy. Successful training

in the communication of empathy also requires training in an adaptive approach based on an ongoing awareness of what truly represents an empathic response for each particular client (Bachelor, 1988).

A constant emphasis on the therapeutic relationship is recommended in continuing education for licensed professionals. Frequent evaluation of relationship factors is vital for experienced clinicians, and such factors should be specifically stressed during ongoing training.

With the contemporary work environment in mental health, many factors could reduce the therapist's ability to relate in an empathic and genuine manner. A short list of such factors could include the increasing influence of managed care, insistence on cost-effective symptom reduction, ascendancy of manual-based therapy, increasing case loads, lower reimbursement per hour, and an increase in paperwork. Such work stressors could easily threaten the therapist's ability to empathize with the client, which in turn could impede the development of a positive alliance and undermine therapeutic progress. Awareness of deterioration in these fundamental areas could alert clinicians to focus on their own personal circumstances and to attend to issues that may impair their therapeutic abilities. For therapists to be effective, it is essential that they take care of themselves so that they are able to care for clients.

RESEARCH IMPLICATIONS

The challenge for science-based psychotherapy is to integrate what is known about the therapeutic relationship, the change process, and specific techniques. Those doing research in integrative and eclectic approaches would do well to place primary focus on the central curative activity of therapy (the therapeutic relationship) while appropriately incorporating the less significant aspects of treatment (techniques) (Lambert, 1992; Mahalik, 1990). In addition to modifying techniques to match the client's diagnosis or presenting problem, the therapist's learning to adapt or tailor his or her interpersonal presentation to match patient styles could also be vital in building a positive alliance and improving client outcome. Continued research in the area of matching clients and therapists or of learning to modify the therapeutic presence according to salient client variables (stage of therapy, client motivation, readiness, attachment style, and so on) could be helpful.

Another essential area of investigation relates to the impact of the individual therapist in psychotherapy outcome. It is clear that some therapists are better than others, at least with some clients (Lambert & Bergin, 1994; Lambert & Okishi, 1997). This is probably related to the therapist's contribution to the therapeutic alliance, especially in working with more severe cases. Further research efforts are needed to clarify the master therapist's contribution to the therapeutic relationship and to client outcome.

We have discussed some of the evidence for the importance of empathy in psychotherapy. An important line of inquiry is to further examine how empathy is perceived and experienced by clients, how it can be most meaningfully assessed, and how and when it is most effectively utilized (Bachelor, 1988; Bohart & Greenberg, 1997; Greenberg, Elliott, & Lietaer, 1994; Lambert, DeJulio, & Stein, 1978).

Research on the therapeutic relationship has shifted from a narrow emphasis on traditional therapist facilitative conditions to an examination of the more collaborative, interactive aspects of the therapeutic relationship exemplified in studies of the therapeutic alliance. Research on the therapeutic alliance has resulted in progress in the conceptualization and operational definition of the therapeutic relationship as well as methods of measuring the meaningful variables (Beutler, Machado, & Neufeldt, 1994). Continued examination of the therapeutic alliance will increase understanding of the qualities of the therapist-client relationship that promote client outcome.

REFERENCES

Ablon, S. T., & Jones, E. E. (1999). Psychotherapy process in the NIMH Collaborative Study of Depression Research Program. *Journal of Consulting and Clinical Psychology, 67,* 64–75.

Agras, W. S., Crow, S. J., Halmi, K. A., Mitchell, J. E., Wilson, G. I., & Kramer, H. C. (2000). Outcome predictors for the cognitive behavior treatment of bulimia nervosa: Data from a multi-site study. *American Journal of Psychiatry, 157,* 1302–1308.

Andrews, G., & Harvey, R. (1981). Does psychotherapy benefit neurotic patients? A re-analysis of the Smith, Glass, and Miller data. *Archives of General Psychiatry, 38,* 1203–1208.

Andrews, G., & Tennant, C. (1978). Life event stress and psychiatric illness. *Psychological Medicine, 8,* 545–549.

Bachelor, A. (1988). How clients perceive therapist empathy: A content analysis of "received" empathy. *Psychotherapy, 25,* 227–240.

Bergin, A. E. (1971). The evaluation of therapeutic outcomes. In A. E. Bergin & S. L. Garfield (Eds.), *Handbook of psychotherapy and behavior change* (pp. 217–270). New York: Wiley.

Bergin, A. E., & Lambert, M. J. (1978). The evaluation of outcomes in psychotherapy. In S. L. Garfield and A. E. Bergin (Eds.), *Handbook of psychotherapy and behavior change: An empirical analysis* (2nd ed., pp. 139–189). New York: Wiley.

Beutler, L. E., Machado, P. P. P., & Neufeldt, S. A. (1994). Therapist variables. In A. E. Bergin & S. L. Garfield (Eds.), *Handbook of psychotherapy and behavior change* (4th ed., pp. 229–269). New York: Wiley.

Bohart, A. C., and Greenberg, L. S. (Eds.). (1997). *Empathy reconsidered: New directions in psychotherapy.* Washington, DC: American Psychological Association.

Bordin, E. S. (1976). The generalizability of the psychoanalytic concept of the working alliance. *Psychotherapy: Theory, Research and Practice, 16,* 252–260.

Bordin, E. S. (1989, April). *Building therapeutic alliances: The base for integration.* Paper presented at the annual meeting of the Society for Exploration of Psychotherapy Integration, Berkeley, CA.

Carkhuff, R. R. (1972). The development of systematic human resource development models. *Counseling Psychologist, 3,* 4–16.

Castonguay, L. G., Goldfried, M. R., Wiser, S., Raue, P. J., & Hayes, A. M. (1996). Predicting the effect of cognitive therapy for depression: A study of unique and common factors. *Journal of Consulting and Clinical Psychology, 65,* 497–504.

Cooley, E. F., & LaJoy, R. (1980). Therapeutic relationship and improvement as perceived by clients and therapists. *Journal of Clinical Psychology, 36,* 562–570.

DeRubeis, R. J., & Feeley, M. (1991). Determinants of change in cognitive therapy for depression. *Cognitive Therapy and Research, 14,* 469–482.

Dobson, K. S. (1989). A meta-analysis of the efficacy of cognitive therapy for depression. *Journal of Consulting and Clinical Psychology, 57,* 414–419.

Dush, D. M., Hirt, M. L., & Schroeder, H. (1983). Self-statement modification with adults: A meta-analysis. *Journal of Consulting and Clinical Psychology, 94,* 408–422.

Elkin, I., Shea, T., Watkins, J. T., Imber, S. D., Sotsky, S. M., Collins, I. F., & Glass, D. R. (1989). National Institute of Mental Health treatment of depression collaborative research program: General effectiveness of treatments. *Archives of General Psychiatry, 46,* 971–982.

Elliott, R., Clark, C., & Kemeny, V. (1991, July). *Analyzing clients' post-session accounts of significant therapy events.* Paper presented at the Society for Psychotherapy Research, Lyon, France.

Fennel, M. J. V., & Teasdale, J. D. (1987). Cognitive therapy for depression: Individual differences and the process of change. *Cognitive Therapy and Research, 11,* 253–271.

Finch, A. E., Lambert M. J., & Brown, J. S. (2000). Attacking anxiety: A naturalistic study of a multimedia self-help program. *Journal of Clinical Psychology, 56,* 1–11.

Garfield, S. L. (1996). Some problems associated with "validated" forms of psychotherapy. *Clinical Psychology: Science and Practice, 3,* 218–229.

Gaston, L. (1990). The concept of the alliance and its role in psychotherapy: Theoretical and empirical considerations. *Psychotherapy, 27,* 143–153.

Gaston, L., Marmar, L. R., Thompson, L., & Gallagher, D. (in press). The importance of the alliance in psychotherapy of elderly depressed patients. *Journal of Gerontology: Psychological Sciences.*

Gloaguen, V., Cottraux, J. K., Cuchert, M., & Blackburn, I. M. (1998). A meta-analysis of the effects of cognitive therapy in depressed patients. *Journal of Affective Disorders, 49,* 59–72.

Goin, M. K., Yamamoto, J., & Silverman, J. (1965). Therapy congruent with class-linked expectations. *Archives of General Psychiatry, 38,* 335–339.

Grawe, K., Caspar, F., & Ambuhl, H. (1990). Differentielle Psychotherapie-Forschung: Vier Therapieformen in Vergleich. [Differential psychotherapy research: A comparison of four forms of therapy.] *Zeitschrift for Klinische Psychologie, 19,* 287–376.

Greenberg, L. S., Elliott, R., & Lietaer, G. (1994). Research on experiential psychotherapies. In A. E. Bergin & S. L. Garfield (Eds.), *Handbook of psychotherapy and behavior change* (4th ed., pp. 509–539). New York: Wiley.

Greenberg, L. S., & Watson, J. (1998). Experiential therapy of depression: Differential effects of client-centered relationship conditions and process experiential interventions. *Psychotherapy Research, 8,* 210–224.

Gurman, A. S. (1977). The patient's perception of the therapeutic relationship. In A. S. Gurman & A. M. Razin (Eds.), *Effective psychotherapy: A handbook of research* (pp. 503–543). New York: Pergamon.

Gurman, A. S., & Razin, A. M. (Eds). (1977). *Effective psychotherapy: A handbook of research.* New York: Pergamon.

Haas, E., Hill, R. D., Lambert, M. J., & Morrell, B. (in press). Do early responders to psychotherapy maintain treatment gains? *Journal of Clinical Psychology.*

Hatcher, R. L., & Barends, A. W. (1996). Patients' view of the alliance in psychotherapy: Exploratory factor analysis of three alliance measures. *Journal of Consulting and Clinical Psychology, 64,* 1326–1336.

Henry, W. P., Strupp, H. H., Butler, S. F., Schacht, T. E., & Binder, J. L. (1993). The effects of training in time-limited dynamic psychotherapy: Changes in therapist behavior. *Journal of Consulting and Clinical Psychology, 61,* 434–440.

Herink, R. (Ed.) (1980). *The psychotherapy handbook: The A to Z guide to more than 250 different therapies in use today.* New York: Meridian.

Hill, C. E., Nutt-Williams, E., Heaton, K., Thompson, B., & Rhodes, R. H. (1996). Therapist retrospective recall of impasses in long-term psychotherapy: A qualitative analysis. *Journal of Counseling Psychology, 43,* 207–217.

Horton, C., & Elliott, R. (1991, November). *The experiential session form: Initial data.* Paper presented at the annual meeting for the Society for Psychotherapy Research, Panama City, FL.

Horvath, A. O., & Greenberg, L. S. (Eds.). (1994). *The working alliance: Theory, research, practice.* New York: Wiley.

Horvath, A. O., & Greenberg, L. S. (1989). Development and validation of the Working Alliance Inventory. *Journal of Counseling Psychology, 36,* 223–233.

Horvath, A. O., & Luborsky, L. (1993). The role of the therapeutic alliance in psychotherapy. *Journal of Consulting and Clinical Psychology, 61,* 561–573.

Horvath, A. O., & Symonds, B. D. (1991). Relation between working alliance and outcome in psychotherapy: A meta-analysis. *Journal of Counseling Psychology, 38,* 139–149.

Ilardi, S. S., & Craighead, W. E. (1999). Rapid early response, cognitive modification, and nonspecific factors in cognitive behavior therapy for depression: A reply to Tang and DeRubeis. *Clinical Psychology: Science and Practice, 6,* 295–299.

Jensen, J. P., Bergin, A. E., & Greaves, D. W. (1990). The meaning of eclecticism: New survey and analysis of components. *Professional Psychology: Research and Practice, 21,* 24–130.

Jones, E. E., Cumming, J. D., & Horowitz, M. J. (1988). Another look at the nonspecific hypotheses of therapeutic effectiveness. *Journal of Consulting and Clinical Psychology, 56,* 48–55.

Krupnick, J. L., Stotsky, S. M., Simmons, S., Moyer, J., Watkins, J., Elkin, I., & Pilkonis, P. A. (1996). The role of the therapeutic alliance in psychotherapy and pharmacotherapy outcome: Findings in the National Institute of Mental Health Treatment of Depression Collaborative Research Program. *Journal of Consulting and Clinical Psychology, 64,* 532–539.

Lafferty, P., Beutler, L. E., & Crago, M. (1991). Differences between more and less effective psychotherapists: A study of select therapist variables. *Journal of Consulting and Clinical Psychology, 57,* 76–80.

Lambert, M. J. (1976). Spontaneous remission in adult neurotic disorders: A revision and summary. *Psychological Bulletin, 83,* 107–119.

Lambert, M. J. (1982). *The effects of psychotherapy* (Vol. 2). New York: Human Sciences.

Lambert, M. J. (1992). Implications of outcome research for psychotherapy integration. In J. C. Norcross & M. R. Goldstein (Eds.), *Handbook of psychotherapy integration.* New York: Basic.

Lambert, M. J., & Anderson, E. M. (1996). Assessment for time-limited psychotherapies. *Annual Review of Psychiatry, 15,* 23–47.

Lambert, M. J., & Bergin, A. E. (1994). The effectiveness of psychotherapy. In A. E. Bergin & S. L. Garfield (Eds.), *Handbook of psychotherapy and behavior change* (4th ed., pp. 143–189). New York: Wiley.

Lambert, M. J., DeJulio, S. S., & Stein, D. M. (1978). Therapist interpersonal skills: Process, outcome, methodological considerations and recommendations for future research. *Psychological Bulletin, 85,* 467–489.

Lambert, M. J., & Ogles, B. M. (in press). The efficacy and effectiveness of psychotherapy. In M. J. Lambert (Ed.). *Handbook of psychotherapy and behavior change* (5th ed.). New York: Wiley.

Lambert, M. J., & Okiishi, J. C. (1997). The effects of the individual psychotherapist and implications for future research. *Clinical Psychology: Science and Practice, 4,* 66–75.

Lambert, M. J., Shapiro, D. A., & Bergin, A. E. (1986). The effectiveness of psychotherapy. In S. L. Garfield & A. E. Bergin (Eds.), *Handbook of psychotherapy and behavior change* (3rd ed., pp. 157–212). New York: Wiley.

Lazarus, A. A. (1971). *Behavior therapy and beyond.* New York: McGraw-Hill.

Levant, R. F., & Shlien, J. M. (Eds.). (1984). *Client-centered therapy and the person-centered approach: New directions in theory, research and practice.* New York: Praeger.

Lewinsohn, P. M., Antonuccio, D. O., Breckenridge, J. S., & Teri, L. (1984). *The coping with depression course.* Eugene, OR: Castalia.

Lipsey, M. W., & Wilson, D. B. (1993). The efficacy of psychological, educational, and behavioral treatment: Confirmation from meta-analysis. *American Psychologist, 48,* 1181–1209.

Lorr, M. (1965). Client perceptions of therapists. *Journal of Consulting Psychology, 29,* 146–149.

Luborsky, L. B. (1994). Therapeutic alliances as predictors of psychotherapy outcomes: Factors explaining the predictive success. In A. O. Horvath & L. S. Greenberg (Eds.), *The working alliance: Theory, research, and practice* (pp. 38–50). New York: Wiley.

Luborsky, L., & Auerbach, A. (1985). The therapeutic relationship in psychodynamic therapy: The research evidence and its meaning for practice. In R. Hales & A. Frances (Eds.), *Psychiatric update annual review* (pp. 550–561). Washington, DC: American Psychiatric Association.

Luborsky, L., Diguer, L., Seligman, D. A., Rosenthal, R., Krause, E. D., Johnson, S., Halperin, G., Bishop, M., Berman, J. S., & Schweizer, E. (1999). The researcher's own therapy allegiances: A "wild card" in comparisons of treatment efficacy. *Clinical Psychology: Science and Practice, 6,* 95–106.

Luborsky, L., McClellan, A. T., Woody, G. E., O'Brien, C. P., & Auerbach, A. (1985). Therapist success and its determinants. *Archives of General Psychiatry, 42,* 602–611.

Luborsky, L., Singer, B., & Luborsky, L. (1975). Comparative studies in psychotherapy. *Archives of General Psychiatry, 32,* 995–1008.

Mahalik, J. R. (1990). Systematic eclectic models. *The Counseling Psychologist, 18,* 655–679.

Mann, A. H., Jenkins, R., & Belsey, E. (1981). The twelve-month outcome of patients with neurotic illness in general practice. *Psychological Medicine, 11,* 535–550.

Martin, D. J., Garske, J. P., & Davis, M. K. (2000). Relation of therapeutic alliance with outcome and other variables: A meta-analytic review. *Journal of Consulting and Clinical Psychology, 68,* 438–450.

Meltzoff, J., & Kornreich, M. (1970). *Research in psychotherapy.* New York: Atherton.

Miller, W. R., Taylor, C. A., & West, J. C. (1980). Focused versus broad-spectrum behavior therapy for problem drinkers. *Journal of Consulting and Clinical Psychology, 48,* 590–601.

Mitchell, K. M., Bozarth, J. D., & Krauft, C. C. (1977). A reappraisal of the therapeutic effectiveness of accurate empathy, non-possessive warmth, and genuineness. In A. S. Gurman & A. M. Razin (Eds.), *Effective psychotherapy: A handbook of research* (pp. 482–502). New York: Pergamon.

Murphy, P. M., Cramer, D., & Lillie, F. J. (1984). The relationship between curative factors perceived by patients in their psychotherapy and treatment outcome: An exploratory study. *British Journal of Medical Psychology, 57,* 187–192.

Najavits, L. M., & Strupp, H. (1994). Differences in the effectiveness of psychodynamic therapists: A process-outcome study. *Psychotherapy, 31,* 114–123.

Nicholson, R. A., & Berman, J. S. (1983). Is follow-up necessary in evaluating psychotherapy? *Psychological Bulletin, 93,* 261–278.

Ogles, B. M., Lambert, M. J., & Craig, D. (1991). A comparison of self-help books for coping with loss: Expectations and attributions. *Journal of Counseling Psychology, 38,* 387–393.

Orlinsky, D. E., Grave, K., & Parks, B. K. (1994). Process and outcome in psychotherapy—Noch einmal. In A. E. Bergin & S. L. Garfield (Eds.), *Handbook of psychotherapy and behavior change* (pp. 257–310). New York: Wiley.

Orlinsky, D. E., & Howard, K. I. (1980). Gender and psychotherapeutic outcome. In A. M. Brodksy & R. T. Hare-Mustin (Eds.), *Women in psychotherapy* (pp. 3–34). New York: Guilford.

Parloff, M., Waskow, I. E., & Wolfe, B. E. (1978). Research on therapist variables in relation to process and outcome. In A. E. Bergin & S. L. Garfield (Eds.), *Handbook of psychotherapy and behavior change* (2d ed., pp. 233–282). New York: Wiley.

Patterson, C. H. (1984). Empathy, warmth, and genuineness: A review of reviews. *Psychotherapy, 21,* 431–438.

Quality Assurance Project. (1983). A treatment outline for depressive disorders. *Australian and New Zealand Journal of Psychiatry, 17,* 129–146.

Rachman, S. (1999). Rapid and not-so-rapid responses to cognitive behavioral therapy. *Clinical Psychology: Science and Practice, 6,* 293–294.

Renaud, J., Brent, D. A., Baugher, M., Birmaher, B., Kolko, D. J., & Bridge, J. (1998). Rapid response to psychosocial treatment for adolescent depression: A two-year follow-up. *Journal of the American Academy of Child and Adolescent Psychiatry, 37,* 1184–1191.

Ricks, D. F. (1974). Supershrink: Methods of a therapist judged successful on the basis of adult outcomes of adolescent patients. In D. F. Ricks, M. Roff, & A. Thomas (Eds.), *Life history research in psychopathology* (pp. 288–308). Minneapolis: University of Minnesota Press.

Robinson, L. A., Berman, J. S., & Neimeyer, R. A. (1990). Psychotherapy for the treatment of depression. A comprehensive review of controlled outcome research. *Psychological Bulletin, 108,* 30–49.

Rogers, C. R. (1957). The necessary and sufficient conditions of therapeutic personality change. *Journal of Consulting Psychology, 22,* 95–103.

Rudolph, J., Langer, I., & Tausch, R. (1980). An investigation of the psychological affects and conditions of person-centered individual psychotherapy. *Zeitschrift für Klinische Psychologie: Forschung und Praxis, 9,* 23–33.

Safran, J. D., Muran, J. C., & Samstag, L. W. (1994). Resolving therapeutic alliance ruptures: A task analytic investigation. In A. O. Horvath & L. S. Greenberg (Eds.), *The working alliance: Theory, research, and practice* (pp. 225–255). New York: Wiley.

Safran, J. D., & Wallner, L. K. (1991). The relative predictive validity of two therapeutic alliance measures in cognitive therapy. *Psychological Assessment: A Journal of Consulting and Clinical Psychology, 3*, 188–195.

Schapira, K., Roth, M., Kerr, T. A., & Gurney, C. (1972). The prognosis of affective disorders: The differentiation of anxiety states from depressive illnesses. *British Journal of Psychiatry, 21*, 175–201.

Shadish, W. R., Navarro, A. M., Matt, G. E., & Phillips, G. (2000). The effects of psychological therapies under clinically representative conditions: A meta-analysis. *Psychological Bulletin, 126*, 512–529.

Shapiro, D. A., & Firth, J. (1987). Prescriptive vs. exploratory psychotherapy: Outcomes of the Sheffield psychotherapy project. *British Journal of Psychiatry, 151*, 790–799.

Shapiro, D. A., Firth-Cozens, J., & Stiles, W. B. (1989). The question of therapists' differential effectiveness: A Sheffield psychotherapy project addendum. *British Journal of Psychiatry, 154*, 383–385.

Shapiro, D. A., & Shapiro, D. (1982). Meta-analysis of comparative therapy outcome studies: A republication and refinement. *Psychological Bulletin, 92*, 581–604.

Silverman, W. H. (1996). Cookbooks, manuals, and paint-by-numbers: Psychotherapy in the 90's. *Psychotherapy, 33*, 207–215.

Sloane, R. B., Staples, F. R., Cristol, A. H., Yorkston, N. J. I., & Whipple, K. (1975). *Short-term analytically oriented psychotherapy vs. behavior therapy.* Cambridge, MA: Harvard University Press.

Smith, M. L., Glass, G. V., & Miller, T. I. (1980). *The benefits of psychotherapy.* Baltimore: Johns Hopkins University Press.

Strupp, H. H., & Anderson, T. (1997). On the limitations of therapy manuals. *Clinical Psychology: Science and Practice, 4*, 76–82.

Strupp, H. H., Fox, R. E., & Lessler, K. (1969). *Patients view their psychotherapy.* Baltimore: Johns Hopkins.

Stuhr, U., & Meyer, A. E. (1991). Hamburg short-term psychotherapy comparison study. In L. Beutler & M. Crago (Eds.), *Psychotherapy research: An international review of programmatic studies.* Washington DC: American Psychological Association.

Tang, T. Z., & DeRubeis, R. J. (1999). Reconsidering rapid early response in cognitive behavioral therapy for depression. *Clinical Psychology: Science and Practice, 6*, 283–288.

Task Force on Promotion and Dissemination of Psychological Procedures (1995). Training in and dissemination of empirically validated therapies. *The Clinical Psychologist, 49*, 3–23.

Truax, C. B. (1971). Effectiveness of counselor and counselor aids: A rejoinder. *Journal of Counseling Psychology, 18*, 365–367.

Truax, C. B., & Carkhuff, R. R. (1967). *Toward effective counseling and psychotherapy: Training and practice.* Chicago: Aldine.

Wampold, B. E., Mondin, G. W., Moody, M., Stich, F., Benson, K., & Ahn, H. (1997). A meta-analysis of outcome studies comparing bona fide psychotherapies: Empirically, "all must have prizes." *Psychological Bulletin, 122*, 203–215.

Weinberger, J. (1995). Common factors aren't so common: The common factors dilemma. *Clinical Psychology: Science and Practice, 2*, 45–69.

Wilson, G. T. (1998). Manual-based treatment and clinical practice. *Clinical Psychology: Science and Practice, 5*, 363–375.

Wilson, G. T. (1999). Rapid response to cognitive behavior therapy. *Clinical Psychology: Science and Practice, 6*, 289–292.

Part II

EFFECTIVE ELEMENTS

A. GENERAL ELEMENTS OF THE THERAPY RELATIONSHIP

3

The Alliance

Adam O. Horvath
Robinder P. Bedi

Over the last three decades, there has been a great surge of interest in the concept of the alliance among both clinicians and researchers. In a recent review Martin (1998) located 1,405 research publications on this topic between 1977 and 1997. Our own search of electronic databases for the years 1998 to 2000 yielded over 650 additional references. What makes this concept so appealing to researchers and clinicians alike? It seems the answer is multilayered.

One reason for this large-scale interest is the response of the therapeutic community to the weight of evidence suggesting that, overall, different psychotherapies produce similar beneficial effect for clients (Luborsky, Singer, & Luborsky, 1975; Smith & Glass, 1977; Stiles, Shapiro, & Elliott, 1986). Although the "Dodo bird interpretation" of the results ("All have won and all must have their prizes") of these meta-analyses has proven somewhat simplistic, most therapists and researchers alike have accepted the notion that a very large part of what is helpful for clients receiving psychotherapy is shared across diverse treatments. It is logical, therefore, that attention should focus on the pantheoretical or generic factors shared by different therapeutic modalities. The therapeutic relationship in general, and the alliance in particular, is the quintessential common ground shared by most psychotherapies.

Another likely reason behind the surge of interest is the impact of Rogers's person-centered theory, which placed the therapeutic relation in the center of the healing process and generated

an important body of literature exploring the interpersonal interior of psychotherapy. Psychodynamic and experiential theories also focused on the curative dynamics of the therapist-client interaction; however, in retrospect, it seems that a combination of the theoretical complexity of the former and a lack of empirical validation by the latter has lessened the impact of these models of the therapeutic relationship.

Lastly, the general move toward theoretical integration and reconciliation of some of the conflicting therapeutic methods had a major impact on the field. The modal theoretical orientation of therapists practicing in North America is eclectic, indicating that the pragmatic "practice wisdom" in the field has shifted from theoretical monism to consideration of useful features arising from a variety of sources. The value of a certain kind of therapist-client relatedness finds strong resonance in most of the "eclectic" sources (e.g., Goldfried, 1980). Parallel to the move toward integration at the practice level, researchers from across the theoretical spectrum have also made a significant effort to develop an empirically supported, integrated framework for therapy (for example, Orlinsky & Howard, 1987). The alliance concept has found ready use and acceptance in these efforts (Castonguay, 2000; Castonguay & Goldfried, 1994).

This chapter will focus on the empirical evidence linking the alliance to outcome in a variety of treatment contexts. The evidence suggests that the impact of the alliance is similar across diverse forms of treatments (Horvath & Symonds, 1991; Martin, Garske, & Davis, 2000), and the organization of this chapter will reflect this level of homogeneity. At the same time, during the last ten years, the focus of this line of research has moved beyond the exploration of the links between alliance and outcome of treatment to investigate the moderators and mediators affecting this relationship. Recent studies have investigated clinically important differences in the way the alliance develops and how these differences have an impact on treatment outcome; there are investigations of the alliance-outcome relation across variables such as time, types of client impairment, and personality variables. As well, there is a recent accumulation of studies of therapist versus client perspectives on the alliance. We will present the available evidence related to these factors. However, before we examine the research literature, the alliance itself needs to be defined.

DEFINITION

The term *alliance* (also *therapeutic alliance, working alliance*, or *helping alliance*) is used in the research literature to refer to a number of related constructs; at this time we do not have a single universally accepted definition of the concept (Horvath & Luborsky, 1993; Saketopoulou, 1999). Simply put, while there are important shared aspects of definitions in the literature (e.g., Bordin, 1980; Gaston et al., 1995; Horvath & Luborsky, 1993), there are also nontrivial differences among authors about the precise meaning of the term. Therefore we will approach the definition of this concept by first reviewing the complex history of the notion of an alliance between therapist and client and its current empirical context.

The Historic Background

The concept of the alliance (though not the term itself) owes its genesis to Freud (1940a). Early in his writings he struggled with the question of what keeps the analysand in therapy in the face of the psyche's unconscious fear and rejection of exploring repressed material. His first formulation suggests that he thought that there was an "analyst" within the patient supporting the healing journey (Freud, 1940a). Later he talked about the reality-based *collaboration* between therapist and client, a conjoint effort to conquer the client's pain. He also referred to this process as the unobjectionable or positive transference (Freud, 1940). Both the wisdom of recognizing the importance of the client's attachment to the therapist, and his ambiguity about the status of this attachment (reality-based and conscious versus transferential and unconscious) has echoed throughout the evolution of the concept.

The term *ego alliance* was coined by Sterba (1934), who conceptualized it as part of the client's ego-observing process that alternates with the experiencing (transferential) process. Zetzel (1956) used the term *therapeutic alliance* to refer to the patient's ability to use the healthy part of her ego to link up or join with the analyst to accomplish the therapeutic tasks. Greenson (1965, 1967) made a distinction between the *working alliance*, the client's ability to align with the tasks of analysis, and the *therapeutic alliance*, which refers to the capacity of therapist and client to form a personal bond.

During the 1970s, efforts were made to move the concept of the alliance from its dynamic roots to encompass the relational elements of all types of helping endeavors. Luborsky (1976) proposed an extension of Zetzel's (1956) and Stone's (1961) concept. He suggested that the alliance between therapist and client developed in two phases. The first phase, Type I alliance, involves the client's belief in the therapist as a potent source of help and the therapist providing a warm, supporting, and caring relationship. This level of alliance results in a secure "holding" relationship within which the work of the therapy can begin. The second phase, Type II alliance, involves the client's investment and faith in the therapeutic process itself, a commitment to some of the concepts undergirding the therapy (such as the nature of the problem and the value of the exploratory process) as well as a willing investment of her or himself and shared ownership of the therapy process. While Luborsky's (1976) assumptions about the therapy process itself are grounded in dynamic theory, the description of the alliance as a therapeutic process was quite general. Luborsky and his team also pioneered an alliance assessment method for raters, using transcripts or audio recordings, to count signs of in-session events indicative of the presence of either type of alliance.

Bordin (1975, 1989, 1994) proposed a different pantheoretical concept of the effective components of the therapeutic relationship, which he called the working alliance. His work utilized some of Greenson's (1965) ideas as a starting point, but departed from the psychodynamic premises even more clearly than Luborsky did. For Bordin, the alliance is fundamentally a collaborative entity and has three components: agreements on the therapeutic goals, consensus with respect to the tasks than make up therapy, and a bond between the client and the therapist. He predicted that different therapies would place different demands on the relationship; thus, the "profile" of the ideal working alliance would be different across therapeutic orientations. He also proposed that as therapy progresses, the strength of the working alliance would build and ebb in the normal course of events; the repair of these ruptures in the alliance would constitute the core task of any helping relationship.

Perhaps the most important and distinguishing feature of the alliance as a conceptualization of the active component of the therapeutic relationship is its emphasis on collaboration and consensus (Bordin, 1980; Hatcher, Barends, Hansell, & Gutfreund, 1995; Luborsky, 1976). Whereas previous formulations of the therapeutic relationship emphasized either the therapist's contributions to the relationship or the unconscious distortions of the relation between therapist and client, modern alliance theory emphasizes the active collaboration between the participants.

More recently, a number of instruments have been developed to measure the alliance. What we know about the alliance and its relation to outcome and other therapy variables has been gleaned from studies which, in practice, define the alliance by the instrument used to measure the concept. In this sense, the instrumentation contributes to the definition of the construct. In the following section, we review the alliance instruments and discuss the differences and similarities of the undergirding alliance definitions among these measures.

Measuring the Alliance

Behind each alliance measure there is an author (or authors) who tries to capture and quantify the alliance using implicit and/or explicit criteria that speak to what properly belongs to the domain of the construct and what is extraneous to it. For example, is the *capacity to engage* in an intimate relationship, such as therapy, part of the alliance itself? Is this a prior ability brought by each participant contributing to the alliance? Or, perhaps capacity to engage is better thought of as a *consequence* of having a positive therapeutic alliance? These decisions, whether made explicitly or implicitly—though often neglected afterward—undergird the nature of each research measure. As our knowledge about the role and function of the alliance is largely based on research studies, these de facto definitions have an important influence on the nature of the findings and the conclusions we can draw from them.

There are more than 24 different alliance scales in use by researchers. Some of these are questionnaires developed for the particular investigation and thus have relatively little impact on how we understand the alliance. In other instances, measures designed to capture a related concept (such as empathy) are used in a study and inferences about the alliance are generated on the bases of the suggested linkage between this construct and the alliance; these techniques also have little impact on the definition of the alliance. We will concentrate on the four important "families" of instruments specifically designed to measure the alliance that are used in the majority of empirical studies.

The earliest of these measures are the Penn Helping Alliance (HA) scales developed by Luborsky and colleagues (Luborsky, Crits-Cristoph, Alexander, Margolis, & Cohen, 1983; Alexander & Luborsky, 1987). These instruments measure Luborsky's (Luborsky, 1976, 1994; Luborsky & Auerbach, 1985) dynamic conceptualization of Type I and Type II helping alliances. This instrument captures the alliance as (1) a warm, supportive, accepting relationship followed by (2) a sense of collaboration, participation, and sharing in therapeutic responsibilities by the client.

The Vanderbilt instruments (Suh, O'Malley, & Strupp, 1986) were developed to measure the process dimensions of the Vanderbilt I project. The original 80-item observer version, Vanderbilt Psychotherapy Process Scale (VPPS), was partly based on the Therapy Session Report (TSR; Orlinsky & Howard, 1986). As the Vanderbilt research team become more specifically interested in the role of the alliance in brief dynamic therapy, a subset of 44 items was extracted from the VPPS to form the bases of the Vanderbilt Therapeutic Alliance Scale (VTAS). This instrument is specifically tailored to dynamic therapies and has items that tap into patient and client contributions to the alliance as well as client-therapist interaction items.

The Working Alliance Inventory (WAI; Horvath, 1981, 1986) was developed to capture Bordin's (1975, 1976, 1980) pantheoretical conceptualization of the alliance comprising collaboration with the therapist in setting goals for the therapy, agreement on and valuing the in-therapy activities (tasks), and a sense of personal bond with the therapist. The original instrument came in client and therapist self-report format. Horvath (1981, 1986) offered evidence of the content and discriminant validity for this instrument. Subsequent reports, however, indicate that clients make relatively little distinction between the task and goal dimensions of the scale (Hatcher & Barends, 1996), while therapists are more able to make the distinctions among these dimensions (Kvilighan & Shaugnessy, 1995; Mallinckrodt, 1993; Paivio & Bahr, 1998). Subsequently, an observer WAI(o) form was developed by Tichenor and Hill (1989), and a 12-item short WAI(s) version was published. This abbreviated scale yields a score that is a close approximation of the total WAI alliance level but not necessarily as reliable at the subscale level (Kokotovic & Tracey, 1989). A couples/family version of the WAI (AI.Co) was recently developed as well (Symonds, 1999). These instruments are theory based, and WAI's relation to Bordin's definition of the alliance has received some support (Horvath & Greenberg, 1986). However, the distinctness of Bordin's three underlying alliance dimensions are undetermined.

The fourth instrument family, the California-Toronto scales, were originally developed by Marmar and colleagues at the Langely Porter Institute (Marmar, Gaston, Gallager, & Thompson, 1989; Marmar, Horowitz, Weiss, & Marziali, 1986; Marziali, 1984; Marziali, Marmar, & Krupnick, 1981). The initial development of these scales appears to have been guided by a dynamic concept of the alliance and, in part, influenced by previous work on the VTAS and the TSR. One version of the scale became the Therapeutic Alliance Rating Scale (TARS; Marziali, 1984), a 42-item instrument assessing both client and therapist positive and negative contributions to the alliance. This instrument focuses mostly on the affective dimensions from a dynamic perspective (Saketopoulou, 1999). Another version of the original scale became the California Therapeutic Alliance Rating Scale (CALTARS; Marmar, Weiss, & Gaston, 1989), and in subsequent revisions, the California Psychotherapy Alliance Scale (CALPAS; Gaston & Marmar, 1994). The CALPAS taps into four alliance dimensions: patient working capacity, patient commitment, therapist understanding, and working strategy consensus.

The most recent version of CALTARS rests on the assumption that the alliance is composed of four parts. Two of these correspond to Bordin's model: the patient's and therapist's bond, and the agreement and collaboration on goals and tasks. In CALTARS the therapist's emphatic attunement is treated as a separate dimension, and the client's working capacity or ego strength to mobilize resources in order to engage with treatment is the fourth dimension (Gaston & Marmar, 1994; Gaston, Marmar, Gallager, & Thompson, 1990). In the underlying model, transference appears to be assumed as part of the relationship but separate from the alliance.

How are these scales similar or different? Cross-scale comparisons of these measures suggest medium to high intercorrelations (ranging from .87 to .34) (Bachelor, 1991; Hatcher, Barends, Hansell, & Gutfreund, 1995; Hatcher & Barends, 1996; Safran & Wallner, 1991; Tichenor & Hill, 1989). Factor analytic examination of the aggregate of the most popular measures suggests that personal bonds, energetic involvement in treatment (collaborative work), and collaboration/agreement on the direction (goal) and substance (tasks) of treatment are each represented, to varying degrees, in these measures (Hatcher, Barends,

Hansell, & Gutfreund, 1995; Hatcher & Barends, 1996).

Does this mean each scale measures the identical construct? The answer is a qualified "no." While the importance of these core elements is almost universally recognized, each measure puts different weight on these central dimensions and assesses some features of the relationship the other measures do not. For example, negative contributions are specifically monitored in some (TARS, CALPAS, and VTAS), but not in others. Client capacities are explicitly included in the CALPAS but not directly in other instruments. Agreement or consensus is weighted most heavily in the WAI; collaboration is emphasized most by the WAI and CALPAS, but less by other scales. The balance between supportive and commitment aspects of the alliance is most clearly identified by the Penn scales, but less likely to be revealed by other instruments.

A Working Definition

The following definition attempts to capture both Bordin's theoretical work and the emerging clinical consensus in the field:

> The alliance refers to the quality and strength of the collaborative relationship between client and therapist in therapy. This concept is inclusive of: the positive affective bonds between client and therapist, such as mutual trust, liking, respect, and caring. Alliance also encompasses the more cognitive aspects of the therapy relationship; consensus about, and active commitment to, the goals of therapy and to the means by which these goals can be reached. Alliance involves a sense of partnership in therapy between therapist and client, in which each participant is actively committed to their specific and appropriate responsibilities in therapy, and believes that the other is likewise enthusiastically engaged in the process. The alliance is a conscious and purposeful aspect of the relation between therapist and client: It is conscious in the sense that the quality of the alliance is within ready grasp of the participants, and it is purposeful in that it is specific to a context in which there is a therapist or helper who accepts some responsibility for providing psychological assistance to a client or clients.

In this definition we speak of the alliance as an "in therapy" and conscious concept. However, we understand that the alliance may be impacted by prior relational history or disposition at several different levels and, though it is conscious, it may be tacit or outside of mindful awareness at any specific time. While the definition we are offering neither specifies the relations among the components that comprise the alliance nor addresses the question of how alliance will differentially manifest in different therapies, it might offer a reasonable starting point to consider important but yet to be answered questions about the limits of this concept (What is *not* alliance?) and the way related concepts (empathy, therapeutic resonance) might be connected to it.

The therapeutic relationship itself, in addition to the alliance, includes elements that represent still active components of past relationships that both the client and the therapist bring to the current encounter. These historical elements are captured by the notion of transference for dynamically oriented clinicians and researchers. Therapists outside the dynamic framework use terms such as *dysfunctional relationship schemas* (Safran, Muran, & Samstag, 1994) or *negative introject* (Henry & Strupp, 1994), or terms borrowed from attachment theory (Hersoug, Monsen, Havik, & Høglend, 2000; Kvilighan, Patton, & Foote, 1998; Tyrrel, Dozier, Teague, & Fallot, 1999).

When researchers study the alliance from the client's perspective, the cognitive elements (goals, tasks, collaboration, and involvement) tend to be highly interrelated but somewhat distinct from personal bonds, which appear to represent the more affective side of the alliance (Hatcher, Barends, Hansell, & Gutfreund, 1995; Hatcher & Barends, 1996). Studies that examined the independent impact of past relationships (such as transference and attachment) and alliance indicate that the impact of the alliance is significant even when these historical factors are controlled (Gaston, Thompson, Gallager, Cournoyer, & Gagnon, 1998; Henry, Strupp, Schacht, & Gaston, 1994). It seems to us that a combination of these two components, the alliance and the past/historical elements, in combination, may provide a useful overarching model of the therapeutically active ingredients of relationship. Obviously there are several other important interpersonal variables active in the therapeutic process; this perspective would imply that these other variables could be most usefully conceptualized as precursors, contributing to, or the resultant of these two major processes.

RESEARCH REVIEW

There is empirical evidence linking the quality of the alliance to therapy outcome. Horvath and Symonds (1991) reported an overall effect size (ES) of .26 between alliance and outcome based on 24 studies. More recently, Martin, Garske, and Davis (2000) published a meta-analysis of the same relationship based on 79 studies and came up with a slightly smaller ES of .22. These two studies relied on similar selection criteria for the inclusion of material in the review and their data are overlapping, but they used a slightly different statistical approach to summarize the results.

We present a summary of the research on the alliance outcome relation in table 3.1. The data are, in part, based on the two studies already mentioned. In addition, we located usable results from 10 studies published since 1997 (the end point of Martin's [1998] original research) and one study prior to that date that meet the selection criteria. These criteria were: (1) the author refers to the therapy process variable as "alliance" (including variants of the term such as helping alliance, working alliance), (2) the research was based on clinical as opposed to analogue data, (3) five or more subjects participated in the study, and (4) the data reported was such that we could extract an index of relation between alliance and outcome. Our data brings the period of the review up to approximately 2000; however, the 1977–2000 portion of the data does not cover the unpublished reports (e.g., theses and dissertations).

The manner we used to analyze the data departs in some minor aspects from the approach taken by Martin and colleagues (2000). They found the relations between alliance and outcome homogeneous overall, and therefore in the published article they did not examine the data for possible mediators, moderators, or interactions with other variables. We, on the other hand, believe that this approach may obscure some of the clinically important relationships within the data

set (Rosenthal & DiMaetto, 2001). Therefore we examined the data in disaggregated form when it was felt that such procedure was warranted on conceptual or statistical grounds.

Both previous meta-analyses examined the reliability of the alliance assessments. Across instruments, Cronbach's alpha was high (client = .84, therapist = .81, observer = .91). Test–retest correlation is a more stringent measure of reliability; these values ranged from .55 (HA) to .73 (WAI). For observer-rated instruments, the interrater reliability ranged from .66 (CALPAS) to .92 (WAI) (Martin, Garske, & Davis, 2000). In general, it appears that alliance assessments are reliable; we did no further analysis on the reliability of the measures.

The Overall Relation Between Alliance and Outcome

Across all studies, the average relation between alliance and outcome was .21 (weighted by sample size). The median effect size was .25. We computed an index of homogeneity (Q statistic; Hedges & Olkin, 1985) and found, in contrast to Martin's recent analysis, that the ESs in our data set were not homogeneous.

One possible reason for such a result is the existence of a subset of research within the larger data set which has distinctly different characteristics than the rest of the data. We inspected the studies and hypothesized that the six substance abuse studies included in the data (Barber et al., 1999; Broome, 1996; Florsheim, Shotorbani, Guest-Warnick, Barratt, & Hwang, 2000; Gerstley et al., 1989; Luborsky, McLellan, Woody, O'Brien, & Auerbach, 1985; Tunis, Deluchi, Schwartz, Banys, & Sees, 1995) might represent such a distinct group. These six studies have a combined ES of .14 and N of 985. Some of these research studies used unique alliance measures (Broome, 1996) and somewhat atypical outcome indices (e.g., drug use, recidivism). The Q statistic without the substance abuse studies in the data set was recomputed; this subset of the data ($N = 86$) was homogeneous. The averaged ES (weighted) of these studies is larger: ES = .23 ($SD = .13$). However, the subset of six substance abuse studies themselves were not homogeneous. Drawing conclusions on the bases of these analy-

Table 3.1. Ninety-Outcome Effect Sizes (1976–2000)

Study	Treatment		Alliance			Outcome			
	Sessions	Type	Rater	Measure	Time	Measure	Rater	ES	N
Adler (1988)	12	Various	C, T	WAI HAq CIS	E, L	TC SCL-90 Self-Esteem Index Inventory of Interpersonal Problems Posttherapy Questionnaire Posttherapy Questionnaire	C C C C C T	0.28	44
Allen et al. (1985)	*	Inpatient	T	ITAS	E, L, A	Overall Outcome GAS Composite Outcome	T T T	0.41	37
Allen et al. (1986)	*	Inpatient	T	ITAS	L, A	Premature Termination	C	0.4	37
Andreoli et al. (1993)	6	Crisis Intervention	T	ITAS	E	Overall Outcome Specific Outcomes Interpersonal Functioning	T T T	0.35	31
Andreoli et al. (1993)	16	Crisis Intervention	T	ITAS	E	Global Change Symptom Severity Specific Outcome Interpersonal Functioning	O O O O	0.24	31
Ankuta (1992)	30	Various	O	CALPAS	E, M, L	SCL-90	C	0.02	44
Barber et al. (1999)	20	Various	C, T C, T	HAq-II CALPAS	E, M E, M	GSI Addiction Severity Index BDI	C C C	0.05	252
Barkham et al. (1993)	12	Interpersonal	O	CALPAS	E	Overall Outcome	C	0.32	12
Bieschke et al. (1995)	7	Various	C	WAI	L	Change in Distress	C	0.3	90
Broome (1996)	46	Drug Counseling, Methadone	C	3-item Alliance Scale	M	Premature Termination Drug Use	C C	0.1	501

(continued)

Table 3.1. (Continued)

Study	Treatment		Alliance			Outcome			N
	Sessions	Type	Rater	Measure	Time	Measure	Rater	ES	
Card (1991)	6	Cognitive-Behavioral	O	CALPAS	E, M, L	STAI BDI HRSD GSI	C C O C	0.07	55
Castonguay et al. (1996)	15	Cognitive, Medication	O	WAI	M	BDI HRSD GAS	C O O	0.49	30
Cislo (1988)	10	Various	C	HAq	A	Sessional Impacts	C	0.3	47
Clarkin et al. (1987)	*	Inpatient Psychiatric Unit	O	ITAS	A	GAS	O	0.39	96
Crits-Christoph et al. (1988)	54	Dynamic	O	HACs	E	Composite Outcome Residual Gain	C, T C, O	0.34	43
Eaton et al. (1988)	*	Various	O	TARS	A	Overall Outcome SCL-90	C, T C	0	40
Feeley (1993)	12	Cognitive	O	HAr	A	BDI	C	0.4	25
Ferleger (1993)	41	Dynamic	O	CALPAS	E	GSI TC Social Adjustment	C C C	0.09	40
Florsheim et al. (2000)	90–100 days	Various (in residential treatment)	C, T	WAI	E, M	Drug Use Teachers' Report Form Youth Self-Report Form Recidivism	C O C O	0.12	78
Forman (1990)	6	Rehabilitation	C, T	WAI	M, L	Global Outcome	C, T	0.27	96
Frank & Gunderson (1990)	56	Various	T	ITAS	M	Premature Termination Specific Symptoms Overall Outcome Symptom Severity Social Relations	C C, O C, O C, O C, O	0.31	143
Gallop et al. (1994)	10	Inpatient Eating Disorders Unit	C, T	WAI	E	Premature Termination	C	0.13	31

Study	Length	Type		Measure	Time	Outcome		ES	N
Gaston et al. (1991)	18	Various	C, T	CALPAS	E, M, L	BDI	C	0.15	54
Gaston et al. (1994)	49	Dynamic	O	CALPAS	A	Depression-Anxiety	O	0.15	32
						Interpersonal Behaviors Scale	C		
Gaston et al. (1998)	18	Various	O	CALPAS	A	BDI	C	0.17	91
						HRSD	C		
Gerstley et al. (1989)	48	Various	C, T	HAq	E	Addictive Severity Index	O	0.27	48
Gomes-Schwartz (1978)	18	Various	O	VPPS	A	Overall Ratings	T, O	0.16	35
						MMPI Maladjustment	C		
						TC	C, T, O		
Greenberg & Webster (1982)	6	Gestalt	C	WAI	E	Scale of Indecision	C	0.62	31
						STAI	C		
						TC	C, T		
Grob & Eisen (1989)	19 weeks	Inpatient	O	ITAS	E, M, L	Overall Improvement	T	0.41	60
Gunderson et al. (1997)	Various	Various	C, T	HAq	E, M, L	SCL-90	C	0.02	33
						Social Adjustment	C		
						GAS	C		
Gunther (1992)	15	Various	O	CALPAS	E, L	SCL-90	C	0.25	41
Gutfreund (1992)	29	Various	O	CALPAS	A	SCL-90	C	0.16	46
						Dynamic outcome	T		
Hansson & Berglund (1992)	4 weeks	Inpatient	C	ITAS	E, L	SCL-90	C, O	0.09	106
						CPRS	C, O		
						DTES	O		
						TC	C		
Hartley & Strupp (1983)	18	Various	O	VTAS	A	Composite Gain Scale	C, T, O	0.15	28
Hatcher & Barends (1996)	51	Dynamic	C	CALPAS HAq WAI	Various	Improvement to Date	C	0.14	229
Hays (1994)	6	Various	C, T	WAI	E	Global Outcome	C, T	0.3	29
						Personal Growth	C		
						Relations with Others	C		

(continued)

45

Table 3.1. (Continued)

Study	Treatment		Alliance			Outcome			
	Sessions	Type	Rater	Measure	Time	Measure	Rater	ES	N
Hilliard et al. (2000)	25	Dynamic	C, T, O	SASB Intrex	M	Interject–best	C	0.16	64
						Interject–worst	C		
						GSI	C		
						Global Outcome	C		
						Global Outcome	T		
						Global Outcome	O		
Hopkins (1988)	12	Various	C, T	WAI	E	SCL-90	C	0.25	15
Horowitz et al. (1984)	12	Dynamic	O	TARS	A	SCL-90	C	0.05	52
						PICS	O		
Horvath (1981)	10	Various	C, T	WAI	E	Posttherapy Questionnaire	C, T	0.47	29
Joyce & Piper (1998)	20	Dynamic	C, T	non-standardized scale	A	General Symptoms	C, T, O	0.26	64
						Individual Objectives	C, T, O		
						Social-Sexual Adjustment	C, T, O		
Jumes (1995)	28 weeks	Inpatient, Medication	C	WAI	E	BPRS	O	0.28	121
						GAS	O		
Kivlighan & Shaughnessy (1995)	12	Various	C, T	WAI	E, M, L	Interpersonal Problems	C	0.17	21
Klee, Abeles, & Muller (1990)	29	Various	O	TARS	E	SCL-90	C	0.23	32
						Global Outcome	C		
Kokotovic & Tracey (1990)	4	Various	C, T	WAI	E	Premature Termination	C	0.09	121
Kolden (1996)	4	Dynamic	C	TBS	E	Mental Health Index	C	0.22	60
Krupnick et al. (1994)	16	Various	O	VTAS	E, A	Global Outcome	C, O	0.15	56
Krupnick et al. (1996)	16	Various	O	VTAS	E, A	HRSD	O	0.3	225
						BDI	C		
Lansford (1986)	12	Dynamic	O	AWR	A	Global Outcome	C, T, O	0.89	6

Study		Treatment		Alliance Measure		Outcome		r	N
Lieberman et al. (1992)	*	Acute Inpatient	C, T	ITGA	E	Symptom Improvement	C	0.1	48
			C	EH	E	GAS	C		
						Premature Termination	C		
						Defense Style	C		
						Self-Esteem Index	C		
Luborsky et al. (1983)	52	Dynamic	O	HAcs	E, L, A	Rated Benefits	C, T	0.42	20
			O	HAr		Residual Gain	C, O		
						Success, Satisfaction, & Improvement	T		
						TC	C		
Luborsky et al. (1985)	14	Various	C	HAq	E	Drug Use	O	0.61	77
						Employment Status	O		
						Legal Status	O		
						Psychological Factors	O		
Mallinckrodt (1993)	12	Various	C, T	WAI	E	Global Outcome	C, T	0.36	61
Mallinckrodt (1996)	15	Brief Interpersonal	C	WAI	E	GSI	O	0.32	34
Marmar, Gaston et al. (1989)	18	Various	C, T	CALPAS	E	BDI	C	0.2	54
Marmar, Weiss, & Gaston (1989)	12	Dynamic	O	CALTARS	A	Patterns of Individual Change Scores	C	0.07	32
						SCL-90	C		
Marshel (1986)	50	Dynamic	C	HAq	E	Premature Termination	C	−0.06	101
			C	TARS	E				
			C	Other	E				
Marziali (1984)	20	Dynamic	C, T, O	TARS	A	Behavioral Symptom Index	C	0.14	42
						Social Adjustment	O		
						Global Outcome	C, T		
Marziali et al. (1981)	12	Dynamic	O	TARS	A	Composite Outcome	C, O	0.45	10
Marziali et al. (1999)	30	Dynamic	C	Therapist behaviors (one subscale of TAS)	E, L	Social Adjustment Scale	C	0.39	18
						BDI	C		
						Object Behaviour Index	C		
						SCL-90	C		
Mohl et al. (1991)	*	Various	C	HAq	E	Premature Termination	C	0.3	80

(continued)

Table 3.1. (Continued)

Study	Treatment		Alliance			Outcome			
	Sessions	Type	Rater	Measure	Time	Measure	Rater	ES	N
Morgan et al. (1982)	52	Dynamic	O	HAr	E, A	Composite Outcome Rated Benefits	C, T, O T	0.5	20
Moseley (1983)	14	Various	C	WAI	E	STAI Self-Concept TC Posttherapy Questionnaire	C C C C	0.28	25
Muran et al. (1995)	20	Cognitive	C	CALPAS	A	SCL-90 Interpersonal Problems GAS TC Overall Outcome	C C T C, T C, T	0.28	53
Ogrodniczuk et al. (2000)	20	Interpretive, Supportive	C, T	non-standardized scale	A	General Symptoms Individual Objectives Social-Sexual Adjustment	C, T, O C, T, O C, T, O	0.07	144
O'Malley et al. (1983)	*	Various	O	VPPS	E	Overall Outcome TC	C, T, O C, T, O	0.39	38
Paivio & Bahr (1998)	12	Experiential	C	WAI	E, L	GSI SASB Introject Unfinished Business Scale	C C C	0.27	33
Piper et al. (1991)	19	Dynamic	C, T	AAS	A	Composite Outcome	C, T, O	0.35	64
Piper et al. (1995)	19	Dynamic	C, T	AAS	A	STAI BDI SCL-90 Overall Usefulness	C C C C, T	0.43	30
Priebe & Gruyters (1993)	20 months	Case management	C	BAS	E	Hospitalization Index Work Axis Accomodation Axis	O O O	0.25	72
Prigatano et al. (1994)	6 months	Neuropsychology Rehabilitation	T	NAS	L	Productivity	O	0.4	37
Pugh (1991)	12	Various	C, T	WAI	E	BSI TC	C C, T	0.18	55

(continued)

Study	Sessions	Treatment	Design	Alliance	Type	Outcome	Source	r	N
Pyne (1991)	6	Various	T	HAr	A	Global Outcome	C, T, O	0.34	29
			O	VPPS	A	Premature Termination	C		
Reiner (1987)	*	Dynamic	C	TBS	E	Overall Outcome	O	0.4	82
Riley (1992)	8	Various	C, T	WAI	E, L	SCL-90	C	0.17	61
			C, T	CALPAS	E, L	TC	C, T		
					T	GAS	T		
Rounsaville et al. (1987)	14	Interpersonal	O	VPPS	E	Schedule for Affective Disorders	O	0.21	35
						Social Adjustment	O		
						Patient Self-Assessment	C		
Safran & Wallner (1991)	20	Cognitive	C	WAI	E	SCL-90	C	0.4	22
			C	CALPAS	E	MCMI	C		
						BDI			
						Global Success	C, T		
						TC	C, T		
Saunders et al. (1989)	26	Dynamic	C	TBS	E	SEQ	C	0.4	113
						Termination Outcome	O		
Sexton (1996)	10	Various	C	WAI-S	E	BOPS	O	0.3	27
						Beck Anxiety Scale	C		
						Social Adjustment	O		
						GAS	O		
						BSI	C		
						Zung	C		
						Global Problem Rating	C		
Solomon et al. (1995)	2 years	Case Management	C, T	WAI	L	Quality of Life	C	0.09	82
						Medication Compliance	C		
						Satisfaction with Treatment	C		
						Other Variables	C, O		
Sonnenberg (1996)	11	Inpatient	C, T	ITAS	E	SCL-90	C	0.03	71
Svartberg & Stiles (1994)	20	Dynamic	C	FAI	M	SCL-90	C	0.36	13
						DAS	C		

Table 3.1. (Continued)

Study	Treatment		Alliance			Outcome			
	Sessions	Type	Rater	Measure	Time	Measure	Rater	ES	N
Tichenor (1989)	16	Various	C, T, O	WAI	A	SCL-90	C	0.16	8
			O	CALPAS	A	Self Concept	C		
			O	HAr	A	TC	C, T		
			O	VTAS	A	HRSD	O		
						HRSA	O		
Tryon & Kane (1990)	19	Various	C, T	HAq	M	Premature Termination	C	0.15	102
Tryon & Kane (1993)	13	Various	C, T	WAI-S	E	Premature Termination	C	0.14	91
Tryon & Kane (1995)	10	Various	C, T	WAI-S	E	Premature Termination	C	0.22	89
Tunis et al. (1995)	180 days	Methadone Detox	C	CALPAS	E, M, L	Premature Termination	C	0.08	29
					A	Opioid Use	C		
						HIV Risk Behaviors	C		
Windholz & Silberschatz (1988)	16	Dynamic	O	VPPS	M	SCL-90	C	0.12	38
						Overall Change	C, T, O		
						TC	C, T, O		
						GAS	T, O		
Yeomans et al. (1994)	230	Dynamic	O	CALPAS	E	Premature Termination	C	0.08	20
Zuroff et al. (2000)	12	Various	O	VTAS	L	DAS	C	0.06	149
						Composite	C		

Note: Data based on Horvath & Symonds (1991), Martin (1998), plus additional research by the authors.

Raters: C = client, T = therapist, O = other

Time: E = early alliance, M = middle alliance, L = late alliance, A = average alliance

Alliance Measures: HAr = Penn Helping Alliance Rating Scale, HAq = Helping Alliance Questionnaire, HAcs = Helping Alliance Counting Signs, VTAS = Vanderbilt Therapeutic Alliance Rating Scale, VPPS = Vanderbilt Psychotherapy Process Scale, TARS = Therapeutic Alliance Rating Scale, WAI = Working Alliance Inventory, WAI-S = Working Alliance Inventory-short version, CALPAS = California Psychotherapy Alliance Scale, CALTARS = California Therapeutic Alliance Rating Scale, TBS = Therapeutic Bond Scale, ITAS = various inpatient therapeutic alliance scales, AWR = Alliance Weakenings and Repairs, ITGA = Inpatient Task and Goal Agreement, CIS = Client Involvement Scale, EH = Patient expectation of helpfulness, AAS = Alberta Alliance Scale, BAS = Berlin Alliance Scale, NAS = Neuropsychology Alliance Scale, FAI = Facilitative Alliance Inventory, SASB = Structural Analysis of Social Behavior, TAS = Therapeutic Alliance Scale. Outcome Measures: BDI = Beck Depression Inventory, BOPS = Brief Outpatient Psychopathology Inventory, BPRS = Brief Psychiatric Rating Scale, CPRS = Comprehensive Psychopathological Rating Scale, DAS = Dysfunctional Attitudes Scale, DTES = Drug Taking Evaluation Scale, GAS = Global Assessment Scale, HRSA = Hamilton Rating Scale for Anxiety, HRSD = Hamilton Rating Scale for Depression, PICS = Pattern of Individual Change Scores, SCL-90 = Symptom Checklist 90, SEQ = Session Quality Scale, STAI = State-Trait Anxiety Inventory, Zung = Zung's Self-Rating of Depression, TC = Target Complaints, BSI = Brief Symptom Index, GSI = Global Severity Index.

Treatment Sessions: * = various length.

ses is premature, but these results suggest that variation across distinct client/problem characteristics certainly warrants further investigation.

Potential Moderators of the Alliance-Outcome Relation

Measures

As noted before, in practice, the alliance measures operationally define the alliance in empirical investigations. There are some expected differences in the magnitudes of the alliance-outcome relation depending on the measure used. Among the more commonly used scales, the alliance-outcome relation was strongest for HA (.27), VTAS/VPPS (.24), and WAI (.24), followed by the CALPAS (.17) and TAS (.17). These instruments account for approximately 70% of the ESs we report. The remaining "other" instruments form a heterogeneous group; the average relation to outcome of these measures is .24. The differences among these relations are not statistically significant; therefore, the impact of these differences on the overall alliance-outcome relation is limited.

Sources of Data

While the alliance is understood to involve collaboration and mutuality, it is *not* a symmetrical relationship. Therapists' responsibilities are different from those of clients, and therapists' phenomenological experience of the relationship is contextualized by their theoretical perspectives and clinical experience. The client's felt experience in therapy is not only the result of the dialectical experience in the therapy room, but is also construed in the light of past relational history. Thus, the link between the alliance and therapeutic efficacy from each of these perspectives throws light on a qualitatively different aspect of the phenomenon. Observers rating the alliance have only inferential information on either of the participants' perspectives; however, they are privy to moment-to-moment behaviors associated with presence or strengthening of the alliance and can gather evidence of objectively verifiable utterances relevant to the status of the alliance. It appears, therefore, that the observer/rater perceptive is not only distinct with respect to the evidence it is based on, but is an aggregation of formative, stochastic aspects of the alliance, in contrast to the participant's report, which is summative. Reports on therapy outcome similarly rely on evidence gathered from these three different perspectives. For the above reasons we have disaggregated the research data in order to look at the alliance-outcome relation from each of these distinct perspectives.

The data in table 3.2 are based on 100 ESs (weighted by sample size) that have been extracted from 60 investigations from which we could confidently obtain ESs specific to one or more combinations of these perspectives. (Some studies yielded more than one ES in the table.) Without regard to the source of the outcome ratings, client- and observer-rated alliance have a similar relation to outcome; therapist-rated alliance and outcome appear to be somewhat less related. Figure 3.1 is a box-and-whisker plot, a visual representation of the relationship of the distributions showing that each of the distributions is overlapping. (Conventional tests of significance are inappropriate to evaluate these relations, since neither the data in the cells nor the marginal values are independent.) In our analysis, without considering the source of the alliance rating, therapist-rated outcome was marginally more related to alliance, followed by observer and client outcome indexes. However, the three distributions were very similar.

Is There a Halo Effect?

The majority of the data in the alliance literature is based on self-report. An important issue in assessing the validity of this body of research is that the relation between alliance and outcome may be exaggerated due to the possibility that the same source of assessment for both the process measure (alliance) and the outcome would inflate the magnitude of the reported ES. The diagonal of table 3.2 represents the "same-source" ESs, while the off-diagonal cells provide all the combinations of process outcome relations that are based on different sources. The average ES of off-diagonal cells was .19 ($n = 59$), which is less than the averaged same-source cells ESs .21 ($n = 41$).

Table 3.2. Effect Sizes (ESs) Sorted by Alliance and Outcome Raters (N = 100 ES)

Outcome Rater	Alliance Rater			
	Client	Therapist	Other	Marginal
Client				
ES	.21	.10	.18	.17
SD	.16	.11	.13	.16
No. of ESs	27	12	17	56
Therapist				
ES	.23	.25	.19	.26
SD	.24	.23	.20	.22
No. of ESs	7	7	6	20
Other				
ES	.26	.19	.39	.24
SD	.15	.16	.19	.15
No. of ESs	10	7	7	24
Marginals				
ES	.22	.15	.22	
SD	.17	.17	.22	
No. of ESs	44	26	30	

The difference between these values is very small indeed, and the two distributions of ESs overlap considerably. These results replicate the conclusion reached by previous analyses (Horvath & Symonds, 1991; Martin, 1998) that the results of these studies do not appear to be biased by a halo factor.

Differential Relations

While the overall relation between alliance and outcome is, of itself, informative, we have examined three specific relations within this larger framework: Is there evidence that alliance measured early in therapy is related to outcome differently than mid-session or over-time (averaged) alliance? Is there evidence that therapists' training affects the alliance–outcome relation? Is there evidence that treatments based on different theoretical assumptions differ in the degree of relation between alliance and outcome?

Time of Alliance Assessment

The majority of the ESs are based on the alliance measured early (between sessions 1–5, or within the first third of treatment). The average ES for these 130 results was .22. The average ES of alliance, measured in midphase of therapy, on outcome was .19 (N = 38), while late alliance correlated with outcome .25 (N = 42). When alliance was measured at multiple occasions and was averaged across treatment, the relation with outcome was .27 (N = 68). The pattern of relations is theoretically interesting; early alliance is a marginally better predictor than midtherapy alliance. Possibly the stress and strain of working through difficult issues has a dampening effect on this value. The higher late alliance figure is likely the result of contamination with therapy benefits. As some studies contributed multiple ESs to this analysis, the data are not independent; therefore the statistical significance of these differences cannot be

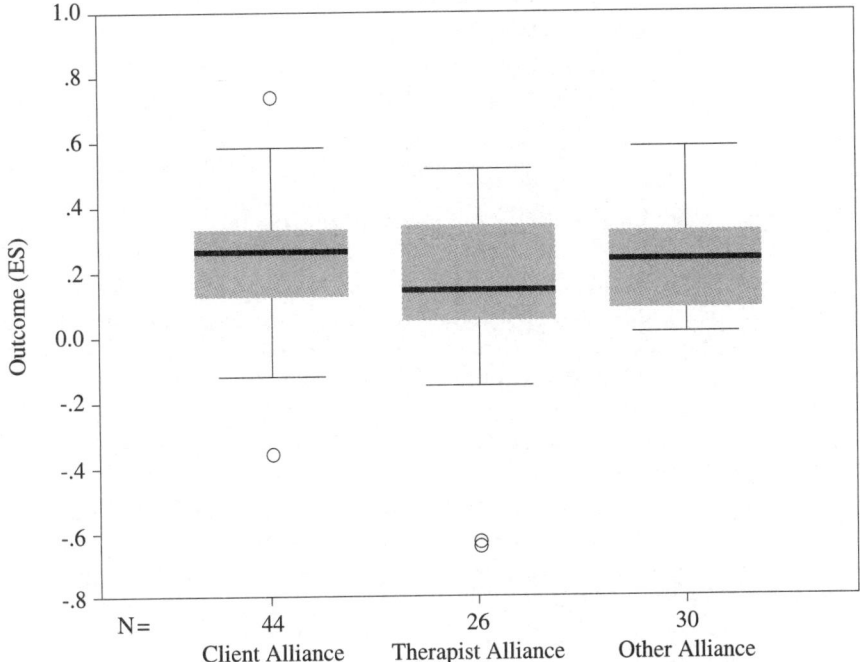

Figure 3.1. Box-and-Whisker Plots of Alliance Outcome Relations (ES) Based on Clients', Therapists', and Observers' Alliance Ratings. Note: O and ⊖ Indicate Outliers.

tested directly. However, later in this chapter we will evaluate the studies where specific comparisons between early and late assessments were available.

Professional Training

Treatment was offered by therapists with a range of training and experience; it was not always possible to differentiate these two variables. The following categories of helpers were specified in sufficient numbers of research reports to summarize the relation between their levels of alliance-outcome correlation and professional categories: psychologists' ES .16 ($N = 17$), other professionals' ES .24 ($N = 71$), and case managers' ES .19 ($N = 2$). These relations are not statistically different ($p > .05$). In addition to data relating to the overall impact of training, there are data from studies that examined the potential impact of training within a particular investigation. These issues will

be taken up later in the discussion of therapists' moderators.

Type of Treatment

Treatment specifications are not standardized in this body of research. To investigate differences across different treatments, we used a conservative grouping that appeared to represent clearly distinctive therapy experiences. Ten studies reported alliance with case managers; the mean ES of these reports was .11. The mean relation between alliance and outcome of 68 studies where some variant of dynamic therapy was used was .23. The remaining ESs were combined under the label "various" and yielded an ES of .22 ($N = 113$). Although the magnitude of these relations showed a substantial range, the differences do not reach statistical significance ($p > .05$). We suspect that at least part of the reason for this result was the lack of homogeneity within these broad categories. Additionally, the type of treatment is very likely confounded with the severity of clients' difficulties. A person treated by a case manager is more likely to experience chronic problems than one receiving short-term dynamic therapy.

MEDIATORS AND MODERATORS

Compared to the numbers of studies examining the links between alliance and outcome, there is less research on factors that mediate or moderate the alliance in therapy; these investigations are also more recent. Researchers have cast a wide net monitoring a broad range of variables with possible relation to alliance; there are relatively few investigations of any specific variable. None of the investigations reviewed offers a prospective as opposed to a retrospective outlook. As a consequence, the review that follows will deal mostly with emergent evidence. Since studies relevant to each specific factor are relatively few, and since the way a variable is operationalized varies across research reports, in this part of the chapter no attempt will be made to numerically synthesize the effect sizes. Rather, the specific studies (and/ or the number of studies) reporting empirical support for a particular relation will be noted. In order to better focus these results, closely linked moderating variables will be discussed under overarching headings.

Client Factors

Client factors that moderate or mediate the alliance will be discussed under two headings: pretherapy variables, that is, experiences, skills, and capacities the client brings to the therapy situation; and clients' in-therapy contributions to the alliance.

Pretherapy Severity of Impairment

There have been a number of investigations of the impact of the severity of the client's disorder on the subsequent development of the alliance in therapy. The findings are somewhat mixed; some reports indicated that more severely disturbed clients have poorer alliances (Gaston, Thompson, Gallager, Cournoyer, & Gagnon, 1998; Yeomans

et al., 1994; Zuroff et al., 2000), while others found little or no difference between more or less severely damaged clients (Gaston, Marmar, Gallager, & Thompson, 1990; Joyce & Piper, 1998; Lieberman, von Rehn, Dickie, Elliott, & Egerter, 1992; Lingiardi, Croce, Fossati, Vanzulli, & Maffei, 2000; Orlinsky, Grawe, & Parks, 1994; Paivio & Bahr, 1998).

It seems that the diversity of findings is linked to four factors. First, the research literature is dominated by reports based on mildly disturbed clients. Second, when reports are available on more severely disturbed clients, such as hospital inpatients, the data do not include contrasting groups of less severely impaired clients; thus the range of severity is still restricted. Third, there are four reports indicating that there is an interaction among the therapist's level of experience, severity of impairment, and quality of alliance, alliance with more difficult clients, but not with less severely handicapped clients (Hayes, 1995; Kivlighan, Patton, & Foote, 1998; Mallinckrodt & Nelson, 1991; Paivio & Bahr, 1998; Rounsaville et al., 1987). Last, there is evidence that clients with poor alliance are more likely to drop out early in therapy (Mohl, Martinez, Ticknor, Huang, & Cordell, 1991; Plotnicov, 1990; Tryon & Kane, 1990, 1993; Yeomans et al., 1994). Therefore it is possible that the relatively weak overall relation between severity and strength of the alliance is, in part, due to the early loss of the more severe cases.

Type of Disorder

There are some reports linking specific psychological problems with difficulties developing the therapeutic alliance. Clients with borderline and other personality disorders, either as the main diagnosis or as a comorbid feature, present a particularly challenging task (Andreoli et al., 1993; Hersoug, Monsen, Havik, & Høglend, 2001b; Lingiardi et al., 2000; Muran et al., 1995). Zuroff and colleagues (2000) report that client alliance has a moderating effect, independent of other aspects of the relationship, between perfectionism and premature termination. Difficulty in developing alliances has also been reported with delinquents, homeless individuals, and some drug-dependent populations (Barber et al., 1999;

Florsheim et al., 2000; Gunderson, Najavits, Leonhard, Sullivan, & Sabo, 1997; Hersoug et al., 2000). However, the challenge of developing an alliance with this group of clients may be confounded by health, legal, economic, and social problems.

Object Relations and Attachment Style

The impact of a client's prior relational experiences, particularly in formative years, has been a subject of a growing number of investigations (Hersoug et al., 2000; Hilliard, Henry, & Strupp, 2000; Kivlighan et al., 1998; Mallinckrodt, 1992, 1996, 2000; Paivio & Bahr, 1998). The most frequently studied variable in this realm has been the quality of the client's object relations (e.g., Piper et al., 1991, 1995) and introject (Henry & Strupp, 1994; Hersoug et al., 2000), closely followed in volume by research on social skills and social support (Mallinckrodt, 1992, 1996; Piper et al., 1991; Piper, DeCarufel, & Szkrumelack, 1985).

There is conflicting evidence on the magnitude of impact of clients' early relational experiences (Hersoug et al., 2001a; Mallinckrodt, 1992); however, there is a confluence of data suggesting that the quality of the alliance as reported by the client in the early phases of therapy is impacted by the quality their attachment style (Eames & Roth, 2000; Hilliard et al., 2000; Joyce & Piper, 1998; Mallinckrodt & Leong, 1992; Ogrodniczuk, Piper, Joyce, & McCallum, 2000; Rubino, Baker, Roth, & Fearon, 2000; Tyrrel et al., 1999). In particular, fearful, anxious, dismissive, and preoccupied styles are correlated with poor initial alliances (Eames & Roth, 2000; Ogrodniczuk et al., 2000; Rubino et al., 2000; Tyrrel et al., 1999).

In-Therapy Variables

Alliance Across Phases of Therapy

There is evidence indicating that establishing a strong alliance early in therapy is important. Alliance measured between the third and fifth session has proven to be a consistent predictor of final therapy outcome (Barber et al., 1999; Castonguay, Goldfried, Wiser, Raue, & Hayes, 1996;

Gaston et al., 1998; Hersoug et al., 2000; Horvath & Symonds, 1991; Krupnick et al., 1996; Sexton, 1996). A number of investigators who compared early and mid-phase alliance assessment as predictor of outcome *within the study* report better outcome prediction based on early rather than later alliance (Barber et al., 1999; Castonguay et al., 1996; Gaston et al., 1998; Hersoug et al., 2001a; Joyce & Piper, 1998; Krupnick et al., 1996; Sexton, 1996), but one study reported the opposite result (Florsheim et al., 2000). Two studies examined the relation of alliance measurements taken at different phases of therapy (Crits-Christoph, Cooper, & Luborsky, 1988; Gaston, Piper, Debbane, Bienvenu, & Garant, 1994). They report that correlation between alliance taken at different times was not significant.

There are reports suggesting that the strength of the alliance at intake or after the first session is a good predictor of premature termination (Barber et al., 1999; Mohl et al., 1991; Plotnicov, 1990; Tryon & Kane, 1993). However, two reports have been published recently which suggest that in some situations high initial alliance, perhaps representing unrealistically high initial expectation, may be related to poor outcome and premature termination. These studies suggest that a somewhat lower but gradually increasing alliance, indicating more realistic expectations, is a more positive outcome predictor (Florsheim et al., 2000; Joyce & Piper, 1998).

Gelso and Carter (1994) hypothesized that successful treatment would typically have a U-shaped (high-low-high) alliance curve, beginning with the establishment of a strong opening relationship, followed by deterioration of this "honeymoon" due to the therapist's increasing focus on the client's dysfunctional relational schemas that surface in the sessions. Toward the end of treatment, a stronger, positive relationship is reestablished. This hypothesis was examined by Kivlighan and Shaughnessy (1995, 2000), and the results are mixed. The U-shaped alliance pattern for successful short-term therapies was not supported, but an increasing alliance pattern appeared as a good prognosticator of positive outcome in brief dynamic therapy. However, the "shape" of a productive alliance over time is far from settled. Some researchers found "flat" as opposed to "sloping" alliance paths positive (Bachelor & Salamé, 2000; Krupnick et al., 1996), while others observed a good fit between a quadratic pattern of alliance and positive outcome in time-limited therapy (Horvath & Marx, 1991).

Raters' Perspective

The majority of early investigators obtained better predictions of outcome based on clients' than therapists' reports and noted significant differences between clients' and therapists' ratings. However, some more recent studies suggest that therapists' assessment of the alliance becomes a better predictor of outcome later in therapy (Hersoug et al., 2000; Kivlighan & Shaughnessy, 1995; Yeomans et al., 1994). Moreover, while earlier analyses suggested that the client's alliance was a uniformly superior outcome predictor than the therapist's, and that therapists' ratings showed poor correlation with clients' (Horvath & Symonds, 1991), more recent investigations monitoring the clients' and therapists' assessment at different phases of therapy found that as therapy progresses, clients' and therapists' assessments become more similar. Further, the degree of similarity between therapist and client alliance rating in mid- and late phases of therapy was positively related to outcome (Gunderson et al., 1997; Hersoug et al., 2000).

Taken together, these findings make clinical sense. When therapy begins, clients respond globally to the therapy experience driven by their own need for safety and desire to actively engage with the therapeutic opportunities the therapist offers. The sense of "being listened to" and "understood," the feeling of a shared purpose (goal), and active collaboration by positive engagement with the therapeutic activities in the session are critical for the client (Diamond, Liddle, Houge, and Dakof, 1999; Jennings & Skovholt, 1999; Lichenberg et al., 1988; Strupp, 1998; Tryon & Kane, 1993). Without these needs being adequately met, there is a risk of early disengagement or the dominance of conflicting feelings about the therapy. The therapist, on the other hand, evaluates the quality of the emerging alliance in light of the theoretical premises of her or his particular orientation. These premises translate to expectations of the kinds of ways a "good" client ought

to respond to therapy (Hersoug et al., 2000). Supporting these hypotheses are the reports indicating that therapists' alliance scores show greater variability than clients' (Hersoug et al., 2000; Kivlighan & Shaughnessy, 1995). Under these circumstances we would expect initial differences between the client's and the therapist's assessment of the quality of the alliance, and it seems logical that, if the client has failed to perceive the relationship as adequate, premature termination or poor outcome would be likely.

Therapist Contributions to the Alliance

Compared to the amount of research available on client moderating or mediating variables, research on the impact of therapist qualities or contributions is less abundant. The available research suggests that the therapist's abilities or qualities that contribute to the development of a good working alliance can be divided into three broad facets: an interpersonal skill component, the intrapersonal element, and interactive components. As was the case with client variables reviewed above, the empirical evidence is based on retrospective, rather than prospective designs, and there is considerable heterogeneity across studies in the way the therapist variables are operationalized. For these reasons the evidence is grouped into conceptually meaningful clusters and the evidence, including specific investigations, is reviewed rather than numerically summed across studies. Moreover, the research on the relation between many of these variables and therapy outcome will be reviewed in detail in subsequent chapters. In the interest of economy and to avoid redundancy, the following review will focus on the relation between these therapist variables and the alliance only.

Interpersonal Skills

The interpersonal dimension is grounded and expressed in the emerging realities of the therapy session. The possession and expression of these skills by the therapist amounts to the capacity to express sensitivity to the client's needs. It results in the therapist expressed responsiveness and the ability to generate a sense of hope. These skills also contribute to the therapist's ability to respond to the challenges represented by the emergence of dysfunctional relationship schemas, negative expectations, and other sources of ruptures and misunderstandings as they occur in therapy (Safran & Muran, 2000; Safran, Muran, Samstag, & Stevens, chap. 12 in this volume).

Communication-Related Skills

Evidence of positive contribution of the therapist's ability to maintain open and clear communication and the quality of the alliance are offered by Kolden (1996), Mohl et al. (1991), Priebe and Gruyters (1993), and Rounsaville et al. (1987). The links between alliance and the therapist's ability to convey understanding or appreciation of the client's phenomenological perspective are supported by several investigators (Bachelor, 1988; Castonguay & Goldfried, 1994; Diamond et al., 1999; Rounsaville et al., 1987; Tryon & Kane, 1993; Windholz & Silberschatz, 1988).

Empathy

Communicated empathy appears to be a contributor to the alliance in general and to the interpersonal bonds between therapist and client in particular. The empirical evidence supporting this relation is complex because some researchers use empathy measures (such as the B-L Relationship Inventory; Barrett-Lennard, 1978) to make inferences about the alliance itself. It seems, however, that the alliance is a broader concept and, when empathy is assessed independently, alliance makes an additional contribution to predicting the outcome of therapy (Zuroff et al., 2000). However, what is empathic for one client might appear to be intrusive to another. Consequently it seems that therapists' ability to place themselves in the client's position is mediated by sensitivity to the client's preference and tolerance of expressions of intimate support of this kind (Lichenberg et al., 1988; Mohl et al., 1991; Windholz & Silberschatz, 1988). To build a good interpersonal bond, therapists need to be able not only to accept and appreciate the client's world, but also to individualize the expression of this understanding and support to suit the client's relationship stance (Bachelor & Horvath, 1999; Bohart, Elliott, Greenberg, & Watson, chap. 5 in this volume).

Openness and Exploration

A number of investigations report positive links between therapist's openness and exploration (Mohl et al., 1991; Priebe & Gruyters, 1993; Rounsaville et al., 1987; Tyrrel et al., 1999). These relations are most often observed in the early phases of treatment. On the opposite side of the coin, Lichenberg and colleagues (1988) report that therapists' "relational control" (taking charge of the session) is negatively correlated with alliance; positive outcome is related to client control.

Experience and Training

The research evidence on the value of the level of the therapists training and experience in relation to alliance is equivocal. Friedlander and her coworkers (Dunkle & Friedlander, 1996) found that experience was not related to the quality of the alliance, while others have reported partial support for such relationship (Bein et al., 2000; Kivlighan et al., 1998; Mallinckrodt & Nelson, 1991). Hersoug (2000, 2001a, 2001b) reports negative correlation between alliance and training but positive correlation with a measure of therapist skill. Perhaps the answer to the seemingly conflicting findings lies in a recent study which found that clients with difficulty forming intimate relationships have stronger alliances with more experienced counselors, while less relationally handicapped patients did not respond differentially to levels of experience (Kivlighan et al., 1998). Another piece of the puzzle may be the finding that experienced therapists are better at identifying deteriorating or poor alliances (Mallinckrodt & Nelson, 1991). The ability to better detect the clients' relational problems in therapy enables these therapists to build and repair their alliances with these difficult clients more efficiently; however, this increased efficacy does not show up in research involving only the less relationally impaired patients.

Negative Therapist Behaviors

There is emerging evidence linking some therapist activities and qualities to poor or deteriorating alliance. These are a "take-charge" attitude in the early phase of therapy (Lichenberg et al., 1988); a therapist whom clients perceive as "cold" (Hersoug et al., 2000); insight or interpretation offered prematurely (Henry et al., 1994); and therapist irritability (Sexton, 1996).

The Intrapersonal Dimension

The therapist participates in the therapeutic relationship as a person and, as such, is vulnerable to experiencing negative or hostile emotions triggered by interaction with certain types of clients or in response to particular interpersonal transactions. Evidence of such dynamics will surface in the form of a therapist's negative or hostile responses to a specific client, or as a negative therapist response triggered by certain kinds of interpersonal challenges in therapy.

There are a number of studies where the relation between a variety of therapist qualities (e.g., attachment, temperament) and alliance was monitored incidentally (Hersoug et al., 2001a, 2001b; Sexton, 1996). The evidence from these studies has yet to converge meaningfully. However, there is one investigation where this question was investigated at a significant depth. Although the result of a single study is insufficient to claim empirical support, we feel that the importance of the topic warrants a discussion.

At the conclusion of the original Vanderbilt study (Strupp & Binder, 1984), Strupp and colleagues shifted the focus of their investigation from specific techniques related to dynamic therapy to the investigation of generic factors, principally the alliance. For the next phase of the Vanderbilt study (Vanderbilt II) a therapy manual was developed for Time-Limited Dynamic Psychotherapy (TLDP), focusing explicitly on the relationship between therapist and client. The clinical trial involved a period of treatment followed by a year of intensive therapist training in TLDP treatment. Subsequent analysis of the data yielded challenging results. Contrary to expectations, the training not only failed to improve therapy outcome, but participating therapists' alliance also did not significantly improve as a result of intensive training. It was still the case, however, that the therapists who managed to develop stronger alliances with their clients were more

likely to generate therapeutic improvement than those who did not develop good alliance.

To explore these unexpected results, Henry and Strupp (1994, p. 66) applied moment-by-moment analysis to the sessions using the SASB method and discovered that "destructive interpersonal process" (therapists' hostility toward themselves, disaffiliative responses, hostile or controlling responses to challenging clients) distinguished therapists with positive alliance and good outcome from those with poor alliance. They concluded, "Taken together, these findings describe a theoretically coherent link between early actions by parents toward the therapist, the therapists' adult introject state, vulnerability countertherapeutic interpersonal process with their patients, and differential outcome."

While these investigations were situated in a specific context (TLDP) and call for replication with other therapies, the findings certainly challenge some of our simple assumptions about the kinds of training therapists need to improve their effectiveness. The TLDP model carefully explicated expected therapist behaviors, and both the manual and the training, measured by criteria, certainly met or exceeded then-current standards. Strupp (1998), among others, suggests that the therapist's own unresolved relational history may be a significant limiting factor in therapeutic potential. This research suggests that we ought to pay more systematic attention to therapists' vulnerabilities.

INTERACTIVE ELEMENTS

Therapist-Client Matching and Complementarity

Complementarity has been investigated from two perspectives: competing versus complementing interpersonal behaviors, and complementing versus similar personality structures of therapists and clients. The hypothesis that greater complementarity in terms of dominance and control would result in more harmonious verbal transactions has received some empirical support (Kiesler & Watkins, 1989; Tracy & Ray, 1984). More clinically meaningful relationship was found between the quality of the alliance and harmonious (friendly and autonomy-enhancing) as opposed to competitive (hostile or controlling) interaction. Harmonious, positive moment-to-moment interactions were closely related to good alliance, and the opposite was true for any form of negative interaction (either participant expressing hostile or negative affect) (Henry & Strupp, 1994; Svartberg & Stiles, 1994). Overall, from the perspective of the alliance, it seems that what is most important is that the therapist-client transactions are not hostile, negative, or competing.

Collaboration

It was noted earlier that collaboration is one of the key features of the alliance concept. Most alliance measures solicit information indicating the degree of *felt* collaboration among the participants. In terms of actual in-therapy behaviors, one would expect to observe sequences of interactions indicating that client and therapist use and build upon each other's verbal contributions. Validation of the sequential and mutual impact of the participants in therapy requires sophisticated design and complex analysis; the results of these kinds of research are just beginning to appear in the literature. Brossart and colleagues (1998) conducted a time series analysis of short-term dynamically informed therapy and came up with a model that demonstrated significant therapist influence on the working alliance both in the short and medium term. No significant reciprocal client effect was found in this study. In a study of supervisory alliance, Chen and Bernstein (2000) found evidence that complementary interaction between supervisor and trainee resulted in better alliance *and* better outcome. The impact of collaborative activity and evidence of the critical role of client-therapist cooperation were demonstrated via time series analysis of therapist-client interaction by Kowalik and colleagues (1997). These studies, taken together, provide preliminary evidence linking collaboration and cooperation to better alliance and more positive outcome. It is important to note, however, that none of the evidence available thus far is sufficient to justify a claim of causal relationship (for example, that collaboration is causally linked to alliance quality or therapy outcome). A more thorough review of the role and impact of collaboration in therapy is provided by Tryon and Winograd in chap. 6 in this volume.

LIMITATIONS OF THE RESEARCH REVIEWED

The overall ecological validity of the data reviewed in this chapter is good; the majority of the studies were based in clinical settings using trained therapists. The average length of treatment, kinds of interventions, types of client problems, and age range of clients are a reasonable reflection of the clinical realities outside of research settings. Nonetheless, some limits of the available data should be noted.

As discussed earlier, the field is moving toward an implicit consensus on the definition of the alliance (Horvath & Luborsky, 1993). However, the lack of concise, explicit agreement on a definition of the alliance clearly makes empirical evidence less clinically meaningful. From our analysis of the data, it is evident that these definitional problems affect the alliance-outcome relation the least; this linkage appears to be stable regardless of how the process is measured. But this conceptual "fuzziness" introduces an additional source of variation that is likely to affect studies involving more specific links between the alliance and the processes that moderate the development or the impact of the alliance in treatment.

A diversity of measurement techniques persist. While some diversity may be essential to accommodate the varied therapeutic contexts and degree of disabilities clients experience, the current situation leads to some ambiguities when the specific clinical implications are discussed. Even more limiting is the persistence of made-for-study alliance measures in a significant number of studies reported in the literature. Such an approach makes the task of detecting convergence of evidence a more difficult task.

Most studies available are correlational designs. Such an approach is suitable for discovery of relations among a broad spectrum of variables. What is needed currently, however, are prospective investigations that would permit the evaluation of more focused hypotheses. Research providing evidence of causal relationships (path-analytic or modeling) between alliance and outcome and the moderators/mediators are just beginning to appear in the literature (e.g., Kolden, 1996; Kivlighan & Shaugnessy, 1995). While such research efforts are difficult to resource, they represent one of the necessary "next steps" in generating clinically meaningful information about the role and function of the alliance.

An exciting recent development in alliance research is the emergence of clinical studies exploring a variety of therapist and client factors that may impact the development of the alliance or the relation between alliance and outcome (that is, mediators and moderators). In contrast to the alliance outcome data, these investigations are yet somewhat uneven, both in design and clinical validity. More investigations of promising variables—such as object relations and the role of training and experience—across different treatments and clients are needed. Moreover, some of the potentially important variables, for example, attachment styles, object relations, and introject need to be more consistently defined by investigators.

Research on therapist intrapersonal variables as they affect the therapist's ability to develop alliance are slowly emerging but are not yet at the stage where the evidence could be considered as empirically reliable. We agree with Wampold (2001) that trustworthy information on therapist variables is the most urgent and clinically needed information.

THERAPEUTIC PRACTICES

Empirical evidence consistently supports the importance of developing a strong alliance early in treatment. What is "early" is obviously relative to the length of therapy, but there is significant convergence of evidence pointing to sessions 3 to 5 as a critical window. If the relationship has failed to solidify by the fifth session, then the outlook for success is threatened.

There are also empirical indications that the danger of early termination is linked to poor initial alliance. Since clients who have difficulty with developing and maintaining relations are particularly vulnerable to early disengagement from therapy, attention should be paid to the develop-

ment of the relationship with these patients at the first session and even at intake.

Clients report that their experience of being understood, supported, and provided with a sense of hope is linked with the strength of the alliance in early stages of therapy. Therapists need to be cautiously curious about the client's perception of therapist activities designed to generate empathy, support, and hope. There is evidence that clients' interpretation of therapist activity, particularly early in treatment, can diverge significantly from what is intended. Moreover, the level and kind of "engagement" with the therapist that a client finds safe also appear to be more varied than previously thought. The empirical evidence suggests that therapists' responsiveness and ability to negotiate interventions flexibly to suit clients' capacities and limits have a positive relation to both the alliance and outcome.

Therapists should anticipate that their initial assessment of the client's relational capacities, preferences, and evaluation of the quality of the alliance may differ from the client's. The task of progressively negotiating the quality of the relationship is an important and urgent challenge for therapists.

There is good empirical support for making the development of the alliance the highest priority in the opening phases of therapy. Technique contributes less to outcome in the early stages of therapy than the quality of the alliance (Gaston et al., 1998; Joyce & Piper, 1998; Krupnick et al., 1996; Kvilighan & Shaughnessy, 2000; Rounsaville et al., 1987; Wampold, 2001). However, this should *not* be interpreted simplemindedly as meaning that the quality of techniques and interventions is inconsequential. Rather, the therapeutic alliance needs to be forged first, including a collaborative agreement about the important strategies to be deployed as a part of the therapeutic work, before therapeutically sound interventions can be usefully implemented.

While the ability to develop positive alliance does not appear to be a direct function of either experience or training, therapists early in their career appear to have more difficulties attuning to relational difficulties with severely impaired clients than their more experienced colleagues. These findings suggest that training and supervision are important resources for persons early in their career, especially if they are working with severely impaired populations.

There is support for therapists assuming a "collaborative stance" as a useful relational position. The value of such a position has been investigated across the theoretical spectrum. However, whether the collaborative process itself *causally* contributes to better alliance or outcome has only circumstantial support.

From the client's perspective, working capacity, quality of object relations, and attachment style each appear to have an impact on alliance development. A related construct, current social skill level or quality of current relations, is also related to initial capacity to develop a therapeutic alliance. The type of psychological impairment influences the client's readiness to form an alliance and might overlap to some extent with the former constructs. The therapist can use information available on these client variables to prepare for the challenges presented by these individuals.

CONCLUSIONS

The overarching message from this body of research is deceptively simple: The quality of the alliance is an important element in successful, effective therapy. Our review suggests that the effect of the alliance on outcome in most therapy situations is somewhere between ES .21 to .25. While the magnitude of this relation may not appear dramatic, in a recent analysis of the literature on psychotherapy effectiveness research Wampold (2001) came to the conclusion that the alliance, along with therapist variables, accounts for most of the systematic outcome variance in psychotherapy. The impact of the alliance across studies, Wampold demonstrated, is far in excess of the outcome variance that can be accounted for by techniques (p. 158).

As we noted before, in the opening phase the therapist faces the challenge of becoming attuned to the phenomenological experience of the client. It seems clear and well supported by evidence that the client's experience of being allied with the person of the therapist, the ritual of therapy, and with the goals of the therapy process plays not only a statistically but also a clinically significant role in helping the client stay in treatment

and in accomplishing positive outcomes. If the therapist is able to assess correctly the status of this early alliance and respond to the client's needs flexibly, positive outcome is more likely to follow.

It seems likely that, in medium- to long-term therapies, effective treatment is accompanied by a convergence of the client's and therapist's assessment of the alliance. This may be a useful clinical guide for therapists during the middle phase of therapy. On the opposite side of the coin, if the therapist has reason to believe that such convergence has failed to occur, it may be a helpful indicator that the therapeutic relation needs more attention at this time. There are some indications that early and later alliance are not necessarily closely related. Thus, while building a "good enough relation" early in therapy is important, a therapist should not assume that the strength of the relationship will hold throughout treatment.

We found some evidence suggesting that, in some cases, high initial alliance ratings by clients may indicate unreasonable expectations. In such cases, these initial high alliance ratings tend to subsequently plummet as a result of discrepancies between these unrealistic expectations and actual experienced benefits.

Overall, the empirical evidence on the alliance supports a contextual rather than a medical model of therapy. Meta-analytic investigations of between-therapy effects suggest that the differences due to the kind of treatment offered across different client dysfunctions are modest. In contrast, across a broad variety of treatment approaches and client concerns, the quality of the therapeutic alliance seems to be linked to therapy outcome. While such conclusions do not in any way negate the importance of finding empirically supported treatment ingredients, the literature seems to justify therapists' emphasis and continuing attention on the alliance as a generic therapy ingredient.

REFERENCES

Adler, J. V. (1988). *A study of the working alliance in psychotherapy.* Unpublished doctoral dissertation, University of British Columbia.

Alexander, L. B., & Luborsky, L. (1987). The Penn Helping Alliance Scales. In L. S. Greenberg &

W. M. Pinsoff (Eds.), *The psychotherapeutic process: A research handbook* (pp. 325–356). New York: Guilford.

Allen, J. G., Tarnoff, G., & Coyne, L. (1985). Therapeutic alliance and long-term hospital treatment outcome. *Comprehensive Psychiatry, 26,* 187–194.

Allen, J. G., Tarnoff, G., Coyne, L., Spohn, H. E., Buskirk, J. R., & Keller, M. W. (1986). An innovative approach to assessing outcome of long-term psychiatric hospitalization. *Hospital and Community Psychiatry, 37,* 376–380.

Andreoli, A., Frances, A., Gex-Mabry, M., Aapro, N., Gerin, P., & Dazord, A. (1993). Crisis intervention in depressed patients with and without DSM-II-R personality disorders. *Journal of Nervous and Mental Disease, 181,* 732–737.

Ankuta, G. Y. (1992). *Initial and later therapeutic alliance and psychotherapy outcome.* Unpublished doctoral dissertation, Michigan State University, East Lansing.

Bachelor, A. (1988). How clients perceive therapist empathy: A content analysis of "received" empathy. *Psychotherapy: Theory Research and Practice, 25,* 227–240.

Bachelor, A. (1991). Comparison and relationship to outcome of diverse dimensions of the helping alliance as seen by client and therapist. *Psychotherapy: Theory, Research and Practice, 28,* 534–539.

Bachelor, A., & Horvath, A. (1999). The therapeutic relationship. In M. A. Hubble, B. L. Duncan, & S. D. Miller (Eds.), *The heart and soul of change: What works in therapy* (pp. 133–179). Washington, DC: American Psychological Association.

Bachelor, A., & Salamé, R. (2000). Participants' perceptions of dimensions of the therapeutic alliance over the course of therapy. *Journal of Psychotherapy Practice and Research, 9,* 39–53.

Barber, J. P., Luborsky, L., Crits-Cristoph, P., Thase, M. E., Weiss, R., Frank, A., Onken, L., & Gallop, R. (1999). Therapeutic alliance as predictor of outcome in treatment of cocaine dependence. *Psychotherapy Research, 9,* 54–73.

Barkham, M., Agnew, R. M., & Culverwell, A. (1993). The California Psychotherapy Alliance Scales: A pilot study of dimensions and elements. *British Journal of Medical Psychology, 66,* 157–165.

Barrett-Lennard, G. T. (1978). The relationship inventory: Later development and adaptations. *JSAS Catalog of Selected Documents in Psychology, 8,* 68.

Bein, E., Anderson, T., Strupp, H. H., Henry, W. P., Schaht, T. E., Binder, J. L., & Butler, S. F. (2000). The effects of training in time limited dynamic psychotherapy: Changes in therapeutic outcome. *Psychotherapy Research, 10,* 119–131.

Bieschke, K. J., Bowman, G. D., Hopkins, M., Levine, H., & McFadden, F. (1995). Improvement and satisfaction in short-term therapy at a university counseling center. *Journal of College Student Development, 36,* 553–559.

Bordin, E. S. (1975, September). *The working alliance: Basis for a general theory of psychotherapy.* Paper presented at the Society for Psychotherapy Research, Washington, DC.

Bordin, E. S. (1976). The generalizability of the psychoanalytic concept of the working alliance. *Psychotherapy: Theory, Research and Practice, 16,* 252–260.

Bordin, E. S. (1980, June). *Of human bonds that bind or free.* Paper presented at the Society for Psychotherapy Research, Pacific Grove, CA.

Bordin, E. S. (1989, June). *Building therapeutic alliances: The base for integration.* Paper presented at the Society for Psychotherapy Research, Berkeley, CA.

Bordin, E. S. (1994). Theory and research on the therapeutic working alliance: New directions. In A. O. Horvath & L. S. Greenberg (Eds.), *The working alliance: Theory, research and practice.* New York: Wiley.

Broome, K. M. (1996). *Antisocial personality and drug abuse treatment process.* Unpublished doctoral dissertation, Texas Christian University, Fort Worth.

Brossart, D. F., Wilson, V. L., Patton, M. P., Kvilighan, D. M., & Multon, K. D. (1998). A time series model of the working alliance: A key process in short-term psychoanalytic counseling. *Psychotherapy, 35,* 197–205.

Card, C. A. (1991). *Therapeutic alliance, complementarity, and distress during stress prevention training after HIV testing.* Unpublished doctoral dissertation, New School for Social Research, New York.

Castonguay, L. G. (2000). A common factors approach to psychotherapy training. *Journal of Psychotherapy Integration, 10,* 263–282.

Castonguay, L. G., & Goldfried, M. R. (1994). Psychotherapy integration: An idea whose time has come. *Applied and Preventative Psychology, 3,* 159–172.

Castonguay, L. G., Goldfried, M. R., Wiser, S., Raue, P. J., & Hayes, A. M. (1996). Predicting the effect of cognitive therapy for depression: A study of unique and common factors. *Journal of Consulting and Clinical Psychology, 64,* 497–504.

Chen, E. C., & Bernstein, B. L. (2000). Relations of complementarity and supervisory issues to supervisory working alliance: A comparative analysis of two cases. *Journal of Counseling Psychology, 47,* 485–497.

Cislo, D. A. (1988). *Client perceptions of the therapeutic alliance and session outcome.* Unpublished doctoral dissertation, University of Toledo, Toledo, OH.

Clarkin, J. F., & Crilly, J. L. (1987). Therapeutic alliance and hospital treatment outcome. *Hospital and Community Psychiatry, 38,* 871–875.

Crits-Cristoph, P., Cooper, A., & Luborsky, L. (1988). The accuracy of therapists' interpretations and the outcome of dynamic psychotherapy. *Archives of General Psychiatry, 56,* 490–495.

Diamond, G. M., Liddle, H. A., Houge, A., & Dakof, G. A. (1999). Alliance-building interventions with adolescents in family therapy: A process study. *Psychotherapy, 36,* 355–368.

Dunkle, J. H., & Friedlander, M. L. (1996). Contribution of therapist experience and personal characteristics to the working alliance. *Journal of Counseling Psychology, 43,* 456–460.

Eames, V., & Roth, A. (2000). Patient attachment orientation and the early working alliance: A study of patient and therapist reports of alliance quality and ruptures. *Journal of Psychotherapy Research, 10,* 421–434.

Eaton, T. T., Abeles, N., & Gutfreund, M. J. (1988). Therapeutic alliance and outcome: Impact of treatment length and pretreatment symptomology. *Psychotherapy: Theory, Research, and Practice, 25,* 536–542.

Feeley, W. M. (1993). *Treatment components of cognitive therapy for major depression: The good, the bad, and the inert.* Unpublished doctoral dissertation, University of Pennsylvania, Philadelphia.

Ferleger, N. A. (1993). *The relationship of dependency and self-criticism to alliance, complementarity, and outcome in short-term dynamic psychotherapy.* Unpublished doctoral dissertation, Fordham University, Bronx, NY.

Florsheim, P., Shotorbani, S., Guest-Warnick, G., Barratt, T., & Hwang, W. (2000). Role of the working alliance in treatment of delinquent boys in community-based programs. *Journal of Clinical Child Psychology, 29,* 94–107.

Forman, N. W. (1990). *The nature of trait empathy in clients with chronic pain and their counselors and its impact on the development of the working alliance and outcome.* Unpublished doctoral dissertation, Ohio State University, Columbus.

Frank, A. F., & Gunderson, J. G. (1990). The role of the therapeutic alliance in the treatment of schizophrenia. *Archives of General Psychiatry, 47,* 228–236.

Freud, S. (1940a). The dynamics of transference. In J. Starchey (Ed.), *The standard edition of the complete psychological works of Sigmund Freud* (Vol. 12, pp. 99–108). London: Hogarth. (Original work published 1912)

Freud, S. (1940b). On the beginning of treatment: Further recommendations on the technique of psychoanalysis. In J. Strachey (Ed.), *Standard edition of the complete psychological works of Sigmund Freud* (Vol. 12, pp. 122–144). London: Hogarth. (Original work published 1913)

Freud, S. (1940c). The technique of psychoanalysis. In J. Strachey (Ed.), *Standard edition of the complete psychological works of Sigmund Freud* (Vol. 23, pp. 172–182). London: Hogarth. (Original work published 1913)

Gallop, R., Kennedy, S. H., & Stern, S. D. (1994). Therapeutic alliance on an inpatient unit for eating disorders. *International Journal of Eating Disorders, 16,* 405–410.

Gaston, L., Goldfried, M. R., Greenberg, L. S., Horvath, A. O., Raue, P. J., & Watson, J. (1995). The therapeutic alliance in psychodynamic, cognitive-behavioral, and experiential therapies. *Journal of Psychotherapy Integration, 15,* 1–26.

Gaston, L., & Marmar, C. (1994). The California Psychotherapy Alliance Scales. In A. O. Horvath & L. S. Greenberg (Eds.), *The working alliance: Theory, research and practice.* New York: Wiley.

Gaston, L., Marmar, C., Gallager, D., & Thompson, L. W. (1990, June). *Alliance prediction of outcome: Beyond initial symptomology and symptomatic change.* Paper presented at the Society for Psychotherapy Research, Philadelphia, PA.

Gaston, L., Marmar, C. R., Thompson, L. W., & Gallager, D. (1991). Alliance prediction of outcome: Beyond in-treatment symptomatic change as psychotherapy progresses. *Psychotherapy Research, 1,* 104–112.

Gaston, L., Piper, W. E., Debbane, E. G., Bienvenu, J. P., & Garant, J. (1994). Alliance and technique for predicting outcome in short- and long-term analytic psychotherapy. *Psychotherapy Research, 4,* 121–135.

Gaston, L., Thompson, L., Gallager, D., Cournoyer, L. G., & Gagnon, R. (1998). Alliance, technique, and their interactions in predicting outcome of behavioral, cognitive, and brief dynamic therapy. *Psychotherapy Research, 8,* 190–209.

Gelso, C. J., & Carter, J. A. (1994). Components of the psychotherapy relationship: Their interaction, and unfolding during treatment. *Journal of Counseling Psychology, 41,* 296–306.

Gerstley, L., McLellan, A. T., Alterman, A. I., Woody, G. E., Luborsky, L., & Prout, M. (1989). Ability to form an alliance with the therapist: A possible marker of prognosis for patients with antisocial personality disorder. *American Journal of Psychiatry, 146,* 508–512.

Goldfried, M. R. (1980). Toward the delineation of therapeutic change principles. *American Psychologist, 35,* 991–999.

Gomes-Schwartz, B. (1978). Effective ingredients in psychotherapy: Prediction of outcome from process variables. *Journal of Consulting and Clinical Psychology, 46,* 1023–1035.

Greenberg, L. S., & Webster, M. C. (1982). Resolving decisional conflict by Gestalt two-chair dialogue: Relating process to outcome. *Journal of Counseling Psychology, 29,* 468–477.

Greenson, R. R. (1965). The working alliance and the transference neuroses. *Psychoanalysis Quarterly, 34,* 155–181.

Greenson, R. R. (1967). *Technique and practice of psychoanalysis.* New York: International University Press.

Grob, M. C., & Eisen, S. V. (1989). Most likely to succeed: Correlates of good versus poor hospital outcome in young adult inpatients. *Psychiatric Hospital, 20,* 23–30.

Gunderson, J. G., Najavits, L. M., Leonhard, C., Sullivan, C. N., & Sabo, A. N. (1997). Ontogeny of the therapeutic alliance in borderline patients. *Psychotherapy Research, 7,* 301–309.

Gunther, G. J. (1992). *Therapeutic alliance, patient object relations and outcome in psychotherapy.* Unpublished doctoral dissertation, Michigan State University, East Lansing.

Gutfreund, M. J. (1992). *Therapist interventions: Their relation to therapeutic alliance and outcome in dynamic psychotherapy.* Unpublished doctoral dissertation, Michigan State University, East Lansing.

Hansson, L., & Berglund, M. (1992). Stability of therapeutic alliance and its relationship to outcome in short-term inpatient psychiatric care. *Scandinavian Journal of Social Medicine, 20,* 45–50.

Hartley, D. E., & Strupp, H. H. (1983). The therapeutic alliance: Its relationship to outcome in brief psychotherapy. In J. Masling (Ed.), *Empirical studies in analytic theories* (Vol. 1, pp. 1–37). Hillside, NJ: Erlbaum.

Hatcher, R. L., & Barends, A. W. (1996). Patient's view of the alliance in psychotherapy: Exploratory factor analysis of three alliance measures. *Journal of Consulting and Clinical Psychology, 64,* 1326–1336.

Hatcher, R. L., Barends, A., Hansell, J., & Gutfreund, M. J. (1995). Patient's and therapist's shared and unique views of the therapeutic alliance: An investigation using confirmatory factor analysis in a nested design. *Psychoanalysis Quarterly, 63,* 636–643.

Hays, V. L. (1994). *The effects of the therapeutic alliance and social support on therapy outcome and mental health of women.* Unpublished doctoral dissertation, University of Wisconsin, Madison.

Hedges, L. V., & Olkin, I. (1985). *Statistical methods for meta-analysis.* New York: Academic.

Henry, W. P., & Strupp, H. H. (1994). The therapeutic alliance as interpersonal process. In A. O. Horvath & L. S. Greenberg (Eds.), *The working alliance: Theory, research and practice.* New York: Wiley.

Henry, W. P., Strupp, H. H., Schacht, T. E., & Gaston, L. (1994). Psychodynamic approaches. In A. E. Bergin & S. L. Garfield (Eds.), *Handbook of psychotherapy and behavior change* (4th ed., pp. 467–508). New York: Wiley.

Hersoug, A. G., Monsen, J. T., Havik, O. E., & Høglend, P. (2000, June). *Prediction of early working alliance: Diagnoses, relationship, and interpsychic variables as predictors.* Paper presented at the Society for Psychotherapy Research, Chicago.

Hersoug, A. G., Monsen, J. T., Havik, O. E., & Høglend, P. (2001a). *Quality of early working alliance in psychotherapy: Diagnoses, relationship, and intrapsychic variables as predictors.* Manuscript submitted for publication.

Hersoug, A. G., Monsen, J. T., Havik, O. E., & Høglend, P. (2001b). *Quality of working alliance in psychotherapy: Therapist variables and patient/therapist similarity as predictors.* Manuscript submitted for publication.

Hilliard, R. B., Henry, W. P., & Strupp, H. H.

(2000). An interpersonal model of psychotherapy: Linking patient and therapist developmental history, therapeutic process, and types of outcome. *Journal of Consulting and Clinical Psychology, 68,* 125–133.

Hopkins, W. E. (1988). *The effects of conceptual level matching on the working alliance and outcome in time-limited counseling.* Unpublished doctoral dissertation, University of Maryland, College Park.

Horowitz, M. J., Marmar, C., Weiss, D. S., De-Witt, K. N., & Rosenbaum, R. (1984). Brief psychotherapy of bereavement reactions: The relationship of process to outcome. *Archives of General Psychiatry, 41,* 438–448.

Horvath, A. O. (1981). *An exploratory study of the working alliance: Its measurement and relationship to outcome.* Unpublished doctoral dissertation, University of British Columbia, Vancouver, Canada.

Horvath, A. O. (1986, April). *Another approach to assess the counseling relationship: The working alliance.* Paper presented at the annual conference of the American Educational Research Association, San Francisco.

Horvath, A. O., & Greenberg, L. S. (1986). Development of the working alliance inventory. In L. S. Greenberg & W. M. Pinsof (Eds.), *The psychotherapeutic process: A research handbook* (pp. 529–556). New York: Guilford.

Horvath, A. O., & Luborsky, L. (1993). The role of the therapeutic alliance in psychotherapy. *Journal of Consulting and Clinical Psychology, 61,* 561–573.

Horvath, A. O., & Marx, R. W. (1991). The development and decay of the working alliance during time-limited counseling. *Canadian Journal of Counselling, 24,* 240–259.

Horvath, A. O., & Symonds, B. D. (1991). Relation between working alliance and outcome in psychotherapy: A meta-analysis. *Journal of Counseling Psychology, 38,* 139–149.

Jennings, L., & Skovholt, T. M. (1999). The cognitive, emotional, and relational characteristics of master therapists. *Journal of Counseling Psychology, 46,* 3–11.

Joyce, A. S., & Piper, W. E. (1998). Expectancy, the therapeutic alliance, and treatment outcome in short-term individual psychotherapy. *Journal of Psychotherapy Practice and Research, 7,* 236–248.

Jumes, M. T. (1995). *The developmental course of the inpatient working alliance in state psychiatric hospital clients.* Unpublished doctoral dissertation, University of Texas Southwestern Medical Center, Dallas.

Kiesler, D. J., & Watkins, L. M. (1989). Interpersonal complementarity and the therapeutic alliance: A study of relationship in psychotherapy. *Psychotherapy, 26,* 183–194.

Kivlighan, D. M., Patton, M. J., & Foote, D. (1998). Moderating effects of client attachment on the counselor experience–working alliance relationship. *Journal of Counseling Psychology, 45,* 274–278.

Kivlighan, D. M., & Shaughnessy, P. (1995). Analysis of the development of the working alliance using hierarchical linear modeling. *Journal of Counseling Psychology, 42,* 338–349.

Kivlighan, D. M., & Shaughnessy, P. (2000). Patterns of working alliance development: A typology of client's working alliance ratings. *Journal of Counseling Psychology, 47,* 362–371.

Klee, M. R., Abeles, N., & Muller, R. T. (1990). Therapeutic alliance: Early indicators, course, and outcome. *Psychotherapy, 27,* 166–174.

Kokotovic, A. M., & Tracey, T. J. (1989, March). *Factor structure of the Working Alliance Inventory.* Paper presented at the American Educational Research Association, San Francisco.

Kolden, G. G. (1996). Change in early sessions of dynamic therapy: Universal processes and the generic model of psychotherapy. *Journal of Consulting and Clinical Psychology, 64,* 489–496.

Kowalik, Z. J., Schiepek, G., Kumpf, K., Roberts, L. E., & Elbeert, T. (1997). Psychotherapy as a chaotic process, II: The application of non linear analysis methods on quasi time-series of the client-therapist interaction: A nonstationary approach. *Psychotherapy Research, 7,* 179–218.

Krupnick, J. L., Elkin, I., Collins, J., Simmens, S., Sotsky, S. M., Pilkonis, A., & Watkings, J. T. (1994). Therapeutic alliance and clinical outcome in the NIMH treatment of depression collaborative research program: Preliminary findings. *Psychotherapy, 31,* 28–35.

Krupnick, J. L., Sotsky, S. M., Simmens, A., Moyer, J., Elkin, I., Watkins, J., & Pilkonis, P. A. (1996). The role of the alliance in psychotherapy and pharmacotherapy outcome: Findings in the National Institute of Mental Health treatment of depression collaborative research program. *Journal of Consulting and Clinical Psychology, 64,* 532–539.

Lansford, E. (1986). Weakenings and repairs of the working alliance in short-term psychotherapy.

Professional Psychology: Research and Practice, 17, 364–366.

Lichenberg, J. W., Wettersten, K. B., Mull, H., Moberly, R. L., Merkey, K. B., & Corey, A. T. (1988). Relationship and control as correlates of psychotherapy quality and outcome. *Journal of Consulting and Clinical Psychology, 45*, 322–337.

Lieberman, P. B., von Rehn, S., Dickie, E., Elliott, B., & Egerter, E. (1992). Therapeutic effects of brief hospitalization: The role of the therapeutic alliance. *Journal of Psychotherapy Practice and Research, 1*, 56–63.

Lingiardi, V., Croce, D., Fossati, A., Vanzulli, L., & Maffei, C. (2000). La valutazione dell'alleanza terapeutica nella psicoterapia dei pazienti con disturbi di personalità (Therapeutic alliance evaluation in psychotherapy of patients with personality disorders). *Ricerca in Psicoterapia, 4*, 63–80.

Luborsky, L. (1976). Helping alliances in psychotherapy. In J. L. Cleghhorn (Ed.), *Successful psychotherapy* (pp. 92–116). New York: Brunner/Mazel.

Luborsky, L. (1994). Therapeutic alliance measures as predictors of future benefits of psychotherapy. In A. O. Horvath & L. S. Greenberg (Eds.), *The working alliance: Theory, research and practice*. New York: Wiley.

Luborsky, L., & Auerbach, A. (1985). The therapeutic relationship in psychodynamic psychotherapy: The research evidence and its meaning for practice. In R. Hales & A. Frances (Eds.), *Psychiatry update annual review* (Vol. 4, pp. 550–561). Washington, DC: American Psychiatric Association.

Luborsky, L., Crits-Cristoph, P., Alexander, L., Margolis, M., & Cohen, M. (1983). Two helping alliance methods for predicting outcomes of psychotherapy: A counting signs vs. a global rating method. *Journal of Nervous and Mental Disease, 171*, 480–491.

Luborsky, L., McLellan, A. T., Woody, G. E., O'Brien, C. P., & Auerbach, A. (1985). Therapist success and its determinants. *Archives of General Psychiatry, 42*, 602–611.

Luborsky, L., Singer, B., & Luborsky, L. (1975). Comparative studies of psychotherapies: "Is it true that everybody has won and all must have prizes?" *Archives of General Psychiatry, 32*, 995–1008.

Mallinckrodt, B. (1992). Client's representations of childhood emotional bonds with parents, social support, and formation of the working alliance. *Journal of Counseling Psychology, 38*, 401–409.

Mallinckrodt, B. (1993). Session impact, working alliance, and treatment outcome in brief counseling. *Journal of Counseling Psychology, 40*, 25–32.

Mallinckrodt, B. (1996). Change in working alliance, social support and psychological symptoms in brief therapy. *Journal of Counseling Psychology, 43*, 448–455.

Mallincrodt, B. (2000). Attachment, social competencies, social support and interpersonal process in psychotherapy. *Psychotherapy Research, 10*, 239–263.

Mallinckrodt, B., & Leong, F. T. L. (1992). Social support in academic programs and family environments: Sex differences and role conflicts for graduate students. *Journal of Counseling and Development, 70*, 716–723.

Mallinckrodt, B., & Nelson, M. L. (1991). Counselor training level and the formation of the therapeutic working alliance. *Journal of Counseling Psychology, 38*, 14–19.

Marmar, C. R., Gaston, L., Gallager, D., & Thompson, L. W. (1989). Therapeutic alliance and outcome in behavioral, cognitive, and brief dynamic psychotherapy in late-life depression. *Journal of Nervous and Mental Disease, 177*, 464–472.

Marmar, C. R., Horowitz, M. J., Weiss, D. S., & Marziali, E. (1986). The development of the therapeutic alliance rating system. In L. S. Greenberg & W. M. Pinsof (Eds.), *The psychotherapeutic process: A research handbook* (pp. 367–390). New York: Guilford.

Marmar, C., Weiss, D. S., & Gaston, L. (1989). Toward the validation of the California Therapeutic Alliance Rating System. *Psychological Assessment, 1*, 46–52.

Marshel, R. L. (1986). *An exploration of the relationship between the therapeutic alliance and premature termination*. Unpublished doctoral dissertation, Northwestern University, Evanston, IL.

Martin, D. J. (1998). *Relation of the therapeutic alliance with outcome and other variables: A meta analytic review*. Unpublished doctoral dissertation, Ohio University.

Martin, D. J., Garske, J. P., & Davis, K. M. (2000). Relation of the therapeutic alliance with outcome and other variables: A meta-analytic review. *Journal of Consulting and Clinical Psychology, 68*, 438–450.

Marziali, E. (1984). Three viewpoints on the therapeutic alliance scales: Similarities, differences, and associations with psychotherapy outcome. *Journal of Nervous and Mental Disease, 172,* 417–423.

Marziali, E., Marmar, C., & Krupnick, J. (1981). Therapeutic alliance scales: Development and relationship to psychotherapy outcome. *American Journal of Psychiatry, 138,* 361–364.

Marziali, E., Munroe-Blum, H., & McClery, L. (1999). The effects of the therapeutic alliance on the outcomes of individual and group psychotherapy with borderline personality disorder. *Psychotherapy Research, 9,* 452–467.

Mohl, P. C., Martinez, D., Ticknor, C., Huang, M., & Cordell, L. (1991). Early dropouts from psychotherapy. *Journal of Nervous and Mental Disease, 179,* 478–481.

Morgan, R., Luborsky, L., Crits-Cristoph, P., Curtis, H., & Solomon, J. (1982). Predicting the outcomes of psychotherapy by the Penn Helping Alliance Rating Method. *Archives of General Psychiatry, 39,* 397–402.

Moseley, D. (1983). *The therapeutic relationship and its association with outcome.* Unpublished master's thesis, University of British Columbia, Vancouver, Canada.

Muran, J. C., Gorman, B. S., Safran, J. D., Twining, L, Samstag, I. W., & Winston, A. (1995). Linking in-session change to overall outcome in short term cognitive therapy. *Journal of Consulting and Clinical Psychology, 63,* 651–657.

Ogrodniczuk, J. S., Piper, W. E., Joyce, A. S., & McCallum, M. (2000). Different perspectives of the therapeutic alliance and therapist technique in 2 forms of dynamically oriented psychotherapy. *Canadian Journal of Psychiatry, 45,* 452–458.

O'Malley, S. S., Suh, C. S., & Strupp, H. H. (1983). The Vanderbilt Psychotherapy Process Scale: A report on the scale development and a process-outcome study. *Journal of Consulting and Clinical Psychology, 51,* 581–586.

Orlinsky, D. E., Grawe, K., & Parks, B. (1994). Process and outcome in psychotherapy— Noch einmal. In A. E. Bergin & S. L. Garfield (Eds.), *Handbook of psychotherapy and behavior change* (4th ed., pp. 270–378). New York: Wiley.

Orlinsky, D. E., & Howard, K. I. (1986). The psychological interior of psychotherapy: Explorations with the Therapy Session Report Questionnaires. In L. S. Greenberg & W. M. Pinsof (Eds.), *The psychotherapeutic process: A research handbook.* New York: Guilford.

Orlinsky, D. E., & Howard, K. I. (1987). A generic model of psychotherapy. *Journal of Integrative and Eclectic Psychotherapy, 6,* 6–27.

Paivio, S. C., & Bahr, L. B. (1998). Interpersonal problems, working alliance, and outcome in short-term experiential therapy. *Psychotherapy Research, 8,* 392–406.

Piper, W. E., Azim, H. F. A., Joyce, A. S., McCallum, M., Nixon, G. W. H., & Segal, P. S. (1991). Quality of object relations vs. interpersonal functioning as predictor of therapeutic alliance and psychotherapy outcome. *Journal of Nervous and Mental Disease, 179,* 432–438.

Piper, W. E., Boroto, D. R., Joyce, A. S., McCallum, M., & Azim, H. F. A. (1995). Pattern of alliance and outcome in short-term individual psychotherapy. *Psychotherapy, 32,* 639–647.

Piper, W. E., DeCarufel, F. L., & Szkrumelack, N. (1985). Patient predictors of process and outcome in short term individual psychotherapy, *Journal of Nervous and Mental Disease, 173,* 726–733.

Plotnicov, K. H. (1990). *Early termination from counseling: The client's perspective.* Unpublished doctoral dissertation, University of Pittsburgh, PA.

Priebe, S., & Gruyters, T. (1993). The role of helping alliance in psychiatric community care: A prospective study. *Journal of Nervous and Mental Disease, 181,* 552–557.

Prigatano, G. P., Klonoff, P. S., O'Brien, K. P., Altman, I. M., Amin, K., Chiapello, D., Shepherd, J., Cunningham, M., & Mora, M. (1994). Productivity after neuropsychologically oriented milieu rehabilitation. *Journal of Head Trauma Rehabilitation, 9,* 91–102.

Pugh, M. A. (1991). *The working alliance, pretherapy interpersonal relationships and therapeutic outcome.* Unpublished doctoral dissertation, Virginia Commonwealth University, Richmond.

Pyne, S. C. (1991). *Therapist's use of countertransference in short-term psychotherapy: A focus on rescuing and counterhostility.* Unpublished doctoral dissertation, University of Colorado, Boulder.

Reiner, P. A. (1987). *The development of the therapeutic alliance.* Unpublished doctoral dissertation, University of North Carolina, Chapel Hill.

Riley, J. D. (1992). *The impact of pre-therapy and extra-therapy role preparation on the development of therapeutic alliance and outcome.* Unpublished doctoral dissertation, Pacific Graduate School of Psychology, Palo Alto, CA.

Rosenthal, R., & DiMaetto, M. R. (2001). Meta-analysis: Recent developments in quantitative methods for literature reviews. *Annual Review of Psychology, 52,* 59–82.

Rounsaville, B. J., Chevron, E. S., Prusoff, B. A., Elkin, I., Imber, S., Sotsky, S., & Watkins, J. (1987). The relation between specific and general dimensions of the psychotherapy process in interpersonal psychotherapy of depression. *Journal of Consulting and Clinical Psychology, 55,* 379–384.

Rubino, G., Baker, C., Roth, T., & Fearon, P. (2000). Therapist empathy and depth of interpretation in response to potential alliance ruptures: The role of therapist and patient attachment styles. *Psychotherapy Research, 10,* 408–420.

Safran, J. D., & Muran, C. (2000). *Negotiating the therapeutic alliance: A relational treatment guide.* New York: Guilford.

Safran, J. D., Muran, J. C., & Samstag, L. W. (1994). Resolving therapeutic ruptures: A task analytic investigation. In A. O. Horvath & L. S. Greenberg (Eds.), *The working alliance: Theory, research and practice.* New York: Wiley.

Safran, J. D., & Wallner, L. K. (1991). The relative predictive validity of two therapeutic alliance measures in cognitive therapy. *Psychological Assessment, 3,* 188–195.

Saketopoulou, A. (1999). The psychotherapeutic alliance in psychodynamic psychotherapy: Theoretical conceptualizations and research findings. *Psychotherapy, 36,* 329–342.

Saunders, S. M., Howard, K. I., & Orlinsky, D. E. (1989). The therapeutic bond scales: Psychometric characteristics and relationship to treatment effeciveness. *Psychological Assessment, 1,* 323–330.

Sexton, H. (1996). Process, life events, and symptomatic change in brief eclectic psychotherapy. *Journal of Consulting and Clinical Psychology, 64,* 1358–1365.

Smith, M. L., & Glass, G. V. (1977). Meta-analysis of psychotherapy outcome studies. *American Psychologist, 32,* 752–760.

Solomon, P., Draine, J., & Delaney, M. A. (1995). The working alliance and consumer case management. *Journal of Mental Health Administration, 22,* 126–134.

Sonnenberg, R. T. (1996). *An examination of the outcome of a brief psychiatric hospitalization with particular reference to the therapeutic alliance and select patient characteristics.* Unpublished doctoral dissertation, University of Nebraska, Lincoln.

Sterba, R. F. (1934). The fate of the ego in analytic therapy. *International Journal of Psychoanalysis, 115,* 117–126.

Stiles, W. B., Shapiro, D., & Elliott, R. (1986). Are all psychotherapies equivalent? *American Psychologist, 41,* 165–180.

Stone, L. (1961). *The psychoanalytic situation: An examination of its development and essential nature.* New York: International Universities Press.

Strupp, H. H. (1998). The Vanderbilt Study I revisited. *Psychotherapy Research, 8,* 17–29.

Strupp, H. H., & Binder, J. L. (1984). *Psychotherapy in a new key: A guide to time-limited dynamic psychotherapy.* New York: Basic.

Suh, C. S., O'Malley, S. S., & Strupp, H. H. (1986). The Vanderbilt Psychotherapy Process Scale (VPPS) and the Negative Indicators Scale (VNIS). In L. S. Greenberg & W. M. Pinsof (Eds.), *The psychotherapeutic process: A research handbook.* New York: Guilford.

Svartberg, M., & Stiles, T. C. (1994). Therapeutic alliance, therapist competence and client change in short-term anxiety-provoking psychotherapy. *Psychotherapy Research, 4,* 20–33.

Symonds, B. D. (1999). *The measurement of alliance in short term couples therapy.* Unpublished doctoral dissertation, Simon Fraser University, Burnaby, British Columbia.

Tichenor, V. (1989). *Working alliance: A measure comparison.* Unpublished doctoral dissertation, University of Maryland.

Tichenor, V., & Hill, C. E. (1989). A comparison of six measures of working alliance. *Psychotherapy: Theory, Research and Practice, 26,* 195–199.

Tracy, T. J., & Ray, P. B. (1984). Stages of successful time-limited counseling: An interactional examination. *Journal of Counseling Psychology, 31,* 13–27.

Tryon, G., & Kane, A. S. (1990). The helping alliance and premature termination. *Canadian Psychologist, 3,* 223–238.

Tryon, G. S., & Kane, A. S. (1993). Relationship of working alliance to mutual and unilateral termination. *Journal of Counseling Psychology, 40,* 33–36.

Tryon, G. S., & Kane, A. S. (1995). Client involvement, working alliance and type of psychotherapy termination. *Psychotherapy Research, 5,* 189–198.

Tunis, S. L., Deluchi, K. L., Schwartz, K., Banys, P., & Sees, K. L. (1995). The relationship of counselor and peer alliance to drug use and

HIV risk behaviors in a six-month methadone detoxification program. *Addictive Behaviors, 20*, 395–405.

Tyrrel, C. L., Dozier, M., Teague, G. B., & Fallot, R. D. (1999). Effective treatment relationships for persons with serious psychiatric disorders: The importance of attachment states of mind. *Journal of Consulting and Clinical Psychology, 67*, 725–733.

Wampold, B. E. (2001). *The great psychotherapy debate: Models, methods, and findings.* Mahwah, NJ: Erlbaum.

Windholz, M. J., & Silberschatz, G. (1988). Vanderbilt psychotherapy process scale: A replication with adult outpatients. *Journal of Consulting and Clinical Psychology, 56*, 56–60.

Yeomans, F. E., Gutfreund, J., Selzer, M. A., Clarkin, J., Hull, J. W., & Smith, T. E. (1994). Factors related to drop-outs by borderline patients: Treatment contract and therapeutic alliance. *Journal of Psychotherapy Practice and Research, 3*, 16–24.

Zetzel, E. R. (1956). Current concepts of transference. *International Journal of Psychoanalysis, 37*, 369–376.

Zuroff, D. C., Blatt, S. J., Sotsky, S. M., Krupnick, J. L., Martin, D. J., Sanislow, C. A., & Simmens, S. (2000). Relation of therapeutic alliance and perfectionism to outcome in brief outpatient treatment for depression. *Journal of Consulting and Clinical Psychology, 68*, 114–124.

4

Cohesion in Group Psychotherapy

Gary M. Burlingame
Addie Fuhriman
Jennifer E. Johnson

Central to the definition of relationship in group psychotherapy is the context in which therapy is to occur. In group psychotherapy, the context is a system of many individuals and relationships, rather than the single relationship between two individuals found in individual therapy (Fuhriman & Burlingame, 1990). As such, the group therapeutic relationship requires a systemic definition, one that captures a multiplicity of relationships and assorted contributing factors that all come together to form a *dynamic* and *complex* influence.

Over time, the construct of cohesion as the essence of relationship in group psychotherapy has advanced. Definitional attempts at cohesion have traveled an evolutionary trail from broad and diffuse (forces that cause members to remain in the group, sticking-togetherness) to concentrated (attractiveness, alliance), from ambiguous to coherent (a tripartite relationship), from an emphasis on the whole to an interplay of parts, and from being described as a small-group phenomenon to a therapeutic factor.

The primary relationships that form cohesion in the group include, from the perspective of the clients, member-to-group, member-to-member, and member-to-leader. This reflects the tripartite definition described by Yalom (1995) and others. More recently, these primary relationships have

been joined by two secondary relationships: leader-to-group, and in the case of a co-therapist participating, leader-to-leader. Cohesion encompasses all these relationship parameters and their interactions with one another.

From the perspective of the therapist, cohesion as relationship requires that attention be directed not only to the therapeutic growth of the individual client members but also to that of the group as a whole. This stems from the further definitional understanding of Crouch, Bloch, and Wanlass (1994), who called for some distinction between the "togetherness" of the group and the belonging or being valued that is sensed by the individual members. The therapeutic processes undergirding cohesion find form in personal (individual member, leader) and interpersonal human dimensions as well as in more structural forms. For example, *intrapersonal* elements of cohesion can be found in a group member's sense of belonging and acceptance and a personal commitment and allegiance to the group (Bloch & Crouch, 1985; Yalom, 1995). *Intragroup* elements include attractiveness and compatibility felt among the group; mutual liking and trust; support, caring, and mutual stimulation that creates learning; and collective commitment to the "work" of the group.

Keeping in mind the involvement of cohesion

with both individual and group, other elements of cohesion are embedded within major structural features that define the boundaries and the processes of the relationships. For example, the size of the group and the composition of its membership are structurally imposed by the therapist and have the potential to affect the quality and process of the therapeutic relationship. Likewise, the group's maturational process involves relationship themes that develop over time (MacKenzie, 1994) and form a major portion of the developmental life of the group. The timing, dosage, and type of therapeutic interventions also qualitatively influence the intrapersonal and interpersonal features of cohesion. Developing a therapeutic alliance is a central role responsibility of the group therapist; in contrast to individual therapy, the alliance embraces multiple relationships.

In summary, in group psychotherapy cohesion is the therapeutic relationship. It involves multiple alliances—member-to-group, member-to-member, member-to-leader, leader-to-group, and leader-to-leader. Its features occur systemically (intrapersonally, interpersonally, and intragroup) and describe a bonding, collaborative, working alliance of the group.

EMPIRICAL BASIS FOR RELATIONSHIP GUIDELINES IN GROUP TREATMENT

There are literally hundreds of articles on how cohesion is valued by psychotherapy groups (see Colijn, Hoencamp, Snijders, Van der Spek, & Duivenvoorden, 1991; MacKenzie, 1987). What follows is a review of the empirical evidence for cohesion as a causal antecedent for client improvement as well as its relationship to salient treatment factors. We then focus on the well-researched dimensions of the group format that have been shown to have an empirical relationship with cohesion: group structure, verbal interaction, and emotional climate. These have been selected because they have a stronger empirical basis and direct implications for clinical practice. For each, we provide a brief synopsis of the research evidence supporting importance of cohesion (what it does), the implications of this research for therapeutic practice (what is its nature), and clinical principles and interventions drawn from this research (how to create it).

Cohesion Predicts Outcome

In a recent study of therapeutic factors, Tschuschke and Dies (1994) declare that group cohesiveness has shown a linear and positive relationship with patient improvement in nearly every published report. However, dissenting voices have been raised on this point (Budman et al., 1989), typically decrying the lack of clarity in definition (Bednar & Kaul, 1994). A representative sample of these varying features of cohesion follows, reflecting the depth and breadth of this construct.

MacKenzie and Tschuschke (1993) contend that the experience of the individual member in the group is an important feature of cohesion. Accordingly, their measure of cohesion as relatedness tapped the sense of acceptance and support that a member felt from his or her group. In systemic terms, this definition of cohesion falls within the member-to-group category and is a good example of the intrapersonal elements of cohesion. The importance of this study is that it is one of a handful that examines cohesion in a longer-term group (six months). These authors found that patients who reported higher levels of relatedness (for example, feeling understood, protected, and comfortable with their group) also reported the most symptomatic improvement, especially if they reported these feelings in the latter half of their group experience.

A minimum level of attraction to the group appears to be important for retaining members, especially in the early phases of group treatment (MacKenzie, 1987). Moreover, higher rates of group attrition have been related to poor outcomes (Hoag & Burlingame, 1997). Patient improvement has also been shown to be related to similar intrapersonal elements, such as liking the group one is in (T. L. Wright & Duncan, 1986), experiencing intimacy (Widra & Amidon, 1987), and being accepted by the group (Rugel & Barry, 1990). Experiencing warmth, empathy, friendliness, consideration, genuineness, and having a good working alliance (intragroup) have all been tied to good group outcomes (see Hurley, 1986; Marziali, Munroe-Blum, & McCleary, 1997; Raskin, 1986).

Budman and colleagues (1989) provide a different perspective on the construct of cohesion that they applied to a 15-session group. The research team, over a five-year period, developed a behavioral rating scale that focused on the experience of the entire group rather than the individual members. Cohesion was defined by five scales that use a positive and negative pole: (1) withdrawal and self-absorption vs. interest and involvement; (2) mistrust vs. trust; (3) disruption vs. cooperation; (4) abusiveness vs. expressing care; and (5) unfocused vs. focused. This definition of cohesion is a good example of the intragroup dimension of cohesion, with raters paying particular attention to member-member relationships. Surprisingly, all five scales of the instrument collapsed to a single dimension. What is important about this study is that group-level cohesion, as rated by an independent observer, was related to patient self-report improvement. Of equal import is that the cohesion exhibited by a group in the first 30 minutes of a session produced the strongest relationship to patient outcome. Thus, high levels of cohesion in early moments of a session predict patient improvement.

A third viewpoint of cohesion, drawn from a study conducted by Sexton (1993), reflects the member-to-leader dimension. Here, patients were asked to provide session ratings including whether they felt warmth, understanding, hope, and being personally valued by their group therapist (leader-member). Sexton also examined negative in-session emotions, interventions (support and advice), therapeutic alliance, and the intensity of positive emotional ties in the group. Group leaders completed a number of in-session process ratings including positive and negative feelings they felt toward group members. Two important findings emerged. Members who experienced warm feelings from their group leader had better therapist-ranked improvement and reported experiencing insight in subsequent sessions. Conversely, patients with poorer outcomes were associated with therapists who reported negative feelings toward these patients.

Cohesion Predicts Process

Cohesion has been related to a number of important group processes that, in turn, may well be related to eventual group outcomes. For instance, Tschuschke and Dies (1994) found that members who reported high levels of cohesion were rated by independent observers as making more self-disclosing statements. This self-report/observational cohesive evidence was especially true in the first 30 minutes of a group session, and independently corroborates the aforementioned findings of Budman and colleagues (1989). Moreover, there was evidence that higher levels of self-disclosure were related to higher levels of interpersonal feedback between members. Thus, high and positive emotional relatedness to other group members appears to promote the propensity to disclose important and meaningful material that, in turn, leads to more frequent and intense feedback from fellow members. The fact that an earlier study (Fuehrer & Keys, 1988) found early group cohesion positively related to later ownership of group functioning further underscores the relationship among cohesion, feedback, self-disclosure, and member responsibility and provides an interesting display of the interplay of intra- and interpersonal facets of cohesion.

The development of early cohesion may also be related to the ability of a group member to tolerate the conflict that often comes in the work stage of group treatment (MacKenzie, 1994). In a well-designed study investigating a 12-session, manualized cognitive-behavioral therapy group for binge eating disorder, Castonguay and colleagues carefully tracked the emotional experience of group members using the member-completed Therapy Session Report (Castonguay, Pincus, Agras, & Hines, 1998). This measure captures both the intra- and interpersonal aspects of cohesion as it taps into the dialogue between participants, emotional experience of each member, the pattern of interaction, and sequential development of the treatment, as well as the therapeutic exchange (client goals and therapist intentions). As predicted by group development theory (MacKenzie), members with the most improvement experienced the group climate (level of engagement or cohesion) in the middle of therapy to be negative (i.e., the work or differentiation stage). However, these same members reported the early phase of group treatment as far more supportive. Thus, Castonguay and colleagues conclude that supportive engagement among group members may help them tolerate the negative emotion and stress associated with the difficulty of therapeutic work that takes place in the middle of successful groups. Collectively, these findings support the position that the group, rather than an individual leader or members, is a most important consideration for the development and maintenance of cohesion (Fuhriman & Burlingame, 1994).

On the other hand, relationships between cohesion and other positive features of group treatment (such as self-disclosure, feedback, listening and empathy, process performance and goal attainment, and support and caring) often make it difficult to determine what is the cause and what is the effect (Braaten, 1990). While some have posited (Kaul & Bednar, 1986) that participants' level of intimacy in self-disclosure was associated with their perceptions of group cohesion, the group literature often fails to meet the scientific standard of cause-and-effect relationships needed for firm conclusions (Cook & Campbell, 1979). With this positive yet guarded context we enter into a review of the literature that can empirically guide clinicians as they manage the therapeutic relationships—cohesion—in their groups.

GROUP STRUCTURE

The impact of leader-initiated structure in small-group treatment is one of the venerable and better researched dimensions in the literature (Kaul & Bednar, 1994; Burlingame & Fuhriman, 1994). Activities typically classified under this rubric include three components: pre-group preparation of a member, leader-initiated early group structure, and the composition of the group. Each has been linked to cohesion and other facilitative group processes.

Pre-Group Preparation

New group members are often apprehensive about joining a treatment group. Guidance and information can minimize their anxiety about the group experience, and pre-group orientation is often the vehicle of delivery. Preparing group members prior to their group experience has been shown to have a positive effect on group cohesion

(Santarsiero, Baker, & McGee, 1995; Neimeyer & Thomas, 1982), as well as increasing members' satisfaction and comfort with the group experience (Couch, 1995). As Bednar and Kaul (1994) note, "pregroup training may be one of the more potent factors involved in creating successful treatment groups" (p. 644).

These findings may partially explain why pre-group preparation has been related to decreased attrition and a sense of members' feeling more empowered, since they often report having a better understanding of their role in the learning process (Santarsiero et al., 1995; Couch, 1995). Indeed, in one study of poorly functioning treatment groups, one of the explanations for the failing groups was that patients were ill prepared to constructively use the group (Karterud, 1988). It should be noted that one paper, while acknowledging the value of pre-group training, questions the magnitude of effect claimed for pre-group preparation in the literature (Piper & Perrault, 1989).

While considerable diversity exists concerning the methods for preparing group members (individual and group interviews, written summaries, media presentations, behavioral practice), five common intervention themes emerge from the research literature to form a guideline that has both intrapersonal and intragroup systemic implications (table 4.1).

Principle I. Conduct pre-group preparation that sets treatment expectations, defines group rules, and instructs members in appropriate roles and skills needed for effective group participation and group cohesion.

Several intrapersonal themes are evident in the goals of extant pre-group interventions (table 4.1). Individual expectations addressing common misconceptions (associating with other patients may make me worse) and unique patient concerns are explicitly addressed. Core group procedures are discussed along with a treatment contract that identifies at least one patient-specific issue to be worked on early in the group (Braaten, 1989). This issue is often linked with the new behaviors that the member might experiment with in the group, as well as the specific skills that will be learned in the group to effect change in the patient's presenting complaint. Process norms

Table 4.1. Empirically Investigated Interventions for Pre-Group Preparation

Goal of Intervention	Intrapersonal	Intragroup
Setting treatment expectations	Set expectations regarding individual fears, rejection, loss of individuality, repeating social failures, and emotional contagion	Describe rationale underlying treatment
Establishing group procedures	Establish individual treatment contract	Discuss group rules, including: group fee, time and place, attendance, absences, tardiness, confidentiality
Role preparation	Discuss personal responsibility and experimenting with new behavior	Initiate reciprocal functioning: member-member and member-leader relations
Skill building	Monitor cognitions and interpersonal skills, for example, self-disclosure, responding to feedback	Provide feedback and conflict resolution experiences. Focus on the here-and-now nature of the emotional exchange
Establishing process norms	Focus on implications of the member as agent of change	Discuss meaning of the group being self-monitoring

(how will I handle highly emotional content?) are explicitly connected to the patient's unique interpersonal style, with fit and misfit discussed.

Pre-group orientation provides an opportune time to set intragroup expectations and inform the client about the group as an entity separate from the personal conflicts they bring to group (table 4.1). Effective protocols convey basic information about the treatment in simple, nontechnical language so that the member understands the change strategy and how treatment will evolve (Couch, 1995). Members should have clear ideas about what can and cannot be accomplished in group therapy. Procedural logistics (fee, time and place, group rules such as confidentiality, planned duration of the group, termination procedures, and the specific nature or purpose of the group) are clearly and explicitly stated, and the member is asked for an initial commitment. The multiplicity of relationships found in the group are explicitly identified (member-member, member-group, and member-leader) and linked to important roles, such as the member being both help-seeker and help-provider (reciprocal functioning), and the group monitoring itself and establishing mechanisms for handling conflict.

Early Group Structure

While pre-group preparation (the first component of structure) sets the stage for group members to participate effectively, they often still feel a predictable level of initial discomfort as the group begins. If the leader does not deal adequately with this discomfort, patient attrition and lower levels of cohesion can result (Neimeyer & Thomas, 1982). To address initial patient discomfort, Bednar, Melnick, and Kaul (1974) articulated the "risk, responsibility and structure" model more than 25 years ago. The primary thesis was that if a leader introduced structured activities in the early sessions of a group (the second component of structure), the decrease in ambiguity would lead to lower levels of anticipatory anxiety and subsequently higher levels of interpersonal risk (such as member self-disclosure). An attendant feature of the model suggests that the leader should gradually diminish structure over time, putting more responsibility on the group members for personal change and monitoring of important group processes.

A significant amount of research testing this model was produced in the 1970s and 1980s

(Kaul & Bednar, 1986). For example, receiving specific behavioral instructions resulted in higher levels of cohesiveness, and high-structure conditions may produce more therapeutically relevant member behavior (Stockton, Rohde, & Haughey, 1992). The structure → disclosure → cohesion hypothesis is not supported in its entirety in the empirical literature (cf. Fuehrer & Keys, 1988; Santarsiero et al., 1995) and incorporates both clinical and analog studies; however, ample evidence exists to warrant its inclusion as a clinical guideline for group practitioners.

Principle II. The group leader should establish clarity regarding group processes in early sessions since higher levels of structure probably lead to higher levels of disclosure and cohesion.

By definition, early group structure exclusively focuses on intragroup considerations. A particularly common form is the use of group exercises at the beginning of a session. Typically this exercise is designed to initiate or facilitate a specific therapeutic process. Such exercises have been associated with increased group cohesion (Stockton et al., 1992), although they have been ineffectual in some applications (Lando & McGovern, 1991). A host of books have been published with exercises purporting to increase group cohesion (for example, Bufe & DeNunzio, 1998). While these exercises are typically used at the beginning of a group, they may be used at any time if matched to the developmental phase or objective of the group. For example, Johnstone (1995) found that exercises designed to address the group developmental task increased the group's cohesiveness more than did neutral structure exercises. Exercises should have a clear conceptual basis and be well timed, whether they are applied during a single session or during the developmental stages of the group. For instance, those involving higher levels of interpersonal intimacy should be held until the group passes through the initial stage of group development (MacKenzie, 1987).

Composition

Identifying the factors that will contribute to a good relationship (such as cohesion) in group therapy is an exponentially more complicated task than in the individual format (Bergin & Garfield, 1994). On the other hand, it can be argued that mismatched patients in group treatment are faced with much higher stakes than those in the individual format, since they run the risk of rejection by a whole group rather than by an individual. Unfortunately, empirical research on this topic in the group literature is in short supply, making this the weakest of the three structure components (pre-group preparation, early structure, and composition).

Homogeneous group composition has been advocated as a structural component that can lead to immediate and higher levels of cohesion. However, the immediate question that comes to mind is, Homogeneous on what dimension? Drawing upon a qualitative investigation, Dacey (1989) has suggested that groups should be homogeneous in terms of members' psychological organization and ability to tolerate anxiety. Others provide evidence for the importance of similarity in diagnosis or gender. For example, there is some evidence that male-only groups avoid intimacy, are more competitive, and have lower levels of cohesion, while men in mixed-gender groups are more self-revealing and demonstrate fewer aggressive behaviors (F. Wright & Gould, 1996; Taylor & Strassberg, 1986). On the other hand, women speak less in a mixed-sex setting, and some argue that they may conform more to expected gender-role behavior in mixed-sex groups, thereby limiting therapeutic growth (F. Wright & Gould, 1996). Siebert and Dorfman (1995) argue from a clinical perspective that groups of AIDS patients are more cohesive when matched for stage of disease.

Others have argued that heterogeneous composition can increase cohesion (De Bosset, 1991). For instance, Stava and Bednar (1979) found that groups balanced in composition on the dimension of dominance and submissiveness produced more therapeutic interaction between members than those that were made up of all submissive or dominant members. Some have asserted that homogeneous groups establish cohesion more rapidly but that heterogeneous groups yield better changes in the long run (Waltman & Zimpfer, 1988).

The diversity of findings underscores the fact that there is no cumulative body of research to support how one should systematically apply client variables to construct groups (Piper, 1994).

Rather, principles drawn from clinical theories that are partially supported in the empirical literature dominate. Therapeutic practice is best summarized by the principle that members who have difficulty relating to each other threaten the development of cohesion (Siebert & Dorfman, 1995).

Principle III. Composition requires clinical judgment that balances intrapersonal and intragroup considerations.

Table 4.2 illustrates a sample of the large number of intrapersonal criteria suggested in the clinical literature (Friedman, 1989; Piper, 1994; Raubolt, 1983; Weiner, 1983; F. Wright & Gould, 1996; Yalom, 1995). Portions of these focus on the individual patient's ability to participate (acuity of pathology) and benefit from the primary task of the group and on the member's capacity to form an adequate member-to-member and member-to-leader relationship. One example is the near-consensus (e.g., Forsyth, 1999; Weiner, 1983; Yalom, 1995) that it is best to avoid putting a member who is different from everyone else in the group (gender, diagnosis, age, etc.), as this increases the likelihood for isolation (F. Wright & Gould, 1996) and decreases the sense of belonging and being a part of the group. The intragroup considerations focus on both member-to-member and member-to-group relationships. Illustrative factors for homogeneity criteria are associated with member-to-member relationships that have been linked to level of cohesion. On the other hand, the illustrative criteria for heterogeneity connect more closely with members

taking on different and important roles in the group (member-to-group relationship). For instance, Friedman (1989) contends that a balance of members who talk about emotions and those who express them creates an important group dynamic.

VERBAL INTERACTION

The study of therapeutic group processes has a long and mixed history (Burlingame, MacKenzie, & Strauss, in press), with many singular attempts to understand an isolated group phenomenon. Nevertheless, there are a few processes that have received consistent empirical attention over several decades, including three that relate to cohesion: leader verbal interaction and style, self-disclosure, and feedback. Each of these has been directly or indirectly related to the development and maintenance of cohesion according to empirically grounded studies and principles.

Leader Interaction

Member-to-member interaction is one of the primary agents of change in small-group treatment (Fuhriman & Burlingame, 2000a) and has been related to the development of trust among group members (Flowers, 1978). While the content and degree of this interaction will vary by treatment and group type, the exchange between members creates the transforming social microcosm within

Table 4.2. Suggested Principles for Group Composition

Intrapersonal	Intragroup
Exclude patients who are • Actively psychotic or organically impaired • Difficult to establish leader-member rapport with • Severely limited in interpersonal skills and impervious to feedback • Unwilling or unable to abide by the contract Include patients who • Define problems as interpersonal • Can give and receive feedback • Have capacity for empathy • Are highly motivated	Seek heterogeneous balance on • Verbal passivity and activity • Intellectualizing and emoting • Risk takers and providers of support • Type of pathology Seek homogeneity on • Ability to provide and accept interpersonal feedback • Intellect, education, and age • Psychological organization and ability to tolerate anxiety • Ability to give and receive help

which change principles operate. In fact, a common position found in the group literature posits member-to-member interaction as the primary change agent in group (Fuhriman & Burlingame, 1994). Accordingly, several theoretically founded coding systems have been developed that categorize verbal interactions, with some touting long and productive empirical histories (for example, the Hill Interaction Matrix; see Fuhriman & Burlingame, 2000b).

While there is insufficient evidence to establish firm guidelines regarding the leader's contribution to interaction, some studies are suggestive. For instance, the leader can set the tone of member-to-member interaction since members are more likely to model their behavior after the leader than themselves (Barlow, Hansen, Fuhriman, & Finley, 1982). Therapist modeling can increase member-to-member interactions, which, in turn, result in more accurate member perceptions (Fromme, Dickey, & Schaefer, 1983). Moreover, the leader can explicitly set norms and reinforce interactional patterns that can lead to increased member-member interactions. These findings result in the question: What interactional style should the leader model?

Higher levels of patient improvement and cohesion can result when group interaction focuses on member-member and member-group relationship themes (Fuhriman & Burlingame, 2000b) and when the content is real time or here-and-now (Slavin, 1993). For instance, Catina and Tschuschke (1993) found confrontive, emotional, and reprimanding group interaction to be associated with therapeutic improvement. Member interaction is not synonymous with turn taking, which has been related to poorly functioning groups in at least one study (Karterud, 1988). Finally, leadership styles that are moderate in directiveness and affiliation have been related to higher levels of cohesion (Kivlighan, Mullison, Flohr, Proudman, & Francis, 1989).

Principle IV. Leader modeling real-time observations, guiding effective interpersonal feedback, and maintaining a moderate level of control and affiliation may positively impact cohesion.

The empirical support for clinical guidelines for leader style and interaction (table 4.3) is modest. Intrapersonal considerations suggest that since leader modeling is critical to group success, a higher level of personal disclosure and transparency may be necessary (Vinogradov & Yalom, 1990). However, leader disclosure should be measured, matched to the stage of group development, and focused on real-time observations that have relevance for the group (Dies, 1994). Given the more egalitarian role of the leader in the group format, leader transparency has been theoretically advocated on both a personal (measured reactions to real-time events in the group) and professional (judicious revelations on processes guiding therapeutic interventions) level. The intragroup considerations given in table 4.3 relate to leader interventions for self-disclosure and feedback.

Member Self-Disclosure

Member self-disclosure is a key ingredient in building intimacy and relationships and in working through problems in the group. While the earlier literature tended to endorse wholesale self-disclosure as beneficial, more recent contributions draw more cautious conclusions. For example, Kirshner, Dies, and Brown (1978) experimentally manipulated self-disclosure and concluded that higher levels of disclosure (intimacy) produced greater group cohesiveness. Flowers, Booraem, and Hartman (1981) reported a similar relationship between self-disclosure and patient improvement. Bunch, Lund, and Wiggins (1983) found that as the personal detail of disclosure increased, the perceived interpersonal distance between members decreased. However, more recently, Slavin (1993) noted that here-and-now disclosure predicted cohesion better than there-and-then disclosure, although she failed to replicate these findings in a later study (Slavin, 1995). Crouch, Bloch, and Wanlass (1994) paint a positive yet conservative portrait regarding the relationship of self-disclosure and cohesion.

The clinical guidelines for self-disclosure delineated in table 4.3 do not solely rest upon an empirical foundation. Rather, they possess a modicum of research support and are grounded in theory and clinical experience. Intrapersonal considerations respect the intentionality of member self-disclosure (volunteered, not pried out) and the reality that individual members often bring concerns and fears that get in the way. On this point, some have suggested that groups should be

Table 4.3. Empirically Investigated Interventions for Verbal Interaction

Dimension	Intrapersonal	Intragroup
Leader verbal style and interaction	• Give and receive personal comments in real time • Model desired member-member behavior and encourage thoughtful member exchange • Prepare to be more personally disclosing • Judiciously use therapist transparency	• Maintain moderate control and affiliation and facilitate member-member interaction • Give specific feedback instruction • Interrupt injurious feedback and reframe; restate member corrective feedback • Accept feedback from members using consensual validation
Self-disclosure	• Emphasize personal responsibility • Identify and discuss fears and concerns • Amount is less important than relationship between discloser and receiver • Reinforce that disclosed issues achieve more resolution than undisclosed issues	• Reinforce here-and-now vs. story-telling disclosure • Interrupt ill-timed or excessive member disclosure • Encourage relationship deepening (such as discussing feelings about one another) over informational disclosures
Feedback	• Consider readiness and openness of receiver before giving corrective feedback • Identify and share personal experience in nonevaluative manner	• Emphasize positive feedback in early sessions • Structure exercises in the beginning stages of the group that focus on emotional expression and exchange • Consider structured feedback exercise in third or fourth session • Balance positive and corrective feedback in later stages • Connect feedback to experiences outside the group

composed of members who easily disclose and can serve as pacesetters (Brown, 1992), or that members should be reminded that progress on issues is directly related to their disclosure. Others suggest that the relational context is more important than the absolute amount of individual self-disclosure (Vinogradov & Yalom, 1990). Thus, a pattern of healthy self-disclosure is based upon the quality of the relationship between discloser and receiver and the relevance of the disclosed content to such.

The intragroup principles emphasizing here-and-now self-disclosures and their timing are based upon limited empirical data. As noted above, real-time disclosures have been related to higher levels of cohesion, and there is some evidence that healthy self-disclosure evolves over time from informational to personal (MacKenzie, 1994). For instance, clinical experience suggests

that the leader should interrupt members who disclose too much too soon, since they tend to drop out of groups (Vinogradov & Yalom, 1990). Depth, timing, and amount should be directly related to the level of the relationships that have developed in the group. Thus, leaders are advised to gently and respectfully try to keep information disclosed by members relevant to the here-and-now in the group (Brown, 1992).

Feedback

An important part of building interpersonal skills and member-member relationships is teaching clients how to give and receive appropriate feedback. Morran, Stockton, and Teed (1998) have recently provided an outstanding summary on this topic. They and others have found feedback to be linked to increased motivation for change, greater insight into how one's behavior affects others, increased comfort with taking interpersonal risks, higher ratings of satisfaction with the group experience, and increased capacity for intimacy (Widra & Amidon, 1987). The acceptance of feedback in group therapy is influenced by psychological closeness, trustworthiness, and attraction between the receiver and giver.

While feedback appears to be both an antecedent and a result of cohesion (Kipper, Bizman, & Einat, 1981), Morran and colleagues' (1998) review suggests several empirically grounded guidelines. The majority of these principles relate to intragroup considerations. For instance, positive feedback should prevail in early sessions, whereas corrective feedback should occur in middle or later sessions. It is often useful to have members share what they hope to gain by receiving feedback early in the group in order to set the tone for later corrective feedback. Corrective feedback is best received when preceded by positive feedback that focuses on specific and observable behaviors. Careful consideration of the readiness and openness of the receiver should be given before corrective feedback is offered. More important, the leader should give instructions on useful feedback procedures and model them as well. One method of doing so is the use of a structured feedback exchange exercise in the third or fourth session (Morran et al., 1998).

Productive negative feedback typically takes place in later sessions (Stockton & Morran, 1981). The therapeutic impact of negative feedback can be increased by the leader restating feedback, asking for consensual validation from group members, or asking the receiver to paraphrase the feedback to ensure understanding. It is important to note that member-member feedback may be more powerful than leader-member feedback. The leader should interrupt negative feedback that is clearly not beneficial or restate the corrective feedback in a way that it can be heard without damaging the interpersonal relationship. Moreover, feedback connected to experiences outside the group can often assist the member is seeing its relevance.

Principle V. The timing and delivery of feedback should be pivotal considerations for leaders as they facilitate this relationship-building process.

Two critical intrapersonal considerations are outlined in table 4.3. The first relates to the receiver's ability and readiness to accept corrective feedback. Positive feedback is readily accepted at any session (Stockton & Morran, 1981), but there is ample evidence to support the leader's active involvement in facilitating the timing, target, and delivery format of corrective feedback. Another consideration relates to delivery format. Corrective feedback that is based upon the giver's personal experience in the group and delivered in a nonevaluative manner rather than an intellectualized evaluation of another's intentions is more likely to be readily received. Once again, the leader has an important role in modeling and monitoring the feedback. The majority of findings described above (Morran et al., 1998) deal with intragroup principles and are based upon both clinical and analog studies.

ESTABLISHING AND MAINTAINING THE EMOTIONAL CLIMATE

Managing the emotional state of the group is of no less import than it is in an individual format. Nevertheless, it is a more complex task that must take into consideration the emotional state of multiple persons, the interactive influence of emotions within the group, and the cumulative affect of the group as a whole. Emotional expression, or catharsis, has long been valued as a chief therapeutic factor or mechanism of change in group (Crouch, Bloch, & Wanlass, 1994); it certainly is viewed as one medium through which the emotional climate emerges, gets conveyed from client members to one another, and is vicariously experienced by the group. While not extensive, the research literature does reveal a variety of contributing attitudes (open, accepting, supportive, responsive) deemed important to the emotional climate of the group (table 4.4). Many of these lie within the therapist's domain, and some are similar to those recognized in individual therapy. Others, again as in individual therapy, are found in the client members themselves; some emerge from the interplay of emotional expression.

Table 4.4. Empirically Investigated Interventions for Creating and Maintaining a Therapeutic Emotional Climate

Dimension	Intrapersonal	Intragroup
Leader contribution	• Maintain some balance in expressions of support and confrontation • Convey understanding of the members and their concerns • Refrain from sharing personal feelings of hostility and anger, either verbally or nonverbally • Avoid being defensive when inappropriate or failed interventions occur, or when confronted by members of the group • Be aware of the effects of your emotional expression on *all* members (direct and vicarious) • Offer empathy, genuineness, and warmth • Maintain an active engagement with the group and its work • Model acceptance by using language that is nonjudgmental and nonevaluative	• Model open and genuine expressions of warmth and personal regard • Encourage active emotional engagement between group members • Promote credibility by conveying an understanding of the members and their concerns • Foster a climate of both support and challenge • Respond at an affective level • Model responsive behavior • Focus on developing relationships with and among group members quickly
Member contribution	• Interrupt evaluative and attacking expressions • Assist members in descriptive expressions of emotion • Encourage reciprocity in emotional expression • Refrain from your own evaluative expression • Assist members in getting emotionally involved • Recognize and respond to the meaning of group members' comments • Encourage members to express and offer meaning • Avoid situations where members feel discounted, misunderstood, attacked, or disconnected	• Block judgmental, exclusionary, and evaluative emotional expression • Emphasize the commitment to the give-and-take (reciprocal) nature of the group process • Facilitate the expression of concerns and motives that accompany members' feelings • Do not avoid conflict, rather involve members in describing and resolving conflict • Elicit the open expression of support among group members • Encourage members to respond to other members' emotional expression (for example, acceptance, belonging) • Help members pay attention to and talk about their emotions

Leader Contribution

The therapist's contributions (intrapersonal) to the relationship are embodied within his or her characteristics, behaviors, and to some extent, attitudes; all lead to the question, how should the leader be? Empirical evidence indicates that positive benefits result from therapists who are warm, accepting, and who convey a positive regard for the individual client member and the group (Braaten, 1989). The relationship also appears to receive positive effects from therapists who are empathic and display genuineness in their interaction with the members (Braaten, 1989). The therapist characteristics of openness, empathic attunement, and tenderness are especially endorsed by various theoretical models. These therapist-offered conditions strike a familiar chord in individual therapy and, perhaps, are constants required in the therapeutic relationship across various formats.

There is some evidence that group members who drop out of therapy experience their therapist as being unsupportive and remote (Roback & Smith, 1987). It is particularly important for the group therapist to exhibit positive relationship-building attitudes and behaviors early on in the group in order to counteract client dropout during the beginning sessions (Klein & Carroll, 1986; Roback & Smith, 1987). Given that client dropout alters the composition and disturbs the cohesive sense of the group-as-a-whole, group clinicians need to be supportive and accepting, convey an interest in the members and their problems and struggles, and convey the underlying rationale of the group experience.

Some have argued (Wessler & Hankin-Wessler, 1989) that the therapist's conveyed expertise, confidence, and belief in the value in the group experience are also contributors to the emotional climate of the group; as well, the leader must be perceived as credible and trustworthy. Interestingly, in group, some manifestation of anxiety and vulnerability on the part of the leader may contribute positively to the relationship (Braaten, 1989), illustrating the more natural here-and-now environment of the group setting, and the more egalitarian nature of the relationships. Perhaps such expression of fallibility lends weight to the leader's credibility. On the other hand, displays of hostility and excessive confronting (versus more supportive responses and actions) by the therapist tend to detract from the cohesiveness of the group (Karterud, 1988).

Principle VI. The group leader's presence not only affects the relationship with individual members, but all group members as they vicariously experience the leader's manner of relating; thus the therapist's managing of his or her own emotional presence in the service of others is important.

Member Contributions

Some of the aforementioned leader contributions to the emotional climate are also useful charac-teristics of the group members. For example, empathy (Braaten, 1990; Trad, 1993), support and caring (Braaten, 1990), acceptance (Bloch & Crouch, 1985), and trust (Roarck & Sharah, 1989) all influence in a positive manner the relationships that exist within the group. Giesekus and Mente (1986) suggest that offering empathy to other group members cures the giver as much as the receiver. Raubolt (1983) suggested that the support members offer to one another helps foster therapeutic relationships for all involved and reduces the initial resistance to the therapeutic enterprise. The lack of such cohesive elements as support, belonging, and mutual understanding appears to contribute to patient dropout (Roback & Smith, 1987).

The basic skills of listening and conveying that one has heard and understands are important patient factors in creating a healthy emotional climate (Braaten, 1990). The commitment of group members to invest themselves in understanding, empathizing with, and trying to help others in the group resolve their problems and conflicts is theorized to play a part in relationship building (Trad, 1993). Members need to feel that the group is protective, supportive, and safe in order to share emotionally their concerns and problems (Farkas-Cameron, 1998). An atmosphere of safety, warmth, support, and pleasure provides many of the members an opportunity to experience affective attunement (Schain, 1989; McKluskey, in press), a positive factor in relationship building. There is some evidence that humor helps foster cohesiveness and increases the members' emotional involvement and investment in the work of the group (Banning & Nelson, 1987).

Some of the members' contributions to the emotional climate find expression in the intra-group features of cohesion. For example, it appears important to the relationship in group that acceptance is mutual or reciprocal and that compatibility (expressed as harmony or liking) exists among the members (Bloch & Crouch, 1985). There is some evidence that the client's acceptance by the other group members may be as important as acceptance by the therapist (Bostwick, 1987). When we add to these intragroup aspects the aforementioned members' commitment to attend to and help others, the emotional climate conducive to cohesion appears to be cooperative, egalitarian, and altruistic in nature—all trademarks of unifying forces.

Doxsee and Kivlighan (1994) found the group relationship to be negatively affected when patients felt they were discounted or misunderstood, or when they felt unconnected to the other members in the group. The feeling of being attacked by other members or merely watching others who are perceived as being attacked also affects the relational quality. Examining critical incidents in low-cohesive group sessions, Braaten (1990) discovered they were dominated by avoiding and defensive member behavior and an atmosphere laced with rebellion and conflict. On the other hand, the high-cohesive incidents had a prevalence of attraction, bonding, empathy, support, and caring. Such examples illustrate the intrapersonal and interpersonal interactions that affect cohesion in both negative and positive ways.

Principle VII. A primary focus of the group leader should be on facilitating group members' emotional expression, the responsiveness of others to that expression, and the shared meaning derived from such expression.

MODERATING OR CONTEXTUAL CONSIDERATIONS

As we have observed elsewhere (Burlingame et al., in press), a considerable gap exists between the clinical literature and the empirical research on group psychotherapy. The theoretical or conceptual papers on the therapeutic relationship surpass the empirical papers in number, but they often fail to test successfully the rich clinical propositions proffered. In many instances we find theoretical propositions in the clinical literature that are never empirically tested (transference/countertransference, co-leadership), while in other instances, there is ample overlap (structure, feedback, pre-group training). While misalignment and gaps between the empirical and clinical literature are to be expected, there is room for improvement. We have taken an unabashedly positive approach in summarizing principles for the therapeutic relationship in group. Nevertheless, at least three important limitations attenuate the empirical support for the aforementioned principles: clinical, conceptual, and methodological.

Clinical

The ubiquitous application of group treatments exacerbates the need for development of uniform clinical guidelines that have widespread applicability. For instance, group models have been developed for populations that vary by setting (inpatient, residential, day treatment, outpatient), disorder (behavioral, medical diseases), theoretical orientation (psychodynamic, cognitive-behavioral, client-centered), and developmental stage (child, adolescent, adult, and elderly). Does the role of the leader in establishing a therapeutic alliance change from setting to setting? Does cohesion manifest itself differently across these distinct clinical populations? While we know of no program of research to cite as "proof positive," it seems conceivable and even plausible that the answer to both questions is yes. The collage of studies that we drew upon in deriving principles necessarily limits our confidence in the universality of the findings.

Conceptual

This chapter proposed a conceptual model of the therapeutic relationship for group treatment that was composed of five distinct dimensions. Unfortunately, the empirically based literature is uneven in its testing of each. Two-thirds of the literature reviewed studied a single dimension, with the most frequent dimension being the member-group followed by the member-leader relationship. Studies investigating the member-to-member relationship were far less frequent, and there was a striking absence of studies investigating the leader. Since the majority of the studies have focused on a single dimension of the proposed model, it is difficult to make strong empirically based conclusions across dimensions.

Methodological

Three methodological factors further limit the strength of our conclusions. The majority of research is correlational. In this type of design, it is impossible to establish causal relationships using standard principles of science (Cook & Campbell, 1979). However, it is not uncommon to read causal conclusions suggesting that therapist warmth will result in higher levels of cohesion. A related problem is that the groups under study not only vary in dosage (ranging from a few hours to more than a year of treatment), but they also differ on when the actual measurement of the relationship was administered. There is growing support that important group processes systematically vary based upon the developmental stage of the group (MacKenzie, 1994). Since the research literature is composed of group treatment that significantly varies in time, we lend caution to the clinical guidelines. Finally, there is considerable variability in the actual instruments used to arrive at the treatment guidelines. Simply put, studies use the same term (cohesion) but rely upon very different definitions, sources (member, leader), and methods (self-report, observation, physical space, sociometry, interviews, statement-by-statement ratings). Thus, even if a common definition (such as cohesion) of a relationship facet existed, undoubtedly different relationships would result depending upon method and source.

CONCLUSION

The construct of cohesion encompasses the multifaceted complexity of the therapeutic relationship in group psychotherapy. The development of cohesion could be conceived of as a complex chemical reaction. In this analogy, the multiple relationships possible in group (member-member, member-group, member-leader, leader-group, and leader-leader) reflect the systemic parameters of the elements to be combined. The research demonstrates that a leader can enhance or attenuate the reaction (cohesion) by intervening at both an intrapersonal and intragroup level and illustrates specific examples of this. In many respects, the leader guards against contamination of the group process by protecting the boundaries of the group and acknowledging the importance of the group as a whole. As with any complex chemical reaction, the combination (composition), dosage (verbal interaction, self-disclosure), and timing (pre-group training, emotional expression) of elements (interventions) can have an important outcome on cohesion and, in turn, the end product (patient improvement). While there is much to be learned about this reaction, research and experience provide a reasonable understanding regarding salutary and deleterious reactions.

REFERENCES

Banning, M. R., & Nelson, D. L. (1987). The effects of activity-elicited humor and group structure on group cohesion and affective responses. *American Journal of Occupational Therapy, 41*, 510–514.

Barlow, S., Hansen, W. D., Fuhriman, A., & Finley, R. (1982). Leader communication style: Effects on members of small groups. *Small Group Behavior, 13*, 518–531.

Bednar, R., & Kaul, T. (1994). Experiential group research: Can the cannon fire? In A. E. Bergin & S. L. Garfield (Eds.), *Handbook of psychotherapy and behavior change* (4th ed., pp. 631–663). New York: Wiley.

Bednar, R., Melnick, J., & Kaul, T. (1974). Risk, responsibility and structure: Ingredients for a conceptual framework for initiating group therapy. *Journal of Counseling Psychology, 21*, 31–37.

Bergin, A. E., & Garfield, S. L. (Eds.) (1994). *Handbook of psychotherapy and behavior change* (4th ed.). New York: Wiley.

Bloch, S., & Crouch, E. (1985). *Therapeutic factors in group psychotherapy.* New York: Oxford University Press.

Bostwick, G. J. (1987). "Where's Mary?" A review of the group treatment dropout literature. *Social Work with Groups, 10*, 117–132.

Braaten, L. J. (1989). Predicting positive goal attainment and symptom reduction from early group climate dimensions. *International Journal of Group Psychotherapy, 39*, 377–387.

Braaten, L. J. (1990). The different patterns of group climate critical incidents in high and low cohesion sessions of group psychotherapy. *International Journal of Group Psychotherapy, 40*, 477–493.

Brown, N. W. (1992). *Teaching group dynamics: Process and practice.* Westport, CT: Praeger.

Budman, S. H., Soldz, S., Demby, A., Feldstein, M., Springer, T., & Davis, S. (1989). Cohesion, alliance and outcome in group psychotherapy. *Psychiatry, 52*, 339–350.

Bufe, C. Q., & DeNunzio, D. (1998). *Exercises for individual and group development: Building blocks* for intimacy, awareness and community. Tucson, AZ: See Sharp.

Bunch, B. J., Lund, N. L., & Wiggins, F. K. (1983, May). Self-disclosure and perceived closeness in the development of group process. *Journal for Specialists in Group Work*, 59–65.

Burlingame, G. M., & Fuhriman, A. (1994). Epilogue. In A. Fuhriman & G. M. Burlingame (Eds.), *Handbook of group psychotherapy: An empirical and clinical synthesis* (pp. 559–562). New York: Wiley.

Burlingame, G. M., MacKenzie, K. R., & Strauss, B. (in press). Evidence-based small group treatments. In M. Lambert, A. E. Bergin, & S. L. Garfield (Eds.), *Handbook of psychotherapy and behavior change* (5th ed.). New York: Wiley.

Castonguay, L. G., Pincus, A. L., Agras, W. S., & Hines, C. E. (1998). The role of emotion in group cognitive-behavioral therapy for binge-eating disorder: When things have to feel worse before they get better. *Psychotherapy Research*, 8, 225–238.

Catina, A., & Tschuschke, V. (1993). A summary of empirical data from the investigation of two psychoanalytic groups by means of a repertory grid technique. *Group Analysis*, 26, 433–447.

Colijn, S., Hoencamp, E., Snijders, H. J. A., Van der Spek, M. W. A., & Duivenvoorden, H. J. (1991). A comparison of curative factors in different types of group psychotherapy. *International Journal of Group Psychotherapy*, 41, 365–377.

Cook, T., & Campbell, D. (1979). *Quasi-Experimentation*. Boston: Houghton-Mifflin.

Couch, D. R. (1995). Four steps for conducting a pre-group screening interview. *Journal for Specialists in Group Work*, 20, 18–25.

Crouch, E., Bloch, S., & Wanlass, J. (1994). Therapeutic factors: Interpersonal and intrapersonal mechanisms. In A. Fuhriman & G. M. Burlingame (Eds.), *Handbook of group psychotherapy: An empirical and clinical synthesis* (pp. 269–315). New York: Wiley.

Dacey, C. M. (1989). Inpatient group psychotherapy: Cohesion facilitates separation. *Group*, 13, 23–30.

De Bosset, F. (1991). Group psychotherapy in chronic psychiatric outpatients: A Toronto model. *International Journal of Group Psychotherapy*, 41, 65–78.

Dies, R. (1994). Therapist variables in group psychotherapy research. In A. Fuhriman & G. M. Burlingame (Eds.), *Handbook of group psycho-*

therapy: An empirical and clinical synthesis (pp. 114–154). New York: Wiley.

Doxsee, D. J., & Kivlighan, D. M. (1994). Hindering events in interpersonal relations groups for counselor trainees. *Journal of Counseling & Development*, 72, 621–626.

Farkas-Cameron, M. M. (1998). Impatient group therapy in a managed health care environment: Application to clinical nursing practice. *Journal of the American Psychiatric Nurses Association*, 4, 145–152.

Flowers, J. V. (1978). The effect of therapist support and encounter on the percentage of client-client interactions in group therapy. *Journal of Community Psychology*, 6, 69–73.

Flowers, J. V., Booraem, C. D., & Hartman, K. A. (1981). Client improvement on higher and lower intensity problems as a function of group cohesiveness. *Psychotherapy: Theory, Research, and Practice*, 18, 246–251.

Forsyth, D. R. (1999). *Group dynamics* (3rd ed.). Belmont, MA: Brooks/Cole.

Friedman, W. H. (1989). *Practical group therapy: A guide for clinicians*. San Francisco: Jossey-Bass.

Fromme, D. K., Dickey, G. V., & Schaefer, J. P. (1983). Group modification of affective verbalizations: Reinforcement and therapist style effects. *Journal of Clinical Psychology*, 39, 893–900.

Fuehrer, A., & Keys, C. (1988). Group development in self-help groups for college students. *Small Group Behavior*, 19, 325–341.

Fuhriman, A., & Burlingame, G. M. (1990). Consistency of matter: A comparative analysis of individual and group process variables. *The Counseling Psychologist*, 18, 6–63.

Fuhriman, A., & Burlingame, G. M. (1994). Group psychotherapy research and practice. In A. Fuhriman & G. M. Burlingame (Eds.), *Handbook of group psychotherapy: An empirical and clinical synthesis* (pp. 3–40). New York: Wiley.

Fuhriman, A., & Burlingame, G. M. (2000a). Group psychotherapy. In A. Kazdin (Ed.), *Encyclopedia of Psychology*. New York: Oxford University Press and Washington, DC: American Psychological Association.

Fuhriman, A., & Burlingame, G. M. (2000b). The Hill Interaction Matrix: Therapy through dialogue. In A. P. Beck & C. Lewis (Eds.), *The process of group psychotherapy: Systems for analyzing change* (pp. 135–174). Washington, DC: American Psychological Association.

Giesekus, U., & Mente, A. (1986). Client empathic understanding in client-centered therapy. *Person-Centered Review*, 1, 163–171.

Hoag, M. J., & Burlingame, G. M. (1997). Evaluating the effectiveness of child and adolescent group treatment. *Journal of Clinical Child Psychology, 26,* 234–246.

Hurley, J. R. (1986). Leader's behavior and group members' interpersonal gains. *Group, 10,* 161–176.

Johnstone, S. B. (1995). Effects of structural conditions and member anxiety on cohesiveness in the early stages of small group development. *Dissertation Abstracts International Section A: Humanities and Social Sciences, 55(7-A),* 1828.

Karterud, S. (1988). The influence of task definition, leadership, and therapeutic style on inpatient group cultures. *International Journal of Therapeutic Communities, 9,* 231–247.

Kaul, T. J., & Bednar, R. L. (1986). Experiential group research: Results, questions, and suggestions. In A. E. Bergin & S. L. Garfield (Eds.), *Handbook of psychotherapy and behavior change.* New York: Wiley.

Kaul, T. J., & Bednar, R. L. (1994). Pretraining and structure: Parallel lines yet to meet. In A. Fuhriman & G. M. Burlingame (Eds.), *Handbook of group psychotherapy.* New York: Wiley.

Kipper, D. A., Bizman, A., & Einat, Y. (1981). Selecting group members: Effects of the content of the feedback and the characteristics of the problem. *Small Group Behavior, 12,* 443–457.

Kirshner, B. J., Dies, R. R., & Brown, R. A. (1978). Effects of experimental manipulation of self-disclosure on group cohesiveness. *Journal of Consulting and Clinical Psychology, 46,* 1171–1177.

Kivlighan, D. M., Mullison, D. D., Flohr, D. F., Proudman, S., & Francis, A. M. (1989, August). *The interpersonal structure of "good" versus "bad" group counseling sessions.* Paper presented at the annual meeting of the American Psychological Association, New Orleans, LA.

Klein, R. H., & Carroll, R. A. (1986). Patient characteristics and attendance patterns in outpatient group psychotherapy. *International Journal of Group Psychotherapy, 36,* 115–132.

Lando, H. A., & McGovern, P. G. (1991). The influence of group cohesion on the behavioral treatment of smoking: A failure to replicate. *Addictive Behaviors, 16,* 111–121.

MacKenzie, K. R. (1987). Therapeutic factors in group psychotherapy: A contemporary view. *Group, 11,* 26–34.

MacKenzie, K. R. (1994). Group development. In A. Fuhriman & G. M. Burlingame (Eds.), *Handbook of group psychotherapy: An empirical and clinical synthesis* (pp. 223–268). New York: Wiley.

MacKenzie, K. R., & Tschuschke, V. (1993). Relatedness, group work, and outcome in long-term inpatient psychotherapy groups. *Journal of Psychotherapy Practice and Research, 2,* 147–156.

Marziali, E., Munroe-Blum, H., & McCleary, L. (1997). The contribution of group cohesion and group alliance to the outcome of group psychotherapy. *International Journal of Group Psychotherapy, 47,* 475–497.

McKluskey, U. (in press). The dynamics of attachment and systems-centered group psychotherapy. *Group Dynamics: Theory, Research, and Practice.*

Morran, D. K., Stockton, R., & Teed, C. (1998). Facilitating feedback exchange in groups: Leader interventions. *Journal for Specialists in Group Work, 23,* 257–268.

Neimeyer, G. J., & Thomas, V. M. (1982). Group structure and group process: Personal construct theory and group development. *Small Group Behavior, 13,* 150–164.

Piper, W. E. (1994). Client variables. In A. Fuhriman & G. M. Burlingame (Eds.), *Handbook of group psychotherapy: An empirical and clinical synthesis* (pp. 83–113). New York: Wiley.

Piper, W. E., & Perrault, E. L. (1989). Pretherapy preparation for group members. *International Journal of Group Psychotherapy, 39,* 17–34.

Raskin, N. J. (1986). Client-centered group psychotherapy, part II: Research on client-centered groups. *Person-Centered Review, 1,* 389–408.

Raubolt, R. R. (1983). Brief, problem-focused group psychotherapy with adolescents. *American Journal of Orthopsychiatry, 53,* 157–165.

Roarck, A. E., & Sharah, H. S. (1989). Factors related to group cohesiveness. *Small Group Behavior, 20,* 62–69.

Roback, H. B., & Smith, M. (1987). Patient attrition in dynamically oriented treatment groups. *American Journal of Psychiatry, 144,* 426–431.

Rugel, R. P., & Barry, D. (1990). Overcoming denial through the group: A test of acceptance theory. *Small Group Research, 21,* 45–58.

Santarsiero, L. J., Baker, R. C., & McGee, T. F. (1995). The effects of cognitive pretraining on cohesion and self-disclosure in small groups: An analog study. *Journal of Clinical Psychology, 51,* 403–409.

Schain, J. (1989). The new infant research: Some

implications for group therapy. *Group, 13,* 112–121.

Sexton, H. (1993). Exploring a psychotherapeutic change sequence: Relating process to intersessional and posttreatment outcome. *Journal of Consulting and Clinical Psychology, 61,* 128–136.

Siebert, M. J., & Dorfman, W. I. (1995). Group composition and its impact on effective group treatment of HIV and AIDS patients. *Journal of Developmental and Physical Disabilities, 7,* 317–334.

Slavin, R. L. (1993). The significance of here-and-now disclosure in promoting cohesion in group psychotherapy. *Group, 17,* 143–150.

Slavin, R. L. (1995). "Here-and-now" and "there-and-then" disclosures on cohesion and on students' attitudes toward specific courses. *Psychological Reports, 76,* 111–121.

Stava, L. J., & Bednar, R. L. (1979). Process and outcome in encounter groups: The effects of group composition. *Small Group Behavior, 10,* 200–213.

Stockton, R., & Morran, D. K. (1981). Feedback exchange in personal growth groups: Receiver acceptance as a function of valence, session, and order of delivery. *Journal of Counseling Psychology, 28,* 490–497.

Stockton, R., Rohde, R. I., & Haughey, J. (1992). The effects of structured group exercises on cohesion, engagement, avoidance, and conflict. *Small Group Research, 23,* 155–168.

Taylor, J. R., & Strassberg, D. S. (1986). The effects of sex composition on cohesiveness and interpersonal learning in short-term personal growth groups. *Psychotherapy, 23,* 267–273.

Tschuschke, V., & Dies, R. R. (1994). Intensive analysis of therapeutic factors and outcome in long-term inpatient groups. *International Journal of Group Psychotherapy, 44,* 185–208.

Trad, P. V. (1993). Using the prospective approach as an adjunct to established models of group psychotherapy. *Group, 17,* 43–60.

Vinogradov, S., & Yalom, I. D. (1990). Self-disclosure in group psychotherapy. In G. Stricker & M. Fisher (Eds.), *Self-disclosure in the therapeutic relationship* (pp. 191–204). New York: Plenum.

Waltman, D. E., & Zimpfer, D. G. (1988). Composition, structure, and duration of treatment: Interacting variables in counseling groups. *Small Group Behavior, 19,* 171–184.

Weiner, M. F. (1983). The assessment and resolution of impasse in group psychotherapy. *International Journal of Group Psychotherapy, 33,* 313–331.

Wessler, R. L., & Hankin-Wessler, S. (1989). Cognitive group therapy. In A. Freeman & K. M. Simon (Eds.), *Comprehensive handbook of cognitive therapy* (pp. 559–581). New York: Plenum.

Widra, J. M., & Amidon, E. (1987). Improving self-concept through intimacy group training. *Small Group Behavior, 18,* 269–279.

Wright, F., & Gould, L. J. (1996). Research on gender-linked aspects of group behaviors: Implications for group psychotherapy. In B. De-Chant (Ed.), *Women and group psychotherapy: Theory and practice* (pp. 333–350). New York: Guilford.

Wright, T. L., & Duncan, D. (1986). Attraction to group, group cohesiveness, and individual outcome: A study of training groups. *Small Group Behavior, 17,* 487–492.

Yalom, I. D. (1995). *The theory and practice of group psychotherapy* (4th ed.). New York: Basic.

5

Empathy

Arthur C. Bohart
Robert Elliott
Leslie S. Greenberg
Jeanne C. Watson

Therapist empathy has had a long and sometimes stormy history in psychotherapy. Proposed and codified by Rogers and his followers in the 1940s and 1950s, it was put forward as the foundation of helping skills training popularized in the 1960s and early 1970s. Claims concerning its universal effectiveness were treated with skepticism and came under intense scrutiny by psychotherapy researchers in the late 1970s and early 1980s. For example, one of us found his research on therapist empathy (Elliott et al., 1982) greeted with intense skepticism when it was submitted for publication in the early 1980s. After that, psychotherapists and psychotherapy researchers paid less attention to the concept. J. C. Watson (2002), Duan and Hill (1996), and others have noted the dearth of research on empathy in the last 20 years.

In contrast, empathy is today a topic of vigorous scientific interest in the fields of developmental and social psychology (e.g., Eisenberg & Fabes, 1990; Feshbach, 1997; Ickes, 1997), particularly because empathy is seen as a major part of "emotional intelligence" (Bar-On & Parker, 2000). As we have argued elsewhere (Bohart & Greenberg, 1997), the time is ripe for the reexamination and rehabilitation of therapist empathy as a key change process in psychotherapy. Indeed, the data we will present clearly support such a conclusion.

CONCEPTUAL DEFINITIONS AND FORMS

The first problem with researching empathy in psychotherapy is that there is no consensual definition (Bohart & Greenberg, 1997; Duan & Hill, 1996). Developmental psychologists have typically emphasized the affective component of empathy, defining it as feeling the feelings of the other person, or as responding in a caring fashion to the feelings of another. Empathy, sympathy, and emotional contagion are not sharply differentiated. By contrast, the two therapeutic approaches which have most emphasized empathy—client-centered therapy and psychoanalytic therapy—have focused on its cognitive aspects. Empathy is understanding the client's frame of reference and way of experiencing the world. Empathy is closer to *perspective-taking* (Selman, 1980), or to what Belenky, Clinchy, Goldberger, and Tarule (1986) have called *connected knowing*. By some accounts, 70% or more of Carl Rogers's responses were to meaning rather than to feeling, despite the fact that his mode of responding was called "reflection of feeling" (Brodley & Brody, 1990; Hayes & Goldfried, 1996; Tausch, 1988). However, understanding clients' frames of reference does include understanding affective experience. In addition, therapists such as Rogers

(Shlien, 1997) have generally repudiated sympathy while prizing empathy.

Following Carl Rogers (1980), we shall define empathy as

the therapist's sensitive ability and willingness to understand the client's thoughts, feelings and struggles from the client's point of view. [It is] this ability to see completely through the client's eyes, to adopt his frame of reference. (p. 85)

It means entering the private perceptual world of the other ... being sensitive, moment by moment, to the changing felt meanings which flow in this other person. . . . It means sensing meanings of which he or she is scarcely aware. (p. 142)

Defined this way, empathy is a higher-order category under which different subcategories can be nested. There are different ways an individual can put him- or herself into the shoes of another: emotionally, cognitively, on a moment-to-moment basis, or by trying to grasp an overall sense of what it is like to be that person. Within these subcategories, different aspects of the client's experience can become the focus of empathy. Similarly, there are many different ways of expressing empathy, including empathic reflections, empathic questions, experience-near interpretations, and empathic conjectures, as well as the responsive use of other therapeutic procedures. Accordingly, empathy is best understood as a complex construct (Gladstein & Associates, 1987; J. C. Watson, 2002) consisting of a variety of acts used in different ways by therapists of different orientations for different purposes.

In particular, we distinguish between three main modes of therapeutic empathy: empathic rapport, communicative attunement, and person empathy. For some therapists, empathy is primarily the establishment of empathic rapport and support. The therapist exhibits a compassionate attitude toward the client and tries to demonstrate that he or she understands the client's experience, often in order to set the context for effective intervention. A second mode of empathy consists of an active, ongoing effort to stay attuned on a moment-to-moment basis with the client's communications and unfolding process.

This kind of "process empathy" has been called communicative attunement (Bohart & Greenberg, 1997; Orlinsky, Grawe, & Parks, 1994). Client-centered and experiential therapists are most likely to emphasize this form of empathy. The therapist's attunement may be expressed in different ways, but most likely in one of several types of empathic responses. But empathic responses do more than merely communicate the therapist's understanding of the client's feelings or message; they are also used to deepen and carry forward the client's exploration (Gendlin, 1968; Greenberg & Elliott, 1997; J. C. Watson, 2002).

Finally, person empathy (Elliott, Watson, Greenberg, Goldman, & Davis, 2001)—also called "experience-near understanding of the client's world" (Bohart & Greenberg , 1997) and "background empathy" (Lerner, 1972)—consists of a sustained effort to understand the client's experiencing, both historically and in the present, that form the background of his or her current experiencing. The question is, How have the client's experiences led him or her to see/feel/think and act as he or she does? This type of empathic understanding is emphasized by psychodynamic therapists. However, empathic rapport, communicative attunement, and person empathy are not mutually exclusive, and the differences are a matter of emphasis.

Empathy has also been seen as a trait or response skill (Egan, 1982; Truax & Carkhuff, 1967), as an identification process of "becoming" the experience of the client (Mahrer, 1997), as a hermeneutic interpretive process that helps clients deconstruct their experience, and as a means of facilitating clients' affect regulation (J. C. Watson, 2002). O'Hara (1984, 1997) argues that empathy is getting inside the "skin of the relationship" as well as inside the skin of the client. Perhaps the most practical conception, and one that we will draw on in our meta-analysis, is Barrett-Lennard's (1981) operational definition of empathy in terms of three different perspectives—that of the therapist ("empathic resonance"), the observer ("expressed empathy"), and the client ("received empathy")—which are organized into a sequential process model.

OPERATIONAL DEFINITIONS AND THE MEASUREMENT

Reflecting the complex, multidimensional nature of empathy, a confusing welter of measures has been developed. We will not review the different measures of empathy that have been used outside the realm of psychotherapy. (See Eisenberg & Fabes, 1990, for a review.)

Within psychotherapy, the most commonly used measures of therapist empathy fall into four categories: empathy rated by objective raters; empathy as rated by clients; therapists rating their own empathy; and predictive empathy (congruence between therapist and client perceptions of the client). Trait measures of empathy exist (for example, Davis, 1994; Mehrabian & Epstein, 1972), but have rarely been used in psychotherapy outcome research.

Types of Measures

Observer-Rated Empathy

Both Truax and Carkhuff (1967) and Carkhuff and Berenson (1967) developed scales for rating empathy. These scales ask the rater to decide if the content of the therapist's response detracts from the client's response, is interchangeable with it, or adds to or carries it forward by responding to feeling. Typically, trained raters listen to two- to five-minute samples from therapy tapes. Samples are usually drawn from the beginning, middle, and/or the end of therapy. Scales such as these do not adequately reflect the client-centered conception of empathy as an attitude because they focus narrowly on a particular kind of response, often empathic reflections. Furthermore, the equation of a particular response form with empathy has made these scales less appropriate for measuring empathy in approaches other than client-centered (Lambert, DeJulio, & Stein, 1978).

More recent empathy measures are based on broader understandings of forms of empathic responding. Elliott and colleagues' (1982) measure breaks empathy down into component elements and has shown good psychometric properties; however, it has not been used in psychotherapy outcome research. J. C. Watson (1999) has developed an observer-rated measure of empathy that assesses therapists' verbal and nonverbal behavior. This new measure is promising because it correlates with client ratings on the Barrett-Lennard Relationship Inventory (J. C. Watson & Prosser, in press).

In addition, the therapist's general empathy can be rated by others who know or have supervised the therapist. For instance, in a study by Miller, Taylor, and West (1980), therapists' empathic capacities were rated by their supervisors. For purposes of our meta-analysis, we lumped together all observer perspective measures of empathy.

Client Ratings

The most widely used client-rated measure is the empathy scale of the Barrett-Lennard Relationship Inventory (BLRI). Other client rating measures have been developed by Lorr (1965), Persons and Burns (1985), Hamilton (2000), and Truax and Carkhuff (1967). Rogers (1957) hypothesized that clients' *perceptions* of therapists' facilitative conditions (positive regard, empathy, and congruence) predict therapeutic outcome. Accordingly, the BLRI, which measures clients' perceptions, is the closest operational definition of Rogers's hypothesis. In earlier reviews, Barrett-Lennard (1981) and Gurman (1977) both concluded that client-perceived empathy predicted outcome better than observer- or therapist-rated empathy.

Therapist Ratings

There are therapist self-rating scales on the BLRI. Earlier reviews (Barrett-Lennard, 1981; Gurman, 1977) found that therapist-rated empathy neither predicted outcome nor correlated with client-rated or observer-rated empathy.

Predictive Empathy

Several studies we reviewed made use of measures of therapist-client congruence. These typically consist of therapists rating clients as they think the clients would rate themselves on various measures, such as personality scales or lists of symptoms, and then comparing these ratings to how clients actually rated themselves. For instance, Landfield (1971) compared how therapists rated clients on Kelly's REP grid with how clients rated themselves. The measure of empathy is the degree of congruence between therapist and client ratings. This is called predictive empathy because the therapist is trying to predict how clients will rate themselves. It is closer to a measure of the therapist's ability to form a global understanding of what it is like to be the client (person empathy) than it is to a process measure of ongoing communicative attunement.

Ickes's (1997) recent work on "empathic accuracy," however, is a variation of this approach that does provide a predictive measure of communicative attunement. He uses a tape-assisted recall procedure in which therapists' or observers' moment-to-moment empathy is measured by comparing their perceptions of client experiences to clients' reports of those experiences. Unfortunately, no process outcome studies using this promising method have been carried out.

Correlations of Different Empathy Measures

Intercorrelations of different types of empathy measures have generally been weak. Low correlations have been reported between cognitive and affective measures (Gladstein et al., 1987) and between predictive measures and the BLRI (Kurtz & Grummon, 1972). Other research has found that tape-rated measures correlate only moderately with client-perceived empathy. Gurman (1977) reports 17 correlations from 10 studies. The range of correlations is from .00 to .88, with a mean of .28. However, the recent observer-rated scale developed by J. C. Watson and Prosser (in press) has been shown to correlate more highly with the BLRI.

These weak correlations are not surprising when one considers what the different instruments are supposed to be measuring. Trying to predict how a client will fill out a symptom checklist is very different from responding sensitively in a way that demonstrates subtle understanding of what the client is trying to communicate. Similarly, clients' ratings of their therapists' understanding may be based on many things other than the ther-

apists' particular skill in empathic reflection. Accordingly, Gladstein and Associates (1987) have suggested that we should not expect different measures of this complex construct to correlate.

Confounding Between Empathy and Other Relationship Variables

A related concern is the distinctiveness of empathy from other relationship constructs. Gurman (1977) reviewed more than 20 studies primarily using the BLRI and found that on average, empathy correlated with congruence .62, with positive regard .53, and with unconditionality .28. Factor analyses reviewed by Gurman (1977) in which scale scores were used found that one global factor typically emerged, with empathy loading on it along with congruence and positive regard. Blatt, Zuroff, Quinlan, and Pilkonis (1996) found that the empathy scale loaded .93 on a global BLRI factor, with positive regard loading .87 and congruence loading .92. Similarly, Salvio, Beutler, Wood, and Engle (1992) found that empathy, regard, and congruence were all highly interrelated, and that they correlated highly with a measure of the strength of the therapeutic alliance. These results suggest that clients' perceptions of empathy are not clearly differentiated from their perceptions of other relationship factors.

On the other hand, Gurman (1977) also reviewed several factor analytic studies where, instead of using scale scores, specific items were used. These studies found empathy emerging as a separate factor. Horvath and Greenberg (1986) found that empathy correlated more highly with the bond component of the therapeutic alliance than with the task and goal components.

The situation is similar with respect to observer-rated empathy. Truax and Carkhuff (1967) reported studies in which empathy, warmth, and genuineness all were interrelated, and other studies where one factor correlated negatively with the other two. Thus, there is evidence both for and against the hypothesis that empathy, positive regard, and congruence are separate and distinct variables. We view empathy as a relationship component that is both conceptually distinct and part of a higher-order evaluative relationship construct.

CLINICAL EXAMPLE

Mark presented to psychotherapy complaining of pervasive anxiety. He was a 30-year-old unmarried man who had been struggling since his early twenties to be successful as a musician. When he entered therapy, he was working as a waiter. He came from a traditional family that lived in the South. His brothers and sisters all had successful careers, were married, and had children. His parents were constantly pestering him about not being married and not having a stable career. His anxiety attacks had begun a few weeks after a visit home for Christmas. When Mark came to his first appointment he was clearly agitated. He had previously called and had sounded desperate over the phone. The therapist initially was concerned that Mark might be in a state of crisis.

The therapist's orientation was an integrative experiential/humanistic approach, based in the principles of client-centered therapy. The therapist tried to understand the client's point of view actively and empathetically and to share that understanding, using his attunement to the client's experience to identify effective interventions and to stay responsively attuned so that therapeutic procedures could be adjusted to maximize learning. Finally, therapist and client worked to develop an ongoing shared frame of reference from which to work collaboratively.

The following are two examples of the therapist's utilization of empathic responding during the first session:

C1: I'm really in a panic [anxious, agitated, looking plaintively at the therapist]. I feel anxious all the time. Sometimes it seems so bad I really worry that I'm on the verge of a psychotic break. I'm actually afraid of completely falling apart. Nothing like this has ever happened to me before. I always felt in charge of myself before, but now I can't seem to get any control over myself at all.

T1: So a real sense of vulnerability—kind of like you don't even know yourself anymore.

C2: Yes! That's it. I don't know myself anymore. I feel totally lost. The anxiety feels like a big cloud that just takes me over, and I can't even find myself in it anymore. I don't even know what I want, what I trust. . . . I'm lost.

T2: Totally lost, like, "Where did Mark go? I can't find myself anymore."

C3: No, I can't [sadly and thoughtfully].

The dialogue continued like this and soon the therapist's empathic recognition provided the client with a sense of being understood. This fostered a sense of safety, and gradually the client moved from agitation into a mode of reflective sadness. The client then began to reflect on his experience in a more productive, exploratory manner. He talked about the basic conflict in his life: whether to continue to pursue an acting career or to find a "real job" and life partner, given the fact that he was now 30 and had shown no signs of making a breakthrough in acting.

Later, the client role-played a dialogue between two sides of himself. One side, his critic or "should" side, said that he should get a stable job and get married and criticized him for not being married. The other side was the "want" side—or in this case, the "don't want" side—which said, "I don't want to live an ordinary life; I want to live a creative life." This side came out in the form of defensive rebellion. Empathic sensitivity was used to help the therapist tune into the client's point of view and to suggest foci for the client's exploratory activities during the role-play activities. What emerged from this role-play was that there was a longing for a "normal" lifestyle underlying Mark's defensive rebellion, in conflict with a desire to do something creative.

During the first few sessions, the client had repeatedly expressed the suspicion that something about his early relationships with his parents had an important component in his current problems. Initially, the therapist had not taken this too seriously, since progress was apparently being made through the collaborative use of other procedures. Because the therapist was not psychodynamic and past-oriented, the therapist had not sensitively enough tuned into this. The therapist's lack of person empathy (that is, not grasping how figural this was for the client within the client's frame of reference) for the larger meaning of the client's interest in this topic had effectively shut off this avenue of exploration.

Finally the therapist listened and responded in an invitational way to the client, and the client began to explore his childhood. This illustrates how empathy not only is permission-giving, but also provides active support for exploration. It illustrates too how sensitive, empathic understanding of the *client's* way of seeing the problem is sometimes crucial for therapeutic progress (Hubble, Duncan, & Miller, 1999). This led to a breakthrough moment. In reviewing his childhood, the client became emotionally aware of how neglected he had felt as a child by his high-achieving parents, who were not mean and cruel, but who were not themselves highly empathic. As a child, the client had always been unusually interested in fantasy activities and was a rather "inner" person, in contrast to his siblings, who were more conventional and high-achieving in school. The parents had not known what to make of their unique child and were unable to respond in an empathic and supportive way to his emerging uniqueness.

The result was that he had had to adopt a kind of defensive "I have a right to be different" attitude. He was never able to genuinely consider whether he wanted to be conventional or not. Underlying this was a longing for conventionality. Accessing this in the context of his family life helped him accept his differentness and to mourn the fact that he was not conventional (and, in effect, mourn that he might never be what his family wanted him to be). Over the course of this work, the anxiety decreased. Eventually he made a decision to continue to pursue a musical career, at least for a while. The crisis abated.

THE RELATIONSHIP OF EMPATHY TO PSYCHOTHERAPY OUTCOME: A META-ANALYSIS

In this section we report the results of a meta-analysis conducted on available research relating empathy to psychotherapy outcome. Because previous reviews (e.g., Orlinsky, Grawe, & Parks, 1994) have used box score methods to assess this relationship, we believe it is important to conduct a more sensitive analysis.

Research Strategy

This meta-analysis addresses the following questions: What is the general association between therapist empathy and client outcome? Do differ-

ent forms of therapy yield different levels of association between empathy and outcome? Does the type of empathy measure predict the level of association between empathy and outcome? What study and sample characteristics (sample size, treatment setting, treatment modality and length, level of client severity, therapist experience, type of outcome measure, unit of process) predict an association between empathy and outcome?

Literature Review

Articles were culled from previous reviews (Beutler, Crago, & Arizmendi, 1986; Gurman, 1977; Lambert, DeJulio, & Stein, 1978; Mitchell, Bozarth, & Krauft, 1977; Orlinsky, Grawe, & Parks, 1994; Orlinsky & Howard, 1986; Parloff, Waskow, & Wolfe, 1978; Truax & Mitchell, 1971; N. Watson, 1984). We also searched PsychInfo and PsychLit forward from 1992 (two years before the publication of the last major review of empathy research in Orlinsky et al., 1994). Additionally, we consulted the indices of relevant journals such as *Psychotherapy*, *Person-Centered Journal*, *Psychotherapy Research*, and *Journal of Humanistic Psychology*.

Our inclusion criteria were that: (1) the study had to include a specific measure of empathy; (2) empathy had to be related to some measure of therapy outcome; (3) the client sample had to involve "real" clinical problems; (4) the average number of sessions had to be greater than two; (5) the study needed to be available in English; (6) the study must have included at least five clients; (7) the study had to be available in published form; or (8) if the study was reported in a shortened form (e.g., in a review article or in a dissertation abstract), enough information had to be available to calculate a weighted effect size.

Characteristics of the Studies Evaluated

In order to examine variables that might moderate the empathy-outcome association, we evaluated the studies on a wide range of sample and method features. For measures of outcome, we included a study if it contained some evaluative assessment of the effects of therapy, even if only at the session level (immediate outcome). For example, we included abstinence from drinking

(Miller et al., 1980), level of depression (Burns & Nolen-Hoeksema, 1992), MMPI scores (Kiesler, Klein, Mathieu, & Schoeninger, 1967), client satisfaction (Lorr, 1965), supervisors' ratings of client improvement (Bergin & Jasper, 1969), client and therapist posttherapy ratings of amount of change (Hamilton, 2000), and session progress (Orlinsky & Howard, 1967). We made no attempt to evaluate the adequacy of the outcome measures used. There is some conceptual overlap between feeling understood and client satisfaction, but this one outcome measure represented only 11 cases out of the 190 specific effects measured.

The resulting sample consisted of 47 studies, encompassing 190 separate tests of the empathy–outcome association and a total of 3026 clients. Study dates ranged from 1961 to 2000, with 68% carried out before 1980. The average study involved 64 clients (range = 8 to 320) seen for slightly less than 30 sessions (range = 3 to 228). Typically, the studies involved mixed, eclectic, or unknown types of therapy (70%); individual treatment (78%); "mixed neurotic" (what today would include primarily affective and anxiety disorders) samples (47%); recent Ph.D. or M.D. therapists (38%); and posttreatment assessment of outcome (60%). Studies contributed between 1 and 42 separate effects (mean = 4.0). Of the 190 separate effects examined, the largest number used client measures (38%; about half of these the BLRI) or observer measures (33%; the vast majority variations of the Truax-Carkhuff scales). Therapist measures were used for 14% of the effects (about half of these the BLRI), while various predictive measures were used 16% of the time (mostly from the Kurtz & Grummon [1972] study). "Therapy to date" was the most common unit for measuring empathy, accounting for 64% of effects.

Estimation of Effect Size

For effect size (ES), we used parametric or nonparametric correlations if available. Otherwise, we used the following conventions to estimate r. First, if we had a significance level, we used the equivalent t value and converted it to r. If the result was nonsignificant, but we had enough information to calculate a t and then convert, we did so. If we had no other information, and the effect was nonsignificant, we set r at .0. If the authors indicated a "nonsignificant trend," but did not report a correlation (for instance, Kiesler and colleagues [1967] indicated several trends on MMPI scales), we estimated the trend by assigning an ES of half the size of a significant r.

Coding Procedure

The following variables were coded: modality of therapy (individual/group); theoretical orientation (client-centered, experiential, psychodynamic, cognitive-behavioral, mixed); experience level of therapists; treatment setting (inpatient, outpatient); number of sessions (typically the mean); type of problems (mixed neurotic, depression, anxiety, severe problems such as psychosis); source of outcome measure (therapist rating, client rating, objective and other measures); when outcome measured (e.g., postsession, posttherapy, follow-up); type of outcome measured (symptom change, improvement, global); source of empathy measure (objective ratings, therapist, client, therapist/client congruence, trait measure); and unit of measure (2–5 minute samples, session, therapy to date).

We conducted two sets of analyses: by effects and by studies. First, we analyzed the 190 separate effects in order to examine the impact of type of empathy and outcome measure. Second, study-level analyses used averaged individual effects (with Fisher r-to-z correction) within studies before calculation, thus avoiding problems of nonindependence and eliminating bias due to variable numbers of effects reported in different studies (for example, one study, Kurtz & Grummon, 1972, contributed 22% of the effects). Finally, in order to correct for small sample and distributional biases, we applied three separate corrections: Fisher's correction for small sample bias (Rosenthal, 1991), weighting by sample size, and Fisher's r-to-z transformation.

Overall Relation Between Therapist Empathy and Outcome

In table 5.1, we report corrected and uncorrected overall effect sizes for separate effects and effects aggregated within studies. Uncorrected and corrected values were around .20 for effect-level anal-

Table 5.1. Empathy-Outcome Correlations: Overall Summary Statistics

	Effect Level (n = 190)		Study Level (n = 47)	
n	M	sd	M	sd
Median r	.18	—	.23	—
Mean r	.20	.28	.26*	.22
Mean unbiased r	.19	.27	.29*	.27
Weighted r	.23	—	.33	—
Weighted unbiased r	.23	—	.32	—

Note: Fisher's r-to-z transformation used to calculate means and sds. Mean unbiased rs use Fisher's correction for small sample bias (Rosenthal, 1991). Weighted rs use sample size as weights.
*Statistically significant (greater than $p < .001$).

yses. Across the 190 analyses represented here, empathy accounted for about 4% of the outcome variance, between a small and a medium effect. Study-level analyses were slightly higher (mean = .26; median = .23). Weighted rs were higher still, because larger studies had slightly larger effects. (Effect sizes for study-level analyses are higher because studies with large numbers of empathy-outcome tests had slightly smaller effects; see Kurtz & Grummon, 1972.) The single best summary value is the study-level, weighted, unbiased r of .32, a medium effect size.

We were surprised by the size of this association. The variance in outcome accounted for by empathy at the study level, therefore, ranges be-

tween 7% and 10%, depending on whether the lowest ES of .26 or the highest estimate of .32 is used. This effect size is on the same order of magnitude as (or slightly larger than) previous analyses of the relationship between therapeutic alliance and outcome (for example, Horvath & Symonds, 1991, with .26; or Martin, Garske & Davis, 2000, with .22). Overall, empathy accounts for as much and probably more outcome variance than does specific intervention (compare to Wampold's [2001] estimate of 1% to 8% for interventions).

Theoretical Orientation as a Moderator Variable

Next, we examined the possibility that different empathy-outcome correlations might be obtained for different theoretical orientations. For example, one might expect the association to be larger in those therapies for which empathy is held to be a key change process (such as experiential therapies). However, our analyses turned up little evidence of such a trend (see table 5.2). On the contrary, there is a hint that empathy might be more important to outcome in cognitive-behavioral therapies than in others. If this finding is reliable, it raises intriguing questions about how empathy functions in therapy. Perhaps empathy is even more important in an intervention-based therapy than in a relational one, in order to provide an effective "ground" for intervention. Or perhaps more active and directive therapists, if they are also sensitive, are perceived as more em-

Table 5.2. Mean Correlations Across Therapy Orientation

Theoretical Orientation	Effect Level			Study Level		
	Mean r	sd	n	Mean r	sd	n
Experiential/humanistic	0.20	0.31	32	0.25	0.21	6
Cognitive-behavioral	0.32	0.38	7	0.49	0.48	4
Psychodynamic	0.16	0.13	15	0.18	0.14	4
Other/unspecified	0.19	0.27	136	0.30	0.27	33
F	.64(d.f. = 3, 186)			.99(d.f. = 3, 37)		

Note: Calculated using unbiased, Fisher's z scores. F represents one-way ANOVA for effect of theoretical orientation on effect sizes (r).

Table 5.3. Mean Correlations Across Empathy Measurement Perspectives

Measurement Perspective	Mean r	sd	n
Observer	0.23	0.3	62
Client	0.25	0.26	72
Therapist	0.18	0.21	26
Predictive	−0.03	0.19	30
F	8.94** (d.f. = 3, 186)		

**$p < .01$

Note: Effect level analyses. Calculated using unbiased, Fisher's z scores, which were then converted back to r.

pathic. Our sample of studies is too small for definite conclusions, so evaluating this finding and what it may mean awaits further research.

Type of Empathy Measure as a Moderator Variable

In table 5.3, we chart relationships between specific types of empathy measures and outcome, using effect-level analyses. As we expected, and as has been noted by previous reviewers (Barrett-Lennard, 1981; Parloff et al., 1978), perspective

of empathy measure made a difference for empathy-outcome correlations. Client measures predicted outcome the best (mean uncorrected $r = .25$), followed closely by observer rated measures (.23) and therapist measures (.18); each of these mean effects was significantly greatly than zero ($p < .001$). In contrast, predictive measures were unrelated to outcome (−.03). Scheffé tests indicated that predictive measures predicted outcome more poorly when compared to each of the other types of measure ($p < .05$). Clarification of these issues also awaits further research; however, for now it seems fair to say the clients' feelings of being understood and observer ratings (and, to a lesser extent, therapist impressions) appear to carry significant weight as far as outcome goes, but that predictive measures do not, in spite of their intuitive appeal.

Other Possible Moderator Variables

Finally, in table 5.4, we consider more specific relationships between empathy and other variables. The most interesting and unexpected finding here is the negative correlation between therapist experience and empathy-outcome association. That is, larger effects are obtained for more junior therapists. Empathy may have a relatively small

Table 5.4. Second-Order Correlations Between Empathy-Outcome Effect Size and Selected Predictor Variables

Predictor	Effect Level		Study Level	
	r	n	r	n
Year of publication	.01	190	.06	47
No. of clients in study	.13	190	.10	47
Setting (1 = outpatient; 2 = inpatient)	.05	189	−.07	46
Modality (1 = individual; 2 = group)	.19*	182	.07	43
Length of therapy (in sessions)	.16*	153	.12	35
Client severity (3-point scale)	.16	145	.19	37
Therapist experience level (6-point scale)	−.24**	171	−.43**	39
Outcome specificity	−.24**	187	—	—
Size of empathy unit (4-point scale)	−.10	190	—	—

*$p < .05$ **$p < .01$

Note: Unbiased, Fisher r-to-z transformed effect sizes used in calculations. Outcome specificity rated on 6-point scale, ranging from 1 (satisfaction measures) to 6 (individualized outcome).

association with outcome for more experienced therapists. There are at least two possible reasons for this finding. First, inexperienced therapists may vary more in empathy, while smaller correlations for experienced therapists may reflect a restriction of range or ceiling effect. Alternatively, experienced therapists may have developed additional skills such as effective problem-solving, so that clients are more likely to forgive empathic misattunements.

There were other findings of note. First, empathy appears to predict improvement in nonspecific measures of outcome (global improvement, client satisfaction) better than it does for more specific, problem-focused outcome measures. This is likely to be due to conceptual confounding between empathy and alliance-linked outcome measures (retrospective change ratings, client satisfaction). Second, group therapy and lengthier therapies produced larger empathy-outcome associations, but only for effect-level analyses. However, both of these effects were fairly small $(r < .2)$.

The Question of Causality

The question of causality—whether empathy causes therapeutic outcome or is a correlate of it—cannot be answered definitively from our data. However data from several studies shed light on the question. First, Burns and Nolen-Hoeksema (1992) used structural equation modeling to demonstrate that empathy bore a causal relationship to outcome. Second, in the Miller and colleagues (1980) study, ratings of therapists' empathy were made by supervisors before and independent of knowing about outcome data. Still, empathy showed a strong $(r = .82)$ relationship to outcome in a cognitive-behavioral program for drinking. Third, Anderson (1999) measured therapists' facilitative interpersonal skills, including accurate empathy, before therapy by having them respond to videotapes of clients who presented interpersonally in difficult ways. Anderson found statistically significant relationships between this prior measure of therapist interpersonal skills and client outcome in subsequent psychotherapy. Based on several studies, Truax and Carkhuff (1967) contended that levels of therapist empathy are primarily determined by the therapist (suggesting a causal relationship).

Further evidence comes from studies which show that client-centered therapy is effective (Elliott, 2002). The mean ES of pre-post differences in client-centered therapy is .97 ($n = 44$ studies). For controlled effects (versus wait-list and no-treatment controls) the mean ES is .80 ($n = 13$). Usually one cannot attribute causal efficacy to a component of a therapy (for example, interpretation in psychoanalysis) because the whole therapy is effective. Although other relational elements are present in client-centered therapy, the vast majority of the time is occupied with therapeutic work in the form of empathic exploration as opposed to supportive prizing or relational dialogue, both of which are relatively rare. For instance, studies have found that more than 90% of Carl Rogers's responses were empathic following responses (see Brodley & Brody, 1990). Given such a heavy weighting of empathy as the major independent variable in client-centered therapy, its effectiveness becomes another piece of supporting (although not definitive) evidence for the causal role of empathy.

None of the above evidence conclusively establishes a causal role. Burns and Nolen-Hoeksema (1992) note that structural equation modeling cannot definitely show causality but only test for it. Miller and colleagues (1980) had supervisors rate supervisees' levels of empathy, and it is possible that these ratings were influenced by the supervisees' reports of how well therapy was going with their clients. In Anderson's (1999) study in which empathy was measured prior to therapy, empathy is confounded with other facilitative interpersonal skills. Even though empathy is the predominant process in client-centered therapy, it is not the only process. Finally, in contrast to Truax and Carkhuff's (1967) contention that empathy is primarily therapist-determined, other studies have indicated that therapists' levels of empathy vary as a function of the client (Beutler, Johnson, Neville, & Workman, 1972; Kiesler et al., 1967; Ham, 1987; Henry, Schacht, & Strupp, 1986; Mitchell, Bozarth, & Krauft, 1977). Further research is needed to clarify this relationship. Nevertheless, empathy is probably better conceived of as a mutually created climate variable rather than as a variable unilaterally "provided" by the therapist.

LIMITATIONS OF THE RESEARCH REVIEWED

J. C. Watson (2002) and others (for example, Patterson, 1984) have discussed problems with the research on empathy. These entail (1) the questionable validity of some of the outcome measures (such as client satisfaction); (2) lack of appropriate, sensitive outcome measures; (3) restricted range of predictor variables; (4) confounds among variations in time of assessment, experience of raters, and sampling methods; (5) reliance on obsolete diagnostic categories; and (6) incomplete reporting of methods and results.

The restricted range of predictor variables is a particular problem. In the Mitchell, Truax, Bozarth, and Krauft (1973) study, for instance, most of the therapists scored below the minimum considered to be sufficient to be effective, and outcome was only modest to moderate in the study. It is not surprising that significant correlations were not found.

Furthermore, in a few cases, results were merely reported as either significant in the positive direction or nonsignificant. It is possible that some of the nonsignificant results were actually in the negative direction. Therefore, it is impossible to say just how this might have affected our results. This is particularly a problem for calculating effect sizes, where assumptions had to be made in order to be able to calculate them at all.

MEDIATORS AND MODERATORS

The section on mediators and moderators of empathy is divided into three parts: (1) therapist factors, (2) client factors, and (3) how empathy leads to outcome.

Therapist Factors

Feshbach (1997) has proposed that two of the skills involved in empathy are those of cognitive perspective-taking and awareness of one's own feelings. Research has in fact found a relationship between various measures of cognitive complexity, such as those of perspective-taking or abstract ability, and empathy in both developmental psychology and in psychotherapy (Eisenberg & Fabes, 1990; Henschel & Bohart, 1981; J. C. Watson, 2002). With respect to awareness of feelings, Peabody and Gelso (1982) found that therapists who were open to conflictual, countertransferential feelings were perceived as more empathic by clients.

The degree of similarity between therapist and client (Duan & Hill, 1996; Gladstein & Associates, 1987; J. C. Watson, 2002) also influences the level of empathy. Another important factor is therapist nonverbal behavior. This includes therapists' posture, vocal quality, ability to encourage exploration using emotion words, and the relative infrequency of engaging in such speech acts as talking too much, advice-giving, and interruption (Duan & Hill, 1996; J. C. Watson, 2002). Other research has shown that responses that are just ahead of the client seem to be more effective than responses that are either at the same level as the client, or at a more global level (Tallman, Robinson, Kay, Harvey, & Bohart, 1994; Sachse, 1990a, 1990b; Truax & Carkhuff, 1967). Myers (2000), in a qualitative study of clients' experience of empathy, found that interrupting, failing to maintain eye contact, and dismissing the client's position while imposing the therapist's own position were perceived as unempathic. Conversely, paying attention to details and being nonjudgmental, attentive, and open to discussing any topic were perceived as empathic.

Finally, empathy is more than simply responding to clients' feelings. J. C. Watson (2002) has noted, "To the extent that empathically understanding others means not only having access to their emotional worlds but also to their goals, intentions, and values, then it seems important to be able to incorporate these in order to adequately capture the multi-faceted and complex nature of the construct" (p. 8). Accordingly, Horvath and Greenberg (1986) found that clients' perceptions of therapists' empathy correlated with the degree to which clients and therapists agreed on the goals and tasks of therapy.

Client Factors

Several authors (for example, Beutler et al., 1972; Beutler et al., 1973; Ham, 1987; Henry et al., 1986) have suggested that the level of empathy provided varies as a function of the client. Kiesler and colleagues (1967) found that levels of empathy were higher with clients who had less pathology and who were brighter, yet were lower in self-esteem. One possible moderator of the degree of empathy a therapist experiences may have to do with the client him- or herself.

Not all clients respond favorably to explicit empathic expressions. Beutler, Crago, and Arizmendi (1986, p. 279) cite evidence that suggests that "patients who are highly sensitive, suspicious, poorly motivated, and reactive against authority perform relatively poorly with therapists who are particularly empathic, involved, and accepting." Another study (Mohr & Woodhouse, 2000) found that some clients prefer businesslike rather than warm, empathic therapists.

More broadly, Duan and Hill (1996) speculate that different types of empathy may be hindering or helpful to clients at different times. Hill and colleagues (Hill, Thompson, & Corbett, 1992; Thompson & Hill, 1991) found that when clients had negative in-session reactions to their therapists, the therapist's awareness of the reaction "led to interventions that were perceived as less helpful than when the awareness was absent" (Thompson & Hill, 1991, p. 269).

Keeping in mind O'Hara's (1984) concept of empathy as not only getting inside the skin of the client, but getting inside the skin of the relationship, it may be that in some cases the therapist is more empathic by not expressing empathy. Martin (2000) notes: "Think of the insensitive irony of a therapist who says, 'I sense the sadness you want to hide. It seems like you don't want to be alone right now but you also don't want somebody talking to you about your sadness'" (pp. 184–185). Martin adds that this might technically seem empathic, but in fact it is unempathic, controlling, and intrusive because it violates the client's personal space.

How Does Empathy Lead
to Good Outcome?

Four factors have been identified as potential mediators between empathy and outcome. Three of these are the processes of empathy (1) as a relationship condition, (2) as a corrective emotional experience, and (3) as a cognitive-affective processing condition. These processes include the mechanisms posited by different theories. The fourth factor has to do with the role of the client as an active self-healer.

Empathy as Relationship Condition

Empathy serves a positive relationship function. Feeling understood increases client satisfaction with therapy and thereby increases compliance (for example, in cognitive-behavioral therapy). Several qualitative studies (Bachelor, 1988; Myers, 2000; Van Kaam, 1959) have found that feeling understood increases feelings of safety in the relationship and makes it easier to self-disclose. Clients also feel safer to approach difficult personal areas. In addition, there is evidence that empathy is correlated with staying in therapy as opposed to premature termination (Altmann, 1973; Landfield, 1971). Chafetz and colleagues (1962, 1964) found that after a single empathic counseling session, alcoholic patients were over 10 times more likely to seek treatment, and 40 to 50 times more likely to stay in treatment.

*Empathy as Corrective
Emotional Experience*

Empathy provides a kind of direct learning or "corrective relational experience." Theoretically, an empathic relationship may help strengthen the self and break isolation (Rowe & MacIsaac, 1989; Jordan, 1997; Bohart & Greenberg, 1997; Zimring, 2000). Empirically, it can help clients learn that they are worthy of respect and of being heard and that their feelings and behaviors make sense, so that they can express their feelings and needs in relationships (Bachelor, 1988; Myers, 2000; Van Kaam, 1959). In addition, empathic attunement may biologically affect both therapist and client (Levenson & Ruef, 1997).

*Empathy and
Cognitive-Affective Processing*

Empathy has been found to promote exploration and meaning creation. This includes helping clients think more productively (Sachse, 1990a, 1990b), raising levels of productive experiencing (Klein & Mathieu-Coughlan, 1986; Rice & Saperia, 1984), and facilitating emotional reprocessing (Greenberg & Paivio, 1997).

Empathy and the Client as Active Self-Healer

Several reviewers have questioned the medical model and its emphasis on primary healing power being located in specific interventions for specific problems. Rather, healing power may primarily reside in clients' active self-healing capacities (Bergin & Garfield, 1994; Bohart & Tallman, 1999; Hubble, Duncan, & Miller, 1999; Wampold, 2001). Accordingly, client active involvement becomes the most important factor in making therapy work (Orlinsky et al., 1994). If so, how does empathy fit into this? First, empathy promotes involvement. Second, empathy provides support for clients' active information-processing efforts; it can provide an "empathic workspace" in which clients mobilize their capacities for self-change (Bohart & Tallman, 1999). Third, empathy helps the therapist choose interventions compatible with the client's frame of reference (Hubble et al., 1999).

THERAPEUTIC PRACTICES

We begin this section with a summary of the implications of the meta-analysis for therapeutic practice. The most consistent evidence is that clients' perceptions that they are understood by their therapists relate to outcome. This suggests it is important that therapists make efforts to understand their clients, and that this understanding be demonstrated through responses that address the needs of the client as the client perceives them on an ongoing basis. This could be contrasted with therapists who respond primarily out of their own agendas. However, this does not imply that therapists must agree with their clients or that they only use reflection responses. Rather, it suggests that a therapist's responses must continue to coordinate with the "moving point" of the focus of the client's concerns as therapy progresses.

In addition, our findings that observer ratings of accurate empathy (generally using the Truax

and Carkhuff scales) predict outcome suggest that therapist responses that add to or carry forward the meaning in the client's communication are useful. While typically this has occurred through the use of empathic responses, it is likely that other responses also carry forward the client's communication. We have identified several different specific types of empathic responses (Greenberg et al., 1993; Greenberg & Elliott, 1997; J. C. Watson, 2002), some of which we illustrate here with a running example.

Empathic understanding responses are simple responses that convey understanding of the client's experiences. For example:

Client: I have been trying to push things away, but every time I sit down to do something it is like I forget what I am doing.

Therapist: Somehow you are not in a space to work, it's hard for you to concentrate.

Empathic affirmations are attempts by the therapist to validate the client's perspective.

C: And my cat is still lost, so we have been staying up at night in case he returns, so last night was another night without sleep . . . and work has been so busy and I have been so tired and P needs my attention. I have been going around in circles and, oh, everything is just a big mess you know?

T: It sounds really hard, being pulled in a million different directions and there hasn't been time for you, everything just seems as if it is falling apart.

Empathic evocations are exploratory responses that try to bring the client's experience alive using rich, evocative, concrete, connotative language. They often have a probing, tentative quality.

C: I don't know what I'm going to do. I have two hundred dollars this month, everything's behind, there isn't enough work, and I have been doing other things, and then my Dad was here. Things are just swirling around me. I don't know how to keep my stuff together enough for me even to survive.

T: You feel so out of control and vulnerable right now that it feels, what?—as if it is hard to keep your boat from capsizing.

Empathic conjectures are attempts by therapists to get at that which is implicit in clients' narratives. They are similar to interpretations but are not an attempt to provide the client with new information. They are grounded in the data, but the information may not be in the foreground.

C: Yeah, yeah, that is it exactly, and P is not helping. One of his friends has needed to use the computer. So he has been over every night this week. I did not want him over Wednesday because I had friends coming over. So he agreed not to come over, but then P brought him over anyway at around midnight and it was difficult for me to get to sleep. Our lives just seem so chaotic right now. We are not eating regularly, we are not sleeping. P and I had Friday alone but then R was over again all day Saturday.

T: It sounds like there is this continual sense of being . . . invaded?

Going beyond specific responses, the empathic therapist's primary task is to understand experiences rather than words. Truly empathic therapists do not parrot clients' words back or reflect only the content of those words; instead, they understand overall goals as well as moment-to-moment experiences, both explicit and implicit. Empathy in part entails capturing the nuances and implications of what people say, and reflecting this back to them for their consideration.

People express themselves on multiple levels. In being empathic, therapists can focus on clients' feelings, perceptions, construals, values, assumptions, and their views of other people and situations. Certain fragile clients may find expressions of empathy too intrusive, while highly resistant clients may find empathy too directive; still other clients may find an empathic focus on feelings too foreign (Kennedy-Moore & Watson, 1999). Therapists therefore need to know when—and when not—to respond empathically. Therapists need to continually engage in process diagnoses to determine when and how to communicate empathic understanding and at what level to focus their empathic responses from one moment to the next. A number of markers for effective empathic

responding have been empirically identified (J. C. Watson, 2002).

Empathic therapists help clients symbolize their experience in words; they track their emotional responses so that clients can deepen their experience and reflexively examine their feelings, values, and goals. Therapists need to help clients access as much internal information as possible. To this end they need to attend to that which is not said, or that which is at the periphery of awareness, as well as that which is said and is in focal awareness (J. C. Watson, 2002).

While conceptually it may be possible to separate empathy from Rogers's other therapeutic conditions of (1) warmth or positive regard and (2) congruence or genuineness, in practice it is not. It is hard to imagine a therapist high in empathy and low in warmth and genuineness. It would seem that the *quality* of the empathy would be different under those circumstances. These three qualities may be analogous to the components of color: hue, brightness, and saturation. While in principle any given color can be dissected into these three qualities, the impact of that particular color depends on all three. With this in mind, it seems clear to us that empathy will have a positive effect only in the context of other positive relationship qualities.

REFERENCES (meta-analysis references are starred)

Altmann, H. A. (1973). Effects of empathy, warmth, and genuineness in the initial counseling interview. *Counselor Education and Supervision, 12,* 225–228.

Anderson, T. (1999). *Specifying non-"specifics" in therapists: The effect of facilitative interpersonal skills in outcome and alliance formation.* Paper presented at the 30th annual meeting of the International Society for Psychotherapy Research, Braga, Portugal.

Bachelor, A. (1988). How clients perceive therapist empathy: A content analysis of "received" empathy. *Psychotherapy, 25,* 227–240.

Bar-On, R., & Parker, J. D. A. (Eds.). (2000). *The handbook of emotional intelligence.* San Francisco, CA: Jossey-Bass.

*Barrett-Lennard, G. (1962). Dimensions of therapist response as causal factors in therapeutic change. *Psychological Monographs, 76*(43, Whole Number 562).

Barrett-Lennard, G. T. (1981). The empathy cycle: Refinement of a nuclear concept. *Journal of Counseling Psychology, 28,* 91–100.

*Barrington, B. L. (1967). The differential effectiveness of therapy as measured by the Thematic Apperception Test. In C. R. Rogers et al. (Eds.), *The therapeutic relationship and its impact* (pp. 337–352). Madison: University of Wisconsin Press. [Combined with Kiesler, Klein, Mathieu, & Schoeninger, 1967, and Van der Veen, 1967.]

Belenky, M. F., Clinchy, B. M., Goldberger, N. R., & Tarule, J. M. (1986). *Women's ways of knowing: The development of self, voice, and mind.* New York: Basic.

Bergin, A. E., & Garfield, S. L. (1994). Overview, trends, and future issues. In A. E. Bergin & S. L. Garfield (Eds.), *Handbook of psychotherapy and behavior change* (4th ed., pp. 821–830). New York: Wiley.

*Bergin, A. E., & Jasper, L. G. (1969). Correlates of empathy in psychotherapy: A replication. *Journal of Abnormal Psychology, 74,* 477–481.

Beutler, L. E., Crago, M., & Arizmendi, T. G. (1986). Research on therapist variables in psychotherapy. In S. L. Garfield & A. E. Bergin (Eds.), *Handbook of psychotherapy and behavior change* (3rd ed., pp. 257–310). New York: Wiley.

*Beutler, L. E., Johnson, D. T., Neville, C. W., & Workman, S. N. (1972). "Accurate empathy" and the AB dichotomy. *Journal of Consulting and Clinical Psychology, 38,* 372–375.

Beutler, L. E., Johnson, D. T., Neville, C. W., Jr., & Workman, S. N. (1973). Some sources of variance in accurate empathy ratings. *Journal of Consulting and Clinical Psychology, 40,* 167–169.

Blatt, S. J., Zuroff, D. C., Quinlan, D. M., & Pilkonis, P. A. (1996). Interpersonal factors in brief treatment of depression: Further analyses of the National Institute of Mental Health Treatment of Depression Collaborative Research Program. *Journal of Consulting and Clinical Psychology, 64,* 162–171.

Bohart, A. C., & Greenberg, L. S. (1997). Empathy: Where are we and where do we go from here? In A. C. Bohart & L. S. Greenberg (Eds.), *Empathy reconsidered: New directions in psychotherapy* (pp. 419–450). Washington, DC: American Psychological Association.

Bohart, A. C., & Tallman, K. (1999). *How clients make therapy work: The process of active self-healing.* Washington, DC: American Psychological Association.

Brodley, B. T., & Brody, A. F. (1990, August). *Understanding client-centered therapy through interviews conducted by Carl Rogers.* Paper presented at the annual convention of the American Psychological Association, Boston, MA.

*Buckley, P., Karasu, T. B., & Charles, E. (1981). Psychotherapists view their personal therapy. *Psychotherapy: Theory, Research and Practice, 18,* 299–305.

*Bugge, I., Hendel, D. D., & Moen, R. (1985). Client evaluations of therapeutic processes and outcomes in a university mental health center. *Journal of American College Health, 33,* 141–146.

*Burns, D. D., & Nolen-Hoeksema, S. (1992). Therapeutic empathy and recovery from depression in cognitive-behavioral therapy: A structural equation model. *Journal of Consulting and Clinical Psychology, 60,* 441–449.

Carkhuff, R. R., & Berenson, B. (1967). *Beyond counseling and therapy.* New York: Holt, Rinehart, & Winston.

*Cartwright, R. D., & Lerner, B. (1965). Empathy, need to change, and improvement in psychotherapy. *Journal of Consulting Psychology, 27,* 138–144.

Chafetz, M. E., Blane, H. T., Abram, H. S., Clark, E., Golner, J., Hastie, E. L., & McCourt, W. F. (1964). Establishing treatment relations with alcoholics: A supplementary report. *Journal of Nervous and Mental Disease, 138,* 390–393.

Chafetz, M. E., Blane, H. T., Abram, H. S., Golner, J., Lacy, E., McCourt, W. F., Clark, E., & Myers, W. (1962). Establishing treatment relations with alcoholics. *Journal of Nervous and Mental Disease, 134,* 395–409.

*Clark, J. V., & Culbert, S. A. (1965). Mutually therapeutic perception and self-awareness in a T-group. *Journal of Applied Behavioral Science, 1,* 180–194.

*Cooley, E. J., & Lajoy, R. (1980). Therapeutic relationship and improvement as perceived by clients and therapists. *Journal of Clinical Psychology, 36,* 562–570.

Davis, M. H. (1994). *Empathy: A social psychological perspective.* Dubuque, IA: Brown & Benchmark.

*Dormaar, J. M., Dijkman, C. I., & de Vries, M. W. (1989). Consensus in patient-therapist interactions: A measure of the therapeutic relationship related to outcome. *Psychotherapy and Psychosomatics, 51,* 69–76.

Duan, C., & Hill, C. E. (1996). A critical review of empathy research. *Journal of Counseling Psychology, 43*, 261–274.

Egan, G. (1982). *The skilled helper* (2nd ed.). Monterey, CA: Brooks/Cole.

Eisenberg, N., & Fabes, R. A. (1990). Empathy: Conceptualization, assessment, and relations to prosocial behavior. *Motivation and Emotion, 14*, 131–149.

Elliott, R. (2002). Research on the effectiveness of humanistic therapies: A meta-analysis. In D. Cain & J. Seeman (Eds.), *Humanistic psychotherapies: Handbook of research and practice* (pp. 57–82). Washington, DC: American Psychological Association.

Elliott, R., Filipovich, H., Harrigan, L., Gaynor, J., Reimschuessel, C., & Zapadka, J. K. (1982). Measuring response empathy: The development of a multi-component rating scale. *Journal of Counseling Psychology, 29*, 379–387.

Elliott, R., Watson, J., Greenberg, L. S., Goldman, R., & Davis, K. (2001). *Learning Process Experiential Therapy: An introduction to emotionally focused therapy*. Unpublished manuscript.

Feshbach, N. D. (1997). Empathy: The formative years—implications for clinical practice. In A. Bohart & L. S. Greenberg (Eds.), *Empathy reconsidered: New directions in psychotherapy* (pp. 33–62). Washington, DC: American Psychological Association.

*Filak, J., & Abeles, N. (1984). Posttherapy congruence on client symptoms and therapy outcome. *Professional Psychology: Research and Practice, 15*, 846–855.

*Fretz, B. R. (1966). Postural movements in a counseling dyad. *Journal of Counseling Psychology, 13*, 335–343.

*Gabbard, C. E., Howard, G. S., & Dunfee, E. J. (1986). Reliability, sensitivity to measuring change, and construct validity of a measure of counselor adaptability. *Journal of Counseling Psychology, 33*, 377–386.

*Garfield, S. L., & Bergin, A. E. (1971). Therapeutic conditions and outcome. *Journal of Abnormal Psychology, 77*, 108–114.

Gendlin, E. T. (1968). The experiential response. In E. Hammer (Ed.), *Use of interpretation in treatment* (pp. 208–227). New York: Grune & Stratton.

Gladstein, G. A., & Associates (1987). *Empathy and counseling: Explorations in theory and research*. New York: Springer-Verlag.

*Goldman, R., Greenberg, L., & Angus, L. (2000, June). *The York II Psychotherapy Study on experiential therapy of depression*. Paper presented at Society for Psychotherapy Research, Chicago, IL.

Greenberg, L. S., & Elliott, R. (1997). Varieties of empathic responding. In A. C. Bohart & L. S. Greenberg (Eds.), *Empathy reconsidered: New directions in psychotherapy* (pp. 167–186). Washington, DC: American Psychological Association.

Greenberg, L. S., & Paivio, S. C. (1997). *Working with emotions in psychotherapy*. New York: Guilford.

*Greenberg, L. S., & Webster, M. (1982). Resolving decisional conflict by means of two-chair dialogue: Relating process to outcome. *Journal of Counseling Psychology, 29*, 468–477.

*Gross, W. F., & DeRidder, L. M. (1966). Significant movement in comparatively short-term counseling. *Journal of Counseling Psychology, 13*, 98–99.

Gurman, A. S. (1977). The patient's perception of the therapeutic relationship. In A. S. Gurman & A. M. Razin (Eds.), *Effective psychotherapy: A handbook of research* (pp. 503–543). New York: Pergamon.

*Hall, J. A., & Davis, M. H. (2000). Dispositional empathy in scientist and practitioner psychologists: Group differences and relationship to self-reported professional effectiveness. *Psychotherapy, 37*, 45–56

Ham, M. A. (1987). Client behavior and counselor empathic performance. In G. A. Gladstein & Associates, *Empathy and counseling: Explorations in theory and research* (pp. 31–50). New York: Springer-Verlag.

*Hamilton, J. C. (2000). Construct validity of the core conditions and factor structure of the Client Evaluation of Counselor Scale. *The Person-Centered Journal, 7*, 40–51.

*Hansen, J. C., Moore, G. D., & Carkhuff, R. R. (1968). The differential relationships of objective and client perceptions of counseling. *Journal of Clinical Psychology, 24*, 244–246.

Hayes, A. M., & Goldfried, M. R. (1996). Rogers' work with Mark: An empirical analysis and cognitive-behavioral perspective. In B. A. Farber, D. C. Brink, & P. M. Raskin (Eds.), *The psychotherapy of Carl Rogers* (pp. 357–374). New York: Guilford.

Henry, W. P., Schacht, T. E., & Strupp, H. H. (1986). Structural analysis of social behavior: Application to a study of interpersonal process in differential psychotherapeutic outcome. *Journal of Consulting and Clinical Psychology, 54*, 27–31.

Henschel, D. N., & Bohart, A. C. (1981, August). *The relationship between the effectiveness of a course in paraprofessional training and level of cognitive functioning.* Paper presented at the American Psychological Association, Los Angeles, CA.

Hill, C. E., Thompson, B. J., & Corbett, M. (1992). The impact of therapist ability to perceive displayed and hidden client reactions on immediate outcome in first sessions of brief therapy. *Psychotherapy Research, 2,* 143–155.

Horvath, A. O., & Greenberg, L. S. (1986). The development of the Working Alliance Inventory. In L. S. Greenberg & W. M. Pinsof (Eds.), *The psychotherapeutic process: A research handbook* (pp. 529–556). New York: Guilford.

*Horvath, A. O., & Greenberg, L. S. (1989). Development and validation of the Working Alliance Inventory. *Journal of Counseling Psychology, 36,* 223–233.

Horvath, A. O., & Symonds, B. D. (1991). Relation between working alliance and outcome in psychotherapy: A meta-analysis. *Journal of Counseling Psychology, 38,* 139–149.

Hubble, M. A., Duncan, B. L., & Miller, S. D. (1999). Directing attention to what works. In M. A. Hubble, B. L. Duncan, & S. D. Miller (Eds.), *The heart and soul of change: What works in therapy* (pp. 407–448). Washington, DC: American Psychological Association.

Ickes, W. (Ed.). (1997). *Empathic accuracy.* New York: Guilford.

Jordan, J. V. (1997). Relational development through mutual empathy. In A. C. Bohart & L. S. Greenberg (Eds.), *Empathy reconsidered: New directions in psychotherapy* (pp. 343–352). Washington, DC: American Psychological Association.

Kennedy-Moore, E., & Watson, J. C. (1999). *Expressing emotion: Myths, realities, and therapeutic strategies.* New York: Guilford.

*Kiesler, D. J., Klein, M. H., Mathieu, P. L., & Schoeninger, D. (1967). Constructive personality change for therapy and control patients. In C. R. Rogers et al. (Eds.), *The therapeutic relationship and its impact* (pp. 251–294). Madison: University of Wisconsin Press. [Combined with Barrington, 1967, and Van der Veen, 1967.]

Klein, M. H., & Mathieu-Coughlan, P. (1986). Measures of client and therapist vocal quality. In L. S. Greenberg & W. M. Pinsof (Eds.), *The psychotherapeutic process: A research handbook* (pp. 21–72). New York: Guilford.

*Kurtz, R. R., & Grummon, D. L. (1972). Different approaches to the measurement of therapist empathy and their relationship to therapy outcomes. *Journal of Consulting and Clinical Psychology, 39,* 106–115.

*Lafferty, P., Beutler, L. E., & Crago, M. (1989). Differences between more and less effective psychotherapists: A study of select therapist variables. *Journal of Consulting and Clinical Psychology, 57,* 76–80.

Lambert, M. J., DeJulio, S. J. & Stein, D. M. (1978). Therapist interpersonal skills: Process, outcome, methodological considerations, and recommendations for future research. *Psychological Bulletin, 85,* 467–489.

Landfield, A. W. (1971). *Personal construct systems in psychotherapy.* Chicago: Rand McNally.

Leitner, L. M. (1995). Optimal therapeutic distance: A therapist's experience of personal construct psychotherapy. In R. A. Neimeyer & M. J. Mahoney (Eds.), *Constructivism in psychotherapy* (pp. 357–370). Washington, DC: American Psychological Association.

*Lerner, B. (1972). *Therapy in the ghetto.* Baltimore: Johns Hopkins University Press.

*Lesser, W. M. (1961). The relationship between counseling progress and empathic understanding. *Journal of Counseling Psychology, 8,* 330–336.

Levenson, R. W., & Ruef, A. M. (1997). Physiological aspects of emotional knowledge and rapport. In W. Ickes (Ed.), *Empathic accuracy* (pp. 44–72). New York: Guilford.

*Lorr, M. (1965). Client perceptions of therapists: A study of therapeutic relation. *Journal of Consulting Psychology, 29,* 146–149.

Mahrer, A. R. (1997). Empathy as therapist-client alignment. In A. C. Bohart & L. S. Greenberg (Eds.), *Empathy reconsidered: New directions in psychotherapy* (pp. 187–216). Washington, DC: American Psychological Association.

Martin, D. G. (2000). *Counseling and therapy skills* (2nd ed.). Prospect Heights, IL: Waveland.

Martin, D. J., Garske, J. P., & Davis, M. D. (2000). Relation of the therapeutic alliance with outcome and other variables: A meta-analytic review. *Journal of Consulting and Clinical Psychology, 68,* 438–450.

*Martin, P. J., & Sterne, A. L. (1976). Post-hospital adjustment as related to therapist's in-therapy behavior. *Psychotherapy: Theory, Research and Practice, 13,* 267–273.

Mehrabian, A., & Epstein, N. A. (1972). A measure of emotional empathy. *Journal of Personality, 40,* 523–543.

*Melnick, B., & Pierce, R. M. (1971). Client evaluation of therapist strength and positive-negative evaluation as related to client dynamics, objective ratings of competence, and outcome. *Journal of Clinical Psychology, 27*, 408–410.

*Miller, W., Taylor, C., & West, J. (1980). Focused versus broad spectrum behavior therapy for problem drinkers. *Journal of Consulting and Clinical Psychology, 48*, 590–601.

Mitchell, K. M., Bozarth, J. D., & Krauft, C. C. (1977). A reappraisal of the therapeutic effectiveness of accurate empathy, nonpossessive warmth, and genuineness. In A. S. Gurman & A. M. Razin (Eds.), *Effective psychotherapy.* New York: Pergamon.

*Mitchell, K. M., Truax, C. B., Bozarth, J. D., & Krauft, C. C. (1973). *Antecedents to psychotherapeutic outcome.* NIMH grant report (12306). Arkansas Rehabilitation Research and Training Center, Arkansas Rehabilitation Services, Hot Springs.

Mohr, J. J., & Woodhouse, S. S. (2000, June). *Clients' visions of helpful and harmful psychotherapy: An approach to measuring individual differences in therapy priorities.* Paper presented at the 31st Annual Meeting of the Society for Psychotherapy Research, Chicago, IL.

*Muller, J., & Abeles, N. (1971). Relationship of liking, empathy, and therapists' experience to outcome in psychotherapy. *Journal of Counseling Psychology, 18*, 39–43.

Myers, S. (2000). Empathic listening: Reports on the experience of being heard. *Journal of Humanistic Psychology, 40*, 148–173.

O'Hara, M. M. (1984). Person-centered gestalt: Towards a holistic synthesis. In R. F. Levant & J. M. Shlien (Eds.), *Client-centered therapy and the person-centered approach: New directions in theory, research and practice* (pp. 203–221). New York: Praeger.

O'Hara, M. M. (1997). Relational empathy: Beyond modernist egocentrism to postmodern holistic contextualism. In A. C. Bohart & L. S. Greenberg (Eds.), *Empathy reconsidered: New directions in psychotherapy* (pp. 295–320). Washington, DC: American Psychological Association.

Orlinsky, D. E., Grawe, K., & Parks, B. K. (1994). Process and outcome in psychotherapy—Noch einmal. In A. E. Bergin & S. L. Garfield (Eds.), *Handbook of psychotherapy and behavior change* (4th ed., pp. 270–378). New York: Wiley.

Orlinsky, D. E., & Howard, K. I. (1967). The good therapy hour: Experiential correlates of patients' and therapists' evaluations of therapy sessions. *Archives of General Psychiatry, 12*, 621–632.

Orlinsky, D. E., & Howard, K. I. (1978). The relation of process to outcome in psychotherapy. In S. L. Garfield & A. E. Bergin (Eds.), *Handbook of psychotherapy and behavior change: An empirical analysis* (2nd ed., pp. 283–330). New York: Wiley.

Orlinsky, D. E., & Howard, K. I. (1986). Process and outcome in psychotherapy. In S. L. Garfield & A. E. Bergin (Eds.), *Handbook of psychotherapy and behavior change* (3rd ed., pp. 311–384). New York: Wiley.

Parloff, M. B., Waskow, I. E., & Wolfe, B. E. (1978). Research on therapist variables in relation to process and outcome. In S. L. Garfield & A. E. Bergin (Eds.), *Handbook of psychotherapy and behavior change: An empirical analysis* (2nd ed., pp. 233–282). New York: Wiley.

Patterson, C. H. (1984). Empathy, warmth, and genuineness: A review of reviews. *Psychotherapy, 21*, 431–438.

Peabody, S. A., & Gelso, C. J. (1982). Countertransference and empathy: The complex relationship between two divergent concepts in counseling. *Journal of Counseling Psychology, 29*, 240–245.

*Peake, T. H. (1979). Therapist-patient agreement and outcome in group therapy. *Journal of Clinical Psychology, 35*, 637–646.

Persons, J. B., & Burns, D. D. (1985). Mechanisms of action of cognitive therapy: Relative contribution of technical and interpersonal intervention. *Cognitive Therapy and Research, 9*, 539–551.

*Rabavilas, A. D., Boulougouris, J. C., & Perissaki, C. (1979). Therapist qualities related to outcome with exposure in vivo in neurotic patients. *Journal of Behaviour Therapy and Experimental Psychiatry, 410*, 293–294.

Rice, L. N., & Saperia, E. P. (1984). Task analysis of the resolution of problematic reactions. In L. N. Rice & L. S. Greenberg (Eds.), *Patterns of change.* New York: Guilford.

*Roback, H. B., & Strassberg, D. S. (1975). Relationship between perceived therapist-offered conditions and therapeutic movement in group psychotherapy with hospitalized mental patients. *Small Group Behavior, 6*, 345–352.

Rogers, C. R. (1957). The necessary and sufficient conditions of therapeutic personality change.

Journal of Consulting Psychology, 21, 95–103.

Rogers, C. R. (1980). *A way of being*. Boston: Houghton Mifflin.

Rosenthal, R. (1991). *Meta-analytic procedures for social research* (rev. ed.). Newbury Park, CA: Sage.

Rowe, C., & MacIsaac, D. (1989). *Empathic attunement: The "technique" of psychoanalytic self-psychology*. Hillsdale, NJ: Aronson.

Sachse, R. (1990a). Concrete interventions are crucial: The influence of the therapist's processing proposals on the client's intrapersonal exploration in client-centered therapy. In G. Lietaer, J. Rombauts, & R. Van Balen (Eds.), *Client-centered and experiential psychotherapy in the nineties* (pp. 295–308). Leuven, Belgium: Leuven University Press.

Sachse, R. (1990b). The influence of therapist processing proposals on the explication process of the client. *Person-Centered Review, 5*, 321–344.

*Saltzman, C., Leutgert, M. J., Roth, C. H., Creaser, J., & Howard, L. (1976). Formation of a therapeutic relationship: Experiences during the initial phase of psychotherapy as predictors of treatment duration and outcome. *Journal of Consulting and Clinical Psychology, 44*, 546–555.

Salvio, M. A., Beutler, L. E., Wood, J. M., & Engle, D. (1992). The strength of the therapeutic alliance in three treatments for depression. *Psychotherapy Research, 2*, 31–36.

*Sapolsky, A. (1965). Relationship between patient-doctor compatibility, mutual perceptions, and outcome of treatment. *Journal of Abnormal Psychology, 70*, 70–76.

*Saunders, S. M. (2000). Examining the relationship between the therapeutic bond and the phases of treatment outcome. *Psychotherapy, 37*(3), 206–218.

Selman, R. I. (1980). *The growth of interpersonal understanding*. Orlando, FL: Academic.

Shlien, J. (1997). Empathy in psychotherapy: A vital mechanism? Yes. Therapist's conceit? All too often. In A. C. Bohart & L. S. Greenberg (Eds.), *Empathy reconsidered: New directions in psychotherapy* (pp. 63–80). Washington, DC: American Psychological Association.

*Staples, F. R., Sloane, R. D., Whipple, K., Cristol, A. H., & Yorkston, N. (1976). Process and outcome in psychotherapy and behavior therapy. *Journal of Consulting and Clinical Psychology, 44*, 340–350.

*Strupp, H. H., Fox, R. E., & Lessler, K. (1969).

Patients view their psychotherapy. Baltimore: Johns Hopkins University Press.

Tallman, K., Robinson, E., Kay, D., Harvey, S., & Bohart, A. (1994, August). *Experiential and non-experiential Rogerian therapy: An analogue study*. Paper presented at the American Psychological Association convention, Los Angeles.

Tausch, R. (1988). The relationship between emotions and cognitions: Implications for therapist empathy. *Person-Centered Review, 3*, 277–291.

Thompson, B., & Hill, C. (1991). Therapist perception of client reactions. *Journal of Counseling and Development, 69*, 261–265.

Trop, J. L., & Stolorow, R. D. (1997). Therapeutic empathy: An intersubjective perspective. In A. C. Bohart & L. S. Greenberg (Eds.), *Empathy reconsidered: New directions in psychotherapy* (pp. 279–294). Washington, DC: American Psychological Association.

*Truax, C. B. (1966). Therapist empathy, warmth, and genuineness and patient personality change in group psychotherapy: A comparison between interaction unit measures, time sample measures, and patient perception measures. *Journal of Clinical Psychology, 22*, 225–229.

Truax, C. B., & Carkhuff, R. R. (1967) *Toward effective counseling and psychotherapy: Training and practice*. Chicago: Aldine.

*Truax, C. B., Carkhuff, R. R., & Kodman, F., Jr. (1965). Relationships between therapist-offered conditions and patient change in group psychotherapy. *Journal of Clinical Psychology, 21*, 327–329.

Truax, C. B., & Mitchell, K. M. (1971). Research on certain therapist interpersonal skills in relation to process and outcome. In A. E. Bergin & S. L. Garfield (Eds.), *Handbook of psychotherapy and behavior change* (pp. 299–344). New York: Wiley.

*Truax, C. B., Wargo, D. G., Frank, J. D., Imber, S. D., Battle, C. C., Hoehn-Saric, R., Nash, E. H., & Stone, A. R. (1966). Therapist empathy, genuineness, and warmth and patient therapeutic outcome. *Journal of Consulting Psychology, 30*, 395–401.

*Truax, C. B., & Wittmer, J. (1971). The effects of therapist focus on patient anxiety source and the interaction with therapist level of accurate empathy. *Journal of Clinical Psychology, 27*, 297–299.

*Truax, C. B., Wittmer, J., & Wargo, D. G. (1971). Effects of the therapeutic conditions of accurate empathy, nonpossessive warmth, and genuineness on hospitalized mental patients during group therapy. *Journal of Clinical Psychology, 27*, 137–142.

*Van der Veen, F. (1967). Basic elements in the process of psychotherapy: A research study. *Journal of Consulting Psychology, 31*, 295–303. [Combined with Barrington, 1967, and Kiesler, Klein, Mathieu, & Schoeninger, 1967.]

Van Kaam, A. L. (1959). Phenomenal analysis: Exemplified by a study of the experience of really feeling understood. *Journal of Individual Psychology, 15*, 66–72.

Wampold, B. E. (2001). *The great psychotherapy debate: Models, methods, and findings.* Mahwah, NJ: Erlbaum.

Watson, J. C. (1999). *Measure of expressed empathy.* Unpublished manuscript. Department of Adult Education, Community Development, and Counseling Psychology, OISE, University of Toronto, Toronto, Ontario, Canada.

Watson, J. C. (2002). Revisioning empathy. In D. Cain & J. Seeman (Eds.), *Humanistic psychotherapies: Handbook of research and practice* (pp. 445–472). Washington, DC: American Psychological Association.

Watson, J. C., & Prosser, M. (in press). The development and validation of a measure of expressed empathy. In J. C. Watson, R. N. Goldman, & M. Warner (Eds.), *Person-centered and experiential psychotherapy in the 21st century: Advances in theory, research, and practice.* London: PCCS.

Watson, N. (1984). The empirical status of Rogers' hypotheses of the necessary and sufficient conditions for effective psychotherapy. In R. F. Levant & J. M. Shlien (Eds.), *Client-centered therapy and the person-centered approach* (pp. 17–40). New York: Praeger.

Zimring, F. (2000). Empathic understanding grows the person. *The Person-Centered Journal, 7*, 101–113.

6

Goal Consensus
and Collaboration

Georgiana Shick Tryon
Greta Winograd

This chapter deals with patient and therapist implementation of the therapeutic contract through goal consensus and collaboration relative to initial engagement in therapy and psychotherapy outcome. After providing definitions of terms used throughout the chapter and giving a clinical example, we briefly describe and summarize results of studies relating therapist-patient goal consensus and collaboration to initial patient engagement in therapy and psychotherapy outcome. We then discuss the limitations of the studies reviewed and provide suggestions for application of results to clinical practice.

DEFINITIONS

Engagement, goal consensus, and collaborative involvement are pantheoretical concepts; that is, they apply to all types of psychotherapies regardless of theoretical orientations and practice settings. The following definitions will be used throughout this chapter.

Engagement is the initial involvement of patient and therapist in the therapeutic process. Successful engagement is operationalized as patient return to the therapist for further therapy after the initial, or intake, interview (Tryon, 1985). Tryon (1985) found that certain therapists had a higher percentage of patients return to them for further therapy after intake than did

other therapists. Therapists who had a higher percentage of initially returning patients also saw a higher percentage of their patients for more than 10 sessions (Tryon, 1985; Tryon & Tryon, 1986). Thus, it appeared that these therapists were involving, or engaging, their patients in an ongoing therapy process during the initial interview.

A therapist's *Engagement Quotient* (EQ) is the percentage of patients who return to the therapist for more than one session. In one study (Tryon, 1999), EQs collected for 85 counseling and clinical psychology practicum students were normally distributed and ranged from 20% to 70%, with a mean of 43.40 ($SD = 10.11$).

Goal consensus is the therapist-patient agreement on therapy goals and expectations (Orlinsky, Grawe, & Parks, 1994). Goal consensus is one aspect of the *working alliance* that is defined by Bordin (1979) as patient-therapist bond and agreement on tasks and goals. A meta-analysis (Martin, Garske, & Davis, 2000) found that the working alliance is itself therapeutic. In other words, patients will improve when they have good working alliances with their therapists.

Collaborative involvement is the mutual involvement of patient and therapist in a helping relationship. It is assessed in various ways that frequently include ratings of patient cooperation or resistance (Colson et al., 1985), homework completion (Schmidt & Woolaway-Bickel, 2000), and involvement in the patient role (Soldz, Budman, & Demby, 1992).

In their extensive review of psychotherapy process and outcome literature, Orlinsky and colleagues (1994) defined the *therapeutic contract* as participants' "understanding about their goals and conditions for engaging each other as patient and therapist" (p. 279). Goal consensus and collaborative involvement are two elements involved in the implementation of this contract.

CLINICAL EXAMPLE

Here is an excerpt from a male undergraduate patient's first session with a female therapist at a college counseling center. Before this point in the interview, the therapist established rapport with the patient and, through the use of questions and encouragement, gathered specific information about his concerns. As the therapist understands the nature of what brought the patient to the clinic, she is able to communicate it back to him in a meaningful way. The "essence" of the interview is revealed toward the end of the session, when the therapist and patient work together to clarify the problem. At this point, the therapist offers the patient information about how the therapy process works, and together they establish treatment goals.

TH: It sounds like the main thing that's bugging you is this career issue—you've spent a lot of time and energy preparing for a career in medicine but now you're having doubts about whether that's what you really want. Is there anything else that is stressing you out or making you feel sad?

PT: Well. I'd like to have a girlfriend, but I'd even be satisfied with one or two close friends to hang out with. I just feel kind of alone a lot of the time, and that's rough.

TH: That does sound difficult. Okay—you're concerned about your major and your social life. Anything else?

PT: That's pretty much it for now.

TH: How would you feel if we spent some time sorting out and talking over your feelings about your career and friendships here at the college? I get the sense that you're pretty self-aware, but sometimes when you talk with someone else, other possibilities come up that you haven't thought of—

PT: Okay.

TH: —and talking sometimes helps you figure out why certain thoughts and experiences make you feel kind of stressed out and depressed.

PT: Yeah.

TH: Does working this way sound like what you were looking for here at the clinic?

PT: Yeah. I think things got to this point and I felt like I would explode, and now it's time to sort things out.

The therapist concludes the session by giving the patient information about the number of sessions he is entitled to and how to make appointments. This patient returned for further therapy. Therefore, this session is categorized as an engagement interview (Tryon, 1985).

RESEARCH REVIEW

This research review is divided into two sections. The first deals with goal consensus and collaborative involvement as they relate to initial engagement (return after intake) of patients in therapy. The second section addresses the implementation of these two elements relative to therapy outcome.

Initial Engagement in Therapy

Patient post-intake return (engagement) is not a therapy outcome, but engagement is important for therapeutic outcome because, with the exception of single-session therapy (Talmon, 1990), most therapies require patient attendance beyond the intake, or initial, session. A substantial number of patients have an intake, or first, session and do not return for further therapy, prompting Odell and Quinn (1998) to conclude "that arguably the largest percentage of clients that drop out of therapy do so after one session" (p. 369). Since Tryon (1985; Tryon & Tryon, 1986) found that patients who return after the initial session tend to stay in therapy until completion, examination of this initial engagement process is important, as initial engagement is the first step in the journey toward outcome.

Goal Consensus

Therapist-patient agreement on patient problems at intake may be the first step toward consensus on therapeutic goals, and patients may be more likely to become engaged, or committed to therapy as indicated by their return for further sessions, when they believe that therapists agree with them about what is wrong. Some investigators (Epperson, Bushway, & Warman, 1983; Kokotovic & Tracey, 1987; Zamostny, Corrigan, & Eggert, 1981) studying problem agreement requested therapists and patients to check or rate categories of problems provided by the researchers either before or after intake. Researchers then compared problem category matches and computed rating difference scores. Using these methods, all three studies found no relationship between patient-therapist problem agreement and patient return for therapy following intake. In therapy, conceptualization of patients' problems usually entails more than a one- or two-word description. A more productive approach to examination of agreement on patients' problems may be to record sessions and rate them for patient-therapist problem agreement. As Kokotovic and Tracey (1987, p. 82) stated, "Perhaps explicit, in-session verbal agreement on the presenting problem between participants and not agreement derived from independent post-session evaluations is the key."

Two studies by Tryon attempted to tap the active process of obtaining goal clarification during intake by asking patients and therapists post-intake questions about problem identification. Tryon (1986) found that engaged patients rated their therapists higher than did nonengaged patients on the item asking, "To what extent did your therapist identify concerns for which you did not initially seek counseling?" In a later study (Tryon, 1989), therapists rated their own intake behavior on a scale composed of the following three items: "To what extent did you identify concerns for which the client did not initially seek therapy?" "To what extent did you provide the patient with new ways of understanding himself/herself?" "How much did you teach the patient about himself/herself?" Higher ratings on these three items were positively related to patient return for therapy after intake. Also, patients rated

the women therapists in this study, who had higher EQs than the men therapists, higher on these items when they were reworded to reflect the patient perspective.

The finding that therapists of engaged patients were better at clarifying patient concerns than therapists of nonengaged patients led Tryon and Tryon (1986) to examine the verbal and diagnostic abilities of higher versus lower engaging trainee therapists. Therapists' EQs correlated positively and significantly with their scores on the Graduate Record Examination Verbal section (GREV), GREV-GRE Quantitative (GREQ), Miller Analogies Test (MAT), and course grades in both a clinical diagnosis and an advanced clinical diagnosis course. Thus, higher engaging trainees were older, more verbally proficient, and better diagnosticians than were lower engaging trainee therapists. Tryon and Tryon (1986) concluded that higher engaging therapists may use their superior verbal skills to extract meaning from things patients tell them and to explain patients' problems. Higher engaging therapists may also use their superior diagnostic skills to recognize problems and to formulate patients' treatment needs. Older therapists have probably had more life experiences on which to draw in clarifying patients' concerns.

Several studies have examined verbal process at intake to investigate the relationship between return for post-intake therapy and goal consensus. Verbalizations, categorized by three psychology doctoral students, of a psychodynamically oriented therapist during engagement interviews showed that the therapist used questions and minimal encouragers during the early interview phases to clarify patient concerns (Tryon, 2002). During the latter part of engagement interviews, the therapist used information verbalizations to communicate diagnostic formulations and treatment plans to patients. In nonengagement interviews, the therapist asked relatively few questions during the early phases of the interviews and communicated little information regarding problems and treatment to patients.

Tracy (1977) investigated the effect of two different types of intake interviews on patient return for therapy—a traditional interview where therapists did not share problem formulations with patients, and a behavioral analysis interview where therapists shared their perceptions of patient problems and negotiated mutual treatment goals with patients. Significantly more patients returned for therapy after behavioral analysis than traditional intakes. In a study by Duehn and Proctor (1977), patient-therapist exchanges were rated from verbatim intake transcripts. There was significantly more response congruence (therapist verbal response that addressed the subject content of a patient's immediately preceding statement) and content relevance (therapists addressed topics that patients indicated were important to them pre-intake) in engagement than in nonengagement interviews. These results indicate that if patients are to return for further therapy after intake, therapists must attend verbally to patients' statements and discuss problems that patients consider relevant.

None of the studies of patient-therapist problem agreement yielded significant engagement results. All studies examining the process of goal clarification, however, found positive relationships between engagement and reformulation of and responsiveness to patients' presenting concerns. Therapists who are higher engagers are those who have greater verbal and diagnostic facility that can be used to communicate with patients about goals and treatment plans. Six of the nine studies, or 67%, in this section found positive associations between goal consensus and engagement.

Collaborative Involvement

Therapists rate some patients as being more attractive therapy candidates than others. Characteristics that therapists identify as attractive in a patient include possessing a motivation to change, being ready and willing to work out problems, admitting weaknesses, being likely to improve, or simply being a patient with whom the therapist would like to work (Davis, Cook, Jennings, & Heck, 1977). Thus, attractive therapy patients appear to be those who have characteristics that may enable them to fill the patient role as cooperative collaborators with therapists.

Tryon (1992) found that patients rated by therapists as more attractive were more likely to become engaged than patients rated as less attractive. In addition, when more attractive patients were paired at intake with high engaging thera-

pists, engagement was much more likely to happen than when less attractive patients were paired with lower engaging therapists. Phillips (1985), Shapiro (1974), and Tryon (1986) found that engaged patients were more likely to have been rated by their therapists as patients with whom the therapist would most like to enter into a therapeutic relationship. Tryon (1990) found that patients who became engaged were more likely to have been rated by their therapists as possessing greater motivation to work on their problems than patients who did not attend more than one session. These studies indicate that therapist-rated patient attractiveness is positively associated with engagement.

Patients may display symptoms that are incompatible with cooperative involvement in relationships. These patients may be difficult to engage. Research at community mental health centers has generally found that more disturbed patients are less likely than less disturbed clients to become engaged in therapy. Relative to engaged patients, nonengaged patients have been found to have a greater incidence of compulsions or phobias (Fiester, Mahrer, Giambra, & Ormiston, 1974), more proneness to hallucinations, unusual thoughts, suicidal ideation, and unusual mannerisms (Richmond, 1992), narcissistic personality disorder and antisocial personality disorder (Hilsenroth, Holdwick, Castlebury, & Blais, 1998), and diagnoses of psychoses (Hoffman, 1985).

In contrast, studies conducted at university counseling centers have generally found that patients rated as more disturbed by therapists were more likely to become engaged (Hilsenroth, Handler, Toman, & Padawer, 1995; Longo, Lent, & Brown, 1992; Tryon, 1986, 1990). One reason for setting differences in engagement of more disturbed patients may be that patients seen at university counseling centers may tend to be generally less disturbed that patients seen at outpatient mental health centers.

Therapists may also behave in ways that make engagement less likely. A study by Mohl, Martinez, Ticknor, Huang, and Cordell (1991) found that one of four intake therapists had a lower engagement rate than the other three therapists. Patients rated this therapist as less verbal and effective than the more engaging therapists.

If patient and therapist are collaboratively involved, patients should be more satisfied with the therapy session than if they are not involved in a positive collaborative endeavor. Satisfaction with the intake interview may facilitate engagement. Earlier studies of patient satisfaction suffered from lack of a uniform measure and yielded mixed results. Schiller (1976) found no relationship between patient-rated satisfaction with intake interviews and patients' return for further therapy to a university counseling center. In contrast, Shueman, Gelso, Mindus, Hunt, and Stevenson (1980) found that engaged counseling center patients were more satisfied with their intake interviews than nonengaged patients. Heilbrun (1972) found no relationship between patient satisfaction with therapist directiveness or nondirectiveness and patient engagement. Fiester and Rudestam (1975) found that the relationship between patient-rated satisfaction and engagement depended on the setting. Patients at a hospital outpatient clinic were more likely to return for further therapy if they gave their therapists higher satisfaction ratings, but this was not true for clients at a state clinic.

More recent studies have found positive associations between patient satisfaction and engagement using either the 3- or 4-item version of the Client Satisfaction Questionnaire (CSQ; see Larsen, Attkisson, Hargreaves, & Nguyen, 1979). Studies using the CSQ (Greenfield, 1983; Kokotovic & Tracey, 1987; Tryon, 1990) found that more satisfied patients were significantly more likely to return for further therapy following intake. This indicates that the CSQ may be a more valid measure than earlier measures of patient satisfaction, because it consistently yields significant relationships with engagement.

Another way to investigate collaborative involvement at intake is to ask participants about the quality of the session. Tryon (1990) found that patients who returned for therapy and their therapists had rated the intake as significantly deeper, more full, more powerful, more valuable, and more special (depth scale items from the Session Evaluation Questionnaire [SEQ]; see Stiles, 1980) than had patients and therapists who did not have further therapy. SEQ smoothness ratings were not related to engagement. Thus, intake interviews do not need to be relaxed, easy, pleasant, smooth, or comfortable (the SEQ smooth-

ness items) experiences for participants to become engaged. In fact, Nash and Garske (1988) speculated that smooth sessions might be more indicative of patient resistance than patient collaboration with the therapist.

Other studies assessed in-session process in relation to engagement. In two studies, Tracey (1986) examined the extent to which a topic initiated by one member of the therapeutic dyad was followed by a response to that topic by the other member of the dyad. Topic determination was "the proportion of topic initiations . . . that were subsequently followed by the other participant" (p. 785). Dyads where the patient did not continue therapy beyond the third session had significantly lower levels of topic determination than continuing dyads. Although this study did not specifically deal with patient return after the initial session, some of the patients left therapy after the first session. Tracey (1986) concluded, "Low levels of topic determination may be a behavioral cue of client resistance because the client is accepting little of what the therapist is offering for discussion" (p. 788).

Beyebach and Carranza (1997) used Tracey's (1986) topic determination coding system and the Family Relational Communication Control Coding Scheme (F-RCCCS; see Watzlawick, Beavin, & Jackson, 1967) to code therapist and patient intake verbalizations. Contrary to Tracey's (1986) findings, they did not find any association between topic determination and patient post-intake return. The FRCCCS coded data showed, however, that nonengaged patients used more domineering communications, interrupted their therapists more often, gave less support to therapists, and engaged in more conflict with therapists than did continuing patients.

In the five studies investigating patient attractiveness, engagement was more likely to occur with patients who are perceived by therapists to be attractive candidates for therapy (that is, motivated to change, ready and willing to work out problems, likely to improve). Half of the eight studies investigating level of patient disturbance found that more disturbed clients were harder to engage. This finding was moderated by setting (clinic vs. counseling center). In one study, patient-rated therapist characteristics were related to engagement. In six of seven studies, patients perceived engagement interviews as more satisfactory than nonengagement interviews. The final three studies found that the patient-therapist interview process had depth, cooperative participant verbal behavior, and less conflict than nonengagement interviews. Taken together, collaborative involvement was positively associated with engagement in 19 of the 24 studies, or 79%.

Therapy Outcome

This section reviews studies relating goal consensus and collaborative involvement to therapy outcome. Assessment of therapy outcome is more complicated than assessment of initial engagement. In contrast to engagement, which is assessed by simply recording patient return for therapy after an initial session, outcome can be evaluated from the perspective of the patient, the therapist, or an outside observer using many different types of assessment methods. Conclusions reached from one perspective and one instrument may differ from those reached by another person or from another questionnaire. Studies reviewed in this section will specify type of outcome measure and outcome evaluator.

Goal Consensus

Patient-therapist agreement on therapeutic goals should influence the way they work together and the outcome of therapy. If patient and therapist are working toward different ends, patient improvement may be hampered.

Rather than assessing outcome of an entire course of therapy, some researchers have examined the relation between goal consensus and outcome of a single session. For example, Eisenthal, Koopman, and Lazare (1983) obtained external observers' ratings of patient-therapist negotiation on a treatment plan from audiotaped intake sessions at a walk-in clinic. Patients' ratings of satisfaction with the interview were positively related to observers' ratings of shared decision making on a treatment plan and clarity of therapist explanation of the plan and its rationale. Therapists' ratings of satisfaction with the interview, however, were not related to any of the observer-rated negotiation variables. In a study of intake at a hospital crisis center, Kirk, Stanley, and Brown (1988)

found that patient-therapist congruence on a measure of patient requests made during the interview was positively associated with reduction in patient-rated post-interview distress as measured by the Stress/Arousal Adjective Checklist (MacKay, Cox, Burrows, & Lazzerini, 1978). Thus, if patient and therapist agreed on goals requested by patients, patients were less distressed at the end of the intake session.

Hoyt (1980) found that sessions from short-term dynamic therapy that were evaluated by raters as being "good" therapy hours were associated with more rater-categorized patient-therapist discussion of the goals and expression of thoughts and feelings than were sessions rated as "poor" therapy hours. The same raters categorized patient-therapist actions and the "goodness/poorness" of the sessions; thus, "goodness" ratings could have been influenced by process ratings and vice versa. In addition, two of the five raters were also therapists of patients in the study, and this may have biased their ratings. In an extension of this study by Hoyt, Xenakis, Marmar, and Horowitz (1983), both therapists and outside raters rated patient-therapist actions and "goodness/poorness" of the session. Hoyt and colleagues (1983) found that patient-therapist discussion of goals and expression of thoughts and feelings were positively associated with "good" therapy sessions in both therapists' and outside raters' assessments.

Other studies have rated both treatment outcome and goal consensus at the same time. Patients in programs at acute day hospitals rated programs as more helpful when they believed that program goals were clearly specified (Goldstein, Cohen, Lewis, & Struening, 1988). In contrast to patients, day hospital staff ratings of clarity of program goals were not significantly related to ratings of helpfulness of the program to patients. In another study of partially hospitalized patients in a month-long day hospital program (Hoge, Farrell, Munchel, & Strauss, 1988), 95% of the patients interviewed by investigators reported that program structure (including routine, receiving directions, regularly scheduled activity, and a clear sense of purpose) was therapeutic. Assessments of both goal clarity and program helpfulness were obtained at the same time from patients during their final days in the program.

Another way to assess the relationship of goal consensus and outcome is by examining goal consensus over the entire course of therapy. In a study by Lansford (1986) of therapist actions in 12-session short-term dynamic therapy, observer ratings of therapists' discussion of the tasks of therapy during the entire course of treatment were not significantly related to observer ratings of therapy outcome. In a study of patients in 12-session dynamic psychotherapy for bereavement, Horowitz, Marmar, Weiss, DeWitt, and Rosenbaum (1984) found that therapists' ratings (taken after each of the 12 sessions) of their actions to clarify the focus of therapy were not related to patient-rated symptom reduction or independent observers' ratings of client change at outcome. Therapists' ratings of their actions to clarify focus during session 4 only were significantly related to independent observer ratings of patient change at outcome. The authors indicate, however, that this latter result "probably represents a chance finding" (Horowitz et al., 1984, p. 444).

By far the most prevalent type of goal consensus-outcome study assesses goal consensus at one or more points before the end of therapy. In a study of 12-session dynamic therapy for bereavement, Jones, Cumming, and Horowitz (1988) found that independent judges' ratings of therapists' explanations of treatment rationale and patients' understanding of the nature and expectations of therapy during the fifth session were positively related to composites of patient-, therapist-, and independent judge-rated outcome scores. Dormaar, Dijkman, and de Vries (1989) studied Dutch outpatient-therapist dyads and found that patient-rated agreement with therapist- and patient-experienced goal consensus, as well as therapist-rated understanding of patient concerns after the second session, predicted reductions in both patient- and therapist-rated target complaints and patient problem endorsement on the Symptom Check List (SCL-90; see Derogatis, 1974) as late as six months after the beginning of treatment. In a study of couples' therapy that averaged 7.2 sessions, Quinn, Dotson, and Jordan (1997) found that wives', but not husbands', scores on the goal consensus scale of the Integrative Psychotherapy Alliance Scale (IPAS; see Pinsof & Catherall, 1986) obtained after the third session were positively correlated with their

ratings of treatment outcome. Mussell and colleagues (2000) studied outcome of a 12-session cognitive-behavioral group therapy for bulimia. They found that pretreatment ratings by patients of their commitment to therapeutic goals were positively related to outcome remission of bulimic symptoms.

Tracey (1988) assessed the relationship of patient-therapist rated responsibility attribution (the extent to which patients' blame for problems was external or internal) congruence and patient-therapist rated problem solution (the extent to which patient responsibility for solving the problem was external or internal) congruence to scores on two patient-rated and two therapist-rated measures of outcome. Treatment was conducted at a university for an average of 13 sessions with clients who had symptoms of anxiety and depression. The problem solving and responsibility attributions questionnaire was completed by patients before the first session and by therapists after the first session. There were no relationships between patient-therapist problem solving congruence and any of the outcome measures. Patient-therapist responsibility attribution congruence was significantly related to therapists' ratings of patient change but to none of the other outcome measures.

In a study at a university clinic (Paivio & Bahr, 1998), patients in 12-session experiential psychotherapy completed the Working Alliance Inventory (WAI; see Horvath & Symonds, 1989) after the third and again after the final session. The Goal Agreement scale scores from the third session were not associated with improvement on any outcome measure. Goal Agreement scale scores at outcome were negatively related to patient outcome change ratings on a scale developed by the authors to measure unresolved relationship issues. Outcome goal agreement, however, did not relate significantly to patient change ratings of symptoms or patient change scores on the Structural Analysis of Social Behavior (SASB; see Benjamin, 1988).

Several studies used the Goal Disagreement scale of the California Psychotherapy Alliance Scales (CALPAS; see Marmar, Horowitz, Weiss, & Marziali, 1986) to assess goal consensus. This scale assesses "the extent to which the patient and therapist are in agreement or at variance regarding the goals of what is to be achieved as a result of treatment" (Marmar, Gaston, Gallagher, & Thompson, 1989, p. 467).

Marmar and colleagues (1989) examined the relationship between goal commitment and outcome for three types of treatments—behavioral, cognitive, and brief dynamic therapy. All therapies were completed in 16 to 20 sessions. They found no statistically significant relationships between patient ratings of goal consensus after the fifth session, assessed using the CALPAS Goal Disagreement scores, and patient change scores on the Beck Depression Inventory (BDI; see Beck, Ward, Mendelson, Mock, & Erbaugh, 1961) at termination. In a replication and extension of this study, Gaston, Marmar, Gallagher, and Thompson (1991) found that the relationship between patient CALPAS Goal Disagreement scores obtained after the fifth, tenth, and fifteenth session and patient change scores on the BDI at termination (after 16 to 20 sessions) did not account for 20% or more of the variance between variables. This indicated that goal consensus from patients' perspectives did not play a substantial role (that is, achieve a large effect size) in alleviation of client depressive symptoms in behavioral, cognitive, or brief dynamic therapy for major depressive disorder. In contrast, in a study of 20-session cognitive therapy for depression, Safran and Wallner (1991) found that patient CALPAS Goal Disagreement scores obtained after the third session were related to patients' improvement as assessed by scores on the BDI and scores on the major depression subscale of the Millon Multiaxial Clinical Inventory (MCMI; see Millon, 1983) at outcome. Thus, in this study goal consensus was significantly related to outcome improvement of depressive symptoms.

In summary, studies relating goal consensus to outcome have produced mixed results. Outcome measures were most frequently based on assessments made by patients. Patient outcome ratings were reported in 14 of the 17 studies, or 82%, and there was a positive relationship between at least one patient-completed outcome measure and goal consensus in 10 of these 14 studies, or 71%. Therapist ratings of outcomes were assessed in only 5 of the 17 studies, or 29%, with positive outcomes associated with at least one therapist-

completed measure in 4 of the 5, or 80%. Observer or staff ratings of outcome were assessed in 6 of the 17 studies, or 35%, with positive outcomes associated with at least one observer-completed measure in 3 of the 6, or 50%. Combining these results from patient, therapist, and outside raters, goal consensus and outcome were significantly, positively related on at least one measure completed by any one of these raters 68% of the time, or by 17 of 25 raters. This provides a rough overall indication of the relationship between goal consensus and outcome. Readers are cautioned that outcome measures were different for different raters. Also, patients, therapists, and outside raters may have different perspectives on what constitutes improvement.

Goal consensus was most frequently (nine studies) based on patients' ratings, followed by outside observers' ratings (five studies), therapists' ratings (three studies), and patient-therapist congruence ratings (two studies; in Hoyt et al., 1983, both therapist and observer ratings of goal consensus were used). While working alliance ratings (of which goal consensus is one component) from these three perspectives are usually positively related, the correlations among them are frequently low (in the .30s), indicating that patient, therapist, and outside rater perceptions of goal consensus differ (Tichenor & Hill, 1989). Thus, results achieved with goal consensus ratings from the patients' perspectives may have been different if goal consensus were assessed from therapists' or outside raters' perspectives.

Positive associations were more likely to occur when goal consensus and outcome were assessed concurrently than when goal consensus was used to predict outcome. For example, both studies of outcome of a single session (Eisenthal et al., 1983; Kirk et al., 1988) attained positive results. On the other hand, two studies (i.e., Gaston et al., 1991; Marmar et al., 1989) assessing goal consensus at earlier points in therapy did not find a positive consensus-outcome association.

Collaborative Involvement

Patients and therapists who are working together rather than opposing or resisting each other should accomplish more in therapy. Thus, collaborative involvement between patient and therapist should result in better outcomes. In a study examining collaboration as it related to session outcome, Orlinsky and Howard (1967) asked therapists and patients to rate the process and outcome of several sessions. In sessions rated as "good," patients indicated a desire for close collaboration with therapists, and therapists sought to increase patients' insight and support patients' self-esteem. "Good" sessions were associated with patient-therapist "deeply felt, actively collaborative engagement . . . in their style of relating, a relationship between equals" (Orlinsky & Howard, 1967, p. 626).

Most studies of collaborative involvement, however, have related it to therapy outcome, and several of these have examined patient resistance. For instance, in a study of medical student patients in psychotherapy by Buckley, Conte, Plutchik, Wild, and Karasu (1984), therapists' ratings of patients' resistance at the beginning, middle, and end of therapy were associated with poorer therapist ratings of outcome. In a study of short-term (no longer than 25 sessions) therapy, Henry, Schacht, and Strupp (1990) found that both patients' and therapists' hostility rated by outside observers from transcripts of the third session were associated with poorer outcomes assessed by patient change scores on the INTREX Introject Questionnaire (Benjamin, 1983). Piper, De-Carufel, and Szkrumelak (1985) found that pretherapy interview ratings by therapists and outside observers of patients' defensive styles were significantly related to patient-, therapist-, and observer-rated changes in target behaviors at the end of short-term psychodynamic psychotherapy. The more resistant and defensive patients were before therapy, the less they had improved at outcome.

Westerman, Frankel, Tanaka, and Kahn (1987) found that resistant patients (rated by observers from intake videos as having a noncoordinating communication style) showed less improvement at termination on observer ratings of general improvement, target behaviors, and stress than did more cooperative patients. This effect was moderated by treatment type, with improvement by patients with noncoordinating styles being greater for those given brief paradoxical treatment com-

pared to those receiving brief behavioral treatment. Westerman and colleagues (1987) indicated that this supports the notion that paradoxical interventions are suited to resistant patients.

Others have investigated the relationship between collaborative involvement and outcome by examining ratings of patient and therapist cooperation and affiliation. Kolb, Beutler, Davis, Crago, and Shanfield (1985) assessed therapist-rated patient cooperation at therapy termination by subtracting ratings of resistance from ratings of participation on the Psychotherapy Process Inventory (PPI; Baer, Dunbar, Hamilton, Guerney, & Beutler, 1980). Patient cooperation was positively related to reductions in patient-rated SCL-90 somatic complaints and paranoid symptoms. Rudy, McLemore, and Gorsuch (1985) found that both patient and therapist ratings of outcome to date were positively related to their perceptions of each other as affiliative.

In a study of 16-session psychodynamically oriented therapy, Windholz and Silberschatz (1988) found that ratings from videotapes of the eighth session of patient involvement and therapist-offered relationship on the Vanderbilt Psychotherapy Process Scale (VPPS; see O'Malley, Suh, & Strupp, 1983) were related to therapists', but not patients', ratings of outcome. Specifically, patient involvement and therapist-offered relationship were positively associated with change scores on the therapist-completed Global Assessment Scale (GAS; see Endicott, Spitzer, Fleiss, & Cohen, 1976), therapist relationship was associated with therapist-rated decreases in target complaints, and patient involvement was positively related to therapists' global change ratings.

In a study of behavioral marital therapy that averaged 23 sessions, couples' ratings of marital satisfaction on the Dyadic Adjustment Scale (DAS; see Spanier, 1976) at termination were positively associated with therapists' ratings of couples' collaboration taken after each session (Holtzworth-Munroe, Jacobson, DeKlyen, & Whisman, 1989). In a study of 16-session therapy, using observers' Q-sorts of therapy process from transcripts of the first, fifth, and fourteenth sessions, patients' increasing commitment to working in therapy and increasingly positive therapy expectations over the three sessions were positively related to patient-, therapist-, and observer-rated outcome (Jones, Parke, & Pulos, 1992).

While most studies of patient resistance/cooperation have been conducted in outpatient settings, two were conducted in hospitals. Using a collaboration scale that they devised, Allen, Deering, Buskirk, and Coyne (1988) found that long-term hospitalized patients' collaboration ratings were positively associated with their own and hospital staff members' ratings of patients' progress during the previous month. Colson and colleagues (1985) found that long-term hospitalized patients who were rated by staff members as more withdrawn and psychotic were also rated by staff as having made poorer progress than less withdrawn patients.

Patients' completion of homework assigned by therapists is another way of assessing collaborative involvement. Worthington (1986) found that completion of homework was positively associated with observer-rated reduction in patient symptoms at outcome. When therapists asked for or patients volunteered information about homework, patients were more likely to comply with homework assignments. In a study of 20- and 40-week behavior therapy with obese patients, Perri, Nezu, Patti, and McCann (1989) found a positive relationship between weight loss and patient-rated homework compliance.

In contrast, Holtzworth-Monroe and colleagues (1989) found no statistically significant relationship between therapists' ratings of homework compliance and couples' ratings of marital satisfaction on the DAS at termination. Results of a study by Hoberman, Lewinsohn, and Tilson (1988) showed no significant relationship between group leaders' records of patient homework completion and patient-rated depressive symptomatology change on the BDI at outcome.

A study of 12-session cognitive-behavioral therapy for panic disorder (Schmidt & Woolaway-Bickel, 2000) found that patients' ratings of the number of days and hours that they spent doing therapy homework was not related to several therapist- and patient-completed outcome inventories. Therapists' and outside evaluators' ratings of the quantity of homework assignments and the quality of patients' compliance, however, predicted improvement on most of the outcome inventories.

David Burns and colleagues conducted a series of studies relating homework completion during cognitive-behavioral therapy to outcome depressive symptomatology after 12 weeks of therapy (Burns & Spangler, 2000; Burns & Nolen-Hoeksema, 1991) or at outcome (Persons, Burns, & Perloff, 1988). They found that both patient- and therapist-rated patient homework compliance were related to reductions in depressive symptomatology assessed by patient ratings on the BDI and/or the SCL-90. Burns and Spangler (2000) also investigated whether or not depressive symptoms interfered with homework completion and found that homework completion was not associated with severity of depressive symptoms.

Kazantzis (2000) believed that inadequate statistical power accounts for conflicting results linking homework to therapy outcome. He calculated the statistical power of 27 cognitive and behavioral psychotherapy outcome studies relating homework to outcome that were published between 1980 and 1998; he found that researchers using multiple groups had only a 9%, 32%, or 58% chance of detecting a small, medium, or large effect size, respectively. Because of the low statistical power of these studies, Kazantzis concluded that the best way to determine homework effects relative to outcome was to aggregate study results in a meta-analysis. The subsequent meta-analysis of these 27 studies showed that both homework assignments and homework compliance were positively related to psychotherapy outcome (Kazantzis, Deane, & Ronan, 2000). These effects were moderated by homework type with more varied types of homework being superior to any one specific type and compliance rater, with therapists' and patients' ratings being more strongly related to outcome than objective measures of compliance. Kazantzis and colleagues (2000, p. 198) concluded that research should now focus on "which types of homework assignments facilitate improvement in therapy for which client problems, and which therapist behaviors can enhance the effects of homework assignments in therapy."

A final way to assess collaborative involvement is to examine ratings of patient role involvement as they relate to outcome. Marmar and colleagues (1989) examined the relationship between patient role involvement and outcome for three types of short-term (16–20 session) treatments—behavioral, cognitive, and brief dynamic therapy. Patient ratings of their role involvement after the fifth session (assessed by CALPAS Patient Commitment scores) were associated with lessening of patients' depression measured by the BDI at outcome for cognitive therapy only. In a replication and extension of this study, Gaston and colleagues (1991) found that the relationship between patient CALPAS Patient Commitment scores obtained after the fifth, tenth, and fifteenth sessions and patient change scores on the BDI at termination (after 16 to 20 sessions) accounted for more than 20% of the variance between variables (i.e., achieved a large effect size) for both behavioral and cognitive treatments.

In a study by Rounsaville, Weissman, and Prusoff (1981), patients' social functioning, emotional health, and aptitude for psychotherapy, rated by independent interviewers pretreatment, were positively related to greater involvement in the patient role, assessed by therapists' ratings after each session, and reductions in depressive symptoms, assessed by the patient-completed Hamilton Depression Scale (Hamilton, 1960) after 16 sessions. In this study, however, patients' characteristics rather than their role involvement were the significant predictors of outcome.

Martin, Martin, Meyer, and Slemon (1986) found that patients' ratings of the amount of effort expended on their role in sessions from the beginning, middle, and end of short-term cognitive-behavioral and client-centered therapy were positively related to patients' and therapists' ratings of both session effectiveness and the effectiveness of therapy to date. Soldz and colleagues (1992) found that independent ratings from videotapes of group therapy patients' participation in the patient role (assessed using the Therapeutic Participation scale of the VPPS) during the course of therapy were positively associated with patient-, therapist-, and observer-ratings of patient benefit from treatment at outcome.

To summarize, we have examined results of 24 studies relating outcome and collaborative involvement (the Holtzworth-Munroe et al. [1989] is counted twice, because it examined cooperation and homework compliance separately). As

assessed by patient cooperation, role involvement, and homework compliance, the results are generally positive. All seven of the studies, or 100%, where outcome was assessed by observer, staff, or other ratings had at least one outcome measure that was positively related to collaborative involvement. In 9 of 10 studies, or 90%, at least one therapist-completed outcome measure was positively related to collaborative involvement. When patients rated outcome, collaborative involvement was associated with at least one patient-completed outcome measure in 16 of 19 studies, or 84%. Combining these results from patient, therapist, and outside raters, collaborative involvement and outcome were significantly, positively related on at least one measure completed by at least one of these raters 89% of the time, by 32 of 36 raters. Therapists and patients rated cooperation, role involvement, and homework compliance in 11 studies each. Observers or hospital staff members rated these things in 9 studies.

Summary

Results of the studies just reviewed tend to support the positive influences of goal consensus and collaborative involvement on psychotherapy outcome. Studies have examined collaborative involvement from different participant and nonparticipant perspectives and defined it in different ways (patient role commitment, homework compliance, and patient cooperation). Results of these studies provide considerable support for the positive impact of collaborative involvement on treatment outcome. Thus, if patients and therapists are involved cooperatively and patients are working hard both in and out of sessions at tasks that are intended to address their problems, outcome is enhanced.

There is also general support for a positive relationship between goal consensus and psychotherapy outcome, but the overall results of these studies were not as positive as those concerning collaborative involvement. Goal consensus is difficult to assess. Patient and therapist may be working on the same goals, but they may talk about them in different ways. In contrast to resistance and homework compliance, it may be more difficult for observers to detect goal consensus.

LIMITATIONS OF THE RESEARCH

There are a number of limitations to the research presented above relating goal consensus and collaborative involvement to initial engagement and psychotherapy outcome. There have been relatively few studies of these important relationship variables, and the ones that have been done are largely correlational studies, which limits the causal conclusions that may be drawn. Also, only one of the studies (Gaston et al., 1991) reported effect sizes.

Regarding engagement, further research is necessary before findings can be generalized to a broader range of settings and populations. Engagement research has generally been conducted with well-educated, middle-class Caucasian patients who were seen by Caucasian therapists. Many of the engagement studies were done at university counseling centers with college student patients. Results of these studies may not be generalizable to other populations.

Further research is also necessary before initial engagement findings can be generalized to therapy relationships involving therapists from diverse theoretical orientations. In many of the engagement studies, therapists' theoretical orientations were not specified. Garfield (1986) pointed out that one problem in research on psychotherapy is that researchers tend to discuss and view psychotherapy without specifying the type of psychotherapy that is being investigated or without describing the actual operations of psychotherapy. Under such conditions, Garfield (1986) states, "It is not surprising that research on client variables may produce conflicting or inconsistent results" (p. 214). Quantitative and qualitative studies of intake verbalizations using patients from various ethnic and socioeconomic backgrounds and therapists from differing theoretical orientations and ethnic backgrounds will clarify further the engagement process.

The outcome studies tended to have patient populations from more diverse backgrounds; however, most studies just reported race/ethnicity and socioeconomic status as patient characteristics and did not investigate their association with the psychotherapy process variables and outcome. The outcome studies usually specified the theoretical orientation of the treatments studied,

but only a few studies compared treatments from different orientations as they related to implementation of goal consensus and collaborative involvement relative to outcome.

While results of psychotherapy outcome studies generally support positive relationships of goal consensus and collaborative involvement to outcome, we endorse the conclusions of Kazantzis and colleagues (2000) that researchers should investigate what particular therapist techniques work with which types of patients. Results of research relating goal consensus and collaboration to outcome would be enhanced if investigators reported not only statistical significance and effect sizes but statistics regarding clinical significance as well. Clinical significance statistics provide information concerning the extent of change for each individual within a sample and enable more precise specification on particular outcome measures of what techniques work for whom (Jacobson & Truax, 1991).

THERAPEUTIC PRACTICES

The engagement and outcome studies yield several suggestions for the practitioner. Patients who have had therapy previously, are self-referred, have less severe personality disturbances, and have already begun to address their problems seem to be easier to engage than other types of clients. Unfortunately, more troubled, more resistant, less motivated patients are perhaps most in need of help and least likely to become engaged in the therapy process or to collaborate with therapists to achieve a positive outcome. Results of the studies just reviewed tend to support the importance of goal consensus and collaborative involvement in facilitating initial patient-therapist therapeutic engagement. Consensus on therapy goals at intake helps this engagement. Patients who are motivated to change and willing to work on their problems are easier to engage. Therapists who verbally attend to patient problems and use their expertise to help patients clarify concerns will engage a high percentage of their patients.

When communicating with patients, therapists should try to address topics of importance to patients and resonate to patients' attributions of blame regarding their problems. When therapists communicate in these ways, patients feel understood and the stage is set for cooperative therapeutic collaboration, a mutual commitment to therapeutic goals, and engagement in the therapeutic process. Providing clients with understanding, sympathetic listeners who attend to topics that patients value is an important ingredient in the engagement process. Engagement occurs when therapists attend to patients' concerns and reformulate them in ways that clarify them to patients and set the stage for patient-therapist agreement on treatment goals. If patients learn something new or develop a new perspective on their problems, they are more likely to return for therapy after intake.

To maximize the possibility of achieving a positive treatment outcome, therapist and patient should be involved throughout therapy in a process of shared decision making, where goals are frequently discussed and agreed upon. Results of the studies reviewed suggest that collaborative involvement throughout therapy that includes friendly, cooperative, affiliative behavior on the part of both participants is associated with better outcomes. Patients who achieve better outcomes are those who are actively involved in the patient role, discussing concerns, feelings, and goals rather than resisting or passively receiving therapists' suggestions. Therapists who give patients homework assignments may achieve better therapy outcomes if they check on these assignments at the next session, and one study (Schmidt & Woolaway-Bickel, 2000) indicated that it is not necessarily the quantity of homework assigned, but the quality of completed homework that leads to better therapy outcomes.

REFERENCES

Allen, J. G., Deering, C. D., Buskirk, J. R., & Coyne, L. (1988). Assessment of therapeutic alliances in the psychiatric hospital milieu. *Psychiatry, 51,* 291–299.

Baer, P. E., Dunbar, P. W., Hamilton, J. E., II, Guerney, L. F., & Beutler, L. E. (1980). Therapists' perceptions of the psychotherapeutic process: Development of a psychotherapy process inventory. *Psychological Reports, 46,* 563–570.

Beck, A., Ward, C., Mendelson, M., Mock, J., & Erbaugh, J. (1961). An inventory for measur-

ing depression. *Archives of General Psychiatry, 4,* 561–571.

Benjamin, L. S. (1983). *The INTREX user's manual, part I and II.* Madison, WI: INTREX Interpersonal Institute.

Benjamin, L. S. (1988). *Manual for coding social interaction in terms of structural analysis of social behavior (SASB).* Madison: University of Wisconsin Press.

Beyebach, M., & Carranza, V. E. (1997). Therapeutic interaction and dropout: Measuring relational communication in solution-focused therapy. *Journal of Family Therapy, 19,* 173–221.

Bordin, E. S. (1979). The generalizability of the psychoanalytic concept of the working alliance. *Psychotherapy: Theory, Research and Practice, 16,* 252–260.

Buckley, P., Conte, H. R., Plutchik, R., Wild, K. V., & Karasu, T. B. (1984). Psychodynamic variables as predictors of psychotherapy outcome. *American Journal of Psychiatry, 141,* 742–748.

Burns, D. D., & Nolen-Hoeksema, S. (1991). Coping styles, homework compliance, and the effectiveness of cognitive-behavioral therapy. *Journal of Consulting and Clinical Psychology, 59,* 305–311.

Burns, D. D., & Spangler, D. L. (2000). Does psychotherapy homework lead to improvements in depression in cognitive-behavioral therapy or does improvement lead to increased homework compliance? *Journal of Consulting and Clinical Psychology, 68,* 46–56.

Colson, D. B., Allen, J. G., Coyne, L., Deering, D., Jehl, N., Kearns, W., & Spohn, H. (1985). Patterns of staff perception of difficult patients in a long-term psychiatric hospital. *Hospital and Community Psychiatry, 36,* 168–172.

Davis, C. S., Cook, D. A, Jennings, R. L., & Heck, E. J. (1977). Differential client attractiveness in a counseling analogue. *Journal of Counseling Psychology, 24,* 472–476.

Derogatis, L. R. (1974). The Hopkins Symptom Checklist (HSCL): A self-report symptom inventory. *Behavioral Science, 19,* 1–15.

Dormaar, M., Dijkman, C. I. M., & de Vries, M. W. (1989). Consensus in patient-therapist interactions: A measure of the therapeutic relationship related to outcome. *Psychotherapy and Psychosomatics, 51,* 69–76.

Duehn, W. D., & Proctor, E. K. (1977). Initial clinical interaction and premature discontinuance in treatment. *American Journal of Orthopsychiatry, 47,* 284–290.

Eisenthal, S., Koopman, C., & Lazare, A. (1983). Process analysis of two dimensions of the negotiated approach in relation to satisfaction in the initial interview. *Journal of Nervous and Mental Disease, 171*, 49–54.

Endicott, J., Spitzer, R. I., Fleiss, J. L, & Cohen, J. (1976). The Global Assessment Scale. *Archives of General Psychiatry, 33*, 766–771.

Epperson, D. L., Bushway, D. J., & Warman, R. E. (1983). Client self-terminations after one counseling session: Effects of problem recognition, counselor gender, and counselor experience. *Journal of Counseling Psychology, 30*, 307–315.

Fiester, A. R., Mahrer, A. R., Giambra, L. J., & Ormiston, D. W. (1974). Shaping a clinic population: The dropout problem reconsidered. *Community Mental Health Journal, 10*, 173–179.

Fiester, A. R., & Rudestam, K. E. (1975). A multivariate analysis of the early dropout process. *Journal of Consulting and Clinical Psychology, 43*, 528–535.

Garfield, S. L. (1986). Research on client variables in psychotherapy. In S. L. Garfield & A. E. Bergin (Eds.), *Handbook of psychotherapy and behavior change* (3rd ed., pp. 213–256). New York: Wiley.

Gaston, L., Marmar, C. R., Gallagher, D., & Thompson, L. W. (1991). Alliance prediction of outcome beyond in-treatment symptomatic change as psychotherapy process. *Psychotherapy Research, 1*, 104–113.

Goldstein, J. M., Cohen, P., Lewis, S. A., & Struening, E. L. (1988). Community treatment environments: Patient vs. staff evaluations. *Journal of Nervous and Mental Disease, 176*, 227–233.

Greenfield, T. K. (1983). The role of client satisfaction in evaluating university counseling services. *Evaluation and Program Planning, 6*, 315–325.

Hamilton, M. (1960). A rating scale for depression. *Journal of Neurological and Neurosurgical Psychiatry, 23*, 56–62.

Heilbrun, A. B., Jr. (1972). Effects of briefing upon client satisfaction with the initial counseling contact. *Journal of Consulting and Clinical Psychology, 38*, 50–66.

Henry, W. P., Schacht, T. E., & Strupp, H. H. (1990). Patient and therapist introject, interpersonal process, and differential psychotherapy outcome. *Journal of Consulting and Clinical Psychology, 58*, 768–774.

Hilsenroth, M., Handler, L., Toman, K., & Padawer, J. (1995). Rorschach and MMPI-2 indices of early psychotherapy termination. *Journal of Consulting and Clinical Psychology, 63*, 956–965.

Hilsenroth, M. J., Holdwick, D. J., Jr., Castlebury, F. D., & Blais, M. A. (1998). The effects of DSM-IV cluster B personality disorder symptoms on the termination and continuation of psychotherapy. *Psychotherapy, 35*, 163–176.

Hoberman, H. H., Lewinsohn, P. M., & Tilson, M. (1988). Group treatment of depression: Individual predictors of outcome. *Journal of Consulting and Clinical Psychology, 56*, 393–398.

Hoffman, J. J. (1985). Client factors related to premature termination of psychotherapy. *Psychotherapy, 22*, 83–85.

Hoge, M. A., Farrell, S. P., Munchel, M. E., & Strauss, J. S. (1988). Therapeutic factors in partial hospitalization. *Psychiatry, 51*, 199–210.

Holtzworth-Munroe, A., Jacobson, N. S., DeKlyen, M., & Whisman, M. A. (1989). Relationship between behavioral marital therapy outcome and process variables. *Journal of Consulting and Clinical Psychology, 57*, 658–662.

Horowitz, M. J., Marmar, C., Weiss, D., DeWitt, D., & Rosenbaum, R. (1984). Brief psychotherapy of bereavement reactions: The relationship of process to outcome. *Archives of General Psychiatry, 41*, 438–448.

Horvath, A. O., & Symonds, B. D. (1989). The development and validation of the Working Alliance Inventory. *Journal of Counseling Psychology, 36*, 223–233.

Hoyt, M. (1980). Therapist and patient actions in "good" psychotherapy sessions. *Archives of General Psychiatry, 37*, 159–161.

Hoyt, M., Xenakis, S., Marmar, C., & Horowitz, M. J. (1983). Therapists' actions that influence their perceptions of "good" psychotherapy sessions. *Journal of Nervous and Mental Disease, 171*, 400–404.

Jacobson, N. S., & Truax, P. (1991). Clinical significance: A statistical approach to defining meaningful change in psychotherapy research. *Journal of Consulting and Clinical Psychology, 59*, 12–19.

Jones, E. E., Cumming, J. D., & Horowitz, M. J. (1988). Another look at the nonspecific hypothesis of therapeutic effectiveness. *Journal of Consulting and Clinical Psychology, 56*, 48–55.

Jones, E. E., Parke, L. A., & Pulos, S. M. (1992). How therapy is conducted in the private consulting room: A multidimensional description of brief psychodynamic treatments. *Psychotherapy Research, 2*, 16–30.

Kazantzis, N. (2000). Power to detect homework effects in psychotherapy outcome research. *Journal of Consulting and Clinical Psychology, 68,* 166–170.

Kazantzis, N., Deane, F. P., & Ronan, K. R. (2000). Homework assignments in cognitive and behavioral therapy: A meta-analysis. *Clinical Psychology: Science and Practice, 7,* 189–202.

Kirk, A. K., Stanley, G. V., & Brown, D. F. (1988). Changes in patients' stress and arousal levels associated with therapists' perception of their requests during crisis intervention. *British Journal of Clinical Psychology, 27,* 363–369.

Kokotovic, A. M., & Tracey, T. J. (1987). Premature termination at a university counseling center. *Journal of Counseling Psychology, 34,* 80–82.

Kolb, D. L., Beutler, L. E., Davis, C. S., Crago, M., & Shanfield, S. B. (1985). Patient and therapy process variables relating to dropout and change in psychotherapy. *Psychotherapy, 22,* 702–710.

Lansford, E. (1986). Weakenings and repairs of the working alliance in short-term psychotherapy. *Professional Psychology: Research and Practice, 17,* 364–366.

Larsen, D. L., Attkisson, C. C., Hargreaves, W. A., & Nguyen, T. D. (1979). Assessment of client/patient satisfaction: Development of a general scale. *Evaluation and Program Planning, 2,* 197–207.

Longo, D. A., Lent, R. W., & Brown, S. D. (1992). Social cognitive variables in the prediction of client motivation and attrition. *Journal of Counseling Psychology, 39,* 447–452.

MacKay, C., Cox, T., Burrows, G., & Lazzerini, T. (1978). An inventory for the measurement of self-reported stress and arousal. *British Journal of Social and Clinical Psychology, 17,* 283–284.

Marmar, C. R., Gaston, L., Gallagher, D., & Thompson, L. W. (1989). Alliance and outcome in late-life depression. *Journal of Nervous and Mental Disease, 177,* 464–472.

Marmar, C. R., Horowitz, M. J., Weiss, D. S., & Marziali, E. (1986). The development of the therapeutic alliance rating system. In L. Greenberg & W. Pinsof (Eds.), *The psychotherapeutic process: A research handbook.* New York: Guilford.

Martin, D. J., Garske, J. P., & Davis, M. K. (2000). Relation of the therapeutic alliance with outcome and other variables: A meta-analytic review. *Journal of Consulting and Clinical Psychology, 68,* 438–450.

Martin, J., Martin, W., Meyer, M., & Slemon, A. (1986). Empirical investigation of the cognitive mediational paradigm for research on counseling. *Journal of Counseling Psychology, 33,* 115–123.

Millon, T. (1983). *Millon Clinical Multiaxial Inventory manual* (3rd ed.). Minneapolis, MN: National Computer Systems.

Mohl, P. C., Martinez, D., Ticknor, C., Huang, M., & Cordell, L. (1991). Early dropouts from psychotherapy. *Journal of Nervous and Mental Disease, 179,* 478–481.

Mussell, M. P., Mitchell, J. E., Crosby, R. D., Fulkerson, J. A., Hoberman, H. M., & Romano, J. L. (2000). Commitment to treatment goals in prediction of group cognitive-behavioral therapy treatment outcome for women with bulimia nervosa. *Journal of Consulting and Clinical Psychology, 68,* 432–437.

Nash, J. M., & Garske, J. P. (1988, August). *Client and process variables as predictors of early counseling dropout.* Paper presented at the annual convention of the American Psychological Association, Atlanta.

Odell, M., & Quinn, W. H. (1998). Therapist and client behaviors in the first interview: Effects on session impact and treatment duration. *Journal of Marital and Family Therapy, 24,* 369–388.

O'Malley, S. S., Suh, C. S., & Strupp, H. H. (1983). The Vanderbilt Psychotherapy Process Scale: A report on the scale development and a process-outcome study. *Journal of Consulting and Clinical Psychology, 51,* 581–586.

Orlinsky, D. E., Grawe, K., & Parks, B. K. (1994). Process and outcome in psychotherapy—Noch einmal. In A. E. Bergin & S. L. Garfield (Eds.), *Handbook of psychotherapy and behavior change* (4th ed.). New York: Wiley.

Orlinsky, D. E., & Howard, K. I. (1967). The good therapy hour. *Archives of General Psychiatry, 16,* 621–632.

Paivio, S. C., & Bahr, L. M. (1998). Interpersonal problems, working alliance, and outcome in short-term experiential therapy. *Psychotherapy Research, 8,* 392–407.

Perri, M. G., Nezu, A. M., Patti, E. T., & McCann, K. L. (1989). Effect of length of treatment on weight loss. *Journal of Consulting and Clinical Psychology, 57,* 450–452.

Persons, J. B., Burns, D. D., & Perloff, J. M. (1988). Predictors of dropout and outcome in cognitive therapy for depression in a private practice setting. *Cognitive Therapy and Research, 12,* 557–575.

Phillips, E. L. (1985). *Psychotherapy revised: New frontiers in research and practice.* Hillsdale, NJ: Erlbaum.

Pinsof, W. H., & Catherall, D. R. (1986). The integrative psychotherapy alliance: Family, couple and individual therapy scales. *Journal of Marital and Family Therapy, 12,* 132–151.

Piper, W. E., DeCarufel, F. L., & Szkrumelak, N. (1985). Patient predictors of process and outcome in short-term individual psychotherapy. *Journal of Nervous and Mental Disease, 173,* 726–733.

Quinn, W. H., Dotson, D., & Jordan, K. (1997). Dimensions of therapeutic alliance and their associations with outcome in family therapy. *Psychotherapy Research, 7,* 429–438.

Richmond, R. (1992). Discriminating variables among psychotherapy dropouts from a psychological training clinic. *Professional Psychology: Research and Practice, 23,* 123–130.

Rounsaville, B. J., Weissman, M. M., & Prusoff, B. A. (1981). Psychotherapy with depressed outpatients: Patient process variables as predictors of outcome. *British Journal of Psychiatry, 138,* 67–74.

Rudy, J. P., McLemore, C. W., & Gorsuch, R. L. (1985). Interpersonal behavior and therapeutic progress: Therapists and clients rate themselves and each other. *Psychiatry, 48,* 264–281.

Safran, J. D., & Wallner, L. K. (1991). The relative predictive validity of two therapeutic alliance measures in cognitive therapy. *Psychological Assessment, 3,* 188–195.

Schiller, L. J. (1976). A comparative study of the differences between client continuers and dropouts at two university counseling centers. *Journal of Counseling Psychology, 23,* 99–102.

Schmidt, N. B., & Woolaway-Bickel, K. (2000). The effects of treatment compliance on outcome in cognitive-behavioral therapy for panic disorder: Quality versus quantity. *Journal of Consulting and Clinical Psychology, 68,* 13–18.

Shapiro, R. J. (1974). Therapist attitudes and premature termination in family and individual therapy. *Journal of Nervous and Mental Disease, 159,* 101–107.

Shueman, S. A., Gelso, C. J., Mindus, L., Hunt, B., & Stevenson, J. (1980). Client satisfaction with intake: Is the waiting list all that matters? *Journal of College Student Personnel, 21,* 114–121.

Soldz, S., Budman, S., & Demby, A. (1992). The relationship between main actor behaviors and treatment outcome in group psychotherapy. *Psychotherapy Research, 2,* 52–62.

Spanier, G. B. (1976). Measuring dyadic adjustment: New scales for assessing the quality of marriage and similar dyads. *Journal of Marriage and the Family, 38,* 15–28.

Stiles, W. B. (1980). Measurement of the impact of psychotherapy sessions. *Journal of Consulting and Clinical Psychology, 48,* 176–185.

Talmon, M. (1990). *Single session therapy.* San Francisco: Jossey-Bass.

Tichenor, V., & Hill, C. E. (1989). A comparison of six measures of working alliance. *Psychotherapy: Theory, Research and Practice, 26,* 195–199.

Tracey, T. J. (1986). Interactional correlates of premature termination. *Journal of Consulting and Clinical Psychology, 54,* 784–788.

Tracey, T. J. (1988). Relationship of responsibility attribution congruence to psychotherapy outcome. *Journal of Clinical and Social Psychology, 7,* 131–146.

Tracy, J. J. (1977). Impact of intake procedures upon client attrition in a community mental health center. *Journal of Consulting and Clinical Psychology, 45,* 192–195.

Tryon, G. S. (1985). The engagement quotient: One index of a basic counseling task. *Journal of College Student Personnel, 26,* 351–354.

Tryon, G. S. (1986). Client and counselor characteristics and engagement in counseling. *Journal of Counseling Psychology, 33,* 471–474.

Tryon, G. S. (1989). Study of variables related to client engagement using practicum trainees and experienced clinicians. *Psychotherapy, 26,* 54–61.

Tryon, G. S. (1990). Session depth and smoothness in relation to the concept of engagement in counseling. *Journal of Counseling Psychology, 37,* 248–253.

Tryon, G. S. (1992). Client attractiveness as related to the concept of engagement in therapy. *Counselling Psychology Quarterly, 5,* 307–314.

Tryon, G. S. (1999). [Engagement quotients for 85 practicum trainees]. Unpublished raw data.

Tryon, G. S. (2002). Engagement in counseling. In G. S. Tryon (Ed.), *Counseling based on process research: Applying what we know* (pp. 1–26). Boston: Allyn & Bacon.

Tryon, G. S., & Tryon, W. W. (1986). Factors associated with clinical practicum trainees' engagement of clients in counseling. *Professional Psychology: Research and Practice, 17,* 586–589.

Watzlawick, P., Beavin, J., & Jackson, D. D.

(1967). *Pragmatics of human communication.* New York: Norton.

Westerman, M. A., Frankel, A. S., Tanaka, J. S., & Kahn, J. (1987). Client cooperative interview and outcome in paradoxical and behavioral brief treatment approaches. *Journal of Counseling Psychology, 34,* 99–102.

Windholz, M. J., & Silberschatz, G. (1988). Vanderbilt Psychotherapy Process Scale: A replication with adult outpatients. *Journal of Consulting and Clinical Psychology, 56,* 56–60.

Worthington, E. L., Jr. (1986). Client compliance with homework directives during counseling. *Journal of Counseling Psychology, 33,* 124–130.

Zamostny, K. P., Corrigan, J. D., & Eggert, M. A. (1981). Replication and extension of social influence processes in counseling: A field study. *Journal of Counseling Psychology, 28,* 481–489.

B. CUSTOMIZING THE THERAPY RELATIONSHIP TO THE INDIVIDUAL PATIENT

7

Resistance

Larry E. Beutler
Carla M. Moleiro
Hani Talebi

While some experts (such as Lambert, 1992; Wampold, 2001) assert that specific techniques offer little advantage over the experience of being understood and affirmed in an environment of safety, in the past decade, evidence of the specific effects of psychotherapy has begun to accumulate. This evidence supports the contention that highly specialized psychotherapies are more powerful than various no-treatment and placebo conditions and add significantly to the effects of a caring and supportive psychotherapy relationship (Chambless & Ollendick, 2001; Kirsch & Sapirstein, 1998). Accordingly, research has begun identifying certain types of therapies that are especially effective at ameliorating different types of symptoms (Barlow, 1994; Nathan & Gorman, 1998).

In spite of the promising evidence that some specific techniques and relationship stances are more effective than others, many authors continue to conclude that there is weak or even negligible evidence that treatment models differ in their relative effects (Wampold et al., 1997; Wampold, 2001). The credibility of the conclusion that all treatments are equivalent, however, suffers from both an inordinately nonspecific definition of psychotherapy and the illusion that the samples from which these studies draw their conclusions are homogeneous (Beutler, 2002).

These difficulties are typical in the randomized clinical trial (RCT) methods that are in vogue for studying psychotherapy effects. This type of research starts with collecting theoretically derived interventions into one or more treatment protocols with the eventual intent of comparing the resulting treatment manuals either to one another or to some form of delayed or no-treatment condition. These manual-based treatments are applied to randomly selected subgroups of patients, all of whom share a common diagnosis. This procedure implicitly assumes that: (1) optimally effective interventions are captured in one theoretical framework, and (2) diagnostic groupings adequately reduce treatment-relevant heterogeneity among patient groups.

For example, it is obvious to most clinicians that interventions from several different theories work, from time to time, and many different personalities and dispositions are represented among patients within any diagnostic group. While it is certainly advantageous to cluster patients into homogeneous groups in order to better observe the effects of treatment, sharing a diagnostic label is probably a poor indicator of how similar or different patients are from one another, especially as pertains to predicting the effects of psychological treatments (Beutler & Malik, 2002). While the assumption that diagnosis is a "good" or "good enough" grouping factor has been useful in psychopharmacological research, there is very little evidence that the effects of different psychotherapy procedures are specific to the various symptoms that define a diagnosis (Beutler, 2002; Beutler, Clarkin, & Bongar, 2000; Kirsch & Sapirstein, 1998). Given the unreliability of most diagnoses (Carson, 1997) and the political nature of diagnostic criteria (Houts, 2002), it is inevitable that when specific treatments are compared to one another, the most defensible conclusion is that all treatments produce similar outcomes (Wampold et al., 1997; Wampold, 2001).

Said another way, just as it is unwise to think that effective methods are all embodied in a single theory, it is equally unwise to think that the qualities that constitute motivation, prognosis, and progress among patients are well captured by diagnostic labels (see Beutler, 1991; Carson, 1997). Logic should convince us that the more refined our distinctions are among both psychotherapy procedures and patient characteristics, the more likely we will be able to identify ways to customize treatments effectively. Thus, the critical question facing mental health treatment remains, "What procedures work for this patient, for this problem, under these circumstances?" (Paul, 1978).

In response to some of the foregoing concerns, contemporary research has begun to look for aptitude by treatment interactions (ATIs). This research largely has investigated how classes of treatment procedures (rather than their brand names) interact with nondiagnostic qualities of patients. This chapter examines the research evidence for one line of investigation, namely patient resistance, a cross-cutting patient dimension.

In clinical practice, evoking patient resistance is often considered to be both a normal and a desired component of therapeutic interventions. Observing it has traditionally been used to help establish a diagnosis, and interpreting it is often assumed to advance one's growth. While invoking and interpreting situational or state-like resistance may have some therapeutic value, its situational specificity makes it of little value as a treatment planning variable. Thus, this review will focus primarily on the enduring aspects of patient resistance that allow treatment planning and outcome enhancement.

DEFINITIONS

Resistant traits are observed and measured by the ease with which resistance to external demands is provoked. A high trait resistant individual is easily stimulated to behave with opposition to a situation. High trait-like resistance may or may not lead to broader psychopathology, but easy arousal of resistance behaviors is likely to be disruptive to relationships and social activities.

The concept of resistance began to take shape in psychology with the development of psychoanalytic theory. Classical psychoanalytic theory characterized resistance as the patient's unconscious avoidance of or distraction from the analytic work (Arlow, 2000). This theoretical perspective assumed that resistance was an effort to repress intrapsychic impulses that conflicted with social expectations and self-perceptions. Resistance was an inherent, unconscious striving to avoid thoughts and feelings that caused discomfort. This concept of resistance has been incorporated into much of contemporary literature and even common parlance.

Outside of psychotherapy and particularly outside of psychoanalytic thought, the concept of resistance has achieved its greatest recognition within the field of social psychology. J. W. Brehm (1966) proposed a theory of "psychological reactance." He defined this term as a "state of mind aroused by a threat to one's perceived legitimate freedom, motivating the individual to restore the thwarted freedom" (S. S. Brehm & J. W. Brehm, 1981, p. 4). Thus, reactance is often considered to be a prototypic, albeit extreme, example of resistance.

Reactance Theory

Reactance theory asserts that any person experiences psychological reactance whenever he or she believes that free behaviors are being threatened with elimination. Thus, even normal reactance tendencies are both differentially responsive to an individual's disposition to perceive threat and motivational in that they direct the individual toward restoring the threatened behaviors. Once activated, reactance is observed in oppositional behavior, noncompliance, and rigidity (Tennen,

Rohrbaugh, Press, & White, 1981). The adolescent whose freedom is restricted thus becomes disposed to rebellion and oppositional behaviors. Whether or not these are actually manifest, however, depends both on the level of reactance disposition and the forcefulness of the external demand.

Unlike psychodynamic theory, reactance theory conceptualizes resistance as a normal process that is designed to protect a sense of personal freedom, rather than as a pathological process of hiding unconscious urges and impulses. From this perspective, reactance theory assumes that: (1) psychotherapy is a process in which the therapist exerts the forces of persuasion and social influence to change the patient's behavior, thoughts, and feelings; (2) freedom (of choice and action) is valued by all human beings; (3) human beings will react negatively to perceived, implied, or actual threats to their "free behaviors"; and (4) the therapist's suggestions or directives may be perceived as threats to the client's freedom (Beutler, 1983; J. W. Brehm, 1966; S. S. Brehm, 1976).

The term resistance, as applied to a client's behavior, implies that refusal to cooperate or change is a form of active opposition to the therapist's influence. However, Kirmayer (1990) points out that clients rarely attribute such active opposition to their own behavior in psychotherapy. Indeed, clients are noted for their failure to self-attribute an active role in their own problems, and this failure to ascribe to personal control over their own behavior leads to the self-view of being victims of circumstance, of disease, or of others' malevolence.

Many of the more recent applications of resistance have broadened the definition of this construct to include both conscious and unconscious processes, to emphasize the role of trait dispositions as well as state responses, and to translate the concepts to clinical conditions and situations (Beutler, 1983; Rohrbaugh, Tennen, Press, & White, 1981; Shoham-Salomon & Hannah, 1991). S. S. Brehm (1976) provided the first recommendations for how to minimize a patient's reactance, based on social persuasion theories. However, most of this latter research was conducted with college students as subjects, and its generalization to clinical settings is not assured.

Most often in this perspective, patient resistance is viewed as a variable that mediates or moderates the effects of therapist level of directiveness. That is, the effectiveness of therapist directives and guidance are considered to be directly dependent on the patient's proneness to resist external control. Viewing resistant behavior as a struggle against loss of freedom and responding by reducing the levels of therapist directiveness may encourage the resistant client to act and may foster the development of self-attributions of control and responsibility.

Social Influence Theory

Acting in opposition to what one is asked to do is only one expression of resistance. Depending upon the client's attributions of causality and control, resistance may be manifest in cognitive dissonance, emotional exacerbation, reactance, or helpless withdrawal. That is, some patients may comply but do so with resentment; others may resist passively rather than actively doing the opposite of what is suggested; still others may simply become angry and drop out of therapy. Strong and colleagues (Strong, 1968; Strong & Matross, 1973) have viewed these reactions through the lens of social influence theory. According to social influence theory, change on the part of the client is considered to be a product of activating and restraining forces that act on the client. The activating forces are direct products of the client's perception of the therapist's influence or power. In this view, one can see some distinctions with the propositions of Brehm's reactance theory. Notably, from a social influence perspective, resistance is not perceived as a protective or defensive response. It is viewed as the product of incongruence in the therapist's behavior and the power and legitimacy ascribed to her. That is, within this perspective, resistance is evoked not by the content of the therapist's interventions but by the client's perception that the therapist's influence is illegitimate. Thus, the patient's resistance represents an internal conflict between the patient's desire to accept the therapist's influence and the patient's reluctance to do so because of the perceived illegitimacy of the therapist's influence.

A modest amount of research on a social influence perspective accumulated during the 1970s and early 1980s (Beutler, 1981; Frank, 1973; Kerr, Olsen, Pace, & Claiborn, 1986). Ruppel and Kaul (1982), for example, asked college students to watch a psychotherapy session via videotape and estimate a counselor's effect on the client's career planning activities, as well as on the congruence of their efforts. The less trustworthy counselor (less legitimate) elicited significantly lower expectations for client instrumentality (compliance) than did the more trustworthy counselor. The interaction between trustworthiness and congruence was also significant; trustworthy counselors who were incongruent in their influence were judged to be less influential with the client and with the subjects themselves than those who were congruent. These analogue results have not been convincingly repeated in clinical settings. The dearth of findings in this area has raised questions about the strength of social persuasion forces, resulting in social influence perspectives gradually losing favor.

Applications of Resistance to Psychotherapy

To anticipate our conclusions, as a general rule, research suggests that patient resistance impedes the achievement of therapeutic goals (Beutler, Clarkin, & Bongar, 2000; Beutler, Goodrich, Fisher, & Williams, 1999). In contrast to the popular view that the manifestation of resistance advances the process, psychotherapy works best if the therapist can avoid raising resistant behaviors. Moreover, resistance does not necessarily reflect pathological behavior. It is advantageous to consider it to be a normal response to stress and threat. Effective psychotherapy may well have the aim to induce as little resistance as possible while still moving the patient toward his or her goals.

Research has also consistently confirmed the presence of certain relationships between those things that are identified as resistant behaviors and the content of therapeutic sessions. Patient resistance, irrespective of its theory of origination, has consistently affected how and what subsequent interventions should be implemented. From the standpoint of planning and tailoring treatment to individual patient needs, for example, clinical researchers have focused on the proposition that the degree of structure and directiveness embodied in treatment can advantageously be adjusted to fit a specific client's level of resistance. For example, this would allow for a clinician to selectively use interventions that vary in such things as the level of therapist control, structure, and directiveness. Some researchers have also suggested that, among patients with especially high levels of resistance traits, the employment of paradoxical interventions may be most effective because they capitalize on the patient's tendency to respond in consistently oppositional manners (Beutler, 1983; Dowd, Milne, & Wise, 1991). By examining how patient resistance may affect specific outcomes when treatments are varied, researchers may be able to clarify patient-treatment relationships and to develop effective models of treatment planning.

CLINICAL EXAMPLE

There are many examples of resistance in psychotherapy: the patient who consistently fails to complete homework assignments, the chronically late patient, the patient who agrees and then disagrees ("yes, but . . . "), and the patient who becomes angry and verbally attacks the therapist's skill or interventions. While any patient may show some of these signs when the therapist moves too fast or makes a tactical error, when such behaviors prove, by their consistency and cross-situational pervasiveness, that they represent an enduring characteristic of the patient, one speaks of the "resistant patient." Whether state or trait, the effective therapist may respond similarly to any specific response by acknowledging the patient's anger or fear, reflecting these feelings, discussing the therapeutic relationship, or re-exploring the therapeutic contract (Beutler & Harwood, 2000).

Lisa was a 37-year-old European-American female in her third marriage. She sought psychotherapy because of mild depressive symptoms. She presented with a matter-of-fact and assertive style. She revealed that she had marital problems and described escalating arguments that lasted several hours. She indicated that her primary goal was to learn how to communicate in a more effective way with her husband. The client admitted that her husband was the one who told her to come to therapy, although he was unwilling to engage in couple or marital therapy.

Lisa defended her decision to undertake psychotherapy by describing the history of her symptoms in detail and reporting her background. She opened the third treatment session by asking, "So, what do we do now?" This was the client's first therapy experience and she declared she wanted to move through the process and find a solution. She expected to be through with therapy in six months.

Although the client's motivation initially appeared to be high, she frequently arrived five minutes late to the sessions. She also "forgot" homework assignments, such as buying a specific book on marital problems, or expressing her wants in an assertive way before becoming angry. The therapist initially considered these instances of passive noncompliance as indications that she was resistant and feared losing control of her free behavior. Her in-session behaviors were consistent with this latter view. She was very active, talking fast, distracting the chain of thought with numerous side stories, while displaying an excitable affect that seemed rather inconsistent with her report of depression.

The therapist ascribed a certain level of "playful" optimism and childishness to the patient's behavior, especially her seeming inability to maintain a topic of conversation for a reasonable period and her inability to reflect on her own experiences. In addition, Lisa frequently asked the therapist about her own week, inquiring how her academic training as a therapist was going, and insisted that her inquiries were due to simple curiosity. The therapist decided to process these behaviors as examples of "resistance" and began this process after the client mentioned a friend who needed psychotherapy but did not want to go.

Therapist: How does that apply to you, and to us?

Client: I guess it makes me feel sad for her [friend]. That she does not have anyone to trust. But, if she did go, it would be a waste of her money, and a waste of two people's time.

Therapist: I do hear what you are saying. . . . You are saying that you are willing to come

here, that you trust me, and that you are willing to put your feelings out there [in session]. . . . And that is important, and I do hear you saying that. On the other hand, I oftentimes feel you're slippery.

Client: Oh, yes!

Therapist: Slipping between my fingers. . . . All the tangent stories and sometimes avoiding what you are feeling.

Client: Oh, yes! I jump around! Oh, yes! That must be frustrating for you! I think a lot about that!

Therapist: I was wondering how aware you were of that . . .

Client: Oh, yes, I am aware. I make you sit through a lot before you get something. I do.

Therapist: What is that like for you?

Client: I thought about this too. That I jump around a lot. It's a defense mechanism. [pause]

Therapist: Defending you from what?

Client: [silent] I guess of being in touch with whatever it is. That has to be the bottom line. Why? Who knows! Probably I don't want to deal with it [topic] at that point in time.

Therapist: So, you want to deal with it, and you are here and you are motivated. And you always show up! But part of you does not want to deal with it. . . .

Client: Yeah, sometimes I come here and I don't know where we are going. . . . And then, sometimes, oops God, we are here [exploring the client's abuse history]! And today . . . [pause]

Therapist: It must be a little frightening because the last two sessions we had were really hard . . . [exploring childhood neglect and abuse in the client's previous marriage]

Client: Oh, yes, they were, weren't they?! So, today, I think I need a little break.

Therapist: I hear that. And it's fine with me. But it is interesting to note and to become aware of your defenses and your own particular ways of doing it.

As this example portrays, the therapist viewed the patient's resistance as an expression of her fear of psychotherapy, not of an unconscious conflict over impulse control. Thus, she attempted to make the session less threatening by providing structure and helping the patient take more control over the process, enrolling her in a joint exploration of her fears. The therapist proceeded into the exploration of such defenses outside the treatment setting and the therapeutic relationship.

RESEARCH REVIEW

Patient Contributions

Overcoming and reducing patient resistance are major objectives of any treatment procedure. Resistant patients experience less benefit and are more prone to prematurely terminate from treatment than those who are cooperative (see reviews by Beutler, Clarkin, & Bongar, 2000; Beutler, Goodrich, Fisher, & Williams, 1999). This evidence seems clear; however, resistance is often defined solely on the basis of the client's failure to improve (Wachtel, 1999). Thus, research has identified those who place more value on self-control than on compliance (Blatt, Sanislow, Zuroff, & Pilkonis, 1996), those who do not become involved in the therapeutic relationship (Last, Thase, Hersen, Bellack, & Himmelhoch, 1984; McCullough et al., 1991), and those who fail to complete homework assignments (Addis & Jacobson, 2000; Edelman & Chambless, 1993; Persons, Burns, & Perloff, 1988) as being poor candidates for treatment. But the behaviors that define resistance in these instances are closely related to outcome itself, making the persistence of symptoms almost synonymous with resistance. Arkowitz (1995) calls attention to this "circularity trap," wherein resistance is defined by absence of therapeutic change and the latter is utilized to define the former.

To escape such circularity, it is important to separately identify levels of patient resistance and their treatment outcome. For example, in an attempt to understand the effects and nature of trait-like resistance, several studies have tried to identify patterns of extratherapy behavior that are associated with the patient's level of trait-like resistance. Dowd, Wallbrown, Sanders, and Yesenosky (1994) found that resistant patients are less concerned about "impression management" and more likely to resist rules and social norms in a variety of contexts than their counterparts. These individuals tend to reject structure and prefer work settings that allow them to exercise personal freedom and initiative. Conversely, less reactant people tend to do best with some degree of guidance and external structure.

Mediators and Moderators

Research has begun to investigate the differential or mediating effects of resistance on different treatments, focusing either on responses to state-like resistance or on the mediating effects of the patient's resistance traits. From the standpoint of planning and tailoring treatment to individual characteristics, the role of trait-like resistance is especially interesting. Drawing from the observation that trait-resistant patients tend to avoid directive guidance, it might follow that the degree of structure and directiveness embodied in the treatment provided should and can be adjusted to fit with the patient's level of resistance.

Table 7.1 provides a summary of empirical research studies that have explored the effects of resistance and outcome as well as the joint interaction of patient resistance and intervention with outcomes. The table separates the studies by the type of relationship observed and notes the way that resistance was measured. Although there are a large number of studies that have addressed various aspects of resistance, we were able to identify 35 different studies that have specifically addressed patient resistance as a factor that either correlated with outcome directly or correlated with the differential value of directive versus nondirective, or paradoxical and nonparadoxical treatments. Eleven of these studies addressed the question of how patient resistance affects outcome, of which nine (82%) found that patient resistance negatively impacted treatment in a variety of ways.

For example, Miller, Benefield, and Tonigan (1993) studied state-like patterns and found that therapist directiveness evoked high levels of patient state-like resistance which subsequently resulted in poorer outcomes than less directive interventions. The same pattern of results was confirmed by Bischoff and Tracey (1995), who emphasized the interactional nature of state-like resistance and the fact that therapist behavior constitutes a mechanism for managing resistance in the psychotherapy session.

More pertinent to the current review are the studies that inspected resistance by treatment interaction effects. It should be noted that these studies inspected both trait and state aspects of resistance, finding similar patterns for both. Twenty studies inspected the differential effects of therapist directiveness as moderated by patient resistance. Sixteen of these studies (80%) found results that were consistent with that suggested by reactance theorists (Beutler & Clarkin, 1990; Brehm & Brehm, 1981; Dowd et al., 1994). Specifically, directive interventions worked best among patients who had relatively low levels of state- or trait-like resistance, while nondirective interventions worked best among patients who had relatively high levels of resistance.

Piper, Joyce, McCallum, and Azim (1998), for example, compared interpretative (directive) and supportive (nondirective) therapies among patients who varied on their interpersonal responsivity and attachment patterns (resistant tendencies). They found that directive interventions evoked higher rates of dropout than supportive ones, as one might expect, and that patient quality of object relations (such as interpersonal receptivity) mediated these treatment effects. Among patients with high receptivity, the application of directive interventions resulted in positive effects, counteracting the tendency for these interventions to be associated with high dropout rates.

In the foregoing study, directive and evocative interventions represented variations of psychodynamic methods. The use of dynamic interpretations by the therapist defined the level of directiveness used. In most studies, however, directive and nondirective interventions have been compared through an assessment of procedures drawn from different models of psychotherapy. Cognitive and behavioral therapies are generally used as the prototypes of directive interventions, while psychodynamic, self-directed, or other relationship-oriented therapies are used as the prototypes of nondirective or evocative interventions. Whether described as variations within therapy models or as differences between these models, the results are generally similar.

For example, in a comparison of cognitive and self-directed therapies, Beutler, Engle, and colleagues (1991) demonstrated that directive therapies (cognitive therapy) and nondirective interventions (self-directed therapy) were differentially effective for reducing depressive symptoms depending on the initial trait-like level of patient resistance. Among very resistant patients, a self-directed therapy regimen surpassed a directive one in affecting therapeutic gain. Conversely, patients who were low on resistance did best with directive, cognitive therapy procedures. These results were cross-validated at one-year follow-up (Beutler, Machado, Engle, & Mohr, 1993) and independently replicated in a cross-cultural sample of depressed patients (Beutler, Mohr, Grawe, Engle, & McDonald, 1991).

This series of studies provided the foundation for a prospective investigation of patient resistance, along with other matching variables, as a mediator of therapist directiveness. Beutler, Moleiro, Malik, and Harwood (in press) found strong support for the use of matching dimensions, across treatments, with from 10% to 40% of the overall outcomes being dependent on the fit of treatment to patient. Among the four matching dimensions studied in this latter investigation, the fit of patient resistance with therapist directiveness was the most consistent predictor of treatment outcome. High resistant patients responded less favorably to treatment overall than their low resistant counterparts, but at least part of this failure to respond could be ameliorated by the application of nondirective interventions.

Reactance theorists have also suggested that, among patients who are especially resistant, paradoxical interventions may be effective since they capitalize on the patient's tendency to respond in oppositional ways. Table 7.1 reveals the results of four studies that have specifically addressed this issue in psychotherapy. All of these studies (100%) supported this proposition. In addition, three meta-analyses (Hampton, 1988; Hill, 1987; Shoham-Salomon & Rosenthal, 1987) have also been conducted in order to inspect the use of paradoxical interventions. None of these meta-analyses specifically investigated patient factors; they restricted their explorations to the direct effects of paradoxical interventions. Nonetheless, two of the three meta-analyses obtained significant findings supporting the value of paradoxical interventions. Specifically, Hampton (1988), using a base of 29 studies, found that paradoxical treatments were generally more effective than nonparadoxi-

Table 7.1. Mediation Between Patient Resistance, Treatment Directiveness, and Outcome

Measure of Resistance	Significant Relationship	Mixed Findings	No Relationship
Direct Relationship Between Resistance and Poor Outcome			
Initial homework noncompliance	Leung & Heimberg (1996); Persons, Burns, & Perloff (1988); Addis & Jacobson (2000)	Edelman & Chambless (1993)	
In-session noncompliance	Bischoff & Tonigan (1993); Miller et al. (1995)	Edelman & Chambless (1993)	
Locus of Control Scale	Leung & Heimberg (1996)		
Therapy involvement	Last et al. (1984)		
Questionnaire for the Measure of Psychological Resistance (QMPR)	Dowd, Wallbrown, Sanders, & Yesenosky (1994)		
Resistance Process Rating			Morgan, Luborsky, Crits-Christoph, Curtis, & Solomon (1982)
Therapeutic Reactance Scale (TRS)	Dowd, Wallbrown, Sanders, & Yesenosky (1994)		
Total Number of Studies $N = 11$	$N = 9$	$N = 1$	$N = 1$
Mediation Effect of Intervention Directiveness on the Relation Between Resistance and Poor Outcome			
Alliances measures		Greenberg & Watson (1998)	
California Psychological Inventory (CPA) subscales	Project MATCH (1996)		
Client Resistance Code (CRC)	Bischoff & Tracey (1995)		
Fundamental Interpersonal Relations Orientation Scale (FIRO-B)			Calvert, Beutler, & Crago (1988)
Locus of Control Index	Beutler & Mitchell (1981)		

Minnesota Multiphasic Personality Inventory (MMPI-2) subscales	Beutler, Engle, et al. (1991); Beutler, Clarkin, & Bongar (2000); Beutler & Mitchell (1981); Beutler, Moleiro, Malik, & Harwood (in press); Beutler, Mohr, et al. (1991); Karno, Beutler, & Harwood (in press)	Beutler, Machado, Engle, & Mohr (1993)	Calvert, Beutler, & Crago (1988)
Process coding system	McCullough et al. (1991)		
Quality of Object Relations (QOR)	Piper, Joyce, McCallum, & Azim (1998)		
Self-evaluation of drinking (motivation for change)	Miller, Benefield, & Tonigan (1993)		
Therapeutic Reactance Scale (TRS)	Beutler, Clarkin, & Bongar (2000); Beutler, Moleiro, Malik, & Harwood (in press); Joyce, Ogrodniczuk, Piper, & McCallum (2000); Tracey, Ellickson, & Sherry (1989)	Joyce & Piper (1996)	
Total Number of Studies $N = 20$	$N = 16$	$N = 3$	$N = 1$

Effect of Paradoxical Interventions on Outcome Among Differentially Resistant Patients

Client noncompliance code	Patterson & Forgatch (1985)		
Questionnaire on procrastination and estimation of personal control	Shoham-Salomon, Avner, & Neeman (1989); Shoham-Salomon, & Hannah (1991)		
Therapeutic Reactance Scale (TRS)	Horvath & Goheen (1990)		
Diverse measures—meta-analysis	Hampton (1988); Hill (1987)	Shoham-Salomon & Rosenthal (1987)	
Total Number of Studies (Excluding Meta-Analyses) $N = 4$	$N = 4$ plus Two Meta-analyses	$N = 1$ Meta-analysis	
Grand Total Number of Studies $N = 35$	$N = 29$	$N = 4$	$N = 2$

Note: Each study was counted only once within each column.

cal, brief treatments. Likewise, Hill (1987), reviewing 15 studies, concluded that on the average paradoxical treatments produced an effect size that was .44 compared to nonparadoxical treatments. Only Shoham-Salomon and Rosenthal (1987) failed to find an overall difference between paradoxical and nonparadoxical treatments. Even they, however, confirmed the need to look at patient moderators and concluded that paradoxical effects were highest among the most severely impaired patients.

Shoham-Salomon, Avner, and Neemen (1989) examined the mechanisms of change under paradoxical interventions (defined as a wide variety of therapeutic injunctions or directives whose common denominator is to attempt to induce change by discouraging it). Although conducted with a nonclinical population, their study revealed that, under paradoxical interventions, subjects who were high on resistance benefited more from intervention than did those low on resistance.

These latter findings were supported by those of Horvath and Goheen (1990), who found that patients with high levels of trait-like resistance improved with paradoxical interventions and maintained their gains beyond the period of active treatment. In opposition, less resistant patients who were exposed to the same paradoxical treatment deteriorated after active treatment was terminated. The reverse pattern was found among those treated with nonparadoxical, stimulus control intervention.

LIMITATIONS OF THE RESEARCH REVIEWED

Because resistance traits cannot be randomly assigned to patients, they are not subject to experimental designs that require random assignment. However, there is a good deal of consistency in the available research, and this supports a modestly strong conclusion about the role of patient resistance traits in mediating treatment effects.

Aside from the correlational nature in studies of treatment effects, the major limitations in studying patient resistance is the absence of consensually accepted and recognized measures of trait-like resistance. We have already drawn attention to the potential circularity of definitions

of resistance, but such a problem would be greatly reduced if there were accepted measures of these traits. Numerous measures have been used, ranging from MMPI-like measures to estimates based on historical review of the patient's problems (see Beutler & Berren, 1995). Clinician-based measures have also been developed (see Fisher, Beutler, & Williams, 1999). In all cases, these measures suffer because of low or inconsistent intercorrelations. The presence of stable and consistent predictive measures would greatly add to the draw that this area has on contemporary researchers.

It is important to note the role played by different theories of psychotherapy in setting the level of therapist direction applied to patients. Much of the research reviewed assumed that different models of treatment are distinguished by definably different levels of directiveness. Thus, it follows that different treatments are more or less appropriate for patients, depending on the level of resistance that these patients evince. Therapies that are thought to be, variously, directive (behavioral and cognitive-behavioral) or nondirective (self-directed or evocative) are assumed to be advantageous for different patients. Indeed, cognitive and behavioral therapies have been found to be most useful for patients who are relatively low in resistance traits, and self-directed and client-centered therapies have been found to be of most value for those who are highly resistant (see Beutler, Engle, et al., 1991; Beutler, Mohr, et al., 1991). Of course, such demonstrations are only interpretable if it can be assured that different models of psychotherapy actually differ in their level of therapist direction.

Beutler, Clarkin, and Bongar (2000) initiated a systematic cross-validation study of the role of patients' resistant traits as indicators of therapist directiveness, using a multisite archival data set in which actual in-therapy levels of directiveness were measured. This data set included three different renditions of cognitive therapy and seven alternative treatments and allowed a direct confirmation of the general directiveness of cognitive models of therapy across treatment sites, manuals, and investigators (Malik, Alimohamed, Holaway, & Beutler, 2000). Using such direct measures of directiveness and resistant traits, Beutler, Clarkin, and Bongar (2000) found strongly supportive evidence of the role of patient trait-like resistance as a negative prognostic indicator and as an indicator for the differential use of directive and nondirective interventions.

THERAPEUTIC PRACTICES

Collectively, the foregoing results provide convincing evidence that low trait-like resistance makes patients especially susceptible to benefit from directive interventions. Conversely, high resistant-like traits make patients vulnerable to interventions that are authoritative and directive, evoke states of resistance that interfere with progress, increase the likelihood of dropout, and reduce effectiveness of treatment.

Clinically, therapists must first learn to recognize the manifestations of resistance both as a state and as a trait. Cues for state-like manifestations of resistance include expressed anger at the therapy or therapist, ranging from simple dissatisfaction with therapeutic progress to overt expressions of resentment and anger. Beutler and Harwood (2000) suggest three responses to these expressions of resistant states: (1) acknowledgment and reflection of the patient's concerns and anger; (2) discussion of the therapeutic relationship; and (3) renegotiation of the therapeutic contract regarding goals and therapeutic roles. These responses are designed to defuse the immediate consequences of resistance and to infuse the patient with some sense of control, as suggested in formulations of reactance theory.

Beutler and Harwood also emphasize the importance of anticipating these state reactions, however, by initially assessing the level of patient trait-like resistance patterns. These are the vulnerability or the dispositions to respond to state-like resistance. These patterns are assessed either by standardized psychological tests that tap interpersonal suspiciousness and distrust, and also by attending to the historical patterns that have characterized the patient's responses to authorities. Patients with high resistance traits are thought to have a history of difficulty taking direction, tendencies toward stubbornness and obstructiveness, and difficulties in working cooperatively in groups. These trait indicators are used to plan a treatment that will de-emphasize therapist au-

thority and guidance, will employ tasks that are designed to bolster patient control and self-direction, and will de-emphasize the use of rigid homework assignments. They recommend that homework assignments be constructed as experiments that require minimal overt action on the part of the patient, in order to avoid failure and to reduce the opportunities for oppositional behavior. The relative amount of listening versus talking should shift more toward the patient, and fewer instructions should be used. Self-directed assignments and reading might replace the usual instructional activities of the therapist.

Paradoxical interventions, such as discouraging rapid change, symptom prescription, and symptom exaggeration are also ways of using the patient's resistance traits in the service of making change. That is, paradoxical interventions are designed to encourage violation of directives. By encouraging the patient to maintain the symptom or slow the rate of change, oppositional impulses may drive the patient to do the opposite of what is suggested and to initiate improvement at an increased rate or frequency.

Specific functional classes of interventions (such as directive versus nondirective, insight-oriented versus symptom-oriented, abreactive versus supportive) are likely to be more conducive to the task of tailoring treatments to individual patients than either selecting among different, global brands of treatment or specific techniques.

Beutler, Clarkin, and Bongar (2000) have suggested that two principles relating to resistance can be applied to clinical practice.

1. Treatment is most effective if the therapist can avoid stimulating the patient's level of resistance.

Based on the current review, we conclude that there is strong and consistent support for the negative relationship between raising patient resistance and therapeutic outcome. While a causal chain cannot be certain, the consistency of the correlational evidence is persuasive.

2. Therapeutic change is greatest when the directiveness of the intervention is either inversely correspondent with the patient's current level of resistance, or authorita-

tively prescribes a continuation of the symptomatic behavior.

This principle is also consistently supported in the current review. A strong majority of studies (83%) that investigated resistance as an indicator for the application of either nondirective or paradoxical interventions found the proposed relationship. This level of evidentiary support has been sufficient to convince some (including Forsyth & Forsyth, 1982) that directive interventions should be proscribed among highly defensive patients. This conclusion may be exaggerated, given the lack of clear evidence that patients actually get worse when therapist level of resistance is mismatched to patient resistance. At least the chances increase under such circumstances that the patient will fail to grow and flourish. Nonetheless, the current review provides strong support for the proposition that trait-like resistance is an indicator for the use of nondirective and paradoxical interventions.

The recognition of both resistant states and traits are directly linked to the therapeutic procedures used. But this procedure also requires that the therapist become skilled in a variety of both directive and nondirective procedures. Most approaches to psychotherapy emphasize a given level of directiveness, and the application of a broader range of interventions may be called for. It appears advisable that therapist learn both the directive and nondirective procedures advocated by their particular approach in order to selectively emphasize one or the other, and to become familiar with some of those that are used in other theories, as well. The integration of these interventions may broaden the therapist's range of effectiveness.

Beutler, Clarkin, and Bongar (2000) conclude that in spite of the consistent results supporting the role of patient resistance in directing treatment directiveness, this relationship might be tempered by other variables. They determined that many variables operate in complex ways and frequently potentiate or suppress each other's effects. While we have not seen this clearly in our review of patient resistance, we must urge consideration of other possible variables by which treatment might be fit to patient needs. Indeed, Beutler, Clarkin, and Bongar (2000) identified six such variables that might be considered in addressing the questions of therapeutic relationship. Further research on how these and other variables interact with patient resistance and with the use of directive, nondirective, and paradoxical interventions is needed.

REFERENCES

Addis, M. E., & Jacobson, N. S. (2000). A closer look at the treatment rationale and homework compliance in cognitive behavioral therapy for depression. *Cognitive Therapy and Research, 24,* 313–326.

Arkowitz, H. (1995). Common factors or processes of change in psychotherapy? *Clinical Psychology: Science and Practice, 2*(1), 94–100.

Arlow, J. A. (2000). Psychoanalysis. In R. J. Corsini & D. Wedding (Eds.), *Current Psychotherapies* (6th ed., pp. 19–62). Itasca, IL: Peacock.

Barlow, D. H. (1994). Psychological interventions in the era of managed competition. *Clinical Psychology: Science and Practice, 1,* 109–122.

Beutler, L. E. (1981). Convergence in counseling and psychotherapy: A current look. *Clinical Psychology Review, 1,* 79–101.

Beutler, L. E. (1983). *Eclectic psychotherapy: A systematic approach.* New York: Pergamon.

Beutler, L. E. (1991). Have all won and must all have prizes? Revisiting Luborsky et al.'s verdict. *Journal of Consulting and Clinical Psychology, 59,* 226–232.

Beutler, L. E. (2000). David and Goliath: When psychotherapy meets health care delivery systems. *American Psychologist, 55*(9), 997–1007.

Beutler, L. E. (2002). The dodo bird really is extinct. *Clinical Psychology: Science and Practice, 9,* 30–34.

Beutler, L. E., & Berren, M. (Eds.). (1995). *Integrative assessment of adult personality.* New York: Guilford.

Beutler, L. E., & Clarkin, J. (1990). *Systematic treatment selection: Toward targeted therapeutic interventions.* New York: Brunner/Mazel.

Beutler, L. E., Clarkin, J. F., & Bongar, B. (2000). *Guidelines for the systematic treatment of the depressed patient.* New York: Oxford University Press.

Beutler, L. E., Engle, D., Mohr, D., Daldrup, R. J., Bergan, J., Meredith, K., & Merry, W. (1991). Predictors of differential and self-directed psychotherapeutic procedures. *Journal of Consulting and Clinical Psychology, 59,* 333–340.

Beutler, L. E., Goodrich, G., Fisher, D., & Williams, O. B. (1999). Use of psychological tests/instruments for treatment planning. In M. E. Maruish (Ed.), *The use of psychological tests for treatment planning and outcome assessment* (2nd ed., pp. 81–113). Hillsdale, NJ: Erlbaum.

Beutler, L. E., & Harwood, M. T. (2000). *Prescriptive therapy: A practical guide to systematic treatment selection.* New York: Oxford University Press.

Beutler, L. E., Machado, P. P., Engle, D., & Mohr, D. (1993). Differential patient X treatment maintenance of treatment effects among cognitive, experiential, and self-directed psychotherapies. *Journal of Psychotherapy Integration, 3*, 15–32.

Beutler, L. E., & Malik, M. (Eds.). (2002). *Rethinking the DSM-IV: Psychological perspectives.* Washington, DC: American Psychological Association.

Beutler, L. E., & Mitchell, R. (1981). Differential psychotherapy outcome among depressed and impulsive patients as a function of analytic and experiential treatment procedures. *Psychiatry: Journal for the Study of Interpersonal Processes, 44*, 297–306.

Beutler, L. E., Mohr, D. C., Grawe, K., Engle, D., & McDonald, R. (1991). Looking for differential effects: Cross-cultural predictors of differential psychotherapy efficacy. *Journal of Psychotherapy Integration, 1*, 121–142.

Beutler, L. E., Moleiro, C., Malik, M., & Harwood, T. M. (in press). UC Santa Barbara: First findings; a new twist on empirically supported treatments. *Revista International de Psicologia clinica y de la Salud.*

Bischoff, M. M., & Tracey, T. J. G. (1995). Client resistance as predicted by therapist behavior: A study of sequential dependence. *Journal of Counseling Psychology, 42*(4), 487–495.

Blatt, S. J., Sanislow, C. A., Zuroff, D. C., & Pilkonis, P. A. (1996). Characteristics of effective therapists: Further analyses of data from the National Institute of Mental Health Treatment of Depression Collaborative Research Program. *Journal of Consulting and Clinical Psychology, 64*, 1276–1284.

Brehm, J. W. (1966). *A theory of psychological reactance.* New York: Academic.

Brehm, S. S. (1976). *The application of social psychology to clinical practice.* Washington, DC: Hemisphere.

Brehm, S. S., & Brehm, J. W. (1981). *Psychological reactance: A theory of freedom and control.* New York: Wiley.

Calvert, S. J., Beutler, L. E., & Crago, M. (1988). Psychotherapy outcome as a function of therapist-patient matching on selected variables. *Journal of Social and Clinical Psychology, 6*, 104–117.

Carson, R. C. (1997). Costly compromises: A critique of the *Diagnostic and Statistical Manual of Mental Disorders.* In S. Fisher & R. P. Greenberg (Eds.), *From placebo to panacea: Putting psychiatric drugs to the test* (pp. 98–112). New York: Wiley.

Chambless, D. L., & Ollendick, T. H. (2001). Empirically supported psychological interventions: Controversies and evidence. *Annual Review of Psychology, 52*, 685–716.

Dowd, E. T., Milne, C. R., & Wise, S. L. (1991). The therapeutic reactance scale: A measure of psychological reactance. *Journal of Counseling and Development, 69*, 541–545.

Dowd, E. T., Wallbrown, F., Sanders, D., & Yesenosky, Y. (1994). Psychological reactance and its relationship to normal personality variables. *Cognitive Therapy and Research, 18*, 601–613.

Edelman, R. E., & Chambless, D. L. (1993). Compliance during sessions and homework in exposure-based treatment of agoraphobia. *Behavior Research and Therapy, 31*, 767–773.

Fisher, D., Beutler, L. E., & Williams, O. B. (1999). Making assessment relevant to treatment planning: The STS Clinician Rating Form. *Journal of Clinical Psychology, 5*, 825–842.

Forsyth, N. L., & Forsyth, D. R. (1982). Internality, controllability, and the effectiveness of attributional interpretations in counseling. *Journal of Counseling Psychology, 29*, 140–150.

Frank, J. D. (1973). *Persuasion and healing: A comparative study of psychotherapy* (rev. ed.). Baltimore: Johns Hopkins University Press.

Greenberg, L. S., & Watson, J. (1998). Experiential therapy of depression: Differential effects of client-centered relationship conditions and process experiential interventions. *Psychotherapy Research, 8*, 210–224.

Hampton, B. R. (1988). The efficacy of paradoxical interventions: A qualitative review of the research evidence. Ph.D. dissertation, University of Texas, Austin. *Dissertation Abstracts International, 49*, 2378–2379.

Hill, K. A. (1987). Meta-analysis of paradoxical interventions. *Psychotherapy, 24*, 266–270.

Horvath, A. O., & Goheen, M. D. (1990). Factors mediating the success of defiance- and compliance-based interventions. *Journal of Counseling Psychology, 37,* 363–371.

Houts, A. C. (2002). Discovery, invention, and the expansion of the modern diagnostic and statistical manuals of mental disorders. In L. E. Beutler and M. Malik (Eds.), *Rethinking the DSM: Psychological perspectives* (pp. 17–68). Washington, DC: American Psychological Association.

Joyce, A. S., Ogrodniczuk, J., Piper, W. E., & McCallum, M. (2000). *Patient characteristics and mid-treatment outcome in two forms of short-term individual psychotherapy.* Presentation at the 31st Annual Meeting of the Society for Psychotherapy Research, Chicago, IL.

Joyce, A. S., & Piper, W. E. (1996). Interpretive work in short-term individual psychotherapy: An analysis using hierarchical linear modeling. *Journal of Consulting and Clinical Psychology, 64,* 505–512.

Karno, M. P., Beutler, L. E., & Harwood, M. (in press). Interactions between psychotherapy process and patient attributes that predict alcohol treatment effectiveness: A preliminary report. *Journal of Alcohol Studies.*

Kerr, B. A., Olson, D. H., Pace, T. M., & Claiborn, C. D. (1986). Understanding client variables in the social influence process. In F. J. Dorn (Ed.), *The social influence process in counseling and psychotherapy.* Springfield, IL: Thomas.

Kirmayer, L. J. (1990). Resistance, reactance, and reluctance to change: A cognitive attributional approach to strategic interventions. *Journal of Cognitive Psychotherapy: An International Quarterly, 4,* 83–103.

Kirsch, I., & Sapirstein, G. (1998). Listening to Prozac by hearing placebo: A meta-analysis of antidepressant medications. *Treatment and Prevention, 1*(1) [On-line], Article 0001c. Available: http://journals.apa.org/prevention/volume 1/pre 0010001c.html.

Lambert, M. J. (1992). Psychotherapy outcome research: Implications for integrative and eclectic therapists. In J. C. Norcross & M. R. Goldfried (Eds.), *Handbook of psychotherapy integration* (pp. 94–129). New York: Basic.

Last, C. G., Thase, M. E., Hersen, M., Bellack, A. S., & Himmelhoch, J. M. (1984). Treatment outcome for solicited versus nonsolicited unipolar depressed female outpatients. *Journal of Consulting and Clinical Psychology, 52,* 134.

Leung, A., & Heimberg, R. G. (1996). Homework compliance, perceptions of control, and outcome of cognitive-behavioral treatment of social phobia. *Behavior Research & Therapy, 34,* 423–432.

Malik, M., Alimohamed, S., Holaway, R., & Beutler, L. E. (2000, June). *Are all cognitive therapies alike? Validation of the TPRS.* Paper presented at the annual meeting of the Society for Psychotherapy Research, Chicago, IL.

McCullough, L., Winston, A., Farber, B. A., Porter, F., Pollack, J., Laikin, M., Vingiano, W., & Trujillo, M. (1991). The relationship of patient-therapist interaction to outcome in brief psychotherapy. *Psychotherapy: Theory, Research, Practice, and Training, 28,* 525–533.

Miller, W. R., Benefield, G., & Tonigan, T. S. (1993). Enhancing motivation for change in problem drinking: A controlled comparison of two therapist styles. *Journal of Consulting and Clinical Psychology, 61,* 455–461.

Morgan, R., Luborsky, L., Crits-Christoph, P., Curtis, H., & Solomon, J. (1982). Predicting the outcomes of psychotherapy by the Penn Helping Alliance Rating Method. *Archives of General Psychiatry, 39,* 397–403.

Nathan, P. E., & Gorman, J. M. (Eds.). (1998). *A guide to treatments that work.* New York: Oxford University Press.

Patterson, G. R., & Forgatch, M. S. (1985). Therapist behavior as a determinant for client noncompliance: A paradox for the behavior modifier. *Journal of Consulting and Clinical Psychology, 53,* 846–851.

Paul, G. L. (1978). The implementation of effective treatment programs for chronic mental patients: Obstacles and recommendations. In J. A. Talbott (Ed.), *The chronic mental patient.* Washington, DC: American Psychiatric Association.

Persons, J. B., Burns, D. D., & Perloff, J. M. (1988). Predictors of dropout and outcome in cognitive therapy for depression in a private practice setting. *Cognitive Therapy and Research, 12,* 557–575.

Piper, W. E., Joyce, A. S., McCallum, M., & Azim, H. F. (1998). Interpretative and supportive forms of psychotherapy and patient personality variables. *Journal of Consulting and Clinical Psychology, 66*(3), 558–567.

Project MATCH Research Team. (1996). Matching alcoholism treatments to client heterogeneity: Project MATCH posttreatment drinking outcomes. *Journal of Studies on Alcohol, 59,* 631–639.

Rohrbaugh, M., Tennen, H., Press, S., & White, L. (1981). Compliance, defiance, and therapeutic paradox: Guidelines for strategic use of paradoxical interventions. *American Journal of Orthopsychiatry, 51*, 454–467.

Ruppel, G., & Kaul, T. J. (1982). Investigation of social influence theory's conception of client resistance. *Journal of Counseling Psychology, 29*(3), 232–239.

Shoham-Salomon, V., Avner, R., & Neemen, R. (1989). You're changed if you do and changed if you don't: Mechanisms underlying paradoxical interventions. *Journal of Consulting and Clinical Psychology, 57*(5), 590–598.

Shoham-Salomon, V., & Hannah, M. T. (1991). Client-treatment interaction in the study of differential change processes. *Journal of Consulting and Clinical Psychology, 59*, 217–225.

Shoham-Salomon, V., & Rosenthal, R. (1987). Paradoxical interventions: A meta-analysis. *Journal of Consulting and Clinical Psychology, 55*, 22–28.

Strong, S. R. (1968). Causal attribution in counseling and psychotherapy. *Journal of Counseling Psychology, 17*(1), 388–399.

Strong, S. R., & Matross, R. P. (1973). Change processes in counseling and psychotherapy. *Journal of Counseling Psychology, 20*(1), 25–37.

Tennen, H., Rohrbaugh, M., Press, S., & White, L. (1981). Reactance theory and therapeutic paradox: A compliance defiance model. *Psychotherapy: Theory, Research and Practice, 18*(1), 14–22.

Tracey, T. J., Ellickson, J. L., & Sherry, P. (1989). Reactance in relation to different supervisory environments and counselor development. *Journal of Counseling Psychology, 36*, 336–344.

Wachtel, P. L. (1999). Resistance as a problem for practice and theory. *Journal of Psychotherapy Integration, 1*, 103–117.

Wampold, B. E. (2001). *The great psychotherapy debate: Models, methods, and findings.* Hillsdale, NJ: Erlbaum.

Wampold, B. E., Mondin, G. W., Moody, M., Stich, F., Benson, K., & Ahn, H. (1997). A meta-analysis of outcome studies comparing bona fide psychotherapies: Empirically, "all must have prizes." *Psychological Bulletin, 122*, 203–215.

8

Functional Impairment and Coping Style

Larry E. Beutler

T. Mark Harwood

Shabia Alimohamed

Mary Malik

The study of how patient attributes interact with psychological treatments (called aptitude by treatment interactions, or ATIs) is a complex and often neglected area of research. The difference between conventional treatment research and ATI research is the inclusion of patient dimensions as covariates or moderators that selectively and predictably alter the effect of various psychotherapies. The potential permutations of patient and treatment dimensions that may be relevant to outcome are staggering in their magnitude, numbering well over one million (Beutler, 1991). Many authors have attempted to identify patient variables that could be used in the selection of different treatments. From these efforts have come treatment planning procedures that range from *technical eclectic* approaches that derive individually tailored menus of techniques for different patients (Beutler, 1983; A. A. Lazarus, 1981) to strategic and prescriptive approaches that identify broad ranging strategies that are applied as a function of complex patient and environmental patterns (Beutler & Harwood, 2000; Goldfried & Padawar, 1982; Prochaska, 1984; Prochaska & DiClemente, 1992).

Numerous studies have explored the role of patient moderators (see Beutler, Clarkin, & Bon-

gar, 2000; Beutler, Goodrich, Fisher, & Williams, 1999). However, most of these research studies have approached the task of identifying the fit between patient and treatment in simplistic ways. Usually they have sought to identify linear relationships that might exist between a single patient quality and a single characteristic of treatment. They seldom have considered either the probability that several different patient moderators are at work at any one time—some potentiating or suppressing the effects of others under some conditions—or the possibility that the relationships of patient "fit" to treatment may be other than linear.

As a result of the simplistic way that these variables have been considered, the process of defining effective patient-therapy matching dimensions has been less than smooth. For example, the most ambitious project to date on patient-therapist fit was Project MATCH (Project Match Research Group, 1997). This study, while carefully designed, produced few results that would indicate that matching patient and treatment works, at least in the case of alcoholism. However, in view of its inconsistency with a large number of other studies and the large number of potential matching variables that were not considered, these negative findings may be viewed as an indictment against the simplicity of the matching hypotheses studied rather than against matching research itself.

In an effort to redress this simplistic view of how treatments may be tailored to fit different patients, Beutler and colleagues initiated an effort to identify and subsequently test the most robust patient and treatment matching dimensions that predict treatment outcomes. Once these variables were extracted from extant literature (Beutler & Berren, 1995; Beutler & Clarkin, 1990; Beutler & Consoli, 1992; Beutler et al., 1999; Beutler & Harwood, 2000), a series of hypotheses about their cascading influences was constructed and a complex, multilevel treatment model was developed. Instruments were developed and then were implemented in a final research step in which the model was independently tested to determine if it yielded better predictions of outcome than the previous, simple systems (Beutler, Clarkin, & Bongar, 2000). The complex model improved predictions notably over simple, single-dimensional systems.

This chapter will focus on two of the dimensions that were identified as moderators of treatment effect by Beutler and colleagues—patient level of functional impairment and patient coping style. It should be understood, however, that these two dimensions for matching patients to treatment cannot be optimally understood without inspecting the complex interactions that characterize the relationships among multiple moderating variables.

DEFINITIONS AND MEASURES

Functional Impairment

Functional impairment is a complex dimension. It reflects the severity of the patient's problem(s) and the range of areas in which reduced functioning is manifest. Research generally confirms the complexity of measuring and understanding patient impairment and, to simplify the issues somewhat, increasingly suggests that it is useful to consider as distinct dimensions objective measures of impairment level and patient self-reported distress (see Strupp, Horowitz, & Lambert, 1997).

Ordinarily, the concept of severity or "functional impairment" derives from ratings of external behaviors, whereas patient "distress" is a term that reflects internal states, usually in the form of self-reports.

The definition of impairment or severity as an estimate of daily functioning is reflected in the ways that this dimensions is typically measured. For example, the Specific Level of Function scale (SLOF; see Schneider & Struening, 1983) identifies functional impairment by deficits in social skills, problem behaviors, self-care deficits, and community living skills; the Social Adjustment Scale–Self-Report (SAS-SR; see Weissman & Bothwell, 1976) focuses on work, home, and leisure role performance as well as economic support; and the Activities of Daily Living scales (Lawton, Moss, Fulcomer, & Kleban, 1982) assess performance of basic life functions (Green et al. 1999).

Beutler, Clarkin, and Bongar (2000) inspected the interrelationships among aspects of observed social and intimate functioning and found them to consolidate around a cluster of variables reflecting low levels of social support, disturbances in social and work relationships, comorbidity, and chronicity. The more chronic and complex the problem and the fewer available social support systems, the higher the level of impairment. Notably, the correlation of this cluster of externally observed variables with patient self-report was modest, confirming the value of restricting the use of the term *impairment* to externally observed behaviors (Fisher, Beutler, & Williams, 1999).

A range of concepts—including disruptions in the immediate family, family of origin, and intimate relationships, as well as problems of social isolation, problems of work, disruptions to home management, and disturbance of leisure activities—have been incorporated into definitions of functional impairment (Beutler, Clarkin, & Bongar, 2000; Judd, Paulus, Wells, & Rapaport, 1996; Ray, Jefferies, & Weir, 1997; Roberts, Kaplan, Shema, & Strawbridge, 1997). Sperry, Brill, Howard, and Grissom (1996) have suggested that impairment level be reduced to a consideration of work, intimate and nonintimate relationships, self-care, and social responsibility.

The Global Assessment of Functioning, or GAF (American Psychiatric Association, 2000) incorporates many of these concepts into a single measure. Anchored at zero through 100, the GAF depends on the ability of a trained clinician to provide an overall indication of the client's abilities to function in social and occupational settings. The primary advantages of the GAF are its ease of administration, which allows clinicians to summarize their overall clinical impression in a single number, and its great breadth, which permits the relative ranking of clients with very severe pathologies in relation to those with minor problems in adjustment. Unfortunately, the GAF also has a number of disadvantages that limit its usefulness in determining the relationship between patient functioning and treatment effects: it suffers from the lack of reliability that is characteristic of all single-item measures; the accuracy of the rating depends heavily on the training and experience of the rater; it confounds symptoms with the patient's level of adjustment or functioning; it does not accord equal weight to all areas of potential deficit (such as intimate relationships, work and social relationships, self-care); and it perpetuates the tendency to confound impairment level with a patient's subjective experience.

Some studies have investigated the inverse of functional impairment, a concept that might be called "quality of life." While a consensual definition of this construct is lacking (Barry & Zissi, 1997; Haas, 1999), the World Health Organization (WHO) has conceptualized quality of life as containing six domains: physical aspects, psychological aspects, level of independence, social relationships, environment, and spirituality or religious beliefs (Koran, 2000).

A review of contemporary research reveals considerable variation in the amount of information available on each of the various aspects of impairment. The most widely studied of these concepts is probably the relationship between social support and patient functioning (for example, see Coyne & Downey, 1991). This literature confirms that the availability of supportive relationships play a role in treatment outcome and also demonstrates that a person's subjective experience of support (or "felt support") is a much better predictor of positive outcomes than objective measures such as the number of relationships available. However, there continues to be disagreement about whether the critical variable in this relationship is the presence of positive supportive relationships or the absence of negative ones (Coyne & Downey, 1991).

Given the complexity of the concept, for this review we have adopted the suggestion that functional impairment be based on observations of external behaviors, rather than internal states (Strupp, Horowitz, & Lambert, 1997). Thus, this review is restricted to studies that used such measures.

Coping Style

Coping style is a term that is used quite differently within different theoretical schools of psychopathology. Latack and Havlovic (1992) identify the most common definition of a coping behavior as a "person-environment transaction that occurs when people appraise a situation as stressful." There is lack of agreement among authors as to the relationship between coping style and personality attributes. While coping style is generally considered to be a more transitory state than personality, this distinction is difficult to hold in practice. Thus, Beutler and Clarkin (1990) resolved the dilemma by including within the term *coping style* a variety of dimensions that are interrelated with one another. This empirical definition removed the requirement that coping styles only be observed during and following stressful situations and thereby eliminated the need to judge the level of stress experienced.

From this broadened perspective, coping styles are habitual and enduring patterns of behavior that characterize the individual when confronting new or problematic situations. Thus, coping styles are not discrete behaviors but a cluster of related behaviors that are distinguished because they are repetitive, enduring, and observable when problems are being addressed. Descriptively, the specific behaviors that form the clusters include both repetitive situational responses such as impulsivity, discrete behaviors, and general temperaments. Unlike more narrow definitions of coping style, definitions based on correlated clusters of behaviors include qualities of personality and exclude judgments of patient stress, but are not explanatory concepts. Given the diversity of measurements used to study coping styles, we will adopt this broad definition as descriptive of behavioral clusters that are enduring, transgenerational, and cross-situational.

This view of coping style as a descriptive, heritable, relatively stable, trait-like cluster of behaviors is generally consistent with other views in both the human and animal literatures (Eysenck, 1990; Koolhaas et al., 1999; McGue & Bouchard, 1998). Accordingly, most factor analytic studies of behavior have found a consistent dimension that varies from introverted/introspective behaviors to extroverted/extratensive behaviors. For example, Eysenck's (1957) initial model of personality included the concept of introversion as one end of this dimension and extroversion at the other. Gray (1981) suggested that Eysenck's two personality dimensions (introversion-extroversion and neuroticism-stability) could be rotated by 45 degrees to form new axes, which he labeled impulsivity and anxiety, respectively, bringing them more into line with the extended concepts of externalization and internalization defined by Beutler and Clarkin (1990).

Within this broad view, introversion is one of several constructs that fit within the broad definition of an internalizing coping style. Other behaviors within this cluster include both general and specific situational behaviors like withdrawal, social restraint, introflexion, self-attribution, self-blame, and self-criticism.

Following the description of Eysenck (1957), the quality that distinguishes internalizing traits and dispositions from other coping styles is that they are governed by the forces of inhibition. In contrast, externalizers are governed by the forces of expression and excitation. The cluster of behavioral traits comprising this latter group include impulsivity, gregariousness, expressiveness, a propensity to blame others, external attributions of cause, and needs for action. Eysenck (1967) proposed that conditioning differed in groups of introverts and extroverts, a view that can be extended to the more general concepts of externalizing and internalizing. Eysenck viewed these differences as reflecting inherent differences in the reticular activating system. Introverts were viewed as having a lower level of inherent arousability and were characterized by traits such as restraint,

inhibition, and introversion. Extroverts, in contrast, were seen as being disposed to high arousal, which was in turn reflected in traits such as impulsivity and other-directedness. Animal behaviorists have extended these qualities to a dimension of active to passive, or proactive versus reactive behaviors (Koolhaas et al., 1999), and others have incorporated similar concepts into the big five personality factors (Costa & McCrae, 1985).

In treatment planning literature, externalizers are defined as those who are impulsive, action or task-oriented, gregarious, aggressive, hedonistic, stimulation-seeking, and lacking in insight. In contrast, internalizers are described as shy, retiring, self-critical, withdrawn, constrained, overcontrolled, self-reflective, worried, and inhibited. While most people can be easily grouped into one of these behavioral groups, coping styles exist at various points between the two extremes that define the prototypic categories.

For research purposes in psychotherapy, patient coping styles are typically assessed using standardized omnibus personality and psychopathology measures such as the Minnesota Multiphasic Personality Inventory (MMPI-2; see Butcher, 1990), supplemented by a review of the patient's past and present reactions to problems. This serves the broad definition used in this literature somewhat better than using many of the measures that are typically identified as measures of coping (see R. S. Lazarus & Folkman, 1984), but whose definition is much narrower than that used in treatment planning. The internalization ratio (IR) formula that has been used by our own research group (see Beutler, Engle, et al., 1991; Beutler & Mitchell, 1981; Beutler, Mohr, Grawe, Engle, & MacDonald, 1991), for example, is a modification of one originally proposed by Welsh (1952) and is based on eight MMPI-2 subscale scores entered as standard T scores:

$$IR = \frac{Hy + Pd + Pa + Ma}{Hs + D + Pt + Si}$$

An IR that favors the numerator suggests that a patient is disposed to use externalizing coping behaviors. These individuals blame others for their feelings (Pa); display active, dependent behaviors (Hy); have high levels of unfocused energy (Ma); are impulsive and frequently have social adjustment problems (Pd).

CLINICAL EXAMPLES

There are many examples of how patient impairment levels and coping styles are manifest in treatment. A patient with comorbid conditions, recurrent depression, and low self-care and social functioning has high levels of functional impairment. This patient may either respond to life crises by withdrawal and self-blame (internalizing) or may fight the stressors by becoming angry, blaming, and avoidant (externalizing).

K. C. was a 42-year-old married (2 years) man who was referred for psychotherapy by his physician, whom he also described as his best friend. The patient's impairment level is indexed by the presence of comorbid and chronic problems related to chemical abuse, depression, and impaired work performance and to deficits in interpersonal functioning. The patient recalled being "very depressed" since the age of 12 and described a family history of abuse, alcohol dependence, and finally abandonment. He was on his own at age 16 and what had begun three years before as recreational marijuana use rapidly developed into extensive cocaine, methamphetamine, and heroin abuse. He held several jobs between the ages of 16 and 40, losing most because of behaviors related to chemical dependency. At age 40 he began his own Internet business in an effort to escape the rigid rules that had frequently led to his termination from other jobs.

Two and a half years before seeking treatment in our center, that patient had become drug-free through a drug detoxification and 12-step program. He had continued to be depressed during this time, however, a condition that was only temporarily alleviated when he married. He relapsed to drug use gradually over a 2-year period, with the final step occurring 6 months prior to his first visit at the clinic. He reported being suicidal after losing his business 3 months before. He sought solace in a visit to his older brother, but this served only to deepen his depression and resulted in his relapse. Stimulated by his brother, the patient recalled a period of severe physical abuse by his father when he was 14 years old; this

memory continued to plague him and cause many self-doubts and preoccupations after his return home. Over the weeks after his return K. C. became severely despondent, advancing to the point of developing a suicide plan and relapsing in the use of heroin and cocaine. He resisted acting out long enough to seek the advice of his physician friend.

The complexity and severity of K.C.'s problems escalated and encroached on other aspects of his life. He began to experience moderate to severe social and marital dysfunction, ostensibly secondary to two drug-related encounters with the law, and began to experience disrupted sexual and intimate attachments, a sense of isolation, and low social support. He reported that he could only turn to two people in his life, his physician and his wife, though relations with his wife were increasingly disrupted.

Though somewhat unusual in such a patient, his history confirmed the presence of an internalizing coping style. This was observed in how he conceptualized both the cause and the consequences of his drug use. He expressed the belief that his drug abuse began because he was weak and defective. He indicated that his problem had continued because he was not strong enough to follow his conscience. While not a religious man, he expressed strong guilt that he had "enticed" his wife into a marriage in which he was unable to take care of her.

His coping style was also seen in how he responded to new events that produced stress and conflict. For example, following the trip to his brother's, he became very self-critical for being unable to "shake off" the memories. He described this as a personal failure. Rather than becoming angry at his parents for their abuse of him or for abandoning him when he was still a teenager, he reflected on his deficits of character and moral definition, which be believed prevented him from keeping things in control. Thus, the patient not only saw the source of the problem in his personal weaknesses but also reacted to crises in his life by self-attributions, self-criticism, and guilt. While taking drugs is an example of acting out, it was clear that this man's dominant pattern of coping once he "fell off the wagon" was one of intropunitive self-demand and self-punishment.

EMPIRICAL RESEARCH REVIEW

Functional Impairment

Patient Contributions

A review of empirical research literature reveals that a variety of patient characteristics predispose an individual to higher levels of functional impairment. Joyce, Ogrodniczuk, Piper, and McCallum (2000) and Piper, McCallum, Joyce, Azim, and Ogrodniczuk (1999) have shown that patients diagnosed with major depression or dysthymia and/or various personality disorders, who also evidence low quality of object relations, show poorer outcomes on measures of overall functioning. Other factors that have been found to influence level of functional impairment include previous history of psychiatric disorder (Cuijpers & Van Lammeren, 1999; Joyce et al., 2000; Roberts et al., 1997), cognitive impairment and impaired self-care (Bartels, Meuser, & Miles, 1997), impaired functioning in previous episodes of disorder (Bilder et al., 2000), the availability of internal psychological resources (Badger & Collins-Joyce, 2000; Zarit, Femia, Gatz, & Johansson, 1999), perceived locus of control (Ray, Jefferies, & Weir, 1997), and available coping strategies (Bussing, Zima, & Perwien, 2000; Rosenblatt & Rosenblatt, 2000; Sanders, 1999). In all cases, impaired functioning at one point in time is predictive of impaired functioning at another, and interferes with treatment response.

One of the most important correlates of functional impairment is level of social support. However, social support appears to be an indirect measure of impairment level and is inversely related to more direct measures of functional impairment (Billings & Moos, 1985; George, Blazer, Hughes, & Fowler, 1989; Godding, McAnulty, Wittrock, Britt, & Khansur, 1995; Hoencamp, Haffmans, Duivenvoorden, Knegtering, & Dijken, 1994; Moos, 1990; Newsom & Schulz, 1996). Low levels of social support, like measures of high impairment, portend subsequent severity of problems and difficulty of treatment.

Conversely, the presence of social support and other indices of low levels of impairment portend good benefits from treatment and lower rates of relapse (Burvill, Hall, Stampfer, & Emmerson, 1991; Gitlin, Swendsen, & Heller, 1995; Gonzales, Lewishon, & Clarke, 1985; Thase, Simons, Cahalane, McGeary, & Harden, 1991; Zlotnick, Shea, Pilkonis, Elkin, & Ryan, 1996). This conclusion is illustrated in table 8.1, in which 10 of the 13 studies (77%) reviewed found that social support was positively related to treatment benefit, indicating that felt social support is positively associated with improvement or maintenance of effects. Patients with good interpersonal contacts, acute problems, and single diagnoses generally are the ones most likely to benefit from treatment and achieve the highest treatment gains.

Though not reviewed in table 8.1, it is worth noting that paucity of social support (high impairment) is also a negative prognostic factor in the development of depression among patients with a variety of medical illnesses (Godding et al., 1995; Koenig, 1998; Littlefield, Rodin, Murray, & Craven, 1990). Likewise, it impedes the course of medical treatment. Oxman, Freeman, and Manheimer (1995), for example, found that absence of social, religious, or community participation and support among patients aged 55 years and over independently predicted post-surgery mortality within 6 months after open-heart surgery.

Likewise, direct measures of functional impairment provide results that parallel those found with respect to social support. Specifically, 22 of the 29 (76%) of the available studies of functional impairment reported in table 8.1 (excluding those based on social support levels alone) found a significant, inverse relationship between level of severity and treatment outcome. Only two studies (Ackerman, Greenland, & Bystritsky, 1994; Lueger, 1996) found that level of impairment enhanced the level of improvement.

Evidence that level of impairment is negatively correlated with degree and rate of improvement is found across a variety of short-term treatments. Studies of patients with dysthymia and/or major depression treated with combinations of tricyclic antidepressants and psychosocial therapy (Sotsky et al., 1991) or with psychosocial interventions alone (Beutler, Kim, Davison, Karno, & Fisher, 1996) variously demonstrate low rate of improvement and poorer outcome for more functionally impaired individuals. This effect transcends the type of treatment and type of disorder.

Table 8.1. Functional Impairment and Outcome

Measure	Significant Relationship	Mixed Findings	Nonsignificant Relationship
Studies Related to Functional Impairment and Outcome			
Direct Relationship Between Level of Social Support and Outcome			
Bedford Life Events & Difficulties Interview	Spangler et al. (1997)		Burvill et al. (1991)
Family Environment Scale (FES; quality of confidant and family support)	Moos (1990)		
Health and Daily Living Form (HDL)	Moos (1990)		
Important People and Activities Form (IPAF)		Longabaugh et al. (1994)	
Index of Social Support (ISS)			Andrew et al. (1993)
Lowenthal-Haven-Kaplan Mannheim Interview on Social Support (MISS)	Vallejo et al. (1991) Veiel et al. (1992)		
Perceived Social Support from Friends (PSS-Fr)	Dadds & McHugh (1992)		
Simulated Social Interaction Test (SSIT)	Mersch et al. (1991)		
Social Adjustment Scale (SAS)	Hoencamp et al. (1994); Sotsky et al. (1991)		
Social Network Form (SNF)	Zlotnick et al. (1996)		
Systematic Treatment Selection–Clinical Rating Form (STS-CRF)	Beutler, Clarkin, & Bongar (2000)		
*Number of studies N = 13	N = 10	N = 1	N = 2
Inverse Relationship Between Level of Functional Impairment and Outcome			
Anxiety Discomfort Scale (ADS)	Keijsers et al. (1994)		
Anxiety Disorders Interview Schedule-Revised (ADIS-R)	Brown & Barlow (1995)		
Beck Depression Inventory (BDI)	Hardy et al. (1995); McLean & Taylor (1992); Shapiro et al. (1995); Thase et al. (1991)	Andrew et al. (1993)	

(continued)

Table 8.1. (Continued)

Measure	Significant Relationship	Mixed Findings	Nonsignificant Relationship
Battelle Quality of Life Scale	Ravindran et al. (1999)		
Bulimic Investigatory Test (BITE)	Fahy & Russell (1993)		
Diagnostic & Statistical Manual-III (DSM-III; Axis I & II)	Mazure et al. (1990)		
Dysfunctional Attitudes Scale (DAS)	Sotsky et al. (1991)		Scogin et al. (1994)
Functional Rating Scale for Symptoms of Dementia (FRSSD)		Fountoulakis et al. (2000)	
Geriatric Depression Scale (GDS)		Fountoulakis et al. (2000)	
Global Assessment of Functioning (GAF-DSM-IV)	Beutler, Clarkin, & Bongar (2000)		
Global Assessment Scale (GAS)	Gitlin et al. (1995); Høglend (1993)		
Global Severity Index (GSI; Brief Symptom Inventory subscale)	Beutler et al. (1996)		
Hamilton Rating Scale for Depression (HRSD)	Hoencamp et al. (1994); Prudic et al. (1993); Sotsky et al. (1991); Shea et al. (1992)	Ackerman et al. (1994)	Burvill et al. (1991); Scogin et al. (1994)
Hamilton Depression Rating Scale (HDRS)	Keijsers et al. (1994)		
Integra Outpatient Tracking Scales (IOTA; Well-Being, Symptoms, Current Life Dysfunction subscales)	Joyce et al. (2000)		
Inventory of Interpersonal Problems (IIP)	Maling et al. (1995)		
Life Events & Difficulties Schedule (LEDS)	Veiel et al. (1992)		
Life stress interview	Ellicott et al. (1990)		
Maudsley Compulsive/Obsessive Scale (MOCI)	Keijsers et al. (1994)		
Personality Assessment Schedule (PAS)	Fahy & Russell (1993)		
Personality Disorders Examination (PDE-A/OC/D; avoidant, obsessive-compulsive, dependent)	Hardy et al. (1995)		
Phobia Questionnaire, Agoraphobia subscale (fear and avoidance)	Basoglu et al. (1994)		

Social Adjustment Scale (SAS)	Sotsky et al. (1991)		
Structured Clinical Interview for DSM-III-Rm axis II (SCID-II)		Hoencamp et al. (1994)	
Symptom Checklist-90-R (SCL-90-R)	Shapiro et al. (1995)	Hoencamp et al. (1994)	
Systematic Treatment Selection–Clinician Rating Form (STS-CRF)	Beutler, Clarkin, & Bongar (2000)		
*Number of studies N = 28	N = 22	N = 4	N = 2
Direct Relationship Between Level of Functional Impairment and Outcome			
Global Assessment Scale (GAS)	Lueger (1996)		
Mental Health Index (Well-Being, Current Symptoms & Current Life Functioning Scales)	Lueger (1996)		
Yale-Brown OC Scale (Y-BOCS)		Ackerman et al. (1994)	
*Number of studies N = 2	N = 1	N = 1	
Total number of studies relating to functional impairment and outcome = 35			

Note: For all columns, studies are counted only once.

It is observed in pharmacotherapy for depression (Hoencamp et al., 1994), combined pharmacotherapy and psychosocial therapies for depression and general mental health conditions (Hardy et al., 1995; Høglend, 1993; Shea et al., 1992), in vivo exposure and relaxation for anxiety disorders (Keijsers, Hoogduin, & Schaap, 1994), and combinations of exposure and relaxation for phobias (Basoglu, Marks, & Swinson, 1994).

When the results for social support are collapsed with other direct measures of severity, 31 of the 42 studies (74%) reviewed found results indicating that level of impairment hampered or attenuated outcomes. These findings provide moderate to strong support for the tempering effects of the patient's impairment level on the power of treatments of any kind.

Moderating Effects

A more interesting and important issue than the relationship between impairment and treatment outcome revolves around how the negative prognosis of impaired patients can be moderated by adjusting and selecting treatments. Three lines of investigation have inspected the differential effects of treatments as a function of patient level of impairment: (1) interactions of functional impairment and type of psychosocial treatment on outcome; (2) interactions of functional impairment and the use of pharmacotherapy on outcome; and (3) interaction between treatment intensity and functional impairment on outcome. These three lines of study are reflected in table 8.2. These studies indicate that the negative effects of functional impairment are moderated by at least the second and third of these aspects of treatment.

Comparisons of the relative impact of different psychosocial treatment models reveal a few effects that seem to be contingent on level of functional impairment (Beutler et al., 1996; Brown & Barlow, 1995; Keijsers et al., 1994; McLellan, Woody, Luborsky, O'Brien, & Druley, 1983; Scogin, Bowman, Jamison, Beutler, & Machado, 1994; Woody et al., 1984). Of the 19 studies on this topic reviewed in table 8.2, only 7 (37%) found evidence of a differential impact of treatments as a function of patient impairment level. The results suggest that both type and intensity of treatment interact in determining the influence of psychosocial treatment.

In a representative study, Hardy and colleagues (1995) compared depressed subjects who varied in severity. Severity was defined by whether participants did or did not present with a comorbid (Cluster C) personality disorder. Participants were randomly assigned to cognitive-behavior therapy (CBT) or to psychodynamic-interpersonal therapy over either 8 or 16 weeks of treatment. They found that initial level of impairment predicted differential effects of treatment type but not treatment length. PD patients and NPD patients produced nonsignificant and generally equivalent outcomes when treated with CBT, but when treated with psychodynamic-interpersonal therapy, NPD patients produced significantly better outcomes than PD patients. The differences between the short (8 weeks) and long (16 weeks) treatment may not have been enough to reveal outcome differences.

Severe patients (those with personality disorder) were, predictably, less improved at one-year follow-up than those with less severe depression, regardless of length of treatment. Overall, the study found support for more structured and directive cognitive and behavioral interventions in the treatment of functionally impaired individuals and improved long-term outcomes in areas of social functioning for initially less depressed and functionally impaired individuals in either psychodynamic or cognitive therapy.

Somewhat stronger results have been obtained in studies of the differential effects of pharmacological treatments. Coinciding with evidence that impaired functioning may be related to various central nervous system impairments (see Garvey & Noyes, 1996; Garvey, Noyes, Woodman, & Laukes, 1995; Garvey, Noyes, Cook, & Blum, 1996; Garvey & Tauson, 1996; Garvey & Underwood, 1997), some evidence has been generated to suggest that impairment level may temper the effects of pharmacological interventions. For example, Fountoulakis, Tsolaki, and Kazis (2000) reported that older, depressed patients with cognitive impairment were responsive to antidepressant medications, particularly if they also suffered cognitive impairment associated with depression. While the response to medical treatment was good, the more severely depressed patients continued to

Table 8.2. Differential Treatment Response to Levels of Functional Impairment

Measure	Significant Relationship	Mixed Findings	Nonsignificant Relationship
Interaction of Impairment and Type of Psychosocial Treatment			
Addiction Severity Index (ASI; Legal, Psychiatric and Family sections)	Project MATCH (1997)		
Anxiety Discomfort Scale (ADS)			Keijsers et al. (1994)
Anxiety Disorders Interview Schedule—Revised (ADIS-R)			Brown & Barlow (1995)
Beck Depression Inventory (BDI)		Shapiro et al. (1995)	Shapiro et al. (1994)
Dysfunctional Attitudes Scale (DAS)			Scogin et al. (1994)
Global Assessment of Functioning (GAF-DSM-IV)			Beutler et al. (1996)
Hamilton Rating Scale for Depression (HRSD)			Thase et al. (1991); Shea et al. (1992); Ogles et al. (1995)
Hospital Intake status	Beutler et al. (1984)		
Important People and Activities Form (IPAF)	Longabaugh et al. (1994)		
Integra Outpatient Tracking Scales (IOTA; Well-Being, Symptoms, Current Life Dysfunction subscales)	Joyce et al. (2000)		
Personality Disorders Examination (PDE-A/OC/D; avoidant, obsessive-compulsive, dependent)	Hardy et al. (1995)		
Quality of Object Relations (QOR) Interview	Joyce & Piper (1996)		
Social Adjustment Scale (SAS; social and work dysfunction)			Imber et al. (1990)
Structured Clinical Interview for DSM-III-Rm axis II (SCID-II; personality disorder)			McClellan et al. (1983); Woody et al. (1984)

(*continued*)

Table 8.2. (Continued)

Measure	Significant Relationship	Mixed Findings	Nonsignificant Relationship
Symptom Checklist-90-R (SCL-90-R; Interpersonal Sensitivity subscale)			Imber et al. (1990)
Systematic Treatment Selection—Clinician Rating Form (STS-CRF)	Beutler, Clarkin, & Bongar (2000)		
*Number of studies N = 19	N = 7	N = 1	N = 11
Interaction of Functional Impairment, Drug Treatment, and Outcome			
Beck Depression Inventory (BDI)	Elkin et al. (1995)		McLean & Taylor (1992); Ogles et al. (1995)
Battelle Quality of Life Scale	Ravindran et al. (1999)		
Clinical rating	Eldredge et al. (1998)		
Dysfunctional Attitudes Scale (DAS)	Sotsky et al. (1991)		
Functional Rating Scale for Symptoms of Dementia (FRSSD)	Fountoulakis et al. (2000)		
Geriatric Depression Scale (GDS)	Fountoulakis et al. (2000)		
Global Assessment Score (GAS)	Elkin et al. (1995)		
Hamilton Rating Scale for Depression (HRSD)	Elkin et al. (1995); Sotsky et al. (1991)		Garvey et al. (1994); Ogles et al. (1995); Shea et al. (1992)
Phobia Questionnaire, Agoraphobia subscale (fear and avoidance)	Basoglu et al. (1994)		
Social Adjustment Scale (SAS; social and work dysfunction)	Sotsky et al. (1991); Mintz et al. (1992)		
Structured Clinical Interview for DSM-III-Rm axis II (SCID-II; personality disorder)	Woody et al. (1984)		
*Number of studies N = 12	N = 8		N = 4

Relationship Between Functional Impairment and Treatment Intensity

Beck Depression Inventory (BDI)	Barkham et al. (1996); Shapiro et al. (1994)	Shapiro et al. (1995)	Hardy et al. (1995)
Family Environment Scale (FES; quality of confidante and family support)	Moos (1990)		
Global Assessment Scale (GAS)	Høglend (1993)		
Global Severity Index (GSI subscale of BSI)	Beutler et al. (1996)		
Hamilton Rating Scale for Depression (HRSD)	Shea et al. (1992)		
Health and Daily Living Form (HDL)	Moos (1990)		
Inventory of Interpersonal Problems (IIP)	Barkham et al. (1996); Maling et al. (1995)		Hardy et al. (1995)
Personality Disorders Examination (PDE-A/OC/D; avoidant, obsessive-compulsive, dependent)			
Social Adjustment Scale (SAS)	Mintz et al. (1992); Shapiro et al. (1994)		
Symptom Checklist-90-R (SCL-90-R)		Shapiro et al. (1995)	
Systematic Treatment Selection-Clinician Rating Form (STS-CRF)	Beutler, Clarkin, & Bongar (2000)		
*Number of studies $N = 10$	$N = 8$	$N = 1$	$N = 1$
Total number of studies relating to differential treatment response = 32			

Note: For all columns, studies are counted only once.

157

evidence residual symptoms at three-month follow-up. Residual symptoms have also been observed among older patients with personality disorders (Abrams, 1996). Pharmacological therapies
have been found to be useful among moderately
and severely impaired young adults and middle-
aged patients who have various depressive symptoms (Friedman, Markowitz, Parides, Gniwesch, &
Kocsis, 1999; Rapaport & Judd, 1998).

Thus, pharmacotherapies appear to be quite
effective among patients with high levels of impairment; however, these studies did not include
a comparison to other types of active treatment
(to avoid confusion, they are not reported in table
8.2). Thus, a clear determination of differential
treatment effects has not been made by these investigations, and the relative effects of medical
treatment cannot be defined.

Table 8.2 reports studies in which a comparison of different types of treatment were possible.
It will be noted that 8 of the 12 (67%) studies
that explored pharmacotherapy found evidence
favoring the use of medication among more severely impaired patients. These studies not only
provide evidence of the benefits of medication
over placebo treatments, but also for the role of
functional impairment as a differential predictor
of drug and psychosocial treatments (Basoglu et
al., 1994; Eldredge, Locke, & Horowitz, 1998;
McLean & Taylor, 1992; Mintz, Mintz, Arruda, &
Hwang, 1992; Shea et al., 1992; Sotsky et al.,
1991; Woody et al., 1984).

Unfortunately, the significance and importance of studies on the differential assignment of
pharmacotherapy to patients who vary in level of
impairment must be tempered by evidence that
the levels and nature of the observed effects of
medication are dependent on how the data are
analyzed. For example, Elkin and colleagues (1995)
reanalyzed data from a previous report of the
NIMH Treatment of Depression Collaborative
Research Program (Elkin et al., 1989) and found
an impairment by treatment interaction effect that
was previously undisclosed. A comparison of CBT,
interpersonal psychotherapy (IPT), imipramine
with clinical management (IMI-CM), and placebo with clinical management (PLA-CM) showed
equivalent treatment effects only among those
whose Global Assessment Scores (GAS) indicated
high initial severity (GAS < 50). Among patients

who evidenced low initial severity (GAS > 50),
differential treatment effects were observed.

The authors concluded that initial severity of
depression and impairment of functioning significantly predicted differential treatment effects
and that psychosocial interventions may be contraindicated for lower levels of impairment. An
analysis of the same NIMH data by Sotsky and
colleagues (1991) gave contradictory results, however. Assessing for cognitive and role impairment,
these researchers found that in cases where social
and cognitive impairment was low, IPT demonstrated superior outcomes over imipramine and
CT, suggesting that tricyclic antidepressants were
contraindicated for low levels of social impairment. This latter finding was generally supported
in a review of 10 studies of work impairment by
Mintz and colleagues (1992).

Several authors (e.g., Gaw & Beutler, 1995;
Keijsers et al., 1994) have suggested that the effects of functional impairment on the selection of
treatment are very complex and cannot be understood without the inclusion of other moderating
and tempering variables. Most promising among
these is that of the intensity of treatment. Indeed,
table 8.2 reveals that of the ten studies that included treatment intensity as a moderating condition, eight (80%) found a complex differential
response.

For example, Barkham and colleagues (1996)
reported that after 8 weeks of treatment, significantly more patients assigned to an 8-week course
of treatment had improved than those assigned to
a 16-week group. The authors suggest that the
shorter time in session may have intensified treatment and allowed change to occur more rapidly,
although larger doses of treatment may result in
negative acceleration of improvement and diminished returns. Reynolds and colleagues (1996), reporting on the same study, confirm these findings;
although no significant differences were found between treatments and durations at treatment end,
the rate of increase in session depth was significantly greater in 8-session vs. 16-session treatment.

Shapiro and colleagues (1994) also found a
two-way interaction between treatment intensity
and functional impairment in affecting outcome.
Patients with high impairment, but not those
with relatively low impairment, responded more
favorably to 16 weeks of behavioral and psycho-

dynamic-interpersonal therapies than to 8 weeks of either treatment. Similar results were reported by Hoglend (1993), who used a wider range of treatment durations (9–53 sessions) to better explore the effects of treatment intensity. Among individuals with personality disorders who received more than 30 sessions, significant effects of treatment intensity were observed on acquisition of insight at 2-year follow-up and on overall psychodynamic change at 4-year follow-up.

Coping Style

Patient Contributions

Coping style is a relatively stable patient quality. Unlike impairment level, however, it has seldom been explored as a predictor of treatment outcome in its own right. We were able to find only one study in which coping style was related to outcome independently of the type of treatment employed. Beutler, Clarkin, and Bongar (2000) explored the prognostic value of coping style, finding that externalizing patients did more poorly than internalizing ones across a range of different treatment and problem types. The preponderance of studies focused on coping style as a moderator of treatment effects.

Moderating Effects

Table 8.3 summarizes the research that has addressed patient coping style as a moderator of treatment outcome. Specifically, the table reveals that 15 of 19 (79%) of the studies on this dimension demonstrated differential effects of symptom-focused and skill-building treatments versus insight-oriented treatments as a function of patient coping style. All of the 15 supportive studies support the conclusion that interpersonal and insight-oriented therapies are most effective among internalizing patients, and symptom-focused and skill-building therapies are most effective among externalizing patients.

In one of the first studies of this relationship, Beutler and Mitchell (1981) treated 40 mixed-diagnosis (depressed and anxious) outpatients with either analytic or experiential treatment techniques. Patient coping style (internalizer or externalizer) was assessed using the MMPI. Patients whose MMPI profiles suggested a preponderance of impulsive (Pd), projective (Pa), and excitable (Ma) symptoms were classified as externalizers. Those whose profiles suggested the presence of self-criticism (D), agitation (Pt), and social withdrawal (Si) were classified as internalizers. The results revealed systematic patient aptitude (coping style) X treatment interaction effects that were independent of diagnoses. Externalizing patients were found to achieve greater benefit from experiential treatment than to analytic-based therapy. Among internalizing patients, however, insight-oriented (analytic) treatment achieved its greatest effects; correspondingly, the behavioral therapies had the least beneficial impact.

In 1984, Beutler, Frank, Scheiber, Calvert, and Gaines compared the effectiveness of three types of group psychotherapy (cognitive-behavioral, experiential-gestalt, and interactive-supportive therapy) to a treatment-as-usual control condition. The patients comprised a group of acutely disturbed mixed-diagnosis psychiatric inpatients who presented for short-term care. Patients who received insight-oriented or abreactive treatment experienced a worsening of symptoms, while those who received interactive-supportive treatment benefited. In a naturalistic follow-up of 108 of these patients, Calvert, Beutler, and Crago (1988) investigated the role of patient coping style on long-term outpatient follow-up treatment. Internalizers were responsive to insight-oriented, individual therapy while externalizers were more responsive to symptom-focused behavioral and cognitive therapies delivered in an individual format.

Pursuing this line of research further, Beutler, Engle, and colleagues (1991) conducted a randomized clinical trial (RCT) on three manualized treatments that were delivered to patients who varied on the dimensions of resistance and coping style. Cognitive therapy (CT; see Yost, Beutler, Corbishley, & Allender, 1986) was symptom-focused, aimed toward the reduction of emotional arousal, and was highly directive. Focused experiential therapy (FEP; see Daldrup, Beutler, Engle, & Greenberg, 1988) was designed to be emotionally arousing, insight-focused, and therapist-directed. A supportive self-directed therapy (S/SD; see Scogin, Hamyblin, & Beutler, 1987) was an insight-focused, nondirective treatment designed to exert little in the way of emotional

Table 8.3. Coping Style

Coping Style Measure	Relationship Consistent with Hypothesis	Mixed Findings	No Relationship
California Psychological Inventory Socialization Scale (CPI-So)	Cooney, Kadden, Litt, & Getter (1991); Litt, Babor, DelBoca, Kadden, & Cooney (1992); Kadden, Cooney, Getter, & Litt (1989)		Project Match (1997)
Client Typology Scale	Lyons, Welte, Brown, Sokolow, & Hynes (1982)		
Defense Mechanism Inventory	Tasca, Russell, & Busby (1994)		
Diagnostic Interview Schedule (Antisocial Personality Status)	Longabaugh, Rubin, Malloy, Beattie, Clifford, & Noel (1994)		
MMPI Index (externalization-internalization defensiveness)	Beutler, Engle, Mohr, Daldrup, Bergan, Meredith, & Merry (1991); Beutler, Machado, Engle, & Mohr (1993); Beutler & Mitchell (1981)		
MMPI scale score combinations (scales 4 & 6)	Beutler, Mohr, Grawe, Engle, & MacDonald (1991)		Karno, Beutler, & Harwood (in press)
MMPI subscale composite results to derive patient internalization ratio	Calvert, Beutler, & Crago (1988)		
MMPI Welsch internalization ratio Object relations Clinician rating	Beutler, Clarkin, & Bongar (2000)*; Ford, Fisher, & Larson (1997)		Karno (1997)
Personality Assessment Form	Barber & Muenz (1996)		
Rotter's Internal-External Locus of Control Scale	Folkman, Lazarus, Dunkel-Schetter, DeLongis, & Gruen (1980)		
Ways of coping			Miller & Joyce (1979)
Totals	N = 15	N = 0	N = 4

Note: This study reflects a combined sample in which coping styles were assessed with a variety of measures (i.e., MMPI, MCMI, Eysenck, or STS-CRF).

arousal. At the conclusion of a 20-week treatment, it was confirmed that internalizing patients responded best to insight-oriented therapies and externalizing patients had better outcomes with symptom-focused therapies.

A one-year analysis of maintenance effects found even stronger results (Beutler, Machado, Engle, & Mohr, 1993). Patients whose coping style matched the level of symptom versus insight focus not only maintained their gains but continued to improve, while those who were mismatched did poorly and frequently relapsed. In still another extension of this, the cross-cultural transportability of the previous findings was demonstrated among a Swiss sample (Beutler, Mohr, et al., 1991). This latter study indicated that internalizing patients who were exposed to insight-focused treatments had better outcomes than those who were exposed to behaviorally focused treatments. Likewise, externalizing patients had better outcomes when provided with behaviorally focused interventions than when exposed to insight-focused treatments.

Kadden, Cooney, Getter, and Litt (1989) utilized the California Personality Inventory (CPI) in an examination of ATI effects that involved 96 inpatients diagnosed with alcohol dependence or abuse. This investigation examined differential patient outcome relative to two contrasting treatments and the patient coping style dimension. That is, outcomes for patients with differing coping styles were compared among those assigned to two differing treatments. Patients in coping skills training (CS), a behaviorally oriented treatment, were contrasted with those assigned to interactional group therapy (IG), an interpersonally oriented treatment. The CPI's Socialization subscale (CPI-SO) was the indicator of externalizing/impulsive or internalizing/introspective coping styles among this patient population. The investigators found that patients' levels of external coping was directly related to the degree of benefit in the behaviorally focused treatment while it was negatively associated with benefit in the interpersonal treatment.

Cooney, Kadden, Litt, and Getter (1991), in a follow-up to Kadden and colleagues' (1989) study, re-examined the ATI effects of behavior therapy (coping skills training; CS) or interpersonal therapy (interactional group therapy; IG)

and coping style at 2 years post-treatment. Impulsive patients who received the behavioral treatment continued their improvement at a greater rate when compared to impulsive patients who received IG. Moreover, patients with introspective and socially sensitive styles continued to respond best to previous interpersonal therapy when compared to patients low on impulsivity who had received CS.

These results have been independently confirmed by three other studies. In a placebo-controlled RCT involving three active treatments (cognitive therapy, interpersonal therapy, and imipramine with clinical management) and 250 outpatients with major depressive disorder, Barber and Muenz (1996) found that cognitive therapy achieved better results among patients who employed direct behavioral avoidance (a coping strategy that is characteristic of externalizers) while patients who utilized obsessive coping (a strategy that is characteristic of internalizers) responded best to interpersonal therapy. Likewise, Longabaugh and colleagues (1994) found that externalizing, alcohol-abusing outpatients showed significantly more reductions of drinking after receiving cognitive-behavioral treatment than after relationship-enhancement therapy. Findings were reversed for alcoholic patients who were low on externalizing traits (that is, patients who were characterized by internalization). These latter patients improved more with relationship enhancement therapy than with cognitive therapy.

Finally, in a study of 40 comorbid depressed and stimulant-abusing patients, Beutler, Moleiro, Malik, and Harwood (2000) found that good matches between patient variables and type of treatment were a positive predictor of outcome. In this study, the contribution of all of the patient matching dimensions (including coping style matched with therapy focus) were explored as a complete rendition of the STS model (Beutler, Clarkin, & Bongar, 2000; Beutler & Harwood, 2000). Although not broken down by actual matching dimension due to the small sample size, patient outcome improved dramatically as adherence to the guidelines proposed by the STS model increased. Based on initial analysis of the full therapy model using patient, treatment, and matching variables together, the prescriptive therapy model accounted for from 80% to 93%

of the variance in six-month follow-up depression scores and for from 57% to 79% of the six-month variance in drug use.

However, not all studies have found significant, confirmatory effects. For example, in the latter study (Beutler, Moleiro, et al., 2000), an effort to develop a treatment that specifically modified the therapist's approach to fit the patient's coping style and functional impairment failed to demonstrate that outcomes favored this treatment. Likewise, in a study involving the treatment of problem drinking delivered in a couples format (Couples Alcoholism Treatment project; CAT), an RCT comparison of a symptom-focused cognitive-behavioral therapy and a theme-focused family systems treatment was conducted on 75 couples. Although other matching dimensions (resistance and distress) were predictive of change, contrary to previous findings among nonalcoholic patients (Beutler, Engle, et al., 1991; Calvert et al., 1988), coping style was not a significant moderator of the effects of behavioral and insight-oriented treatments (Karno, Beutler, & Harwood, in press).

Similarly, the largest RCT in the exploration of matching dimension to date (Project Match Research Group, 1997) also found few effects. In Project MATCH, 952 outpatients and 774 inpatients diagnosed as alcohol dependent were assigned to one of three 12-week, manual-guided treatments (cognitive-behavioral coping skills therapy, motivational enhancement therapy, or 12-step facilitation therapy). Coping style was defined by the CPI and follow-up was for a period of 1 year post-treatment. The earlier analyses involving coping style yielded nonsignificant results; however, additional analyses that may yield different findings are ongoing. The failure to find significant ATI effects for coping style among this large population of alcoholic patients, as of yet, is surprising given the consistency of significant findings from previous well-designed studies based on similar populations.

LIMITATIONS OF THE RESEARCH REVIEWED

Functional impairment and coping style are not qualities that can be randomly assigned to pa-

tients, and thus it is difficult to conclude that the observed correlation between degree of fit between patient quality and treatment condition is causal. This is a decided weakness in the current results.

Moreover, only one controlled clinical trial has been conducted in which an effort was made to specifically modify the particular treatment to attend to the patient's level of functional impairment or coping style (Beutler, Moleiro, et al., 2000). While this study provided strong support for the matching dimensions, it did not indicate that differential use of the procedures could be taught to therapists. This was especially true of those procedures that varied from insight to symptom focus. While the number of studies support the value of functional impairment and coping style as differential treatment predictors, weaknesses in current methodologies have failed to demonstrate how one might teach therapists to use this information effectively and consistently in planning and carrying out treatment.

THERAPEUTIC PRACTICES

Both patient coping style and patient level of functional impairment are promising moderators of treatment outcomes. They positively impact on outcome when appropriately matched with treatment variables. Moreover, at least patient impairment level is a prognostic indicator that attenuates treatment outcome. Clinicians should take advantage of the information provided by studies that explore patient-level and treatment-level variables and adjust their treatments accordingly. Patients who have little support from other people and who manifest impairment in two or more areas of functioning (family, social, intimate, work, etc.) may benefit from treatment that includes a medication component and increases the intensity of interventions by lengthening treatment. Likewise, patients who manifest externalizing tendencies might be provided with treatments that are focused on skill building and on symptom change. In contrast, those who manifest patterns of self-criticism and emotional avoidance are likely to benefit from an interpersonally focused and insight-oriented treatment.

The effective clinician will be one who is able to modify interventions and treatment plans to fit the level of impairment and the coping style of the patient. Unfortunately, the evidence is still unclear as to how this can best be done. While the evidence is reasonably clear that all patients do not respond equivalently to a given intervention and that patient factors moderate treatment response, exact cut-off points on measures and exact procedures for implementing treatment variations are not certain. At least the level of care, in the form of intensity and the use of adjunctive medications, and the differential use of behavioral versus interpersonal/insight procedures may facilitate treatment outcomes when appropriately applied to patients who differ in impairment levels and coping styles.

Assessment of these patient attributes need not be time-consuming or tedious; cues for the identification of a variety of patient attributes are included in Beutler and Harwood (2000) to enable the clinician to make any necessary in-session treatment matching adjustments. These procedures combine self-report and clinician ratings to define areas in which the patient's functioning is impaired and characteristic ways that the patient responds to acute stress. Investigators, as well as clinicians, who are interested in psychotherapy outcome research are encouraged to continue with, or begin, the exploration of therapy process relevant ATIs in the hopes of developing treatments that outperform extant conventional treatment packages.

In support of this effort, Beutler, Clarkin, and Bongar (2000) have extracted four principles from extant research literature that they believe may be useful in helping practicing clinicians to, first, recognize relevant patient characteristics and, second, select and apply an effective treatment.

1. The likelihood of improvement (prognosis) is a positive function of social support level and a negative function of functional impairment.

There is *moderately strong support* for this conclusion, with confirming results in over 70% of the studies reviewed. Level of impairment is most directly reflected in impaired social relationships, work performance, the inability to attach to loved ones, and a sense of emotional alienation. These things portend the development of future problems, are predictive of depression, and impede the effects of treatment. The presence of social supportive relationships, intimate attachments, and friendships, however, buffers the patient against these effects. Thus, interventions that provide or enhance patient social support (such as family therapy, group therapy, etc.) may be indicated for those who lack attachments.

2. Amount of benefit from psychoactive medication is greatest among those patients with high functional impairment and low social support.

The support for this principle is *moderately strong*, with 67% of the available studies supporting this conclusion. The evidence is not as supportive of this proposition, however, as it is for the use of functional impairment as a predictor of treatment response. Because there are some limitations in the research on psychoactive medication, more research is needed in order to determine the conditions that potentiate and suppress the relative effects of psychoactive drugs and psychological interventions.

It should be noted that the results reviewed here, as well as those reviewed by Beutler, Clarkin, and Bongar (2000), failed to support a differential effect of impairment level on the selection of psychosocial treatments. Most psychosocial treatments appear to produce similar levels of responses among patients whose problems range widely in severity.

3. Benefit corresponds with treatment intensity among functionally impaired patients.

The research reviewed on this topic provides *moderate to strong support*, with 80% of studies showing this effect. While the results are promising, there are still too few studies available to make this case strongly. The studies on treatment intensity are imbued with problems in defining treatment intensity; the better the distinction between intensive and nonintensive treatment, the clearer the results. The best evidence indicates that long-term treatment of more than six months, and probably a year or more, is indicated among patients who have significant disturbances in multiple areas of functioning, are comorbid, or whose problems are chronic.

4. Therapeutic change is greatest when the internal or external focus of the selected interventions parallel the external or internal methods of avoidance that are characteristically used by the patient to cope with stressors.

The evidence for this principle is *moderate to strong*, with 80% of available studies providing support for the principle. A promising number of studies support the conclusion that task- and symptom-focused interventions are more effective than insight-oriented ones among patients who are impulsive, extroverted, and noninsightful. The converse also appears to be true. Insight-oriented and interpersonally focused interventions are most effective among patients who are introspective, introverted, and self-critical. These patients seem to do less well with behavioral and skill-focused interventions.

REFERENCES

Abrams, R. C. (1996). Personality disorders in the elderly. *International Journal of Geriatric Psychiatry, 11*(9), 759–763.

Ackerman, D. L., Greenland, S., & Bystritsky, A. (1994). Predictors of treatment response in obsessive-compulsive disorder: Multivariate analyses from a multicenter trial of comipramine. *Journal of Clinical Psychopharmacology, 14,* 247–253.

American Psychiatric Association. (2000). *Diagnostic and statistical manual of mental disorders* (4th ed.). Washington, DC: American Psychiatric Association.

Andrew, B., Hawton, K., Fagg, J., & Westbrook, D. (1993). Do psychosocial factors influence outcome in severely depressed female psychiatric in-patients? *British Journal of Psychiatry, 163,* 747–754.

Badger, T. A., & Collins-Joyce, P. (2000). Depression, psychosocial resources, and functional ability in older adults. *Clinical Nursing Research, 9*(3), 238–255.

Barber, J. P., & Meunz, L. R. (1996). The role of avoidance and obsessiveness in matching pa-tients to cognitive and interpersonal psychotherapy: Empirical findings for the treatment for depression collaborative research program. *Journal of Consulting and Clinical Psychology, 64,* 951–958.

Barkham, M., Rees, A., Stiles, W. B., Shapiro, D. A., Hardy, G. E., & Reynolds, S. (1996). Dose-effect relations in time-limited psychotherapy for depression. *Journal of Consulting and Clinical Psychology, 64*(5), 927–935.

Barry, M. M., & Zissi, A. (1997). Quality of life as an outcome measure in evaluating mental health services: A review of the empirical evidence. *Social Psychiatry and Psychiatric Epidemiology, 32,* 37–47.

Bartels, S. J., Mueser, K. T., & Miles, K. M. (1997). A comparative study of elderly patients with schizophrenia and bipolar disorder in nursing homes and the community. *Schizophrenia Research, 27*(2–3), 181–190.

Basoglu, M., Marks, I. M., & Swinson, R. P. (1994). Pre-treatment predictors of treatment outcome in panic disorder and agoraphobia treated with alprazolam and exposure. *Journal of Affective Disorders, 30,* 123–132.

Beutler, L. E. (1983). *Eclectic psychotherapy: A systematic approach.* New York: Pergamon.

Beutler, L. E. (1991). Have all won and must all have prizes? Revisiting Luborsky et al.'s verdict. *Journal of Consulting and Clinical Psychology, 59,* 226–232.

Beutler, L. E., & Berren, M. R. (1995). *Integrative assessment of adult personality.* New York: Guilford.

Beutler, L. E., & Clarkin, J. F. (1990). *Systematic treatment selection: Toward targeted therapeutic interventions.* New York: Brunner/Mazel.

Beutler, L. E., Clarkin, J. F., & Bongar, B. (2000). *Guidelines for the systematic treatment of the depressed patient.* New York: Oxford University Press.

Beutler, L. E., & Consoli, A. J. (1992). Systematic eclectic psychotherapy. In J. C. Norcross & M. R. Goldfried (Eds.), *Handbook of psychotherapy integration* (pp. 264–299). New York: Basic.

Beutler, L. E., Engle, D., Mohr, D., Daldrup, R. J., Bergan, J., Meredith, K., & Merry, W. (1991). Predictors of differential response to cognitive, experiential, and self-directed psychotherapeutic techniques. *Journal of Consulting and Clinical Psychology, 59,* 333–340.

Beutler, L. E., Frank, M., Scheiber, S. C., Calvert, S., & Gaines, J. (1984). Comparative effects of group psychotherapies in a short-term in-patient setting: An experience with deterioration effects. *Psychiatry, 47,* 66–76.

Beutler, L. E., Goodrich, G., Fisher, D., & Williams, O. B. (1999). Use of psychological tests/instruments for treatment planning. In M. E. Maruish (Ed.), *The use of psychological tests for treatment planning and outcome assessment* (2nd ed., pp. 81–113). Hillsdale, NJ: Erlbaum.

Beutler, L. E., & Harwood, T. M. (2000). *Prescriptive psychotherapy: A practical guide to systematic treatment selection.* New York: Oxford University Press.

Beutler, L. E., Kim, E. J., Davison, E., Karno, M., & Fisher, D. (1996). Research contributions to improving managed health care outcomes. *Psychotherapy, 33,* 197–206.

Beutler, L. E., Machado, P. P. P., Engle, D., & Mohr, D. (1993). Differential patient X treatment maintenance of treatment effects among cognitive, experiential, and self-directed psychotherapies. *Journal of Psychotherapy Integration, 3,* 15–31.

Beutler, L. E., & Mitchell, R. (1981). Differential psychotherapy outcome among depressed and impulsive patients as a function of analytic and experiential treatment procedures. *Psychiatry, 44,* 297–306.

Beutler, L. E., Mohr, D. C., Grawe, K., Engle, D., & MacDonald, R. (1991). Looking for differential treatment effects: Cross-cultural predictors of differential psychotherapy efficacy. *Journal of Psychotherapy Integration, 1,* 121–141.

Beutler, L. E., Moleiro, C., Malik, M., & Harwood, T. M. (2000, June). *The UC Santa Barbara study of fitting therapy to patients: First results.* Paper presented at the International Society for Psychotherapy Research, Chicago.

Bilder, R. M., Goldman, R. S., Robinson, D., Reiter, G., Bell, L., Bates, J. A., Pappadopulos, E., Willson, D. F., Alvir, J. M. J., Woerner, M. G., Geisler, S., Kane, J. M., & Lieberman, J. A. (2000). Neuropsychology of first-episode schizophrenia: Initial characterization and clinical correlates. *American Journal of Psychiatry, 157* (4), 549–559.

Billings, A. G., & Moos, R. H. (1985). Life stressors and social resources affect posttreatment outcomes among depressed patients. *Journal of Abnormal Psychology, 94,* 140–153.

Brown, T. A., & Barlow, D. H. (1995). Long-term outcome in cognitive-behavioral treatment of panic disorder: Clinical predictors and alternative strategies for assessment. *Journal of Consulting and Clinical Psychology, 63,* 754–765.

Burvill, P. W., Hall, W. D., Stampfer, H. G., & Emmerson, J. P. (1991). The prognosis of depression in old age. *British Journal of Psychiatry, 158,* 64–71.

Bussing, R., Zima, B. T., & Perwien, A. R. (2000). Self-esteem in special education children with ADHD: Relationship to disorder characteristics and medication use. *Journal of the American Academy of Child and Adolescent Psychiatry, 39*(10), 1260–1269.

Butcher, J. N. (1990). *The MMPI-2 in psychological treatment.* New York: Oxford University Press.

Calvert, S. J., Beutler, L. E., & Crago, M. (1988). Psychotherapy outcomes as a function of therapist-patient matching on selected variables. *Journal of Social and Clinical Psychology, 6,* 104–117.

Cooney, N. L., Kadden, R. M., Litt, M. D., & Getter, H. (1991). Matching alcoholics to coping skills or interactional therapies: Two-year follow-up results. *Journal of Consulting and Clinical Psychology, 59,* 598–601.

Costa, P. T., Jr., & McCrae, R. R. (1985). *The NEO Personality Inventory manual.* Odessa, FL: Psychological Assessment Resources.

Coyne, J. C., & Downey, G. (1991). Social factors and psychopathology: Stress, social support, and coping process. *Annual Review of Psychology, 42,* 401–425.

Cuijpers, P., & Van Lammeren, P. (1999). Depressive symptoms in chronically ill elderly people in residential homes. *Aging and Mental Health, 3*(3), 221–226.

Dadds, M. R., & McHugh, T. A. (1992). Social support and treatment outcome in behavioral family therapy for child conduct problems. *Journal of Consulting and Clinical Psychology, 60,* 252–259.

Daldrup, R. J., Beutler, L. E., Engle, D., & Greenberg, L. S. (1988). *Focused expressive psychotherapy.* New York: Guilford.

Eldredge, K. L., Locke, K. D., & Horowitz, L. M. (1998). Patterns in interpersonal problems associated with binge eating disorder. *International Journal of Eating Disorders, 23*(4), 383–389.

Elkin, I., Gibbons, R. D., Shea, M. T., Sotsky, S. M., Watkins, J. T., Pilkonis, P. A., & Hedeker, D. (1995). Initial severity and differential treatment outcome in the National Institute of Mental Health Treatment of Depression Collaborative Research Program. *Journal of Con-*

sulting and Clinical Psychology, *63*(5), 841–847.

Elkin, I., Shea, T., Watkins, J. T., Imber, S. D., Sotsky, S. M., Collins, J. F., Glass, D. R., Pilkonis, P. A., Leber, W. R., Docherty, J. P., Fiester, S. J., & Parloff, M. B. (1989). National Institute of Mental Health Treatment of Depression Collaborative Research Program. *Archives of General Psychiatry*, *46*, 971–982.

Ellicott, A., Hammen, C., Gitlin, M., Brown, G., & Jamison, K. (1990). Life events and the course of bipolar disorder. *American Journal of Psychiatry*, *147*, 1194–1198.

Eysenck, H. J. (1957). *The dynamics of anxiety and hysteria*. New York: Praeger.

Eysenck, H. J. (1967). *The biological basis of personality*. Springfield, IL: Thomas.

Eysenck, H. J. (1990). Genetic and environmental contributions to individual differences: The three major dimensions of personality. *Journal of Personality*, *58*, 245–261.

Fahy, T. A., & Russell, G. F. M. (1993). Outcome and prognostic variables in bulimia-nervosa. *International Journal of Eating Disorders*, *14*, 135–145.

Fisher, D., Beutler, L. E., & Williams, O. B. (1999). STS Clinician Rating Form: Patient assessment and treatment planning. *Journal of Clinical Psychology*, *55*, 825–842.

Folkman, S., Lazarus, R. S., Dunkel-Schetter, C., DeLongis, A., & Gruen, R. J. (1980). Dynamics of a stressful encounter: Cognitive appraisal, coping, and encounter outcomes. *Journal of Personality and Social Psychology*, *50*, 992–1003.

Ford, J. D., Fisher, P., & Larson, L. (1997). Object relations as a predictor of treatment outcome with chronic posttraumatic stress disorder. *Journal of Consulting and Clinical Psychology*, *65*, 547–559.

Fountoulakis, K. N., Tsolaki, M., & Kazis, A. (2000). Target symptoms for fluvoxamine in old-age depression. *International Journal of Psychiatry in Clinical Practice*, *4*(2), 127–134.

Fremouw, W. J., & Zitter, R. E. (1978). A comparison of skills training and cognitive restructuring-relaxation for the treatment of speech anxiety. *Behavior Therapy*, *9*, 248–259.

Friedman, R. A., Markowitz, J. C., Parides, M., Gniwesch, L., & Kocsis, J. H. (1999). Six months of desipramine for dysthymia: Can dysthymic patients achieve normal social functioning? *Journal of Affective Disorders*, *54*(3), 283–286.

Garvey, M. J., Hollon, S. D., & DeRubies, R. J. (1994). Do depressed patients with higher pretreatment stress levels respond better to cognitive therapy than imipramine? *Journal of Affective Disorders*, *32*(1), 45–50.

Garvey, M. J., & Noyes, R. (1996). Association of levels of N-acetyl-beta-glucosaminidase with severity of psychiatric symptoms in panic disorder. *Psychiatry Research*, *60*(2–3), 185–190.

Garvey, M. J., Noyes, R., Cook, B., & Blum, N. (1996). Preliminary confirmation of the proposed link between reward-dependence traits and norepinephrine. *Psychiatry Research*, *65*(1), 61–64.

Garvey, M. J., Noyes, R., Woodman, C., & Laukes, C. (1995). Relationship of generalized anxiety symptoms to urinary 5-hydroxyindoleacetic acid and vanillylmandelic acid. *Psychiatric Research*, *57*(1), 1–5.

Garvey, M. J., & Tauson, V. B. (1996). Urinary levels of 3-methoxy-4-hydroxyphenylglycol predict symptom severity in selected patients with unipolar depression. *Psychiatry Research*, *62*(2), 171–177.

Garvey, M. J., & Underwood, K. (1997). Association of N-acetyl-beta-glucosaminidase levels with seriousness of suicide attempts. *Biological Psychiatry*, *42*(4), 286–289.

Gaw, K. F., & Beutler, L. E. (1995). Integrating treatment recommendations. In L. E. Beutler & M. Berren (Eds.), *Integrative assessment of adult personality* (pp. 280–319). New York: Guilford.

George, L. K., Blazer, D. G., Hughes, D. C., & Fowler, N. (1989). Social support and the outcome of major depression. *British Journal of Psychiatry*, *154*, 478–485.

Gitlin, M. J., Swendsen, J., & Heller, T. L. (1995). Relapse and impairment in bipolar disorder. *American Journal of Psychiatry*, *152*, 1635–1640.

Godding, P. R., McAnulty, R. D., Wittrock, D. A., Britt, D. M., & Khansur, T. (1995). Predictors of depression among male cancer patients. *Journal of Nervous and Mental Disease*, *183*(2), 95–98.

Goldfried, M. R., & Padawar, W. (1982). Current status and future direction in psychotherapy. In M. R. Goldfried (Ed.), *Converging themes in psychotherapy* (pp. 3–52). New York: Springer.

Gonzales, L. R., Lewishon, P. M., & Clarke, G. N. (1985). Longitudinal follow-up of unipolar depressives: An investigation of predictors of relapse. *Journal of Consulting and Clinical Psychology, 53,* 401–469.

Gray, J. A. (1981). A critique of Eysenck's theory of personality. In H. J. Eysenck (Ed.), *A model for personality* (pp. 246–276). New York: Springer.

Green, C. R., Marin, D. B., Mohs, R. C., Schmeidler, M. A., Fine, E., & Davis, K. L. (1999). The impact of behavioral impairment of functional ability in Alzheimer's disease. *International Journal of Geriatric Psychiatry, 14,* 307–316.

Haas, B. K. (1999). Clarification and integration of similar quality of life concepts. *Image: Journal of Nursing Scholarship, 31,* 215–220.

Hardy, G. E., Barkham, M., Shapiro, D. A., Stiles, W. B., Rees, A., & Reynolds, S. (1995). Impact of Cluster C personality disorders on outcomes of contrasting brief psychotherapies for depression. *Journal of Consulting and Clinical Psychology, 63,* 997–1004.

Hoencamp, E., Haffmans, P. M. J., Duivenvoorden, H., Knegtering, H., & Dijken, W. A. (1994). Predictors of (non)-response in depressed outpatients treated with a three-phase sequential medication strategy. *Journal of Affective Disorders, 31,* 235–246.

Høglend, P. (1993). Personality disorders and long-term outcome after brief dynamic psychotherapy. *Journal of Personality Disorders, 7*(2), 168–181.

Imber, S. D., Pilkonis, P. A., Sotsky, S. M., Elkin, I., Watkins, J. T., Collins, J. F., Shea, M. T., Leber, W. R., & Glass, D. R. (1990). Mode-specific effects among three treatments for depression. *Journal of Consulting and Clinical Psychology, 58,* 352–359.

Joyce, A. S., Ogrodniczuk, J., Piper, W. E., & McCallum, M. (2000, June). Patient characteristics and mid-treatment outcome in two forms of short-term individual psychotherapy. Presentation at the 31st annual meeting of the Society for Psychotherapy Research, Chicago, IL.

Joyce, A. S., & Piper, W. E. (1996). Interpretative work in short-term individual psychotherapy: An analysis using hierarchical linear modeling. *Journal of Consulting and Clinical Psychology, 64,* 505–512.

Judd, L. L., Paulus, M. P., Wells, K. B., & Rapaport, M. H. (1996). Socioeconomic burden of subsyndromal depressive symptoms and major depression in a sample of the general population. *American Journal of Psychiatry, 153*(11), 1411–1417.

Kadden, R. M., Cooney, N. L., Getter, H., & Litt, M. D. (1989). Matching alcoholics to coping skills or interactional therapies: Posttreatment results. *Journal of Consulting and Clinical Psychology, 57,* 698–704.

Karno, M. (1997). *Identifying patient attributes and elements of psychotherapy that impact the effectiveness of alcoholism treatment.* Unpublished doctoral dissertation, University of California, Santa Barbara.

Karno, M., Beutler, L. E., & Harwood, T. M. (in press). Interactions between psychotherapy process and patient attributes that predict alcohol treatment effectiveness: A preliminary report. *Addictive Behavior.*

Keijsers, G. P. J., Hoogduin, C. A. L., & Schaap, C. P. D. R. (1994). Predictors of treatment outcome in the behavioral treatment of obsessive-compulsive disorder. *British Journal of Psychiatry, 165,* 781–786.

Koenig, H. (1998). Depression in hospitalized older patients with congestive heart failure. *General Hospital Psychiatry, 20*(1), 29–43.

Koolhaas, J. M., Korte, S. M., De Boer, S. F., Van der Vegt, B. J., Van Reenan, C. G., Hopster, H., De Jong, I. C., Ruis, M. A. W., & Blokhuis, H. J. (1999). Coping style in animals: Current status in behavior and stress-physiology. *Neuroscience and Biobehavioral Reviews, 23,* 925–935.

Koran, L. M. (2000). Quality of life in obsessive-compulsive disorder. *The Psychiatric Clinics of North America, 23,* 509–517.

Latack, J. C., & Havlovic, S. J. (1992). Coping with job stress: A conceptual evaluation framework for coping measures. *Journal of Organizational Behavior, 13,* 479–508.

Lawton, M., Moss, M., Fulcomer, M., & Kleban, M. (1982). A research and service oriented multi-level assessment instrument. *Journal of Gerontology, 37,* 91–99.

Lazarus, A. A. (1981). *The practice of multi-modal therapy.* New York: McGraw-Hill.

Lazarus, R. S., & Folkman, S. (1984). *Stress, arousal, and coping.* New York: Springer.

Litt, M. D., Babor, T. F., DelBoca, F. K., Kadden, R. M., & Cooney, N. L. (1992). Type of alcoholics: II. Application of an empirically derived typology to treatment matching. *Archives of General Psychiatry, 49,* 609–614.

Littlefield, C. H., Rodin, G. M., Murray, M. A., & Craven, J. L. (1990). Influence of functional impairment and social support on depressive symptoms in persons with diabetes. *Health Psychology, 9*(6), 737–749.

Longabaugh, R., Rubin, G. M., Malloy, P., Beattie,

M., Clifford, P. R., & Noel, N. (1994). Drinking outcomes of alcohol abusers diagnosed as antisocial personality disorder. *Alcoholism: Clinical and Experimental Research, 18*, 778–785.

Lueger, R. J. (1996). Using feedback on patient progress to predict the outcome of psychotherapy. *Journal of Clinical Psychology, 55*, 1–27.

Lyons, J. P., Welte, J. W., Brown, J., Sokolow, L., & Hynes, G. (1982). Variation in alcoholism treatment orientation: Differential impact upon specific subpopulations. *Alcoholism: Clinical and Experimental Research, 6*, 333–343.

Maling, M. S., Gurtman, M. B., & Howard, K. I. (1995). The response of interpersonal problems to varying doses of psychotherapy. *Psychotherapy Research, 5*, 63–75.

Mazure, C. M., Nelson, J. C., & Jatlow, P. I. (1990). Predictors of hospital outcome without antidepressants in major depression. *Psychiatry Research, 33*, 51–58.

McGue, M., & Bouchard Jr., T. J. (1998). Genetics and environmental influences on human behavioral differences. *Annual Review of Neuroscience, 21*, 1–24.

McLean, P. D., & Taylor, S. (1992). Severity of unipolar depression and choice of treatment. *Behavior Research and Therapy, 30*, 443–451.

McLellan, A. T., Woody, G. E., Luborsky, L., O'Brien, C. P., & Druley, K. A. (1983). Increased effectiveness of substance abuse treatment: A prospective study of patient-treatment "matching." *Journal of Nervous and Mental Disease, 171*, 597–605.

Mersch, P. P. A., Emmelkamp, P. M. G., & Lips, C. (1991). Social phobia: Individual response patterns and cognitive interventions. A follow-up study. *Behavioral Research and Therapy, 29*, 357–362.

Miller, W. R., & Joyce, M. A. (1979). Prediction of abstinence, controlled drinking, and heavy drinking outcomes following behavioral self-control training. *Journal of Consulting and Clinical Psychology, 47*, 773–775.

Mintz, J., Mintz, L. I., Arruda, M. J., & Hwang, S. S. (1992). Treatments of depression and the functional capacity to work. *Archives of General Psychiatry, 49*, 761–768.

Moos, R. H. (1990). Depressed outpatients' life contexts, amount of treatment, and treatment outcome. *Journal of Nervous and Mental Diseases, 178*, 105–112.

Newsom, J. T., & Schulz, R. (1996). Social support as a mediator in the relation between functional status and quality of life in older adults. *Psychology and Aging, 11*(1), 34–44.

Ogles, B. M., Sawyer, J. D., & Lambert, M. J. (1995). Clinical significance of the National Institute of Mental Health Treatment of Depression Collaborative Research Program data. *Journal of Consulting and Clinical Psychology, 63*, 321–326.

Oxman, T. E., Freeman, D. H., & Manheimer, E. D. (1995). Lack of social participation or religious strength and comfort as risk factors for death after cardiac surgery in the elderly. *Psychosomatic Medicine, 57*, 5–15.

Piper, W. E., McCallum, M., Joyce, A. S., Azim, H. F., & Ogrodniczuk, J. S. (1999). Follow-up findings for interpretive and supportive forms of psychotherapy and patient personality variables. *Journal of Consulting and Clinical Psychology, 67*(2), 267–273.

Prochaska, J. O. (1984). *Systems of psychotherapy: A transtheoretical analysis* (2d ed.). Homewood, IL: Dorsey.

Prochaska, J. O., & DiClemente, C. C. (1992). The transtheoretical approach. In J. C. Norcross & M. R. Goldfried (Eds.), *Handbook of psychotherapy integration* (pp. 300–334). New York: Basic.

Project Match Research Group. (1997). Matching alcoholism treatments to client heterogeneity: Project Match posttreatment drinking outcomes. *Journal of Studies in Alcoholism, 58*, 7–29.

Prudic, J., Sackeim, H. A., Davanand, D. P., & Kiersky, J. E. (1993). The efficacy of ECT in double depression. *Depression, 1*, 38–44.

Rapaport, M. H., & Judd, L. L. (1998). Minor depressive disorder and subsyndromal depressive symptoms: Functional impairment and response to treatment. *Journal of Affective Disorders, 48*(2–3), 227–232.

Ravindran, A. V., Anisman, H., Merali, Z., Charbonneau, Y., Telner, J., Bialik, R. J., Wiens, A., Ellis, J., & Griffiths, J. (1999). Treatment of primary dysthymia with group cognitive therapy and pharmacotherapy: Clinical symptoms and functional impairment. *American Journal of Psychiatry, 156*, 1608–1617.

Ray, C., Jefferies, S., & Weir, W. R. C. (1997). Coping and other predictors of outcome in chronic fatigue syndrome: A 1-year follow-up. *Journal of Psychosomatic Research, 43*(4), 405–415.

Reynolds, S., Stiles, W. B., Barkham, M., Shapiro, D. A., Hardy, G. E., & Rees, A. (1996). Acceleration of changes in session impact during contrasting time-limited psychotherapies. *Journal of Consulting and Clinical Psychology, 64,* 577–586.

Roberts, R., Kaplan, G., Shema, S., & Strawbridge, W. (1997). Does growing old increase the risk for depression? *American Journal of Psychiatry, 154*(10), 1384–1390.

Rosenblatt, A., & Rosenblatt, J. (2000). Demographic, clinical, and functional characteristics of youth enrolled in six California systems of care. *Journal of Child and Family Studies, 9*(1), 51–66.

Sanders, N. E. J. (1999). An assessment of coping and adjustment in individuals with Parkinson's disease and their caregivers. *Dissertation Abstracts International, 60,* 842.

Schneider, L. C., & Struening, E. L. (1983). SLOF: A behavioral rating scale for assessing the mentally ill. *Social Work Research and Abstracts, 19*(3), 9–21.

Scogin, F., Bowman, D., Jamison, C., Beutler, L. E., & Machado, P. P. (1994). Effects of initial severity of dysfunctional thinking on the outcome of cognitive therapy. *Clinical Psychology and Psychotherapy, 1,* 179–184.

Scogin, F., Hamblin, D., & Beutler, L. (1987). Bibliotherapy for depressed older adults: A self-help alternative. *Gerontologist, 27,* 383–387.

Shapiro, D. A., Barkham, M., Rees, A., Hardy, G. E., Reynolds, S., & Startup, M. (1994). Effects of treatment duration and severity of depression on the effectiveness of cognitive-behavioral and psychodynamic-interpersonal psychotherapy. *Journal of Consulting and Clinical Psychology, 62,* 522–534.

Shapiro, D. A., Rees, A., Barkham, M., Hardy, G., Reynolds, S., & Startup, M. (1995). Effects of treatment duration and severity of depression on the maintenance of gains after cognitive-behavioral and psychodynamic-interpersonal therapy. *Journal of Consulting and Clinical Psychology, 63,* 378–387.

Shea, M. T., Elkin, I., Imber, S. D., Sotsky, S. M., Watkins, J. T., Collins, J. F., Pilkonis, P. A., Beckham, E., Glass, D. R., Dolan, R. T., & Parloff, M. B. (1992). Course of depressive symptoms over follow-up: Findings from the National Institute of Mental Health Treatment of Depression Collaborative Research Program. *Archives of General Psychiatry, 49,* 782–787.

Sotsky, S. M., Glass, D. R., Shea, T. M., Pilkonis, P. A., Collins, J. F., Elkin, I., Watkins, J. T.,

Imber, S. D., Leber, W. R., Moyer, J., & Oliveri, M. E. (1991). Patient predictors of response to psychotherapy and pharmacotherapy: Findings in the NIMH Treatment of Depression Collaborative Research Program. *American Journal of Psychiatry, 148,* 997–1008.

Spangler, D. L., Simons, A. D., Thase, M. E., & Monroe, S. M. (1997). Response to cognitive-behavioral therapy in depression: Effects of pretreatment cognitive dysfunction and life stress. *Journal of Consulting and Clinical Psychology, 65,* 568–575.

Sperry, L., Brill, P. L., Howard, K. L., & Grissom, G. R. (1996). *Treatment outcomes in psychotherapy and psychiatric interventions.* New York: Brunner/Mazel.

Strupp, H. H., Horowitz, L. J., & Lambert, M. J. (Eds.). (1997). *Measuring patient change after treatment for mood, anxiety, and personality disorders: Toward a core battery.* Washington, DC: American Psychological Association.

Tasca, G. A., Russell, V., & Busby, K. (1994). Characteristics of patients who chose between two types of group psychotherapy. *International Journal of Group Psychotherapy, 44,* 499–508.

Thase, M. E., Simons, A. D., Cahalane, J., McGeary, J., & Harden, T. (1991). Severity of depression and response to cognitive behavior therapy. *American Journal of Psychiatry, 148,* 784–789.

Vallejo, J., Gasto, C., Catalan, R., Bulbena, A., & Menchon, J. M. (1991). Predictors of antidepressant treatment outcome in melancholia: Psychosocial, clinical and biological indicators. *Journal of Affective Disorders, 21,* 151–162.

Veiel, H. O., Kuhner, C., Brill, G., & Ihle, W. (1992). Psychosocial correlates of clinical depression after psychiatric in-patient treatment: Methodological issue and baseline differences between recovered and non-recovered patients. *Psychological Medicine, 22,* 425–427.

Weissman, M. M., & Bothwell, S. (1976). Assessment of social adjustment by patient self-report. *Archives of General Psychiatry, 33,* 111–115.

Welsh, G. S. (1952). An anxiety index and an internalization ratio for the MMPI. *Journal of Consulting Psychology, 16,* 65–72.

Woody, G. E., McLellan, A. T., Luborsky, L., O'Brien, C. P., Blaine, J., Fox, S., Herman, I., & Beck, A. T. (1984). Severity of psychiatric symptoms as a predictor of benefits from psychotherapy: The Veterans Administration–Penn Study. *American Journal of Psychiatry, 141,* 1172–1177.

Yost, E., Beutler, L. E., Corbishley, A., & Allender, J. (1986). *Group cognitive therapy: A treatment approach for depressed older adults*. New York: Pergamon.

Zarit, S. H., Femia, E. E., Gatz, M., & Johansson, B. (1999). Prevalence, incidence and correlates of depression in the oldest old: The OCTO study. *Aging and Mental Health, 3*(2), 119–128.

Zlotnick, C., Shea, M. T., Pilkonis, P., Elkin, I., & Ryan, C. (1996). Gender, dysfunctional attitudes, social support, life events, and depressive symptoms over naturalistic follow-up. *American Journal of Psychiatry, 153*, 1021–1027.

Part III

Promising Elements

A. GENERAL ELEMENTS OF THE THERAPY RELATIONSHIP

9

Positive Regard

Barry A. Farber
Jodie S. Lane

The book [*Client-centered Therapy*] . . . expresses, I trust, our conviction that though science can never make therapists, it can help therapy; that though the scientific finding is cold and abstract, it may assist us in releasing forces that are warm, personal, and complex; and that though science is slow and fumbling, it represents the best road we know to the truth, even in so delicately intricate an area as that of human relationships.

—Carl Rogers (1951, p. xi)

Nearly 45 years ago, in what is now considered a classic paper, Carl Rogers (1957) posited that therapists' provision of positive regard (nonpossessive warmth), congruence (genuineness), and empathy were the necessary and sufficient conditions for therapeutic change. Rogers had been developing these views for many years, some of which were expressed in his seminal (1942) work, *Counseling and Psychotherapy*. Still, the publication of the 1957 article seems to have catalyzed a shift in the way that many thought about the putative mechanisms of psychotherapeutic change. The prevailing view at the time—and still an enormously influential one, though currently cast in somewhat different terms—was that technical expertise on the part of the therapist, especially in terms of choice and timing of interventions, is the essential discriminating factor between effective and noneffective therapy. Under the sway of Rogers's burgeoning influence in the late 1950s and throughout the 1960s, the notion that the relationship per se was the critical factor in determining therapeutic success took hold.

Moreover, this new way of conceptualizing the essence of psychotherapy influenced both the conduct of psychotherapy and the nature of investigations into therapeutic effectiveness. Therapists of varying persuasions, even those from theoretical camps that had traditionally eschewed an emphasis on relational factors, began to consider the importance of the relationship. Behaviorists and cognitive-behaviorists suggested that a good relationship could facilitate the provision of their technical interventions (Beck, 1995), and many psychoanalysts shifted their clinical perspective to emphasize "relational" factors (Mitchell & Aron, 1999). On the research front, even the first edition of Bergin and Garfield's (1971) psychotherapy research "bible," *Handbook of Psychotherapy and Behavior Change*, contained a chapter (Truax & Mitchell, 1971) on the relationship of "therapist interpersonal skills" to process and outcome. By the mid-1990s, the persistent demonstration that relational factors were significantly associated with outcome prompted Marvin Goldfried, a past president of the Society of Psychotherapy Research (SPR), to half-jokingly suggest the creation of an official SPR bumper sticker: "It's the relationship, stupid!"

Over the years, a great many studies have attempted to investigate Rogers's claims regarding the necessary and sufficient conditions of therapy.

There is, then, a substantial body of research to draw upon in looking at the association between the therapist's positive regard for his or her patients and therapeutic outcome. However, as will be detailed below, drawing firm conclusions from these efforts has been difficult. The problems that typically plague the investigation of complex psychological issues have been played out in this area as well: inconsistent findings, small sample sizes, lack of standardized measures, and lack of operational definitions of the concepts themselves. In addition, as the Rogerian influence on psychotherapeutic practice has waned in the last two decades—or, more accurately, has been incorporated into the mainstream with little awareness or explicit acknowledgment—empirical studies based on Rogerian concepts have also waned. Similarly, the focus of empirical research in recent years has shifted away from the individual contributions of each of the participants in therapy toward a consideration of the alliance or therapeutic relationship. And although Rogers's facilitative conditions are "very similar to contemporary, psychodynamic conceptualizations of the 'working,' 'helping,' or 'therapeutic' alliance" (Beutler, Machado, & Neufeldt, 1994, p. 243), it remains difficult to "translate" the findings of the extensive empirical research on the alliance to conclusions regarding the contributions of the therapist's relational qualities (such as positive regard) into effective psychotherapy.

This chapter focuses on one of Rogers's stated conditions: positive regard. It reviews Rogers's original discussions of the concept and traces how it has changed in meaning, terminology, description, and measurement. It also discusses how the use of multiple terms (including positive regard, unconditional positive regard, affirmation, respect, acceptance, warmth, support, caring, and prizing) has led to conceptual confusion as well as empirical difficulties in determining the link between the basic phenomenon and therapeutic outcome. The emphasis of this chapter, however, is on reviewing the findings of those empirical studies that have investigated the relationship between this variable and outcome in individual psychotherapy. Although much of this discussion and many of the studies of positive regard are framed within a Rogerian (person-centered) or broad-based humanistic-existential paradigm, virtually all schools of therapy either explicitly or implicitly promote the value of this basic attitude toward patients. Thus, the results of these studies have implications for the conduct not only of person-centered therapists, but for virtually all psychotherapists.

DEFINITIONS

To the extent that the therapist finds himself experiencing a warm acceptance of each aspect of the client's experience as being a part of that client, he is experiencing unconditional positive regard. . . . It means there are no conditions of acceptance . . . it means a "prizing" of the person . . . it means a caring for the client as a separate person.—Carl Rogers (1957, p. 101)

From the beginning of his efforts to explicate the essential elements of client-centered therapy, Rogers focused on positive regard and warmth: "Do we tend to treat individuals as persons of worth, or do we subtly devalue them by our attitudes and behavior? Is our philosophy one in which respect for the individual is uppermost?" (1951, p. 20). Implicit in this statement is his disapproval of what he perceived as the arrogance of the psychoanalytic community at that time. Rogers did not believe that anyone, including a therapist, could be more expert or knowledgeable about a client than the client him- or herself. He did not believe that a therapist's neutrality, dispassionate stance, or psychological distance from his or her client could facilitate a client's growth— no matter how brilliant the interpretations in such a therapy might be. Instead, he believed that treating clients in a consistently warm, highly regarding manner would inevitably allow them to grow psychologically, to fulfill their potential. Rogers framed these desirable attitudes of the therapist within the overarching concept of positive regard: "Can I let myself experience positive attitudes toward this other person—attitudes of warmth, caring, liking, interest, respect?" (1958, p. 12).

To this day, agreeing on a single phrase to refer to this basic positive attitude remains problematic. It is most often termed "positive regard," but early studies and theoretical writings preferred the phrase "nonpossessive warmth." As recently as 1994, Orlinsky, Grawe, and Parks, in reviewing studies on "acceptance, nonpossessive warmth, or positive regard" (p. 326), grouped them under the category of "therapist affirmation." For the most part, we will use the phrase "positive regard" to refer to the general constellation of attitudes encompassed by this and similar phrases.

Early in his career, Rogers (1951) viewed positive regard and acceptance as separate: "Still another issue is whether I can be acceptant of each facet of this other person which he presents to me. Can I receive him as he is?" (p. 122). Later, he combined these attributes into one of his basic conditions: "The second attitude of importance [after genuineness] in creating a climate for change is acceptance, or caring, or prizing—unconditional positive regard" (1986, p. 198).

Further confusing the conceptual issues at play here, Rogers's focus on accepting and affirming the client has, from the outset, been conflated with an emphasis on empathy. That is, the therapist's attempt to "provide deep understanding and acceptance of the attitudes consciously held at the moment by the client" could only be accomplished by the therapist's "struggle to achieve the client's internal frame of reference, to gain the center of his own perceptual field and see with him as perceiver" (1951, pp. 30–31). Rogers seems to be suggesting here that positive regard (including the component of acceptance) can best—and perhaps only—be achieved through empathic identification with one's client. And conversely, as Truax and Carkhuff (1967, p. 32) noted, "Deep empathic understanding can scarcely exist without a prior or concomitant feeling of nonpossessive warmth."

Yet another problem with attempts to focus exclusively on positive regard is the overlap between this concept and that of genuineness. In fact, Rogers suggested that the therapist's genuineness or congruence was not only a prerequisite for his or her experience of positive regard and empathy (Rogers & Truax, 1967) but that this attitude of genuineness was, of all the facilitative conditions, most basic to a helping relationship. Others (including Lietaer, 1984; Truax & Carkhuff, 1967) have considered that positive regard and genuineness should be understood as parts of a more basic attitude of "openness." As Lietaer explained: "The more I accept myself and am able to be present in a comfortable way with everything that bubbles up in me, without fear or defense, the more I can be receptive to everything that lives in my client" (p. 44).

Further problems with the concept of unconditional positive regard have been reviewed by Lietaer (1984). He notes that there may be an inherent tension between genuineness and unconditionality (for example, that therapists' own issues inevitably affect what they can and cannot truly accept in others); that it is unlikely that any therapist can provide constant doses of unconditional positive regard (that is, we all reinforce selectively); and that therapists' attempts to adopt a consistent attitude of unconditional positive regard may, paradoxically, lead to client self-confrontation (that is, a therapist's acceptance can lead to a deep and painful process of client awareness and self-confrontation). To a certain extent, Rogers himself anticipated such criticism. In a footnote to his 1957 article, "On the Necessary and Sufficient Conditions of Therapeutic Personality Change," he noted the following:

> The phrase "unconditional positive regard" may be an unfortunate one, since it sounds like an absolute, an all-or-nothing dispositional concept. . . . From a clinical and experiential point of view I believe the most accurate statement is that the effective therapist experiences unconditional positive regard for the client during many moments of his contact with him, yet from time to time he experiences only a conditional positive regard—and perhaps at times a negative regard, though this is not likely in effective therapy. It is in this sense that unconditional positive regard exists as a matter of degree in any relationship. (p. 101)

In short, there has been a historical confounding in Rogers's (and his followers') writings among the concepts of "warmth," "respect," "acceptance," "openness," "genuineness," and "empathy." How can one, then, assess a therapist's level of warmth or positive regard without implicitly measuring a concept like empathy as well? In fact, reading transcripts of Rogers's work (see Farber, Brink, & Raskin, 1996) makes clear how difficult it is to tease out pure examples of positive regard. Rogers is consistently "with" his clients, testing his understanding, reframing, clarifying, intent on entering and "getting" as much as possible the client's experiential world. The process is inevitably and necessarily suffused with empathy.

MEASUREMENT

As previously noted, there is an array of terms that are essentially used as synonyms in the literature. While it might be possible to delineate relatively unalloyed examples of each, in actual clinical situations these apparent distinctions blur. It is because of this that almost all research efforts focused on the effects of therapist positive regard have used measurement instruments, typically either the Barrett-Lennard Relationship Inventory (BLRI; see Barrett-Lennard, 1964, 1986) or the Truax Relationship Questionnaire (Truax & Carkhuff, 1967), that have included items reflecting each of these elements.

The BLRI consists of 64 items across four domains (level of regard, empathic understanding, unconditionality of regard, and congruence). Eight items are worded positively and eight negatively in each domain; each item is answered on a +3 (yes, strongly felt agreement) to -3 (no, strongly felt disagreement) basis. This instrument can be used by the client, the therapist, or both. Both level of regard and unconditionality have been used in research studies to investigate the influence of positive regard. Level of regard, according to Barrett-Lennard (1986, p. 440–441), "is concerned in various ways with warmth, liking/caring, and 'being drawn toward.'" Positive items include "She respects me as a person," "I feel appreciated by her," and "She is friendly and warm toward me." Representative negative items include "I feel that she disapproves of me," "She is impatient with me," and "At times she feels contempt for me."

Unconditionality of regard is explained by Barrett-Lennard (1986, p. 443) in terms of its stability "in the sense that it is not experienced as varying with or otherwise dependently linked to particular attributes of the person being regarded." Examples of positively worded items are: "How

much he likes or dislikes me is not altered by anything that I tell him about myself"; "I can (or could) be openly critical or appreciative of him without really making him feel any differently about me." Examples of negatively worded items are: "Depending on my behavior, he has a better opinion of me sometimes than he has at other times"; "Sometimes I am more worthwhile in his eyes than I am at other times."

Truax developed two separate instruments for the measurement of Rogers's facilitative conditions. One was a set of scales (with definitions and clinical examples) to be used by raters in their assessment of these conditions as manifest in either live observations or through tape recordings of sessions. There are five stages on the scale to measure nonpossessive warmth. At Stage 1, the therapist is "actively offering advice or giving clear negative regard" (Truax & Carkhuff, 1967, p. 60); at stage 5, the therapist "communicates warmth without restriction. There is a deep respect for the patient's worth as a person and his rights as a free individual" (p. 66).

Truax also developed a survey instrument to be used by clients, the Relationship Questionnaire. This measure consists of 141 items marked "true" or "false" by the client. Of these items, 73 are keyed to the concept of nonpossessive warmth; it is noteworthy, however, that many of these items are also keyed to the other two facilitative conditions of genuineness and empathy. That is, a "true" response on one item may count toward a higher score on more than one subscale. Representative items on the nonpossessive warmth scale are: "He seems to like me no matter what I say to him" (this item is also on the "genuineness" scale); "He almost always seems very concerned about me"; "He appreciates me"; "I feel that he really thinks I am worthwhile"; "Even if I were to criticize him, he would still like me"; and "Whatever I talk about is okay with him."

In addition to these scales, therapist positive regard has been assessed via instruments primarily designed to measure the strength of the alliance. In particular, the Vanderbilt Psychotherapy Process Scale (VPPS) has been used in this manner. The VPPS is "a general-purpose instrument designed to assess both positive and negative aspects of the patient's and the therapist's behavior and attitudes that are expected to facilitate or impede progress in therapy" (Suh, Strupp, & O'Malley, 1986, p. 287). Each of 80 items is rated by clinical observers on a 5-point, Likert-type scale, either from the actual therapy sessions or from video- or audiotapes of therapy. Factor analyses of these items have yielded 8 subscales, one of which, therapist warmth and friendliness, closely approximates the concept of positive regard. The specific therapist attributes rated in this subscale include "involvement" (the therapist's engagement in the patient's experience), "acceptance" (the therapist's ability to help the patient feel accepted), "warmth and friendliness," and "supportiveness" (the therapist's ability to bolster the patient's self-esteem, confidence, and hope).

CLINICAL EXAMPLES

The examples below of a therapist exhibiting positive regard and/or support must be viewed within the context of an interpersonal relationship in which mutuality of respect and caring is often present. Supporting this idea, Najavits and Strupp (1994) found that therapists with higher scores on the Helping Alliance Scale displayed more warmth and friendliness and more affirmation and understanding than therapists with lower alliance scores. Some of the case examples below are based on the transcripts of Rogers's actual sessions with clients (Farber et al., 1996). Others are written from the perspective of a more psychodynamically oriented treatment.

Case Example 1

Client: I don't know why I feel that way, I feel like everyone there is expecting me to be the life of the party and I'm the only one who isn't. I feel like none of my jokes come off right and everyone is looking at me like I've said something stupid. I always end up saying something stupid.

Therapist: It sounds like you're pretty hard on yourself.

Client: It makes me feel pathetic, that I can't just go to a party and have fun and talk to people. That I have to watch every word I say and then I end up not saying anything.

Therapist: It sounds more like you're scared than pathetic.

Client: [Pause] I'm afraid that I'll say something wrong. I feel like everyone else knows how to act socially except for me, like I didn't get the handbook or something.

Therapist: My guess is that most everyone has felt that way at some time.

In this case, the therapist responds to one self-debasing remark ("I always end up saying something stupid") with a gentle reframe and statement of support ("It sounds like you're pretty hard on yourself"). Similarly, he clarifies (or perhaps interprets) another of the client's remarks in a supportive, positively regarding way, stating that the client seemed "scared" rather than "pathetic." In addition, the therapist's final comment here ("My guess . . . ") is supportive by way of universalizing the patient's experience, stating that most everyone has felt this way at one time or another.

Case Example 2

Client: That's okay, I can outsmart people. I won't be taken advantage of. I call the shots.

Therapist: It seems important for you to be dominant in every relationship.

Client: Yes. I don't show emotion and I don't put up with it in anyone else. I don't want someone to get all hysterical and crying with me. I don't like it.

Therapist: How did you learn that being emotional is a sign of weakness?

Client: I don't know.

Therapist: What if you meet your intellectual match, if you can't "outsmart" them?

Client: [silence]

Therapist: Okay, what if someone got to you through your feelings?

Client: Last week you did. It bothered me all day.

Therapist: That you were weak?

Client: Yeah.

Therapist: I didn't see you as submissive or weak. In fact, since showing emotion is so difficult for you I saw it as quite the opposite.

In this example, the therapist initially tries to get the patient to open up about his past and discuss his "faulty strategy" of dominating relationships; it appears as if they are about to discuss transference issues. However, the therapist shifts at the end, perhaps intuitively sensing that what would be most effective for this patient (at least at this moment) is a statement of true positive regard. Thus, the therapist is affirming, suggesting that she views the client not as weak or submissive but rather the opposite, as perhaps brave for doing something that was difficult for him.

Whereas both these first two vignettes fall under the general rubric of positive regard, they also reflect aspects of what a number of authors view as therapist "support." According to Jones, Cummings, and Horowitz (1988, p. 52), in this style of interaction, the therapist offers "direct reassurance in an attempt to allay the patient's troubled feelings and to instill the hope that matters would improve, sometimes assuming a didactic or teacher-like role in relation to the patient." Similarly, Hayes and Strauss (1998, p. 942) state that support (or stabilization) may include a therapist's providing "a sense of safety, trust, respect, and security; augmenting the client's strengths, self-esteem, coping resources and social support; providing a sense of hope."

Case Example 3

Client: I feel like I won't know what to do without him. He was the only person in my life for so long.

Therapist: And there's a real ache in your heart with his dying and leaving you alone.

Client: Yes, I tried to protect him from things in life that are so bad, but I couldn't. What I did didn't matter in the end.

Therapist: The world can be a hard place.

Client: Um-hmm.

Therapist: And you wanted to protect him from it.

Client: Yes, to make it perfect, like if a bully picked on him at school, or if he fell down and scraped his knee, I wanted to have it not hurt him. Anything but hurt him.

Therapist: I guess it's hard to face that you couldn't make it better.

Client: [Begins to cry]

Therapist: It's very hard.

In some cases, reflecting back is simply a means of confirming the therapist's understanding of the patient's experience, of "checking in" with the patient in order to be sure he or she has been understood. In this case, the therapist's reflections also convey a deep sense of caring and support. The therapist's comments are devoid of judgment or interpretation of the patient's dependence on her son; rather, they communicate the therapist's warmth and understanding.

Warmth is often communicated by nonverbal behavior, for example, through such therapist gestures as smiling, vocal intonation, and body orientation. But verbal aspects of warmth, like in this case example, may include statements that indicate interest, encouragement, acceptance, concern, and generally positive affect.

Case Example 4

Client: If I OD'd right now, not a soul would shed a tear.

Therapist: That sounds like a desolate and lonely feeling. [Pause] Is it inconceivable that people might care about you?

Client: You might.

Therapist: What makes me the exception?

Client: Well, I don't know if you really are. I mean, I know that I come here for free, so you're not in it for the financial gain.

Therapist: Umm hmm.

Client: Maybe you thought I was interesting and you'd write a book about me someday and be famous. I'm a good specimen.

Therapist: Hmmm, I've been in practice for quite a while.

Client: I guess you've seen it all.

Therapist: I suppose you'll have to come up with another reason. Why do I "bother" with you?

Client: I guess I'm confused. [Pause] I find it hard to believe that you would care.

Therapist: What makes you think that?

Client: I mean, we just meet here, in your office, once a week for a set amount of time and then you can forget about me for the rest of the week.

Therapist: While it's true that our relationship has a certain structure and boundaries that I think are important, it doesn't mean that I don't care about you. And it certainly wouldn't prevent me from being very affected if you hurt yourself.

Client: I'm surprised. [Pause] I don't really know what to make of it.

Therapist: That's important because this is a crucial issue for you. Because maybe, just maybe if I, if one person can care about you, maybe another can, and just maybe, one or two more.

Here, positive regard is both subtle and manifest. The therapist states directly to the patient that he (the therapist) cares about him. Simultaneously, he is also communicating respect for the patient by remaining nonjudgmental about the patient's drug abuse. Both of these actions clearly imply that the patient is worth caring about and worthy of respect.

Case Example 5

Client: I don't know if I did the right thing, I mean he's so angry at me now. Maybe he doesn't belong in that school, but I thought it was the best thing for him.

Therapist: It sounds like it was a very difficult decision to make.

Client: It was. I don't think I've ever had to make a decision like this before, not one this important. I mean, I interviewed everyone, I talked to all the teachers, administrators . . .

Therapist: It seems like you put a lot of thought into it, considered it from many angles.

Client: Yes. It's been a terrible time. And now I feel like he trusted me and I've betrayed him.

Therapist: I can see how you might feel that way. He is too young to understand how you agonized over the choice.

Client: No, you're right, he doesn't understand yet.

In this example, the therapist decides that interpreting the patient's ambivalence about sending her son away to school would not be useful, at least at this time. Instead, the therapist senses it would be more important to express to the patient that he recognizes her effort and her fears, and that he trusts her decision making process. The therapist is being supportive of the patient's decision but also, and perhaps more importantly, conveying that she is capable of making difficult choices.

Case Example 6

Client: I feel like there are people who do care and accept me. I do, but . . .

Therapist: But the person that can't accept and value you, is actually you.

Client: Yes, mostly.

Therapist: It seems the person who is hardest on you is you.

Client: Yes. No one else would be as cruel to me as I am.

Therapist: And make such harsh judgments, you're pretty tough on yourself.

Client: Yes, I wouldn't judge my friends the way I judge myself.

Therapist: No, you're not a very good friend to yourself.

Client: No, I wouldn't treat anyone the way I treat me.

Therapist: Maybe because you can see what is lovable in them, but not in yourself. To you, you're unlovable.

Client: Maybe there are small pieces of me that are lovable.

Therapist: [pause] So there are parts of you that you see as OK, as worthy of being loved.

Client: Yes, I guess. The child in me, the child that struggled and survived. She, I, can still be playful and fun and warm.

Therapist: Those are very wonderful qualities.

Client: She's strong, a survivor.

Therapist: She's a part of you that you can hold on to.

Client: Yes.

Therapist: Do you think she'd judge you so harshly?

Client: No, she loves me.

Therapist: To this special child part of you, none of you is unforgivable.

Client: No, she loves all of me.

In this final example, the therapist is clearly conveying to the patient that she is worthy of respect and love. The therapist's positive regard for the patient may allow her to begin to view herself as the therapist does. These last two examples are good illustrations of the multiple aspects of positive regard, including affirmation, trust, understanding, warmth, interest, empathy, and respect.

RESEARCH REVIEW

Several reviews of the relationship between Rogers's three facilitative conditions and outcome have been conducted. Each bears relevance for the specific issue of how positive regard and outcome are related. The following six are among the most influential and incisive of these reviews.

1. The first review of Rogers's facilitative conditions was conducted by Truax and Carkhuff (1967) in their book, *Toward Effective Counseling and Psychotherapy*. Many of the studies they cited failed to report the associations of each of the facilitative conditions to outcome, focusing instead on the aggregate results of all three facilitative conditions taken together. However, among the early studies they reviewed that did provide data on positive regard alone was Barrett-Lennard (1962). He found a significant relationship between nonpossessive warmth and personality change among a subsample of more disturbed patients in his sample of 42. What is also noteworthy about this study is that he constructed scales for this research (actually, his doctoral dissertation) that emerged as a widely used assessment instrument for the facilitative conditions: The Barrett-Lennard Relationship Inventory.

Another seminal study that was reviewed extensively in this book was that of the Wisconsin Schizophrenic Project, a comprehensive study of 16 hospitalized schizophrenic patients begun under the aegis of Carl Rogers in 1958. Multiple publications and a wealth of data emerged from this project (including Truax & Carkhuff, 1963; Truax, Wargo, Frank, Imber, Battle, Hoehn-Saric, Nash, & Stone, 1966). However, for purposes of our review what is most relevant is the publication (Truax & Carkhuff, 1967) of simple correlations between raters' evaluations of therapists' unconditional positive regard and an aggre-gate measure of outcome (including psychological test change data, diagnostic evaluations of personality change, and measure of time spent in the hospital since initial evaluation), $r = .73$, $p < .01$. Based solely on the evaluations of test change, the correlation was determined to be .47, $p < 05$.

In all, Truax and Carkhuff (1967) reviewed 10 studies that focused on individual psychotherapy for which conclusions could be drawn on the effects of positive regard alone on therapeutic outcome. They evaluated 8 of these 10 as offering statistical evidence in favor of the hypothesis that nonpossessive warmth (the preferred term at that time for what is now more commonly called positive regard) is significantly associated with therapeutic improvement.

2. Truax and Mitchell's (1971) chapter, "Research on Certain Therapist Interpersonal Skills in Relation to Process and Outcome," was predicated on their view that "some therapists produce positive client change, but that the majority of therapists either effect no change or client deterioration" (p. 300). The table that focused on nonpossessive warmth (positive regard) summarized the results of 12 studies (across 925 clients), 10 of which were either authored or coauthored by Truax. Aggregated across all studies, the authors found a statistically significant relationship (at $p < .05$ or greater) between nonpossessive warmth and a total of 34 specific outcome measures. No study provided statistical evidence of a negative relationship between therapist-provided warmth and any outcome measure.

In one case, however, a study of 40 outpatients treated by psychiatrists in individual therapy (Truax et al., 1966), the evidence indicated a negative relationship between therapist warmth and a combined outcome measure. Somewhat surprisingly, in this study there was evidence of positive relationships between outcome and levels of both accurate empathy and genuineness. Despite the results of this one study, the overall evidence reported by Truax and Mitchell was quite positive in regard to the empirical relationship between respect/warmth and therapeutic outcome.

Nevertheless, it is important to reiterate what others (Mitchell, Bozarth, Truax, & Krauft, 1973; Parloff, Waskow, & Wolfe, 1978) later pointed out—namely, that there are multiple ways of understanding the tabulation of these data. For example, of 108 correlations between warmth/positive regard and specific outcomes noted in Truax and Mitchell's (1971) report, only 34 were reported as significantly positive. That is, while none of these correlations were significantly negative, relatively few were significantly positive.

3. In a follow-up review, Mitchell, Bozarth, and Krauft (1977) identified 15 studies that met their criteria for consideration. Somewhat surprisingly, one of their criteria was that only raters' assessments of tape segments or transcripts of sessions were to be used, not client or therapist perceptions. This position, consistent with that proposed earlier by Truax and Carkhuff (1967), holds that patients are unable to accurately perceive the affective quality of the therapeutic relationship—that is, their perceptions of the therapist are necessarily distorted. Eleven of these studies investigated the relationship between positive regard (here termed nonpossessive warmth) and outcome. According to Mitchell and colleagues (1977), at most four of these studies offered support for the proposition that higher levels of therapist-provided warmth lead to better outcome. However, according to the authors, none of the studies provided evidence either for or against the more cogent hypothesis that minimally facilitative levels of positive regard lead to positive outcome.

4. To the eleven studies on the relationship of warmth/positive regard to outcome reviewed by Truax and Mitchell (1971), Orlinsky and Howard (1978) added 12 more. They showed that approximately two-thirds of the studies on warmth indicated a significant positive association with therapeutic outcome, with the remaining one-third showing mostly null results. But they also added several caveats, notably that the uneven quality and methodological flaws in the research made any firm conclusions suspect.

5. As part of a remarkably comprehensive review of process and outcome in psychotherapy, Orlinsky and Howard (1986) conducted separate reviews of studies evaluating the effects of "therapist support" and "therapist affirmation." As others (such as Beutler, Crago, & Arizmendi, 1986; Gurman, 1977) had advocated, they too strongly endorsed a position that evaluation of any process-outcome study must include consideration of rater perspective on both the process and outcome variables. Thus, in the case of therapist positive regard, it becomes critical to understand whether this variable was evaluated from the perspective of client, therapist, or nonparticipant observer/rater and whether the chosen outcome variables were evaluated from these perspectives or, alternatively, via an objective score (e.g., MMPI).

The variable of therapist support does not directly stem from a Rogerian perspective, although it does share many common elements with positive regard. Therapist support implies a sense of active encouragement on the part of the therapist—more of an "I'm here for you," "I believe in you," or "I think you can do the work and achieve some good results here." Orlinsky and Howard (1986) identified 11 studies that included a support/encouragement variable; within this group of studies they focused on 25 separate findings. That is, some of these studies included multiple process and/or outcome perspectives that were evaluated independently. Their conclusion was, "Although 6 of the 25 are significantly positive findings and none are negative, more than three-quarters show a null association between specific therapist efforts to give support and patient outcome. Thus, while it may be occasionally helpful, this mode of intervention does not appear to have much consistent impact" (p. 326).

The authors identified 94 findings on the association between "therapist affirmation" (essentially warmth, caring, and acceptance) and outcome, with more than half (53%) demonstrating a significant relationship between these sets of variables. Underscoring their emphasis on considering the perspective of raters, they noted that "the proportion of positive findings is highest across all outcome categories when therapist warmth and acceptance are observed from the patient's process perspective" (p. 348). That is, in 30 cases where the patient's ratings of therapist positive regard were used, 20 outcome scores were positively correlated with these ratings (aggregated over the outcome perspectives of patient, therapist, rater, and objective score), and no outcome scores (regardless of the source) were significantly negatively correlated with patient ratings of therapist positive regard. They also noted that, in the 12 cases when therapists rated both their own level of positive regard and patient outcome, significant associations were obtained all 12 times. As Orlinsky and Howard noted, "When therapists feel they are being especially warm, they tend to be more satisfied with the outcome of their treatment" (p. 352).

6. The most recent review of therapist positive regard was conducted by Orlinsky and colleagues (1994) in the fourth edition of *Handbook of Psychotherapy and Behavior Change*. The relevant studies were again organized here under the rubric of "therapist affirmation," explained by the authors as a variable that includes aspects of acceptance, nonpossessive warmth, or positive regard. The authors summarized the results of 154 findings (including those already noted in the earlier Orlinsky & Howard [1986] review), drawn from a total of 76 studies. They found that 56% of the findings were positive, and that, again, the findings based on the patients' process perspective (that is, the patient's sense of the therapist's positive regard) yielded even a higher rate of positive therapeutic outcomes, 65%.

When patients rated the therapist's positive regard and also rated outcome, a significant positive association was found almost 74% of the time (14 of 19 times); when patients rated the therapist's positive regard but therapists rated outcome, a significant positive association was found an even higher percentage (80%) of the time (12/15). However, when patients rated the therapist's positive regard and an objective score (e.g., MMPI) was used to assess outcome, a positive association was found only 43% of the time (12/21).

In fact, when the findings for patient ratings of the therapist are removed from consideration, the association between therapist positive regard (as assessed by either the therapist or an outside rater) and outcome (regardless of source) is surprisingly mixed. Therapist ratings and outcome were found to be positively associated in 19 studies, but in 19 other studies the association was found to be nonsignificant, and in one study the association was found to be significantly negative. Therapist ratings of their own positive regard were far more likely to be positively associated with outcome when therapists also rated outcome; under these conditions, a positive finding occurred 75% of the time (12 of 16 studies). Similarly, observer ratings and outcome were found to be positively associated in 27 studies, but in 24

other studies the association was nonsignificant, and in one study the association was significantly negative.

"Overall," Orlinsky and colleagues (1994, p. 326) concluded, "nearly 90 findings indicate that therapist affirmation is a significant factor, but considerable variation in ES [effect size] suggests that the contribution of this factor to outcome differs according to specific conditions." Indeed, among the 42 effect sizes reported in this 1994 review (18 were either not reported or not computed), 40 were below .50, and 28 were below .20.

RECENT STUDIES ON POSITIVE REGARD

In table 9.1, we summarize the results of 16 studies published since 1990 in which the therapist's positive regard of the patient has been analyzed in terms of its association to therapeutic outcome. Perhaps what is most surprising is the paucity of studies that have examined this relationship. As noted earlier, in the last decades, the focus of attention has shifted toward an examination of a related concept, that of the therapeutic alliance (see Horvath & Bedi, chap. 3 in this volume). That is, both theoretically and empirically, psychotherapy has shifted to what many have termed a "two-person" field. Similarly, because the direct influence of person-centered therapy seems to have waned, researchers are substituting measures of therapeutic alliance (seen by most researchers as essentially pantheoretical) for measures of therapist positive regard (seen as more directly embedded in the theoretical tradition espoused by Rogers and his followers). Thus, use of either the Barrett-Lennard Scales or the Truax Scales—instruments that explicitly measure therapist warmth or positive regard—have been far less widely used in studies in the past decade than in the first several decades of psychotherapy research.

One consequence of this trend is that it becomes more difficult to tease out the specific contribution of therapist regard in studies that use instruments that assess the alliance. Even those alliance measures such as the VPPS (Suh et al., 1986) that have subscales (such as therapist warmth and friendliness) that seem to tap the same construct as positive regard may be problematic as a measure of this variable. In completing the entire scale, patients may be far more cued to thinking about the nature of the relationship than the nature of the therapist's characteristics per se. Parenthetically, we would also add that other alliance subscales (for example, the Helping Alliance Type I of the Penn Helping Alliance Rating Method; see Morgan, Luborsky, Crits-Christoph, Curtis, & Solomon, 1982) are problematic in that items that comprise the subscale reflect not only the therapist's helpful attitude but also positive outcome (the patient's experience of receiving help), thereby confounding results of analyses investigating the relationship between warmth/positive regard and outcome.

In examining the box score at the bottom of table 9.1, several patterns stand out. First, no recent study has found a negative relationship between positive regard and outcome. Second, the results are essentially evenly split between positive and nonsignificant effects. That is, 49% (27/55) of all reported associations were significantly positive, while 51% (28/55) did not achieve significance. It is important to note, however, that the majority of nonsignificant findings occur when an objective rater evaluates therapeutic outcome. For example, when patients rate positive regard but an objective rater evaluates outcome, there are two positive findings but five nonsignificant findings. Conversely, when patients rate their own outcome, there are 10 positive findings and only two nonsignificant findings. Thus, the results of positive regard can be considered more definitive and encouraging when we take the patient's perspective on outcome. Third, and as noted by previous reviewers, when the patient rates both the therapist's positive regard and treatment outcome, a positive association between these variables is especially likely. Among studies that have been conducted since 1990, this has occurred in 7 of 8 data points. Lastly, the effect sizes for the significant results tend to be modest, with the larger effect sizes occurring when positive regard is assessed in terms of its association to length of stay in therapy rather than outcome per se (see, for example, Najavits & Strupp, 1994). If this finding continues to hold across future studies, it would suggest that the effectiveness of positive regard might lie especially in its ability to

facilitate a long-term working relationship. Among the studies in this table, two merit particular attention in that they address the relationship between positive regard and outcome relatively directly: Najavits and Strupp (1994) and Conte, Ratto, Clutz, and Karasu (1995). Najavits and Strupp, using a group of 16 experienced psychodynamic therapists treating 80 patients once weekly for 25 weeks, distinguished between "more effective" and "less effective" therapists based on specific behaviors associated with each. Effectiveness was defined in terms of outcome scores on a variety of measures, including the Symptom Check List (SCL)–90, and in terms of length of stay. Therapist behaviors were assessed via multiple measures (including the Luborsky Helping Alliance Scale, the VPPS, the Vanderbilt Negative Indicators Scale, and the BLRI) and from multiple perspectives (therapist, patient, independent observers, and supervisors). None of the 34 process variables studied was significant in regard to outcome when outcome was summed across sessions 3, 8, 16, and 22. That is, none of the subscale nor total scale scores discriminated significantly between more and less effective therapists in terms of outcome across these sessions. However, 8 of these 34 variables were significant in regard to length of stay, including the Warmth and Friendliness subscale of the VPPS, and the Structural Analysis of Social Behavior (SASB) cluster, Affirming and Understanding from both patient and therapist perspectives.

Conte et al. (1995) surveyed 138 outpatients who had already terminated therapy. Among other survey items, these ex-clients were asked to indicate the extent to which they continued to experience their presenting problems at discharge, the extent to which they believed they were generally helped, and the extent to which they were satisfied with their therapist. A fourth outcome measure used was the Psychiatric Outpatient Rating Scale (PORS), a scale completed by therapists. The terminated patients in this study were also asked to rate 18 characteristics of their therapist, including the extent to which he or she "respected me," "accepted me," "liked me," and "was encouraging." The correlations between "respected me" and the four outcome measures (symptom improvement, felt generally helped, satisfaction with therapist, and PORS score) were .40,

Table 9.1. Recent Studies Investigating the Association of Therapist Positive Regard or Support to Outcome (1991–2001)

Author	Sample	Sample Description	Independent Variable (Scale)	Perspective
Bachelor (1991)	$N = 47$	University outpatient service Multiple theoretical orientations	Penn Helping Alliance Rating Method: Therapist Warmth & Friendliness Scale	P
Coady (1991)	$N = 9$ 5 "good" outcome vs. 4 "poor" outcome	Outpatient clinic Time limited individual psychodynamic psychotherapy	SASB: Helping & Protecting Subscale SASB: Affirmation & Understanding Subscale	R
Conte, Ratto, Clutz, & Karasu (1995)	$N = 138$	Discharged outpatients w/ affective disorders, schizophrenia, substance abuse, 95% in individual psychotherapy	Therapist Satisfaction Scale created for this study, relevant variables: Respected me, liked me, accepted me, gave me full attention	P
Chisholm (1988)	$N = 150$	University clinic outpatients	VPPS: Therapist Warmth & Friendliness Subscale, Negative Therapist Attitude Subscale VNIS: Therapist lack of respect subscale CALPAS: Therapist Understanding & Involvement Subscale	R R R
Cramer & Takens (1992)	$N = 63$	Individual long-term psychotherapy, predominantly psychoanalytically oriented and person-centered	Questionnaires: 6 items assessing therapist acceptance (measured at sessions 2 and 6)	P (2) (6)
Gaston et al. (1991)	$N = 91$	Patients with major depressive disorder ages 60 to 80 in cognitive, behavioral, and brief dynamic treatment	CALPAS: Therapist Negative Contribution Subscale.	P
Green & Herget (1991)	$N = 22$	Clients: selected as "difficult," most had been in tx before w/problems lasting 3 yrs/+	6-point Likert scale created for this study measuring therapist warmth	R

Dependent Variable (Scale)	Perspective	Outcome	Effect Size[a]
Global Rating Scale	R	Therapist Warmth and Friendliness (P)/Global Rating Scale (R): +	Therapist Warmth and Friendliness (P)/Global Rating Scale (R): .53
Derogatis's Symptom Index Beck's Mood Scale Weissman's Social Adjustment Scale	(R P R) = C	Helping & Protecting (R)/(C): + Affirming & Understanding (R)/(C): 0	Helping & Protecting (R)/(C): .75[c] Affirming & Understanding (R)/(C): A/C
Symptoms and Problems Questionnaire (sx quest.) PORS GAS	P T R	Liked me (P)/sx quest. (P): + Liked me (P)/PORS (T): + Liked me (P)/GAS (R): 0 Accepted me (P)/sx quest. (P): + Accepted me (P)/PORS (T): + Accepted me (P)/GAS (R): 0 Respected me (P)/sx quest. (P): + Respected me (P)/PORS (T): + Repected me (P)/GAS (R): 0 Gave me full attention (P)/sx quest. (P): + Gave me full attention (P)/PORS (T): 0 Gave me full attention (P)/GAS (R): 0	Liked me (P)/sx quest. (P): .44 Liked me (P)/PORS (T): .22 Like me/GAS (R): .07 Accepted me (P)/sx quest. (P): .44 Accepted me (P)/PORS (T): .23 Accepted me (P)/GAS (R): .01 Respected me (P)/sx quest. (P): .40 Respected me (P)/PORS (T): .40 Respected me (P)/GAS (R): .00 Gave me full attention (P)/sx quest. (P): .27 Gave me full attention (P)/PORS (T): .12 Gave me full attention (P)/GAS (R): .00
Early termination vs. completers	I	Therapist warmth & friendliness scale (R)/Completers (I): + Therapist negative attitudes (R)/Completers (I): 0 Therapist lack of respect (R)/Completers (I): 0 Therapist Understanding & Involvement (R)/Premature terminators (I): 0	Therapist warmth & friendliness scale (R)/Completers (I): .59[c] Therapist negative attitudes (R)/Completers (I): .54 Therapist lack of respect (R)/Completers (I): .39 Therapist Understanding & Involvement (R)/Premature terminators (I): −.14
Questionnaires: regarding therapeutic progress (measured at sessions 2 and 6)	P (2) (6) T (2) (6)	Acceptance (P2)/Progress (P2) = + Acceptance (P2)/Progress (P6) = 0 Acceptance (P2)/Progress (T2) = 0 Acceptance (P2)/Progress (T6) = 0 Acceptance (P6)/Progress (P2) = + Acceptance (P6)/Progress (P6) = + Acceptance (P6)/Progress (T2) = 0 Acceptance (P6)/Progress (T6) = +	Acceptance (P2)/Progress (P2) = .45 Acceptance (P2)/Progress (P6) = .26 Acceptance (P2)/Progress (T2) = .10 Acceptance (P2)/Progress (T6) = .22 Acceptance (P6)/Progress (P2) = .52 Acceptance (P6)/Progress (P6) = .49 Acceptance (P6)/Progress (T2) = .07 Acceptance (P6)/Progress (T6) = .45
Beck Depression Inventory (BDI)	S	Therapist negative contribution (P)/BDI (S) = 0	Therapist negative contribution (P)/BDI (S) = A/C
Goal Attainment Scaling (GAS) Global Outcome Ratings: Patient, rater and therapist outcome ratings. (both measured at 1 month and 3 yrs)	P P T R	Therapist warmth (R)/GAS (P) at 1 month: + Therapist warmth (R)/GAS (P) at 3 years: + Therapist warmth (R)/GOR (P) at 1 month: + Therapist warmth (R)/GOR (T) at 1 month: +	Therapist warmth (R)/GAS (P) at 1 month: .58 Therapist warmth (R)/GAS (P) at 3 years: .79 Therapist warmth (R)/GOR (P) at 1 month: .63 Therapist warmth (R)/GOR (T) at 1 month: .63

Table 9.1. (Continued)

Author	Sample	Sample Description	Independent Variable (Scale)	Perspective
Hayes & Strauss (1998)	$N = 32$	Depressed outpatients	The Rating Scale of Therapy Change Processes: Support/Stabilization	R
Henry, Schacht, & Strupp (1990)	$N = 7$	Outpatients "Good" vs. "Poor" outcome	SASB: Affirming & Understanding Subscale, Helping & Protecting Subscale	R
Hynan (1990)	$N = 31$	University counseling center Primarily patients w/anxiety and depression	Questionnaire: Reasons for term (including client perceptions of therapist attributes and behaviors warmth, and respect)	P
Meyer (1990)		Cited in Orlinsky et al. (1994)		R R
Najavits & Strupp (1994)	$N = 80$	Outpatients Ages 24–64 87% axis I 67% axis II	SASB: Affirmation & Understanding LHAS (HA): Warmth VPPS: Warmth & Friendliness	P T R R
Quintana & Meara (1990)	$N = 48$	University clinic outpatients	SASB: Cluster "focus on other" (e.g., Affirmation & Understanding Subscale)	P
Russell, Bryant, Estrada (1996)	$N = 5$	5 Children, diagnosed with dysthymia, PTSD, ODD, PDD Predominantly psychodynamic orientation	LCPPS: Positive evaluation SICS: Positive affect	R R
Schindler (1991)		Cited in Orlinsky et al. (1994)		P
Williams & Chambless (1990)	$N = 33$	Patients diagnosed with agoraphobia w/panic attacks treated with *in vivo* exposure	Therapist Rating Scale (TRS): Unconditionally accepting Subscale, Caring & Involved Subscale	P

Dependent Variable (Scale)	Perspective	Outcome	Effect Size[a]
GAS BDI & HRSD composite score	T P	Support (R)/GAS (T): 0 Support (R)/composite (P): 0	Support (R)/GAS (T): .29 Support (R)/composite (P): .24
SLC-90	S	Affirming & Understanding (R)/SLC-90 (S): 0 Helping & Protecting (R)/SLC-90 (S): 0	Affirming & Understanding (R)/SLC-90 (S): A/C Helping & Protecting (R)/SLC-90 (S): 0
Early vs. Late Terminators	S	Therapist respect for client (P)/Late Terminators (S): + Therapist warmth (P)/Late Terminators (S): +	Therapist respect for client (P)/Late Terminators (S): .60 Therapist warmth (P)/Late Terminators (S): .62
	S S	(R/S): + (R/S): 0	Affirmation (R/S): .66 Affirmation (R/S): .22
Length of treatment SLC-90 GAS PSS GOR (Outcome Composite)	I (P T, R P P, T, R) = C	(Across sessions: 3,8,16,22): Warmth, LHAS (HA) (R)/Outcome (C): = 0 Warmth & Friendliness, VPPS (R)/Outcome (C): = 0 Affirmation & Understanding SASB, (P)/Outcome (C): = 0 Affirmation & Understanding, SASB (T)/Outcome (C): = 0 (Across sessions: 3,8,16,22): Warmth, LHAS (HA) (R)/Length of stay (I): = + Warmth & Friendliness, VPPS (R)/Length of stay (I): = + Affirmation & Understanding, SASB, (P)/Length of stay (I): = + Affirmation & Understanding, SASB (T)/Length of stay (I): = +	(Across sessions: 3,8,16,22):[c] Warmth, LHAS (R)/Outcome (C): = NA Warmth & Friendliness, VPPS (R)/Outcome (C): = NA Affirmation & Understanding SASB, (P)/Outcome (C): = NA Affirmation & Understanding, SASB (T)/Outcome (C): = NA (Across sessions: 3,8,16,22): Warmth, LHAS (R)/Length of stay (I): = .78 Warmth & Friendliness, VPPS (R)/Length of stay (I): = .78 Affirmation & Understanding, SASB, (P)/Length of stay (I): = .77 Affirmation & Understanding, SASB (T)/Length of stay (I): = .82
SASB: Cluster "focus on self" (e.g., Disclosing & Expressing)	S	Focus on other–Affirmation (P)/Focus on Self-Disclosing (S): +	Affirmation (P)/Disclosing (S): .54[c]
High vs. low quality sessions by "objective rating systems"	R	Positive evaluation, LCPPS (R)/Rating system (R): 0 Positive affect, SICS (R)/Rating system (R): 0	Positive evaluation, LCPPS (R)/Rating system (R): 0 Positive affect, SICS (R)/Rating system (R): 0
	S	(P/S): 0	Affirmation (P/S): .35
Behavioral Avoidance Test (BAT)	R	Unconditionally accepting (P)/BAT (R): 0 Caring & Involved (P)/BAT (R): +	Unconditionally accepting (P)/BAT (R): .05 Caring & Involved (P)/BAT (R): .17

(*continued*)

Table 9.1. (Continued)

| | OUTCOME | | | | | | | | | | | | | | | | | | | | |
| PROCESS | Patient (P) | | | Therapist (T) | | | Rater (R) | | | Objectively determined index (I) | | | Psychometric score (S) | | | Combined/ composite score (C) | | | Total | | |
	−	0	+	−	0	+	−	0	+	−	0	+	−	0	+	−	0	+	−	0	+
Patient	0	1	7	0	4	4	0	5	2	0	1	1	0	2	3	0	1	0	0	14	17
Therapist	0	0	0	0	0	0	0	0	0	0	0	1	0	0	0	0	1	0	0	1	1
Rater	0	1	3	0	1	1	0	2	0	0	3	3	0	3	1	0	3	1	0	13	9
Total	0	2	10	0	5	5	0	7	2	0	4	5	0	5	4	0	5	1	0	28	27

Scale Abbreviations: BAT: Behavioral Avoidance Test; BDI: Beck Depression Inventory; BSI: Brief Symptom Inventory; CALPAS: California Psychotherapy Process Scale; GAS: Global Adjustment Scale; GOR: Global Outcome Rating; HRSD: Hamilton Rating Scale for Depression; LCPPS: Loyola Child Psychotherapy Process Scales; LHAS (HA): Luborsky Helping Alliance Scale; PSS: Problem Severity Scale; PORS: Psychiatric Outpatient Rating Scale; SASB: Structural Analysis of Social Behavior; SICS: Stuttgart Interactional Category System; SLC-90: Symptom Check list 90; TRS: Therapist Rating Scale; TSS: Therapist Satisfaction Scale; VPPS: Vanderbilt Psychotherapy Project Scales; WAI: Working Alliance Inventory; VNIS: Vanderbilt Negative Indicators Scale

P = Patient ratings; T = Therapist ratings; R = Ratings by nonparticipant raters; I = Objectively determined index; S = Psychometric test score; C = Combined perspectives; + = Positively related to outcome; − = Negatively related to outcome; 0 = No significant association; A/C = Effect size not available

[a]As per current convention, effect size was calculated as r rather than r^2.

[b]Data were also presented for session 3; however, it was our judgment that including these findings in addition to the ones presented here would have overrepresented the same datebase.

[c]Effect sizes are based on F-tests.

.48, .66, and .40, all significant at the .001 level. The correlations between "accepted me" and these four outcome measures were .44, .53, .65, and .23, respectively; the first three associations significant at the .001 level, the last one significant at .01. The correlations for "liked me" were .44, .48, .64, and .22, respectively; the first three of these were significant at the .001 level, the last correlation was significant at the .05 level. And lastly, the correlations for "was encouraging": .41, .56, .75, and .18; again the first three of these analyses were significant at the .001 level, the last analysis was significant at the .05 level. While several authors (for example, Sirles, 1984) have noted that those who are most satisfied with their therapy are most likely to return surveys, these results nevertheless suggest that therapist characteristics akin to positive regard are at least moderately associated with ex-clients' perceptions of improvement.

LIMITATIONS OF THE RESEARCH REVIEWED

Among the first group of researchers to point out significant methodological flaws in studies attempting to validate the purported relationship between Rogers's three facilitative conditions and outcome was Mitchell et al. (1977). They noted, for example, that in many studies the number of therapists was quite small and that some therapists may have been aware of the research hypotheses. They also suggested that some of the studies had employed instruments of questionable validity. Their most potent criticism, however, was that, in most studies, it was impossible to determine how many of the therapists were functioning at even minimally facilitative levels and that the proportions of truly high and truly low therapists (in regard to these facilitative conditions) were unknown in every study to date. Their argument was that the true hypothesis of interest—one that had yet to be tested sufficiently—was that *high* (or at least minimally facilitative) levels of these conditions lead to client improvement and that inspecting simple correlations between outcome and these facilitative conditions was irrelevant to the testing of Rogers's postulates. They contended, therefore, that the relationship between empathy, warmth, genuineness, and outcome is "exceedingly more complex than was thought earlier . . . it may be that the interpersonal skills are related differentially to client change as a function of the different stages of therapy, the nature of the client's problems, and the integration of the interpersonal skills with other therapist variables" (p. 486).

Gurman (1977) also pointed to substantial flaws in the research linking the three facilitative conditions to outcome. His position was that virtually all studies in the area were inappropriate in that they were based on nonparticipant observers' ratings of these conditions. This empirical perspective, argued Gurman, failed to honor one of Rogers's basic assumptions: that whatever relational conditions the therapist provides must be communicated to (and assumedly experienced by) the client. As Gurman noted, "The theoretical inappropriateness of much of this empirical literature is all the more striking in that the majority of it has been conducted by Rogers's own students and by others who adhere to client-centered therapy" (p. 505). Thus, client perceptions of these conditions must be assessed for a true test of the facilitative conditions-outcome hypothesis. Gurman demonstrated that there is "little convincing evidence of agreement" between patients' and therapists' perceptions of the therapeutic relationship, and that there is "inconsistent evidence" regarding the presumed positive relationship between ratings of the therapeutic relationship by patients and trained judges (pp. 517–518). Gurman also argued, as did Bergin and Jaspar (1969), that the instruments use to assess any of Rogers's facilitative conditions were appropriate primarily, if not exclusively, for those practicing within a client-centered mode.

Parloff, Waskow, and Wolfe (1978) cast doubt on Truax and Mitchell's (1971) earlier, positive conclusions regarding the relationship between Rogers's three variables and therapeutic outcome. Indeed, they regarded these conclusions as "somewhat injudicious" in that they "failed to give sufficient weight to the obvious inconsistencies among the reports they cited" (p. 245). Among other specific criticisms leveled, they suggested that no attempt had yet been made—either by these authors or others investigating this area—to delineate what specific outcomes might be expected as a consequence of the provision of each of these conditions. As Gurman (1977) did, they also criticized the methodology of many of these studies,

specifically the measurement of these conditions by outside raters rather than by patients themselves—a measurement decision, they noted, that was in direct contradiction to Rogers's original contention that what mattered most was clients' perceptions of these conditions. Similarly, they noted that measuring any of these conditions is complicated by the fact that the "levels" of each may vary by patient as well as by what point in therapy these units are measured. "It must be concluded," they noted, "that the unqualified claim that 'high' levels (absolute or relative) of accurate empathy, warmth, and genuineness (independent of the source of rating or the nature of the instrument) represent the 'necessary and sufficient' conditions for effective therapy (independent of the outcome measures or criterion) is not supported" (p. 249).

In the third edition of Handbook of Psychotherapy and Behavior Change, Beutler et al. (1986) reviewed therapist variables in psychotherapy, echoing some methodological concerns that had been raised previously. One point of emphasis in their review was that outcome measures based on patient ratings might reflect a halo effect. That is, as Gurman (1977) pointed out previously, patient ratings of therapist variables are invariably more strongly related to positive outcomes than are independent raters' evaluations.

THERAPEUTIC PRACTICES

The therapist's ability to provide positive regard seems to be significantly associated with therapeutic success—at least when we take the patient's perspective on therapeutic outcome. However, virtually all the significant findings bear relatively modest effect sizes, suggestive of the fact that, like the therapeutic alliance, it is a significant but not exhaustive part of the process-outcome equation. Extrapolating somewhat from the data, we conclude that therapists' provision of positive regard is strongly indicated in clinical practice. We assume that, at a minimum, it "sets the stage" for other mutative interventions and that, at least in some cases, it may be sufficient by itself to effect positive change. Moreover, there seems to be virtually no empirically supported reason to withhold positive regard. In this vein, we are reminded of the oft-heard sentiment in contemporary psychoanalytic circles that one of Kohut's major contributions to the field was to provide a theoretical justification for being kind to one's patients.

Results from several decades of studies in this area also suggest that, similar to the situation with the therapeutic alliance, it is the patient's perspective of the therapist's positive regard that is most often associated with good outcome. One simple clinical conclusion we can draw from this finding is that therapists should not be content with feeling good about their patients but instead should ensure that their positive feelings are communicated to them. This does not have to translate to a stream of compliments nor to a gushing of positive sentiment that, in fact, may overwhelm or even terrify some clients; rather, it speaks to the need for therapists to communicate a caring, respectful, positive attitude that serves to affirm a client's basic sense of worth. To many, if not most, clients the inner conviction that "my therapist really cares about me" likely serves a critical function, especially in times of stress.

That there is considerable variance in the findings linking positive regard to outcome suggests that, in addition to methodological inconsistencies, (1) therapists vary in the extent to which they are able to convey positive regard to their patient (some therapists are better at providing this condition than others); (2) clients vary in the extent to which they need and/or benefit from a therapist's positive regard; and (3) whatever level of positive regard a particular therapist generally functions at is influenced by characteristics of his or her patients as well as by the current state of that particular therapy. Thus, virtually all therapists, whether or not they are naturally skilled at providing positive regard to patients, need to self-monitor this tendency and adjust as a function of the needs of particular patients and particular clinical situations. In this regard, too, we suspect that the inevitable ruptures in the therapeutic alliance (Safran, Crocker, McMain, & Murray, 1990) that occur over the course of therapy are the result not only of a therapist's technical errors but also of the therapist's occasional inability to demonstrate minimally facilitative levels of positive regard.

We believe that, consistent with much of the current research in psychotherapy, future studies in this field should be concerned with the question of specificity: for which patients, presenting with which types of problems, is the provision of therapist regard most important, and for which is this variable of relatively minor import? Similarly, investigations should focus on the interaction between modes of therapy and positive regard (for example, is there a more potent interaction, in terms of effect on outcome, between psychodynamic therapy and positive regard than there is between cognitive-behavioral therapy and positive regard?).

Despite the current zeitgeist emphasizing more technical (technique-oriented, manually driven) therapeutic interventions, it is difficult to envision the future of psychotherapy without imagining therapists who are deeply caring, compassionate, supportive, and affirming of their patients. The research indicating a positive, albeit modest, association between therapist positive regard for patients and outcome is testament to the importance of a therapist's humanity and also testament to the importance of relational factors in the outcome of psychotherapy.

REFERENCES

Bachelor, A. (1991). Comparison and relationship to outcome of diverse dimensions of the helping alliance as seen by client and therapist. *Psychotherapy, 28*(4), 534–549.

Barrett-Lennard, G. T. (1962). Dimensions of the client's experience of his therapist associated with personality change. *Psychological Monographs, 76*(43, Whole number 562).

Barrett-Lennard, G. T. (1964). *The Relationship Inventory. Form OS-M-64 and OS-F-64 Form MO-M-64 and MO-F-64.* University of New England, Australia.

Barrett-Lennard, G. (1986). The relationship inventory now: Issues and advances in theory, method and use. In L. S. Greenberg & W. M. Pinsof (Eds.), *The psychotherapeutic process: A research handbook* (pp. 439–476). New York: Guilford.

Beck, J. S. (1995). *Cognitive therapy: Basics and beyond.* New York: Guilford.

Bergin, A. E., & Garfield, S. L. (Eds.) (1971). *Handbook of psychotherapy and behavior change: An empirical analysis.* New York: Wiley.

Bergin, A. E., & Jaspar, L. G. (1969). Correlates of empathy in psychotherapy: A replication. *Journal of Abnormal Psychology, 74*, 447–481.

Beutler, L. E., Crago, M., & Arizmendi, T. G. (1986). Therapist variables in psychotherapy process and outcome. In S. L. Garfield and A. E. Bergin (Eds.), *Handbook of psychotherapy and behavior change* (3rd ed., pp. 257–310). New York: Wiley.

Beutler, L. E., Machado, P. P. P., & Neufeldt, S. A. (1994). Therapist variables. In S. L. Garfield and A. E. Bergin (Eds.), *Handbook of psychotherapy and behavior change* (4th ed., pp. 229–269). New York: Wiley.

Chisholm, S. M. (1998). *A comparison of the therapeutic alliances of premature terminators versus therapy completers.* Unpublished doctoral dissertation, Kent State University, Kent, OH.

Coady, N. F. (1991). The association between client and therapist interpersonal processes and outcomes in psychodynamic psychotherapy. *Research on Social Work Practice, 1*(2), 122–138.

Conte, H. R., Ratto, R., Clutz, K., & Karasu, T. B. (1995). Determinants of outpatients' satisfaction with therapists. *The Journal of Psychotherapy Practice and Research, 4*, 43–51.

Cramer, D., & Takens, R. J. (1992). Therapeutic relationship and progress in the first six sessions of individual psychotherapy: A panel analysis. *Counseling Psychology Quarterly, 5*(1), 25–36.

Farber, B. A., Brink, D. C., & Raskin, P. M. (1996). *The psychotherapy of Carl Rogers: Cases and commentary.* New York: Guilford.

Gaston, L., Marmar, C. R., Gallagher, D., & Thompson, L. W. (1991). Alliance prediction of outcome beyond in-treatment symptomatic change as psychotherapy processes. *Psychotherapy Research, 1*, 104–113.

Green, R. J., & Herget, M. (1991). Outcomes of systemic/strategic team consultation: The importance of therapist warmth and active structuring. *Family Process, 30*, 321–336.

Gurman, A. (1977). The patient's perception of the therapeutic relationship. In A. S. Gurman & A. M. Razin (Eds.), *Effective psychotherapy* (pp. 503–543). New York: Pergamon.

Hayes, A. M., & Strauss, J. L. (1998). Dynamic systems theory as a paradigm for the study of change in psychotherapy: An application to cognitive therapy for depression. *Journal of Consulting and Clinical Psychology, 66*(6), 939–947.

Henry, W. P., Schacht, T. E., & Strupp, H. H. (1990). Patient and therapist introject, interpersonal process, and differential psychotherapy outcome. *Journal of Consulting and Clinical Psychology, 58*(6), 768–774.

Hynan, D. J. (1990). Client reasons and experiences in treatment that influence termination of psychotherapy. *Journal of Clinical Psychology, 46*(6), 891–895.

Jones, E. E., Cummings, J. D., & Horowitz, M. J. (1988). Another look at the nonspecific hypothesis of therapeutic effectiveness. *Journal of Consulting and Clinical Psychology, 56*, 48–55.

Lietaer, G. (1984). Unconditional positive regard: A controversial basic attitude in client-centered therapy. In R. F. Levant & J. M. Shlien (Eds.), *Client-centered therapy and the person-centered approach: New directions in theory, research, and practice* (pp. 41–58). New York: Praeger.

Meyer, A. E. (1990). *Nonspecific and common factors in treatment outcome: Another myth?* Paper presented at the annual meeting of the Society for Psychotherapy Research, Wintergreen, VA.

Mitchell, S. A., & Aron, L. (1999). *Relational psychoanalysis.* New York: Analytic.

Mitchell, K., Bozarth, J., & Krauft, C. (1977). A reappraisal of the therapeutic effectiveness of accurate empathy, non-possessive warmth and genuineness. In A. S. Gurman & A. M. Razin (Eds.), *Effective psychotherapy* (pp. 482–502). New York: Pergamon.

Mitchell, K., Bozarth, J., Truax, C., & Krauft, C. (1973). *Antecedents to psychotherapeutic outcome.* Arkansas Rehabilitation Research and Training Center, University of Arkansas (NIMH Final Report, MH 12306).

Morgan, R., Luborsky, L., Crits-Christoph, P., Curtis, H., & Solomon, J. (1982). Predicting the outcomes of psychotherapy by the Penn Helping Alliance Rating Method. *Archives of General Psychiatry, 39*, 397–402.

Najavits, L. M., & Strupp, H. H. (1994). Differences in the effectiveness of psychodynamic therapists: A process-outcome study. *Psychotherapy, 31*, 114–123.

Orlinsky, D. E., Grawe, K., & Parks, B. K. (1994). Process and outcome in psychotherapy—Noch einmal. In A. E. Bergin & S. L. Garfield (Eds.), *Handbook of psychotherapy and behavior change* (4th ed., pp. 270–376). New York: Wiley.

Orlinsky, D. E., & Howard, K. (1978). The relation

of process to outcome in psychotherapy. In S. L. Garfield & A. E. Bergin (Eds.), *Handbook of psychotherapy and behavior change* (2nd ed., pp. 283–329). New York: Wiley.

Orlinsky, D. E., & Howard, K. (1986). Process and outcome in psychotherapy. In S. L. Garfield & A. E. Bergin (Eds.), *Handbook of psychological behavior and change* (3rd ed., pp. 311–381). New York: Wiley.

Parloff, M. B., Waskow, I. E., & Wolfe, B. E. (1978). Research on therapist variables in relation to process and outcome. In S. L. Garfield & A. E. Bergin (Eds.), *Handbook of psychotherapy and behavior change* (2nd ed., pp. 233–282). New York: Wiley.

Quintana, S. M., & Meara, N. M. (1990). Internalization of therapeutic relationships in short-term psychotherapy. *Journal of Counseling Psychology, 2,* 123–130.

Rogers, C. R. (1942). *Counseling and psychotherapy.* Boston: Houghton Mifflin.

Rogers, C. R. (1951). *Client-centered therapy.* Boston: Houghton Mifflin.

Rogers, C. R. (1957). The necessary and sufficient conditions of therapeutic personality change. *Journal of Consulting Psychology, 21,* 95–103.

Rogers, C. R. (1958). The characteristics of a helping relationship. *Personnel and Guidance Journal, 37,* 6–16.

Rogers, C. R. (1986). A client-centered/person-centered approach to therapy. In I. Kutash & A. Wolf (Eds.), *Psychotherapist's casebook* (pp. 197–208). San Francisco: Jossey-Bass.

Rogers, C. R., & Truax, C. B. (1967). The therapeutic conditions antecedent to change: A theoretical view. In C. R. Rogers, E. T. Gendlin, D. J. Kiesler, & C. B. Truax (Eds.), *The therapeutic relationship and its impact: A study of psychotherapy with schizophrenics.* Madison: University of Wisconsin Press.

Russell, R. L., Bryant, F. B., & Estrada, A. U. (1996). Confirmatory P-technique analysis of therapist discourse: High- versus low-quality child therapy sessions. *Journal of Consulting and Clinical Psychology, 64*(6), 1366–1376.

Safran, J., Crocker, P., McMain, S., & Murray, P. (1990). Therapeutic alliance rupture as therapy event for empirical investigation. *Psychotherapy, 27,* 154–165.

Schindler, L . (1991). *Die empirische Analyse der therapeutischen Beziehung. Beiträge zur Prozessforschung in der Verhaltenstherapie* [The empirical analysis of the therapeutic relation: Contribution to process research in behavior therapy]. Berlin: Springer-Verlag.

Sirles, E. A. (1984, June). Who responds to follow-up studies? *Social Casework: Journal of Contemporary Social Work,* 354–356.

Suh, C. S., Strupp, H. H., & O'Malley, S. S. (1986). The Vanderbilt Process Measures: The Psychotherapy Process Scale (VPPS) and the Negative Indicators Scale (VNIS). In L. S. Greenberg & W. M. Pinsof (Eds.), *The psychotherapeutic process: A research handbook* (pp. 285–323). New York: Guilford.

Truax, C. B., & Carkhuff, R. R. (1963, June). *For better or for worse: The process of psychotherapeutic personality change.* Paper presented at the Academic Assembly of Clinical Psychology, Montreal, Canada.

Truax, C. B., & Carkhuff, R. R. (1967). *Toward effective counseling and psychotherapy: Training and practice.* Chicago: Aldine.

Truax, C. B., & Mitchell, K. (1971). Research on certain therapist interpersonal skills in relation to process and outcome. In A. E. Bergin & S. L. Garfield (Eds.), *Handbook of psychotherapy and behavior change: An empirical analysis* (pp. 299–344). New York: Wiley.

Truax, C. B., Wargo, D. G., Frank, J. D., Imber, S. D., Battle, C. C., Hoehn-Saric, R., Nash, E. H., & Stone, A. R. (1966). Therapist empathy, genuineness, and warmth and patient therapeutic outcome. *Journal of Consulting Psychology, 30,* 395–401.

Williams, K. E., & Chambless, D. L. (1990). The relationship between therapist characteristics and outcome of in vivo exposure treatment for agoraphobia. *Behavior Therapy, 21,* 111–116.

10

Congruence

Marjorie H. Klein
Gregory G. Kolden
Jennifer L. Michels
Sarah Chisholm-Stockard

In 1957, Carl Rogers characterized the necessary and sufficient conditions of therapeutic change as the client and therapist being in "psychological contact." The client is in a "state of incongruence, being vulnerable or anxious" (p. 96). The therapist, on the other hand, "is congruent or integrated in the relationship" while also experiencing "unconditional positive regard for the client" and "an empathic understanding of the client's internal frame of reference" (p. 96). He assumed that these facilitative conditions are communicated to the client.

While Rogers (1957) stated that all three of the conditions must be present for constructive personality change to take place in the client, congruence plays a special role in his system in that neither empathy nor regard can be conveyed in the therapeutic relationship unless the therapist comes across as genuine. Thus, congruence is a basic element in the facilitative conditions triad.

In this chapter, we first review the definitions and measurement of congruence or genuineness and then consider its relation to psychotherapy outcome. We conclude with the limitations of the empirical research and the therapeutic practices that emanate from the 40 years of research on the construct.

DEFINITIONS

There are two facets to congruence. The first characterizes the therapist's personal integration in the relationship, that "he is freely and deeply himself, with his actual experience accurately represented by his awareness of himself" (Rogers, 1957, p. 97). By emphasizing the relationship, Rogers does not require the therapist to be well-integrated in all aspects of his life, but at least be "accurately himself in this hour of this relationship . . . in this moment of time" (p. 97). The second facet characterizes the therapist's capacity to communicate his or her personhood *to* the client, as appropriate. While the aim is not for the therapist to indulge in indiscriminant self-disclosure or ventilation of feelings, the therapist must not deceive the client about his or her feelings, especially if they stand in the way of achieving unconditional positive regard and/or empathic understanding.

Lest the concept of congruence seem elusive, think of how we react to people in everyday life. Some people seem to be operating from behind a front or to be playing a role; they are incongruent. Other people seem more open and transparent so that we sense that we are in contact with the real person; they are congruent. In therapy, this means that the therapist is openly "being the feelings and attitudes which at the moment are flowing within him" (Rogers et al., 1967, p. 100) and not hiding behind a professional role or holding back feelings that are obvious. Congruence thus involves both a self-awareness on the part of the therapist, and a willingness to share this awareness in the moment. To quote Rogers, the congruent therapist "comes into a direct personal encounter with his client by meeting him on a person-to-person basis. It means that he is *being* himself, not denying himself" (p. 101).

One reason why congruence plays so central a role in Rogers's thinking about therapy is that he defines the problems that clients bring to therapy in terms of their incongruence and sees the therapy process as helping the client to become more congruent; that is, to become more able to own and express feelings without fear. Thus, therapist congruence can serve as a model for the client in the sense that the client's recognition of the "realness" of the therapist may enable the client to become more open to his own experiencing; this makes the therapist-client relationship deeper and the psychological contact more immediate.

The first systematic investigations of the therapeutic conditions took place at the University of Chicago Counseling Center, where Rogers and others refined the client-centered approach (Rogers, 1951) and pioneered the development of outcome measures (Rogers & Dymond, 1954) and process research (Gendlin, Jenny, & Shlein, 1960; Rogers, 1959; Tomlinson & Hart, 1962; A. Walker, Rablen, & Rogers, 1960; see also Barrett-Lennard [1998] for an excellent history of Rogers's career and the research). After his move to the University of Wisconsin, Rogers broadened the scope of his research to see if the conditions hypothesis could be supported in psychotherapy with hospitalized schizophrenics. Analyses of tape recordings of many therapy sessions showed that two of the three conditions—accurate empathy as rated from the therapy sessions, and congruence as perceived by the patients on the Relationship Inventory—were associated with greater improvement in the small sample of schizophrenics. These relationships, however, were moderated by factors such as the patient's socioeconomic status, verbal ability, and expressive capacity at the beginning of therapy, and by the level of in-session experiencing exhibited by the patient throughout the therapy course. This led the group to propose an interactive view of the therapy process in which the "best therapy relationship develops between a therapist who is understanding and real, and a client or patient who is able to be somewhat expressive, who is not too remote from his own experiencing" (Rogers, Gendlin, Kiesler, & Truax, 1967, p. 92).

The conception of the *therapist real relationship* (Gelso & Carter, 1985; Gelso & Hayes, 1998) is conceptually very similar to congruence/genuineness and is consistent with ideas initially offered by Greenson (1967). The real relationship is seen as primarily undistorted by transferential material and comprised of two defining features: genuineness and realistic perceptions. Genuineness is viewed as "the ability to and willingness to be what one truly is in the relationship" (Gelso & Carter, 1994, p. 297). Gelso and Hayes (1998) observed that genuineness in their scheme is related to other terms such as "authenticity, openness, honesty, nonphoniness, or Carl Rogers's (1957) concept, congruence" (p. 109).

Another source of emphasis on congruence/genuineness in the current conceptual literature can be found in Lietaer's (1993) work on client-centered/experiential psychotherapy. He asserts that genuineness is the most important of the three Rogerian relationship conditions. He conceptualizes genuineness as composed of an internal aspect and an external aspect. The internal aspect "refers to therapists' own internal experiencing with their clients. . . . To the extent that therapists are able to be in touch with their own experience they may be termed congruent" (J. C. Watson, Greenberg, & Lietaer, 1998, p. 9). The external aspect "refers to the therapists' ability to reveal their experience to their clients. This is termed transparency. . . . It is not necessary to share every aspect of their experience but only those that they feel would be facilitative of their clients' work. Transparency is always used in an empathic climate" (p. 9).

MEASUREMENT

The first measures of the conditions variables were developed at the University of Chicago Counseling Center. Halkides (1958) designed separate scales for each condition for use by independent raters. This groundbreaking study was followed by numerous studies examining the relationship between judges' ratings of the core conditions and patient outcomes (Barrett-Lennard, 1998).

Barrett-Lennard (1959) developed what has become the most recognized and validated therapist- or patient-self-report assessment of the core conditions, the Barrett-Lennard Relationship Inventory (BLRI; see Barrett-Lennard, 1962). Parallel forms of the BLRI ask the therapist to describe his or her feelings toward the client while in session (for example, "I am willing to tell him my own thoughts and feelings") or the patient to describe his or her experience of the therapist ("He is willing to tell me his own thoughts and feelings").

The original 92-item version of the BLRI included five scales: level of regard, empathic understanding, unconditionality, genuineness, and willingness to be known. This last scale was merged into the congruence scale in the 64-item 1964 revision (Barrett-Lennard, 1978). Likert scaling ranging from −3 (I strongly feel that it is not true) to +3 (I strongly feel that it is true) is used to rate each question (table 10.1). Gurman (1973a, 1973b) later developed a 30-item version of the Relationship Inventory. Truax also developed another version of the BLRI entitled the Truax Relationship Questionnaire (TRQ; see Truax & Carkhuff, 1967) as a self-report assessment of the core conditions. While Truax (1968) stated that client self-report was less valid for assessing the core conditions and impractical with certain populations (such as psychotic patients), the economical and wide-ranging uses for the instrument justified its development.

As Barrett-Lennard was developing and revising the BLRI, Rogers's group at the University of Wisconsin was engaged in more extensive development of scales for raters to assess the conditions from tape recordings of therapy sessions. Early versions by Hart (1960) and Gendlin and Geist (1962) were followed by Truax's development of the 1962 Self-Congruence Scale (Rogers et al., 1967) for use in the Wisconsin Schizophrenia Project. Independent observers rate how the therapist "appears" in tape-recorded session samples; table 10.1 lists the descriptors for the five stages (Truax, 1966a). Kiesler made further revisions of the measure for the final ratings of the Wisconsin Schizophrenia Project (Rogers et al., 1967) because of difficulties obtaining good reliability with the Truax version. This modification consisted of a five-point scale ranging from "a point where there is an obvious discrepancy between the therapist's feelings about the patient and his concurrent communication to the patient (stage 1) to a point where the therapist communicates both his positive and negative feelings about the patient openly and freely, without traces of defensiveness or retreat into professionalism (stage 5)" (Kiesler, 1973, p. 229; Rogers et al., 1967, pp. 581–583). In contrast to the Truax version, ratings in the Kiesler scale were only applied to session segments in which the client either "explicitly or implicitly questioned the therapist's feelings or opinions about him" (Rogers et al., 1967, p. 140). Carkhuff (1969) also developed a scale of genuineness derived from the Truax scale for broad application to interpersonal interactions beyond those occurring between a therapist and client. Aside from its broader application, the Carkhuff scale differs from Truax's version in that it includes more of an emphasis on negative reactions resulting from moderate to low levels of genuineness.

The reliability of the two most frequently cited measures of the core conditions—the BLRI and the Truax scale—has generally been adequate. Barrett-Lennard (1998) reports that most internal and test-retest reliability coefficients for the BLRI range between .75 and .95 with most exceeding .80. In an extensive review, Gurman (1977) reported split-half reliability coefficients for congruence ranging from .76 to .92 with a mean coefficient of .89.

Reliability coefficients have also been adequate for independent raters using the Truax scales. Correlations among ratings of congruence on the same samples of therapeutic interactions have ranged between .25 and .95 with the majority above .45 and a median of .72 (Truax & Carkhuff, 1967). Mitchell, Bozarth, and Krauft (1977) reviewed 15 studies and reported adequate reliability coefficients for congruence/genuineness, ranging from .34 and .85 with the majority over .65.

Table 10.1. Rating Scales for Congruence

Congruence Items on the BLRI[a]

Positively Valenced Items

He is comfortable and at ease in our relationship.
I feel that he is real and genuine with me
I nearly always feel that what he says expresses exactly what he is feeling and thinking as he says it.
He does not avoid anything that is important for our relationship.
He expresses his true impressions and feelings with me.
He is willing to express whatever is actually in his mind with me, including any feelings about himself or about me.
He is openly himself in our relationship.
I have not felt he tries to hide anything from himself that he feels with me.

Negatively Valenced Items

I feel that he puts on a role or front with me.
It makes him uneasy when I ask or talk about certain things.
He wanted me to think that he likes me or understands me more than he really does.
Sometimes he is not at all comfortable but we go on, outwardly ignoring it.
At times I sense that he is not aware of what he is really feeling with me.
There are times when I feel that his outward response to me is quite different from the way he feels underneath.
What he says to me often gives a wrong impression of his whole thought or feeling at the time.
I believe that he has feelings he does not tell me about that are causing difficulty in our relationship.

Stages of the Truax Self-Congruence Scale[b]

Stage 1

The therapist is clearly defensive in the interaction, and there is explicit evidence of a very considerable discrepancy between what he says and what he experiences. There may be striking contradictions in the therapist's statements; the content of his verbalization may contradict the voice qualities or nonverbal cues (for example, the upset therapist stating in a strained voice that he is "not bothered at all" by the patient's anger).

Stage 2

The therapist responds appropriately but in a professional rather than a personal manner, giving the impression that his responses are said because they sound good from a distance but do not express what he really feels or means. There is a somewhat contrived or rehearsed quality or an air of professionalism present.

Stage 3

The therapist is implicitly either defensive or professional, although there is no explicit evidence.

Stage 4

There is neither implicit nor explicit evidence of defensiveness or the presence of a façade. The therapist shows no self-incongruence.

Stage 5

The therapist is freely and deeply himself in the relationship. He is open to experiences and feeling of all types—both pleasant and hurtful—without traces of defensiveness or retreat into professionalism. Although there may be contradictory feelings, these are accepted or recognized. The therapist is clearly being himself in all of his responses, whether they are personally meaningful or trite. At stage 5 the therapist need not express personal feelings, but whether he is giving advice, reflecting, interpreting, or sharing experiences, it is clear that he is being very much himself, so that his verbalizations match his inner experiences.

[a]Barrett-Lennard (1962)
[b]Truax (1966b, pp. 68–72)

Relations Among the
Facilitative Conditions

Observer Ratings

While it appears that genuineness can be reliably rated from session tapes, one must ask whether or not a discrete therapy variable is being measured when assessing genuineness. Rogers's view of the core conditions suggested that empathy, unconditional regard, and genuineness should be highly interrelated. Research over the decades has not overwhelmingly supported this assertion. With respect to conditions rated from therapy tapes, Bozarth and Grace (1970) reported correlations between accurate empathy (AE) and congruence (C) and between unconditional positive regard (UPR) and congruence (C) of .03 and .10 respectively. Other studies reveal similarly low associations (Rogers et al., 1967; Truax, 1961). In contrast, other investigations have revealed relatively high correlations among conditions (for example, Anthony, 1971/1972). However, Garfield and Bergin (1971) reported correlations with C of −.66 and −.65 for AE and UPR, respectively. The variability in this data makes it difficult to render more definitive conclusions about interrelations among the facilitative conditions. The fact that few studies report these interrelations introduces the possibility that the available data may not be an accurate representation of these associations.

Participant Ratings

With respect to patient or therapist relationship perceptions, Gurman (1977) reported intercorrelations among scales within the BLRI or the TRQ for studies conducted between 1962 and 1974. Correlations between empathy and congruence ranged from .26 to .85 with a mean of .62. Correlations between regard and congruence ranged from .27 to .84 with a mean of .67. Correlations between unconditionality and congruence ranged from −.16 to .77 with a mean of .36. Gurman (1977) initially summarized this data by stating that empathy, regard, and congruence appear to be moderately dependent constructs. However, Gurman went on to compare these correlations with internal reliability data for these same scales and noted that the reliability data uniformly ex-

ceeded intercorrelations among the conditions; he therefore concluded, "These scales, while overlapping to some extent, are consistently measuring different dimensions of the patient's perceptions of the therapeutic relationship" (1977, p. 511).

Relations Among
Measurement Perspectives

Do clients and therapists rate the therapy session in similar ways? While there are limited published data addressing this question, Gurman (1977) reviewed eight studies in which correlations between patient and therapist ratings of congruence on the BLRI ranged from −.67 to .40 with only one statistically significant. Rogers and colleagues (1967) reported similar findings, with all correlations between therapist- and client-rated congruence falling below .25. Both studies also noted that therapists tend to rate themselves more favorably on the core conditions than do clients. Thus, clients and therapists do not appear to share highly similar perceptions of therapist congruence/genuineness.

The discrepancy among measurement perspectives on the BLRI also holds for observer and client ratings. Gurman (1977) reported five studies in which observer ratings and client ratings of congruence on the BLRI were compared. Correlations ranged from .04 to .42. None were significant. Moreover, two additional studies, not reported by Gurman, revealed correlations between observer ratings and client ratings of .27 and .49 (Rogers et al., 1967; Van der Veen, 1967b).

Discrepancies among client, therapist, and observer ratings suggest that each may be evaluating therapist congruence/genuineness from a slightly different perspective. This highlights the importance of cautious interpretation of research findings using different rating perspectives as well as consideration of evaluating congruence/genuineness from multiple perspectives.

CLINICAL EXAMPLES

Therapist Perspectives

The following excerpts from Rogers and colleagues (1967) are examples of Rogers's description of how his work with individuals who are schizophrenic led him to refine the experiential component of client-centered therapy.

In the first example, Rogers explains how he may use his feelings about the difficulty ending a session to provide the "vehicle for therapeutic responding" (p. 389):

> Some of my feelings about him [the patient] in the situation are a good source of responses, if I tell them in a personal, detailed way. . . . One whole set of feelings I have for others in situations comes at first as discomfort. As I look to see why I am uncomfortable I find content relevant to the person I am with, to what we just did or said. Often it is quite personal. I was stupid, rude, hurrying, embarrassed, avoidant, on the spot: I wished I didn't have to go since he wants me to stay. I wish I hadn't hurried him out. Or, "I guess you're mad at me because I'm leaving. I don't feel very good about it either. It just never feels right to me to go away and leave you in here [a hospital ward]. I have to go, or else I'll be late for everything I have to do all day today, and I'll feel lousy about that." Silence. "In a way, I'm glad you don't want me to go. I wouldn't like it at all if you didn't care one way or the other." (pp. 389–390)

In reflecting on these moments, Rogers explains that:

> These . . . have in common that I express feelings of mine which are at first troublesome or difficult, the sort I would at first tend to ignore in myself. It requires a kind of *doubling back*. When I first notice it, I have *already* ignored, avoided, or belied my feelings—only now do I notice what it was or is. I must double back to express it. At first, this seems a sheer impossibility! How can I express this all-tied-up, troublesome, puzzling feeling? Never! But a moment later I see that it is only another perfectly human way to feel, and in fact includes much concern for the patient, and empathic sensitivity to him. It is him I feel unhappy about—or what I just did to him.
> A very warm and open kind of interaction is created in telling my feelings this way. I am not greatly superior, wiser, or better than the other people in the patient's life. I have as many weaknesses, needs, and stupidities. But

the other people in his life rarely extend him this kind of response. (p. 390)

Another example shows how Rogers uses an "openness to what comes next" to increase his sensitivity, even to repair a breach in the interaction. He notes that by being open to what comes next, a positive feeling will usually emerge:

> I used to ponder whether I was about to say a right or wrong thing. Then, if it was wrong (as I could tell from the patient's reaction), I would not know what to do. Now I spend moments letting my feelings clarify themselves, but once they feel clear, I no longer wonder so much whether it is right or wrong to express them. Rather, I have open curiosity, sensitivity, and a readiness to meet whatever reaction I will get. This may tell me what I said was "wrong," but all will be well if *now* I respond sensitively to what I have stirred. I now say whatever I now sense which *makes* what I said before "wrong." (It is not my admission that I was wrong which matters here. I rarely make a point of having been wrong. That matters only to me. I am the only one who cares how often I am right or wrong. But whatever it is in him which I now sense and which *makes* what I said wrong—I now see it in his further reaction—*that* is what I have to respond to in the next moment.) (p. 391)

The final example illustrates the key role of the therapist's self-experiencing in building mutual congruence:

> We tend to express the *outer* edges of our feelings. That leaves *us* protected and makes the other person unsafe. We say, "This and this (which *you* did) hurt me." We do not say, "This and this weakness of mine *made me* be hurt when you did this and this."
> To find this inward edge of my feelings, I need only ask myself, "Why?" When I find myself bored, angry, tense, hurt, at a loss, or worried, I ask myself, "Why?" Then, instead of "You bore me," or "This makes me mad," I find the "why" *in me* which makes it so. That is always more personal and positive, and much safer to express. Instead of "You bore me," I find, "I want to hear more personally from you," or, "You tell me what happened, but I want to hear also what it all meant to you." (pp. 390–391)

Patient Perspectives

How is this openness on the part of the therapist perceived by the patient? One way to capture this is to review the genuineness items that a patient would endorse in the BLRI (table 10.1). The patient's experience of the highly self-congruent therapist is that the therapist is fully at ease within the relationship and is openly himself or herself. Being attuned to his or her experience in the moment, the therapist is open to honestly sharing this experience with the patient and does not avoid sharing uncomfortable feelings and impressions that are important to the therapy. Because of this personal attunement and genuineness, the therapist's words accurately capture his or her momentary experience.

Observer Perspectives

A third perspective on genuineness is provided by some samples from transcripts. The following two examples of high congruence come from the training material for the Truax (1966b) scale and from Rogers's filmed therapy session with the client "Gloria" (Shostrum, 1966). The first example represents Stage 5, the highest level on the Truax scale.

C: I guess you realize that, too, don't you? Or do you? [Laughs]

T: Do I realize that? You *bet* I do! Sure yeah—I always wanted somebody to take *care of me*, you know, but I also wanted them to let me do what I wanted to do! Well, if you have somebody taking care of you, then you've got to do what *they* want you to do.

C: That's right. [Pause]

T: So, I never could kind of get it so that I'd have both, you know, *both* things at once: either I'm doing what I want to do and taking care of myself or, you know, I used to have somebody taking care of me and then I'd do what *they* wanted to do. And I'd think, "Aw, hell!" It just—never works out, you know.

C: Always somebody there, isn't there? [Laughs]

T: Yeah, just somebody goofing up the works all the time. [Pause] Yeah, if you're dependent on somebody else, you're under their control, sort of.

C: To a certain extent . . . T: Yeah, that's what I was going to say—yeah, you're right. [Pause] So you just sit around the ward and you read a little bit, and then you go out and play horseshoes and—boy, that sounds like a *drag*! (Truax, 1966b, p. 72).

The next high-level example comes from the transcripts of Carl Rogers's demonstration therapy session with the client Gloria (Shostrom, 1966) where he clearly expresses his feeling of closeness to Gloria:

Gloria: That is why I like substitutes. Like I like talking to you and I like men that I can respect—Doctors, and I keep sort of underneath feeling like we are real close, you know, sort of like a substitute father.

Rogers: I don't feel that is pretending.

Gloria: Well, you are not really my father.

Rogers: No. I meant about the real close business.

Gloria: Well, see, I sort of feel that's pretending too because I can't expect you to feel very close to me. You don't know me that well.

Rogers: All I can know is what I am feeling and that is I feel close to you in this moment.

RESEARCH REVIEW

Congruence and Outcome

The empirical evidence for the relationship between therapist congruence or genuineness and patient outcome has been previously reviewed by Meltzoff and Kornreich (1970); Truax and Mitchell (1971); Luborsky, Chandler, Auerbach, Cohen, and Bachrach (1971); Kiesler (1973); Lambert, DeJulio, and Stein (1978); Parloff, Waskow, and Wolfe (1978); Orlinsky and Howard (1978, 1986); Mitchell et al. (1977); N. Watson (1984); and Orlinsky, Grawe, and Parks (1994). The consensus of these reviews is that support for the contribution of congruence to patient outcome is mixed.

In order to identify studies to include in the present review, we decided to focus on published studies (in English) or dissertation research on individual or group therapy with adults or adolescents (thereby excluding studies of psychotherapy with children and unpublished research reports). In the case of multiple reports from the same study, such as the Rogers et al. (1967) Wisconsin Schizophrenia Project and Truax's group psychotherapy studies, we tabled only the final or most comprehensive reports in order to limit bias due to multiple reporting; thus, we excluded positive findings from Truax (1961, 1963, 1970) and Van der Veen (1967a), and mixed results from Van der Veen and Stoler (1965). In addition to the studies meeting these criteria in the previous reviews, we conducted PSYCHINFO and MEDLINE searches using the keywords "congruence," "genuineness," and "psychotherapy."

Twenty studies meeting these criteria are summarized in table 10.2. They are classified with respect to (1) type and perspective of congruence measure, (2) timing within the therapy course for the congruence measure, and (3) type and perspective of outcome measure. Most of the tabled studies included multiple measures of outcome. When a study that employed multiple measures summarized their results in a test composite or overall outcome measure, we only tabled the results for the composite. Multiple measures in studies without composite scoring were tabled separately. We also did not include studies that analyzed outcomes only for combined scores of the three conditions, thus omitting positive results from Blatt, Zuroff, Quinlan, & Pilkonis (1996), Cain (1972/1973), Dickenson and Truax (1966), and McNally (1972) and null results from Beutler, Johnson, Neville, and Workman (1973). All results tabled as positive (+) were significant at the .05 level or less.

Except for one preliminary report from Truax's study of group therapy with psychiatric inpatients (Truax, Carkhuff, & Kodman, 1965) not tabled because it overlaps with the more comprehensive data presented in Truax, 1966a, there were no negative results. Among the 77 results from the 20 studies tabled, 26 (34%) were positive results and 51 (66%) were null results. It is interesting that the most consistent pattern of positive findings within a single study was from Barrett-Lennard's (1962) first BLRI study at the University of Chicago clinic where client-centered therapy was developed (Barrett-Lennard, 1998). Indeed, 17 (65%) of the 26 positive findings were

reported by researchers either associated with Rogers's Chicago or Wisconsin research groups (Barrett-Lennard, 1962; Halkides, 1958; Rogers et al., 1967; Truax, 1966a, 1971, Truax et al., 1971) or from client-centered clinics or student counseling centers (Athay, 1973/1974; Fretz, 1966; Hansen, Moore & Carkhuff, 1968; Melnick & Pierce, 1971; Schauble & Pierce, 1974). It is also noteworthy that the vast majority of the studies are from the 1960s (7 studies) or 1970s (11 studies), with only 2 from the 1980s, and none after 1989.

Table 10.3 summarizes the "box scores" by congruence measure, timing of congruence measurement during therapy episode, outcome measure, congruence perspective, outcome perspective, and congruence by outcome perspective match. There is some indication that more positive results were found when patients were rating the relationship using either the BLRI or the TRQ. Results were also somewhat more positive when patients or therapists reported congruence and when global therapist ratings were used to assess outcomes (6 positive results out of 8 findings; all reported by researchers associated with Rogers's Chicago or Wisconsin research groups). These patterns underscore the subjective or phenomenological nature of the congruence concept and suggest that congruence may be best captured by self-report; they also raise the possibility of researcher or participant bias or halo effects.

Before concluding that congruence/genuineness *has not* convincingly been shown to be associated with therapy outcome, it is reasonable to consider whether this result is unique to congruence or is also true for the other Rogerian facilitative conditions. Rogers and colleagues' (1967) original formulation specified that all three conditions—congruence, accurate empathy, and unconditional positive regard—would have to be present in effective therapy. When we looked at the associations with outcomes found for 59 results that also assessed accurate empathy or positive regard, we found that most of the results were consistent; that is, when congruence was positively associated with outcome, there was either a positive association with at least one of the other conditions (21 times), or all were null (19 times). There were 18 instances when congruence was not associated with outcome but either

Table 10.2. Summary of Findings: Therapist's Congruence and Outcome in Psychotherapy

	Congruence Measure[a]	Outcome Measure[b]	Finding[c]
Outcome Type: Symptoms			
Buckley et al. (1981)	Honesty-L-P	Symptoms-P	0
Buckley et al. (1981)	Genuineness-L-P	Symptoms-P	0
Garfield & Bergin (1971)	Truax-EML-O	MMPI change-P	0
Garfield & Bergin (1971)	Truax-EML-O	Fear survey-P	0
Jones & Zoppel (1982)	Formality-L-P	Symptoms-P	0
Jones & Zoppel (1982)	Neutrality-L-P	Symptoms-P	+
Jones & Zoppel (1982)	Formality-L-P	Anxiety-P	0
Jones & Zoppel (1982)	Neutrality-L-P	Anxiety-P	+
Lafferty et al. (1989)	RI-L-P	SCL-90 change-P	0
Melnick & Pierce (1971)	Carkhuff-EML-O	MMPI change-P	+[d]
Rogers et al. (1967)	Kiesler-EML-O	Wittenborn Psychiatric Rating Scale-O	0
Rogers et al. (1967)	RI-EL-P	Wittenborn Psychiatric Rating Scale-O	0
Schauble & Pierce (1974)	Truax-EL-O	MMPI profile improvement-O	+
Sloane et al. (1975)	Truax-E-O	Target symptom improvement-O	0
Sloane et al. (1975)	TRQ-L-P	Target symptom improvement-O	0
Staples & Sloane (1976)	Truax-E-O	Target symptom improvement-O	0
Truax et al. (1966a)	Truax-EML-O	Discomfort scale change-P	0
Truax et al. (1966a)	Truax-EML-O	Target symptom improvement-P	0
Outcome Type: Patient Functioning			
Buckley et al. (1981)	Honesty-L-P	Social/sex life-P	+
Buckley et al. (1981)	Genuineness-L-P	Social/sex life-P	0
Buckley et al. (1981)	Honesty-L-P	Work function-P	0
Buckley et al. (1981)	Genuineness-L-P	Work function-P	0
Garfield & Bergin (1971)	Truax-EML-O	Social adjustment-P	0
Rogers et al. (1967)	Kiesler-EML-O	Days out of hospital first year	0
Rogers et al. (1967)	RI-EL-P	Days out of hospital first year	+
Truax et al. (1966)	Truax-EML-O	Change in social ineffectiveness-O	0
VandenBos (1970)	Kiesler-M-O	IQ improvement (4 indices)	0
VandenBos (1970)	Kiesler-M-O	Days out of hospital	−
Outcome Type: Well Being			
Abramovitz & Abramovitz (1974)	RI-E-P	Improvement on 11 scales-P	0
Buckley et al. (1981)	Honesty-L-P	Self-esteem-P	0
Buckley et al. (1981)	Genuineness-L-P	Self-esteem-P	0
Hansen et al. (1968)	Truax-EML-O	Change in self-ideal self-concept-P	+
Hansen et al. (1968)	RI-L-P	Change in self-ideal self-concept-P	0
Jones & Zoppel (1982)	Formality-L-P	Happiness-P	0
Jones & Zoppel (1982)	Neutrality-L-P	Happiness-P	0
Jones & Zoppel (1982)	Formality-L-P	Enjoyment of life-P	0
Jones & Zoppel (1982)	Neutality-L-P	Enjoyment of life-P	0
Jones & Zoppel (1982)	Formality-L-P	Energy-P	0
Jones & Zoppel (1982)	Neutrality-L-P	Energy-P	0

(*continued*)

Table 10.2. (Continued)

	Congruence Measure[a]	Outcome Measure[b]	Finding[c]
Outcome Type: Global			
Athay (1973/1974)	TRQ-L-P	Student improvement-P	+
Athay (1973/1974)	TRQ-L-P	Semantic differential for change-P	+
Athay (1973/1974)	TRQ-L-P	Counseling effectiveness-TP	+
Barrett-Lennard (1962)	RI-E-P	General adjustment change-T	+[e]
Barrett-Lennard (1962)	RI-E-T	General adjustment change-T	0[e]
Barrett-Lennard (1962)	RI-E-P	Change index-T	+
Barrett-Lennard (1962)	RI-E-T	Change index-T	+
Barrett-Lennard (1962)	RI-L-P	Change index-T	+
Barrett-Lennard (1962)	RI-L-T	Change index-T	+
Buckley et al. (1981)	Honesty-L-P	Character change-P	0
Buckley et al. (1981)	Genuineness-L-P	Character change-P	+
Garfield & Bergin (1971)	Truax-EML-O	Rating of change-T	0
Garfield & Bergin (1971)	Truax-EML-O	Rating of change-P	0
Garfield & Bergin (1971)	Truax-EML-O	Rating of change-O	0
Halkides (1958)	Rogers-EL-O	Composite rating of outcome-O	+
Jones & Zoppel (1982)	Formality-L-P	Global outcome-P	0
Jones & Zoppel (1982)	Formality-L-P	Global change-P	+
Jones & Zoppel (1982)	Neutrality-L-P	Global outcome-P	0
Jones & Zoppel (1982)	Neutrality-L-P	Global change-P	0
Rogers et al. (1967)	Kiesler-EML-O	Overall assessment of change-O	0
Rogers et al. (1967)	RI-EL-P	Overall assessment of change-O	+
Rogers et al. (1967)	Kiesler-EML-O	Outcome and personality change-T	0
Rogers et al. (1967)	RI-EL-P	Outcome and personality change-T	0
Truax (1966)	RI-EML-P	Composite of multiple measures-P	+[f]
Truax (1966)	Truax-EML-O	Composite of multiple measures-P	+[g]
Truax et al. (1966)	Truax-EML-O	Global improvement-P	+
Truax et al. (1966)	Truax-EML-O	Global improvement-T	+
Truax (1971)	TRQ-E-P	Composite of multiple measures-P	0[h]
Truax (1971)	TRQ-E-P	Composite of multiple measures-P	+[i]
Truax (1971)	TRQ-E-P	Composite of multiple measures-P	0[j]
Truax et al. (1971)	Truax-EML-O	Composite of multiple measures-P	0[k]
VandenBos (1970)	Kiesler-M-O	Global functioning-O	0
Outcome Type: Other			
Fretz (1966)	RI-M-P	Satisfaction with therapy-P	0
Fretz (1966)	RI-L-P	Satisfaction with therapy-P	0
Jones & Zoppel (1982)	Formality-L-P	Satisfaction with therapy-P	0
Jones & Zoppel (1982)	Neutrality-L-P	Satisfaction with therapy-P	0
VandenBos (1970)	Kiesler-M-O	TAT emotional health-O	+
VandenBos (1970)	Kiesler-M-O	Rorschach emotional health-O	+

[a]Letter after congruence measure indicates when the measures were completed in therapy (E = early or initial session, M = middle of therapy, L = late or at or after termination, EML = multiple measures over therapy course) and who completed the measure or made the ratings (P = patient made the ratings, T = therapist made the ratings, O = observer made the ratings from tapes).

(continued)

Table 10.2. (Continued)

[b]Letter after the outcome measure indicates who completed the measure (P = patient, T = therapist, O = independent clinician or interviewer).

[c]Findings reported as "+" (therapist congruence was found to be significantly positively related to outcome), "0" (no significant difference), "−" (therapist congruence was significantly negatively related to outcome).

[d]They analyzed nine MMPI scales and found positive correlations with congruence change on three.

[e]General adjustment change was analyzed only for the more disturbed half of the sample.

[f]Truax (1966a) combines 40 schizophrenics from Mendota State Hospital with 40 juvenile delinquents from two Wisconsin State facilities.

[g]An earlier report for the Mendota schizophrenic sample (Truax, Carkhuff, & Kodman, 1965) found rated congruence negatively related to MMPI change. Truax (1966a) combined the 40 Mendota schizophrenics with 40 juvenile delinquents and reported positive findings for congruence, but these were probably carried by the pattern for the delinquents. The Truax (1968) report (not tabled) on the Mendota schizophrenics found congruence-outcome relationships to be mediated by the "differential reinforcement" of congruence on self-exploration.

[h]TRQ = Truax Relationship Questionnaire (Truax version of BLRI); possibly the same inpatients as in Truax et al. (1971).

[i]Juvenile delinquents, N = 40; it is not clear if these are the same juvenile delinquents for whom Relationship Inventory results were presented in Truax (1966a).

[j]Sample of neurotic outpatients.

[k]Truax et al. (1971) combines results from the Mendota schizophrenic inpatients with inpatients from various hospitals in Kentucky, so there may be some overlap with Truax (1966a).

accurate empathy or regard was, and only 1 instance where congruence was positively associated with outcome and the other conditions were not. Thus the findings for conditions were consistent in 68% of the instances where at least one of the other conditions was tested and inconsistent in 32%. This seems to support Rogers's (1957) contention that the conditions "act together," but again, the regression analyses that could characterize their interactions have never been performed. It may also be due to the bias, noted previously, in studies that used the same raters to rate one or more of the conditions.

These findings raised questions about the extent to which patient perceptions of the relationship and therapist perceptions of patient outcome may be accounted for by a third variable such as therapist empathy or patient expressiveness. This highlights the importance of examining these relations with more sophisticated statistical techniques (for example, multiple regression or structural equation modeling).

The trend for diminishing interest in research examining congruence-outcome relationships parallels the development of consensus about the lack of robustness of the findings from the original studies. Table 10.4 summarizes the ratios of positive to null and negative results reported in the major reviews of psychotherapy process-outcome relationships. The first review of this research by Truax and Mitchell (1971) reported

very favorable box scores (100% positive for overall outcome ratings; 77% for specific outcome measures; 81% in total), but these findings must be tempered by the fact that all of the studies reviewed were conducted by Truax and colleagues. A later review by Mitchell and colleagues (1977) yielded a rate of 50% positive findings for the 9 studies tabled, and a much lower rate of 9% if all multiple measures are considered. When Lambert, DeJulio, and Stein (1978) reviewed an updated list of studies, they found evidence of a positive association of congruence and outcome in 8 (62%) of the 13 studies. They noted that the relationship may only exist "in certain settings" (p. 469) and was most "prevalent in the research conducted by Truax" (p. 471). Not only was the evidence for conditions-outcome relationships "modest" at best (p. 472), but they noted this research has been beset by methodological problems such as failure to deliver sufficiently high levels of conditions, the restricted range of conditions, concerns about whose perspective (patient, therapist, or observer) is the more valid, inadequate sampling, and the numerous issues involved in the selection of samples for rating (see also N. Watson, 1984; Kiesler, Mathieu, & Klein, 1967a; Meltzoff & Kornreich, 1970; Parloff, Waskow, & Wolfe, 1978).

Orlinsky and Howard (1978) reviewed 26 studies of congruence or genuineness. They distinguished between results based on ratings of

Table 10.3. Box Scores for Positive and Null Results

	Outcome n (% total)		Row % Positive
	Null	Positive	
Total	51 (66)	26 (34)	34
Congruence Measure			
Observer Rated[a]	19 (25)	9 (12)	32
BLRI/TRQ	11 (14)	12 (16)	52
Other	21 (27)	5 (6)	19
Timing of Congruence Measurement			
Early only	6 (8)	5 (7)	46
Middle only	4 (5)	2 (3)	33
Late only	25 (33)	10 (13)	29
Early and late	2 (3)	3 (4)	60
Early, middle, late	14 (18)	6 (8)	30
Outcome Measure			
Symptoms	13 (17)	4 (5)	24
Functioning	8 (10)	2 (3)	20
Well-being	10 (13)	1 (1)	9
Global	15 (20)	17 (22)	53
Other	5 (7)	2 (3)	29
Congruence Perspective			
Patient	31 (40)	15 (20)	33
Therapist	1 (1)	2 (3)	67
Rater	19 (25)	9 (12)	32
Outcome Perspective			
Patient	36 (47)	13 (17)	27
Therapist	4 (5)	7 (9)	64
Other	11 (14)	6 (8)	35
Congruence by Outcome Perspective Match			
Patient : Patient	29 (38)	9 (12)	24
Therapist : Therapist	1 (1)	2 (3)	67
Other : Other	10 (13)	4 (5)	29
Mismatches	11 (14)	11 (14)	50
Congruence by Therapist Global Outcome			
Patient	1 (1)	4 (5)	80
Therapist	1 (1)	2 (3)	67
Other	2 (3)	1 (1)	33
Total	4 (5)	7 (9)	64

[a]Observer rated scales by Truax, Kiesler, Carkhuff, or Rogers.

BLRI = Barrett-Lennard Relationship Inventory; TRQ = Truax Relationship Questionnaire.

session tapes and ratings made by patients, the former under the heading of "Therapy as Dramatic Interpretation" (p. 307), and the latter under "Therapy as Experience" (pp. 299–300). Of the 6 studies reviewed that considered the relationship of patient ratings of therapist genuineness to patient outcome, 5 (83%) were positive, compared with the 14 (58%) positive when genuineness was rated from therapy tapes. After noting that the conditions are difficult to distinguish from one another and that for patient's ratings, their "commonality may outweigh the nuances of difference" (p. 298), they concluded that "cumulatively, these studies seem to warrant the conclusion that therapist genuineness is at least innocuous, however, it is probably neither a necessary nor a sufficient condition of therapeutic benefit" (p. 307). In their 1986 review, Orlinsky and Howard added only two studies to their earlier list, used a scoring method that tallied the results by the process perspective (patient, therapist, or other) and outcome perspective (patient, therapist, or other), and counted multiple outcome measures separately. Among the 53 results tabled from the 28 studies, 20 (38%) were positive, 32 (60%) null, and 1 (1%) negative. They also noted that "therapist-process by therapist-outcome was the only cell in which therapists' perceptions of their own genuineness showed any relationship to outcome" (p. 339) and that "genuineness was significantly related to outcome about half the time when patients' perceptions of genuineness were used, but only one-third of the time when nonparticipant observations of therapist perceptions were used" (p. 340).

In their most recent, review Orlinsky and colleagues (1994) added results from five more studies conducted in the 1980s. They found the same ratio of positive to negative and null results (38%) and concluded that "this factor may contribute to therapeutic success under some conditions" (p. 343). Thus, the results of the last two comprehensive reviews are very close to the 34% positive results obtained in the present, more selective review.

N. Watson (1984) also reviewed many of the same studies while considering the degree to which each rigorously tested Rogers's original hypothsis, namely, whether they included clients who were initially incongruent, whether the cli-

Table 10.4. Ratios of Positive to Null or Negative from Major Reviews

Review	No. of Studies	No. of Results	No. of Positive	% Positive
Truax & Mitchell (1971)	8	32	26	81
Mitchell et al. (1977)	6	6	3	50[a]
Lambert et al. (1978)	13	13	8	62
Orlinsky & Howard (1978)	26	26	19	73
N. Watson (1984)	12	17	11	65
Orlinsky & Howard (1986)	28	53	20	38
Orlinsky et al. (1994)	33	60	23	38
Klein et al. (2002)	20	77	26	34

[a]Mitchell et al. (1977) tabled box scores for 19 studies with 52 (7%) positive; 560 of these "analyses" were from an unpublished report by Mitchell, Bozarth, Truax, & Krauft (1973). Without access to the report, it does not seem reasonable to table such a discrepant finding.

ent's perception was used to measure congruence, whether outcomes were rated by multiple sources, and whether the design allowed interpretation of the results as causal as contrasted with purely correlational results. Watson observed that *none* of the studies reviewed met this degree of rigor and concluded that "correlations between the hypothesized conditions and outcome . . . are necessary but not sufficient evidence for Rogers' hypotheses" (p. 35). However, he noted that the consistency of the patterns for congruence and empathy across the correlational studies when patients were rating the conditions, despite methodological flaws, does not refute Rogers's view, and regrets that many of the studies failed to report the data that would be needed to either support or refute the conditions hypothesis.

Consistent with the diminishing empirical support for the concept of congruence or genuineness, it is relevant to note that the concept, under the heading of Therapist Self-Relatedness, plays a marginal role in the Generic Model of Psychotherapy proposed by Orlinsky and his colleagues (Orlinsky & Howard, 1986, 1987; Orlinsky et al., 1994). This model places more emphasis on the complex interplay between patient and therapist behaviors and suggests that genuineness, as one component of the Therapist's Self-Relatedness, exerts its influence on outcome indirectly through its contribution to the key variable of Therapeutic Bond.

This more dynamic interpretation echoes the "interactive view" offered by Kiesler, Mathieu, and Klein (1967b) as an alternate view of the findings of Rogers's Wisconsin Schizophrenia Project (Rogers et al., 1967). In this interpretation, when a patient enters therapy with a

> fair degree of expressive capacity and/or motivation for self-exploration, the therapist's corresponding involvement may be enhanced. The more motivated the patient for the therapeutic process, the easier it will be for the therapist to become correspondingly involved in, and committed to, the relationship. The more responsive the patient, the more likely it will be that the therapist can communicate the genuineness of his concern for, and interest in the patient as a person. (pp. 308–309)

Thus, while the empirical evidence for congruence as an independent condition for therapy outcome is mixed, there remains both empirical and theoretical support for it to continue to be considered as an important component of a more complex conception of the psychotherapy relationship.

Input Characteristics, Other Therapy Processes, and Congruence

In the course of our review of the empirical literature examining the relationship between congruence/genuineness and psychotherapy outcome, we came across several studies that documented associations of congruence with characteristics that patients and therapists bring to therapy—input characteristics—as well as relations with other therapy processes. The summary of results that follows is somewhat selective; we report only significant findings due to space limitations.

Input Characteristics

Tepper (1972) demonstrated an association between observer-rated genuineness and therapist nonverbal behaviors indicative of therapist involvement including a forward trunk lean, maintenance of direct eye contact, concerned vocal intonation, and facial expression. Lin (1973) showed that patient-perceived congruence was related to counselor-rated self-confidence. Abramovitz and Abramovitz (1974) found an association between congruence and patient psychological mindedness, however, only in the insight-oriented therapy examined in their study. Contrasting this is Sloane, Staples, Cristol, Yorkson, and Whipple (1975), who found that congruence was rated higher in behavior therapists than analytic therapists; they speculated that this was presumably due to behavior therapists being more active and directive about information giving in their therapy interactions.

Ziemelis (1974) demonstrated a relation between patient-rated congruence and perceptions of having been assigned to a preferred or nonpreferred counselor type. While no differences were observed on congruence ratings between those actually receiving therapy from preferred versus nonpreferred counselors, patients rated counselors as more congruent when they were told they were receiving their preferred counselor type (as opposed to those told they were not being assigned to their preferred type). This speaks to the relation between patient expectations and the experience of congruence.

The relation between genuineness and patient and therapist mood is another area that has received some attention. With respect to patient mood, Janowsky, Kraft, Clopton, and Huey (1984) demonstrated that irrespective of diagnosis, patients reported lower levels of genuineness when also reporting dysphoric mood. Rogers and colleagues (1967) also found that patient-rated genuineness was negatively impacted by patient elevations on the MMPI mania and schizophrenia clinical scales at entry into their study. Thus, patient mood and self-rated pathology, as well as expectations, appear to influence their ratings

of their therapist's congruence. Finally, Gurman (1973a) found a trend for therapists rated as high on facilitative conditions to exhibit higher genuineness when therapist pre-session mood was low and lower genuineness when pre-session therapist mood was better. Conversely, therapists rated as low on facilitative conditions exhibited higher genuineness when therapist pre-session mood was better and lower genuineness when therapist pre-session mood was lower. He speculated that high-conditions therapists are more likely to be aware of their moods and are able to prevent them from interfering with the therapy process.

Other Therapy Processes

The relation of congruence to the nature and quality of the verbal exchange that occurs in psychotherapy is an area that has been examined in several studies. Barrington (1961) discovered a trend for an association between congruence and greater integration/smoothness of speaking exchanges (such as fewer breaks in responses). Rogers and colleagues (1967) showed a relation between congruence and patient verbal facility. Staples and Sloane (1976) demonstrated associations between congruence, on the one hand, and patient and therapist speech measures on the other. Therapists rated high on congruence were observed to react more quickly to patient comments, and patients, in turn, responded more quickly. Moreover, this study showed that congruence was related to the match between patient and therapist measures of the pace of the exchange. Nagy (1972/1973) tapped a variable that is conceptually close to congruence, personally relevant concreteness, and found that patient anxiety was more likely to decrease in counseling clients who received high levels of this condition. Together, these studies highlight the relation between congruence/genuineness and active or involved therapeutic interactions.

Rogers's (1957) original theory held that the effect of facilitative conditions on patient outcome was due to their facilitation of the depth of patient involvement and experiencing in the therapy sessions. Numerous studies have carefully examined the association between genuineness and experiencing as well as the related concept of depth of self-exploration. Van der Veen

(1963) found a relation between genuineness and change in experiencing over the course of two interviews offered to inpatients on an *ad lib* basis (that is, therapists were available for patients to talk with as requested). Gross and DeRidder (1966) showed that genuineness was positively related to experiencing level as well as to change in experiencing over the course of a short-term counseling episode. Rogers and colleagues (1967) demonstrated that genuineness was positively related to patient experiencing level. However, they found no relation between genuineness and either patient or therapist experiencing change.

Truax and Carkhuff (1965) demonstrated a relation between rated therapist congruence and depth of patient self-exploration in group therapy with hospitalized schizophrenics and incarcerated juvenile delinquents. In a separate analysis of the schizophrenia data, Truax (1968) showed that when therapist congruence was associated with deeper patient self-exploration, patient outcome was better. This suggests that self-exploration may be a mediator of congruence-outcome relationships.

Eugster and Wampold (1996) examined the relation between therapy processes and global session evaluations by patients and therapists. They identified a process that is conceptually very similar to congruence/genuineness. "The therapist real relationship taps the therapist's willingness to be known through degree of transparency or disclosure, liking for the patient, and strictly role-defined versus natural or spontaneous behavior" (p. 1021). "The real relationship . . . is based on accurate perceptions and genuineness" (p. 1025). They found that the therapist real relationship was positively associated with session evaluation from both therapist and patient perspectives. When included along with other process variables in multiple regression analyses, the patient-rated therapist real relationship was the strongest contributor to patient session evaluation. Interestingly, however, therapist-rated therapist real relationship demonstrated a negative association with therapist session evaluation in the context of the other process variables. They contended that this supports the notion that patients most highly value the genuine human relationship with the therapist, while the therapist perceives this negatively. For the therapist, self-perceptions of expertise appear to be more highly

valued. This study underscores the importance of rating perspective (by patient, therapist, or rater) for understanding empirical relations of congruence/genuineness as well as the complexity among psychotherapy processes (especially between therapy relationship variables); it also underscores the critical importance of examining these relations with modern statistical techniques.

LIMITATIONS OF THE RESEARCH

What can be concluded from this review of the congruence/genuineness empirical literature? Any inferences must be made with the methodological limitations of the studies reviewed clearly in mind. Parloff and colleagues (1978), Patterson (1984), Lambert and colleagues (1978), and N. Watson (1984) provide a very comprehensive listing of the limitations: studies not limited to clients who are in need of change (that is, who are incongruent), low levels of conditions, restricted ranges of conditions variables, low reliability of conditions and/or outcome, variability in experience levels of therapists (trainees vs. master therapists), and different rating perspectives. They also noted the limitations of ratings from audiotapes that do not allow nonverbal behaviors to be rated, varying qualifications and/or training of raters, inadequate and variable sampling methods (sessions vs. segments; one interview vs. several sessions), small sample sizes in most studies, and small amounts of variance accounted for by conditions-outcome/criterion measures.

These methodological limitations, together with evidence for positive correlational findings in several studies, as many or more null findings, and very few negative findings leads us to conclude that the evidence is likely to be more strongly supportive than appears at first glance of a positive relation between congruence/genuineness and psychotherapy outcome. Orlinsky and Howard (1978) noted, "If study after flawed study seemed to point in the same general direction, we could not help believing that somewhere in all that variance there must be a reliable effect" (pp. 288–289). Similarly, Patterson (1984) argued, "Considering the statistical factors militating against the obtaining of significant positive results, it is concluded that the evidence for the effectiveness of the therapist variables is far greater than is recognized by many reviewers" (p. 431); to obtain "positive results against such handicaps [methodological limitations of studies] is an indication of the strength of the relationships" (p. 437). A consistent pattern of positive findings is very unlikely to be explained by study flaws. A pattern of null findings could be, and perhaps is even likely to be, explainable by study inadequacies.

Aside from modeling the congruence that the therapist is attempting to foster in the client, congruence can be seen as providing "therapist-supplied affective meaning" that helps the patient express his feelings more openly in the "felt mesh of a shared experiencing" (p. 399). Through his commitment to truthfulness, the therapist can "help patients live with, in, and through what does confront them" (p. 398).

THERAPEUTIC PRACTICES

As a psychotherapy treatment parameter, congruence/genuineness has both *intrapersonal* and *interpersonal* facets. As noted by Rogers in Rogers and colleagues (1967), it can be seen as a *personal characteristic* (intrapersonal) of the therapist as well as a *mutual, experiential quality* of the relationship (interpersonal). Congruence may also arise as an *issue* that patients raise in therapy sessions when, for example, they directly question the therapist's genuineness (a mix of interpersonal and intrapersonal). In our view, congruence/genuineness should be recognized as a key psychotherapy treatment parameter and a potent change process with both interpersonal and intrapersonal dimensions.

Psychotherapy change processes are antecedent factors that either temporally or logically precede outcome targets of interest. Change processes may directly contribute to change and/or they may indirectly mediate the effects of other change processes (such as facilitative conditions and interventions) on outcomes. Congruence might directly contribute to outcome by eliciting positive affect and promoting attachment as well as corrective relational experiences. Indirectly, congruence might contribute to change by mediating the impact of positive regard and perceived empathy as well as interventions.

Given this framework for understanding the nature and influence of congruence/genuineness, what tactics can therapists use to achieve and maintain congruence/genuineness in their therapy sessions? Descriptively, congruent responses may involve self-disclosure by therapists of personal information and life experiences. They may also entail articulation of thoughts and feelings, opinions, feedback on behavior, and pointed questions. Genuine responses require mindful attention and self-reflection. Congruent responses are honest. Genuine responses are not disrespectful, overly intellectualized, or insincere (although they may involve irreverence). They are authentic and consistent with the therapist as a real person with likes, dislikes, preferences, beliefs, and opinions. Congruent responses are flexibly guided by normative therapist role behavior and yet they are not rigidly role bound. Genuine therapist responses are cast in the language of personal pronouns (I feel, My view is, This is how I experience).

The intrapersonal experiential facet of congruence has been discussed in the Clinical Examples section. It involves the therapist being in touch with and receptive to his or her experiencing of the client as well as a willingness to use this as material relevant for therapy. This "experiential stance" plays a major role in promoting and maintaining the therapeutic bond. Moreover, it also serves as a vehicle for communicating empathy and regard.

Although most of Rogers's examples of congruence are expressed in experiential terms, in his discussion of therapeutic procedures, he outlines techniques that may be used to enhance genuineness in the course of therapeutic interactions (Rogers et al., 1967). For example, he suggests that the therapist engage "himself directly and spontaneously" (p. 375) in the service of patient experiencing. In addition, the congruent therapist is "self-grounded," he or she owns and is responsible for his or her feelings and reactions, and this "ownership of feelings is specified" (p. 377) so that the patient clearly knows when the therapist is pointing to what he thinks the patient is feeling (accurate empathy) in contrast to what the therapist is feeling (congruence). This requires the therapist to attend to his or her actual train of thought and feeling as a source of responses to the patient, which might include the therapist's thinking "out loud" about why he or she said or did something. Rogers refers to this as "doubling back" or "retroactive responding." The congruent therapist may own up to feelings of discomfort which, when reflected upon by the therapist, may reveal issues relevant to the patient. Rogers also suggests that therapists adopt an attitude of "openness to what comes next" (p. 391) that involves curiosity, sensitivity, and readiness to receive client reactions to therapist verbalizations so that "almost anything is an opportunity for further interaction" (p. 391).

The maintenance of congruence in the therapeutic relationship requires that therapists be aware of instances when congruence falters. Rogers speaks of feeling "twisted . . . perhaps I am responding socially, smiling, while actually I know we are avoiding something . . . or perhaps I have promised something I do not wish" (p. 396) and then using the twisted feeling as a cue for the need for self-examination and a return to a more genuine and direct way of relating. A corollary is that there are "no unmentionables . . . as anything that seems unmentionable is really an opportunity for more direct relating" (p. 396). This may involve what Rogers terms the "two-sided compound" that may emphasize appreciation of the positive and negative aspects of the situation. As Rogers illustrates:

> For example, to say just, "I think maybe you're very scared that you really are crazy" might scare him because he might feel that *I* think he is. Actually he often makes very good sense about a lot of things, and if I express that too . . . the first sentence becomes a safe one. This therapist expression becomes possible for me as I decide to voice that which first stopped me from expressing my feeling. Another example, "I don't like it when you do that, and I don't want you to do it anymore. *But I think you do it to* . . . and I like *that.*" (p. 397)

It is important, however, for therapists to recognize the importance of identifying and being aware of their congruence style. (This is an aspect of what Lampropoulos [2000] and Lazarus [1993]

have referred to as relationship style or stance.) Furthermore, therapists must be able to discern the differing needs and expectations that clients have with regard to genuineness. For example, some need and expect greater formality than others. Thus, therapist effectiveness in this realm requires tailoring of *congruence style* according to client needs and expectations in order to maintain genuineness.

REFERENCES

Abramovitz, S. I., & Abramovitz, C. V. (1974). Psychological-mindedness and benefit from insight oriented group therapy. *Archives of General Psychiatry, 30,* 610–615.

Anthony, J. J. (1971/1972). A comparison of measured and perceived conditions of empathy, warmth, and genuineness in secondary school counseling. (Doctoral dissertation, University of Florida, 1971). *Dissertation Abstracts International, 33,* 562A.

Athay, A. L. (1973/1974). The relationship between counselor self-concept, empathy, warmth, and genuineness, and client rated improvement. (Doctoral dissertation, University of Utah, 1973). *Dissertation Abstracts International, 34,* 3976A.

Barrett-Lennard, G. T. (1959). Dimensions of perceived therapist response related to therapeutic change. Unpublished doctoral dissertation, University of Chicago.

Barrett-Lennard, G. T. (1962). Dimensions of therapist response as causal factors in therapeutic change. *Psychological Monographs: General and Applied, 76*(43, Whole No. 562).

Barrett-Lennard, G. T. (1978). The Relationship Inventory: Later development and adaptations. *JSAS Catalogue of Selected Documents in Psychology, 8,* 68 (MS 1732).

Barrett-Lennard, G. T. (1998). *Carl Rogers' helping system: Journey and substance.* Beverly Hills, CA: Sage.

Barrington, B. L., (1961) Prediction from counselor behavior of client perception and of case outcome. *Journal of Clinical Psychology, 8,* 37–42.

Beutler, L. E., Johnson, D. T., Neville, C. W., & Workman, S. N. (1973). The A-B therapy-type distinction, accurate empathy, nonpossessive warmth, and therapist genuineness in psychotherapy. *Journal of Abnormal Psychology, 82,* 273–277.

Blatt, S. J., Zuroff, D. C., Quinlan, D. M., & Pilkonis, P. A. (1996). Interpersonal factors in brief treatment of depression: Further analyses of the National Institute of Mental Health Treatment of Depression Collaborative Research Program. *Journal of Consulting and Clinical Psychology*, 64, 162–171.

Bozarth, J. D., & Grace, D. P. (1970). Objective ratings and client perceptions of therapeutic conditions with university counseling center clients. *Journal of Clinical Psychology*, 26, 117–118.

Buckley, P., Karasu, T. B., & Charles, E. (1981). Psychotherapists view their personal therapy. *Psychotherapy: Theory, Research and Practice*, 18, 299–305.

Cain, D. J. (1972/1973). The therapists' and clients' perceptions of therapeutic conditions in relation to perceived interview outcome. (Doctoral dissertation, University of Wyoming, 1972). *Doctoral Dissertations International*, 1973, 33, 6071B.

Carkhuff, R. R. (1969). *Helping and human relations: A primer for lay and professional helpers.* New York: Holt, Rinehart, and Winston.

Dickenson, W. A., & Truax, C. B. (1966). Group counseling with college underachievers. *Personnel and Guidance Journal*, 45, 243–247.

Eugster, S. L., & Wampold, B. E. (1996). Systematic effects of participant role on evaluation of the psychotherapy session. *Journal of Consulting and Clinical Psychology*, 64, 1020–1028.

Fretz, B. R. (1966). Postural movements in a counseling dyad. *Journal of Counseling Psychology*, 13, 335–343.

Garfield, S. L., & Bergin, A. E. (1971). Therapeutic conditions and outcome. *Journal of Abnormal Psychology*, 77, 106–114.

Gelso, C. J., & Carter, J. A. (1985). The relationship in counseling and psychotherapy: Components, consequences, and theoretical antecedents. *The Counseling Psychologist*, 13, 155–244.

Gelso, C. J., & Carter, J. A. (1994). Components of the psychotherapy relationship: Their interaction and unfolding during treatment. *Journal of Counseling Psychology*, 41, 296–306.

Gelso, C. J., & Hayes, J. A. (1998). *The psychotherapy relationship: Theory, research, and practice.* New York: Wiley.

Gendlin, E. T., & Geist, M. (1962). The relationship of therapist congruence to psychological test evaluations of personality change. Wisconsin Psychiatric Institute, *Brief Research Reports*, 24.

Gendlin, E. T., Jenny, R. H., & Schlein, J. M. (1960). Counselor ratings of process and outcome in client-centered therapy. *Journal of Clinical Psychology*, 16, 210–213.

Greenson, R. R. (1967). *The technique and practice of psychoanalysis* (Vol. 1). Madison, CT: International Universities Press.

Gross, W. F., & DeRidder, L. M. (1966). Significant movement in comparatively short-term counseling. *Journal of Counseling Psychology*, 13, 98–99.

Gurman, A. S. (1973a). Effects of the therapist and patient mood on the therapeutic functioning of high and low-facilitative therapists. *Journal of Consulting and Clinical Psychology*, 40, 48–58.

Gurman, A. S. (1973b). Instability of the therapeutic conditions in psychotherapy. *Journal of Counseling Psychology*, 20, 16–24.

Gurman, A. S. (1977). The patient's perception of the therapeutic relationship. In A. S. Gurman & A. M. Razin (Eds.), *Effective psychotherapy: A handbook of research.* (pp. 503–543). New York: Pergamon.

Halkides, G. (1958). *An experimental study of four conditions necessary for therapeutic change.* Unpublished doctoral dissertation, University of Chicago.

Hansen, J. C., Moore, G. D., & Carkhuff, R. R. (1968). The differential relationships objective and client perceptions of counseling. *Journal of Counseling Psychology*, 24, 244–246.

Hart, J. T. (1960). *A replication of the Halkides study.* Unpublished manuscript, University of Wisconsin.

Janowsky, D. S., Kraft, A., Clopton, P., & Huey, L. (1984). Relationships of mood and interpersonal perceptions. *Comprehensive Psychiatry*, 25, 546–555.

Jones, E. E., & Zoppel, C. L. (1982). Impact of client and therapist gender on psychotherapy process and outcome. *Journal of Consulting and Clinical Psychology*, 50, 259–272.

Kiesler, D. J. (1973). *The process of psychotherapy: Empirical foundations and systems of analysis.* Chicago: Aldine.

Kiesler, D. J., Mathieu, P. L., & Klein, M. H. (1967a). Measurement of conditions and process variables. In C. R. Rogers, E. T. Gendlin, D. J. Kiesler, & C. B. Truax (Eds.), *The therapeutic relationship and its impact: A study of psychotherapy with schizophrenics* (pp. 135–186). Madison: University of Wisconsin Press.

Kiesler, D. J., Mathieu, P. L., & Klein, M. H. (1967b). A summary of the issues and conclusions. In C. R. Rogers, E. T. Gendlin, D. J. Kiesler, & C. B. Truax (Eds.), *The therapeutic relationship and its impact: A study of psychotherapy with schizophrenics* (pp. 135–186). Madison: University of Wisconsin Press.

Klein, M. H., Kolden, G. G., Michels, J. L., & Chisholm-Stockard, S. (2002). Congruence or genuineness. *Psychotherapy: Theory/Research/Practice/Training, 38*, 396–400.

Lafferty, P., Beutler, L. E., & Crago, M. (1989). Differences between more and less effective psychotherapists: A study of select therapist variables. *Journal of Consulting and Clinical Psychology, 57*, 76–80.

Lambert, M. J., DeJulio, S. S., & Stein, D. M. (1978). Therapist interpersonal skills: Process, outcome, methodological considerations, and recommendations for future research. *Psychological Bulletin, 85*, 467–489.

Lampropoulos, G. K. (2000). Evolving psychotherapy integration: Eclectic selection and prescriptive applications of common factors in therapy. *Psychotherapy, 37*, 285–297.

Lazarus, A. A. (1993). Tailoring the therapeutic relationship or being an authentic chameleon. *Psychotherapy, 30*, 404–416.

Lietaer. G. (1993). Authenticity, congruence, and transparency. In D. Brazier (Ed.), *Beyond Carl Rogers: Towards a psychotherapy for the twenty-first century* (pp. 17–46). London: Constable.

Lin, T. T. (1973). Revision and validation of the Truax-Carkhuff relationship questionnaire. *Measurement and Evaluation in Guidance, 6*, 82–86.

Linehan, M. M. (1993). *Cognitive-behavioral treatment of borderline personality disorder*. New York: Guilford.

Luborsky, L. B., Chandler, M., Auerbach, A. H., Cohen, J., & Bachrach, H. M. (1971). Factors influencing the outcome of psychotherapy: A review of quantitative research. *Psychological Bulletin, 75*, 145–185.

McNally, H. A. (1972) An investigation of selected counselor and client characteristics as possible predictors of counseling effectiveness. (Doctoral dissertation, University of Maine, 1972). *Dissertation Abstracts International, 33*, 6672–6673A.

Melnick, B., & Pierce, R. M. (1971). Client evaluation of therapist strength and positive-negative evaluation as related to client dynamics, objective ratings of competency and outcome. *Journal of Clinical Psychology, 27*, 408–411.

Meltzoff, J., & Kornreich, M. (1970). *Research in psychotherapy*. New York: Atherton.

Mitchell, K. M., Bozarth, J. D., & Krauft, C. C. (1977). A reappraisal of the therapeutic effectiveness of accurate empathy, nonpossessive warmth, and genuineness. In A. S. Gurman and A. M. Razin (Eds.), *Effective psychotherapy: A handbook of research* (pp. 503–543). Oxford: Pergamon.

Mitchell, K. M., Truax, C. B., Bozarth, J. D., & Krauft, C. C. (1973, March). *Antecedents to psychotherapeutic outcome*. (NIMH Grant Report No. 12306). Arkansas Rehabilitation Research and Training Center, Arkansas Rehabilitation Services, Hot Springs.

Nagy, T. F. (1972/1973). Therapist level of functioning and change in clients' quantifiable anxiety level and verbal behavior. (Doctoral dissertation, University of Illinois, 1972). *Dissertation Abstracts International, 34*(2), 878–879.

Orlinsky, D. E., Grawe, K., & Parks, B. K. (1994). Process and outcome in psychotherapy—Noch einmal. In A. E. Bergin & S. L. Garfield (Eds.), *Handbook of psychotherapy and behavior change* (4th ed., pp. 270–376). New York: Wiley.

Orlinsky, D. E, & Howard, K. I. (1978). The relation of process to outcome in psychotherapy. In S. L. Garfield & A. E. Bergin (Eds.), *Handbook of psychotherapy and behavior change* (2nd ed., pp. 283–329). New York: Wiley.

Orlinsky, D. E, & Howard, K. I. (1986). Process and outcome in psychotherapy. In S. L. Garfield & A. E. Bergin (Eds.), *Handbook of psychotherapy and behavior change* (3nd ed., pp. 311–381). New York: Wiley.

Orlinsky, D. E, & Howard, K. I. (1987). A generic model of psychotherapy. *Journal of Integrative and Eclectic Psychotherapy, 6*, 6–27.

Parloff, M. B., Waskow, I. E., & Wolfe, B. E. (1978). Research on therapist variables in relation to process and outcome. In S. L. Garfield & A. E. Bergin (Eds.), *Handbook of psychotherapy and behavior change* (2nd ed., pp. 233–282). New York: Wiley.

Patterson, C. H. (1984). Empathy, warmth, and genuineness in psychotherapy: A review of reviews. *Psychotherapy: Theory, Research, Practice, and Training, 21*, 431–438.

Rogers, C. R. (1951). *Client-centered psychotherapy*. Boston: Houghton Mifflin.

Rogers, C. R. (1957). The necessary and sufficient conditions of therapeutic personality change. *Journal of Consulting Psychology, 21*, 95–103.

Rogers, C. R. (1959). A tentative scale for the measurement of process in psychotherapy. In A. R. Rubenstein & M. B. Parloff (Eds.), *Research in psychotherapy* (Vol. 1, pp. 96–107). Washington, DC: American Psychological Association.

Rogers, C. R., & Dymond, R. F. (Eds.). (1954). *Psychotherapy and personality change*. Chicago: University of Chicago Press.

Rogers, C. R., Gendlin, E. T., Kiesler, D. J., & Truax, C. B. (Eds.). (1967). *The therapeutic relationship and its impact: A study of psychotherapy with schizophrenics.* Madison: University of Wisconsin Press.

Schauble, P. G., & Pierce, R. M. (1974). Client in-therapy behavior: A therapist guide to process. *Psychotherapy, 11,* 229–234.

Shostrum, E. L. (Producer). (1966). *Three approaches to psychotherapy.* [Film]. (Available from Psychological and Educational Files, Santa Ana, CA.)

Sloane, R. B., Staples, F. R., Cristol, A. H., Yorkson, N. J., & Whipple, K. (1975). *Psychotherapy versus behavior therapy.* Cambridge, MA: Harvard University Press.

Staples, F. R., & Sloane, R. B. (1976). Truax factors, speech characteristics, and therapeutic outcome. *Journal of Nervous and Mental Disease, 163,* 135–140.

Tepper, D. T. (1972). The communication of counselor empathy, respect, and genuineness through verbal and non-verbal channels. *Dissertation Abstracts International, 33*(9-A), 4858.

Tomlinson, T. M., & Hart, J. T., Jr. (1962). A validation of the process scale. *Journal of Consulting Psychology, 26,* 74–78.

Truax, C. B. (1961). The process of group psychotherapy: Relationships between hypothesized therapeutic conditions and intrapersonal exploration. *Psychological Monographs: General and Applied, 75*(7) (Whole No. 511, 1–35).

Truax, C. B. (1963). Effective ingredients in psychotherapy: An approach to unraveling the patient-therapist interaction. *Journal of Counseling Psychology, 10,* 256–263.

Truax, C. B. (1966a). Therapist empathy, warmth and genuineness and patient personality change in group psychotherapy: A comparison between interaction unit measures, time sample measures, patient perception measures. *Journal of Clinical Psychology, 22,* 225–229.

Truax, C. B. (1966b). *Toward a tentative measurement of the central therapeutic ingredients.* Arkansas Rehabilitation Research and Training Center and University of Arkansas, Fayetteville.

Truax, C. B. (1968). Therapist interpersonal reinforcement of client self-exploration and therapeutic outcome in group psychotherapy. *Journal of Counseling Psychology, 15,* 225–231.

Truax, C. B. (1970). Effects of client-centered psychotherapy with schizophrenic patients: Nine years pretherapy and nine years posttherapy hospitalization. *Journal of Consulting and Clinical Psychology, 35,* 417–422.

Truax, C. B. (1971). Perceived therapeutic conditions and client outcome. *Comparative Group Studies, 2,* 301–310.

Truax, C. B., & Carkhuff, R. R. (1965). Client and therapist transparency in the psychotherapeutic encounter. *Journal of Counseling Psychology, 12,* 3–9.

Truax, C. B., & Carkhuff, R. R. (1967). *Toward effective counseling and psychotherapy: Training and practice.* Chicago: Aldine.

Truax, C. B., Carkhuff, R. R., & Kodman, F. (1965). Relationships between therapist-offered condition and patient change in group psychotherapy. *Journal of Clinical Psychology, 21,* 327–329.

Truax, C. B., & Mitchell, K. M. (1971). Research on certain therapist interpersonal skills in relation to process and outcome. In A. E. Bergin & S. L Garfield (Eds.), *Handbook of psychotherapy and behavior change* (pp. 99–344). New York: Wiley.

Truax, C. B., Wargo, D. G., Frank, J. G., Imber, S. D., Battle, C. C., Hoen-Saric, R., Nash, E. H., & Stone, A. R. (1966). Therapist empathy, genuineness, and warmth and patient therapeutic outcome. *Journal of Consulting Psychology, 30,* 395–401.

Truax, C. B., Wittmer, J., & Wargo, D. G. (1971). Effects of the therapeutic conditions of accurate empathy, non-possessive warmth, and genuineness on hospitalized mental patients during group therapy. *Journal of Clinical Psychology, 27,* 137–142.

VandenBos, G. R. (1970, June). *Rogerian therapist conditions in psychoanalytic psychotherapy.* Paper presented at the meeting of the Society for Psychotherapy Research, Chicago, IL.

Van der Veen, F. (1963, August). *The effects of the therapist and the patient on each other's therapeutic behavior early in therapy: A study of the beginning interviews of three patients with each of five therapists.* Paper presented at the meeting of the American Psychological Association, Philadelphia, PA.

Van der Veen, F. (1967a). Basic elements in the process of psychotherapy. *Journal of Consulting Psychology, 31,* 295–303.

Van der Veen, F. (1967b). The effects of the therapist and the patient on each other. In C. R. Rogers, E. T. Gendlin, D. J. Kiesler, & C. B. Truax (Eds.), *The therapeutic relationship and its impact* (pp. 353–366). Madison: University of Wisconsin Press.

Van der Veen, F., & Stoler, N. (1965). Therapists' judgments, interview behavior, and case outcome. *Psychotherapy, 2,* 158–163.

Walker, A., Rablen, R. A., & Rogers, C. R. (1960). Development of a scale to measure process change in psychotherapy. *Journal of Clinical Psychology, 16,* 79–85.

Walker, B. S., & Little, D. F. (1969). Factor analysis of the Barrett-Lennard Relationship Inventory. *Journal of Counseling Psychology, 16,* 516–521.

Watson, J. C., Greenberg, L. S., & Lietaer, G. (1998). The experiential paradigm unfolding: Relationship and experiencing in therapy. In L. S. Greenberg, J. C. Watson, & G. Lietaer (Eds.), *Handbook of experiential psychotherapy* (pp. 3–27). New York: Guilford.

Watson, N. (1984). The empirical status of Rogers' hypotheses of the necessary and sufficient conditions for effective psychotherapy. In R. F. Levant & J. M. Schlein (Eds.), *Client-centered therapy and the person-centered approach: New directions in theory, research, and practice* (pp. 17–40). New York: Praeger.

Ziemelis, A. (1974). Effects of client preference and expectancy upon the initial interview. *Journal of Counseling Psychology, 21,* 23–30.

11

Feedback

Charles D. Claiborn
Rodney K. Goodyear
Pamela A. Horner

DEFINITION AND OVERVIEW

Feedback is a ubiquitous feature of the psychotherapeutic process, just as it is of everyday life. Used as a deliberate, focused intervention, it is a powerful tool for changing client behavior as well as the perceptions and cognitions with which the client construes the self and the environment. Feedback as a concept and as an intervention does not have its origin in psychotherapy, nor even in psychology, but it has become so much a part of the therapeutic enterprise that it is now hard to imagine conducting therapy, talking about therapy, or training therapists without referring to feedback. As is often the case with concepts that are so widely applied, however, feedback is at once a simple and straightforward idea, yet also a complex set of processes that require understanding and skill to apply for maximum effect.

Basic definitions of feedback in psychology tend to stress that it is (1) information provided to a person (2) from an external source (3) about the person's behavior or the effects of that behavior. In the field of performance appraisal, feedback tends to be about how a person performs a task, and how well, relative to some goal or standard (Kluger & DeNisi, 1996). Thus, feedback has descriptive and evaluative components, though the proportion of these components can vary across situations. Giving feedback also implies that the giver has done some kind of assessment of the

receiver's behavior. In many cases, of course, the assessment is informal and ongoing, consisting of one person's perception of and reaction to another's behavior in the moment. Thus, according to the definition of Benne, Bradford, and Lippitt (1964), which has been widely used in the group process literature, "feedback . . . signifies verbal and nonverbal responses from others to a unit of behavior provided as close in time to the behavior as possible, and capable of being perceived and utilized by the individual initiating the behavior [that is, the receiver of the feedback]" (p. 24). In other cases, the assessment is much more formal and requires that the person giving the feedback applies some expertise to its formulation and delivery. In this regard, Dana and Graham (1976) defined feedback in clinical assessment as "client-relevant information resultant from interview or test-technique administration that is communicated directly to the client" (p. 464). Just as therapists employ both formal and informal assessments throughout psychotherapy, so does their feedback draw upon these various sources of information.

The form and content of feedback vary according to the nature and goals of the situation. Jacobs (1974) noted four general types of feedback content, all of which are common in psychotherapy. The first is an observation or description of the client's behavior, as for example in a role play involving assertion skills: "Your voice is halting here, and you're not maintaining eye contact." The second type is an emotional reaction to the client's behavior, as in this comment on a client's incongruent communication: "I think I'm getting a mixed message again, and I feel frustrated, like my hands are tied." The distinction between behavioral and emotional feedback has been very prominent in the literature (see Robison & Hardt, 1992), for these two types of feedback have been found to have different effects on receivers in interaction with other variables.

The third type of feedback is an inference about something that is not directly observable in the client, such as a trait or internal experience. This is an example from psychological assessment: "You seem to enjoy people and social situations, and tend to feel re-energized from interacting with others." Of course, personality assessment makes extensive use of inferential feedback, but all kinds of feedback, even the most simply descriptive, employ inference to some extent. This raises the question about the difference between feedback and interpretation, an issue that is addressed later in the chapter.

Jacobs (1974) referred to the fourth type of feedback as mirroring. This type is different from the others in that rather than receiving a message about his or her behavior, the client is presented with a sample of that behavior. A common example is the use of videotape in family therapy to show the family how it goes about making a decision.

A number of variables affect the functioning and impact of feedback. These variables have been the subject of considerable research, much of which is reviewed subsequently in this chapter. Such variables include the specificity versus generality of description, valence (positivity versus negativity), sequencing of positive and negative feedback, and the interpersonal context within which feedback is exchanged.

Feedback is a multifaceted intervention, and different facets have been highlighted by different writers. Sometimes these facets also suggest mechanisms by which feedback produces its effects in therapy. Researchers in group work have distinguished between the informational and motivational aspects of feedback and emphasized the importance of both. Morran, Robison, and Stockton (1985) described the informational aspect of

feedback as "a directive to modify behavior or keep it on course" (p. 57), referring to negative or positive feedback, respectively. They described the motivational aspect of feedback as "stimulat[ing] an emotional response that may enhance or hinder the corrective potential of the feedback process" (p. 57). Whereas the informational aspect of feedback points to its role in influencing the client toward therapeutic goals, the motivational aspect stresses that the emotion aroused by feedback is not invariably therapeutic, and that indeed, according to Morran and colleagues, "such emotion . . . [may] introduce distortion and resistance into the feedback exchange" (p. 57). It is the therapist's task as influence agent to manage feedback delivery, including contextual variables, so that the emotion aroused by feedback does not impair its clarity or contribute to client resistance.

Some of the facets of feedback make it resemble—and function like—other therapeutic interventions. Given its variable content, it is not surprising that feedback can have supportive or confrontive aspects. For example, in a weight-control clinic, Chang (1994) employed positive feedback as affirmative statements about clients' behavior. In their treatment of an agoraphobic client, DeVoge, Minor, and Karoly (1981) combined positive feedback of the affirmative sort with negative feedback about the client's unhealthy choices, which had a clearly confrontive edge: for example, "I have to hand it to you, Mr. Y, you sure *are* getting good at being sick" (p. 598).

The interpretive aspect of feedback has already been noted. Feedback becomes more interpretive as it moves away from the raw data of observation (descriptive feedback) and toward inferences based on those data (inferential feedback). But feedback is also interpretive for another reason; it offers the client not only new information, but a new perspective on the self and the world (Claiborn, 1982). Thus, Finn and Tonsager (1992), in their study of MMPI-2 interpretation as a therapeutic intervention, referred to feedback as interpretation by stating that the communication of test results "exposed [clients] to additional ways of thinking about themselves that were new but not in conflict with their existing self-definition" (p. 285). Feedback is similarly interpretive in ongoing therapy, which always includes ongoing assessment and the inferences that arise from it.

This last example illustrates one additional facet of feedback, namely, the reciprocal nature of feedback exchange (Strong & Claiborn, 1982). Though this chapter is concerned with the therapist's feedback to the client, it is important to emphasize that even this cannot be thought of as an isolated one-way communication. Any instance of feedback begins with an observation, or assessment, of another person's behavior. Thus, the therapist's feedback to the client is a response to the prior behavior of the client. In addition, the client, upon receiving the feedback, responds to it in some way—by attending to it, reflecting upon it, agreeing or disagreeing with it, correcting it, distorting it, incorporating it, and so on. Any such responses by the client, in turn, constitute feedback to the therapist about the feedback the therapist has just delivered. And so each instance of feedback is sandwiched between behaviors of the feedback receiver, and the behaviors of the feedback receiver are themselves feedback sent, in reciprocal fashion, to the giver. This makes both parties in the exchange simultaneously givers and receivers of feedback.

In this chapter, we focus primarily on feedback used by therapists in psychotherapy. We also describe feedback as delivered by group members to one another, inasmuch as it informs our general understanding of feedback. The chapter draws upon research from both basic and applied areas of psychology; however, our main purpose is to review the empirical research on the links between feedback and therapy outcome. Though a good bit of feedback research has involved the delivery of false feedback—including the so-called Barnum studies—this research is largely ignored in the chapter, except in a few instances. The effects of deliberately giving false feedback seem particularly irrelevant to clinical situations, in which the accuracy of information and the honesty of the therapist are paramount concerns (Claiborn & Hanson, 1999; Dana & Graham, 1976; Furnham & Schofield, 1987).

Before turning to research on feedback in psychotherapy, however, we want to place the concept of feedback in a larger psychological context. Thus, we examine feedback as a concept in psychology and psychotherapy theory.

FEEDBACK AS A CONSTRUCT IN PSYCHOLOGY AND PSYCHOTHERAPY

Though feedback has become a common concept in psychotherapy, it is relatively new as a construct in psychology. The social psychologist Kurt Lewin, who borrowed the term *feedback* from the field of electrical engineering, was the first to apply it in the behavioral sciences, particularly group dynamics (Yalom, 1995). Lewin employed the concept in small-group human relations training, the so-called T-groups. He theorized that behavior is a function of the person and the situation, and that in groups, the situation consists primarily of other members' behavior. He conceptualized the impact of others' behavior as feedback. Lewin's sense of the term *feedback* has been generally accepted in group work and, by extension, in other areas of applied psychology, including psychotherapy. Most of what is described as feedback in this chapter has its roots in Lewin's conceptualization of the term.

Another influential source of the concept of feedback is the field of cybernetics, which is concerned with the functioning of informational systems. In the case of psychology, the systems in question are human systems, such as dyadic relationships, groups, and families. According to Bateson (1968), feedback is the process by which one element of a system passes information to another element, with the result that the latter element changes its value. If the element is a person, as it is in human systems, then the change in value amounts to a change in the rate or type of behavior. According to a cybernetic definition, positive feedback has the effect of continuing or amplifying the person's behavior, essentially directing the person to "do more of the same." If the person is a family member who suddenly flies into a rage, then positive feedback (in the cybernetic sense) is any behavior on the part of other family members that maintains or escalates the rage.

Negative feedback, according to a cybernetic definition, has the effect of changing the person's behavior in the direction of its original state, or homeostasis. It directs the person to "behave as usual." Thus, in the example of the raging family member, negative feedback (in the cybernetic sense) is any behavior that discourages or de-escalates the rage and returns the family member to "normal"—that is, how the family expects this member to behave. Negative feedback maintains the stability or steady state of the system; however, "stability" (like "normal" in the previous sentence) does not necessarily connote psychological health, but rather the usual functioning of the system. We introduce the cybernetic definitions of feedback to emphasize how different they are from the other senses in which feedback is used in this chapter, but also because these definitions and related cybernetic concepts are so prominent in family therapy (see Watzlawick, Beavin, & Jackson, 1967). For the most part, however, these definitions of feedback are not used in this chapter.

In psychotherapy, feedback, like other interventions, can be usefully conceptualized as an influence process (Strong & Claiborn, 1982). According to this view, the therapist establishes a degree of social power in the relationship with the client, based on the therapist's possession of resources, such as expertise or similarity to the client, that the client can make use of in his or her change efforts (Strong & Matross, 1973). The therapist's social power translates into an ability to influence the client's behavior through the delivery of discrepant, change-promoting messages, such as feedback. Important variables in this process include therapist, message (feedback), client, and context characteristics. The impact of these variables as mediators and moderators of feedback in therapy are considered later in the chapter.

In contrast to the traditional view of feedback as a primarily discrepant, corrective intervention in psychotherapy, Kelly (2000) has argued, with some research support, for a different role of feedback in therapy. This is illustrated in the following sequence:

(a) Clients describe themselves in various ways (i.e., perform various self-presentations) to their therapists; (b) therapists then offer feedback to their clients based on those self-presentations; (c) this feedback can lead to the clients' shifting their self-beliefs in the direction of the feedback, particularly because the feedback is from an expert [i.e., the therapist]; and (d) this shifting of self-beliefs followed by similar self-presentations and feedback may eventually lead to changes in the clients' self-

concepts [i.e., in their relatively stable collections of self-beliefs]. (p. 476)

Kelly's model is controversial because it posits that the process is therapeutic even though—perhaps because—the clients have chosen *not* to disclose highly objectionable aspects of themselves, an idea that runs counter to the traditional wisdom about therapeutic disclosure and change. However, Kelly has argued that as long as clients present aspects of themselves that they believe in—the more positive self-beliefs from a range of possible self-beliefs—the therapist's feedback affirms those aspects and encourages their incorporation.

RESEARCH REVIEW

General Effects

The problem with exploring feedback effects in psychotherapy is that they are the focus of much less outcome research than their widespread use would warrant. One reason for this is that feedback takes so many different forms that it is often called by other names: praise, reinforcement, immediacy, confrontation, and interpretation. As form varies, so does function; feedback performs different functions in the change process, and therefore it is used to achieve different outcomes.

Though feedback is part of the common parlance in psychotherapy, it often does not appear as a category of therapist response in researchers' coding systems. Nevertheless, feedback is implicitly present in these systems, because feedback functions cut across several response categories. Elliott's (1985) taxonomy clusters therapist behavior according to its function, yet feedback seems to fall both in the new perspective category and in the reassurance category. Goldfried, Newman, and Hayes's Coding Scheme of Therapeutic Focus has a number of focus categories that are served by feedback (for a published description, see Goldsamt, Goldfried, Hayes, & Kerr, 1992). These include (1) the reality focus, in which the therapist helps the client see things more "objectively," that is, as a disinterested observer might see them; (2) the support focus, or therapist reassurance; (3) the change focus, in which the therapist describes the client's progress; (4) the pattern focus, in which the therapist points out patterns in the client's interpersonal behavior; and (5) the consequence focus, in which the therapist calls attention to the effects of the client's behavior.

As the coding systems suggest, feedback seems to have both interpretive and supportive functions. Its interpretive functions have already been described. On the supportive side, feedback contributes to a strong therapeutic relationship, one in which the client is engaged as a collaborator (Finn & Tonsager, 1992) and in which the client engages in the sorts of behaviors that make for effective therapy, because the therapist's feedback reinforces these behaviors (Chang, 1994). The supportive nature of feedback also contributes to important therapeutic outcomes. Thus, Kelly (2000) has emphasized the importance of positive feedback in shaping positive self-presentations in the client and thereby strengthening the client's self-concept.

In a different way, McNulty and Swann (1991) have described the use of positive feedback in *disconfirming* the specific negative self-perceptions of the client, despite the client's desire that these negative views be confirmed (as predicted by self-verification theory). They have also proposed an indirect way of changing self-concept through "noncontingent positive feedback" (p. 226), feedback that teaches and reinforces effective behavior in the client without connecting the behavior to negative self-perceptions the client wishes to maintain. Over time, the effective behaviors accumulate to impel changes in the client's self-perceptions and, in turn, self-concept. This approach illustrates the value of feedback in combating client resistance.

We turn now to examining the effects of feedback as a therapeutic intervention in specific clinical situations. We look in turn at individual therapy, couple and family therapy, group therapy, and personality assessment and test feedback. Table 11.1 summarizes the outcomes of this research (positive, mixed, or negative) by the four areas reviewed.

Individual Therapy

The four studies of individual therapy in which feedback has been studied as a separate intervention have dealt with assertion training and the treatment of phobia. In assertion training for women, Thelen and Lasoski (1980) examined the separate and combined effects of video playback, therapist focusing, and behavioral rehearsal. Both video playback and therapist focusing are feedback interventions, according to Jacobs's (1974) typology; video playback is mirroring, and therapist focusing is behavioral description. Results indicated that therapist focusing—providing direct performance feedback—was particularly effective in shaping assertive behavior, both alone and in combination with behavioral rehearsal. Therapist focusing in this study is a typical example of the sort of performance feedback that often accompanies skill development in therapy. It is probably one of the most common uses of feedback in individual therapy.

Leitenberg, Agras, Allen, Butz, and Edwards (1975) reported on five single case studies of treatment for phobic anxiety, in which the use of specific performance feedback was systematically added to and withdrawn from the use of praise. The performance feedback was purely informa-

Table 11.1. Summary of Outcomes of Feedback Studies

Treatment Type	Number of Studies	Number of Outcomes		
		Positive	Mixed	Negative
Individual therapy	4	4	0	0
Couple/family therapy	2	2	0	0
Group therapy	2	0	2	0
Personality assessment/test feedback	3	2	1	0

tional; it had to do with, for example, the time spent looking at or being in the presence of the feared stimulus. Praise consisted of positive evaluations ("excellent") following performance. Across the five cases, the application of performance feedback produced considerable change in approach behavior. Moreover, withdrawal of this feedback did not produce the decrement in behavior often observed in single case studies.

In another single case study, DeVoge and colleagues (1981) examined the use of interpersonal feedback as well as a number of other cognitive and behavioral interventions in the treatment of an agoraphobic client. The feedback here was more evaluative than descriptive; it confronted the client with the consequences of his behavior, positive and negative, and communicated the therapist's belief in the client's capabilities. The researchers reported that the use of feedback produced the most marked behavior change of any of the interventions.

Rapee and Hayman (1996) experimentally examined video playback in a treatment of social anxiety and found it to be effective in reducing anxiety. They reasoned that since socially anxious clients tend to evaluate their own social behavior very negatively, video feedback—confrontation with more "objective" data—lessened this tendency.

In summary, it is probably unwise to draw too many conclusions from such limited research. However, these studies demonstrate the power of feedback interventions, as the outcomes observed in each of the four studies was fairly dramatic and quite positive. In addition, the studies illustrate the diversity of the form and function of feedback in actual therapeutic situations.

Couple and Family Therapy

Though the use of feedback in couple and family therapy is extremely common, only two studies have focused specifically on this technique. In the practice of therapy with couples, there has been a growing use of test feedback as an intervention to promote mutual understanding and facilitate problem solving. In the one study of test feedback with couples conducted to date, Worthington and colleagues (1995) found that giving test feedback to couples, based on an extensive battery of instruments, produced gains in dyadic satisfaction and commitment to working on the relationship, as compared with the no-feedback control.

With respect to family therapy, one study has focused on feedback as a central component of treatment. Kemenoff, Worchel, Prevatt, and Willson (1995) conducted a study of family therapy that was based on the Milan approach. They compared video playback and therapist verbal feedback following a task assigned by the therapist. The task was videotaped in both conditions, but in the former condition the family viewed the tape itself, and in the latter condition, the therapist viewed the tape and gave the family verbal feedback. Results indicated that the video playback condition instilled a greater sense of responsibility among family members for the problem, as well as greater symptomatic improvement.

Obviously, no conclusions can be drawn from one study each of couple and family therapy, despite the fact that both studies used rigorous research designs and both produced positive outcomes. We include them here primarily as illustrations of the sorts of feedback practices used in these treatment modalities. Neither use of feedback is unique, of course, as test and video feedback are common techniques in individual treatment, as well.

Group Therapy

The group therapist's primary role with respect to feedback is to establish the climate and norms for feedback exchange by group members. Not surprisingly, the nature of the feedback exchanged in the group changes as the group moves through different stages and faces different goals. Research on feedback at different stages of group development has consistently shown that positive feedback is important (and prevalent) early in group development in order to establish trust and cohesion, whereas a combination of negative and positive feedback is more useful (and again, prevalent) later on, where it contributes powerfully to interpersonal learning (see Morran et al., 1985; Stockton & Morran, 1981).

In their review of research on group therapist behavior, Bednar, Melnick, and Kaul (1974) stressed the importance of therapist structuring in shaping such group tasks as feedback exchange.

Two studies have focused specifically on the impact of structuring on feedback in groups. Robison and Hardt (1992) experimented with providing growth group members with cognitive and behavioral structure for giving feedback. Cognitive structure, as they defined it, concerns the rationale for giving feedback, such as how it contributes to group process and interpersonal learning. Behavioral structure consists of specific guidelines for giving and receiving feedback. They found that a combination of these two kinds of structure, accompanied by actual practice in feedback, increased the amount of corrective (and therefore, risky) feedback exchanged in the group. Rose and Bednar (1980), noting the difficulty of exchanging negative feedback in groups, also found structuring to be helpful in establishing more effective feedback sequences (particularly, positive-to-negative sequences) in group members. They recommended that group therapists and facilitators provide such structuring in early group sessions. As Bednar and colleagues (1974) concluded in their review, providing sufficient structure to groups early on reduces members' unreasonable sense of responsibility for feedback outcomes and increases feedback exchange.

In summary, a small amount of research has pointed to the role of therapist structuring in enhancing feedback exchange in group therapy. Specifically, we found two such studies, each with mixed results. No studies have focused specifically on the therapist's delivery of feedback in the group, though considerable research has concerned factors affecting feedback effectiveness in group process; this latter research can apply (with due caution) to therapist-delivered feedback as well as to feedback exchanged by group members. This research is reviewed in the section on mediators and moderators.

Personality Assessment and Test Feedback

Ideas about giving clients feedback based on personality assessment has changed dramatically in the field of psychotherapy. Not so long ago, test results and other diagnostic information were generally not shared with clients, but more recently, test feedback has come to be seen as beneficial for clients. Goodyear and Lichtenberg (1999)

have suggested three reasons to give clients test feedback. The first is to respond to an ethical imperative: Because psychological tests are invasive and their results can have real consequences, test takers have a right to their results. Principle 2.09 of the American Psychological Association's Ethical Principles and Code of Conduct (1992) states that psychologists are to explain test results "using language that is reasonably understandable to the person assessed or to another legally authorized person on behalf of the client" (p. 1604). The second reason is to help clients monitor treatment progress. Clients can be given the results of the same test—say, the Beck Depression Inventory or Brief Symptom Inventory—taken at multiple points during therapy. Such feedback can provide encouragement and consolidate changes.

The third reason is the one that receives primary focus in this chapter—namely, that test results can be discussed with clients in the course of therapy as an aspect of treatment. In some ways test feedback can offer the client information that other feedback from the therapist cannot. To begin with, the use of tests provides observations with established reliability and validity. To tell a client that she or he scored at the 73rd percentile on a well-developed measure of achievement motivation conveys more information than if the therapist simply shared the impression that the client seemed driven to achieve. In addition, most psychological tests have multiple scales that together provide a useful conceptual framework for clients to organize their thinking about themselves. Finally, just as the therapist has credibility as a source of valid information, so may tests have credibility. Therefore, the client who receives test feedback in therapy has exposure to two sources of information and influence, which in turn can make the impact of the information all the more powerful (Claiborn & Hanson, 1999).

Test Feedback Outcomes

Fischer (1970) deserves credit for the original blending of what might be considered the clinical and counseling assessment traditions. She advocated involving the client as a collaborator during the assessment process and the writing of psychological reports. Finn and Tonsager (1997), the researchers currently most associated with this blending, have acknowledged Fischer's influence on their conceptualization of "therapeutic assessment."

To date, three studies have attempted to connect test feedback to psychotherapy outcomes. In an experimental study, Finn and Tonsager (1992) demonstrated that interpreting MMPI-2 test results to clients can have a therapeutic effect, namely, reduction in symptomatic distress, increased self-esteem, and increased optimism about overcoming problems. They claim that their study was the "first empirical test of personality test feedback as a therapeutic aid to brief, time-limited psychotherapy" (p. 279).

Newman and Greenway (1997) have since replicated their work with methodological improvements. Whereas Finn and Tonsager (1992) administered the MMPI-2 only to clients who were to receive feedback, Newman and Greenway administered the test to clients in feedback and non-feedback conditions, so that the effect of simply taking the test could be controlled. They found that clients receiving feedback showed increased self-esteem immediately after the feedback session and greater symptomatic improvement two weeks after the session, compared with clients not receiving feedback. These findings were entirely consistent with those of Finn and Tonsager, but stronger, given the inclusion of a non-feedback condition. A limitation of both studies, however, was the use of a single therapist who was also one of the researchers.

Miller, Benefield, and Tonigan (1993) demonstrated the effectiveness of test feedback with alcoholic clients. They examined two styles of giving feedback about results from two alcoholism screening instruments. In one style the therapist was directive-confrontive; in the other the therapist was nondirective. Clients who participated in either test feedback condition showed greater reduction in drinking than a control group at both 6-week and 1-year follow-ups. However, the directive-confrontive style aroused more resistance and predicted poorer outcomes after a year than did the nondirective style.

Test Feedback Process

One important issue in test feedback is the extent to which the client is actively involved in finding meaning in the test results versus being a more passive receiver of the information (Goodyear, 1990). Only two studies have examined this issue, both of which isolated test feedback in very brief counseling. Hanson, Claiborn, and Kerr (1997) experimentally compared two methods of delivering test (Personality Research Form and Vocational Preference Inventory) feedback to clients. They designed the first method to be "interactive," in that therapist and client were collaborative and the client was invited to offer specific examples of the interpretation. In the second method the feedback was "delivered," meaning that the client was given the interpretation and an opportunity to ask questions about it, but was otherwise not invited to interact about the interpretation. In this published study, in which test feedback was given to undergraduate honors student clients, they found the interactive approach to be superior. However, in a subsequent study with non-honors students (Claiborn, Hanson, Burgess, & Mathews, 2000), the delivered approach was more effective. Thus, it is possible feedback style interacts with either the ability or motivation of the client in affecting test interpretation outcomes, though this hypothesis has not been tested directly.

In summary, the research on test feedback to clients is surprisingly scant (Goodyear, 1990). It is hard to draw many conclusions from the research other than that, first, giving test feedback to clients can be quite beneficial, and second, a collaborative or interactive approach to providing feedback may be more effective than a more directive style. With respect to test feedback outcomes—the first conclusion—two of the studies produced generally positive outcomes (Finn & Tonsager, 1992; Newman & Greenway, 1997), and the third a mixed outcome, given the resistance aroused by one of the feedback conditions (Miller, Benefield, & Tonigan, 1993).

MEDIATORS AND MODERATORS

In studying the influence process, psychologists have generally designated variables as having to do with the *source* of influential messages, the *message* itself, the *receiver* of the message, and the *context* in which influence takes place. We adopt the same approach here in describing the important variables in the feedback process in therapy. In the use of feedback in therapy, the primary source of feedback is the therapist, though in formal assessment situations, assessment instruments, such as the MMPI-2 or the Strong Interest Inventory, are additional sources of feedback (Claiborn & Hanson, 1999). Many of the same variables that affect therapist social power also affect the credibility of the test. The influential messages are, of course, the feedback interventions, and in this chapter we include both content and stylistic variables as message variables. The receiver of the feedback is the client, and therefore client variables are those characteristics of the client that affect his or her responses to the feedback, from seeking it (which initiates the feedback process) to incorporating it and making behavior changes based on it (which completes the feedback process). The context of feedback delivery includes both the therapeutic relationship within which the feedback is exchanged, as well as the specific framing or structure the feedback situation is given. Therapist, message, client, and context variables in the feedback process are each examined in turn.

Therapist Variables

Researchers in both social psychology and psychotherapy stress the importance of the source's social power, particularly source credibility, in affecting responses to feedback. Therapist credibility is generally based in the client's perception that the therapist is knowledgeable and skilled in the areas relevant to the client's need (Strong & Matross, 1973), and in a specific instance of feedback, it is probably also important that the client see the therapist as having sufficient information on which to base the feedback. In discussing the implications of self-verification theory for psychotherapy, McNulty and Swann (1991) especially emphasized the importance of therapist social power in giving disconfirming feedback to clients, which is of course feedback that clients are most likely to resist. In his review of feedback in group work, including feedback provided by group therapists or group leaders, Kivlighan (1985) concluded that the social power of the giver is the most important variable affecting the

acceptance of feedback by the receiver. In both cases, social power is likely to be based in the therapist's credibility, but sometimes it may be based in the therapist's social attractiveness, or likeability, as well.

Chang's (1994) research has called attention to reciprocal relations between the giving of feedback and the credibility of the giver. In his study, interviewers provided positive (accepting, encouraging) or neutral feedback to clients in a weight-control clinic. Clients who received positive feedback complied more with interviewer requests than those in the neutral condition. Since compliance is one outcome of influence, this effect suggests that providing positive feedback enhances one's social power in a therapeutic context like this one. In addition, since the positive feedback in this study was of a supportive sort, the social power that resulted from it was as likely to be social attractiveness as it was credibility.

In summary, establishing social power is an important prerequisite to delivering feedback in therapy, if the therapist wishes to increase the probability that the client will accept the feedback or otherwise respond to it in accordance with the goals of therapy. The social power is likely to be credibility, based on the therapist's credentials as a professional (including expertise in the need areas of the client), but it can also include social attractiveness, as the therapist creates a supportive and collaborative relationship with the client. In addition, the therapist is likely to draw upon the credibility of any assessment instruments he or she might use in providing feedback to the client based on these instruments.

Message Variables

By far the most research on feedback has dealt with the content and style of the message. Much of this research has been conducted in naturalistic interpersonal situations, such as dyads and small groups, though these have not necessarily been therapeutic in aim. Only occasionally has the research been done in therapeutic situations. Even so, this body of research has much to offer the practicing therapist, as long as the findings are considered with appropriate caution. The message variables reviewed here are feedback valence and sequencing.

Valence

Valence refers to the direction of feedback, that is, the extent to which it is positive or negative. Positive feedback in this sense refers to communication that praises, supports, and encourages the client or that describes the client's behavior as effective relative to some specific criterion. "You have really improved in your ability to label your feelings" is an example of positive feedback. Negative, or corrective, feedback describes the client's behavior as ineffective relative to a criterion. An example of negative feedback is, "I notice that you tend to smile when you talk about being angry." Feedback such as "You seem to be presenting yourself as a very logical person" is ambiguous with respect to valence, since its evaluative cues are minimal and the criterion for effectiveness is not implicitly clear. The valence of feedback dramatically affects its acceptability to the receiver, whether alone or in interaction with other variables. Thus, understanding and managing valence is essential to the feedback deliverer's effectiveness.

The most consistent finding in this literature is that positive feedback is more acceptable to receivers than is negative feedback (see Jacobs, 1974; Kivlighan, 1985). This is the so-called credibility gap (Jacobs, p. 431) in group dynamics. Comparing it to negative feedback, participants in various small group studies have rated positive feedback as more credible, desirable, helpful, and meaningful—the four most common outcome criteria for feedback effectiveness (Martin & Jacobs, 1980; Morran et al., 1985; Morran & Stockton, 1980; Robinson, 1970; Rotheram, LaCour, & Jacobs, 1982). In a non-group setting of students receiving personality feedback, Davies (1997) also found that positive feedback was considered more accurate than negative feedback. This suggests that the effect generalizes to other feedback situations. Davies also examined the way his participants processed feedback differing in valence. He found that positive feedback produced more consistent than inconsistent cognitive processing, whereas negative feedback produced no difference in processing.

The variable of valence has been found to interact with the variable of time in small groups. The effect of this is that the credibility gap is wider in early group sessions and diminishes substantially in later sessions, after trust and cohesion have been established (Morran et al., 1985; Stockton & Morran, 1981). Rotheram and colleagues (1982) also found that positive feedback was more effective than negative in producing group cohesion and trust, thus setting the stage for richer feedback exchange in subsequent sessions.

Extrapolating these results to therapy generally, one might expect that positive feedback is more likely to be seen as accurate and useful by clients, especially early on in the relationship. As the working alliance becomes established and the goals of the client (and thus the criteria for judging the effectiveness of the client's behavior) are clear, negative feedback is likely to be accepted as accurate and useful, as well. The client may even come to desire such feedback because it relates to the goals for change, and it may be effective in setting the direction for change.

Sequencing

Sequencing of positive and negative feedback is important especially to the acceptability of negative feedback. Negative feedback is generally more acceptable when it is preceded by positive feedback (Rose & Bednar, 1980; Stockton & Morran, 1981) or "sandwiched" between positive feedback statements (Morran, Stockton, Cline, & Teed, 1998). As a particularly good illustrative study, Schaible and Jacobs (1975) examined the sequencing of positive and negative feedback in small groups. Results indicated that participants rated negative feedback more acceptable and desirable when it was preceded by positive feedback than when it was not. On the other hand, positive feedback was rated less desirable when it was preceded by negative feedback. Given these sequencing effects, they recommended a strategy of delivering positive feedback in the early part of an intervention in order to increase the acceptability of negative feedback delivered subsequently. Rose and Bednar (1980) cautiously concurred with this recommendation. Finally, in his review of the literature on feedback in group therapy, Kivlighan (1985) concluded that clients view the positive-to-negative sequence of feed-back as more credible, desirable, and meaningful than other combinations. We may generalize this conclusion, with due caution, to feedback sequencing in therapy generally.

Client Variables

As the receiver of the therapist's feedback, the client plays an active role throughout the feedback process. The client solicits feedback through self-presentations, problem presentations, and direct requests for feedback. In addition, the client must fully attend to and cognitively process the therapist's feedback in order for the feedback to *begin* to have an impact on the client's self-perceptions and behavior. Most important, the client plays an active role in responding to the feedback with a full range of possible responses, including such positive outcomes as acceptance and incorporation and such negative outcomes as distortion, denial, or outright rejection. Certain personal characteristics of the client contribute to the feedback process by affecting the client's participation in it. These include the client's self-esteem, mood, and desire for feedback.

Self-Esteem

Many clients exhibit low self-esteem, so that research relating self-esteem to feedback is especially relevant to psychotherapy, even though the research has generally been conducted in social psychological settings. In a series of studies, Baumgardner, Kaufman, and Levy (1989) arranged for participants to receive feedback from a personality test or from another person; in each case, participants believed the feedback to be valid, though it was in fact false. High self-esteem participants judged the positive feedback to be more accurate than negative feedback—a common finding among people in general (Jacobs, 1974; Kivlighan, 1985). Low self-esteem participants, however, judged neither type of feedback to be more accurate. The results seem to support the self-verification hypothesis (McNulty & Swann, 1991). Low self-esteem participants did not judge positive feedback to be especially accurate, since it did not confirm their beliefs about themselves.

Tafarodi (1998), using a similar false-feedback procedure, studied participants with "paradoxical" self-esteem, that is, participants whose self-efficacy was high but self-liking was low, or vice versa. The outcome in this study was memory, rather than perception, of personality feedback. Results indicated that participants who were paradoxically low or high in self-esteem were more negatively and positively biased in their memory of feedback, respectively, than subjects who were simply low or high in self-esteem. Thus, the self-liking portion of paradoxical self-esteem predicted the bias in feedback processing: If self-liking was low, bias was negative; if self-liking was high, bias was positive.

Finally, Morran and Stockton (1980) conducted a self-esteem study more directly related to actual therapy, a study that in addition involved valid, rather than false, feedback. Participants in ongoing counseling groups exchanged feedback in the sixth session of the groups. Results indicated that participants with high self-esteem rated negative feedback as more desirable than did participants with moderate self-esteem. Desirability is one of several indices of feedback acceptability. This finding is not really inconsistent with the study by Baumgardner and colleagues (1989), since desirability is a different variable than accuracy; even though the high-self esteem participants rated negative feedback as more desirable than other participants did, they nevertheless rated positive feedback as more desirable than negative.

Mood

Another variable that has particular relevance to psychotherapy is the mood of the person receiving feedback. Dysphoria, or depressed mood, has been examined in feedback studies using widely differing procedures. Nelson and Craighead (1977) studied performance feedback in a learning paradigm—a situation admittedly remote from therapy. Using the Beck Depression Inventory to differentiate between depressed and nondepressed participants, they found that depressed participants recalled more negative and less positive feedback than nondepressed participants. In addition, depressed participants were more accurate in recalling the amount of negative feedback they had received than nondepressed participants, who underestimated the amount. The researchers related their findings to Beck's (1967) cognitive theory of depression, in particular to the negative cognitive processing that characterizes depression.

MacFarland and Morris (1998) also differentiated participants on the Beck Depression Inventory and administered negative performance feedback to them in a memory paradigm. Compared with nondepressed participants, depressed participants were more suggestible after receiving negative feedback—that is, they were more likely than nondepressed participants to shift their responses in the direction of the leading questions of the interviewers.

Finally, in a study that involved group interaction, Dykman, Horowitz, Abramson, and Usher (1991) examined the respective roles that depressive schemata, or self-beliefs, and social skill deficits play in responses to ambiguous, disconfirming feedback. The study used a false-feedback procedure. Depressed participants (again, assessed by the Beck Depression Inventory) were more negative than nondepressed participants in interpreting the ambiguous feedback. In addition, the fact that they were less socially skillful in the interaction seemed to contribute to their negative processing somewhat independently of their negative schemata. This suggests that biased processing is based not simply in the negative beliefs depressed clients have about themselves, but in their accurate awareness of their own social performance, as well. This finding is consistent with that of Nelson and Craighead (1977) in drawing attention to the realistic basis of negative cognitive processing in depressed people.

Desire for Feedback

The receiver's desire for feedback was explored in a series of studies by Snyder, Ingram, Handelsman, Wells, and Huweiler (1982). They measured desire for feedback with a single item that serves as a definition of the variable:

Individuals vary in the extent to which they want to have feedback about themselves from other people. For example, people differ in their desire to know "how they are doing" in school performance, social activities, work settings, psychological tests, etc. *Generally speaking, to what extent do you like to get feedback about yourself?* (p. 318)

In a false-feedback study of test interpretation, the researchers found that participants high in desire for feedback were more differentially accepting of positive versus negative feedback (that is, showing greater acceptance of positive feedback) than were clients low in this desire. In a study of help-seeking attitudes, they found that desire for feedback was modestly correlated with positive therapeutic expectancies. Participants low in desire for feedback, however, indicated that they were less willing to seek help for psychological problems than those high in this desire. Finally, in a study comparing client and nonclient samples, they found that though both samples were generally interested in receiving feedback, nonclient participants showed a higher desire for feedback than participants who were clients.

In summary, the literature on receiver variables in the feedback process is suggestive of ways in which the client actively contributes to the process. The client's level of self-esteem and mood may be especially predictive of the client's cognitive processing and incorporation of feedback. The client's desire for feedback may relate to many aspects of the feedback process, from his or her willingness to seek feedback opportunities, to the differential acceptance of positive and negative feedback. The therapist's sensitivity to and consideration of such client variables in planning feedback interventions may be crucial in their success.

Context Variables

Context refers to the relationship that the therapist must create in order to use feedback to therapeutic effect. It also refers to the specific ways in which the therapist prepares the client to receive feedback—the framing or structuring the therapist provides for the feedback process. The therapist certainly wants the client to make good use of the information in the feedback and to extend or modify that information to enhance its applicability. The therapist also wants to minimize the possibility that the client will misunderstand, distort, or resist the feedback.

Context variables have not been the subject of as much research as other aspects of the feedback process; rather our understanding of context has been informed primarily by clinical observation and assumption. In addition, discussion of context has focused on feedback that accompanies formal assessment, such as test interpretation; nevertheless, with minimal modification it can be generalized to most feedback situations in therapy.

A collaborative relationship seems to be especially important for effective feedback exchange (Berg, 1985; Clair & Prendergast, 1994). The procedure described by Finn (1996) for MMPI-2 interpretation is based on collaboration: The client sets goals for the assessment by coming up with the questions that he or she would like the test results to address. The therapist makes clear that the while the MMPI-2 is a valuable source of information about personality, particularly in problematic areas, the client is the expert with regard to his or her own life. The client is therefore invited to be an active partner in the interpretation process, to apply the results to specific circumstances and issues and to correct the results when they do not seem to fit. Finn and Tonsager (1992) further noted that the feedback process itself serves a rapport-building function in that it establishes collaboration in the assessment phases of therapy that may be continued throughout therapy.

According to Pope (1992), structuring the relationship for assessment and feedback is an ethical imperative as well. Formal assessment and subsequent feedback rely on informed consent, in which (1) the goals and procedures are made clear in advance, so that the client knows what to expect; (2) the roles and responsibilities of the therapist and client are explained; and (3) possible outcomes of the process are explored, especially how the feedback will be used in therapy. Pope also cautioned therapists to acknowledge the possible error in feedback (for example, psychometric limitations of formal assessment instruments) and to guard against using feedback against the client (for example, harsh treatment recommendations for a client with whom the therapist is angry). Finally, he stressed the importance of follow-through in the feedback process. The therapist must allow the client an opportunity to explore emotional reactions to the feedback.

In summary, though there is not much research evidence for the effects of context variables in the feedback process, there seems to be a clinical consensus that (1) the relationship be collaborative, so that therapist and client can inform each other; (2) the feedback situation be carefully framed, so that the client knows what to expect; and (3) the feedback itself be made clear, understandable, and relevant to the client, given the client's own needs and goals. As constructive as the context is, however, client resistance to feedback, like resistance to other aspects of therapy, is to be expected as a natural part of the client's response to a challenging intervention. Effective feedback delivery therefore includes anticipation of the likely responses of the client to the feedback, positive and negative, as well as sensitive and thorough follow-through, whatever these responses turn out to be.

THERAPEUTIC PRACTICES

The literature on feedback is rich and diverse and does not contribute to a single conceptualization of feedback. The literature is perhaps most usefully summarized as a set of recommendations for therapists, with the proviso that the usefulness of the recommendations may vary considerably depending on the circumstances of the case, the particular approach to treatment, and therapy goals. Most of the recommendations have moderate to strong research support, though as we have noted throughout the chapter, the research has not always been conducted in clinical settings with participants who are actual clients. When it has not, we have nevertheless included it when the circumstances of the research seemed to resemble therapeutic interactions reasonably closely. Still, caution must be exercised in extrapolating these findings to actual therapy. Our clinical recommendations regarding feedback are as follows:

1. Feedback ranges from descriptive to inferential, a continuum that reflects its closeness to the raw data of observation. Generally, feedback is more useful when it is descriptive, though feedback based on formal assessments like psychological tests are necessarily descriptive and inferential.

2. Positive feedback is generally more acceptable to clients than negative feedback. The acceptability of negative feedback can be increased, however, through establishing a safe and trusting relationship and by preceding negative feedback with positive feedback.

3. Positive and negative feedback have different roles in the change process. Positive feedback affirms client self-perceptions and shapes and cements the client's self-concept. Negative feedback serves as a corrective in shaping client attitudes and behaviors.

4. The optimal therapeutic relationship for feedback exchange seems to be a collaborative one. Such a relationship is not only important for feedback exchange, but exchanging feedback—particularly positive feedback—also contributes to the establishment of that relationship.

5. Structuring the situation for feedback is important in shaping client expectancies for feedback and in preparing the client to receive and make use of the feedback. Therapists do this by describing the feedback process and goals in a clear way. Therapists may additionally train clients in the skills of giving and receiving feedback.

6. The social power of the therapist, based on a combination of expertise and social attractiveness, contributes importantly to the acceptability of feedback.

7. The client's low self-esteem and negative mood may bias processing of feedback in a negative direction. It is essential that the therapist keep these client characteristics in mind in planning, carrying out, and following through on feedback interventions.

8. Feedback can be in error, and the client's response may be necessary to correct it. In addition, feedback can arouse client resistance, including the dismissal or distortion of the feedback. Berg (1985) offered a list of possible defensive responses clients might make to the feedback they receive: (1) "helpless perplexity" (p. 65), indicating a lack of responsibility for their behavior and their problems; (2) counterargument, attempting to prove the assessment wrong; (3) disinterest; (4) "glib acceptance" (p. 66); and (5) unwillingness to end the session, suggesting a dependence on the therapist. Of course, whether or not such responses are defensive in nature or appropriate responses to the feedback—which may have indeed been confusing, incorrect, or irrelevant—is a judgment that calls for therapist sensitivity and expertise. In any case, to allow for the possibility of feedback error or client resistance, it is important that the therapist allow for the feedback to be discussed and worked through.

9. In relationship, family, and group therapy, the therapist is responsible not only for his or her own feedback but for the feedback the members exchange. Therapist structuring increases the effectiveness of members' feedback and diminishes the possibility of detrimental effects.

10. Test feedback seems more effective when preceded by a goal-setting or question-generating discussion. This allows the test results to be framed in terms of client needs and interests.

In addition to these general recommendations, Morran and colleagues (1998) offered specific suggestions for group therapists and facilitators. These included (1) modeling appropriate feedback delivery; (2) instructing group members in giving effective feedback; (3) inviting group members to discuss their feelings about giving and receiving feedback; (4) using structured feedback exchanges, especially when feedback is not being offered spontaneously; (5) cutting off feedback when it seems unhelpful (for example, the receiver is not ready for it or the message is too harshly worded); (6) reinforcing some feedback through consensual validation, that is, asking if other members of the group also experience the receiver in a particular way; and (7) inviting the receiver to connect the feedback to his or her experiences in the group or everyday life.

REFERENCES

American Psychological Association (1992). Ethical principles of psychologists and code of conduct. *American Psychologist, 47,* 1597–1611.

Bateson, G. (1968). The biosocial integration of behavior in the schizophrenic family. In D. D. Jackson (Ed.), *Therapy, communication, and change* (pp. 9–15). Palo Alto, CA: Science and Behavior.

Baumgardner, A. H., Kaufman, C. M., & Levy, P. E. (1989). Regulating affect interpersonally when low esteem leads to greater enhancement. *Journal of Personality and Social Psychology, 56,* 907–921.

Beck, A. T. (1967). *Depression: Causes and treatment.* Philadelphia: University of Pennsylvania Press.

Bednar, R. L., Melnick, J., & Kaul, T. J. (1974). Risk, responsibility, and structure: A conceptual framework for initiating group counseling and psychotherapy. *Journal of Counseling Psychology, 21,* 31–37.

Benne, K. D., Bradford, L. P., & Lippitt, R. (1964). The laboratory method. In L. P. Bradford, J. R. Gibb, & K. D. Benne (Eds.), *T-group theory and laboratory method* (pp. 15–44). New York: Wiley.

Berg, M. (1985). The feedback process in diagnostic psychological testing. *Bulletin of the Menninger Clinic, 49,* 52–69.

Chang, P. (1994). Effects of interview questions and response type on compliance: An analogue study. *Journal of Counseling Psychology, 41,* 74–82.

Claiborn, C. D. (1982). Interpretation and change in counseling. *Journal of Counseling Psychology, 29,* 439–453.

Claiborn, C. D., & Hanson, W. E. (1999). Test interpretation: A social influence perspective. In J. W. Lichtenberg & R. K. Goodyear (Eds.), *Scientist-practitioner perspectives on test interpretation* (pp. 151–166). Needham Heights, MA: Allyn & Bacon.

Claiborn, C. D., Hanson, W. E., Burgess, D. H., & Mathews, T. (2000, August). Test interpretations in the counseling process: A research agenda. In T. Vacha-Haase (Chair), *Improving test interpretation and feedback: Guidelines for practical application.* Symposium conducted at the meeting of the American Psychological Association, Washington, DC.

Clair, D., & Prendergast, D. (1994). Brief psychotherapy and psychological assessments: Entering a relationship, establishing a focus, and providing feedback. *Professional Psychology: Research and Practice, 25,* 46–49.

Dana, R. H., & Graham, E. D. (1976). Feedback of client-relevant information and clinical practice. *Journal of Personality Assessment, 40,* 464–469.

Davies, M. F. (1997). Positive test strategies and confirmatory retrieval processes in the evaluation of personality feedback. *Journal of Personality and Social Psychology, 73,* 574–583.

DeVoge, J. T., Minor, T., & Karoly, P. (1981). Effects of behavioral intervention and interpersonal feedback on fear and avoidance components of severe agoraphobia: A case analysis. *Psychological Reports, 49,* 595–605.

Dykman, B. M., Horowitz, L. M., Abramson, L. Y., & Usher, M. (1991). Schematic and situational determinants of depressed and nondepressed students' interpretation of feedback. *Journal of Abnormal Psychology, 100,* 45–55.

Elliott, R. (1985). Helpful and nonhelpful events in brief counseling interviews: An empirical taxonomy. *Journal of Counseling Psychology, 32,* 307–322.

Finn, S. E. (1996). *Manual for using the MMPI-2 as a therapeutic intervention.* Minneapolis: University of Minnesota Press.

Finn, S. E., & Tonsager, M. E. (1992). Therapeutic effects of providing MMPI-2 test feedback to college students awaiting therapy. *Psychological Assessment, 4,* 278–287.

Finn, S. E., & Tonsager, M. E. (1997). Information-gathering and therapeutic models of assessment: Complementary paradigms. *Psychological Assessment, 9,* 374–385.

Fischer, C. T. (1970). The testee as co-evaluator. *Journal of Counseling Psychology, 17,* 70–76.

Furnham, A., & Schofield, S. (1987). Accepting personality test feedback: A review of the Barnum effect. *Current Psychological Research and Reviews, 6,* 162–178.

Goldsamt, L. A., Goldfried, M. R., Hayes, A. M., & Kerr, S. (1992). Beck, Meichenbaum, and Strupp: A comparison of three therapies on the dimension of therapeutic feedback. *Psychotherapy Research, 29,* 167–176.

Goodyear, R. K. (1990). Research on the effects of test interpretation: A review. *The Counseling Psychologist, 18,* 240–257.

Goodyear, R. K., & Lichtenberg, J. W. (1999). A scientist-practitioner perspective on test interpretation. In J. W. Lichtenberg & R. K. Goodyear (Eds.), *Scientist-practitioner perspectives on test interpretation* (pp. 1–14). Needham Heights, MA: Allyn & Bacon.

Hanson, W. E., Claiborn, C. D., & Kerr, B. (1997). Differential effects of two test-interpretation styles in counseling: A field study. *Journal of Counseling Psychology, 44,* 400–405.

Jacobs, A. (1974). The use of feedback in groups. In A. Jacobs and W. E. Spradlin (Eds.), *The group as an agent of change* (pp. 408–448). New York: Behavioral Publications.

Kelly, A. E. (2000). Helping construct desirable identities: A self-presentational view of psychotherapy. *Psychological Bulletin, 126,* 475–494.

Kemenoff, S., Worchel, F., Prevatt, B., & Willson, V. (1995). The effects of video feedback in the context of Milan Systemic therapy. *Journal of Family Psychology, 9,* 446–450.

Kivlighan, D. M. (1985). Feedback in group psychotherapy: Review and implications. *Small Group Behavior, 16,* 373–385.

Kluger, A. N., & DeNisi, A. (1996). The effects of feedback interventions on performance: A historical review, a meta-analysis, and a preliminary feedback intervention theory. *Psychological Bulletin, 119,* 254–284.

Leitenberg, H., Agras, W. S., Allen, R., Butz, R., & Edwards, J. (1975). Feedback and therapist praise during treatment of phobia. *Journal of Consulting and Clinical Psychology, 43,* 396–404.

MacFarland, W. L., & Morris, S. J. (1998). Are dysphoric individuals more suggestible or less suggestible than nondysphoric individuals? *Journal of Counseling Psychology 45,* 225–229.

Martin, L., & Jacobs, M. (1980). Structured feedback delivered in small groups. *Small Group Behavior, 11,* 88–107.

McNulty, S. E., & Swann, W. B. (1991). Psychotherapy, self-concept change, and self-verification. In R. C. Curtis (Ed.), *The relational self* (pp. 213–237). New York: Guilford.

Miller, W. R., Benefield, R. G., & Tonigan, J. S. (1993). Enhancing motivation for change in problem drinking: A controlled comparison of two therapist styles. *Journal of Consulting and Clinical Psychology, 61,* 455–461.

Morran, D. K., Robison, F., & Stockton, R. (1985). Feedback exchange in counseling groups: An analysis of message content and receiver acceptance as a function of leader versus member delivery, session, and valence. *Journal of Counseling Psychology, 32,* 57–67.

Morran, D. K., & Stockton, R. (1980). Effect of self-concept on group member reception of positive and negative feedback. *Journal of Counseling Psychology, 27,* 260–267.

Morran, D. K., Stockton, R., Cline, R. J., & Teed, C. (1998). Facilitating feedback exchange in groups: Leader interventions. *Journal for Specialists in Group Work, 23,* 257–268.

Nelson, R. E., & Craighead, W. E. (1977). Selective recall of positive and negative feedback, self-control behaviors, and depression. *Journal of Abnormal Psychology, 86,* 379–388.

Newman, M. L., & Greenway, P. (1997). Therapeutic effects of providing MMPI-2 test feedback to clients at a university counseling service. *Psychological Assessment, 9,* 122–131.

Pope, K. S. (1992). Responsibilities in providing psychological test feedback to clients. *Psychological Assessment, 4,* 268–271.

Rapee, R. M., & Hayman, K. (1996). The effects of video feedback on the self-evaluation of performance in socially anxious subjects. *Behaviour Research and Therapy, 34,* 315–322.

Robinson, M. B. (1970). A study of the effects of focused videotaped feedback in group counseling. *Comparative Group Studies, 1,* 47–75.

Robison, F. F., & Hardt, D. A. (1992). Effects of cognitive and behavioral structure and discussion of corrective feedback outcomes on counseling group development. *Journal of Counseling Psychology, 39,* 473–481.

Rose, G. S., & Bednar, R. L. (1980). Effects of positive and negative self-disclosure and feedback on early group development. *Journal of Counseling Psychology, 27,* 63–70.

Rotheram, M., LaCour, J., & Jacobs, A. (1982). Variations in group process due to valence, response mode, and directness of feedback. *Group and Organizational Studies, 7,* 67–75.

Schaible, T. D., & Jacobs, A. (1975). Feedback III. Sequence effects: Enhancement of feedback acceptance and group attractiveness by manipulation of the sequence and valence of feedback. *Small Group Behavior, 6,* 151–173.

Snyder, C. R., Ingram, R. E., Handelsman, M. M., Wells, D. S., & Huweiler, R. (1982). Desire for personal feedback: Who wants it and what does it mean for psychotherapy? *Journal of Personality, 50,* 316–330.

Stockton, R., & Morran, D. K. (1981). Feedback exchange in personal growth groups: Receiver acceptance as a function of valence, session, and order of delivery. *Journal of Counseling Psychology, 28,* 490–497.

Strong, S. R., & Claiborn, C. D. (1982). *Change through interaction: Social psychological processes of counseling and psychotherapy.* New York: Wiley.

Strong, S. R., & Matross, R. P. (1973) Change processes in counseling and psychotherapy. *Journal of Counseling Psychology, 20,* 25–37.

Tafarodi, R. W. (1998). Paradoxical self-esteem and selectivity in the processing of social information. *Journal of Personality and Social Psychology, 74,* 1181–1196.

Thelen, M. H., & Lasoski, M. C. (1980). The separate and combined effects of focusing information and videotape self-confrontation feedback. *Journal of Behavior Therapy and Experimental Psychiatry, 11,* 173–178.

Watzlawick, P., Beavin, J., & Jackson, D. D. (1967). *Pragmatics of human communication.* New York: Norton.

Worthington, E. L., McCullough, M. E., Shortz, J. L., Mindes, E. J., Sandage, S. J., & Chartrand, J. M. (1995). Can couples assessment and feedback improve relationships? Assessment as a brief relationship enrichment procedure. *Journal of Counseling Psychology, 42,* 466–475.

Yalom, I. D. (1995). *The theory and practice of group psychotherapy* (4th ed.). New York: Basic.

12

Repairing Alliance Ruptures

Jeremy D. Safran
J. Christopher Muran
Lisa Wallner Samstag
Christopher Stevens

One of the most consistent findings emerging from psychotherapy research is that the quality of the therapeutic alliance is one of the better predictors of outcome across the range of different treatment modalities (Horvath & Symonds, 1991; Martin, Garske, & Davis, 2000). Much of the original research on the therapeutic alliance focused on providing empirical evidence for what had long been established clinical wisdom, namely, that a strong alliance is a prerequisite for change in psychotherapy. In the last decade or so, a second generation of alliance research has emerged that attempts to clarify the factors leading to the development of the alliance, as well as those processes involved in repairing strains or ruptures in the alliance when they occur. In this chapter, we review the recent research in this second generation of alliance research and spell out what we consider the emerging practice guidelines.

The concept of the therapeutic alliance has a long and controversial history in the psychoanalytic tradition (see Safran & Muran, 2000a, for a detailed discussion). In the past two decades, the concept has spread to other traditions as well, in large part due to its prominence in the psychotherapy research literature. One of the important factors leading to the flourishing of the topic in psychotherapy research was Bordin's (1979) seminal reformulation of the alliance in transtheoretical terms. Bordin theorized that there are three

components to the alliance: agreement on tasks, agreement on goals, and the bond. For him, quality of the alliance is a function of the degree of agreement between therapist and patient about the tasks and goals of treatment, as well as the quality of the affective bond between them. These three components influence one another in an ongoing fashion. For example, an initial agreement about tasks or goals will tend to enhance the quality of the bond. Alternatively, when there are disagreements, the existence of an adequate bond will facilitate the negotiation of tasks and goals.

The idea that this type of negotiation is central to the change process is implicit in Bordin's (1979) original thinking but is brought out more explicitly in the final article he wrote on the alliance concept (Bordin, 1994). His conceptualization of the alliance influenced our earliest thinking on the topic of therapeutic alliance ruptures (Safran, Crocker, McMain, & Murray, 1990), but it is only with hindsight that we have come to see more clearly how prescient his thinking was.

It is not difficult to make an argument on pragmatic grounds that if the quality of the alliance is critical to treatment outcome, then it makes sense to do research on the question of how best to address alliance ruptures when they occur. At a more general theoretical level, however, it has become increasingly clear to us that the negotiation of ruptures in the alliance is at the heart of the change process, and Bordin's formulation helps to provide a theoretical framework for clarifying how and why this is the case.

Traditional psychoanalytic conceptualizations of the alliance give priority to one type of goal or task over others (see Greenson, 1967; Sterba, 1934; Zetzel, 1956). Although they emphasized the importance of the therapist acting in a supportive fashion in order to facilitate the development of the alliance, ultimately they assumed that the patient would identify with the therapist and adapt to his or her conceptualization of the tasks or goals of therapy (for example, the use of interpretation in order to gain insight). In contrast, Bordin's conceptualization is more dynamic and mutual. It assumes that there will be an ongoing negotiation between therapist and patient at both conscious and unconscious levels concerning the tasks and goals of therapy, and that this process of negotiation both establishes the necessary conditions for change to take place and is an intrinsic part of the change process.

This conceptualization is consistent with an increasingly influential way of thinking about the therapeutic process that is emerging from contemporary relational psychoanalytic thinking (Mitchell & Aron, 1999). This perspective holds that learning to negotiate the needs of the self versus the needs of others is both a critical developmental task and an ongoing challenge of human existence. Many of the problems that people bring into therapy are thus influenced, at least in part, by difficulties they have in negotiating this tension in a constructive fashion. The development of a relationship with the therapist inevitably involves this type of ongoing negotiation between two different subjectivities at both conscious and unconscious levels. This process can have an important impact upon the patient's fundamental sense of the extent to which he or she lives in a potentially negotiable world or needs to compromise his or her own sense of integrity in order to hold onto relationships (J. Benjamin, 1990; Mitchell, 1993).

What we are thus arguing is that therapeutic tasks and goals, in Bordin's terms, provide an important part of the substance of the negotiation that inevitably takes place in any therapy. This negotiation is always taking place, sometimes explicitly and sometimes implicitly. When things are running smoothly, the negotiation may take place without conscious awareness. For example, the therapist may decide, without thinking, to not use a particular intervention because he or she has a sense that the patient will not find it helpful, or the patient may give the therapist the benefit of the doubt and try on an interpretation for size, or try a behavioral assignment even though he or she is initially skeptical. But when things break down and there is an overt rupture in the therapeutic alliance, this process of negotiation moves into the foreground.

It should be emphasized that as we see it, this process of negotiation is not a superficial negotiation toward consensus, but rather a genuine confrontation between individuals with conflicting views, needs, or agendas. Both patient and therapist struggle to sort out how much they can accommodate the other's view without compromising themselves in some important way. This conceptualization is thus less vulnerable to the previously mentioned criticism, which equates the alliance with compliance.

DEFINITION AND TAXONOMY

A rupture in the therapeutic alliance can be defined as a tension or breakdown in the collaborative relationship between patient and therapist. These ruptures vary in intensity from relatively minor tensions, of which one or both of the participants may be only vaguely aware, to major breakdowns in understanding and communication. The latter, if not addressed, may lead to premature termination or treatment failure.

Following Bordin's understanding of the alliance, we find it useful to conceptualize ruptures in the alliance as consisting of (1) disagreements about the tasks of treatment, (2) disagreements about the goals of treatment, or (3) strains in the bond. An example of a disagreement about the goal dimension would be a situation in which the patient begins treatment seeking immediate relief from his or her panic symptoms, but the therapist believes the goal should be one of obtaining insight rather than immediate symptom relief. An example of a disagreement about the task dimension would be a situation in which the patient believes that it is important to spend time reviewing and making sense of his or her history, but the therapist has a present-focused, pragmatic orientation. An example of a strain in the bond dimension would be a situation in which the patient feels patronized or misunderstood by the therapist. These three types of ruptures are, of course, not mutually exclusive. For example, the patient whose therapist is unwilling to negotiate the tasks or goals of treatment may feel misunderstood or disrespected. Conversely, a patient who feels mistrusting of his or her therapist will be more likely to disagree with the therapist about a therapeutic task or goal.

Elsewhere, we have outlined a taxonomy for schematizing different types of interventions for addressing or resolving alliance ruptures, which follows from the above conceptualization (Safran & Muran, 2000a, 2000b). This taxonomy emerged out of our attempts to synthesize the contributions of theorists from a range of different therapeutic orientations. In table 12.1 and in the following discussion, we describe this taxonomy in brief, in order to provide the reader with a broad overview of the range of different types of alliance rupture interventions.

Dimension 1: Directness versus indirectness of intervention. Each of the three types of ruptures (*disagreements about task, disagreements about goals,* or *strains in the bond*) can be addressed by the therapist either directly or indirectly. For example, if the patient questions the relevance of completing homework between sessions, the therapist may respond directly by providing a therapeutic rationale or indirectly by changing the therapeutic task (in this case abandoning the task of completing homework assignments).

Dimension 2: Surface versus underlying level of meaning. In addition, interventions may be targeted either at a surface or manifest level of meaning or at an underlying level of meaning that requires some degree of inference. For example, a disagreement about the task of therapy (for example, reporting whatever comes to mind) can be explored in its own terms (discussing the rationale underlying the task) or in terms of an underlying relational theme (the patient feels pressured to perform, which is a common theme in relationships with others, and can be traced back to features of his or her developmental history). In everyday practice, many of the most common alliance building or repairing interventions are directed to the surface level. For example, without giving it much conscious thought, but intuitively gauging that it will have a positive impact on the alliance, a therapist may answer a patient's questions about the purpose of an intervention or apologize for a mistake. At the same time, some of the more important alliance mending interventions are addressed at the level of underlying meaning.

CLINICAL EXAMPLES

In accordance with the taxonomy just outlined and represented in table 12.1, alliance rupture interventions can take the following forms:

Providing therapeutic rationale. Outlining the therapeutic rationale at the beginning of treatment can play an important role in developing the alliance at the outset. Reiterating the rationale can help to repair a strained alliance. For example, the therapist can help to repair an alliance

Table 12.1. Therapeutic Alliance Rupture Intervention Strategies

Disagreements on Tasks and Goals		Strains in the Bond	
Direct	Indirect	Direct	Indirect
Surface Level Providing therapeutic rationale	Reframing the meaning of tasks and goals	Clarifying misunderstandings	Allying with the resistance
Underlying Meaning Exploring core relational themes I	Changing tasks and goals	Exploring core relational themes II	New relational experience

Table 12.2. Detecting Ruptures Studies

Study	N	Method	Analysis	Outcome
Rennie (1994)	14	Psychotherapy clients in a variety of settings and treatment lengths.	Tape-assisted recalls of 14 patients, gathered immediately following an hour of therapy, analyzed using the grounded theory form of qualitative analysis.	Patient deference to therapists was the major category derived with 7 lower-level categories emerging: (1) concerns about the therapist's approach, (2) fear of criticizing the therapist, (3) understanding the therapist's frame of reference, (4) meeting the perceived expectations of the therapist, (5) accepting the therapist's limitations, (6) threatening the therapist's self-esteem, and (7) indebtedness to the therapist.
Regan & Hill (1992)	24	Six-session psychotherapy.	Patients and therapists reported on thoughts or feelings that they were unable to express in treatment using the Things Left Unsaid Inventory, the Session Evaluation Questionnaire, and the Personal Questionnaire. They asked the therapists to guess what patients had left unsaid and then matched the results.	Results indicated that for both patients and therapists, most things left unsaid were negative. In addition, therapists were only aware of 17% of the things patients left unsaid.
Rhodes et al. (1994)	19	Retrospective analysis of client satisfaction with past therapies (not from a single source).	Qualitative analysis comparing client satisfaction measured by Client Satisfaction Questionnaire and addressed vs. unaddressed misunderstanding events measured by Retrospective Misunderstanding Event Questionnaire.	Comparison of 11 resolved and 8 unresolved misunderstanding events suggested that a good relationship, patients' willingness to assert negative feelings about being misunderstood, and therapists' facilitation of a mutual repair effort led to resolution, whereas unwillingness or inability to engage in this process led to unresolved misunderstandings and unilateral termination.

| Hill, Thompson, Cogar, & Denman (1993) | 26 | Patients in long-term psychotherapy | Audio- and videotaped reviews of sessions in which patients and therapists talked about the helpfulness of interventions, described their own covert processes, and guessed the processes of the other. Written evaluations were also conducted. Eight measures and independent judges were used to evaluate and match the recalls. | Therapists were often unaware of patients' unexpressed reactions. They also found that patients are particularly likely to hide negative feelings. Therapists were only able to guess patients' hidden negative feelings 45% of the time; 65% of the patients in the study left something unsaid (most often negative), and only 27% of the therapists were accurate in their guesses about what their patients were withholding. |
| Hill, Nutt-Williams, Heaton, Thompson, & Rhodes (1996) | 12 | Therapists who had experienced impasse events ending in termination of therapy | Qualitative analysis of therapists' recall of impasse events ending in termination. | Variables associated with impasses include patient's history of interpersonal problems, lack of agreement about the tasks and goals of therapy, interference with therapy from the outside, transference, possible therapist mistakes, and therapists' personal issues. Additionally, they found that therapists were often unaware of their patients' dissatisfaction until they announced unilateral termination. |

rupture resulting from his or her attempt to make a transference interpretation by reiterating that exploring parallels between the therapeutic relationship and other relationships can help the patient to become aware of self-defeating patterns.

Exploring core relational themes I. In some situations, the process of clarifying factors leading to disagreements about tasks or goals of therapy will lead to the exploration of core relational themes. For example, a patient may experience the therapist's questions about her inner experience as intrusive. Exploring the meaning and nature of this experience for the patient may reveal that it is related to a more general experience on her part of feeling intruded upon by others. A patient who fails to do his homework assignments in cognitive therapy may have a particular sensitivity to feeling dominated and controlled by others.

Reframing the meaning of tasks or goals. Reframing the meaning of therapeutic tasks or goals in terms that are acceptable to the patient is a type of joining intervention commonly used by strategic and systemic approaches. For example, a patient who was receiving a cognitive-behavioral treatment for social anxiety was initially reluctant to complete any between-session assignments that involved increasing social contact because of a fear of rejection. When the therapist reframed the meaning of the assignment as one of "putting yourself into the anxiety-provoking situation in order to self-monitor your cognitive processes," she was willing to complete the assignment.

Changing task or goals. In this type of intervention, the therapist attempts to work on tasks or goals that seem relevant to the patient rather than exploring factors underlying such disagreements. The therapist's willingness to accommodate the patient by working in terms that are more meaningful to him or her can play an important role in building the alliance in the immediate context, and in helping the patient to develop trust in the possibility of getting his or her needs met in other relationships. For example, treating the patient's phobia at a symptomatic level may help him to develop sufficient trust to engage in the task of self-exploration later on.

Clarifying misunderstandings at a surface level. For example, a therapist notices that her patient seems withdrawn and initiates an exploration of what is going on in the here-and-now of the therapeutic relationship. The patient admits to feeling criticized by the therapist. The therapist responds in a nondefensive fashion and acknowledges that she can see how the patient might have felt criticized by what she said.

Exploring core relational themes II. Just as the exploration of disagreements about tasks or goals can lead to an exploration of important underlying themes, the exploration of strains in the bond dimension of the alliance can ultimately lead to a working through of core relational themes. For example, a patient's feeling of not being understood by the therapist may reflect a narcissistic sensitivity which becomes a major focus of the treatment.

Allying with the resistance. For example, a patient withdraws from the therapist because she experiences the attempt to explore her painful feelings as too threatening. The therapist retreats from the attempt to explore avoided feelings and emphasizes that the patient's current efforts to "protect herself" are understandable.

New relational experience. The therapist acts in a way that he or she hypothesizes will provide the patient with an important new relational experience without explicitly exploring the underlying meaning of the interaction. This type of intervention is particularly important when the patient has difficulty exploring the therapeutic relationship in the here-and-now. For example, a therapist decides to answer a patient's request for advice because she formulates the situation as one in which the decision to do so will provide an important contrast to the patient's abandoning mother.

REVIEW OF EMPIRICAL EVIDENCE

In this section, we first review the research most relevant to the topic of alliance rupture and repair. The relevant studies are summarized in tables 12.2, 12.3, 12.4, and 12.5. Our own research program on the topic is reviewed subsequently.

One of the most consistent findings coming out of research on the therapeutic alliance is that a strong or improving therapeutic alliance contributes to a positive treatment outcome (Horvath & Symonds 1991; Martin, Garske, & Davis,

Table 12.3. Qualitative Analyses of Alliance Problems and Negative Therapist Response

Study	N	Method	Analysis	Outcome
Castonguay et al. (1996)	30	Brief cognitive therapy (average 14.4 sessions)	The outcome measure (Beck Depression Inventory) and the WAI, Experiencing Scales, and Coding System of Therapist Feedback were correlated.	Alliance and patients' emotional involvement predicted client improvement, but the therapist focus on the impact of distorted cognitions of depressive affect was found to be negatively correlated with outcome. Qualitative analysis suggests that therapists may attempt to address alliance strains by increasing their adherence to the cognitive model with the opposite result.
Piper, Azim, Joyce, & McCallum (1991)	64	20 sessions of short-term individual psychotherapy in a controlled clinical trial investigation of manualized approaches based on Malan, Strupp & Binder	Therapists Intervention Rating System was used to categorize interventions. A series of six 7-point items were used to assess alliance, and a comprehensive set of outcome measures was provided by patients, therapists, and independent assessors.	An inverse relationship was found between proportion of transference interpretations and measures of therapeutic alliance and favorable outcome. Additionally, qualitative analysis suggested that there may have been attempts by therapists to address weaknesses in the alliance by increasing transference interpretations and possibly becoming engaged in a vicious cycle.
Piper, Ogrodniczuk, Joyce, McCallum, Rosie, O'Kelly, & Steinberg (1999)	44	22 dropouts with 22 matched completers	Therapeutic alliance was measured using a series of six 7-point items. The Vanderbilt Psychotherapy Process Scale was used to assess positive and negative aspects of both therapist and patient behavior and attitudes. Process variables were assessed using a team of external raters. A qualitative analysis was done on the last session prior to termination.	No pretherapy predictors (demographics, diagnostic, initial disturbance) differentiated the dropouts from the completers. Dropouts were found to have weaker alliances, less exploration, less work, and a greater focus on transference. The qualitative analysis of the last session indicates a pattern of resistance and increased transference interpretation.

2000; see also Muran et al., 1995; Safran & Wallner, 1991, from our own research program). Similarly, there is ample evidence that weakened alliances are correlated with unilateral termination (Tryon & Kane, 1990, 1993, 1995). These findings suggest that the process of recognizing and addressing weakness or ruptures in the therapeutic alliance may play an important role in successful therapy.

In practice, however, this is a task that often proves difficult for even experienced therapists (see table 12.2). Patients are not always able or willing to reveal when they are uncomfortable or disagree with their therapist. Rennie (1994), us-

Table 12.4. Directly Addressing and Repairing Ruptures Studies

Study	N	Method	Analysis	Outcome
Foreman & Marmar (1985)	6	12-week dynamic psychotherapy of bereavement.	California Therapeutic Alliance Scale was correlated with patient, therapist, and independent ratings of outcome and compared to a list of therapist actions.	Interpretive actions which directly addressed weak alliances were related to cases with good outcome. Interpretive work that did not address alliance weakness did not improve alliance or result in good outcome.
Lansford (1986)	6	12-session, short-term psychotherapy	Measures of initial alliance, alliance weakness, and repair were correlated with observer ratings of outcome.	Raters were able to predict outcome from weakening and repair excerpts. Direct action by therapists to repair weakened alliances were followed by the highest levels of patient alliance ratings. Success in addressing weaknesses was predictive of outcome.

ing a qualitative research methodology, discovered that patients' deference to their therapists played a significant role in therapeutic interactions. He found a number of factors to be associated with patient deference, including fear of criticizing the therapist, need to meet the therapist's perceived expectations, acceptance of the therapist's limitations, fear of threatening the therapist's self-esteem, and a sense of indebtedness to the therapist, among others.

If, as Rennie's findings suggest, patients believe protecting their therapists is the best way to maintain the relationship, it is understandable that they would be reluctant to talk openly with them about their concerns regarding treatment. It is thus critical for therapists to be able to pick up on cues that the alliance is in trouble and address them in a way that allows the patient to participate without undue anxiety. Unfortunately, research has shown that even experienced therapists may have considerable difficulty recognizing such moments.

Regan and Hill (1992) asked patients and therapists to report on thoughts or feelings that they were unable to express in treatment. They then asked the therapists to guess what patients had left unsaid. Results indicated that for both

patients and therapists, most things left unsaid were negative. In addition, therapists were only aware of 17% of the things patients left unsaid. Taking a different tack, Rhodes, Hill, Thompson, and Elliott (1994), in another study, asked therapists and therapists-in-training to recall events from their own treatment and performed a qualitative analysis of the events. Although some of the patients were able to talk openly about their negative feelings toward the therapist, patients who felt uncomfortable addressing misunderstanding events were able to conceal them from their therapists so that the misunderstandings remained unaddressed, often leading to termination.

Hill, Thompson, Cogar, and Denman (1993) extended the investigation into patient covert processes (reactions to in-session events) to include things left unsaid and secrets. As in their previous studies, they found that therapists were often unaware of patients' unexpressed reactions. They also found that patients were particularly likely to hide negative feelings and that even experienced, long-term therapists were only able to guess when patients had hidden negative feelings 45% of the time. Furthermore, 65% of the patients in the study left something unsaid (most

Table 12.5. Patterns of Alliance Development Studies

Study	N	Method	Analysis	Outcome
Golden & Robbins (1990)	2	Single-case analysis	Vanderbilt Psychotherapy Process Scales and the WAI scores were examined to determine patterns of alliance development.	WAI scores were found to be lowest in the middle phase of treatment in both cases studied.
Patton, Kivlighan, & Multon (1997)	13	Psychoanalytic college counseling over two semesters	Hierarchical linear model analyzed 4 factors: psychoanalytic technique, working alliance, client resistance, and client transference, for patterns of development and change.	The significant t tests for the quadratic coefficient indicated that client outcome was significantly related to a high-low-high pattern of alliance development.
Nagy, Safran, Muran, & Winston (1998)	75	Patients and therapists complete post-session questionnaire in three short-term psychotherapies	Patients and therapists reported on ruptures, the extent they were resolved, and the WAI after every session, as well as pre- and post-treatment measures regarding outcome.	Percentage of ruptures reported by patients ranged from 11% (cognitive-behavioral) to 38% (psychodynamic) and by therapists ranged from 25% (cognitive-behavioral) to 53% (psychodynamic). More ruptures were evidenced early in treatment. Patient-reported ruptures were negatively related to patient-rated alliance early in treatment. Correspondence between patient and therapist reportings of ruptures predicted outcome. Patient-rated rupture resolution predicted patient-rated alliance.
Kivlighan & Shaughnessy (2000)	38	Four-session college counseling with volunteer subjects	Cluster analysis was used to determine patterns of alliance development, which were then correlated with the Inventory of Interpersonal Problems and the Battery of Interpersonal Capabilities.	Three patterns of working alliance development were found: the stable alliance, linear alliance growth, and quadratic alliance growth. The high-low-high quadratic pattern was found to have the greatest association with treatment outcome.

often negative), and only 27% of the therapists were accurate in their guesses about what their patients were withholding.

In a later study, Hill, Nutt-Williams, Heaton, Thompson, and Rhodes (1996) conducted a qualitative analysis of therapists' recollections of impasse events that had ended in termination. In retrospect, therapists identified multiple variables they associated with the impasses, including lack of agreement about the tasks and goals of therapy, transference, possible therapist mistakes, and therapists' personal issues, among others. Perhaps most significant, however, was the finding that, as in the Rhodes, Hill, Thompson, and Elliott (1994) study, patients did not reveal their dissatisfaction until they quit therapy. Moreover, therapists reported that they became aware of patients' dissatisfaction only with the announcement of termination and were often taken by surprise.

Even if therapists do become aware of their patients' reservations, it may prove quite difficult to address them in a way that is beneficial to the treatment. A number of studies have suggested that therapists' awareness of patients' negative reactions can be detrimental to outcome (see Fuller & Hill, 1985; Martin, Martin, Meyer, & Slemon, 1986; Martin, Martin, & Slemon, 1987). There is empirical evidence (see table 12.3 and below) to support various interpretations of this type of finding. One is that therapists may increase their adherence to their preferred treatment model in a rigid fashion, rather than responding flexibly to a perceived rupture in the alliance. Another is that therapists may respond to patients' negative feelings by expressing their own negative feelings in a defensive fashion.

In an investigation of the process of change in cognitive therapy, Castonguay, Goldfried, Wiser, Raue, and Hayes (1996) found that while alliance and patients' emotional involvement predicted improvement, therapists' focus on distorted cognitions was *negatively* correlated with outcome. Using qualitative analysis in an attempt to understand these counterintuitive findings, they found that in poor outcome cases, therapists often attempted to address alliance ruptures by increasing their adherence to the cognitive model (challenging distorted cognitions), rather than responding more flexibly.

Piper, Azim, Joyce, and McCallum (1991) found an inverse relationship between the proportion of transference interpretations and both alliance and outcome for patients with a history of high-quality object relations. Examining the findings, they hypothesized that increased concentrations of transference interpretations may have been attempts to repair weakened alliances. They observed an alternating pattern of silences and transference interpretations and found that the inverse relationship between transference interpretations and alliance strengthened over the course of the treatment. This suggests that the patients and therapists may have been engaged in

a vicious cycle in which, as therapists intensified their transference interpretations in a counterproductive attempt to remedy the situation, the alliance continued to weaken. They concluded, "The continuation of the cycle during the course of therapy suggests that the use of increased transference interpretations was not successful in resolving the impasse in the working relationship" (p. 951).

In a later study, Piper, Ogrodniczuk, Joyce, McCallum, Rosie, O'Kelly, and Steinberg (1999) compared a sample of 22 dropouts with 22 matched completers on pretherapy and therapy process variables. In addition to assessing patient hostility and patient and therapist exploration and focus on transference, they examined the last session prior to dropout for typical patterns. Qualitative analysis of the therapeutic process indicated that these sessions typically started with patients expressing dissatisfaction or disappointment with treatment, to which therapists responded with transference interpretations. As the patients continued to withdraw or express resistance, therapists often continued to focus on transference issues. Sessions often ended with patients agreeing to continue treatment at the recommendation of the therapist, but never returning.

The findings in these studies are consistent with those of the Vanderbilt II study conducted by Strupp and colleagues (Henry, Schacht, Strupp, Butler, & Binder, 1993; Henry, Strupp, Butler, Schacht, & Binder 1993; Strupp, 1993). In this study, a group of experienced therapists treated a cohort of patients and were subsequently given a year of intensive training in a manualized form of psychodynamic treatment. The training paid special attention to helping therapists detect and manage maladaptive interpersonal patterns as they are enacted in the therapeutic relationship. Following their training, the therapists treated a second cohort of patients. Evaluation of the differences in the therapeutic process and outcome showed that therapists were, in fact, able to shift their work to correspond more closely with the treatment manual. At the same time, however, the researchers found that rather than being able to treat their patients more skillfully, therapists displayed more hostile negative interactions and complex communications (interpretations that can be seen as both helpful and critical). Thus, even when therapists recognize patients' negative feelings about the treatment, they often respond defensively by adhering rigidly to their preferred treatment model or by acting out their own counterhostility.

In contrast, several studies suggest that when therapists *are* able to respond nondefensively, attend directly to the alliance, adjust their behavior, and address rifts as they occur, the alliance improves. Foreman and Marmar (1985), for example, in a small sample study, found that when therapists directly addressed the patient's defenses against feelings toward the therapist, problematic therapeutic relationship patterns, and negative feelings toward the therapist, the alliance improved. Interpretive actions that directly addressed weak alliances were related to good outcome, but interpretive actions that did not address alliance weakness did not improve alliance or result in good outcome.

A year later, Lansford (1986) looked at six short-term therapy cases, identifying weakening and repairs in the alliance. Independent raters were able to predict outcome by observing excerpts showing weakening and repair of the alliance even though these segments made up a small proportion of the therapy (as little as 8%). Analysis showed that segments when therapists and patients took direct action to repair weakened alliances were followed by the highest levels of patient alliance ratings and that the degree of success in addressing weaknesses was predictive of outcome. In the previously discussed study by Rhodes and colleagues (1994) of patients' recollection of misunderstanding events, the investigators found that patients' willingness to assert negative feelings about being misunderstood and therapists' willingness to engage in a mutual effort to repair the rupture led to the resolution of impasses. Unilateral terminations by patients tended to take place when these processes did not occur.

There is also a growing body of evidence suggesting that the importance of dealing effectively with alliance ruptures may extend beyond allowing the treatment to continue and the technical aspects of treatment to work; it may actually be an intrinsic part of the change process. Based to a large degree on the work of Mann (1973) and Gelso and Carter (1994), these studies have examined the notion that there are identifiable stages of alliance development. According to this view, the initial stage of treatment is a period when patients become mobilized and hopeful. They then experience a phase of ambivalence when they may begin to question what therapy can provide. If this phase is successfully negotiated, the alliance is strengthened and termination can be worked through. To date, the investigations into patterns of alliance development provide some support for the idea that therapeutic dyads which go through a period of decreased alliance followed by improved alliance may do as well, and possibly even better than, dyads with steady or increasing alliance levels.

Golden and Robbins (1990) hypothesized that despite consistent therapist action during the therapy, patients would go through a period in mid-treatment of increased negative affect, attitudes, and behavior. They analyzed two successful therapy cases, finding that therapists exhibited a fair amount of warmth and friendliness and high levels of exploration consistently throughout both treatments. The patients' alliance ratings increased, dropped, and then increased again during the course of the therapy, suggesting that patients went through the phases of alliance development predicted by Mann (1973). Patton, Kivlighan, and Multon (1997) videotaped 16 patients and 6 therapists over two semesters. Analysis indicated that a quadratic high-low-high pattern of alliance development was present and related to improved outcome. While a significant linear increase across sessions was also observed, it was found to be unrelated to client outcome. In a later study Kivlighan and Shaughnessy (2000) used cluster analysis to examine patterns of alliance development in 79 therapist-patient dyads across four counseling sessions. They found three distinct patterns of alliance development: stable alliance, linear alliance growth, and quadratic alliance growth. While average level of alliance did predict outcome, the quadratic pattern of alliance development was associated with the greatest improvement compared to other patterns of alliance development. While the results from the studies on patterns of alliance development are far from conclusive, they seem to point toward the possible therapeutic benefits of alliance rupture development and repair over the course of the treatment.

It is important to distinguish between the development of the alliance at a more global level versus shifts in the alliance at a more molecular level. Although the studies of Golden and Robbins (1990); Patton, Kivlighan, and Multon (1997); and Kivlighan and Shaughnessy (2000) are relevant to the first phenomenon, Nagy, Safran, Muran, and Winston (1998) investigated patients' and therapists' perceptions of shifts in the quality of the alliance within session. In a sample of 75 short-term therapy cases consisting of three different treatment modalities, we found that patients reported the presence of alliance ruptures in 11 to 38% of the sessions, depending on the treatment modality. Therapists reported alliance ruptures in 25 to 53% of the sessions. This indicates that the perception of ruptures, while varying according to treatment modality, is a fairly common occurrence and that therapists are more likely to perceive (or at least report) ruptures than patients. Early in treatment, frequency of patient-reported ruptures was significantly negatively correlated with their ratings of alliance at the session level (that is, ratings of the quality of the alliance of the session as a whole, irrespective of whether a rupture had taken place). This was not true later in treatment and not true for therapist-reported ruptures. This suggests that for patients, once the therapeutic relationship has had a chance to develop, a momentary rupture is less likely to impact on their perceptions of the alliance at a more global level. It also suggests that therapists, even early in treatment, are less likely to allow a momentary rupture to affect their evaluation of the alliance at a more global level. Finally, we found that patient and therapist agreement about the presence of ruptures within sessions was positively related to ultimate outcome.

Our Research Program Investigating Rupture Repair

Our research program, which has been primarily aimed at the study of therapeutic alliance ruptures and their resolution or repair, can be conceptualized as consisting of four recursive stages: model development, model testing, treatment development, and treatment evaluation. In the first stage, a change-process model is developed through a series of intensive analyses of single cases identified as including ruptures and resolution processes. In the second stage, the model is tested by evaluating whether the presence of the processes described in the model distinguishes rupture resolution and nonresolution events. In the third stage, treatment interventions are developed and refined in response to the findings emerging from the model development and model testing stages of the research program. In the final stage, the efficacy of treatment intervention is evaluated. This stage of the research serves simultaneously as a treatment outcome study and as a model verification study.

The stages of our research program that involve model development and verification have been greatly influenced by the task analytic paradigm for psychotherapy research, which integrates quantitative and qualitative strategies to analyze the process involved in the performance of an in-session "task" or change event (Greenberg, 1986; Rice & Greenberg, 1984; Safran, Greenberg, & Rice, 1988). An important component of our research has been the development and use of parallel forms of a questionnaire completed by both patient and therapist for every session of treatment. The post-session questionnaire (PSQ) serves the function of facilitating the identification of critical in-session processes and verifying their relationship to overall outcome. Over the course of the past decade, we have conducted several studies demonstrating the psychometric properties of our PSQ, including its sensitivity to detect ruptures and resolutions, as well as its predictive validity (Muran et al., 1995; Nagy et al., 1998; Safran & Wallner, 1991; Samstag, Batchelder, Muran, Safran, & Winston, 1998; Winkelman, Safran, & Muran, 1998; see Muran, in press, for a review). Table 12.6 summarizes our research efforts regarding rupture resolution.

Our first model of the rupture resolution process, Stage-Process Model I, was developed from a qualitative analysis of 15 psychotherapy sessions in which alliance ruptures had appeared to reach some degree of resolution (Safran et al., 1990).

Table 12.6. Rupture Resolution: Model Testing Studies

Studies	Subjects	Selection Criteria	Coding Scheme	Method of Analysis	Results
Stage-Process Model I ~ *Qualitative Analysis* (Safran, Crocker, McMain, & Murray, 1990)	29 cases 15 sessions	Patient & therapist rated sessions by thirds on an alliance measure. Resolution sessions indicated 20% increases by both patient & therapist.	N/A	Qualitative analysis	*Proposed model:* Attending to Rupture (1), Exploring Rupture Experience (2), Exploring Avoidance (3), Exploring Interpersonal Schema (4)
Stage-Process Model I ~ *Preliminary Test* (Safran, Muran, & Samstag, 1994)	5 cases 7 sessions (4 resolution + 3 nonresolution)	Patient & therapist rated sessions by thirds on an alliance measure. Resolution sessions indicated 20% increases by both patient & therapist.	Structural Analysis of Social Behavior (SASB), Experiencing Scales (EXP), Client Vocal Quality (CVQ)	Frequency analysis of model stages	1. Higher frequency of model stages in resolution sessions, but 4th stage only evident in 2/4 sessions. 2. *Refined model:* attending to rupture (1), exploring rupture experience (2), exploring avoidance (3), self-assertion (4)
Stage-Process Model II ~ *Small-Scale Verification Study* (Safran & Muran, 1996)	4 cases 8 sessions (4 resolution + 4 nonresolution)	Patient & therapist rated sessions by thirds on an alliance measure. Resolution sessions indicated 20% increases by both patient & therapist.	SASB EXP CVQ	Lag 1 sequential analyses of hypothesized sequences	Significant differences between resolution and nonresolution sessions, consistent with hypotheses
Stage-Process Model II ~ *Replication Study* (Safran & Muran, 1996)	3 cases 6 sessions (3 resolution + 3 nonresolution)	Patient & therapist reported tension in all six sessions. Resolution sessions required resolution ratings of ≥3 on 5-point scale by both patient & therapist.	SASB EXP CVQ	Lag 1 sequential analyses of hypothesized sequences	1. Significant differences consistent with hypotheses 2. *Refined model:* Stage-Process Model III (4th stage redefined with the CCRT method as Emergence of Wish/Need)

We selected these sessions from a pool of 29 cases based on patient and therapist post-session ratings of the therapeutic alliance. The proposed model from this exploratory analysis included four stages involving patient and therapist interactions: (1) attending to the rupture marker, (2) exploring the rupture experience, (3) exploring the avoidance, and (4) exploring the interpersonal schema (the patient's generalized representations of self and other). We then conducted a preliminary test of this model on a new sample that compared four rupture resolution and three nonresolution sessions (Safran et al., 1994). In this preliminary test, we applied various measures of psychotherapy process (such as the Structural Analysis of Social Behavior [SASB; see Benjamin, 1974], Experiencing Scales [EXP: see Klein, Mathieu-Coughlan, & Kiesler, 1986], and Client Vocal Quality [CVQ: see Rice & Kerr, 1986]) to operationalize multiple dimensions (that is, interpersonal behavior, emotional involvement, and vocal quality) of each patient and therapist position in the resolution process. The results generally indicated a higher frequency of model components in the resolution sessions than in the nonresolution sessions.

Although the results of this test provided some verification of the proposed model, it also resulted in a refinement of our rupture resolution model. First, we found it more useful to distinguish between two types of patient communications or behaviors that mark a rupture—withdrawal and confrontation markers—as opposed to our original definition of seven types (Safran et al., 1990). In withdrawal markers, the patient withdraws or partially disengages from the therapist, his or her own emotions, or some aspect of the therapeutic process. In confrontation ruptures, the patient directly expresses anger, resentment, or dissatisfaction with the therapist or some aspect of the therapy in an attempt to control the therapist. In some instances, the marker can be characterized as a mix of confrontation and withdrawal. Second, finding that Stage 4 (exploration of the interpersonal schema) did not occur consistently, we eliminated it from our model, but included instead as the fourth stage, "self-assertion," which we observed as an elaboration of Stage 2 (exploration of the rupture experi-

ence). This refinement resulted in Stage-Process Model II.

Our next step was to conduct a verification study of this revised model, in which we compared matched resolution and nonresolution sessions from four different cases (8 sessions in total). We followed this analysis with a replication study involving matched resolution and nonresolution sessions from another three cases (six sessions in total). In both studies, we operationalized the various stages of the model, using a coding scheme that included the SASB, EXP, and CVQ. We then conducted a series of lag one sequential analyses to confirm the hypothesized sequences and demonstrate a difference between resolution and nonresolution sessions. In sum, the results indicated support for the hypothesized sequences of the model and demonstrated differences between resolution and nonresolution sessions, particularly with regard to the "exploring avoidance" pathway and the pathway from "exploring the rupture" to "self-assertion." These processes were more evident in resolution sessions.

Further qualitative analysis of the seven new rupture resolution sessions led to further revision of the model in the form of Stage-Process Model III (see figure 12.1). Probably the most noteworthy revision concerned the definition of the fourth stage. We found the Core Conflictual Relationship Theme (CCRT; see Luborsky, 1984) method to understanding tranferential dynamics (Safran & Muran, 1996) and the distinction between primary and secondary emotions (Greenberg & Safran, 1987) to be especially helpful in refining our understanding of the patient state that emerges upon the resolution of a rupture. Specifically, we observed that the fourth stage of the resolution process invariably involves the expression of the patient's underlying wish/need or the primary emotion associated with that wish/need, and so came to define this stage as the Emergence of the Wish/Need. This can sometimes take the form of asserting negative feelings, but it can also take other forms (the assertion of a desire for more help, direction, or nurturance, or the expression of an underlying vulnerability). Further, we observed that the type of rupture marker (withdrawal versus confrontation) is associated with some important differences in the res-

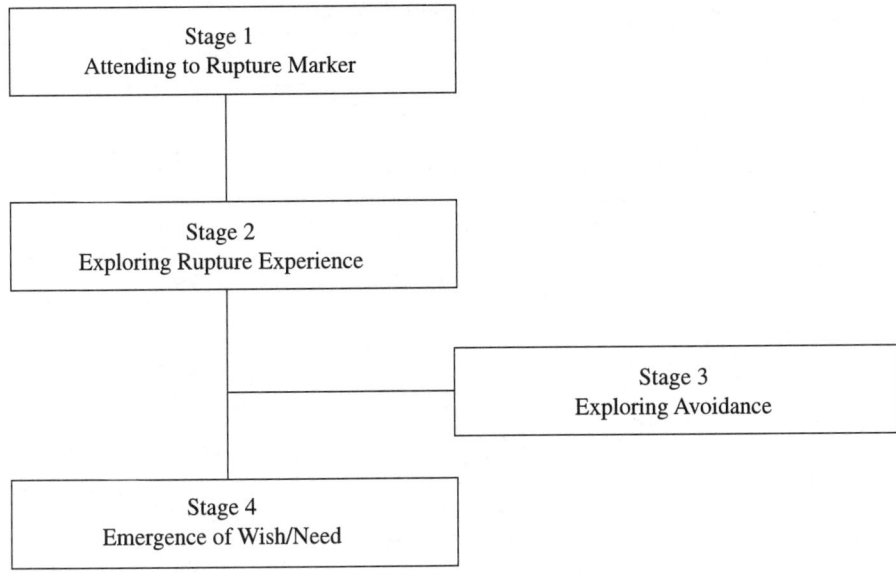

Figure 12.1. Stage-Process Model III of Rupture Resolution

olution process, especially in the transition from Stage 2 (exploration of the rupture experience) to Stage 4 (emergence of the wish/need). For example, the common progression in the resolution of withdrawal ruptures consists of moving through increasingly clearer articulations of discontent to self-assertion, in which the need for agency is realized and validated by the therapist (Stage 4). The progression in the resolution of confrontation ruptures consists of moving through feelings of anger, to feelings of disappointment and hurt over having been failed by the therapist, to contacting vulnerability and the wish to be nurtured and taken care of (Stage 4). Typical avoidant operations that emerge, regardless of rupture type, concern anxieties and self-doubts resulting from the fear of being too aggressive or too vulnerable. These concerns are associated with the expectation of retaliation or rejection by the therapist (Stage 3).

Our study of the rupture resolution process has enabled us to develop and manualize a treatment model that includes interventions that we have found facilitative of the resolution process (see Muran & Safran, in press; Safran, 2002a, 2000b; Safran & Muran, 2000a). The model has been manualized as a short-term treatment in or-

der to facilitate clinical trial research, but it is not intrinsically a short-term model. This approach (referred to as Brief Relational Therapy, or BRT) synthesizes principles derived from our research program with principles derived from relational psychoanalysis (see Mitchell & Aron, 1999), humanistic/experiential psychotherapy (see Greenberg, Watson, & Lietaer, 1998), and contemporary theories on cognition and emotion (see Greenberg & Safran, 1987; Safran & Greenberg, 1991).

In a treatment study of 128 personality disordered patients presenting with comorbid symptomatology (Muran & Safran, 2002), we compared BRT to two traditional short-term psychotherapies: one psychodynamic, the other cognitive-behavioral (see table 12.7). In one set of analyses involving traditional statistical tests of between-group differences on multiples measures of change, the results indicated equivalent efficacy among the three models for those who completed treatment, although there was a nearly significant ($p <$ .10), medium effect that suggested a difference, at termination, in favor of BRT and the cognitive-behavioral model. In a second set of analyses, we tried to examine clinical significance and found both BRT and the cognitive-behavioral model to be significantly superior to the psychodynamic

Table 12.7. Rupture Resolution: Treatment Evaluation Studies

Study	Subjects	Design	Results
Muran & Safran (2002)	128 patients Personality disordered patients with comorbid symptomatology randomly assigned	*Comparative Treatment Study:* Relational treatment model (BRT) (based on process research) versus two traditional short-term models (one psychodynamic, the other cognitive-behavioral)	1. All three treatments are equally effective for patients who completed, based on traditional statistical analyses 2. BRT cognitive-behavioral models are superior for those who completed, based on clinical significance 3. BRT is superior based on dropout rates
Safran & Muran (2002)	59 patients randomly assigned 18 patients determined to be at risk for treatment failure (based on in-session performance variable) and offered random reassignment	*Comparative Treatment Study:* Comparison of same three treatments: relational treatment as experimental condition, other two as control condition Patients were selected for reassignment to an alternative treatment based on inability to establish a working alliance with previously assigned therapist	1. Of the 18 cases, only 10 elected to be reassigned. 2. Of the five cases reassigned to experimental condition, three completed with good outcome, one moved out of state, and one dropped out. 3. Of the five reassigned to the control condition, all dropped out.

treatment. Finally, in a third take on efficacy, we examined dropout rates and found a significant difference, with BRT (20%) superior to the cognitive-behavioral (37%) and psychodynamic (46%) models.

In another effort to evaluate the efficacy of our integrated treatment model, we have been conducting a small-scale clinical trial funded by the National Institute of Mental Health (NIMH) that employs a methodology designed to overcome an important obstacle to finding differences in treatment efficacy and to be maximally sensitive to any real treatment effects that occur (Safran & Muran, 2002). The assumption guiding our proposed research strategy is that a major obstacle to finding treatment differences is a lack of contextual specificity (Beutler, 1991; Greenberg, 1986). To the extent that patients can be grouped together on the basis of a variable that in theory is particularly relevant to a specific intervention, the possibility of finding treatment differences should be increased. Following this line of reasoning, we hypothesized that selecting patients for

treatment specifically on the basis of difficulties they are having in establishing a therapeutic alliance with their therapists should increase the possibility that an intervention designed specifically to resolve problems or ruptures in the alliance would have more impact than one which is not. This type of patient selection strategy goes beyond the more traditional factorial design of clustering patients on the basis of a static characteristic (such as diagnostic category) by selecting on the basis of a relevant in-session performance variable (ability or failure to establish an adequate therapeutic alliance). This should increase the power of the design by reducing the slippage resulting from selecting on the basis of the type of trait variable, which has been shown to have limited predictive validity.

The NIMH study has consisted of two phases (see table 12.7). In the first phase, patients are randomly assigned to either the psychodynamic or cognitive-behavioral treatment model. The patients are tracked early in treatment; and on the basis of a number of empirically derived criteria from patient and therapist perspectives, a subgroup is identified with whom therapists are having difficulty establishing an alliance and who are at risk for treatment failure or dropout. These patients are then offered the option of transferring to another treatment condition. Those who choose to be transferred are randomly reassigned to BRT or the control for their previous treatment, that is, the psychodynamic therapy if they are coming from the cognitive-behavioral therapy, or the cognitive-behavioral therapy if they are coming from the psychodynamic therapy. In the second phase of the study, they undergo another treatment. Of the 59 patients admitted thus far into this study, 18 (31%) met criteria for risk of treatment failure and were offered the opportunity to be randomly reassigned to the experimental condition or one of the two control conditions. Ten agreed to the offer, and eight chose to remain in the treatment they were receiving (seven of whom eventually dropped out). Of the five assigned to BRT, three completed treatment with indication of good outcome, one moved out of state after completing midphase (with good outcome), and one dropped out. Of the five assigned to the control conditions, all dropped out.

Evaluation of the Empirical Evidence

Although research on alliance rupture and repair is promising, in many respects it is in its early stages. Much of it consists of small sample and/or qualitative studies. Some of the studies lack ecological validity in that they use graduate student therapists to administer analogue treatments (for example, four sessions). Moreover, the number of relevant studies available is limited. At this point in time, our impression is that the following conclusions can be drawn:

1. Given the fact that the quality of the therapeutic alliance is one of the most robust predictors of treatment outcome, it can be inferred that the process of repairing alliance ruptures is an important one. Direct evidence in support of this proposition exists but is limited. This absence of evidence is a function, however, of the limited number of studies available addressing this proposition and should not be confused with the presence of negative findings.

2. There is preliminary evidence available supporting the role that specific processes (e.g., patient expression of negative feelings, therapists' nondefensive behavior) play in resolving ruptures in the therapeutic alliance. Some of this evidence demonstrates the relationship between specific resolution processes within a session and improvements of the alliance within that session. Other evidence demonstrates the relationship between these processes and both improved alliances and outcome over the course of treatment. This evidence is based primarily on small samples and qualitative research, and there is clearly a need to complement the available research with larger samples and more traditional hypothesis testing approaches. Nevertheless, the consistency of the research findings regarding the relevant rupture repair processes, combined with the consistent evidence of the importance of the therapeutic alliance, provides sufficient grounds for proposing provisional guidelines for therapeutic practice.

3. There is preliminary evidence indicating that for some patients a "tear-and-repair" pattern of alliance development over the course of treatment is associated with positive outcome. There is also evidence to suggest that both average level of alliance over the course of treatment and a linear increase in quality of alliance over the course of treatment both predict outcome. This suggests that while the process of developing and repairing alliance ruptures over the course of time is not necessarily an essential aspect of the treatment process for all patients, it may play an important role in the treatment process for some patients. It may, in fact, be the case that different types of alliance development are important for different types of patients. It may also be the case that different patterns of alliance development are associated with different types of change processes and different types of outcome.

4. There is evidence to suggest that poor outcome cases are distinguished by a pattern of patient-therapist complementarity (vicious cycles) in which therapists respond to patients' hostile communications with hostile communications of their own.

5. There is preliminary evidence indicating that ruptures in the alliance occur fairly frequently and that frequency of ruptures (or willingness to report them) is influenced by factors

such as treatment modality and the observer's (that is, the therapist's or patient's) perspective.

THERAPEUTIC PRACTICES

In this section, we summarize provisional practice implications of the foregoing research, bearing in mind the limitations of the research discussed previously.

1. Therapists should be aware that patients often have negative feelings about the therapy or the therapeutic relationship which they are reluctant to broach for fear of the therapist's reactions. It is thus important for therapists to be attuned to subtle indications of ruptures in the alliance and to take the initiative in exploring what is transpiring in the therapeutic relationship when they suspect that a rupture has occurred.

2. It appears to be important for patients to have the experience of expressing negative feelings about the therapy to the therapist should such feelings emerge, or to assert their perspective on what is going on when it differs from the therapist's.

3. When this take place, it is important for therapists to attempt to respond in an open or nondefensive fashion, and to accept responsibility for their contribution to the interaction.

4. There is some evidence to suggest that the process of exploring patient fears and expectations that make it difficult for them to assert their negative feelings about the treatment may contribute to the process of resolving the alliance rupture.

5. Notwithstanding the evidence suggesting that patients' expression of their negative feelings toward their therapists is an important component of the resolution process, there is also evidence to suggest that cases in which therapists are aware of their patient's negative feelings toward them are more likely to result in poor outcome. This may reflect the possibility that therapists in such cases are responding in a hostile or defensive fashion to their patient's negative communications.

6. There is some empirical evidence to suggest that it is difficult to train therapists to deal in a constructive fashion with vicious cycles of this type. This suggests that it is important to place greater emphasis on clarifying the factors mediating the acquisition of the relevant skills by therapists.

REFERENCES

Benjamin, J. (1990). An outline of intersubjectivity: The development of recognition. *Psychoanalytic Psychology, 7*, 33–46.

Benjamin, L. S. (1974). Structural analysis of social behavior. *Psychological Review, 81*, 392–425.

Beutler, L. E. (1991). Have all won and must all have prizes? Revisiting Luborsky et al.'s verdict. *Journal of Consulting and Clinical Psychology, 59*, 226–232.

Bordin, E. (1979). The generalizability of the psychoanalytic concept of the working alliance. *Psychotherapy: Theory, Research and Practice, 16*, 252–260.

Bordin, E. (1994). Theory and research on the therapeutic working alliance: New directions. In A. O. Horvath & L. S. Greenberg (Eds.), *The working alliance: Theory, research, and practice* (pp. 13–37). New York: Wiley.

Castonguay, L. G., Goldfried, M. R., Wiser, S., Raue, P. J., & Hayes, A. M. (1996). Predicting the effect of cognitive therapy for depression: A study of unique and common factors. *Journal of Consulting and Clinical Psychology, 64*(3), 497–504.

Foreman, S. A., & Marmar, C. R. (1985). Therapist actions that address initially poor therapeutic alliances in psychotherapy. *American Journal of Psychiatry, 142*(8), 922–926.

Fuller, F., & Hill, C. E. (1985). Counselor and helpee perceptions of counselor intentions in relation to outcome in a single counseling session. *Journal of Counseling Psychology, 32*(3), 329–338.

Gelso, C. J., & Carter, J. A. (1994). Components of the psychotherapy relationship: Their interaction and unfolding during treatment. *Journal of Counseling Psychology, 41*, 296–306.

Golden, B. R., & Robbins, S. B. (1990). The working alliance within time-limited therapy. *Professional Psychology: Research and Practice, 21*(6), 476–481.

Greenberg, L. S. (1986). Change process research. *Journal of Consulting and Clinical Psychology, 54*, 4–9.

Greenberg, L. S., & Safran, J. D. (1987). *Emotion in psychotherapy*. New York: Guilford.

Greenberg, L. S., Watson, J. C., & Lietaer, G. (Eds.). (1998). *Handbook of experiential psychotherapy*. New York: Guilford.

Greenson, R. (1967). *The technique and practice of psychoanalysis*. New York: International Universities Press.

Henry, W. P., Schacht, T. E., Strupp, H. H., Butler, S. F., & Binder, J. L. (1993). Effects of training in time-limited dynamic psychotherapy: Mediators of therapists' responses to training. *Journal of Consulting and Clinical Psychology*, 61, 441–447.

Henry, W. P., Strupp, H. H., Butler, S. F., Schacht, T. E., & Binder, J. L. (1993). Effects of training in time-limited psychotherapy: Changes in therapist behavior. *Journal of Consulting and Clinical Psychology*, 61, 434–440.

Hill, C. E., Nutt-Williams, E., Heaton, K. J., Thompson, B. J., & Rhodes, R. H. (1996). Therapist retrospective recall impasses in long-term psychotherapy: A qualitative analysis. *Journal of Counseling Psychology*, 43(2), 207–217.

Hill, C. E., Thompson, B. J., Cogar, M. C., & Denman, D. W. (1993). Beneath the surface of long-term therapy: Therapist and client report of their own and each other's covert processes. *Journal of Counseling Psychology*, 40(3), 278–287.

Horvath, A. O., & Symonds, B. D. (1991). Relation between working alliance and outcome in psychotherapy: A meta-analysis. *Journal of Counseling Psychology*, 38, 139–149.

Kivlighan, D. M., & Shaughnessy, P. (2000). Patterns of working alliance development: A typology of client's working alliance ratings. *Journal of Counseling Psychology*, 47(3), 362–371.

Klein, M. H., Mathieu-Coughlan, P., & Kiesler, D. J. (1986). *The psychotherapeutic process: A research handbook*. New York: Guilford.

Lansford, E. (1986). Weakenings and repairs of the working alliance in short-term psychotherapy. *Professional Psychology: Research and Practice*, 17(4), 364–366.

Luborsky, L. (1984). *Principles of psychoanalytic psychotherapy: A manual for supportive-expressive treatment*. New York: Basic.

Mann, J. (1973). *Time-limited psychotherapy*. Cambridge, MA: Harvard University Press.

Martin, D. J., Garske, J. P., & Davis, M. K. (2000). Relation of the therapeutic alliance with outcome and other variables: A meta-analytic review. *Journal of Consulting and Clinical Psychology*, 68(3), 438–450.

Martin, J., Martin, W., Meyer, M., & Slemon, A. (1986). Empirical investigation of the cognitive mediational paradigm for research on counseling. *Journal of Counseling Psychology*, 33(2), 115–123.

Martin, J., Martin, W., & Slemon, A. G. (1987). Cognitive mediation in person-centered and rational-emotive therapy. *Journal of Counseling Psychology*, 34(3), 251–260.

Mitchell, S. A. (1993). *Hope and dread in psychoanalysis*. New York: Basic.

Mitchell, S. A., & Aron, L. (Eds.). (1999). *Relational psychoanalysis: The emergence of a tradition*. New York: Analytic.

Muran, J. C. (in press). A relational approach to understanding change: Multiplicity and contextualism in a psychotherapy research program. *Psychotherapy Research*.

Muran, J. C., Gorman, B., Safran, J. D., Twining, L., Samstag, L. W., & Winston, A. (1995). Linking in-session change to overall outcome in short-term cognitive therapy. *Journal of Consulting and Clinical Psychology*, 63, 651–657.

Muran, J. C., & Safran, J. D. (2002). *A comparative treatment study of personality disorders*. Paper presented at the international meeting of the Society for Psychotherapy Research, Santa Barbara, CA.

Muran, J. C., & Safran, J. D. (in press). A relational approach to psychotherapy: Resolving ruptures in the therapeutic alliance. In F. W. Kaslow (Ed.), *Comprehensive handbook of psychotherapy*. New York: Wiley.

Nagy, J., Safran, J. D., Muran, J. C., & Winston, A. (1998). *A comparative analysis of treatment process and therapeutic ruptures*. Paper presented at the international meeting of the Society for Psychotherapy Research, Snowbird, UT.

Patton, M. J., Kivlighan, D. M., & Multon, K. D. (1997). The Missouri Psychoanalytic Research Project: Relation of change in counseling process to client outcomes. *Journal of Counseling Psychology*, 44(2), 189–208.

Piper, W. E., Azim, H., Joyce, A. S., & McCallum, M. (1991). Transference interpretations, therapeutic alliance, and outcome in short term individual psychotherapy. *Archives of General Psychiatry*, 48, 946–953.

Piper, W. E., Ogrodniczuk, J. S., Joyce, A. S., McCallum, M., Rosie, J. S., O'Kelly, J. G., & Steinberg, P. I. (1999). Prediction of dropping out in time-limited, interpretive individual psychotherapy. *Psychotherapy*, 36(2), 114–122.

Regan, A. M., & Hill, C. E. (1992). Investigation of what clients and counselors do not say in brief therapy. *Journal of Counseling Psychology, 39,* 168–174.

Rennie, D. L. (1994). Clients' deference in psychotherapy. *Journal of Counseling Psychology, 41*(4), 427–437.

Rhodes, R. H., Hill, C. E., Thompson, B. J., & Elliott, R. (1994). Client retrospective recall of resolved and unresolved misunderstanding events. *Journal of Counseling Psychology, 41*(4), 473–483.

Rice, L. N., & Greenberg, L. S. (1984). *Patterns of change: Intensive analysis of psychotherapy process.* New York: Guilford.

Rice, L. N., & Kerr, G. P. (1986). Measures of client and therapist voice quality. In L. S. Greenberg & W. M. Pinsof (Eds.), *The psychotherapeutic process: A research handbook* (pp. 73–105). New York: Guilford.

Safran, J. D. (2002a). Brief relational psychoanalytic treatment. *Psychoanalytic Dialogues, 12*(2), 171–195.

Safran, J. D. (2002b). Reply to commentaries by Warren, Wachtel, and Rosica. *Psychoanalytic Dialogues, 12*(2), 235–258.

Safran, J. D., Crocker, P., McMain, S., & Murray, P. (1990). Therapeutic alliance rupture as a therapy event for empirical investigation. *Psychotherapy, 27,* 154–165.

Safran, J. D., & Greenberg, L. S. (Eds.). (1991). *Emotion, psychotherapy, and change.* New York: Guilford.

Safran, J. D., Greenberg, L. S., & Rice, L. N. (1988). Integrating psychotherapy research and practice: Modeling the change process. *Psychotherapy, 25*(1), 1–17.

Safran, J. D., & Muran, J. C. (1996). The resolution of ruptures in the therapeutic alliance. *Journal of Consulting and Clinical Psychology, 64,* 447–458.

Safran, J. D., & Muran, J. C. (2000a). *Negotiating the therapeutic alliance: A relational treatment guide.* New York: Guilford.

Safran, J. D., & Muran, J. C. (2000b). Resolving therapeutic alliance ruptures: Diversity and integration. *Journal of Clinical Psychology, 56*(2), 233–243.

Safran, J. D., & Muran, J. C. (2002). *A comparative treatment study of potential treatment failures.* Paper presented at the annual meeting of the Society for Psychotherapy Research, Santa Barbara, CA.

Safran, J. D., Muran, J. C., & Samstag, L. W. (1994). Resolving therapeutic alliance ruptures: A task analytic investigation. In A. O. Horvath & L. S. Greenberg (Eds.), *The working alliance: Theory, research, and practice* (pp. 225–255). New York: Wiley.

Safran, J. D., & Wallner, L. K. (1991). The relative predictive validity of two therapeutic alliance measures in cognitive therapy. *Psychological Assessment: A Journal of Clinical and Consulting Psychology, 3,* 188–195.

Samstag, L. W., Batchelder, S., Muran, J. C., Safran, J. D., & Winston, A. (1998). Predicting treatment failure from in-session interpersonal variables. *Journal of Psychotherapy Practice and Research, 5,* 126–143.

Sterba, R. (1934). The fate of the ego in analytic therapy. *International Journal of Psycho-Analysis, 15,* 117–126.

Strupp, H. H. (1993). The Vanderbilt Psychotherapy Studies: Synopsis. *Journal of Consulting and Clinical Psychology, 61,* 431–433.

Tryon, G. S., & Kane, A. S. (1990). The helping alliance and premature termination. *Counseling Psychology Quarterly, 3,* 233–238.

Tryon, G. S., & Kane, A. S. (1993). Relationship of working alliance to mutual and unilateral termination. *Journal of Counseling Psychology, 40*(1), 33–36.

Tryon, G. S., & Kane, A. S. (1995). Client involvement, working alliance, and type of therapy termination. *Psychotherapy Research, 5*(3), 189–198.

Winkelman, E., Safran, J. D., & Muran, J. C. (1998). *The development and validation of the rupture resolution questionnaire.* Unpublished manuscript.

Zetzel, E. (1956). Current concepts of transference. *International Journal of Psycho-Analysis, 37,* 369–375.

13

Self-Disclosure

Clara E. Hill
Sarah Knox

Self-disclosure is one of the most controversial therapist interventions, with some theorists enthusiastically promoting it and others adamantly opposing its use in therapy. The purpose of this chapter is to review the empirical evidence about the effectiveness of therapist self-disclosure in individual therapy and propose guidelines for using it in practice. But first, we define therapist self-disclosure and discuss the theoretical positions about its use.

DEFINITION

We define therapist self-disclosure as therapist statements that reveal something personal about the therapist. Note that this definition excludes disclosures that are nonverbal (that is, based on observations of dress, office decor, and surroundings) because these nonverbal disclosures are not voiced or offered discretely at one point in time and hence are qualitatively different from verbal disclosures. Most of the literature about therapist self-disclosure leaves the definition at this broad, inclusive level, although some have defined self-disclosure more narrowly. For example, McCarthy and Betz (1978) distinguished between self-disclosing disclosures (henceforth called just self-disclosures) and self-involving disclosures (which have also been called immediacy). Similarly, Hill and O'Brien (1999, p. 369) defined self-disclosure as a statement that "reveals something personal about the helper's nonimmediate experiences or feel-

ings," such as "When I'm not seeing clients, I like to fish." They defined immediacy as "immediate feelings about self in relation to the client, about the client, or about the therapeutic relationship" (p. 369), for example, "I'm feeling anxious right now with you."

Hill and O'Brien (1999) further recommended subdividing therapist self-disclosure into four subtypes: *disclosures of facts* ("I got my degree from Southern Illinois University"), *disclosures of feelings* ("When I have been in that situation, I felt angry"), *disclosures of insights* ("When I was in a similar situation adjusting to college, I realized that what made it so difficult was that I felt guilty leaving my mother all by herself"), or *disclosures of strategies* ("When I was in that situation, I forced myself to brush my teeth as soon as I finished lunch"). Therapists likely use each subtype for a different intention in the therapy process, and each probably also has a different outcome.

Another distinction in the literature is between positive or negative disclosures. This distinction has sometimes referred to positive or negative experiences or personal characteristics of the therapist (e.g., Hoffman-Graff, 1977) and at other times has referred to the therapist's positive or negative feelings or reactions to the client (Andersen & Anderson, 1985; Remer, Roffey, & Buckholtz, 1983; Reynolds & Fischer, 1983). Hill, Mahalik, and Thompson (1989) argued that the positive/negative dimension was too value-laden and suggested instead a reassuring/challenging dimension to capture the intent behind the positive/negative distinction. For Hill and colleagues (1989), reassuring disclosures support, reinforce, or legitimize the client's perspective, way of thinking, feeling, or behaving; whereas challenging disclosures challenge the client's perspective, way of thinking, feeling, or behaving.

Furthermore, self-disclosures can be categorized in terms of whether or not the disclosure is reciprocal, that is, in response to a similar client disclosure (Barrett & Berman, in press). Finally, from the literature on client self-disclosure (see Cozby, 1973), we know that disclosures can be evaluated in terms of the breadth or amount of information disclosed, the depth or level of intimacy of information disclosed, and the duration or time spent in disclosure.

Therapist self-disclosure, then, has been defined variously in the literature, but one theme that unites these definitions is that therapist self-disclosure involves a therapist's personal self-revelatory statement. Hence, unless otherwise specified, the reader should assume that we are using this broad definition of self-disclosure in this chapter.

THEORETICAL POSITIONS ON THERAPIST SELF-DISCLOSURE

Psychoanalytic/Psychodynamic Theories

Although Freud is reputed to have used self-disclosure with his patients, including showing them pictures of himself and discussing personal activities and interests (Cornett, 1991), his writings warn other analysts against such practices. Following Freud's directives, psychoanalytic therapists have been trained to be neutral, anonymous, abstinent, and non-self-disclosing in therapy. Such a neutral approach is deemed necessary for uncovering, interpreting, and resolving client transference, which psychoanalysts assert must remain unhampered by information about the therapist as a real person (Goldstein, 1997). As Jackson stated, "The point of the therapist's revealing little . . . is so that the patient may reveal more" (1990, p. 94). In fact, psychoanalytic therapists have asserted an inverse relationship between a client's knowledge of a therapist's personal life, thoughts, and feelings, and a client's capacity to develop transference to the therapist (Freud, 1958). Psychoanalysts generally acknowledge, however, that total anonymity on the part of therapists is impossible. Nevertheless, many assert that therapists should strive for relative anonymity, confining self-disclosure to information implicit in the therapy setting, such as revelations inherent in therapists' offices and appearances (Lane & Hull, 1990).

Many psychodynamic therapists, though clearly rooted in the psychoanalytic tradition, have tempered their view of therapist self-disclosure. For example, Lane and Hull (1990) stated that clients may become more aware of the effects of their behaviors on others when therapists disclose their reactions to clients. Likewise, Goldstein (1997) and Palombo (1987) argued that thoughtful use of therapist self-disclosure can reinforce the empathic attunement and responsiveness necessary for successful engagement and treatment of some clients.

Humanistic Theories

Humanistic theorists more openly embrace therapist self-disclosure, asserting that such interventions demonstrate therapists' genuineness and positive regard for clients (Robitschek & McCarthy, 1991) and demystify the therapeutic process (Kaslow, Cooper, & Linsenberg, 1979). Proponents of this approach advocate therapist authenticity, realness, and mutuality (Goldstein, 1997), regarding these as necessary prerequisites for client openness, trust, intimacy, gains in self-understanding, and change (Rogers, 1951; Truax & Carkhuff, 1967). Therapist transparency is believed to make the therapist more humane, to bind therapist and client together, to enable therapists to serve as models of personal growth for clients (Lane & Hull, 1990), and to equalize the control over the therapy relationship while simultaneously correcting client transference misconceptions (Jourard, 1971). In addition, therapist self-disclosure is believed to help clients feel less alone with their painful experiences and emotions, thereby confirming the essential humanness and universality of clients' experiences (Cornett, 1991).

Behavioral/Cognitive/ Cognitive-Behavioral Theories

It is likely that therapists with behavioral and cognitive orientations would view therapist self-disclosures positively, especially when these interventions are intended to serve as a model for client self-disclosure. We found nothing in the literature, however, that describes how therapist self-disclosure is viewed by these orientations.

Feminist Theories

Feminist therapists have supported the appropriate use of therapist self-disclosure (Mahalik, VanOrmer, & Simi, 2000), believing that this intervention can serve several therapeutic goals. Therapist self-disclosure may, for example, serve as a vehicle for transmitting feminist values, equalize power in the therapy relationship, facilitate client growth, foster a sense of solidarity between therapist and client, help clients view their own situations with less shame, encourage clients' feelings of liberation, and acknowledge the importance of the real relationship between therapist and client. In addition, feminist therapists believe that therapist revelation can enable clients to make informed decisions about whether or not they choose to work with a therapist. For clients to make such decisions, appropriate content for therapist self-disclosure includes therapists' beliefs and lifestyle, religious and class background, sexual orientation, political views, and feelings toward clients.

Multicultural Theories

Multicultural theories, which are now considered the fourth force in psychotherapy, also advocate using self-disclosure, particularly with clients from different sociocultural backgrounds and alternative lifestyles (Goldstein, 1994; Jenkins, 1990; Sue & Sue, 1999). Because mental health services often occur within a biased historical and social context (Jenkins, 1990), therapists working with clients who are culturally different from themselves may need to self-disclose to prove themselves worthy of trust (Sue & Sue, 1999). The client stance of "Prove that you can be trusted" or

"Before I open up to you, I want to know where you are coming from" is nevertheless difficult for therapists because of the implied demand for self-disclosure, an intervention many are still trained to avoid. Some clients, however, may not open up until the therapist first discloses.

CLINICAL EXAMPLES

The following two clinical examples are taken from a qualitative study (Knox, Hess, Petersen, & Hill, 1997) in which clients were interviewed about their experiences of therapist self-disclosure and its effects. These examples were selected because they were clear illustrations of therapist self-disclosure (as opposed to immediacy) and because they had a positive impact on the clients.

"Ann," a 35-year-old White woman who sought therapy for depression and an eating disorder, had been in therapy with "Dr. S," a 45-year-old White male therapist, for almost 7 years. A helpful self-disclosure that Ann vividly remembered was when Dr. S revealed that he spent his childhood summers at the beach. This disclosure made Ann feel that Dr. S could understand her because she, too, had spent summers at the shore. She also viewed Dr. S's disclosure as evidence that he trusted her, which increased Ann's self-esteem, comfort, and sense of importance. As a result of the ensuing discussions of days spent at the shore, Ann was able to recall the good times of her childhood and see her parents as not entirely evil, but as ill. This realization allowed Ann to forgive her parents before they died and also helped her feel less guilty about her own children. Furthermore, the disclosure equalized the therapy relationship and enabled Ann to see Dr. S as a real person. Ann credited Dr. S's disclosure with having allowed her to feel more comfortable and open with him and with fostering her trust in him.

"Susan," a 44-year-old White woman with dissociative identity disorder, had been seeing "Dr. A," a 58-year-old White male therapist, for almost four years. She described their early relationship as uncomfortable and distrusting, "rocky" enough that she used his comments and reactions as reasons to consider leaving therapy. Dr. A's consistency and persistence, however, allowed Susan to feel more safe and open to revealing her feelings, and so she stayed in therapy. Susan, who was interested in AIDS research, brought in a song about a young man dying of AIDS and gave it to Dr. A. When Dr. A returned the tape, he disclosed that one of his family members had died of AIDS. Susan was initially surprised by the personal nature of his disclosure and then felt sympathy for Dr. A. She said that this disclosure enabled her to be more open, more present, and less protective in therapy. She viewed the disclosure as a gift, which made her feel safer, closer, and special that someone like Dr. A would share such a personal and emotional experience with her. The disclosure validated her feelings about the trauma of loss, which she could connect to recent losses in her own family. Dr. A's disclosure also changed how Susan saw him: It made him easier for her to talk to, equalized their relationship, and helped her feel better outside of therapy.

RESEARCH REVIEW

Perceptions of Therapist
Self-Disclosure by Nonclients

The existing research on how therapist self-disclosure is experienced has been primarily analogue in design (that is, involving simulations of therapy rather than actual therapy). Subjects (usually undergraduate psychology students participating for course credit) are typically presented with a stimulus of a disclosure embedded in a written transcript, audiotape, or videotape of a hypothetical therapy session. After reading, listening to, or watching the stimulus, participants rate their perceptions of the disclosure and/or of the therapist.

Generally, these studies have shown that nonclients perceived both therapist self-disclosing and self-involving disclosures favorably. Of 18 studies of therapist self-disclosure in individual therapy, 14 reported positive perceptions of therapist self-disclosure (Bundza & Simonson, 1973; Doster & Brooks, 1974; Dowd & Boroto, 1982; Feigenbaum, 1977; Fox, Strum, & Walters, 1984; Hoffman-Graff, 1977; Myrick, 1969; Nilsson, Strassberg, & Bannon, 1979; Peca-Baker & Fried-

lander, 1987; Simonson, 1976; Simonson & Bahr, 1974; VandeCreek & Angstadt, 1985; Watkins & Schneider, 1989; Wetzel & Wright-Buckley, 1988), three reported negative perceptions (Carter & Motta, 1988; Cherbosque, 1987; Curtis, 1982), and one reported mixed findings (Goodyear & Shumate, 1996). Of seven studies investigating therapist self-involving statements in individual therapy, six reported positive perceptions (Andersen & Anderson, 1985; Dowd & Boroto, 1982; McCarthy & Betz, 1978; Remer, Roffey, & Buckholtz, 1983; Reynolds & Fischer, 1983; Watkins & Schneider, 1989), whereas one reported negative perceptions (Cherbosque, 1987).

In his review of this analogue literature on therapist self-disclosure, Watkins (1990) concluded that therapists who self-disclosed in a moderate or nonintimate way have been viewed more favorably and elicited more client self-disclosure than therapists who did not disclose at all, who disclosed a lot, or who disclosed personal and intimate material. This analogue research provides some useful information, suggesting that therapist self-disclosure is experienced positively by nonclients who read it, listened to it, or observed it. Because of their analogue design, however, the findings may not be generalizable to real clients in real therapy relationships. Only one of the analogue studies, for example, investigated the effects of therapist self-disclosure with current therapy clients rather than nonclients (Curtis, 1982). Similarly, we are limited in our understanding of how these results may apply to nonmajority populations, for only Cherbosque (1987) specifically targeted such participants.

Frequency of Therapist Self-Disclosure
in Psychotherapy

According to a number of different sources (judges, clients, and therapists), therapist self-disclosure is a low-frequency intervention in therapy. For example, across several studies where judges coded therapist behavior in transcripts of therapy sessions, 1 to 13% (with an average of 3.5% across studies) of all therapist interventions in individual therapy were self-disclosures (Barkham & Shapiro, 1986; Elliott et al., 1987; Hill, 1978; Hill, Thames, & Rardin, 1979; Hill et al., 1988; Stiles, Shapiro, & Firth-Cozens, 1988). In a study conducted by Ramsdell and Ramsdell (1993) of former clients (surveyed up to 14 years after therapy ended) who had been seen at least six times by therapists from a wide variety of orientations, 58% said that their therapist had self-disclosed at least once. Specifically, 9% said their therapist had disclosed once, 34% indicated 3–4 times, 9% indicated 4–9 times, and 6% said their therapist had disclosed 10 or more times. Given that Ramsdell and Ramsdell assessed clients' memories of how much therapists had disclosed rather than having judges code disclosure behavior in sessions, this study probably captured more of clients' perceptions of memorable self-disclosures or their overall sense of the therapists' disclosing style. Finally, in a survey of therapists from a wide range of orientations (Edwards & Murdock, 1994), therapists reported that they generally disclosed a moderate amount (3 on a 5-point scale), with only 6% indicating that they never disclosed.

A few studies have examined how often different types of therapist self-disclosures have been used. Therapists reported that they disclosed most often about their professional background (e.g., therapy style and training) and rarely about sexual practices and beliefs (Edwards & Murdock, 1994; Geller & Farber, 1997; Robitschek & McCarthy, 1991). Clients reported more helpful than unhelpful therapist disclosures in a study of individual therapy (Knox et al., 1997).

Furthermore, humanistic/experiential therapists reported disclosing more often than did psychoanalytic therapists (Edwards & Murdock, 1994; Simon, 1990) and were also judged by experienced clinical psychologist raters as having a more disclosing style than analytic therapists (Beutler & Mitchell, 1981), which fits with their stated theoretical orientations. No differences in disclosure were reported, however, between male and female therapists (Edwards & Murdock, 1994; Robitschek & McCarthy, 1991), nor among therapists of different racial/ethnic origins (Edwards & Murdock, 1994).

Why Do Therapists Disclose?

On the basis of reviewing videotapes of their sessions, therapists indicated that they had disclosed to give information and to resolve their own needs (Hill et al., 1988). In surveys (Edwards & Murdock, 1994; Geller & Farber, 1997; Simon, 1990), therapists indicated that they most often disclosed to increase perceived similarity between themselves and their clients, to model appropriate behavior for clients, to foster the therapeutic alliance, to validate reality or normalize client experiences, to offer alternative ways to think and act, and because clients wanted therapist disclosure. Similarly, when clients were asked why they thought their therapists disclosed, they indicated that they believed therapists disclosed to normalize their experiences, reassure them, and help them make constructive changes (Knox et al., 1997). Hence, there is some overlap between therapist and client perceptions of why therapists disclose (to normalize experiences, reassure clients, and help clients change).

Therapists indicated on surveys that they generally *avoided* self-disclosure when the disclosure would fulfil their own needs, move the focus from the client to the therapist, interfere with the client's flow of material, burden or confuse the client, be intrusive for the client, blur the boundaries between the therapist and client, overstimulate the client, or contaminate the transference (Edwards & Murdock, 1994; Geller & Farber, 1997; Simon, 1990). These results suggest that therapists are very aware about possible negative consequences on outcome of disclosing in therapy.

The Effects of Therapist Self-Disclosure

The effects of therapist self-disclosure have been investigated both in terms of immediate outcome in the session (for example, what happens in the session right after a therapist self-discloses) and in terms of distal outcome (for example, changes after treatment).

Immediate Outcome

Given that the frequent reasons for using therapist self-disclosures are immediate goals for the therapy process rather than long-term goals for symptom change, it makes sense to examine immediate rather than ultimate outcome. Indeed, the studies (three studies on two data sets) that have examined the immediate outcome of therapist self-disclosures on clients have found positive effects. Hill and colleagues (1988) found that clients gave the highest ratings of helpfulness and had the highest subsequent experiencing levels (such as involvement with their feelings) in response to therapist self-disclosures. In contrast, therapists gave the lowest ratings of helpfulness to self-disclosures, which Hill and colleagues speculated may have been because disclosures made therapists feel vulnerable. In a further analysis of the same data, Hill, Mahalik, and Thompson (1989) found that reassuring disclosures were viewed as more helpful than challenging disclosures in terms of both client and therapist helpfulness ratings and subsequent client experiencing levels.

In a qualitative study of helpful therapist self-disclosures (Knox et al., 1997), clients noted several major impacts of helpful therapist self-disclosures (not including immediacy statements). Knox and colleagues (1997) noted that therapist self-disclosures led to client insight and made the therapist seem more real and human. Feeling that the therapist was more real and human in turn improved the therapeutic relationship and helped clients feel reassured and normal. The improved therapeutic relationship and feeling reassured and normal in turn made clients feel better and served as a model for positive changes and for being open and honest in therapy. It is interesting to note here that the effects of therapist self-disclosure were part of a complicated sequence of events combining both immediate and distal outcome.

Treatment (Distal) Outcome

The results of studies of the effects of therapist self-disclosure on ultimate outcome have been mixed. Of studies using a correlational method, no relationship was found between the frequency of therapist self-disclosures and client, therapist, and/or observer judgments of treatment outcome in six studies (Beutler & Mitchell, 1981; Braswell, Kendall, Braith, Carey, & Vye, 1985; Coady, 1991; Hill et al., 1988; Kushner, Bordin, & Ryan, 1979; Williams & Chambless, 1990), and a negative relationship was found between frequency of therapist self-disclosure and therapists' ratings of client improvement in another study (Braswell et al., 1985). We should note, however, that the definitions of and ways of assessing self-disclosure in these studies were vague and inconsistent.

In contrast to the previous neutral or negative results, two other studies using other methodologies found positive effects of therapist self-disclosure on treatment outcome. A survey of former clients who had received at least six sessions of treatment found that clients rated therapists' sharing personal information as having a beneficial effect on therapy (Ramsdell & Ramsdell, 1993). Another study found that clients who received more *reciprocal* therapist self-disclosures (that is, self-disclosures in response to similar client self-disclosures) liked their therapists more and had less symptom distress after treatment, although they did not increase in the number or intimacy of their own self-disclosures (Barrett & Berman, 2001).

The Barrett and Berman study involved an experimental manipulation such that graduate-student therapists increased the number of reciprocal self-disclosures in brief therapy with one client and refrained from using them with another client. Importantly, therapists gave only about five disclosures per session in the high-disclosure condition, suggesting that disclosures were still infrequent.

Summary of Empirical Research

So what do we know? A summary of the analogue literature suggests that nonclients generally have positive perceptions of therapist self-disclosure. They liked therapists who moderately disclosed personal information about themselves. A summary of the literature about actual therapy indicates that humanistic/experiential therapists disclosed more than psychoanalytic therapists, therapists disclosed infrequently in therapy, and therapists disclosed mostly about professional background and rarely about sexual practices and beliefs. Furthermore, in actual therapy, disclosures were perceived as helpful rather than unhelpful in terms of immediate outcome, although the effects on the ultimate outcome of therapy remain unclear. Finally, therapists had many therapeutic reasons for disclosing (to give information, to normalize client's experiences), as well as several indications of when they would avoid disclosing (to meet their own needs, to move the focus from client to therapist).

LIMITATIONS OF THE RESEARCH

Although the research evidence on therapist self-disclosure is provocative and interesting, it must be viewed with caution. Studies have rarely used similar definitions or methods to study self-disclosure, and results have not been replicated across studies in actual therapy. In what follows, we briefly identify several problems in hopes of improving future research.

Definitional Issues

Many different definitions of therapist self-disclosure have been used in the empirical literature, making it difficult to compare results across studies. For example, is "willingness to be known" the same as "revealing something personal about oneself"? Clearly, a therapist disclosure of a superficial past positive experience in response to a similar client disclosure (such as, "I also felt anxious when I took tests in college") would be viewed very differently from a deep therapist disclosure of immediate feelings in the therapeutic relationship ("I am feeling angry at you right now because it feels like you're belittling me"). Hence, we stress that researchers must clearly define what they mean by therapist self-disclosure. Preferably researchers should use definitions consistent with those used by other researchers so that results can be compared across studies. Furthermore, we strongly encourage researchers to differentiate between self-disclosures and immediacy, and to differentiate subtypes of disclosures (of facts, of feelings, of insight, and of strategies) given that different types of disclosures probably have different effects on therapy.

Focus on Frequency

Much of the research investigating the effects of therapist self-disclosure in actual therapy has correlated the frequency of self-disclosures with treatment outcome. Clearly, there is no compelling reason to believe that more disclosures should lead to better outcome. It may even be that therapist self-disclosure yields its positive effects because it typically occurs so infrequently. In fact, therapists may disclose more in particularly difficult cases where the client has trouble making a connection with the therapist. Such cases may have worse outcomes not because of the greater number of therapist self-disclosures, but because of the clients' initial disturbance level. Similarly, Stiles, Honos-Webb, and Surko (1998) identified a problem in the entire process-outcome literature that they called "responsiveness." They noted that therapists give clients what they perceive they need at a particular time. If therapists are indeed responsive to client needs, it is unlikely that there would be a relationship between therapist self-disclosure and outcome; one client might need one disclosure, whereas another might need ten. Hence, frequency is not the right thing to be examining; rather, researchers should be examining types of disclosures, timing of disclosures, quality of disclosures, and client readiness for disclosures. Furthermore, it strains the imagination to think that any single self-disclosure would lead to client change at the end of treatment. Rather, it makes sense that self-disclosures influence the immediate process, which then indirectly influences treatment outcome.

Lack of Theoretical Basis for Research

Another important issue to note is that despite the rich theoretical literature on therapist self-disclosure, most of the research has been atheoretical. Hence, we do not know if therapist self-disclosure contaminates the transference as asserted by psychoanalytic theorists, or whether it is particularly appropriate with culturally different clients as asserted by multicultural theorists. Given the provocative and widely divergent claims by the different theoretical orientations, research is needed to determine to test these propositions.

Methodology and Analysis

The analogue design of many of the studies presents limitations because they are not realistic and have limited applicability to real clients, real therapists, and real therapy, where the evolving context and relationship are crucial. In addition, most of the participants in the analogue studies were undergraduates participating for research credit, and these students may differ in meaningful ways from actual therapy clients. Furthermore, the therapist self-disclosure stimulus used in these studies was often provided with minimal context, instead of emerging out of an ongoing interaction between therapist and client. In fact, a study that compared therapists' responses to filmed clients (an analogue) with their actual behavior in intake sessions with real clients found that therapists did not disclose the same amount in the analogue situation as they did in real intake sessions (Kushner et al., 1979).

In addition, the most typical methods for analyzing the effects of therapist self-disclosures in ongoing therapy have been the correlational method mentioned above (in which the frequency of therapist self-disclosures is related to session or treatment outcome), sequential analyses (in which the effects of self-disclosure are tested in terms of the immediate client behavior), surveys (in which therapists and clients are asked about their experiences of giving or receiving therapist self-disclosures), and qualitative methods (in which participants are interviewed and data are coded using words rather than numbers). Each method for studying self-disclosure has its advantages and disadvantages (see Hill & Lambert, in press), and none is ideal for studying therapist self-disclosure. We suggest that new models need to be built that combine sequential analyses of immediate outcome with analyses of longer-term outcome, incorporating mediating variables such as how the client thought about and acted upon the disclosures outside of therapy.

Thus, particular types of disclosures (for example, reassuring and reciprocal) done at the optimal time in therapy might help to build the therapeutic alliance, which in turn might allow clients to benefit further from other interventions and feel confident to explore themselves more thoroughly and make changes, which in turn may lead them to disclose more to significant others outside therapy and receive positive feedback, which in turn might lead to better treatment outcome. This more complicated pathway of influence needs to be investigated using new methodologies designed specifically for this purpose.

THERAPEUTIC PRACTICES

In crossing the threshold of anonymity, therapists may powerfully affect their clients with self-disclosures. It is incumbent upon therapists, then, to understand the potential impact of their disclosures and to use this intervention appropriately. On the basis of the empirical literature, we suggest several practice guidelines (note that these guidelines are for self-disclosure and not for immediacy).

1. *Therapists should generally disclose infrequently.* A number of studies show that therapists disclose only infrequently. It may be that self-disclosure is helpful because it occurs so infrequently.

2. *The most appropriate topic for therapist self-disclosure involves professional background, whereas the least appropriate topics include sexual practices and beliefs.* Disclosing about professional background seems particularly important so that therapists can inform clients about their credentials and build trust. Such disclosures are also relatively benign and not deeply intimate. Disclosing about sexual practices and beliefs, in contrast, is not typically necessary for therapy and may be much too intimate for the therapeutic setting. Research has indicated that therapists who disclosed nonintimate material were viewed more favorably than those who disclosed intimate material.

3. *Therapists should generally use disclosures to validate reality, normalize, model, strengthen the alliance, or offer alternative ways to think or act.* These reasons for disclosing appear to be helpful in therapy and to enhance the therapeutic relationship.

4. *Therapists should generally avoid using disclosures that are for their own needs, remove the focus from the client, interfere with the flow of the session, burden or confuse the client, are intrusive, blur the boundaries between the therapist and client, overstimulate the client, or contaminate the transference.* Disclosures used for each of these reasons can have a deleterious effect on the therapy relationship and process. In addition, disclosures used for these reasons may signal that the therapist is struggling with unresolved conflicts, which should be addressed in supervision and/or personal therapy.

5. *Therapist self-disclosure might be particularly effective when it is in response to similar client self-disclosure.* Therapist self-disclosure used in response to similar client self-disclosure may be effective because it helps clients feel normal and reassured.

6. *Therapists should observe carefully how clients respond to their disclosures, ask the clients about their reactions, and use that information to conceptualize their clients and decide how to intervene next.* Therapist self-disclosure is a provocative and potentially powerful intervention, so therapists need to monitor how clients react to it (how they feel when they hear it, whether it influences their view of the therapist, and whether it affects the therapy relationship).

7. *It may be especially important for therapists to disclose with some clients more than others.* Therapists may need to use self-disclosure in some cases to build trust. Without therapist self-disclosure, some clients might not persist in therapy.

REFERENCES

Andersen, B., & Anderson, W. (1985). Client perceptions of counselors using positive and negative self-involving statements. *Journal of Counseling Psychology, 32,* 462–465.

Barkham, M., & Shapiro, D. A. (1986). Counselor verbal response modes and experienced empathy. *Journal of Counseling Psychology, 33,* 3–10.

Barrett, M. S., & Berman, J. S. (2001). Is psychotherapy more effective when therapists disclose information about themselves? *Journal of Consulting and Clinical Psychology, 69,* 597–603.

Beutler, L. E., & Mitchell, R. (1981). Psychotherapy outcome in depressed and impulsive patients as a function of analytic and experiential treatment procedures. *Psychiatry, 44,* 297–306.

Braswell, L., Kendall, P. C., Braith, J., Carey, M. P., & Vye, C. S. (1985). "Involvement" in cognitive-behavioral therapy with children: Process and its relationship to outcome. *Cognitive Therapy and Research, 9,* 611–630.

Bundza, K. A., & Simonson, N. R. (1973). Therapist self-disclosure: Its effect on impressions of therapist and willingness to disclose. *Psychotherapy: Theory, Research, and Practice, 10,* 215–217.

Carter, R. I., & Motta, R. W. (1988). Effects of intimacy of therapist's self-disclosure and formality on perceptions of credibility in an initial interview. *Perceptual and Motor Skills, 66,* 167–173.

Cherbosque, J. (1987). Differential effects of counselor self-disclosure statements on perception of the counselor and willingness to disclose: A cross-cultural study. *Psychotherapy, 24,* 434–437.

Coady, N. F. (1991). The association between complex types of therapist interventions and outcomes in psychodynamic psychotherapy. *Research on Social Work Practice, 1,* 122–138.

Cornett, C. (1991). The "risky" intervention: Twinship self-object impasses and therapist self-disclosure in psychodynamic psychotherapy. *Clinical Social Work Journal, 19,* 49–61.

Cozby, P. C. (1973). Self-disclosure: A literature review. *Psychological Bulletin, 79,* 73–91.

Curtis, J. M. (1982). The effect of therapist self-disclosure on patients' perceptions of empathy, competence and trust in an analogue psychotherapeutic interaction. *Psychotherapy: Theory, Research, and Practice, 19,* 54–62.

Doster, J. A., & Brooks, S. J. (1974). Interviewer disclosure modeling, information revealed, and interviewee verbal behavior. *Journal of Consulting and Clinical Psychology, 42,* 420–426.

Dowd, E. T., & Boroto, D. R. (1982). Differential effects of counselor self-disclosure, self-involving statements, and interpretation. *Journal of Counseling Psychology, 29,* 8–13.

Edwards, C. E., & Murdock, N. L. (1994). Characteristics of therapist self-disclosure in the counseling process. *Journal of Counseling and Development, 72,* 384–389.

Elliott, R., Hill, C. E., Stiles, W. B., Friedlander, M. L., Mahrer, A. R., & Margison, F. R. (1987). Primary therapist response modes: Comparison of six rating systems. *Journal of Consulting and Clinical Psychology, 55,* 218–223.

Feigenbaum, W. M. (1977). Reciprocity in self-disclosure within the psychological interview. *Psychological Reports, 40,* 15–26.

Fox, S. G., Strum, C., & Walters, H. A. (1984). Perceptions of therapist disclosure of previous experience as a client. *Journal of Clinical Psychology, 40,* 496–498.

Freud, S. (1958). *The dynamics of the transference.* In J. Strachey (Ed.), The standard edition of the complete works of Sigmund Freud (Vol. 12, pp. 97–109). London: Hogarth. (Originally published in 1912)

Geller, J. D., & Farber, B. A. (1997, August). *Why therapists do and don't disclose*. Paper presented at the annual meeting of the American Psychological Association, Chicago, IL.

Goldstein, E. G., (1994). Self-disclosure in treatment: What therapists do and don't talk about. *Clinical Social Work Journal, 22*, 417–433.

Goldstein, E. G. (1997). To tell or not to tell: The disclosure of events in the therapist's life to the patient. *Clinical Social Work Journal, 25*, 41–58.

Goodyear, R. K., & Shumate, J. L. (1996). Perceived effects of therapist self-disclosure of attraction to clients. *Professional Psychology: Research and Practice, 27*, 613–616.

Hill, C. E. (1978). Development of a counselor verbal response category system. *Journal of Counseling Psychology, 25*, 461–468.

Hill, C. E., Helms, J. E., Tichenor, V., Spiegel, S. B., O'Grady, K. E., & Perry, E. S. (1988). The effects of therapist response modes in brief psychotherapy. *Journal of Counseling Psychology, 35*, 222–233.

Hill, C. E., & Lambert, M. J. (in press). Methodological issues in studying psychotherapy processes and outcomes. In M. J. Lambert (Ed.), *Handbook of psychotherapy and behavior change* (5th ed.). New York: Wiley.

Hill, C. E., Mahalik, J. R., & Thompson, B. J. (1989). Therapist self-disclosure. *Psychotherapy, 26*, 290–295.

Hill, C. E., & O'Brien, K. (1999). *Helping skills: Facilitating exploration, insight, and action*. Washington, DC: American Psychological Association.

Hill, C. E., Thames, T. B., & Rardin, D. (1979). A comparison of Rogers, Perls, and Ellis on The Hill Counselor Verbal Response Category System. *Journal of Counseling Psychology, 26*, 198–203.

Hoffman-Graff, M. A. (1977). Interviewer use of positive and negative self-disclosure and interviewer-subject sex pairing. *Journal of Counseling Psychology, 24*, 184–190.

Jackson, J. M. (1990). The role of implicit communication in therapist self-disclosure. In G. Stricker & M. Fisher (Eds.), *Self-disclosure in the therapeutic relationship* (pp. 93–102). New York: Plenum.

Jenkins, A. H. (1990). Self-disclosure and the non-white ethnic minority patient. In G. Stricker & M. Fisher (Eds.), *Self-disclosure in the therapeutic relationship* (pp. 117–134). New York: Plenum.

Jourard, S. M. (1971). *The transparent self*. New York: Van Nostrand Reinhold.

Kaslow, F., Cooper, B., & Linsenberg, M. (1979). Family therapist authenticity as a key factor in outcome. *International Journal of Family Therapy, 1*, 194–199.

Knox, S., Hess, S., Petersen, D., & Hill, C. E. (1997). A qualitative analysis of client perceptions of the effects of helpful therapist self-disclosure in long-term therapy. *Journal of Counseling Psychology, 44*, 274–283.

Kushner, K., Bordin, E. S., & Ryan, E. (1979). Comparison of Strupp and Jenkins' audiovisual psychotherapy analogues and real psychotherapy interviews. *Journal of Consulting and Clinical Psychology, 47*, 765–767.

Lane, R. C., & Hull, J. W. (1990). Self-disclosure and classical psychoanalysis. In G. Stricker & M. Fisher (Eds.), *Self-disclosure in the therapeutic relationship* (pp. 31–46). New York: Plenum.

Mahalik, J. R., VanOrmer, E. A., & Simi, N. L. (2000). Ethical issues in using self-disclosure in feminist therapy. In M. M. Brabeck (Ed.), *Practicing feminist ethics in psychology* (pp. 189–201). Washington, DC: American Psychological Association.

McCarthy, P. R., & Betz, N. E. (1978). Differential effects of self-disclosing versus self-involving counselor statements. *Journal of Counseling Psychology, 25*, 251–256.

Myrick, R. D. (1969). Effect of a model on verbal behavior in counseling. *Journal of Counseling Psychology, 16*, 185–190.

Nilsson, D. E., Strassberg, D. S., & Bannon, J. (1979). Perceptions of counselor self-disclosure: An analogue study. *Journal of Counseling Psychology, 26*, 399–404.

Palombo, J. (1987). Spontaneous self-disclosures in psychotherapy. *Clinical Social Work Journal, 15*, 107–120.

Peca-Baker, T. A., & Friedlander, M. L. (1987). Effects of role expectations on clients' perceptions of disclosing and nondisclosing counselors. *Journal of Counseling and Development, 66*, 78–81.

Ramsdell, P. S., & Ramsdell, E. R. (1993). Dual relationships: Client perceptions of the effect of client-counselor relationship on the therapeutic process. *Clinical Social Work Journal, 21*, 195–212.

Remer, P., Roffey, B. H., & Buckholtz, A. (1983). Differential effects of positive versus negative self-involving counselor responses. *Journal of Counseling Psychology, 30*, 121–125.

Reynolds, C. L., & Fischer, C. H. (1983). Personal

versus professional evaluations of self-disclosing and self-involving counselors. *Journal of Counseling Psychology, 30,* 451–454.

Robitschek, C. G., & McCarthy, P. R. (1991). Prevalence of counselor self-reference in the therapeutic dyad. *Journal of Counseling and Development, 69,* 218–221.

Rogers, C. (1951). *On becoming a person.* Boston: Houghton Mifflin.

Simon, J. C. (1990). Criteria for therapist self-disclosure. In G. Stricker & M. Fisher (Eds.), *Self-disclosure in the therapeutic relationship* (pp. 207–225). New York: Plenum.

Simonson, N. R. (1976). The impact of therapist disclosure on patient disclosure. *Journal of Counseling Psychology, 23,* 3–6.

Simonson, N. R., & Bahr, S. (1974). Self-disclosure by the professional and paraprofessional therapist. *Journal of Consulting and Clinical Psychology, 42,* 359–363.

Stiles, W. B., Honos-Webb, L., & Surko, M. (1998). Responsiveness in psychotherapy. *Clinical Psychology: Science and Practice, 5,* 439–458.

Stiles, W. B., Shapiro, D. A., & Firth-Cozens, J. A. (1988). Do sessions of different treatments have different impacts? *Journal of Counseling Psychology, 35,* 391–396.

Sue, D. W. & Sue, D. (1999). *Counseling the culturally different: Theory and practice* (3rd ed.). New York: Wiley.

Truax, C. B., & Carkhuff, R. R. (1967). *Toward effective counseling and psychotherapy.* Chicago: Aldine.

VandeCreek, L., & Angstadt, L. (1985). Client preferences and anticipations about counselor self-disclosure. *Journal of Counseling Psychology, 32,* 206–214.

Watkins, C. E., Jr. (1990). The effects of counselor self-disclosure: A research review. *The Counseling Psychologist, 18,* 477–500.

Watkins, C. E., Jr., & Schneider, L. J. (1989). Self-involving versus self-disclosing counselor statements during an initial interview. *Journal of Counseling and Development, 67,* 345–349.

Wetzel, C. G., & Wright-Buckley, C. (1988). Reciprocity of self-disclosure: Breakdowns of trust in cross-racial dyads. *Basic and Applied Social Psychology, 9,* 277–288.

Williams, K. E., & Chambless, D. L. (1990). The relationship between therapist characteristics and outcome of in vivo exposure treatment for agoraphobia. *Behavior Therapy, 21,* 111–116.

14

The Management of Countertransference

Charles J. Gelso
Jeffrey A. Hayes

The concept of countertransference is about as old as the fields of psychotherapy and psychoanalysis themselves. Like so many fundamental constructs in psychotherapy, the term was created by Freud shortly after the turn of the twentieth century. Although Freud never wrote extensively about countertransference, it was clear that he viewed it as problematic. For example, in the *Future Prospects of Psychoanalytic Therapy*, originally published in 1910, Freud (1957, pp. 144–145) commented, "We have begun to consider the 'counter transference,' which arises in the physician as a result of the patient's influence on his unconscious feelings, and have nearly come to the point of requiring the physician to recognize and overcome this countertransference in himself."

He then went on to note, "Anyone who fails to produce results in a self-analysis of this kind may at once give up any idea of being able to treat patients by analysis" (pp. 144–145). This view of countertransference as a pejorative was likely a major influence in the field's neglect of the topic for many decades. It became simply something to be done away with, not something to be examined. The good analyst was, in fact, capable of maintaining objectivity and of keeping his or her personal conflicts out of the therapeutic relationship. During those early days, one might even say that countertransference attained the status of a taboo topic.

As models of psychoanalysis moved beyond classical drive and ego analytic theory and toward greater receptivity to more relational and interpersonal models, conceptions of countertransference also changed. Countertransference was increasingly viewed as an inevitability that could be for better or worse, depending on how the therapist dealt with it.

The newer conceptions of countertransference, to be discussed subsequently, began emerging in the 1950s. During this decade, the first empirical studies on the topic also emerged (for example, Fiedler, 1951; Cutler, 1958). From that point on, there has been a steady increase of clinical and theoretical writing on countertransference. As is so often the case, however, empirical efforts lagged sadly behind theoretical work, although studies did appear occasionally.

The likely reasons for the slow pace of research were twofold. First, countertransference originated from and was firmly embedded in psychoanalysis, a discipline containing a decidedly anti-empirical bent and strongly opposed to the simplification that appears to be an inherent part of scientific research. Second, and perhaps more telling, the construct itself is awesomely complex, focusing as it does on unconscious processes, defense mechanisms, and indeed often one person's unconscious reactions to another person's unconscious reactions. Add to these the definitional ambiguity that seems to be a part of virtually all high-level constructs, and the research road was filled with obstacles.

In recent years, however, significant changes have occurred. Countertransference has been theorized to be a key part of all therapy relationships, and theoretical propositions have been offered about its operation across various approaches to treatment (Gelso & Hayes, 1998). This, along with the fact that psychoanalysis is itself more receptive to research than in the past, has likely been responsible for some of the increase in research in recent years. In addition, laboratory analogue studies have sought to reduce this high-level construct to more scientifically manageable proportions and have paved the way for more clinically meaningful studies.

In the present chapter, we review empirical research on countertransference (CT) and examine its relation to treatment outcome. Our review incorporates studies conducted within all research traditions: field, laboratory, survey, experimental, and correlational. Also, in recent years efforts have been made to study psychotherapy using qualitative methods. Such qualitative studies, too, have shed light on CT phenomena and shall be reviewed in the chapter. We begin the review by describing varying conceptions and definitions of CT and then examine research as it bears upon the question of the effects of CT on treatment process and, especially, outcome.

DEFINITIONS

As Epstein and Feiner (1988) have noted, three conceptions of CT have been most prominent over the years: the *classical*, the *totalistic*, and what may be termed the *complementary* view. Let us examine each of these.

The classical view was originated by Freud (1957). This view has been stated most forcefully by Annie Reich (1951, 1960). CT is seen as the therapist's unconscious, conflict-based reaction to the patient's transference. In this sense, CT is the therapist's transference to the patient's transference. Although it contains both neurotic and non-neurotic elements (Epstein & Feiner, 1988), the neurotic elements are what make this form of CT undesirable. Unresolved conflicts originating

in the therapist's early childhood are triggered by the patient's transference, and are acted out by the therapist in one way or another. Thus, the CT may serve to cloud the therapist's understanding, create distortions in the therapist of the patient's psyche and self, and/or cause the therapist to behave in antitherapeutic ways. Advocates of this view of CT see little or no benefit to CT. They do not generally believe CT can be used to enhance understanding or to promote therapeutic gain. What needs to occur is that the therapist works through his or her unresolved issues so that CT does not happen or happens minimally.

The totalistic conception of CT originated in the 1950s and was further developed in subsequent years (Heimann, 1950; Kernberg, 1965; Little, 1951). According to this conception, CT represents *all* of the therapist's emotional reactions to the patient. All reactions are important, all should be studied and understood, and all are usefully placed under the broad umbrella of CT. This definition served to legitimate CT and make it an object of the therapist's self-investigation and use. Accordingly, as the totalistic view gained ascendancy, CT became seen more and more as something that could greatly benefit the work, if the therapist studied his or her internal reactions and used them to further understanding of patients, these patients' impact on others, and hidden aspects of patients' internal lives.

It is significant that the totalistic position gained popularity as psychodynamic therapists began doing more work with severely disturbed patients, such as those with borderline and narcissistic disorders. In such cases, therapists usually (perhaps inevitably) experience intense emotional reactions. For example, there has been much writing about hate and rage in the therapist when working with borderlines (see early papers by Winnicott, 1949, and Kernberg, 1965). If intense emotional reactions are natural and expected when working with certain classes of profoundly troubled patients, then, so the reasoning goes, it is helpful to think of CT as a more general process—as something that is inevitable and that can be helpful if understood.

The view of CT as an inevitable reaction to the patient's transference or style overlaps with the third conception: CT as complement or counterpart to the patient's transference or style of relating. Early on, this conception was powerfully stated by Heinrich Racker (1957, 1968) and is also clearly evident in more current interpersonal, relational, and object relations theory (Anchin & Kiesler, 1982; Butler, Flasher, & Strupp, 1993; Cashdan, 1988; Levenson, 1995; Mitchell, 1993; Strupp & Binder, 1984; Teyber, 1997). According to the complementary conception, the patient exhibits certain "pulls" on the therapist. Racker, for example, posited a "law of tallion" dictating that every positive transference is met with a positive CT, whereas every negative transference is met with a negative CT. The well-functioning therapist, however, does not act out *lex talionis* ("an eye for an eye, a tooth for a tooth"), even though it is the "normal" reaction. The good therapist, instead, restrains his or her "eye for an eye" impulse, and seeks to understand what the patient is doing to stir up these reactions. This allows for an understanding of the transference-CT matrix and for the effective framing of therapeutic interventions.

An Integrative Conception

In the literature, as well as in everyday clinical dialogue, the three conceptions of CT that we have described above are all used. The problem is that it is often unclear which of the three, or which combination, is intended at any given time. We have also noticed that the conception often shifts, even within the same discussion!

Beyond ambiguity of usage, it is important to note that each of the three views of CT possesses fundamental limitations. The classical view is overly restrictive in several ways. For example, it construes CT in almost exclusively negative terms; it closes the door to exploration because of its very negativity; it ignores the almost inevitable reactions of the therapist that are tied to powerful "pulls" by the patient; and it focuses almost exclusively on transference (the patient's and the therapist's). Similarly, the totalistic position, in its attempt to encompass all of the therapist's emotional reactions, may render the concept of CT meaningless. If all emotional reactions are CT, then there is nothing else, and the need for the term CT is eliminated. We can simply refer to therapist emotional reactions. However, if this were the case, we would then surely become

aware that there are varying kinds of therapist reactions and that it would be helpful to divide therapist emotional reactions into types. At least some of those types most certainly would be very similar to conceptions of CT that involve therapists' unresolved issues. Many years ago, Winnicott (1949), for example, differentiated what he termed "objective" CT from the more deleterious types. Objective CT included the analyst's love and hate reactions that were largely created by the patient's pathological defenses. These internal reactions were essentially inevitable—for example, one naturally feels hateful affects when working intensely with a highly aggressive, hateful borderline patient—they would occur in anyone working intensively with certain types of patients.

In regard to the complementary or counterpart conception, it is limited in the sense that, in its focus on CT as "pulls" on the therapist stemming from the patient's material or style, it does not take into enough account the therapist's defenses and unresolved conflicts. To use Winnicott's term, it pays too much attention to objective CT and not enough to all that goes on inside the therapist that determines his or her emotional reaction.

Although each of the common conceptions is seriously limited, all three point to extremely important elements of and issues related to CT. An integrated definition best includes learnings from all three. Elsewhere (Gelso & Hayes, 1998; Hayes & Gelso, 2001) we have discussed how it is important to limit the definition of CT to internal and external reactions in which unresolved conflicts of the therapist, usually but not always unconscious, are implicated. All of the therapist's emotional reactions are important and worthy of investigation, clinically and empirically; but the definition of CT must be narrower than the totalistic one if it is to be scientifically useful and clinically meaningful. Our conception of CT is similar to the classical in its focus on the therapist's unresolved conflicts as the source of CT, but it is different in that CT is seen as a potentially useful phenomenon if the therapist successfully understands his or her reactions and uses them to help understand the patient. In this sense, the therapist follows Freud's (1958 [1912], p. 115) suggestion that the therapist "must turn his own unconscious like a receptive organ towards the transmitting unconscious of the patient" as the best way of deeply understanding the patient.

Thus, in seeing CT as both a hindrance and a potential aid to treatment, an integrative definition picks up on the two thematic constructs that Epstein and Feiner (1988) note have been intertwined, like a double helix, throughout the history of thought about CT. In addition, like the totalistic position, it is suggested that CT is inevitable. This is so because all therapists have unresolved issues and unconscious "soft spots" that are touched upon in the work. Furthermore, we suspect that in many or even most cases in which the therapist's intense emotional reaction is a "natural" response to the patient, therapist unresolved conflicts are implicated. An example from a therapist supervisee of the first author helps illustrate this point:

> The therapist-trainee was in her fourth practicum of a doctoral training program, and by every indication appeared to have extraordinary potential as a therapist. In the early part of her work with a 20-year-old male patient, she experienced continued strong irritation, and she reacted to the patient in a controlled, muted, and metallic manner. For his part, the patient was an angry, obsessional young man who had many borderline features. He negated the therapist's attempts to help him understand how his issues might be causing his ongoing problems with women, and he denied that the treatment could have any impact. Also, he usually negated the therapist's observations about what he might be feeling. Clearly the therapist's emotional reactions were "natural," given this patient's negativity and hostility. Yet this therapist's unresolved issues about not being good enough, about fearing that she could not take care of others sufficiently, and about some transference-based fears of her supervisor's evaluation of her were clearly implicated in her irritation and her muted reaction to the patient. As she came to understand these issues, her irritation with the patient lessened, and she was able to empathically grasp the terrifying affects that were underlying much of his negativity.

Finally, like the complementary view, an integrative conception of CT does not simply focus on the therapist's reaction to the patient's transference. Rather, it incorporates the therapist's reaction to both transference and non-transference material presented by the patient. The latter includes the patient's personality style, the actual content that the patient is presenting, and even the patient's appearance.

Two Key Distinctions

Despite the definitional inconsistency, most empirical studies on CT, implicitly or explicitly, use a definition that involves the therapist's unresolved conflicts as the source, and one or more characteristics of the patient as the trigger. Before delving into the empirical literature, however, a few additional distinctions need to be made.

Chronic Versus Acute Countertransference

This distinction was first made by Reich (1951) and has become part of most conceptions of CT over the years. Acute CT includes therapist responses occurring "under specific circumstances with specific patients" (Reich, 1951, p. 26). Reich believed acute CT was based on an identification with the patient. The therapist so identifies because he or she gets some gratification from doing so; for example, the therapist reinforces the patient's assertiveness as a way of satisfying her own wishes to be more assertive. Although Reich's focus was identification, acute CT may reflect myriad needs. For example, the therapist may reinforce submissiveness out of his need or wish to be dominant; the therapist may stop listening because the patient's material is touching on a painful and unresolved current or repressed issue; or the therapist may fall silent and become depressed when working with an assaultive patient due to the therapist's issues with an assaultive father.

In contrast, chronic CT reflects a need of the therapist's that is so habitual that it has become part of his or her personality structure. For example, the therapist may be chronically oversupportive as a means of unconsciously gaining the support that was not sufficiently provided to her; he may see aggression in all clients as a projection of unresolved aggressive needs of his own; or she may be highly active and promote activity in all patients because of fears of her own passive side. Although there may be patient triggers for chronic CT, the trigger itself is less significant than is the case for acute CT. A wide range of patient material will trigger CT that is on the chronic side. In this sense, chronic CT is a "reaction waiting to happen."

CT as Internal State Versus Overt Expression

As an internal state, CT may be reflected in therapist anxiety, failure to recall events and material accurately, feeling states ranging from highly negative to highly positive, and varying degrees of emotional intensity (from very high intensity to under intensity). In terms of overt behavior, generally CT has been studied as withdrawal, underinvolvement, or avoidance of the client's material, or at times as overinvolvement. Generally, CT behavior is seen as hindering because it represents acting out on the patient. Internal CT, on the other hand, is seen as potentially helpful. If the therapist is able to understand these reactions and how they may relate to the patient's inner life and behavior, then this understanding may aid the therapist in his or her work with the patient.

RESEARCH REVIEW

In the following sections, we examine research findings on the effects of CT. We explore patient, therapist, and patient-therapist interaction factors. For the sake of convenience, studies are classified as laboratory, quantitative field, and qualitative investigations. Subsequently we review the empirical literature on CT management.

The Causes of Countertransference

Several studies have examined patient factors that may serve as triggers of CT. An example of such work is the series of laboratory studies on therapist-trainees' CT reactions to seductive or hostile client-actresses in contrast to those who were neutral with respect to sex and aggression, but who appeared to come across as insecure and dependent (Hayes & Gelso, 1991; Peabody &

Gelso, 1982; Robbins & Jolkovski, 1987; Yulis & Kiesler, 1968). The basic hypothesis behind these studies was that clients exhibiting sexual and aggressive responses in relation to the therapist would be responded to with greater CT than those whose responses were neutral with respect to sex and aggression. Each of these studies followed a paradigm developed by Yulis and Kiesler, in which therapists responded to an audiotaped "client" by selecting from two alternatives what their responses would be to the client at several stopping points in the tape. At each stopping point, alternative responses either addressed the client's reaction to the therapist (effective response) or avoided it (indication of CT). The general conclusion from this line of work is that patient factors, in and of themselves, do not affect CT. This conclusion is consistent with other CT studies done in the laboratory (such as Gelso, Fassinger, Gomez, & Latts, 1995; Hayes & Gelso, 1993) and field situations. In regard to the latter, an intensive qualitative analysis of eight cases of therapy lasting from 12 to 20 sessions supports the laboratory findings. Expert therapists were interviewed after every session regarding their reactions to clients, including CT reactions. No evidence emerged to support the idea that particular triggers (client behaviors or material) would tend to stimulate CT.

Turning to the therapist's contribution, research has demonstrated numerous specific origins within the therapist. CT, for example, may stem from conflicts revolving around the therapist's family background, sex roles, parenting roles and responsibilities, unmet needs, professional self-concept, homophobia, and so on (see review by Hayes & Gelso, 2001). In certain ways, listing such origins is like mixing apples and oranges. Each of these represents a different point on a developmental path. Some reflect more current issues (for example, professional self-esteem), whereas others relate to earlier conflicts that we would view as more basic (family background). Developmentally, it is useful to consider the roots of any given CT reaction as residing in unresolved issues from the therapist's childhood. Thus, while any given CT reaction may be viewed as stemming from an immediate issue within the therapist (for example, not being a good enough caretaker), it is likely a derivative of an earlier issue (not feeling cared for sufficiently as a child, not feeling worthy of care as a child).

Based on their review of the early theoretical and empirical literature, Singer and Luborsky (1977, p. 449) concluded that "more experienced and competent therapists tend to be aware of their countertransference feelings and are more able to prevent them from influencing their behavior with their patients." Thus, therapist experience and overall competence tend to be inversely related to the acting out of CT and positively related to understanding of CT feelings. Another therapist quality that has shown up in several studies is anxiety, when conceptualized as a trait (an enduring aspect of the person) or a state (transitory, situational anxiety). For example, early studies by Bandura (1956), Yulis and Kiesler (1968), and Milliken and Kirchner (1971), as well as more recent research (Hayes & Gelso, 1991), all point to the deleterious effects of therapist anxiety. Therapists who experience greater anxiety are more likely than those who are less anxious to avoid patient affect, inaccurately recall material from the session, and ignore patients' feelings about the therapist. Although these studies of therapist anxiety have all been conducted in laboratory settings, they are robust and they do appear to support what has been long held clinically, that is, that ongoing and unresolved therapist anxiety is both a part of CT (when experienced in the session) and a precipitant of other responses indicative of CT.

Although patient and therapist factors, taken separately, appear to have some role in CT, clinical experience suggests that it is the interaction of patient material with therapist unresolved conflicts that more powerfully stimulates CT reactions. In keeping with this conception, several empirical studies to date have supported an interaction hypothesis. In a pair of laboratory studies, counselor-trainees' verbal responses to videotaped client-actors and actresses exhibiting relational and sexual problems, contrary to expectation, did not reflect greater CT when these clients were gay (Hayes & Gelso, 1993) or lesbian (Gelso et al., 1995) than when they were heterosexual. However, these counselors' levels of homophobia predicted avoidance of client material in their responses to gay and lesbian, but not heterosexual, client-actors/actresses.

Both field and laboratory studies have examined the ways in which CT may result from an interaction of patient material and therapist unresolved issues. In a classic field study, one that seemed far ahead of its time, Cutler (1958) intensively studied two therapist-trainees, and found that when patient material was related to areas of unresolved conflict in the therapist, reports by the therapist of his own and his patient's behavior were much less accurate than when patient material was related to areas in which the therapist was not conflicted. For example, when the therapists had measured issues around dominance, rejection, or submissiveness, they tended to misperceive their patients' issues around these areas—either over reporting or under reporting patients' behavior in the same areas. These therapists' interventions with their patients were also affected by CT. Thus, when patient material touched upon areas of conflict for the therapist, the therapist's interventions were judged by supervisors to be less effective.

In another early study, Bandura, Lipsher, and Miller (1960) found that therapists' CT reactions to a hostile client were inversely related to the therapists' need for approval. Thus, therapists who had stronger needs for approval were more likely to avoid clients' expression of hostility. Similarly, in a laboratory study, Sharkin and Gelso (1993) found that counselors who were high on anger proneness and discomfort had greater anxiety when dealing with an angry client.

Mohr, Gelso, and Hill (2002) investigated first counseling sessions to determine if CT behaviors resulted from an interaction of therapist-trainees' and their clients' attachment styles. Nineteen therapists interviewed 65 clients, and CT behavior ratings were made of the 11 supervisors of those therapists. It was found that therapists with dismissing attachment styles were more likely to exhibit hostile CT with clients possessing preoccupied attachment styles, whereas preoccupied therapists were more likely to exhibit hostile CT with dismissing clients. In addition, clients who had preoccupied attachment styles appeared to elicit withdrawing CT in therapists whose attachment styles were dismissing, but not in therapists with other attachment styles. In sum, this study provides clear evidence that, at least in an initial session conducted by therapist-trainees, the effect of clients' attachment styles on CT behavior depends upon the attachment styles of their therapists.

In the aforementioned study by Gelso and colleagues (1995), there was also some indication that therapist gender interacted with sexual orientation. As theorized, when responding to a videotaped lesbian client, female counselors exhibited greater CT than males, whereas when responding to a female heterosexual client, male and female counselors did not differ in CT. Interestingly, the measure of CT that differentiated male and female counselors when interacting with lesbian and heterosexual client-actresses was the recall of sexual words that the client expressed on the tape. Females had a poorer recall of the number of sexual words than males when responding to lesbian clients (but not with heterosexual clients). These findings are part of an emerging literature on the complex ways in which gender relates to CT (Hayes & Gelso, 1991; Howard, Orlinsky, & Hill, 1969; Latts & Gelso, 1995; Lecours, Bouchard, & Normandin, 1995). Although space considerations do not permit a full exploration of these findings, the early field study by Howard and colleagues seems especially noteworthy because it highlights complex interactions. These investigators examined the subjective experience of therapists and female clients in actual therapy dyads and found that female therapists were likely to be threatened by dependency needs of their female clients, whereas male therapists were not. Male therapists, however, experienced unpleasant affect more frequently than females when working with female clients and were also more likely to withdraw emotionally.

The Consequences of Countertransference

As we examine the effects of CT, it should be noted that outcomes are seen as existing on a continuum from immediate to distal. Immediate outcomes pertain to the effects of or on a given phenomenon within the hour, whereas distal outcomes address the effects of treatment on indices of client behavior at the end of treatment. The latter includes outcomes assessed at various points after termination, such as follow-up studies of varying lengths. In between immediate and distal outcomes resides a wide range of what might be called proximate outcomes—those outcomes that pertain to a given session or series of sessions, as well as outcomes that are presumed to be the way station for more distal outcomes; for example, change in patient experiencing may be seen as proximal to change in level of psychopathology, itself a more distal outcome. One aspect of CT should be noted at the outset, since it is related importantly to the effects of this construct. That is, certain manifestations of CT in and of themselves reflect a negative impact or effect on treatment. This is particularly so for the behavioral manifestations. Thus, avoiding what patients are expressing, seen as a behavioral manifestation of CT in the research literature, is in and of itself a negative effect. This applies also to behaviors that are judged to be overly positive (being "too nice") or negative (being rejecting). Although naturally the final judgment about such behaviors must await research that links them to more distal outcomes, it would be hard to imagine effective psychotherapy in situations in which the therapist enacted such behaviors in greater than minimal ways.

A striking feature of the empirical CT literature is the near absence of research seeking to connect CT to more distal outcomes. We shall have more to say about this later, but for now we simply note that nearly all research on CT effects focuses on immediate or proximate outcomes.

Quantitative Studies

Cutler's (1958) classic study was relevant to outcome in that when patient's material touched upon therapists' unresolved conflicts, therapists' interventions were more likely to be judged by their supervisor to be inadequate. Although this represents clear evidence for the negative immediate effects of CT, the fact that only two therapists were studied must be kept in mind. Also, like many of the CT studies, the therapists were in training, although one of them was quite advanced.

In an investigation that examined a more cognitive manifestation of CT, McClure and Hodge (1987) studied 12 therapists (possessing a range of experience) and 36 clients. They found that when therapists possessed very strong positive or negative affect toward clients (an indication of

CT), they were likely to manifest perceptual distortion of the client. When this intense affect was positive, therapists distorted clients' personality in such a way that it seemed more similar to the therapist's personality than was the case, based on personality measures. When the therapists had strong negative affect, they distorted clients in such a way that these clients were seen as more dissimilar from therapists than they were. In contrast, when therapists were free from strong affect, there were no indications of distortions of the client's personality. Although the authors viewed strong affect as the CT basis for therapist distortion of client personality, both variables (strong affect and perceptual distortion) have been viewed in the literature as indications of CT. It is plausible that some other variable(s) caused both strong affect and distortion.

Fauth and Hayes (2002), in another study that examined relations among different indicators of CT, found that in a therapy analogue, therapists (both trainees and experienced professionals) who felt more threatened and less efficacious in response to a videotaped client were more hesitant (greater delay) in framing their verbal responses to the client. On the other hand, therapists who felt more positively challenged and efficacious were less hesitant and exhibited less verbal avoidance.

In a recent field study, Ligiero and Gelso (in press) sampled 51 psychology doctoral students and their clinical supervisors. Supervisors evaluated therapists on a new measure of CT behavior (Friedman & Gelso, 2000) over a three-session block in the middle phase of treatment. Both supervisors and therapists rated the working alliance between these therapists and their clients. Results indicated that negative CT behavior was significantly and negatively related to both supervisor ($r = -.58$) and therapist ($r = -.34$) ratings of the working alliance and each of its components (therapist-client agreement on tasks and goals of treatment, and the bond between participants). Also, positive CT (too much and/or inappropriate support, friendliness, deference) related negatively to supervisors' ratings of the bond aspect of the alliance ($r = -.36$). Thus, negative CT behavior, and perhaps positive CT as well, are related to the development of weaker alliances. Similarly,

Rosenberger and Hayes (in press) conducted a quantitative case study (13 therapy sessions, experienced female therapist) and discovered an inverse relation between CT behavior and working alliance. Specifically, the more avoidance behavior the therapist exhibited in the work, the lower were her ratings of the overall alliance. Also, trained judges' ratings of negative CT behavior in sessions were related to the bond aspect of the working alliance, as assessed by both the therapist and the client. The greater the amount of negative CT behavior, the weaker was both participants' experience of their working alliance bond.

Despite the fact that no clear causal direction has been established by these two studies, it does appear that when therapists exhibit CT behavior, the working alliance becomes weakened. Although the working alliance is not a distal outcome, it has been consistently shown to contribute to distal outcomes (Martin, Garske, & Davis, 2000). Thus, the link of CT behavior to working alliance provides an important hint that CT may well have an impact on outcomes.

In the only study to date that examined the relation of CT to outcome, Hayes, Riker, and Ingram (1997) studied 20 cases of brief therapy (M = eight sessions) conducted by therapist-trainees. Supervisors observed (via video camera) each session and rated CT. For the less successful cases, a strong negative relationship was found between CT behavior as rated by both supervisor ($r = -.87$) and counselor ($r = -.69$) and a composite measure of outcome rated by therapists, supervisors, and clients. For the more successful cases, however, no relationship was found. The authors speculated that in the more successful cases, a strong working alliance mitigated the negative effect of CT.

Qualitative Studies

Four qualitative studies have examined the reported effects of CT. All have employed the consensual qualitative research (CQR) approach developed by Hill, Thompson, and Williams (1997), and all contain results that have a bearing on the effects of CT. In the first of these studies (Hill, Nutt-Williams, Heaton, Thompson, & Rhodes, 1996), the investigators examined the in-therapy factors that cause impasses that end in termination. Impasses were understood to be disagreements between clients and therapists that result in premature ending. The researchers studied 12 experienced therapists of varying theoretical persuasions, and each reported on one case with such an impasse. As expected, many factors were found to be implicated in the impasses, and CT was among the most prominent. Most of the therapists indicated that their own personal conflicts were involved in the impasses. Family-of-origin issues were prominent in this respect; for example, two of the therapists had a parent who had committed suicide, which led the therapists to feel especially vulnerable when their clients threatened suicide. Such a finding is consistent with the CT-relevant quantitative study by Boyer and Hoffman (1993), who discovered that therapists with significant losses in their backgrounds were more likely to feel depressed during termination with their cases. In sum, therapists in the study by Hill and colleagues reported difficulties with clients when they felt the clients behaved in a way that was similar to the therapists' parents, or when the issues hit on one of their personal soft spots.

An example of a long-term case (300 weekly sessions) reported in this study is instructive. The impasse revolved around a feeling that the therapy was going in circles. At the time of the impasse, the client had a strong wish that the therapist would give him advice about whether to get married again. But the client consistently rejected the therapist's perspective on his issues and life. This was a difficult client by any yardstick. More to the point of the CT, as the impasse was unfolding:

> Dr. K. felt frustrated, trapped, and disappointed by the impasse. She wondered if she had been too passive, avoiding a more confrontive, active, directive stance out of fear of becoming controlling like the client's mother. *She also recognized that she had her own personal issues about aggression (e.g., she became defensive and felt like running out of the room when the client verbally attacked her).* (italics added; Hill et al., 1996, p. 213)

This example is typical of the clinical literature in that CT problems result from a difficult case in conjunction with material that connects to the therapist's unresolved feelings and conflicts. The findings of this study were also consistent with the clinical literature on therapy impasses in that CT appears to be implicated in a central way (for example, see Elkind, 1992; Nathanson, 1992).

Gelso, Hill, Mohr, Rochlen, and Zack (1999) sampled 11 experienced psychodynamic therapists in an effort to examine the operation of, and therapist responses to, transference in successful long-term therapy. The researchers conducted one-hour phone interviews (and follow-up interviews) focused on a recently terminated case that fit the study's selection criteria. It was found that, even within these successful cases, there were many CT reactions that therapists reported. Notably, positive CT appeared to involve underlying issues just as much as did more negative CT. An example of positive CT that appeared to be problematic was a case in which the "therapist reported that he admired the client for doing things in his life that the therapist could not do, and at the same time enjoyed being idealized by the client. Tied to these reactions, the therapist felt he did not give the client enough permission to express negative transference feelings" (p. 264).

The two previous studies involved seasoned therapists. In a study of neophyte therapists (Williams, Judge, Hill, & Hoffman, 1997), seven prepracticum students in a counseling psychology doctoral program were participants. During this prepracticum, trainees worked with about three clients for approximately three 50-minute sessions each. Based on a range of measures completed after each session and at the end of the semester by trainees, clients, and supervisors, qualitative analyses were conducted to determine the personal reactions trainees experience during sessions and the strategies trainees use to manage their reactions. The data suggested that, although the trainees' skills and confidence grew considerably during the training, trainees' feelings and personal conflicts did at times interfere with their effectiveness with clients. For example, supervisors noted negative behaviors often were the source of interference—displaying annoyance or anger, pushing one's own agenda, becoming very directive, talking a lot, and shutting down. Trainees' difficulties managing their feelings and reactions included avoidance and overinvolvement, typical indications of CT in the literature. All of these CT-based difficulties, according to supervisors, tended to impede counselor effectiveness.

In the three prior qualitative studies, CT and its effects were only one of the elements studied. In a study by Hayes and colleagues (1998), the focus was entirely on CT. The aim of the study was to explore the causes, manifestations, and effects of CT (explicitly defined as reactions originating from unresolved intrapsychic conflict). Eight experienced therapists identified as experts by peers each treated one patient for between 12 and 20 sessions. Despite the conservative definition of CT, therapists identified CT as operative in fully 80% of their 127 sessions, and it appeared that CT was prominent in each case. Such findings support the proposition offered by Gelso and Carter (1994) and Gelso and Hayes (1998) that CT is a universal phenomenon in therapy, even when defined from an integrative rather than totalistic perspective. The findings, of course, run counter to what may be seen as the Freudian myth that good therapists do not experience CT (Spence, 1987).

As regards the effects of CT on treatment outcome, Hayes and colleagues (1998) believed that the data contained evidence for both hindering and facilitative effects. For example, they noted one therapist who was too immersed in her CT issues of strength and independence to connect with her dependent client and help her work through her problems. On the other hand, they point to another therapist who was able to make use of her CT-based needs to nurture and be a good parent by appropriately supporting and being patient with her client. The researchers reflected upon what determines whether CT will be facilitative or hindering, and offered the idea that "the more resolved an intrapsychic conflict is for a therapist, the greater the likelihood that the therapist will be able to use his or her countertransference therapeutically (that is, to deepen one's understanding of the client)" (p. 478). Conversely, they offered that the less resolved the conflict, the greater the likelihood that CT will have antitherapeutic effects.

In sum, the results of the six quantitative and four qualitative studies support the idea that CT does affect treatment outcomes. The evidence at this point, however, is admittedly suggestive, or "soft" (see "Limitations of the Research," later in this chapter).

Managing Countertransference

Over the past two decades, the clinical literature on CT has been replete with writing about its potential to aid the treatment process. A fundamental concept in this literature is that if CT is to be a help rather than a hindrance, the therapist must do something to, with, or about the CT, other than acting it out in the treatment. A significant aspect of all of this may be termed CT management. During the past decade a small body of literature has emerged on CT management; it is reviewed here.

Reich observed many years ago (Reich, 1951, 1960) that therapy involves a partial identification with the patient. In this identification, the therapist absorbs the patient's material into his or her own mind. In this way, then, the therapist's internal experience is an important clue to what is going on with the patient beyond the surface. If the process is to work effectively, however, the therapist has to swing to an "outside" position and inspect what is being experienced. In Reich's (1960) words, therapists "should be alert to our own feelings, stop to investigate them, and analyze what is going on" (p. 392). In this statement, three factors are highlighted that may be fundamental to CT management: therapist empathy (partial identification), awareness of CT feelings, and the ability to make sense of these feelings.

Initial empirical work on CT management addressed these three factors. Peabody and Gelso (1982) studied the interrelations of therapist empathy, CT behavior, and awareness of CT. Using a sample of 20 therapist-trainees, these researchers found that the therapist's general empathic ability related negatively to CT behavior (withdrawal of personal involvement) under conditions the researchers speculated to be the most threatening to therapists. Further, the greater the empathic ability, the more openness these therapists had to their CT feelings. Empathic ability and openness to CT feelings (two of Reich's factors) appear to be interrelated as expected, and empathy may prevent CT behavior when the therapist deals with threatening material.

Robbins and Jolkovski (1987) similarly reasoned that CT management would be aided by therapists' openness to CT feelings (referred to as CT awareness). However, they also theorized that another of Reich's factors—ability to analyze and make sense of these feelings—was implicated. They operationalized the latter as what they called the "theoretical framework"—the extent to which the therapist uses a formal or informal theoretical framework to explain the events of the hour, or make them intelligible. Using 58 therapist-trainees in an analogue situation in which trainees listened and responded to audiotaped clients (as in Yulis and Kiesler, 1968), it was found that awareness of CT feelings, as expected, was associated with fewer CT behaviors. Also, CT awareness and theoretical framework interacted, in such a way that high awareness and high theoretical framework resulted in the least amount of CT behavior, whereas use of theory in conjunction with low awareness resulted in the greatest amount of CT behavior. Thus, it appeared that therapist-trainees who were most aware and had a theory upon which to rely displayed the least CT (had the best CT management). But the use of theory alone—in the absence of awareness—is a negative factor.

The Robbins and Jolkovski (1987) study was replicated by Latts and Gelso (1995), despite their use of a different stimulus situation. Forty-seven therapist-trainees viewed a video of a client-actress playing the role of a rape survivor. The therapists responded verbally at certain stopping points in the tape as they would if they were working with the client. Using verbal avoidance responses as the measure of CT behavior, Latts and Gelso precisely replicated the interaction effect found by Robbins and Jolkovski (1987); awareness of CT feelings along with the use of a theory fostered CT management (that is, prevented CT behavior), whereas the use of a theory without CT awareness produced the most CT behavior.

Five Factors in CT Management

Based on the empirical work of Robbins and Jolkovski (1987) and Peabody and Gelso (1982), as well as several clinical papers, a formal theoretical statement of CT management was offered by Van-Wagoner, Gelso, Hayes, and Diemer (1991). The management of CT was theorized as consisting of five interrelated factors: self-insight, self-integration, empathy, anxiety management, and conceptualizing ability (Hayes, Gelso, VanWagoner, & Diemer, 1991; VanWagoner et al., 1991). The five factors can be summarized as follows.

Therapist *self-insight* refers to the extent to which the therapist is aware of his or her own feelings, including CT feelings, and understands their basis. Therapist *self-integration* refers to the therapist's possession of an intact, basically healthy character structure. In the therapy interaction, such self-integration manifests itself as a recognition of ego boundaries or an ability to differentiate self from other. *Anxiety management* refers to therapists allowing themselves to experience anxiety and but also possessing the internal skill to control and understand anxiety so that it does not bleed over into their responses to patients. *Empathy*, or the ability to partially identify with and put one's self in the other's shoes, permits the therapist to focus on the patient's needs despite difficulties he or she may be experiencing with the work and the pulls to attend to his or her own needs. Also, empathic ability may be part of sensitivity to one's own feelings, including CT feelings, which in turn ought to prevent acting out of CT (Peabody & Gelso, 1982; Robbins & Jolkovski, 1987). Finally, *conceptualizing ability* reflects the therapist's ability to draw on theory in the work and grasp theoretically the patient's dynamics in terms of the therapeutic relationship.

Research on the Five-Factor Theory

Several empirical efforts have related CT management, as defined in these five factors, to aspects of therapy relevant to outcomes. All studies employed a measure designed to assess the five factors—the Countertransference Factors Inventory (CFI; see VanWagoner et al., 1991; Hayes et al., 1991) or a psychometrically improved version (CFI-R; see Latts, 1996). In the original study, VanWagoner et al. (1991) asked 122 psychologist-therapists to rate either a particular therapist whom they considered to be excellent or therapists in general on the CFI. Excellent therapists were rated more favorably on all five CFI factors than therapists in general. In addition, in a laboratory study, Gelso and colleagues (1995) found that two aspects of CT management (self-integration and anxiety management) appeared to reduce CT feelings when therapist-trainees made verbal responses to a videotape of an actress portraying a lesbian client with relationship and sexual problems. Thus, trainees who were rated more favorably by clinical supervisors on self-integration and anxiety management in their overall clinical work reported less anxiety when responding to the taped client.

Three additional studies linked CT management to the ability to refrain from CT behavior. Friedman and Gelso (2000) found that clinical supervisors' ratings of their supervisees' overall ability to manage CT (on the CFI-R) was negatively related to supervisees' CT behavior in their most recent therapy session. Similarly, inspection by the authors of unpublished data from the aforementioned Hayes and colleagues (1997) study indicated an inverse relationship between past clinical supervisors' ratings of therapist-trainees' CT management ability on the CFI and current supervisors' ratings of CT behavior in observed therapy sessions. The third study to link CT management to therapists' refraining from acting out CT was the aforementioned quantitative case study by Rosenberger and Hayes (2001). The therapist's self-ratings on the CFI were found to relate to the client's ratings of both the working alliance and the depth of the session. Higher CT management ratings by the therapist were predictive of stronger alliance and session depth ratings by the client. Thus, taken together, these three studies suggest that, overall, measured CT management ability aids therapists in containing their CT responses in sessions.

Although the CT management studies cited above present results that appear to be relevant to outcome, only one study to date has directly assessed the relation of CT management to outcome. Gelso, Latts, Gomez, and Fassinger (in press) had 32 therapist-trainees and their clinical supervisors rate treatment outcomes of one case, while the supervisors also evaluated the supervisees' CT management ability on the CFI. Outcome ratings by both therapists and supervisors (controlling for initial level of client disturbance) were positively related to supervisor-rated CFI scores overall and on three of the five subscales.

Taken together, the quantitative findings on CT management are promising. It appears that such management is a characteristic of therapists seen as excellent by their peers, aids in controlling the manifestation of CT, and may be related to treatment outcome. In addition to these quantitative studies, four previously reviewed qualitative investigations (Gelso et al., 1999; Hayes et al., 1998; Hill et al., 1996; Williams et al., 1997) all point to the importance of CT management in the judgment of therapists whose views about particular clients were studied. These qualitative studies are especially significant in that three of them sampled highly experienced therapists, with two focusing on very long-term therapy.

Although the empirical literature on CT management is promising, this line of work is in its early stages. In the final section of this chapter, we explore potentially useful directions for CT management research and for CT research more generally.

LIMITATIONS OF THE RESEARCH

In their review of a quarter of a century ago, Singer and Luborsky (1977) reflected upon the contributions of CT research, as well as its limitations. With regard to contributions, they noted that much of the existing research tended to confirm what was written in the clinical literature, although the research also added somewhat to clinical theory. One of the major additions was the importance of the actual stimulus value of the client. The literature was consistent in finding that certain patient behaviors elicited corresponding therapist behaviors; for example, patient hostility elicited therapist hostility. Singer and Luborsky thus concluded, "More than the clinical literature would suggest, the patient influences the therapist to a marked degree and in predictable ways" (1977, p. 449).

It appears that we have moved beyond this conclusion by determining, at least in a preliminary way, how patient and therapist factors, separately and interactively, influence therapist countertransference reactions (where CT is usually assumed to reflect unresolved issues in the therapist). Further, research has continued to explore the ways in which CT affects outcome-relevant aspects of treatment. The evidence has very slowly accumulated to support another conclusion offered by Singer and Luborsky (1977):

> Perhaps the most clear-cut and important area of congruence between the clinical and quantitative literatures is the widely agreed-upon position that uncontrolled countertransference has an adverse effect on therapy outcome. Not only does it have a markedly detrimental influence on the therapist's technique and interventions, but it also interferes with the optimal understanding of the patient. (p. 449)

As we have reviewed the research literature, investigations since this earlier review have served to solidify these conclusions. It must be noted, however, that the link of CT behavior to treatment outcome is a tenuous one. Effects of CT on outcome may be inferred from the data. However, there is precious little *direct* empirical support for such conclusions. In other words, it seems obvious that if CT is part of avoiding the patient's feelings, recalling the content of sessions inaccurately, and becoming overinvolved in the patient's problems, then it is a good bet that its effects on the treatment outcome are negative. Further, if CT behavior is negatively related to sound working alliances and to supervisors' evaluations of effectiveness, then it also seems safe to suggest that uncontrolled CT is harmful to treatment. On the other hand, we could locate only one study (Hayes et al., 1997) seeking to connect CT behavior to treatment outcomes beyond immediate or proximate outcomes, and the results of that study only partially support the link of CT to outcome.

Clearly research is needed on how CT is related to treatment outcome, not only in terms of main effects (relating aspects of CT to outcome) but also in terms of the conditions under which CT affects varying indices of outcome. For example, does the effect depend upon patient qualities (such as personality, degree and type of disturbance), therapist qualities (overall competence, experience), and the qualities of CT itself (positive vs. negative, CT feelings vs. CT behavior, mild vs. extreme CT)? Also of interest are the ways in which CT may directly versus indirectly influence outcome. For example, it may be that degree of CT in a given therapy directly affects

working alliance, which in turn directly influences outcome. In this instance, CT may not directly relate to outcome, but instead affects outcome *through* its influence on alliance. Currently popular path-analytic models might be fruitfully applied to CT research in order to examine such direct and indirect effects.

With respect to limitations of the early CT research noted by Singer and Luborsky, these reviewers pointed out that because of the enormous complexity of countertransference, researchers had been unable "to work very well with the more subtle, yet substantial, aspects of countertransference. Rather, these studies have been limited to more simplified and superficial problems, and restricted in terms of what could be measured" (1977, p. 448). Have we progressed beyond this point? Our evaluation leads to a yes-and-no answer. On the positive side, although many of the studies conducted since the earlier review continue to be laboratory manipulations, these investigations have moved forward in terms of both realism and the complexity. For example, videotapes have replaced audiotapes as client stimuli; rather than choosing from predetermined written responses, therapist participants usually are asked to generate their own verbal responses to the client stimulus. Also, CT is more likely in recent laboratory studies to be operationalized multidimensionally, that is, in terms of affective, cognitive, and behavioral manifestations.

A further advance has been the development of a line of research on CT management. Such work moves the field toward studying the ways in which CT may be beneficially used—what we have called the other strand of the double helix of countertransference. Such work, however, is barely past its infancy. Clearly more work on the ways in which CT may be managed, including how effective clinicians go about this, is needed. There is a great need to study experienced therapists, specific ways of managing and using CT, and the connection of CT management to treatment outcome.

On the negative side, the laboratory studies conducted since Singer and Luborsky's review do possess the limitations inherent to this methodology. Such manipulations inevitably are highly simplified. Clinical meaningfulness and external validity are sacrificed for experimental control and viability. However, we would offer that such simplifications are a reasonable and helpful way to proceed, as long as a sufficient number of field studies are done to complement the analogues and to allow for methodological triangulation. Herein lies one of the most serious limitations of CT research: Field studies have accumulated at a strikingly slow pace over the years. It is true that the emergence of qualitative research may be resulting in significant changes. Four such studies have appeared within the past few years, and have served to advance knowledge valuably. Still, there is a great need for more controlled, quantitative field research in the CT area.

THERAPEUTIC PRACTICES

In terms of the effects of CT on outcome, the evidence points to the likely conclusion that the acting out of CT is harmful and that CT management is helpful. It follows that the effective therapist must work at preventing such acting out and must manage internal CT reactions in a way that benefits the work. The five factors we have discussed appear to be a useful part of this process. Using two of these factors (self-insight and self-integration) as an example, the therapist's struggle to gain self-understanding, especially within the treatment situation (self-insight) and the therapist's work on his or her own psychological health, including boundary issues between the therapist and the patient (self-integration) are fundamental to managing and effectively using one's internal reactions. These two factors allow the therapist to pay attention to what client behaviors are affecting the therapist in what ways, and why. Such understanding is the first step in the process of arriving at ways in which CT may be useful to the client. As the therapist seeks to understand what internal conflicts are being stirred by the patient's material, the therapist also considers how this process may relate to the patient's life outside the consulting room—both the patient's earlier life and current life. Then the therapist may be in a good position to devise responses that will be helpful to the patient. The specific nature of such responses will depend heavily upon the therapist's theoretical orientation; psychoanalytic therapists tend to interpret, whereas cognitive-behavioral therapists offer suggestions. But the therapist's awareness of underlying CT conflicts forms a basis for the effectiveness of these responses.

One aspect of CT management—self-integration—relates to the therapist's own psychological organization, including strengths and conflicts. This factor underscores the importance of the therapist resolving his or her major issues, which in turn points to the potential value of personal therapy for the psychotherapist. Personal therapy for the therapist seems especially important when dealing with chronic countertransference problems. Although we believe the evidence supports the pervasive nature of CT, it seems obvious that chronic CT problems (see earlier discussion) need to be dealt with by the therapist, and that personal therapy is a likely vehicle for such resolutions. Naturally, clinical supervision, for experienced therapists as well as trainees, is another key factor in understanding and managing CT and in using it to benefit the work of therapy.

An area that has not been addressed by researchers but that must be continually addressed in clinical practice is how the therapist should deal with CT that has in fact been acted out in the work—that is, with mistakes therapists make due to having their unresolved conflicts stirred up. It is important for the therapist to understand that indeed he or she was acting out personal conflicts; in addition, some research (Hill et al., 1996) points to the value of therapists' admitting that a mistake was made and that the therapists' conflicts were the source. Therapists need not go into detail about just what those problems were, for we suggest that doing so more often than not serves therapists' needs more than the patient's. Yet the simple admission does appear to benefit the work and to diminish potential impasses. At the same time, the topic of how the therapist should best address CT behavior once it has occurred is one that should capture researchers in the years ahead.

Finally, the evidence suggests that if CT is to be managed and used for the benefit of the work, having and using a theory is not enough. Theory alone may be used defensively, but the evidence suggests that theory in conjunction with personal awareness is a key to the therapeutic use of countertransference.

REFERENCES

Anchin, J. C., & Kiesler, D. J. (Eds.) (1982). *Handbook of interpersonal psychotherapy*. New York: Pergamon.

Bandura, A. (1956). Psychotherapists' anxiety level, self-insight, and psychotherapeutic competence. *Journal of Abnormal and Social Psychology, 52*, 333–337.

Bandura, A., Lipsher, D. H., & Miller, P. E. (1960). Psychotherapists' approach-avoidance reactions to patients' expressions of hostility. *Journal of Consulting Psychology, 24*, 1–8.

Boyer, S. P., & Hoffman, M. A. (1993). Therapists' affective reactions to termination: Impact of therapist loss history and client sensitivity to loss. *Journal of Counseling Psychology, 40*, 271–277.

Butler, S. F., Flasher, L. V., & Strupp, H. H. (1993). Countertransference and qualities of the psychotherapist. In N. E. Miller, L. Luborsky, J. P. Barber, & J. P. Docherty (Eds.), *Psychodynamic treatment research: A handbook for clinical practice* (pp. 342–360). New York: Basic.

Cashdan, S. (1988). *Object relations therapy*. New York: Norton.

Cutler, R. L. (1958). Countertransference effects in psychotherapy. *Journal of Consulting Psychology, 22*, 349–356.

Elkind, S. N. (1992). *Resolving impasses in therapeutic relationships*. New York: Guilford.

Epstein, L., & Feiner, A. H. (1988). Countertransference: The therapist's contribution to treatment. In B. Wolstein (Ed.), *Essential papers on countertransference* (pp. 282–303). New York: New York University Press.

Fauth, J., & Hayes, J. A. (2002). *Therapists' male gender role attitudes and stress appraisals as predictors of countertransference behavior with male clients*. Manuscript submitted for publication.

Fiedler, F. E. (1951). On different types of countertransference. *Journal of Clinical Psychology, 7*, 101–107.

Freud, S. (1957). Future prospects of psychoanalytic therapy. In J. Strachey (Ed.), *The standard edition of the complete works of Sigmund Freud* (Vol. 11, pp. 139–151). London: Hogarth.

Freud, S. (1958). Recommendations to physicians practicing psychoanalysis. In J. Strachey (Ed.), *The standard edition of the complete psychological works of Sigmund Freud* (Vol. 12, pp. 111–120). London: Hogarth.

Friedman, S. C., & Gelso, C. J. (2000). The development of the Inventory of Countertransference Behavior. *Journal of Clinical Psychology, 56*, 1221–1235.

Gelso, C. J., & Carter, J. (1994). Components of the psychotherapy relationship: Their interaction and unfolding during treatment. *Journal of Counseling Psychology, 41*, 296–306.

Gelso, C. J., Fassinger, R. E., Gomez, M. J., & Latts, M. G. (1995). Countertransference reactions to lesbian clients: The role of homophobia, counselor gender, and countertransference management. *Journal of Counseling Psychology, 42*, 356–364.

Gelso, C. J., & Hayes, J. A. (1998). *The psychotherapy relationship: Theory, research, and practice*. New York: Wiley.

Gelso, C. J., Hill, C. E., Mohr, J. J., Rochlen, A., & Zack, J. (1999). Describing the face of transference: Psychodynamic therapists' recollections about transference in cases of successful long-term therapy. *Journal of Counseling Psychology, 46*, 257–267.

Gelso, C. J., Latts, M., Gomez, M., & Fassinger, R. E. (in press). Countertransference management and therapy outcome: An initial evaluation. *Journal of Clinical Psychology*.

Gorkin, M. (1987). *The uses of countertransference*. New York: Aronson.

Hayes, J. A., & Gelso, C. J. (1991). Effects of therapist-trainees' anxiety and empathy on countertransference behavior. *Journal of Clinical Psychology, 47*, 284–290.

Hayes, J. A., & Gelso, C. J. (1993). Counselors' discomfort with gay and HIV-infected clients. *Journal of Counseling Psychology, 40*, 86–93.

Hayes, J. A., & Gelso, C. J. (2001). Clinical implications of research on countertransference: Science informing practice. *In Session/Journal of Clinical Psychology, 57*, 1041–1052.

Hayes, J. A., Gelso, C. J., VanWagoner, S. L., & Diemer, R. (1991). Managing countertransference: What the experts think. *Psychological Reports, 69*, 139–148.

Hayes, J. A., McCracken, J. E., McClanahan, M. K., Hill, C. E., Harp, J. S., & Carozzoni, P. (1998). Therapist perspectives on countertransference: Qualitative date in search of a theory. *Journal of Counseling Psychology, 45*, 468–482.

Hayes, J. A., Riker, J. B., & Ingram, K. M. (1997). Countertransference behavior and management in brief counseling: A field study. *Psychotherapy Research, 7*, 145–154.

Heimann, P. (1950). Countertransference. *British Journal of Medical Psychology, 33*, 9–15.

Hill, C. E., Nutt-Williams, E., Heaton, K. J., Thompson, B. J., & Rhodes, R. H. (1996). Therapist retrospective recall of impasses in long-term psychotherapy: A qualitative analysis. *Journal of Counseling Psychology, 43,* 201–217.

Hill, C. E., Thompson, B. J., & Williams, E. (1997). A guide to conducting consensual qualitative research. *The Counseling Psychologist, 25,* 517–572.

Howard, K., Orlinsky, D., & Hill, J. (1969). The therapist's feelings in the therapeutic process. *Journal of Clinical Psychology, 25,* 83–93.

Kernberg, O. (1965). Notes on countertransference. *Journal of the American Psychoanalytic Association, 13,* 38–56.

Latts, M. G. (1996). *A revision and validation of the Countertransference Factors Inventory.* Unpublished doctoral dissertation, University of Maryland, College Park.

Latts, M. G., & Gelso, C. J. (1995). Countertransference behavior and management with survivors of sexual assault. *Psychotherapy, 32,* 405–415.

Lecours, S., Bouchard, M. A., & Normandin, L. (1995). Countertransference as the therapist's mental activity: Experience and gender differences among psychoanalytically oriented psychologists. *Psychoanalytic Psychology, 12,* 259–279.

Levenson, H. (1995). *Time-limited dynamic psychotherapy.* New York: Basic.

Ligiero, D., & Gelso, C. J. (in press). The therapist's contribution: Countertransference, attachment, and the working alliance. *Psychotherapy.*

Little, M. (1951). Countertransference and the patient's response to it. *International Journal of Psychoanalysis, 32,* 32–40.

Luborsky, L., & Crits-Christoph, P. (1990). *Understanding transference.* New York: Basic.

Martin, D. J., Garske, J. O., & Davis, M. K. (2000). Relation of therapeutic alliance with outcome and other variables: A meta-analytic review. *Journal of Consulting and Clinical Psychology, 68,* 438–450.

McClure, B. A., & Hodge, R. W. (1987). Measuring countertransference and attitude in therapeutic relationships. *Psychotherapy, 24,* 325–335.

Milliken, R. L., & Kirchner, R. (1971). Counselors' understanding of students' communication as a function of the counselor's perceptual defense. *Journal of Counseling Psychology, 18,* 14–18.

Mitchell, S. A. (1993). *Hope and dread in psychoanalysis.* New York: Basic.

Mohr, J. J., Gelso, C. J., & Hill, C. E. (2002). *Client and therapist attachment in the first session: Testing a two-person perspective on countertransference and session outcome.* Manuscript in preparation.

Nathanson, D. L. (1992). The nature of therapeutic impasse. *Psychiatric Annals, 22,* 509–513.

Peabody, S. A., & Gelso, C. J. (1982). Countertransference and empathy: The complex relationship between two divergent concepts in counseling. *Journal of Counseling Psychology, 29,* 240–245.

Pine, F. (1990). *Drive, ego, object, and self: A synthesis for clinical work.* New York: Basic.

Racker, H. (1957). The meanings and uses of countertransference. *Psychoanalytic Quarterly, 26,* 303–357.

Racker, H. (1968). *Transference and countertransference.* New York: International Universities Press.

Reich, A. (1951). On countertransference. *International Journal of Psychoanalysis, 32,* 25–31.

Reich, A. (1960). Further remarks on countertransference. *International Journal of Psychoanalysis, 41,* 389–395.

Robbins, S. B., & Jolkovski, M. P. (1987). Managing countertransference feelings: An interactional model using awareness of feeling and theoretical framework. *Journal of Counseling Psychology, 34,* 276–282.

Rosenberger, E. W., & Hayes, J. A. (in press). Causes, consequences, and management of countertransference: A case study. *Journal of Counseling Psychology.*

Sharkin, B., & Gelso, C. J. (1993). The influence of counselor-trainee anger proneness on reactions to an angry client. *Journal of Counseling Psychology, 71,* 483–487.

Singer, B. A., & Luborsky, L. (1977). Countertransference: The status of clinical versus quantitative research. In A. S. Gurman & A. M. Razin (Eds.), *Effective psychotherapy: A handbook of research* (pp. 433–451). New York: Pergamon.

Spence, D. (1987). *The Freudian metaphor.* New York: Norton.

Strupp, H. H., & Binder, J. L. (1984). *Psychotherapy in a new key: A guide to time-limited dynamic psychotherapy.* New York: Basic.

Teyber, E. (1997). *Interpersonal process in psychotherapy: A relational approach.* Pacific Grove, CA: Brooks/Cole.

VanWagoner, S. L., Gelso, C. J., Hayes, J. A., & Diemer, R. (1991). Countertransference and the reputedly excellent psychotherapist. *Psychotherapy: Theory, Research, and Practice, 28*, 411–421.

Williams, E. N., Judge, A. B., Hill, C. E., & Hoffman, M. A. (1997). Experiences of novice therapists in prepracticum: Trainees', clients', and supervisors' perceptions of therapists' personal reactions and management strategies. *Journal of Counseling Psychology, 44*, 390–399.

Winnicott, D. W. (1949). Hate in the countertransference. *International Journal of Psycho-Analysis, 30*, 69–74.

Yulis, S., & Kiesler, D. J. (1968). Countertransference response as a function of therapist anxiety and content of patient talk. *Journal of Consulting and Clinical Psychology, 32*, 414–419.

15

Relational Interpretations

Paul Crits-Christoph
Mary Beth Connolly Gibbons

The overall focus of this book is on the relational aspects of psychotherapy. As such, the volume serves as a counterpoint to those that overly emphasize the technical components of psychotherapy. This chapter, however, stands midway between these two perspectives. Our goal is to examine the research evidence regarding relationship-oriented interpretations. On the one hand, interpretations are typically categorized as technical interventions, and thus a review of research on interpretation might be seen as highlighting the "technical" elements of psychotherapy. On the other hand, such interpretations occur in the context of the therapeutic relationship and influence this relationship. Moreover, a class of such interpretations ("transference interpretations") are concerned specifically with what's going on between the patient and therapist. Thus, we view an examination of "relational interpretations" as relevant both to an understanding of psychotherapy techniques and to an understanding of the importance of the therapeutic relationship.

To understand the concept of relational interpretation, a brief historical review of the concept of interpretation and transference interpretation will first be presented. We then review data on the frequency of interpretations in diverse psychotherapies, followed by an illustration of the concept through the presentation of numerous clinical examples. Empirical studies of the impact of interpretations on the therapeutic alliance and treatment outcome are then reviewed, including the examination of patient variables that may be

mediators and moderators of these relationships. Within the context of limitations of the empirical evidence, we conclude with the potential clinical implications.

DEFINITIONS

Interpretation Within Psychoanalysis and Psychodynamic Therapy

The concept of interpretation originated with Freud. While listening to patients' flow of associations, Freud noticed that there were gaps in memory. Freud's initial treatment approach emphasized the uncovering of early memories and the reconstruction of the past. However, when Freud directly asked his patients to fill in apparent gaps in their discourses, he found that they often deflected his efforts in various ways. Freud hypothesized that forgetting of certain memories resulted from an active force, repression, which was activated by the patient's efforts to avoid anxiety and other emotions that arise from unacceptable impulses. To the extent that ideas entered conscious awareness, they were distorted or disguised by the power of repression. The goal of interpretation in early psychoanalysis was to distill the underlying repressed thought or feeling from the overt, disguised free association material. In order to achieve this goal, analysts interpreted not only free associations, but also slips of the tongue, dreams, and symptoms. Interpretations were the main vehicle through which patients gain insight, and such insight resulted in therapeutic change.

Freud (1953) emphasized the importance of interpretations that address aspects of the patient-therapist relationship. Such interpretations are generally referred to as "transference interpretations," an expression that should be defined carefully. The term *transference* refers to desires, thoughts, feelings, and associated behaviors originating from an early (for example, parental) relationship that are projected or "transferred" onto a current interpersonal relationship. It is used in clinical writings, however, as shorthand for these issues as they arise in the patient-therapist relationship in particular. Thus, "transference interpretation" is used to describe interpretations that address the patient-therapist relationship, and we follow that convention here. We use the term "relational interpretation" to refer to interpretations that address relationships in general. Transference interpretations are therefore a subset of relational interpretations.

Over time, psychoanalysts such as Fenichel (1945) and others placed more weight on interpretations that addressed the active resistances that prevent a patient from accessing repressed material and experiencing a sense of conviction regarding the reality of disavowed desires. Thus, according to this psychoanalytic perspective, defenses and resistances needed to be interpreted before interpreting the underlying impulses and conflicts.

Also within the psychoanalytic camp, Bibring (1954) provided definitions of different types of therapeutic interventions. Interpretation was defined as going beyond the descriptive-phenomenological data and elucidating how the patient's behaviors were determined by certain anxiety-provoking, but gratifying, wishes and thoughts, which formerly were out of awareness. According to this definition, addressing the patient's behavior toward the therapist would not be an interpretation unless some aspect of the behavior outside the patient's conscious awareness was pointed out. In contrast, Lowenstein (1951) defined interpretation more broadly as "those explanations, given to patients by the analyst, which add to their knowledge about themselves" (p. 4).

A number of factors have contributed to an altered view of interpretations in the context of psychodynamically oriented psychotherapy and psychotherapy is general. One factor has been the development of brief, time-limited psychodynamic treatments. These brief dynamic therapies (e.g., Davanloo, 1980; Luborsky, 1984; Malan, 1976a; Mann, 1973; Sifneos, 1992; Strupp & Binder, 1984) typically limit treatment to a central focal theme that could be addressed within the time contraints of short-term therapy. While some (such as Davlanloo, 1980) emphasize interpretation of defenses and resistance and others (such as Luborsky, 1984; Strupp & Binder, 1984) emphasize interpretation of relationship themes, most of these treatments have a greater focus on the here-and-now as opposed to reconstruction of the past. The view of Freud and many of his followers that interpretation could be used as a mechanism for reconstructing the past has been criticized on the basis that the actual past is less important than the individual's reconstruction of the past (Strupp & Binder, 1984). Moreover, the truth of the events in the past cannot be determined in psychotherapy (Spence, 1982).

A second factor influencing the reconceptualization of interpretations in modern psychotherapy was the development of the interpersonal perspective. Within the psychodynamic literature, the interpersonal school can be traced to Sullivan (1953). A variety of "relational" theories have emerged within psychoanalysis since Sullivan. One important aspect of these relational approaches is the view that the relational meaning of interpretations is more crucial than the content (Mitchell, 1988).

While an interpersonal emphasis remains a major school within the psychodynamic perspective, the advent of a specific form of manual-based interpersonal psychotherapy—Klerman, Weissman, Rounsaville, & Chevron's (1984) Interpersonal Therapy (IPT)—further popularized the interpersonal perspective, at least within the context of the research/academic writings on psychotherapy. IPT is distinguished from many forms of psychodynamic psychotherapy in that it does not advocate the frequent use of transference interpretations. Moreover, interpersonal factors are seen as contributing to psychopathology through the difficulties encountered when one or more of four interpersonal experiences occur: (1) interpersonal role transitions, (2) interpersonal role disputes, (3) interpersonal loss (grief), and (4) interpersonal deficits. Thus, relative to traditional psychodynamic therapy, there is a de-emphasis on early childhood experiences, unconscious processes, and defenses. Although no formal definition of "relational interpretation" exists within IPT or the interpersonal psychodynamic perspective, such a definition would likely be similar to Lowenstein's (1951) broad definition mentioned earlier, and include any explanation given by the therapist that adds to the patient's knowledge of their thoughts, feelings, and behaviors in interpersonal relationships.

Research Definitions

The broader and evolving definition of interpretation was also inherent in most research studies of interpretation. As reviewed above, the psychoanalytic literature originally defined interpretations as interventions that bring material to consciousness that was previously out of awareness. Research on interpretation in psychotherapy is almost always accomplished through examination of tapes or transcripts of therapy sessions. Unfortunately, it is difficult, if not impossible, to determine whether or not a patient was unaware of certain material. Researchers have therefore needed to define interpretation in a way that does not include a judgment about whether the patient was aware of something. Moreover, in order to investigate other forms of psychotherapy besides psychoanalytic therapy, there was a need for broader definitions of interpretation.

Interpretations have been examined in research studies as one type of "verbal response mode" for coding therapist speech during sessions. For these systems, trained raters evaluate transcripts or video/audiotapes of psychotherapy sessions and categorize each therapist statement. A variety of such pantheoretical coding systems have been developed, including those by Hill (1978), Stiles (1979), Friedlander (1982), Mahrer (1983), Goldberg et al. (1984), Elliott (1985), and Connolly et al. (2000). Elliott et al. (1987) compared the first six of these systems and concluded that there

was strong convergence regarding six major modes: question, information, advisement, reflection, interpretation, and self-disclosure. The definitions of interpretation in these systems are similar. For example, Hill (1978) defines interpretation as going beyond what the client has overtly recognized, including establishing connections between statements or events, pointing out themes, patterns, or causal relationships in the patient's behavior or personality, or giving alternative meanings for old behaviors or issues. Stiles (1979) defines interpretation as making connections, explaining, or drawing conclusions.

In the context of short-term psychodynamic psychotherapy, investigators have defined interpretations as those interventions that address interpersonal themes or make important links (for example, between themes with significant others and themes with the therapist). Piper, Debbane, de Carufel, and Bienvenu (1987) specifically define an interpretation as a therapist statement that refers to an internal conflict of the patient. To be rated as an interpretation in the system developed by Piper and colleagues, the statement must make reference to one or more dynamic components. The authors define a dynamic component as encompassing impulses, anxiety, defenses, and dynamic expressions, as a part of the patient's conflict that exerts an internal force on another aspect of the patient.

FREQUENCY OF INTERPRETATIONS

Data on the frequency of interpretation in diverse psychotherapies are available from two recent reports examining therapist responses in a relatively large number of psychotherapy sessions. Connolly, Crits-Christoph, Shappell, Barber, and Luborsky (1998) and Connolly and colleagues (2000) present data on the coding of therapist response modes in transcripts of 260 sessions of cognitive therapy (CT; see Beck, Rush, Shaw, & Emery, 1979) and 240 sessions of IPT drawn from the Treatments for Depression Collaborative Research Program (TDCRP; see Elkin et al., 1989), as well as transcripts of 98 sessions of supportive-expressive (SE) psychodynamic therapy (Luborsky, 1984). Another study (Piper, Azim, Joyce, & McCallum, 1991) on brief psychodynamic therapy based upon the approaches of Malan (1976a) and Strupp and Binder (1984) reports frequency of interpretation for 64 patients (8 sessions coded per patient). The overall proportion of therapist statements that were classified as "learning statements" or interpretations was similar across CT and IPT (Connolly et al., 2000). Therapists made an average of 10 ± 7 per session in CT and 11 ± 8 in IPT. Similarly, the Piper and colleagues (1991) study reports an average of 11 ± 4 interpretations per treatment session. For SE therapy, the average number of interpretations per session was 5 ± 3 (Connolly et al., 1998). The lower number of interpretations in SE may be a function of generally lower therapist activity in SE (125 statements per sessions in SE versus 263 in CT and 233 in IPT) or may be an artifact of the different coding schemes applied to the studies. Given that there are about half as many therapist statements in SE, and half as many interpretations, the proportion of therapists statements that are interpretations across SE, CT, and IPT are roughly the same (4–5%). These coding schemes, however, include brief acknowledgments (such as "Uh-huh") that are classified as "other statements" and represent 36–64% of all therapist statements. Eliminating these other statements, approximately 10% of therapist statements in SE, IPT, and CT are typically interpretations. For the Piper and colleagues (1991) study that utilized a more traditional transference-focused dynamic therapy, the average number of therapist statements per sessions was only 44. Thus, interpretations represented 25% of all interventions in this study, although the raw frequency was comparable to the IPT and CT sessions from the investigation of Connolly and colleagues (2000).

Within SE therapy, 9% of all interpretations make reference to the therapist "transference interpretations" (Connolly et al., 1998). In IPT and CT, the comparable figures are 5% and 5%, respectively (Connolly et al., 2000). Consistent with the move away from the psychoanalytic emphasis on the use of interpretation as a vehicle for reconstruction of the past, 85% of interpretations in SE make reference to the present, while only 6% make any reference to childhood, and 32% to recent adult past (these numbers add up to more

than 100% because interpretations sometimes link present and past) (Connolly et al., 1998).

In contrast to the Connolly and colleagues (1998) study of brief dynamic SE therapy, Piper and colleagues (1991) report that 45% of all interpretations were transference interpretations. These numbers serve to illustrate the diversity among treatments labeled psychodynamic therapy. Several psychodynamic therapies (for example, Malan, 1976a; Piper et al., 1991) have a strong emphasis on transference interpretation, while in others, such as SE, the frequency of transference interpretation is similar to non-dynamic therapies.

CLINICAL EXAMPLES

In order to further understand the nature of common interpretations within psychotherapy, we present in table 15.1 an extended list of interpretations drawn from actual transcripts of psychotherapy sessions for patients receiving brief psychodynamic, interpersonal, or cognitive therapy. Because these interpretations were drawn from sessions of actual patients in psychotherapy, we have deleted any identifying information and altered some of the content of the actual therapist statements so that confidentiality is protected. In making these modifications, however, we retained the essence of the interpersonal message in each interpretation. While these interpretations are only a sample of the therapist statements made within these treatments, they serve to illustrate the types of interpersonally oriented interpretative interventions made by therapists of diverse orientations. Most of such interpretations, even within supportive-expressive psychodynamic psychotherapy, focus on relatively observable interpersonal behavior and felt needs and emotions.

RESEARCH REVIEW

Tables 15.2, 15.3, 15.4, 15.5, and 15.6 summarize the findings of all investigations that we could locate that examine the relationship of interpretations to psychotherapy outcome and alliance. Studies that examined only the immediate impact (in session or after session) of interpretations

Table 15.1. Sample Interpretations from Supportive-Expressive, Interpersonal, and Cognitive Therapies

Brief Supportive-Expressive Psychotherapy: Sample Interpretations
1. "On one hand you want to be taken care of, but on another hand you want to be your own person. I think that's part of you resenting your boyfriend after a while."
2. "Well, that's the area she becomes larger than life, and her power. And it's like a seesaw effect. As she gets more power, you become smaller and less powerful and feel like you have no power at all. The only power is, at that point, or the way to get out for the moment, is to give in, and that makes you feel smaller. And so it boomerangs; the whole thing begins to really collapse and fold onto itself."
3. "Yeah, there's two parts to it though. One is a wish to get very close, make sure you care for the person, help them care for you. But on the other side of the wish is the fear that if you got really close to someone you would depend on them and then there is the fear that they would leave."

Brief Supportive-Expressive Psychotherapy: Sample Transference Interpretations
1. "When you were young you already had hated affection because you felt it made you weak. So already you're having to deny that you have any desire to belong, to be loved, to get affection. But you came up with the solution: to hide it at all costs. I can't imagine you coming into therapy without that same kind of feeling."
2. "I bring up the idea that you are uncomfortable when people offer support because it crossed my mind that possibly the same thing might have gone on here. When I think about the last time we met, I had offered you at that time, saying if you need it, come twice a week or whatever, or call. In the same way, I wonder if that offer you more times for more support, if that also was something that made you uncomfortable."

Interpersonal Psychotherapy: Sample Interpretations
1. "Your tendency is to like those men who don't like you, and not like men who do like you. I wonder if it has something to do with fear of intimacy, fear of closeness."
2. "Because if your mother gets angry and sulks, I think what, at some level you used to do as a child was to blame yourself. There's something wrong with you because mother is sulking or mother is unhappy, or mother is angry.—And to some extent that was transferred to your relationships with all women. If something went wrong, it was your fault, or there was something wrong with you as a man or you weren't good enough."
3. "The kind of theme that you keep coming back to is that you can't win. I hear you keep saying over and over again as you relate to your girlfriend and to other people that, uh, is that somehow if you take that risk and really open up and assert yourself that you're going to get knocked on the head and beaten back down again."

Interpersonal Therapy: Sample Transference Interpretations
1. "Do you notice as we're talking about issues of intimacy between you and your boyfriend your mind goes blank? Is it hard to talk about it? Maybe it's safer to go blank than to drop your guard with me."
2. "It sounds like you feel as though I'm being critical of you for making that statement."

Cognitive Therapy: Sample Interpretations
1. "You know, that sort of feeds on itself in a cycle you know, every time you blow up you feel rotten and guilty and, and the more rotten and guilty you feel the less it takes to make you blow up again. You know, and so it's just a cycle and if you can learn to forgive yourself I guess—or learn to look at your own behavior more realistically."
2. "So I mean, you know, you felt very dependent and very much like you should be in the relationship, and therefore you feel very pressured, and that it makes it pretty hard to want to be there."
3. "And one of the things that happened as you begin to get close to people is they ask you for more.—And I think one of *your* reactions is, 'Don't put demands on me.' And to say that in an angry way."

Cognitive Therapy: Sample Transference Interpretations
1. "And in here, when I ask you to do things. Frequently the sequence that happens is I'll say, 'Let's do this,' and you get angry and get very resentful about the demands, and then you won't do it."
2. "I wonder if you don't feel a little embarrassed, we'd been talking earlier about how you worry about speaking up and you spoke up a little more to me today. I wonder if you felt that you opened up too much."

Table 15.2. Studies of the Frequency of Interpretation Predicting Psychotherapy Outcome

Study	Treatment	Sample Size	Measure of Interpretation	Findings
Interpretations				
Foreman & Marmar (1985)	Time-limited dynamic psychotherapy	6	Frequency of interventions that addressed defenses	3 improved cases had relatively more interpretations
Hill et al. (1988)	12–20 sessions of brief (mostly dynamic) therapy	8	Proportion of therapist statements that were interpretations	$r = .17$ with change in anxiety $r = .38$ with change in depression $r = .55$ with change in self-concept
Piper et al. (1987)	22 sessions of short-term dynamic therapy	21	Proportion of therapist statements that contained dynamic components	$r = .61^{**}$ for proportion of statements with 2 dynamic components in prediction of therapist's rating of overall usefulness of therapy $r = .53^*$ for proportion of statements with 3 dynamic components
Piper et al. (1991)	20 sessions of brief dynamic therapy	64	Proportion of therapist interventions that were transference interpretations	$r = .34^{**}$ with general symptoms and dysfunction $r = .17$ with individualized patient objectives for therapy $r = .09$ with social-sexual functioning
Piper et al. (1986)	Average of 23 sessions of brief dynamic therapy	21	Proportion of interpretations that made reference to the therapist	17 outcome measures; 1 significant finding in opposite direction than expected. Actual correlations with outcome given for 5 of 17 outcome measures; average $r = .05$
Connolly et al. (1999)	16 sessions of supportive-expressive dynamic psychotherapy	29	Percentage of interpretations that include the therapist as object	F change = 2.05, ns, for prediction of change in Hamilton Depression Rating Scale (HAMD) F change = .46, ns, for prediction of change in Beck Depression Inventory (BDI)
Malan (1976b) Study 1	Brief dynamic psychotherapy	21	Frequency of interpretation of negative transference; frequency of statements that link transference and patient's relationship with parents	Greater frequency of interpretation of negative transference not associated with positive outcome. Greater number of links associated with positive outcome (Kendall's rank correlation coefficient = .55^{**})
Malan (1976b) Study 2	Brief dynamic psychotherapy	22	Frequency of interpretation of negative transference; frequency of statements that link transference and patient's relationship with parents	Frequency of interpretation of negative transference not correlated with outcome. Frequency of links associated with outcome ($r = .40^*$ for first judge and $r = .35$ [$p = .06$] for second judge)

$^*p < 0.05$
$^{**}p < 0.01$

Table 15.3. Studies of Frequency of Interpretation Predicting the Alliance

Study	Treatment	Sample Size	Finding
Interpretations No studies			
Transference Interpretations			
Piper et al. (1991)	20 sessions of brief dynamic therapy	64	$r = -.21$ with patient-rated alliance; $r = -.33^{**}$ with therapist-rated immediate impression of alliance; $r = -.32^{**}$ with therapist-rated reflective impression of alliance; average $r = -.29$
Piper, Azim, et al. (1993)	20 sessions of brief dynamic therapy	64	High proportions of transference interpretations linked with better alliance for males ($r = .60^*$) but poorer alliance for females ($r = -.53^*$) across patients with high quality of interpersonal relationships
Connolly et al. (1997)	16 sessions of supportive-expressive dynamic psychotherapy	29	$F = .24$, $p = .63$ for prediction of change in the alliance from the proportion of transference interpretations. $F = 1.80$, $p = .19$ for prediction of change in the alliance from crossproduct of proportion of transference interpretations and quality of interpersonal relationships

$^*p < 0.05$
$^{**}p < 0.01$

Table 15.4. Studies of Quality of Interpretations Predicting the Outcome of Psychotherapy

Study	Treatment	Sample Size	Measure of Interpretation	Findings
Interpretations				
Crits-Christoph et al. (1988)	naturalistic dynamic therapy	43	Accuracy of interpretations relative to patient's core conflictual relationship themes (CCRT)	$r_p = .36^*$ with ratings of improvement. $r_p = .43^{**}$ with residual change in general adjustment (controlling for alliance and general errors in technique)
Piper, Joyce, et al. (1993)	20 sessions of brief dynamic therapy	64	Correspondence of therapist transference interpretation with therapist's initial dynamic formulation	$r = -.22^*$ for general symptoms and dysfunction across entire sample; $r = .08$ for individualized objectives across the entire sample; $r = .11$ for social-sexual adjustment across the entire sample
Norville et al. (1996)	16 sessions of dynamic psychotherapy	7	Compatibility of interpretations with specific theory-guided formulation	$r = .69^*$ with plan attainment; $r = .48$ with composite outcome

$^*p < 0.05$
$^{**}p < 0.01$

Table 15.5. Studies of Quality of Interpretation Predicting the Alliance

Study	Treatment	Sample Size	Measure of Interpretation	Findings
Piper, Joyce, et al. (1993)	20 sessions brief dynamic therapy	64	Correspondence of therapist transference interpretation with therapist's initial dynamic formulation	For entire sample: $r = -.10$ with patient impressions factor; $r = -.14$ with therapist impressions factor; $r = -.23^*$ with therapist reflective impressions factor. For patients with low quality of object relations: $r = -.37^{**}$ with patient impressions factor; $r = -.04$ with therapist impressions factor; $r = -.37^*$ with therapist reflective impressions factor
Crits-Christoph et al. (1993)	Dynamic therapy	33	Accuracy of therapist interpretations with patient's core conflictual relationship theme (CCRT)	$r_p = .51^{**}$ for accuracy on wish plus response from other predicting the development of the alliance. $r_p = -.05$, ns, for accuracy on response of self predicting the development of the alliance.

$^*p < 0.05$
$^{**}p < 0.01$

were not included. In addition, studies that assessed broader categories of therapist behavior (for example, use of exploratory techniques) but did not specifically assess interpretations were excluded. Studies of nonclinical samples were excluded as well.

In our review, we first examine studies that used measures of the frequency/proportion of interpretations, followed by a review of studies of the quality of interpretations. We look at the relation of interpretations to both treatment outcome and the therapeutic alliance. Within the context of each study, we also present any findings on moderator variables (that is, pretreatment patient characteristics that might affect the relation between interpretation and outcome/alliance). A final section examines studies of how interpretations interact with the quality of the patient-therapist relationship in predicting outcome.

Frequency of Interpretation and Outcome

One of the earliest empirical investigations of interpretations in relation to outcome was provided by Malan (1976b). He describes two studies in which he examined correlations between measures of technique and the outcome of brief psychodynamic therapy. In one study, greater frequency of interpretation of negative transference and greater number of links between the transference and the patient's relationships with parents were associated with positive treatment outcome. In the second study, frequency of interpretation of negative transference was not significantly correlated with outcome, but frequency of links between the transference and the patient's relationships with parents was again positively associated with outcome.

Foreman and Marmar (1985) examined the frequency of use of different psychodynamic interventions of six patients with initially poor alliances, three of whom subsequently improved and three of whom did not improve in terms of alliance and outcome. All patients were in time-limited dynamic therapy. Because of the small sample size, no statistical analysis of the data was presented. The improved cases, however, were predominantly characterized by relatively greater use of interventions that addressed defenses the

Table 15.6. Studies of Moderators on Interpretation-Outcome Relationships

Study	Treatment	Sample Size	Finding
Piper et al. (1991)	20 sessions of brief dynamic therapy	64	For patients with better quality of object relations: $r = .58^{**}$ with general symptoms and dysfunction; $r = .47^{**}$ with individualized patient objectives for therapy; $r = .23$ with social-sexual functioning. For patients with poorer object relations: $r = .16$ with general symptoms and dysfunction; $r = -.02$ with individualized patient objectives for therapy; $r = -.04$ with social-sexual functioning
Høglend (1993)	9–53 sessions of dynamically oriented psychotherapy	43	R^2 change = $.31^{***}$ for prediction of 4-year follow-up dynamic change from program assignment to high versus low use of transference interpretation only for patients with high quality of interpersonal relations
Connolly et al. (1999)	16 sessions of supportive-expressive dynamic psychotherapy	26	F change = 5.41^{**} for prediction of change in HAMD from interaction of quality of interpersonal relations and percentage of transference interpretation. F change = 4.74^{*} for prediction of BDI change. F change = 4.92^{*} for prediction of subsequent change in BDI controlling for prior symptom change
Crits-Christoph et al. (1988)	naturalistic dynamic therapy averaging 1 year	43	No significant interaction between accuracy of interpretation and alliance in predicting outcome

$^{*}p < .05$
$^{**}p < .01$
$^{***}p < .001$

patient used to cope with feelings in relation to the therapist and others.

Piper, Debbane, Bienvenu, deCarufel, and Garant (1986) examined the proportion of interpretations that made reference to the therapist for 21 patients who received an average of 23 sessions of brief dynamic therapy. The average correlation between proportion of transference interpretations and outcome, across 17 outcome measures, was .05.

Piper and colleagues (1987) examined the frequency of different types of interpretations for 21 patients in short-term (22 sessions) dynamic therapy. Eight sessions, or approximately every third treatment session, were analyzed for each patient. The proportion of interpretations that contained two dynamic components ($r = .61$, $p < .01$), as

well as the proportion that contained three dynamic components ($r = .53$, $p < .02$), were associated with positive therapeutic outcome.

Hill, Helms, Tichnor, and Spiegel (1988) coded all treatment sessions for eight anxious-depressed patients who received from 12 to 20 sessions of brief (mostly psychodynamic) therapy. The authors failed to find any statistically significant relationships between the proportion of therapist statements that were interpretations and treatment outcome. However, some correlations were moderately large ($r = .55$ between proportion of statements that were interpretations and change in self-concept), although significance was limited by the very low statistical power.

Høglend (1993) evaluated the frequency of transference interpretations for 43 diagnostically heterogeneous patients with varying (9 to 53) numbers of sessions of dynamically oriented psychotherapy. Patients ($n = 22$) judged suitable for dynamic psychotherapy received treatment with a relatively high frequency of transference interpretations. Patients ($n = 21$) judged less suitable received dynamic psychotherapy without transference interpretations. Adjusting for pretreatment suitability and number of sessions, an inverse relation between frequency of transference interpretations and treatment outcome was found; that is, greater use of transference interpretation was associated with relatively poorer outcome. Contrary to what might be expected, this inverse relation was statistically significant only for patients with relatively high quality of object relations.

In the largest study of frequency of interpretation, Piper and colleagues (1991) examined the proportion of transference interpretations in relation to outcome for 64 patients treated with short-term (20-session) dynamic therapy. Therapist interventions were rated for sessions 4, 7, 9, 11, 14, 16, and 18. Analyses were conducted separately for patients with high versus low quality of object relations. High rates of transference interpretation were associated with poor outcome for patients who had a history of high quality of object relations ($r = .58$, $p < .001$).

Connolly and colleagues (1999) explored the role of transference interpretations in the early sessions of 33 patients treated with Supportive-Expressive (SE) psychotherapy for depression. This study found that high levels of transference interpretations were significantly associated with poor treatment outcome for patients with poor interpersonal functioning. The authors suggest that their results may in fact be consistent with the results reported by Piper and colleagues (1991) and Høglend (1993), since the investigations evaluated treatments with different ranges of transference interpretations. Piper and colleagues (1991) found that patients with low quality of object relations had poor outcomes across moderate to high levels of transference interpretations, while patients with high quality of object relations had good outcomes at moderate levels and poor outcomes at high levels of transference interpretations. Connolly and colleagues (1999) found that patients with high quality of interpersonal rela-

tionships had good outcomes across the range of low to moderate proportions of transference interpretations, while patients with low quality of interpersonal relationships did well at low levels but poorly at moderate levels of transference interpretations. Thus, these research studies complement each other, suggesting that low quality of object relations patients have good outcomes only at very low levels of transference interpretation. Patients with high quality of object relations can benefit from low to moderate levels but have problems with high levels of transference interpretation.

In general, studies of direct correlations between frequency of interpretations and outcome have yielded mixed findings. However, studies specifically of transference interpretations have recently converged toward the conclusion that high rates of transference interpretations can lead to poor outcome, particularly for patients with low quality of object relations.

Quality of Interpretations and Treatment Outcome

At least three studies have empirically evaluated the relation between quality of interpretations and outcome. These are summarized in table 15.4. Piper, Joyce, McCallum, and Azim (1993) investigated the quality of interpretations while also controlling for the quantity of interpretations. Quality of interpretation was defined in this study as the correspondence of therapist transference interpretations with the therapist's initial dynamic formulation of each case. This measure was rated on each interpretation in selected sessions; it captures the extent to which the therapist's interpretations maintained an ongoing focus on the patient's central dynamic issues. In the same study reported earlier that examined proportion of transference interpretations, Piper, Joyce, and colleagues (1993) applied this measure of "correspondence" to 8 of the 20 therapy sessions for each of the 64 patients treated with short-term dynamic therapy. Across the sample as a whole, there were no significant correlations of "correspondence" with treatment outcome. However, for patients with high quality of object relations, the authors found an interaction between proportion of transference interpretations and quality of transference interpretations in the prediction of six-month follow-up outcomes. Better outcome was associated with a relatively low proportion of transference interpretations, but a high level of correspondence with the dynamic formulation. No such significant interactions were found for low object quality patients.

Two other studies have investigated the quality of interpretations in terms of accuracy relative to a formulation of each patient's central dynamic themes. In contrast to the study of Piper, Joyce, and colleagues (1993), who based "correspondence" on the content of interpretations relative to therapists' own case formulations, these studies assessed patients' dynamic themes through the use of independent judges.

Silberschatz, Fretter, and Curtis (1986) reported that, for three patients, interpretations that addressed a specific theory-guided formulation of each case (based upon the patient's unconscious "plan") were more common for the patient that had the best outcome and relatively less common for the patient that had the worst outcome. Norville, Sampson, and Weiss (1996) further evaluated the compatibility of therapist's interpretations across the three cases described by Silberschatz and colleagues (1986), plus an additional four cases. Across the seven subjects, the authors report a significant association between the average compatibility of interpretations and the patient's plan attainment ($r = .69$, $p = .043$).

Crits-Christoph, Cooper, and Luborsky (1988) examined the accuracy of therapists' interpretations in relation to treatment outcome for 43 patients in naturalistic psychodynamic treatment averaging about one year in duration. Judges rated whether therapist interpretations were congruent with the patient's core conflictual relationship theme (CCRT), consisting of a wish, a perceived response from other, and a response of self. The findings indicated that therapist accuracy on the wish and response from other components (combined into a composite measure) significantly predicted treatment outcome.

In summary, studies of the quality of interpretations have yielded consistent findings suggesting that relatively more favorable treatment outcomes are produced when therapists accurately address central aspects of patients' interpersonal dynamics.

Interpretations and the Therapeutic Alliance

Only a few investigations have directly evaluated the relation between interpretations and the therapeutic alliance, as shown in table 15.3. Piper and colleagues (1991) found that a high proportion of transference interpretations was associated with poorer alliance. Although this relation was strongest for patients with high quality of object relations, a regression analysis indicated that quality of object relations was not a statistically significant moderator of the relation between transference interpretations and outcome. An attempt to unravel the causal relation between these variables failed to find evidence that the primary causal direction was from interpretation to alliance, or the reverse (Piper, Azim, Joyce, & McCallum, 1993). Moreover, some gender effects qualified the relations between proportion of transference interpretations and alliance, with high proportion of transference interpretation linked with better alliance for males but poorer alliance for females (Piper, Azim, et al., 1993) across patients with a high quality of object relations.

Crits-Christoph, Barber, and Kurcias (1993) evaluated the relation between the accuracy of therapist's interpretations and alliance in a sample of 33 patients treated in psychoanalytic psychotherapy. Using the same methodology described in the Crits-Christoph et al. (1988) study of accuracy and treatment outcome, the authors reported that accuracy on the wish and response from other dimensions significantly predicted the development (change) in the alliance from early to later in treatment ($r_p = .51$, $p = .004$), while accuracy on the response of self was not a significant predictor of change in the alliance ($r_p = -.05$).

Connolly, Crits-Christoph, Shappell, Barber, and Luborsky (1997) evaluated the relation of the proportion of transference interpretations to the therapeutic alliance for a sample of 33 patients treated with 16 sessions of supportive-expressive dynamic psychotherapy. The authors found that the proportion of transference interpretations was not significantly related to subsequent changes in the therapeutic alliance for patients across levels of quality of interpersonal relationships.

There are too few studies that have examined the relation between interpretations and the therapeutic alliance to draw any meaningful conclusions at this time.

Interaction of Interpretation and Alliance in Predicting Outcome

Most models of psychotherapy adhere to the belief that techniques will have maximum impact in the context of a good patient-therapist relationship (the "alliance"). Studies by Gaston and Ring (1992), Gaston, Piper, Debbane, and Garant (1994), and Gaston, Thompson, Gallagher, Cournoyer, and Gagnon (1998) investigated session ratings of the use of exploratory techniques in interaction with alliance but did not directly focus on interpretations. Crits-Christoph et al. (1988) failed to find a significant interaction between accuracy of interpretation and the alliance in the prediction of outcome of dynamic psychotherapy. Thus, this common clinical assumption has received very little attention in the empirical literature.

LIMITATIONS OF RESEARCH REVIEWED

Correlational Designs

All of the studies reviewed were generally of the same design. Measures of interpretations coded from treatment sessions were correlated with therapy outcome. As a consequence, this literature suffers from the limitations inherent in all correlational research in attempting to establish a causal role for a predictor variable: issues of time precedence and spuriousness ("third variables" explaining the obtained correlation).

In psychotherapy process-outcome correlational studies, early patient improvement will likely influence therapist behavior during the session. The direction of such an effect may vary depending upon the process variable coded and the types of changes occurring or not occurring in the patient. This is the general issue of "therapist responsiveness" described by Stiles, Honos-Webb, and Surko (1998). For example, if a patient has made much progress between intake and, say,

session five, including reduced symptom levels, greater understanding of interpersonal issues, and lowered resistance, the therapist may see less of a need to make frequent interpretations, allowing the patient instead to successfully make connections on their own, with the therapist providing general support for the changes that have been made to date. This patient continues to show highly positive outcomes at the termination of brief therapy. (In fact, research has documented that early treatment outcomes are highly related to end-of-treatment outcomes in diverse psychotherapies; Crits-Christoph et al., 2001). Conversely, with a highly resistant, difficult patient who has made little progress by session five, a therapist may increase the use of interpretations in order to attempt to make initial progress. This difficult patient, however, is somewhat likely to demonstrate relatively less change by termination.

If an investigator attempts to correlate frequency of interpretation at session 5 with therapeutic change from intake to termination (outcome), these particular patients would contribute to a negative association (such as low frequency of interpretation associated with good outcome, or high frequency of interpretation associated with bad outcome). By this process a spurious inverse relation can result in the sample for a whole, or a "true" positive relationship may be obscured.

Therapist responsiveness may also operate in the opposite direction as given in the above example. With highly cooperative patients who are likely to improve over the course of treatment, the patient and therapist may find it easy to "play the game" of therapy. Therapists may make frequency interpretations with such patients, and these patients cooperate by providing more material relevant to the interpretation, or praise the therapist, thereby encouraging more work along the same lines. In contrast, difficult, noncooperative patients may pull therapists out of their preferred mode of operation, so that they spend most therapy time discussing crisis issues or providing emotional support if the patient is highly distressed. When an investigator then correlates frequency of interpretation to outcome, a significant spurious positive association is found. This time a pre-existing patient variable (patient cooperativeness/difficulty) is responsible for the obtained process-outcome correlation.

There are, however, several reasons to believe that such therapist responsiveness is unlikely to be affecting all of the reported process-outcome correlations reviewed. First of all, many of the studies examined therapist interpretations during relatively early stages (sessions 3–5) of treatment. At this very early stage, a therapist is not likely to believe that the patient themes and problems have been adequately and fully interpreted and, therefore, is likely to continue to use interpretations even if the patient has shown progress (particularly only symptomatic change) to date. Several studies, however, examined process over the full course of treatment (and averaged frequencies across these sessions). These studies may be particularly prone to spurious correlations introduced by therapist responsiveness. Second, most of the studies reviewed involved a manual-based psychotherapy. Although there is some degree of therapist flexibility in such manual-based therapies, therapists are generally inclined to continue to implement the protocol (interpret the transference) regardless of changes that have occurred in the patient. Third, studies of quality of interpretation are less likely to be influenced by therapist responsiveness compared to studies of frequency of interpretation. If a patient has made significant progress in treatment, therapists might decrease the frequency of interpretations, but the accuracy of the infrequent interpretations that remain is not likely to be affected.

We know of only two studies (Barber, Crits-Christoph, & Luborsky, 1996; Connolly et al., 1999) that have successfully ruled out early improvement as a factor in explaining the relationship between therapist actions and treatment outcome. The Barber and colleagues (1996) study did not assess interpretations per se. In the Connolly and colleagues (1999) study, the interaction of quality of interpersonal relationship and proportion of transference interpretations in predicting outcome was significant even controlling for early improvement.

The impact of other "third variables," such as patient cooperativeness, also needs further attention in research. Experimental studies in which patients are randomly assigned, for example, to a treatment with a high level of transference interpretations versus a treatment with a low level of transference interpretation could help overcome the limitations inherent in correlational research.

Small Sample Sizes

Most studies of therapist interpretation have relatively small sample sizes (20–30 patients). Although the Piper, Joyce, and colleagues (1993) study had a sample of 64 patients, the data were analyzed by dividing the sample into those low versus high in quality of object relations. Even though statistically significant findings were reported in some of these studies with small sample sizes, the confidence interval around such correlations is very large. Ultimately, the goal of such research is to understand the size of the relationship between interpretation and outcome, rather than statistical significance per se. Only through knowledge of the size of the relationship can such empirical results be translated into clinical usefulness, but the broad confidence intervals that are inherent in small sample research prevents accurate identification of the size of specific effects. Unfortunately, practical issues in coding large numbers of psychotherapy sessions make it unlikely that large sample sizes will be routinely available in this field of inquiry.

Limited Assessment of Interpretation

Most studies have focused on a single aspect of interpretation, such as the quantity of transference interpretation or the accuracy of interpretations. It is likely that there are a variety of facets of interpretations that influence the impact of these relational interventions. Interpretations have to be on target (accurate), but also have to be well timed in terms of the patient's readiness to hear and work with the material addressed. Moreover, the particular phrasing of an interpretation is likely to be crucial. The same thematic content can be communicated in an empathic way or a critical way, depending upon not only the choice of words but also the tone of voice. For example, in a small study that compared five good outcome therapy cases with four poor outcomes, Coady (1991) reported that, excluding therapist statements that focused on the therapist-patient relationship or on patient affects, the poor outcome cases had significantly more disaffiliative communications (interpretations plus confrontations). Caspar and colleagues (2000) have demonstrated that raters can reliably distinguish content from process in evaluating interpretation, and that both appear important to understanding the immediate impact of interpretations.

Other than the studies by Piper and colleagues that at least examined both quantity and quality of interpretation, no attention has been given to the set of variables that probably affect the impact of interpretations. When examined in isolation, it is unlikely that any one aspect of interpretations will explain more than a small outcome of variance in patient outcomes or alliance. Moreover, based upon the clinical literature on interpretation, it is naïve to assume that frequency of interpretation per se is likely to be a meaningful determinant of outcome. Future research, therefore, needs to place greater emphasis on the more clinically important facets of interpretation, such as quality and timing, rather than frequency.

Restriction in Range of Relevant Process Variables

Most studies of interpretation in relation to outcome have been performed using therapists who were carefully selected and trained, generally in brief dynamic therapy methods. In contrast, purely naturalistic samples are likely to have greater variability in both therapist skill and the quality of the therapeutic relationship. The restriction in range of therapist technique and therapeutic alliances that is somewhat inherent in carefully designed research studies limits the size of relationships that can emerge between these variables and outcome. In particular, the clinical idea that exploratory techniques will have less impact when the alliance is poor, and greater impact when the alliance is positive, might need to be tested within naturalistic samples that have a wide range of alliances, including some very poor alliances.

THERAPEUTIC PRACTICES

Because of these substantial limitations to the empirical literature on relational interpretation, caution must be applied in attempting to draw implications for clinical practice. Several of the methodological limitations (including small sam-

ple sizes, restriction in range of variables) would tend to make it more difficult to find real effects. Thus, one danger is prematurely closing the book on a hypothesis before it has been adequately tested. Other methodological limitations (for example, correlational studies) raise questions about the validity of reported findings. Our own view is that without larger scale studies that address causation and likely third variables, only findings that have been consistent across multiple studies should be used as a basis for clinical recommendations. However, even basing recommendations on replicated findings is risky if all of the studies are correlational. It is possible, indeed likely, that a finding that has been replicated across several studies may be due to an uncontrolled third variable in all of the studies (for example, failure to control for improvement up to the point of measuring interpretations).

With these caveats in mind, we propose two preliminary practice implications from the literature on interpretation:

1. High levels of transference interpretations should be avoided. This finding has emerged in three correlational studies. One of these studies (Connolly et al., 1999) ruled out at least one potential third-variable explanation for the relationship. Moreover, high levels of transference interpretations appear to be particularly problematic for patients with low levels of object relations.

2. In brief therapy, interpretations should primarily focus on the central interpersonal themes for each patient, namely, the quality or accuracy of such interpretations. While this recommendation may seem obvious to many clinicians, it is noteworthy that it is based upon empirical research. This finding has emerged in three studies, but the methods employed in the three studies were different.

Both of these recommendations apply primarily to therapies that have an interpersonal or psychodynamic focus. However, as reviewed in our section on frequency of interpretation, such interpersonally oriented interpretations occur in diverse psychotherapies, including cognitive therapy. Whether such interpersonal interpretations are important determinants of outcome in cognitive-behavioral psychotherapies has not been directly addressed.

REFERENCES

Barber, J. P., Crits-Christoph, P., & Luborsky, L. (1996). Effects of therapist adherence and competence on patient outcome in brief dynamic therapy. *Journal of Consulting and Clinical Psychology, 64*(3), 619–622.

Beck, A. T., Rush, A. J., Shaw, B. F., & Emery, G. (1979). *Cognitive therapy of depression.* New York: Guilford.

Bibring, E. (1954). Psychoanalysis and the dynamic psychotherapies. *Journal of the American Psychoanalytic Association, 2*, 745–770.

Caspar, F., Pessier, J., Stuart, J., Safran, J. D., Samstag, L. W., & Guirguis, M. (2000). One step further in assessing how interpretations influence the process of psychotherapy. *Psychotherapy Research, 10*, 309–320.

Coady, N. (1991). The association between complex types of therapist interventions and outcomes in psychodynamic psychotherapy. *Research on Social Work Practice, 1*, 257–277.

Connolly, M. B., Crits-Christoph, P., Levinson, J., Gladis, L., Siqueland, L., Barber, J. P., & Elkin, I. (2000). *Therapist interventions in the Interpersonal and Cognitive Therapy Sessions of the Treatment of Depression Collaborative Research Program (TDCRP).* Manuscript submitted for publication.

Connolly, M. B., Crits-Christoph, P., Shappell, S., Barber, J. P., & Luborsky, L. (1997, June). *The role of transference interpretations in brief supportive-expressive psychotherapy for depression.* Paper presented at the annual meeting of the Society for Psychotherapy Research, Geilo, Norway.

Connolly, M. B., Crits-Christoph, P., Shappell, S., Barber, J. P., & Luborsky, L. (1998). Therapist interventions in early sessions of brief supportive-expressive psychotherapy for depression. *Journal of Psychotherapy Practice and Research, 7*, 290–300.

Connolly, M. B., Crits-Christoph, P., Shappell, S., Barber, J. P., Luborsky, L., & Shaffer, C. (1999). Relation of transference interpretations to outcome in the early sessions of brief supportive-expressive psychotherapy. *Psychotherapy Research, 9*, 485–495.

Crits-Christoph, P., Barber, J., & Kurcias, J. (1993). The accuracy of therapists' interpretations and the development of the therapeutic alliance. *Psychotherapy Research, 3*, 25–35.

Crits-Christoph, P., Connolly, M. B., Gallop, R., Barber, J. P., Tu, X., Gladis, M., & Siqueland, L. (2001). Early improvement during manual-guided cognitive and dynamic psychotherapies predicts 16-week remission status. *Journal of Psychotherapy Practice and Research, 10*, 145–154.

Crits-Christoph, P., Cooper, A., & Luborsky, L. (1988). The accuracy of therapists' interpretations and the outcome of dynamic psychotherapy. *Journal of Consulting and Clinical Psychology, 56*, 490–495.

Davanloo, H. (1980). *Short-term dynamic psychotherapy.* New York: Aronson.

Elkin, I., Shea, M. T., Watkins, J. T., Imber, S. D., Sotsky, S. M., Collins, J. F., Glass, D. R., Pilkonis, P. A., Leber, W. R., Docherty, J. P., Fiester, S. J., & Parloff, M. B. (1989). National Institute of Mental Health Treatment of Depression Collaborative Research Program: General effectiveness of treatments. *Archives of General Psychiatry, 46*, 971–982.

Elliott, R. (1985). Helpful and nonhelpful events in brief counseling interviews: An empirical taxonomy. *Journal of Counseling Psychology, 32*, 307–322.

Elliott, R., Hill, C. E., Stiles, W. B., Friedlander, M. L., Mahrer, A. R., & Margison, F. R. (1987). Primary therapist response modes: Comparison of six rating systems. *Journal of Consulting and Clinical Psychology, 55*(2), 218–223.

Fenichel, D. (1945). *The psychoanalytic theory of neurosis.* New York: Norton.

Foreman, S. A., & Marmar, C. R. (1985). Therapist actions that address initially poor therapeutic alliances in psychotherapy. *American Journal of Psychiatry, 142*, 922–926.

Freud, S. (1953). Fragment of an analysis of a case of hysteria. In J. Strachey (Ed.), *The standard edition of the complete psychological works of Sigmund Freud* (Vol. 7). London: Hogarth. (Originally published from 1901 to 1905)

Friedlander, M. L. (1982). Counseling discourse as a speech event: Revision and extension of the Hill Counselor Verbal Response Category System. *Journal of Counseling Psychology, 29*, 425–429.

Gaston, L., Piper, W. E., Debbane, E. G., & Garant, J. (1994). Alliance and technique for predicting outcome in short-and long-term analytic psychotherapy. *Psychotherapy Research, 4*, 121–135.

Gaston, L., & Ring, J. M. (1992). Preliminary results on the inventory of therapeutic strategies. *Journal of Psychotherapy Practice and Research, 1,* 135–146.

Gaston, L., Thompson, L., Gallagher, D., Cournoyer, L., & Gagnon, R. (1998). Alliance, technique, and their interaction in predicting outcome of behavioral, cognitive, and brief dynamic therapy. *Psychotherapy Research, 8,* 190–209.

Goldberg, D. P., Hobson, R. F., Maguire, G. P., Margison, F. R., O'Dowd, T., Osborn, M., & Moss, S. (1984). The clarification and assessment of a method of psychotherapy. *British Journal of Psychiatry, 144,* 567–580.

Hill, C. E. (1978). Development of a counselor verbal response category system. *Journal of Counseling Psychology, 25*(5), 461–468.

Hill, C. E., Helms, J. E., Tichenor, V., & Spiegel, S. B. (1988). Effects of therapist response modes in brief psychotherapy. *Journal of Counseling Psychology, 35*(3), 222–233.

Høglend, P. (1993). Transference interpretations and long-term change after dynamic psychotherapy of brief to moderate length. *American Journal of Psychotherapy, 47*(4), 494–507.

Klerman, G. L., Weissman, M. M., Rounsaville, B. J., & Chevron, E. (1984). *Interpersonal psychotherapy of depression.* New York: Basic.

Lowenstein, R. M. (1951). The problem of interpretation. *Psychoanalytic Quarterly, 20,* 1–14.

Luborsky, L. (1984). *Principles of psychoanalytic psychotherapy: A manual for supportive-expressive treatment.* New York: Basic.

Mahrer, A. R. (1983). *Taxonomy of procedures and operations in psychotherapy.* Unpublished manuscript, University of Ottawa, Canada.

Malan, D. H. (1976a). *The frontier of brief psychotherapy: An example of the convergence of research and clinical practice.* New York: Plenum.

Malan, D. H. (1976b). *Towards the validation of dynamic psychotherapy: Replication.* New York: Plenum.

Mann, J. (1973). *Time-limited psychotherapy.* Cambridge, MA: Harvard University Press.

Mitchell, S. A. (1988). *Relational concepts in psychoanalysis.* Cambridge, MA: Harvard University Press.

Norville, R., Sampson, H., & Weiss, J. (1996). Accurate interpretations and brief psychotherapy outcome. *Psychotherapy Research, 6,* 16–29.

Piper, W. E., Azim, H. F., Joyce, A. S., & McCallum, M. (1991). Transference interpretations, therapeutic alliance, and outcome in short-term individual psychotherapy. *Archives of General Psychiatry, 48,* 946–953.

Piper, W. E., Azim, H. F. A., Joyce, A. S., & McCallum, M. (1993). Reply to "Transference interpretations, patients' gender, and dropout rates." *Archives of General Psychiatry, 50,* 1002.

Piper, W. E., Debbane, E. G., Bienvenu, J. P., de Carufel, F., & Garant, J. (1986). Relationships between the object focus of therapist interpretations and outcome in short-term individual psychotherapy. *British Journal of Medical Psychology, 59,* 1–11.

Piper, W. E., Debbane, E. G., de Carufel, F. L., & Bienvenu, J. P. (1987). A system for differentiating therapist interpretations from other interventions. *Bulletin of the Menninger Clinic, 51,* 532–550.

Piper, W. E., Joyce, A. S., McCallum, M., & Azim, H. F. A. (1993). Concentration and correspondence of transference interpretations in short-term psychotherapy. *Journal of Consulting and Clinical Psychology, 61,* 586–595.

Sifneos, P. W. (1992). *Short-term anxiety-provoking psychotherapy: A treatment manual.* New York: Basic.

Silberschatz, G., Fretter, P. B., & Curtis, J. T. (1986). How do interpretations influence the process of psychotherapy? *Journal of Consulting and Clinical Psychology, 54,* 646–652.

Spence, D. (1982). *Narrative truth and historical truth.* New York: Norton.

Stiles, W. B. (1979). Verbal response modes and psychotherapeutic technique. *Psychiatry, 42,* 49–62.

Stiles, W. B., Honos-Webb, L., & Surko, M. (1998). Responsiveness in psychotherapy. *Clinical Psychology: Science and Practice, 5,* 439–458.

Strupp, H. H., & Binder, J. L. (1984). *Psychotherapy in a new key: A guide to time-limited dynamic psychotherapy.* New York: Basic.

Sullivan, H. S. (1953). *The interpersonal theory of psychiatry.* New York: Norton.

B. CUSTOMIZING THE THERAPY RELATIONSHIP TO THE INDIVIDUAL PATIENT

16

Stages of Change

James O. Prochaska
John C. Norcross

In the transtheoretical model, behavior change is conceptualized as a process that unfolds over time and involves progression through a series of six stages: precontemplation, contemplation, preparation, action, maintenance, and termination. At each stage, different processes of change optimally produce progress. Matching change processes to the respective stages requires that the therapy relationship be matched to the client's stage of change. Furthermore, as clients progress from one stage to the next, the therapy relationship also progresses.

In this chapter, we review the nascent research evidence on how matching the therapy relationship to stage of change can enhance outcome, specifically in the percentage of patients completing therapy and in the ultimate success of intervention. Then we briefly address the future of psychotherapy and how our field can relate to patient populations so that we can produce stage-matched impacts with entire patient populations.

DEFINITIONS

Stages of Change

Following are brief descriptions of each of the six stages of change. Each stage represents a period of time as well as a set of tasks needed for movement to the next stage. Although the time an individual spends in each stage may vary, the tasks to be accomplished are assumed to be invariant.

Precontemplation is the stage at which there is no intention to change behavior in the foreseeable future. Most individuals in this stage are unaware or under-aware of their problems. Families, friends, neighbors, or employees, however, are often well aware that the precontemplators have problems. When precontemplators present for psychotherapy, they often do so because of pressure from others. Usually they feel coerced into changing by a spouse who threatens to leave, an employer who threatens to dismiss them, parents who threaten to disown them, or courts that threaten to punish them.

There are multiple ways to measure stage of change. In our studies employing the discrete categorization measurement of stages of change, we ask if the individual is seriously intending to change the problem behavior in the near future, typically within the next six months. If not, they are classified as precontemplators. Even precontemplators can wish to change, but this is quite different from intending or seriously considering change. Items that are used to identify precontemplation on the continuous stage of change measure (McConnaughy, DiClemente, Prochaska, & Velicer, 1989; McConnaughy, Prochaska, & Velicer, 1983) include: "As far as I'm concerned, I don't have any problems that need changing," and "I guess I have faults but there's nothing that I really need to change." Resistance to recognizing or modifying a problem is the hallmark of precontemplation.

Contemplation is the stage in which people are aware that a problem exists and are seriously thinking about overcoming it but have not yet made a commitment to take action. People can remain stuck in the contemplation stage for long periods. In one study of self-changers, we followed a group of 200 smokers in the contemplation stage for two years. The modal response of this group was to remain in the contemplation stage for the entire two years of the project without ever moving to significant action (Prochaska & DiClemente, 1983).

Contemplators struggle with their positive evaluations of their dysfunctional behavior and the amount of effort, energy, and loss it will cost to overcome it. On discrete measures, individuals who state that they are seriously considering changing the problem behavior in the next six months are classified as contemplators. On the continuous measure, these individuals would be endorsing such items as "I have a problem and I really think I should work on it," and "I've been thinking that I might want to change something about myself." Serious consideration of problem resolution is the central element of contemplation.

Preparation is a stage that combines intention and behavioral criteria. Individuals in this stage are intending to take action in the next month and have unsuccessfully taken action in the past year. As a group, individuals who are prepared for action report some small behavioral changes—"baby steps," so to speak. Although they have made some reductions in their problem behaviors, individuals in the preparation stage have not yet reached a criterion for effective action, such as abstinence from smoking, alcohol abuse, or heroin use. They are intending, however, to take such action in the very near future. On the continuous measure they score high on both the contemplation and action scales.

Action is the stage in which individuals modify their behavior, experiences, and/or environment in order to overcome their problems. Action involves the most overt behavioral changes and requires considerable commitment of time and energy. Modifications of the problem behavior made in the action stage tend to be most visible and receive the greatest external recognition. Individuals are classified in the action stage if they have successfully altered the dysfunctional behavior for a period from 1 day to 6 months. On the

continuous measure, individuals in the action stage endorse statements like "I am really working hard to change," and "Anyone can talk about changing; I am actually doing something about it." They score high on the action scale and lower on the other scales. Modification of the target behavior to an acceptable criterion and significant overt efforts to change are the hallmarks of action.

Maintenance is the stage in which people work to prevent relapse and consolidate the gains attained during action. For addictive behaviors this stage extends from 6 months to an indeterminate period past the initial action. For some behaviors, maintenance can be considered to last a lifetime. Being able to remain free of the problem behavior and/or to consistently engage in a new incompatible behavior for more than 6 months are the criteria for considering someone to be in the maintenance stage. On the continuous measure, representative maintenance items are "I may need a boost right now to help me maintain the changes I've already made," and "I'm here to prevent myself from having a relapse of my problem." Stabilizing behavior change and avoiding relapse are the hallmarks of maintenance.

Termination is the stage in which people have completed the change process and no longer have to work to prevent relapse. Termination is defined as total confidence or self-efficacy across all high-risk situations and zero temptation to relapse. Whether people are depressed, angry, anxious, or lonely, they now feel totally confident they will never go back. And they have no urges to rely on their dysfunctional behavior. They have exited from the cycle of change.

As relapse is the rule rather than the exception across virtually all behavioral disorders, change is not a linear progression through the stages. Rather, it is typically a spiral. Most clients actually move through the stages of change in a spiral pattern: they progress from contemplation to preparation to action to maintenance, but most will relapse. During relapse, individuals regress to an earlier stage. Some relapsers feel like failures—embarrassed, ashamed, and guilty. These individuals become demoralized and resist thinking about behavior change. As a result, they return to the precontemplation stage and can remain there for various periods of time.

Processes of Change

The processes of change represent an intermediate level of abstraction between metatheoretical assumptions and specific techniques spawned by those theories. While there are more than 400 ostensibly different psychotherapies, we have been able to identify only 7 to 10 different processes of change based on principal components analysis. We prefer to conceptualize change mechanisms as processes, not as specific techniques.

Change processes are overt and covert activities that individuals engage in when they attempt to modify problem behaviors. Each process is a broad category encompassing multiple techniques, methods, and relationship stances traditionally associated with disparate theoretical orientations.

Table 16.1 presents the processes receiving the most theoretical and empirical support in our work, along with their definitions and representative interventions. A common and finite set of change processes has been repeatedly identified across diverse disorders.

Stages × Processes

The transtheoretical model posits that different processes of change are differentially effective in certain stages of change. In general terms, change processes traditionally associated with the experiential, cognitive, and psychoanalytic persuasions are most useful during the earlier precontemplation and contemplation stages. Change processes traditionally associated with the existential and behavioral traditions, by contrast, are most useful during action and maintenance.

Research has shown which processes of change work best in each stage to facilitate stage progression. *Consciousness raising* will help clients progress from precontemplation to contemplation. In particular, patients need to increase their awareness of the advantages to changing and the multiple benefits of psychotherapy.

Contemplation can be a safe haven for clients and therapists alike. Clients are intending to make major changes, but not right now. First they need to increase consciousness more and more and more. Reflecting, feeling, and re-evaluating how they have been and what they might become can be hard work at times. But it can also be very meaningful and even fun. Such sharing builds a therapeutic bond that can be hard to let go. Who wants to give up such a close relationship? How can you fail as a therapist by having such a good therapeutic relationship? By allowing your client to stay stuck in contemplation.

The process of *dramatic relief* can include anticipatory grieving, the sadness and loss of letting

Table 16.1. Definitions and Representative Interventions of Change Processes

Process	Definition and Interventions
Consciousness raising	Increasing information about self and problem: observations; confrontations; interpretations; bibliotherapy
Self-reevaluation	Assessing how one feels and thinks about oneself with respect to a problem: value clarification; imagery, corrective emotional experience
Dramatic relief (or emotional arousal)	Experiencing and expressing feelings about one's problems and solutions: psychodrama; grieving losses; role-playing
Self-liberation	Choosing and commitment to act or belief in ability to change: decision-making therapy; logotherapy techniques; commitment-enhancing techniques
Counterconditioning	Substituting alternatives for problem behaviors: relaxation; desensitization; assertion; positive self-statements
Stimulus control	Avoiding or controlling stimuli that elicit problem behaviors: restructuring one's environment (e.g., removing alcohol or fattening foods); avoiding high-risk cues; fading techniques
Reinforcement	Rewarding oneself or being rewarded by others for making changes: contingency contracts; overt and covert reinforcement; self-reward

go of a best friend in a bottle, a childlike way of relating that encourages others to take care of us, or a sense of self-worth based on suffering and self-sacrifice. Dramatic relief can also include facing the fear, guilt, or regret that would come from not changing. If I hold on to safe and secure patterns of behaviors that are also self-defeating and self-destructive, how will I feel about myself in the future?

As people progress from precontemplation to contemplation, they rely more on the process of *self-reevaluation*. "How do I think and feel about myself as a couch potato or a passive person? How will I think and feel about myself as a more active or proactive person?" Many couch potatoes perceive joggers as road hazards, public nuisances. Why would they want to become one of them? The lesson learned here is that therapy needs to help people find positive images that can draw them into a healthier future just as the tobacco industry provides attractive images that draw young people into an unhealthy future.

As people progress into the preparation stage, they have to rely more on the process of *self-liberation*. This is the belief that we have the personal determinism to change our behavior and the commitment and recommitment to act on that belief. This process is what the public calls willpower. People often over-rely on this process. And when they relapse because of over-reliance on one change process, they attribute their failure to lack of willpower.

Self-liberation can be enhanced via many routes. First, as with each change process relevant to a particular stage of change, we try to provide expert guidance as to whether clients are over-utilizing, underutilizing, or appropriately utilizing willpower compared to their peers who have been most successful in progressing from preparation to action. Such feedback requires scientific assessments with adequate reliability and validity. Another way to enhance self-liberation is to give clients choices. If we only give them one choice (go to AA), they won't be as committed as they would be if we gave them two choices (AA or motivational interviewing). Two choices won't enhance willpower as much as three choices (AA or motivation interviewing or cognitive-behavioral therapy).

During action, clients also need to receive adequate *reinforcement* for their action efforts. One problem is they expect to be reinforced by others much more than others will actually reinforce them. Average acquaintances are good for one or two reinforcements before they start to take the change for granted. Therefore, clients need to be prepared to rely much more on self rather than social reinforcements.

Clients also need to apply *counterconditioning* or response substitution as they replace their problem behaviors with healthier and happier behaviors. This includes assertion training, relaxation, and cognitive substitutions to replace negative thinking with more positive patterns.

As clients progress into the maintenance stage, they do not have to work as hard, but they still have to apply change processes to prevent relapse. They particularly have to be prepared for the situations that are most likely to induce relapse.

But for all, therapy has to terminate before the problem is terminated. This is one reason why therapists and clients alike can feel anxiety or concerns about termination. They both know that under certain conditions the risk of relapse is real. Of course, clients can return for brief therapy if they lapse or relapse. They can analyze what they did right, what mistakes they made, and what they need to do differently to keep moving ahead.

Because of anxieties about relapse, clients can become dependent on therapists for social support and the helping relationship. We find that it works best to fade out the therapeutic relationship, just as one may fade out substances that clients have depended upon.

CLINICAL EXAMPLE

The following exchange from a psychotherapy session demonstrates the relational stance a transtheoretical therapist (Prochaska) would adopt with a patient in the precontemplation stage. The client is a 32-year-old stockbroker in precontemplation for chronic cocaine abuse. The stages of change were briefly outlined and then the client, Donald, was given feedback that his assessment indicated he was in the precontemplation stage. Did he concur? "Yeh, probably."

Therapist: We know that individuals in the precontemplation stage often feel coerced into entering therapy rather than being there by choice. What pressures were there on you to seek therapy?

Client: Lots of people have been on my back. My girlfriend, my mother. My job may be in jeopardy. They all think it's caused by cocaine. But I've been using it for years and it's never been a problem.

Therapist: How do you react when people pressure you to quit cocaine when you're not ready?

Client: I get angry. I tell them to mind their own business.

Therapist: You get defensive.

Client: Sure, wouldn't you? Nobody likes to be told what to do, to be treated like a kid.

Therapist: How would you react if I told you to quit cocaine?

Client: I would get angry. I would tell myself you're just like all the others—think you know better than me how to run my life.

Therapist: Would you want to drop out of therapy?

Client: Probably. I don't react well to being controlled.

Therapist: I appreciate you sharing your reactions with me. Let me share my main concern. I am concerned that you might drop out of therapy before I have a chance to make a significant difference in your life.

I don't want to coerce or control you. I do want to help you to be freer to do what is best for your life. So will you let me know if I am pressuring you or parenting you?

Client: You'll know.

Historically, confrontation was one of the recommended ways of relating to defensive and resistant clients. By consistently confronting patients' defenses and resistance, therapists expected to be able to break through their denial and other defenses. Miller and Rollnick's (1991; also see DiClemente, 1991) research has shown, however, that a confrontational style of relating drives many patients away and increases premature termination.

Later, in the same session, the therapist adopts an affirming, Socratic style and relies primarily on consciousness-raising strategies that the research evidence suggests will assist clients' progress from precontemplation to contemplation. This entails increasing awareness of the pros of changing and the multiple benefits of sticking with therapy.

Therapist: We know people are likely to complete therapy if they appreciate the many benefits they can get from therapy. Donald, how do you think people benefit from therapy?

Client: It makes the therapist better off.

Therapist: That's good! And how about the client?

Client: I expect it helps them solve their problems.

Therapist: That's true. And would that help them to feel better about themselves?

Client: Yeh, it should.

Therapist: And would that improve their moods?

Client: Sure.

Therapist: Would that improve their relationships?

Client: It should.

Therapist: And be more open and less defensive.

Client: I can see that.

Therapist: And do better in their job and make more money.

Client: I don't know about that.

Therapist: It's true. How about we make a deal. If your income goes up 10%, my fee goes up 10%?

Client: That would be worth it.

Therapist: You might not believe this, but there's only one other thing you could do for an hour a week that would give you more benefits than therapy.

Client: What's that?

Therapist: I'm not going to tell you because you might invest in that instead.

[Client laughs.]

The therapist's stance at different stages can be characterized as follows. With clients in precontemplation, often the role is like that of a *nur-*

turing parent joining with a resistant and defensive youngster who is both drawn to and repelled by the prospects of becoming more independent. With patients in contemplation, the role is akin to a *Socratic* teacher who encourages clients to achieve their own insights into their condition. With clients who are in the preparation stage, the stance is more like that of an *experienced coach* who has been through many crucial matches and can provide a fine game plan or can review the participant's own plan. With clients who are progressing into action and maintenance, the psychotherapist becomes more of a *consultant* who is available to provide expert advice and support when action is not progressing as smoothly as expected. As termination approaches in lengthier treatment, the transtheoretical therapist is consulted less and less often as the client experiences greater autonomy and ability to live a life freer from previously disabling problems.

RESEARCH REVIEW

Empirical research on the stages and processes of change has taken a number of tacks over the past 20 years (for reviews, see Prochaska, DiClemente, & Norcross, 1992; Prochaska & Norcross, 2002; Prochaska, Redding, & Evers, 2001). In this section, we review only those published research studies that have directly examined the stages and processes of change as they relate to treatment outcome, broadly defined.

Stages × Processes

Twenty years of research in behavioral medicine and psychotherapy converge in showing that different processes of change are differentially effective in certain stages of change. Rosen (2000) recently published a meta-analysis of 47 cross-sectional studies examining the relationships of the stages and the processes of change. The studies involved smoking, substance abuse, exercise, diet, and psychotherapy. The mean effect size was .11 for variation in cognitive-affective processes by stage and .14 for variation in behavioral processes by stage, both moderate to large effects (corresponding to $d = .70$ and .80, respectively). At the same time, the sequencing of change processes by stage varied somewhat by disorder or

sample. Of particular interest was the finding that "use of helping relationships was strongly related to stages in studies of psychotherapy" (Rosen, 2000, p. 601).

Predicting Dropout

When people present for psychotherapy, the initial challenge is to help them continue. A meta-analysis across 126 studies found that the dropout rate was about 50% (Wierzbicki & Pekarik, 1993).

Research has identified stage of change-related variables as the best predictor of dropout across a growing number of problems, such as heroin addiction, cocaine abuse, alcoholism, domestic violence, obesity, smoking, rehabilitation for chronic mental illness, and a variety of mental health diagnoses. In one of our studies we were able to predict psychotherapy dropout with over 90% accuracy among clients with a variety of mental health problems (Brogan, Prochaska, & Prochaska, 1999). The 40% of the patients who terminated quickly (fewer than three sessions) and prematurely, as judged by their therapists, had a group profile representing the precontemplation stage. The 20% of patients who terminated quickly but appropriately had a group profile representing the action stage. The 40% who continued in therapy had a mixed profile with the majority being in the contemplation stage.

Stage as an Outcome Predictor

The amount of progress clients make during treatment tends to be a function of their pretreatment stage of change. For example, an intensive action- and maintenance-oriented smoking cessation program for cardiac patients achieved success for 22% of precontemplators and 43% of the contemplators. Fully 76% of those in action or prepared for action at the start of the study were not smoking 6 months later (Ockene, Kristellar, Ockene, & Goldberg, 1992).

If clients progress from one stage to the next during the first month of treatment, they can double their chances of taking action in the next 6 months. Among smokers, for example, of the precontemplators who were still in precontemplation at 1-month follow-up, only 3% took action by 6 months. For the precontemplators who progressed to contemplation at 1 month, 7% took action by 6 months. Similarly, of the contemplators who remained in contemplation at 1 month, only 20% took action by 6 months. At 1 month, 41% of the contemplators who progressed to the preparation stage attempted to quit by 6 months (Prochaska, DiClemente, Velicer, Ginpil, & Norcross, 1985). These data indicate that treatment programs designed to help people progress just one stage in a month may be able to double the chances of participants taking action on their own in the near future.

Proactive Treatment

Psychotherapy has traditionally taken a passive and narrow perspective on its relationship to patient populations. Like most health care providers, psychotherapists initially relate to patient populations in a reactive pattern. Therapists passively wait for patients to seek their services, and then they react. Passive and reactive relating is appropriate when practicing acute care—when patients are acutely ill, in pain, or distressed. Such patients are likely to seek professional services to treat their acute conditions. But the major killers, cripplers, and cost-drivers of the twentieth century were chronic conditions. When our field has evaluated the efficacy of psychotherapy, we implicitly have colluded to ignore the majority of populations we fail to serve.

A revolution in therapeutic relating requires a transformation from passive approach for acute care to a proactive approach for chronic conditions. One of our most recent studies investigated the results of reaching out to patient populations.

With a representative sample of 5,000 smokers, we proactively offered therapeutic services. Because we knew less than 20% of this population would be ready to take action on their smoking, we let them know the services were designed for smokers at every stage of change: the 20% or less in the preparation stage who were ready to act in the next month; the 40% in the contemplation stage who were getting ready to quit in the next 6 months; and the 40% in the precontemplation stage who were not ready to quit.

By proactively reaching out to this patient population and customizing our clinical communications to their stage of change, we were able to have 80% participate in our clinical services (Prochaska, Velicer, Fava, Rossi, & Tsoh, 2001). That results in a quantum increase in our ability to care for this deadly and costly addiction. We replicated these results with an HMO population of about 4,000 smokers (Prochaska et al., 2000) and a teenage population of about 4,000 teenagers with multiple behavior risks and their parents (Prochaska, Redding, Velicer, et al., 2001).

Two transformations in therapeutic relating can increase the percentage of high-risk and suffering people receiving clinical services. The first is to proactively reach out and offer them therapeutic services. The second is to match the services to each individual's stage of change.

Stage-Matched Treatments

A series of clinical trials applying stage-matched interventions have been conducted. In our first large-scale clinical trial, we compared four treatments: a home-based action-oriented cessation program (standardized); stage-matched manuals (individualized); expert system computer reports plus manuals (interactive); and counselors plus computers and manuals (personalized). We randomly assigned by stage 739 smokers to one of the four treatments (Prochaska, DiClemente, Velicer, & Rossi, 1993).

In the computer condition, participants completed by mail or telephone 40 questions that were entered into our central computers, which generated feedback reports. These reports informed participants about their stage of change, the pros and cons of changing, and their use of change processes appropriate to their stages. At the beginning of treatment, participants were given positive feedback on what they were doing correctly and guidance on which processes they needed to apply more in order to progress. In two progress reports delivered over the next 6 months, participants also received positive feedback on any improvement they made on any of the variables relevant to progressing.

In the personalized condition, smokers received four proactive counselor calls over the 6-month intervention period. Three of the calls were based on the computer reports. Counselors reported much more difficulty in interacting with participants without any progress data. Without scientific assessments, it was harder for both clients and counselors to tell whether any significant progress had occurred since their last interaction.

Point prevalence abstinence rates were compared for each of the four treatment groups over 18 months, with treatment ending at 6 months. The two self-help manual conditions paralleled each other for 12 months. At 18 months, the stage-matched manuals moved ahead (18% vs. 11% abstinent). This is an example of a delayed action effect, which we often observe with stage-matched programs specifically and others have observed with self-help programs generally. It takes time for participants in early stages to progress all the way to action. Therefore, some treatment effects as measured by action will be observed only after considerable delay.

The computer alone and computer plus counselor conditions paralleled each other for 12 months. Then, the effects of the counselor condition flattened out (18% abstinent) while the computer condition effects continued to increase (25% abstinent). We can only speculate as to the delayed differences between these two conditions. Participants in the personalized condition may have become somewhat dependent on the social support and social control of the counselor calling. The last call was after the 6-months' assessment, and benefits would be observed at 12 months. Termination of the counselors could result in no further progress because of the loss of social support and control. The classic pattern for therapies for all addictions is rapid relapse beginning as soon as the treatment is terminated. Some of this rapid relapse could well be due to the sudden loss of social support or social control provided by the counselors and other participants in therapy programs.

The next test was to demonstrate the efficacy of the expert system when applied to an entire population recruited proactively. With over 80% of 5,170 smokers participating and fewer than 20% in the preparation stage, we demonstrated significant benefit of the expert system at each 6-month follow-up (Prochaska, Velicer, Fava, Rossi, & Tsoh, 2001). The point-prevalent abstinence rates for expert systems versus assessment alone were: 9.7% vs. 7.4%; 18.0% vs. 14.5%; 21.7% vs. 16.6%, and 25.6% vs. 19.7% at 6, 12, 18, and 24 months, respectively. The advantages over proactive assessment alone increased at each follow-up for the full 2 years assessed. The implications are that stage-matched expert system interventions in a population can continue to demonstrate benefits long after the intervention has ended.

The expert system's efficacy was replicated in an HMO population of 4,000 smokers with 85% participation (Prochaska et al., 2000). In the first population-based study, the expert system was 34% more effective than assessment alone; in the second it was 31% more effective (23.2% abstinent vs. 17.5%). These replicated differences were clinically significant as well. While working on a population basis, we were able to produce the level of success normally found only in intense clinic-based programs with low participation rates of much more selected samples of smokers, namely about 25% abstinence at long-term follow-up.

Enhancing Expert Systems and Counselor Interventions

In recent benchmarking research, we have been trying to create enhancements to our expert system to produce even greater outcomes. In the first enhancement in an HMO population, we added a personal hand-held computer designed to bring the behavior under stimulus control (Prochaska et al., 2000). This commercially successful innovation was an action-oriented intervention that did not enhance our expert system program on a population basis. In fact, our expert system alone was twice as effective as the system plus the enhancement. There are two major implications here: more is not necessarily better; and providing interventions that are mismatched to stage can make outcomes markedly worse.

In the HMO population, counselors plus expert system computers were outperforming expert systems alone at 12 months (25.6% vs. 20.6%). But at 18 months the counselor enhancement had declined while the benefit of computers alone had increased. Both interventions were producing identical outcomes of 23% abstinence, which are excellent for an entire population (Prochaska et al., 2000).

Why did the effect of the counselor condition drop after the intervention? As indicated, our leading hypothesis is that people become dependent on the counselors for the social support and social monitoring that they provide. Once these social influences were withdrawn, people may do worse. The expert system computers, on the other hand, may maximize self-reliance.

In a recent clinical trial we faded out the counselor relationship over time as a method for dealing with dependency on the counselor. If fading is as effective as it appears to be, it will have implications for how the therapy relationship should be terminated: gradually over time rather than suddenly. The research to date indicates that the most powerful change programs will combine the personalized benefits of therapy with the stage-matched, interactive, and data-based benefits of expert systems.

LIMITATIONS OF THE RESEARCH REVIEWED

Although at least a hundred empirical studies have been conducted on the stages of change, none have directly and prospectively matched and mismatched the therapist's relational style in psychotherapy outcome studies. Rather, the available research concerns the predictive utility of the stages of change in terms of outcomes and dropouts, the differential use of the processes of change at various stages of change, and the relative efficacy of diverse forms of service delivery. Further, the majority of published research concerns self-help interventions for addictive behaviors, as contrasted to psychotherapy for a wide range of neurotic disorders.

THERAPEUTIC PRACTICES

1. *Assess the client's stage of change.* Probably the most obvious and direct implication is the need to assess the stage of a client's readiness for change and to tailor interventions accordingly.

2. *Beware treating all patients as though they are in action.* Professionals frequently design excellent action-oriented treatment and self-help programs, but then are disappointed when only a small percentage of populations participate in therapy. The vast majority of patients are *not* in the action stage. Aggregating across studies and populations, we estimate that 10% to 20% are prepared for ac-

tion, approximately 30% to 40% are in the contemplation stage, and 50 to 60% in the precontemplation stage. Thus, those professionals who only use action-oriented programs are likely to underserve or misserve the majority of their target population. The therapeutic recommendation is to move from an action paradigm to a stage paradigm.

3. *Set realistic goals; move one stage at a time.* A realistic goal for many patients, particularly in a time-limited managed-care environment, is to set realistic goals, such as helping patients progress from precontemplation to contemplation. If we view change as a process that unfolds over time, through a series of stages, such progress means that patients are changing. Helping patients break out of that chronic, stuck phase of precontemplation is a therapeutic success, since it about doubles the chances that patients will take effective action in the next 6 months. If we can help them progress two stages with brief therapy, we triple to quadruple the chances they will take effective action.

4. *Tailor the processes to the stages.* We know that across every disorder that has been studied, people in precontemplation underestimate the benefits of changing, they overestimate the drawbacks, and they are not particularly conscious that they are making such mistakes (Prochaska et al., 1994). Compared to their peers in other stages, precontemplators rate the drawbacks of changing—and of therapy—as higher than the benefits. It is no wonder that they are at a high risk for dropping out. If therapists try to impose action on these individuals, they will drive them away, and then the therapists will blame the clients for being resistant, unmotivated, noncompliant, or not ready for therapy. Historically it has been therapists who were not ready for these clients, who were not motivated to match their relationship and interactions to the clients' needs, and were resistant to trying new approaches in order to retain more clients.

5. *Prescribe stage-matched "relationships of choice" as well as "treatments of choice."* We conceptualize this practice, paralleling the notion of "treatments of choice" in terms of techniques, as offering "therapeutic relationships of choice" in terms of interpersonal stances (Norcross, 1993; Norcross & Beutler, 1997). The integration of stages

of change and relationships of choice is an important practical guide for psychotherapists. Once the therapist knows a patient's stage of change, then it will be clear which relationship stances to apply in order to help him or her progress to the next stage and eventually maintenance. Rather than apply the relationship stances in a haphazard or trial-and-error manner, practitioners can use them in a more systematic and efficient style across the course of psychotherapy.

6. *Avoid mismatching stages and processes.* A person's stage of change provides proscriptive as well as prescriptive information on treatments of choice. Action-oriented therapies may be quite effective with individuals who are in the preparation or action stages. These same programs may be ineffective or detrimental, however, with individuals in precontemplation or contemplation stages.

We have observed two frequent mismatches (Prochaska, Norcross, & DiClemente, 1995). First, some therapists and self-changers appear to rely primarily on change processes most indicated for the contemplation stage—consciousness raising, self-evaluation—while they are moving into the action stage. They try to modify behaviors by becoming more aware, a common criticism of classical psychoanalysis: insight alone does not necessarily bring about behavior change. Second, other therapists and self-changers rely primarily on change processes most indicated for the action stage—reinforcement management, stimulus control, counterconditioning—without the requisite awareness, decision making, and readiness provided in the contemplation and preparation stages. They try to modify behavior without awareness, a common criticism of radical behaviorism: overt action without insight is likely to lead to temporary change.

7. *Shift to proactive recruitment in population-based treatments.* If these results continue to be replicated, treatment programs will be able to produce unprecedented impacts on entire populations.

REFERENCES

Brogan, M. M., Prochaska, J. O., & Prochaska, J. M. (1999). Predicting termination and continuation status in psychotherapy using the transtheoretical model. *Psychotherapy, 36,* 105–113.

DiClemente, C. C. (1991). Motivational interviewing and the stages of change. In W. R. Miller & S. Rollnick (Eds.), *Motivational interviewing: Preparing people for change.* New York: Guilford.

McConnaughy, E. A., DiClemente, C. C., Prochaska, J. O., & Velicer, W. F. (1989). Stages of change in psychotherapy: A follow-up report. *Psychotherapy, 26,* 494–503.

McConnaughy, E. A., Prochaska, J. O., & Velicer, W. F. (1983). Stages of change in psychotherapy: Measurement and sample profiles. *Psychotherapy, 20,* 368–375.

Miller, W. R., & Rollnick, S. (Eds.). (1991). *Motivational interviewing: Preparing people for change.* New York: Guilford.

Norcross, J. C. (1993). The relationship of choice: Matching the therapist's stance to individual clients. *Psychotherapy, 30,* 402–403.

Norcross, J. C., & Beutler, L. E. (1997). Determining the therapeutic relationship of choice in brief therapy. In J. N. Butcher (Ed.), *Objective psychological assessment in managed health care: A practitioner's guide.* New York: Oxford University Press.

Ockene, J., Kristellar, J., Ockene, I., & Goldberg, R. (1992). Smoking cessation and severity of illness. *Health Psychology, 11,* 119–126

Prochaska, J. O., & DiClemente, C. C. (1983). Stages and processes of self-change in smoking: Toward an integrative model of change. *Journal of Consulting and Clinical Psychology, 5,* 390–395.

Prochaska, J. O., DiClemente, C. C., & Norcross, J. C. (1992). In search of how people change: Applications to addictive behaviors. *American Psychologist, 47,* 1102–1114.

Prochaska, J. O., DiClemente, C. C., Velicer, W. F., Ginpil, S., & Norcross, J. C. (1985). Predicting change in smoking status for self-changers. *Addictive Behaviors, 10,* 395–406.

Prochaska, J. O., DiClemente, C. C., Velicer, W. F., & Rossi, J. S. (1993). Standardized, individualized, interactive, and personalized self-help programs for smoking cessation. *Health Psychology, 13,* 39–46.

Prochaska, J. O., & Norcross, J. C. (2002). *Systems of psychotherapy: A transtheoretical analysis* (5th ed.). Pacific Grove, CA: Brooks/Cole.

Prochaska, J. O., Norcross, J. C., & DiClemente, C. C. (1995). *Changing for good.* New York: Avon.

Prochaska, J. O., Norcross, J. C., Fowler, J., Follick, M., & Abrams, D. B. (1992). Attendance and outcome in a work-site weight control program: Processes and stages of change as process and predictor variables. *Addictive Behaviors, 17,* 35–45.

Prochaska, J. O., Redding, C. A., & Evers, K. (2001). The transtheoretical model and stages of change. In K. Glanz, F. M. Lewis, & B. K. Rimer (Eds.), *Health behavior and health education* (3rd ed.). San Francisco, CA: Jossey-Bass.

Prochaska, J. O., Redding, C. A., Velicer, W. F., Rossi, J. S., Fava, J. L., Sun, X., Rossi, S. R., Greene, G. W., & Plummer, B. A. (2001). *Stage-based expert systems to help a population of parents to quit smoking, eat healthier, and prevent skin cancer.* Manuscript submitted for publication.

Prochaska, J. O., Velicer, W. F., Fava, J. L., Rossi, J. S., & Tsoh, J. Y. (2001). Evaluating a population-based recruitment approach and a stage-based expert system intervention for smoking cessation. *Addictive Behaviors, 26,* 583–602.

Prochaska, J. O., Velicer, W. F., Fava, J. L., Ruggiero, L., Laforge, R., Rossi, J. S., Johnson, S. S., & Lee, P. A. (2000). Counselor and stimulus control enhancements of a stage-matched expert system intervention for smokers in a managed care setting. *Preventive Medicine, 32,* 23–32.

Prochaska, J. O., Velicer, W. F., Rossi, J. S., Goldstein, M. G., Marcus, B. H., Rakowski, W., Fiore, C., Harlow, L., Redding, C. A., Rosenbloom, D., & Rossi, S. R. (1994). Stages of change and decisional balance for twelve problem behaviors. *Health Psychology, 13,* 39–46.

Rosen, C. S. (2000). Is the sequencing of change processes by stage consistent across health problems? A meta-analysis. *Health Psychology, 19,* 593–604.

Wierzbicki, M., & Pekarik, G. (1993). A meta-analysis of psychotherapy dropout. *Professional Psychology: Research and Practice, 29,* 190–195.

17

Anaclitic/Sociotropic and Introjective/Autonomous Dimensions

Sidney J. Blatt
Golan Shahar
David C. Zuroff

Efforts to identify empirically supported treatments (ESTs) are often seriously flawed for two fundamental reasons: (1) they focus on differences in the techniques of treatment and ignore interpersonal dimensions in the treatment process, and (2) they focus on symptom reduction and neglect change in vulnerability as a primary criteria of therapeutic gain (Blatt, Zuroff, Bondi, & Sanislow, 2000). We illustrate these criticisms by reviewing the empirical research on the impact of anaclitic and introjective personality dimensions on the interpersonal dynamics of the therapeutic process in three research projects: the Riggs-Yale Project (R-YP), additional analyses of data from the Menninger Psychotherapy Research Project (MPRP), and further analyses of data from the National Institute of Mental Health (NIMH)-sponsored Treatment of Depression Collaborative Research Program (TDCRP).

LIMITATIONS OF CURRENT ATTEMPTS TO IDENTIFY ESTS

The focus on comparing relative efficacy of different interventions for focal symptoms has resulted in a relatively unproductive research agenda.

Findings in these comparisons usually indicate that active treatments are better than waiting list controls or "treatment as usual" (TAU)—but these are weak and imprecise contrast groups. Waiting list controls demonstrate that some contact is better than no contact but provide no information about the effective therapeutic agents. Treatment as usual, as defined by contemporary community standards, is often an imprecise control because it usually includes a diversity of therapists, at varying levels of training, in a wide range of orientations, who usually work in relative isolation. Comparison among active treatments is a much stronger experimental design, but few significant differences are usually found among these treatments. The frequently observed "dodo bird effect" (Luborsky, 1975; Luborsky, Diguer, McLellan, & Woody, 1995, Wampold, Mondin, Moody, Stich, Benson, & Ahn, 1997) is suggested by extensive meta-analyses that indicate few differences between alternative treatments (American Psychiatric Association, 1982; Frank, 1979; Shapiro & Shapiro, 1982; M. L. Smith, Glass, & Miller, 1980). These similarities in outcome suggest that either common processes are shared by various therapeutic techniques (Frank, 1982; Strupp & Binder, 1984) so that they are functionally equivalent (Lambert, Shapiro, & Bergin, 1986; Stiles, Shapiro, & Elliott, 1986), or that this research has not adequately addressed major methodological issues (Kazdin, 1986; VandenBos & Pino, 1980; Wortman, 1983).

A possible factor underlying the dodo bird effect is the use of manifest symptoms as the primary criterion of therapeutic outcome. Symptom reduction can be realized in ways other than therapy, including general support from family and friends (Brown & Harris, 1978; Cohen & Wills, 1985) and writing about stressful experiences (Pennebaker, 1997). Symptom reduction may be a ubiquitous effect that can occur to some degree in many supportive experiences. In addition, patients frequently seek therapy for broader reasons—to find more effective ways of dealing with difficult life circumstances and personal limitations. Consequently, differences among therapies may be more fully expressed in a reduction of vulnerability that facilitates patients' ability to cope with life stresses.

This point has been demonstrated recently in further analyses (Blatt et al., 2000; Zuroff, Blatt, Krupnick, & Sotsky, 2001) of data collected as part of the NIMH-TDCRP. Previous analyses of the TDCRP found no differences in the degree of symptom reduction after 16 weeks of treatment (for example, Elkin, 1994) among the three active treatments evaluated in this study—Cognitive-Behavioral Therapy (CBT), Interpersonal Therapy (IPT), and Imipramine with clinical management (IMI-CM)—as well as at a follow-up assessment 18 months after termination (Blatt et al., 2000). Further analyses of the TDCRP data set (Blatt et al., 2000; Zuroff et al., 2001), however, revealed significant treatment differences in patients' ratings of their capacity to cope during the follow-up period, beginning at the first follow-up evaluation conducted 6 months after termination. Specifically, patients in IPT reported greater satisfaction with treatment than patients who received medication (IMI-CM), and patients in both CBT and IPT reported significantly greater capacity to establish and maintain interpersonal relationships and to recognize, understand, and cope with their symptoms of depression than patients receiving IMI-CM. Further analyses (Zuroff et al., 2001) highlight the importance of this impact of treatment on patients' adaptive capacities.

Patients who reported that treatment contributed subtantially to their capacity to cope at the 6-month follow-up assessment had significantly fewer depressive symptoms in response to stressful life events during the remainder of the follow-up period. Thus, an enhanced capacity to cope, reported early in the follow-up period, reduced patients' subsequent vulnerability to stressful life events.

Recent observations of Luborsky and colleagues (1999) of the extensive impact of the investigator's theoretical allegiance on treatment outcome also raise questions about the limitations of randomized clinical trials (RCTs) in psychotherapy research. RCTs are also limited because attrition during treatment distorts the random assignment and alters the sample being studied. Important differences exist between the patients who begin treatment, those who participate partially, and those who complete treatment. Even further, differences between experimental and more open-ended treatment conditions may have different effects on patients. Assignment to a treatment condition can influence the patient's sense of personal responsibility and commitment to the treatment process. Findings from further analyses of the data from the TDCRP suggest that an arbitrary fixed termination date (for example, 16 weeks) has a negative affect on patients with elevated pretreatment scores on the Dysfunctional Attitudes Scale (DAS) Perfectionism factor (Blatt, Zuroff, Bondi, Sanislow, & Pilkonis, 1998). Even further, the entire research context of systematic evaluations conducted before, during, and after treatment may have very different meanings for self-critical patients who are concerned with self-worth and who tend to avoid intimacy (Zuroff & de Lorimer, 1989) and self-disclosure (Zuroff & Fitzpatrick, 1995) than for dependent patients who seek the attention and concern of others (R. Sills-Shahar, personal communication, 6/2001). A more productive research strategy than comparative RCTs might be to seek to understand more fully the nonspecific factors, such as the quality of the therapeutic alliance, that contribute to effective outcome in various forms of treatment. Despite many findings that consistently indicate that the therapeutic alliance is a major factor in treatment outcome, much effort in contemporary psychotherapy research continues to contrast differences in therapeutic technique in manualized treatments rather than study the contributions of interpersonal dimensions to the treatment process.

The investigation of brief treatment of a specific symptom by relatively inexperienced therapists whose treatment is directed by a treatment manual contributes little to understanding the complex interpersonal processes that occur in psychotherapy (Blatt, 1995a). Rather, research needs to venture beyond contrasting the effects of different manualized treatments on specific focal symptoms and begin to explore the complex interpersonal dimensions that facilitate change. Psychotherapy research also needs to differentiate among patients and to examine systematically the patient's contributions to the treatment process. As noted by Cronbach (1953) almost a half century ago, and by many others since (for example, Beutler, 1991), differences in therapeutic outcome may be a function of the congruence of patient characteristics with aspects of the treatment process. Different types of patients may respond more effectively to different types of treatment or respond to the same type of treatment in different ways (Blatt & Felsen, 1993). Frank (1979, p. 312), for example, noted that research consistently suggests that "major determinants of therapeutic success appear to lie in aspects of the patients' personality and style of life."

Patient characteristics are also pertinent to psychotherapy research because one of the major issues in evaluating treatments is the differential extent to which various types of patients remain vulnerable to adverse life circumstances (Blatt et al., 2000; Zuroff et al., 2001). Unfortunately, this issue of differential vulnerability has rarely been addressed in psychotherapy research; however, it has assumed a major role in other fields of research, particularly the study of the interaction between personality and reactivity to stress and the capacity to cope with stressful situations. Evidence consistently demonstrates that patients' clinical functioning is affected by disruptive life circumstances such as the loss of a spouse or chronic marital difficulties (Brown & Harris, 1978; Coyne, 1994). Individuals differ in their vulnerability to particular adverse circumstances. Consistent with the "stress-diathesis model" (Monroe & Simons, 1991; Zubin & Spring, 1977), psychopathology results from a co-occurrence of external

stress and personal vulnerability, be it biological or psychological. More recent derivatives of this "stress-diathesis" model postulate that psychological disturbances result from an interaction between particular personality characteristics and congruent contextual circumstances. Thus, individuals with elevated levels of dependency, who have strong needs for maintaining close and nurturing interpersonal relations, reacted with distress primarily to disruptive interpersonal events (Blatt & Zuroff, 1992; Robins, 1995; but see criticism in Coyne & Whiffen, 1995).

Vulnerability, however, may be a more active rather than a passive process, in which individuals contribute to the construction of particular stressful life events. An "action theory" perspective (Brandstater, 1998; Lerner, 1983) stresses that individuals actively shape their environment (Blatt & Zuroff, 1992; Buss, 1987; Mongrain, Vettese, Shuster, & Kendal, 1998; Mongrain & Zuroff, 1994; Priel & Shahar, 2000; Zuroff, 1992; Zuroff & Duncan, 1999). Findings (Coyne, 1976; Hammen, 1991; Potthoff, Holahan, & Joiner, 1995; Priel & Besser, 2001; Priel & Shahar, 2000) indicate that individuals contribute actively to the construction of social and interpersonal conditions that are implicated in their psychological distress. Little is known about the extent to which therapy alleviates patients' vulnerability to the stressful life events that contribute to the formation, exacerbation, and recurrence of their symptoms or the tendency to repeatedly contribute to the construction of stressful events. The emphasis on symptom reduction often neglects the investigation of these issues of vulnerability. Recent research (Hollon, DeRubeis, & Evans, 1996), consistent with the later findings of Blatt et al. (2000), indicates that one of the advantages of CBT over medication is the reduction of patients' vulnerability to depression. These findings suggest that treatment differences may be more discernible in the reduction in vulnerability than in the reduction of symptoms. But different types of patients may contribute in different ways to the construction of various types of life stress.

The interaction of patient characteristics with treatment variables, identified by Cronbach (Cronbach, 1953, 1957; Cronbach & Gleser, 1953; Edwards & Cronbach, 1952) as "Aptitude-Treatment Interactions" (ATIs), suggests a new research paradigm for psychotherapy research (Dance & Neufeld, 1988). Different types of treatment may not only be more or less effective with different individuals, but therapeutic progress may be expressed in different but equally desirable outcomes with the same therapeutic intervention (Shoham-Salomon & Hannah, 1991). Nevertheless, a major limitation in studying ATIs is often the lack of a coherent, comprehensive, theoretical framework that links patients' characteristics with central aspects of the therapeutic process and treatment outcome. Research not guided by theoretically derived considerations and previous exploratory research will lead researchers into a "hall of mirrors" (Cronbach, 1975) because of the complexity of the potential interactions. "One can avoid entering (this) hall of mirrors by exploring the interactions between theoretically meaningful . . . variables" (Beutler, 1991, p. 222) that are grounded in conceptual models. The choice of which patient qualities to include in psychotherapy research needs to be theory driven and include dimensions thought to be relevant to the processes that are assumed to underlie psychological change (Beutler, 1991; B. Smith & Sechrest, 1991; Snow, 1991).

DEFINITIONS

Blatt and colleagues (Blatt, 1974, 1991, 1995b; Blatt & Blass, 1990, 1996; Blatt & Shichman, 1983) proposed a model of personality development and psychopathology that is theoretically derived and empirically supported, and thus has the potential to facilitate the introduction of patient variables into psychotherapy research. Blatt and colleagues conceptualized personality development as involving two fundamental developmental lines—(1) a relatedness or anaclitic line that involves the development of the capacity to establish increasingly mature and mutually satisfying interpersonal relationships, and (2) a self-definitional or introjective line that involves the development of a consolidated, realistic, essentially positive, differentiated, and integrated self-identity. These two developmental lines normally evolve throughout life in a reciprocal or dialectic transaction. An increasingly differentiated, integrated, and mature sense of self is contingent on

establishing satisfying interpersonal relationships, and, conversely, the continued development of increasingly mature and satisfying interpersonal relationships is contingent on the development of a more mature self-concept and identity. In normal personality development, these two developmental processes evolve in an interactive, reciprocally balanced, mutually facilitating fashion.

These formulations are consistent with a wide range of personality theories ranging from fundamental psychoanalytic conceptualizations to basic empirical investigations of personality development. Freud (1957), for example, observed in *Civilization and Its Discontents* that "the development of the individual seems . . . to be a product of the interaction between two urges, the urge toward happiness, which we usually call 'egoistic,' and the urge toward union with others in the community, which we call 'altruistic' (p. 140). . . . The man who is predominantly erotic will give the first preference to his emotional relationship to other people; the narcissistic man, who inclines to be self-sufficient, will seek his main satisfactions in his internal mental processes" (p. 83–84). Loewald (1962, p. 490) noted that the exploration of "these various modes of separation and union . . . [identify a] polarity inherent in individual existence of individuation and 'primary narcissistic union'—a polarity that Freud attempted to conceptualize by various approaches but that he recognized and insisted upon from beginning to end by his dualistic conception of instincts, of human nature, and of life itself." Shor and Sanville (1978) discussed psychological development as involving a fundamental oscillation between "necessary connectedness" and "inevitable separations," or between "intimacy and autonomy." Personality development involves "a dialectical spiral or helix which interweaves these two dimensions of development." A wide range of more general, nonpsychoanalytic personality theorists (for example, Angyal, 1951; Bakan, 1966; Benjamin, 1974, 1995; McAdams, 1985; McClelland; 1986; Wiggins, 1991) have also discussed relatedness and self-definition as two primary dimensions of personality.

Various forms of psychopathology can be conceptualized as involving an overemphasis and exaggeration of one of these developmental lines and the defensive avoidance of the other. This distorted overemphasis defines two distinct configurations of psychopathology, each containing several types of disordered behavior that range from relatively severe to relatively mild forms of psychopathology. Anaclitic psychopathologies are those disorders in which patients are primarily preoccupied with issues of relatedness, ranging from more dependent to more reciprocal and mature relationships, and utilize primarily avoidant defenses (such as withdrawal, denial, and repression) to cope with psychological conflict and stress. Anaclitic disorders involve a preoccupation with interpersonal relations and issues of trust, caring, intimacy, and sexuality; they range from more to less disturbed and include nonparanoid schizophrenia, borderline personality disorder, infantile (or dependent) character disorder, anaclitic depression, and hysterical disorders.

In contrast, introjective psychopathology includes disorders in which the patients are concerned with establishing and maintaining a viable sense of self, ranging from a basic sense of separateness through concerns about autonomy and control to more complex internalized issues of self-worth. These patients utilize counteractive defenses (projection, rationalization, intellectualization, doing and undoing, reaction formation, overcompensation) to cope with conflict and stress. Introjective patients are more ideational and more concerned with establishing, protecting, and maintaining a viable self-concept than they are about the quality of interpersonal relations and achieving feelings of trust, warmth, and affection. Issues of anger and aggression, directed toward the self or others, are usually central to their difficulties. Introjective disorders, ranging from more to less severely disturbed, include paranoid schizophrenia, the overideational borderline, paranoia, obsessive-compulsive personality disorders, introjective (guilt-ridden) depression, and phallic narcissism (Blatt, 1974, 1991, 1995b; Blatt & Shichman, 1983).

ASSESSMENT

The distinction between these two broad configurations of psychopathology can be made reliably from clinical case records. In contrast to the atheoretical *Diagnostic and Statistical Manual of Mental Disorders* diagnostic systems developed by the American Psychiatric Association based primarily on differences in manifest symptoms, the diagnostic differentiation between anaclitic and introjective pathologies is based on dynamic considerations, including differences in primary instinctual focus (libidinal versus aggressive), types of defensive organization (avoidant versus counteractive), and predominant character style (emphasis on an object versus self-orientation, and on affects versus cognition).

In the analyses of two of the three data sets discussed below, clinical judges reliably classified patients as either anaclitic or introjective based on descriptions of the patients in clinical case reports prepared at admission to the treatment programs. Comparisons were made of the differential response of these two groups of patients to long-term intensive treatment. The distinction between these two groups of patients (anaclitic and introjective) was made with a high degree of inter-rater reliability (94% and 80% agreement) by judges in two different studies. This distinction facilitated the identification of important differences in the processes of clinical change in long-term intensive treatment with both inpatients and outpatients. Importantly, analyses of the data in these two studies based on more conventional diagnostic differentiations (such as psychotic, severe borderline, and neurotic psychopathology) were not as effective in understanding differences over the course of treatment.

The distinction between anaclitic and introjective patients has also been useful in defining subtypes of depression (see Blatt, 1974, 1998; Blatt, D'Afflitti, & Quinlan, 1976; Blatt, Quinlan, Chevron, McDonald, & Zuroff, 1982). Dissatisfaction with symptomatic classifications of depression has led several groups of clinical investigators to differentiate types of depression on the basis of the fundamental concerns that lead individuals to become depressed. Depression in these approaches is considered more than a clinical disorder, but rather an affect state that ranges from a relatively mild and appropriate transient reaction to difficult life circumstances, to a profound, sustained, and disabling clinical disorder involving intense dysphoria, distorted cognition, and neurovegetative disturbances like loss of libido and sleep and weight loss (Blatt, 1974). Investigators from different theoretical positions have discussed two major types of experiences that result in depression: (1) disruptions of gratifying interpersonal relationships (for example, object loss), and (2) disruptions of an effective and essentially positive sense of self (for example, failure). Depressed patients who are primarily responsive to one or the other of these two types of experiences have been characterized by several psychoanalytic investigators as anaclitic and introjective (Blatt, 1974, 1998; Blatt & Shichman, 1983) or dependent and self-critical (Blatt, D'Afflitti, & Quinlan, 1976; Blatt et al., 1982), as dominant other and dominant goal (Arieti & Bemporad, 1978, 1980), and anxiously attached and compulsively self-reliant (Bowlby, 1980). More recent formulations from a cognitive-behavioral perspective in which Beck (1983) differentiated between a socially dependent (sociotropic) and an autonomous type of depression are highly congruent with these formulations about depression from three different strands of psychoanalytic theory. These formulations, derived from both clinical experience and research findings, suggest impressive agreement about the nature of depression among various theoretical perspectives, at least on a descriptive level (Blatt & Maroudas, 1992).

Four procedures have been developed that assess the anaclitic or sociotropic and introjective or autonomous types of depression.

1. The Depressive Experiences Questionnaire (DEQ; see Blatt et al., 1976), a 66-item questionnaire on which individuals rate themselves on a 7-point scale, assesses a wide range of experiences frequently associated with depression but that are not in their own right symptoms of depression. Factor analysis (Blatt et al., 1976; Zuroff, Quinlan, & Blatt, 1990) yielded three orthogonal factors which were labeled Dependency (corresponding to the anaclitic mode of depression), Self-Criticism (corresponding to the introjective mode of depression), and Efficacy (a resilience-related factor).

2. The Sociotropy-Autonomy Scale (SAS; see Beck, Epstein, Harrison, & Emery, 1983) is a questionnaire containing two 30-item self-report scales. The Sociotropy Scale taps concerns about disapproval, attachment, and pleasing others. The Autonomy Scale assesses the need for achieve-

ment, freedom from control, and preference for solitude.

3. The Personal Style Inventory (PSI; see Robins & Luten, 1991; Robins, Ladd, Welkowitz, Blaney, Diaz, & Kutcher, 1994) is a 48-item integration of the DEQ and the SAS, with improved internal consistency and better convergent, discriminant, and construct validity.

4. The Dysfunctional Attitudes Scale (DAS; see Weissman & Beck, 1978), a 40-item questionnaire, assesses attitudes presumed to predispose an individual to depression. Factor analyses of the DAS (e.g., Cane, Olinger, Gotlib, & Kuiper, 1986) identified two principal factors, labeled Need for Approval and Perfectionism. The first factor, which taps patients' need for approval by others, corresponds to the anaclitic or dependent form of depression. The second factor, which taps patients' tendency to set extremely high and unrealistic self-standards and to adopt a punitive attitude toward the self, corresponds to the introjective or self-critical form of depression.

RESEARCH REVIEW

The Riggs-Yale Project

Therapeutic change was studied in a sample ($N = 90$) of seriously disturbed, treatment-resistant patients who, after a number of years of unsuccessful outpatient and brief inpatient treatment, participated in long-term, intensive, psychoanalytically oriented inpatient treatment in an open therapeutic facility (Blatt & Ford, 1994; Blatt, Ford, Berman, Cook, & Meyer, 1988). Systematic differences were found in independent measures of psychological change after, on average, 15 months of intensive inpatient treatment (including at least four times weekly psychoanalytically oriented psychotherapy) between patients preoccupied with concerns about disruptions of interpersonal relatedness (anaclitic patients) and those preoccupied with issues of self-definition, autonomy, self-control, and self-worth (introjective patients). Introjective patients seemed to change more readily and to express their change primarily in the intensity of clinical symptoms, as reliably rated from case reports, and in cognitive functioning, as reliably assessed on psychological tests administered at the beginning and toward the end of treatment (thought disorder on the Rorschach and measures of intelligence). Therapeutic change seemed to occur more slowly and in more subtle form in anaclitic patients, expressed primarily in changes in the quality of interpersonal relationships, as reliably rated from case reports, and in representations of the human figure on the Rorschach. Thus, anaclitic and introjective patients changed primarily in the modalities of their basic concerns and preoccupations. These differential outcomes for the two types of patients suggested that the two types of patients might have a differential response to different forms of therapy or to different aspects of the therapeutic process.

The Menninger Psychotherapy Research Project

The second study, based on further analyses of data from the MPRP, compared the effects of psychoanalysis and long-term supportive-expressive psychotherapy with outpatients (Blatt, 1992). Despite many prior analyses of data from the clinical evaluations and psychological testing conducted before and after treatment in the MPRP, the results repeatedly failed to discern any differences in outcome between the two types of therapeutic intervention (Wallerstein, 1986). Further analyses of these data utilizing the distinction between the two configurations of psychopathology, however, indicated that anaclitic and introjective patients were differentially responsive to psychotherapy and psychoanalysis. Based on procedures for reliably evaluating object representation on the Rorschach (Blatt, 1990; Blatt & Berman, 1984; Urist, 1973, 1980), analysis of the psychological test data gathered at the beginning and at the end of treatment revealed that anaclitic patients had significantly greater positive change in psychotherapy than in psychoanalysis, while introjective patients had significantly greater positive change in psychoanalysis than in psychotherapy. Thus, the relative therapeutic efficacy of psychoanalysis versus psychotherapy seems contingent to a significant degree upon the patient's pretreatment pathology and character

structure. It seems consistent that more dependent, interpersonally oriented, anaclitic patients would respond more effectively in a therapeutic context in which there is more direct interaction with the therapist. It also seems consistent that more ideational introjective patients, who stress separation, autonomy, and independence, would respond more effectively in psychoanalysis. These statistically significant ($p < .001$) patient-by-treatment interactions indicate the importance of differentiating between these two types of patients in studies of therapeutic outcome and of therapeutic process; they further suggest that congruence between patients' character style and important aspects of the therapeutic situation contribute to the nature and efficacy of treatment outcome. Patients come to treatment with different types of problems, different character styles, and different needs, and they are responsive in different ways to different types of therapeutic intervention.

Treatment of Depression Collaborative Research Program

The differential response of anaclitic and introjective patients in the study of therapeutic change and outcome in long-term, intensive treatment in the Riggs-Yale and Menninger data sets suggested that the anaclitic-introjective distinction might be useful when evaluating the differential effectiveness of various forms of brief psychotherapy (for example, cognitive-behavioral compared to interpersonal therapy) and medication in treating depression. The NIMH-sponsored TDCRP (Elkin et al., 1989) compared three forms of treatment for depression: interpersonal therapy (IPT), cognitive-behavioral therapy (CBT), and imipramine plus clinical management (IMI-CM). In the primary analyses of their data, the TDCRP investigators found "no evidence of greater effectiveness of one of the psychotherapies as compared with the other and no evidence that either of the psychotherapies was significantly less effective than . . . imipramine plus clinical management" (Elkin, 1994, p. 971). Interpersonal psychotherapy and imipramine plus clinical management, however, were more effective than cognitive-behavioral therapy with severely depressed patients who were functionally impaired.

Patient Characteristics in Brief Treatment of Depression

In an attempt to bring greater precision to their data analyses, Imber and his TDCRP colleagues (Imber et al., 1990) argued for the need to develop measures of change that were directly relevant to possible treatment-specific effects. They stressed the need to develop precisely specified, appropriately applied outcome measures "selected for presumed sensitivity to different treatments." Though these investigators carefully derived outcome measures based on the rationales and procedures of three types of treatment for depression (IPT, CBT, and IMI-CM), their results provided little support for their basic hypothesis: "None of the therapies produced consistent effects on measures related to its theoretical origins" (Imber et al., 1990, p. 352). Their findings, consistent with the dodo bird hypothesis, appear to support the contention (Butler & Strupp, 1986) that the search for specific treatment effects is unproductive and that psychotherapy research should move on to more productive areas.

Further analyses of data from the TDCRP conducted by Blatt and colleagues, however, provide support for the contribution of patients' characteristics to therapeutic outcome. Anaclitic and introjective dimensions were introduced into analyses of the TDCRP data by patients' pretreatment scores on the two subscales of the DAS. The DAS was administered to the patients in the TDCRP as part of the intake procedure, as well as several times during treatment and during follow-up assessments. Factor analysis conducted on the DAS data obtained at intake in the TDCRP (Imber et al., 1990), consistent with previous analyses of the DAS (for example, Cane et al., 1986), identified two principal factors, Need for Approval and Perfectionism. Previous studies have shown links between these two DAS scales and the anaclitic (dependent) and introjective (self-critical) personality configurations, respectively (Blaney & Kutcher, 1991; Rude & Burnham, 1995; Segal, Shaw, & Vella, 1987). More recent analyses, however, indicate that while the Perfectionism factor of the DAS taps the introjec-

tive dimension, the Need for Approval factor is less specific and taps both introjective and anaclitic vulnerabilities (Shahar, 1999; Shahar & Priel, 2001).

Blatt and colleagues (Blatt, Quinlan, Pilkonis, & Shea, 1995; Blatt, Zuroff, Quinlan, & Pilkonis, 1996; Blatt, Zuroff, Bondi, Sanislow & Pilkonis, 1998; Zuroff, Blatt, et al., 2000) examined the contributions of patients' pretreatment DAS levels of Need for Approval and Perfectionism to therapeutic outcome in the TDCRP. While Need for Approval seemed to facilitate treatment outcome, these results failed to reach statistical significance ($p < .11$). However, consistent significant effects were found in analyses involving Perfectionism. Specifically, patients' pretreatment perfectionism predicted poorer outcome at termination (that is, after 16 weeks of treatment), as well as at the follow-up assessment conducted 18 months after the termination of treatment (Blatt et al., 1995; Blatt et al., 1998). Further analyses revealed that patients' pretreatment perfectionism significantly impeded therapeutic progress in two-thirds of the sample primarily in the latter half of treatment, beginning between the ninth and the twelfth treatment session (Blatt et al., 1998).

Additional analyses indicated that pretreatment level of perfectionism impacted on therapeutic outcome primarily by disrupting the patients' quality of interpersonal relations both in the treatment process and in social relationships outside of treatment. Zuroff et al. (2000), utilizing ratings of the therapeutic alliance in the TDCRP developed by Krupnick and colleagues (1996), which was in turn based on a modified version of the Vanderbilt Therapeutic Alliance Scale (VTAS; Hartley & Strupp, 1983), found that patients' (but not the therapists') contributions to the therapeutic alliance mediated the effect of pretreatment perfectionism on treatment outcome at termination. More perfectionist patients failed to continue to participate actively in the development of the therapeutic alliance especially in the latter half of the treatment process; the disrupted therapeutic alliance led to poorer therapeutic response (Zuroff et al., 2000, p. 121).

Shahar, Blatt, Zuroff, Krupnick, and Sotsky (2001) found that pretreatment perfectionism was also related to impaired social network outside of treatment, and this impaired social network also significantly mediated the relationship of perfectionism to treatment outcome. Clinical evaluators in the TDCRP used the Social Network Form (Elkin, Parloff, Hadley, & Autry, 1985) to assess patients' social network, and patients with high levels of pretreatment perfectionism reported less satisfying social relationships over the course of treatment, which in turn predicted poorer therapeutic outcome. Thus, perfectionist patients appear to have greater interpersonal difficulty within, and external to, the treatment process. Perfectionist patients have poorer therapeutic alliance (Zuroff et al., 2000) and a more limited social network (Shahar et al., 2001) during treatment. Even further, patients with higher pretreatment levels of perfectionism are also more vulnerable to stressful life events during the follow-up period, leading to increased depression, because they failed at termination to develop a capacity to cope with stressful life events (Zuroff et al., 2001). Their findings also suggest that patients' development of enhanced capacities to cope with aspects of their lives is a more discriminating measure of therapeutic progress than a reduction in symptoms (Blatt et al., 2000; Shahar et al., 2001).

These findings are particularly pertinent to our evaluation of the attempts to identify ESTs. They demonstrate that therapeutic response, even in a research design ideal for identifying ESTs (a randomized clinical trial using manualized treatments for a clearly defined and specific symptom), appears to be determined more by the impact of particular pretreatment characteristics of patients on the quality of their interpersonal relations both in the treatment process and in their general social relations during treatment than by the specific therapeutic techniques.

Therapist Characteristics in Brief Treatment of Depression

Blatt, Zuroff, and colleagues (1996) sought to identify treatment factors that served to mitigate the disruptive effects of pretreatment perfectionism on treatment outcome. Patients at the end of the second treatment session in the TDCRP, using the Barrett-Lennard Relationship Inventory (BLRI; see Barrett-Lennard, 1962, 1985), rated their perceptions of their therapist's empathy, positive regard, and congruence, characteristics that Carl Rogers (1957) considered the necessary and sufficient conditions for therapeutic change. Patients who, at the end of the second treatment session, had a more positive view of their therapist, had significantly ($p < .05$) greater therapeutic gain at termination. This more positive view of the therapist significantly moderated the disruptive effects of perfectionism on therapeutic outcome, but only at the middle level of perfectionism. At high and low levels, perfectionism was not moderated by the patient's perception of the therapist; but at moderate levels, the impact of pretreatment perfectionism on therapeutic outcome was significantly ($p < .001$) determined by the patient's perception of the therapist.

The TDCRP design allowed for a comparison of more and less effective therapists. Blatt, Sanislow, Zuroff, and Pilkonis (1996), using a composite outcome measure that integrated the five primary outcome variables employed in the TDCRP, aggregated the outcome scores at termination of all the patients seen by each of the 28 therapists who had participated in the TDCRP (10 each providing IPT and pharmacotherapy and 8 providing CBT). The therapists were either M.D.- or Ph.D.-level clinicians with an average of 11 years of clinical experience. All the therapists received training in the treatment they provided in the TDCRP, and only therapists who met competency criteria participated in the study. Tapes of sessions were reviewed periodically to assure adherence to treatment protocols, and therapists received consultation during the study (Elkin, 1994).

To explore the therapists' contributions to treatment outcome, Blatt, Sanislow, and colleagues (1996) identified more and less effective therapists as defined by the average therapeutic gain achieved by the patients that each therapist had seen in active treatment in the TDCRP. Significant differences were found among three groups of therapists (more, moderate, and less effective), independent of the type of treatment they provided. Differences in therapeutic efficacy were associated with basic clinical orientation, especially about the treatment process. More effective therapists had a more psychological than a biological orientation and reported that in their general clinical practice they predominantly used psychotherapy with depressed patients and rarely used biological interventions (such as medication and ECT). These highly experienced M.D.- and Ph.D.-level therapists in the TDCRP were asked to describe their general clinical practice in terms of the percentage of their time they usually devoted to psychotherapy alone, medication alone, and to a combination of psychotherapy and medication. Less effective therapists, somewhat like the more effective therapists, reported that they primarily tended to use psychotherapy alone in their clinical practice (42.1% of the time) but, more often than the more effective therapists, they combined their psychotherapeutic efforts with medication almost half (48.6%) of the time. More effective therapists, in contrast, primarily use psychotherapy alone (73.8% of the time) and only occasionally (19.6%) combine their psychotherapy with medication. Moderately effective therapists use primarily medication, either alone (14.4% of the time) or in combination with psychotherapy (56.1%) and relatively rarely use psychotherapy alone (29.4%) in their clinical practice. Thus, the moderately effective therapists appear to be more biologically oriented. Less effective therapists, like the more effective therapists, are primarily interested in psychotherapy but they combine their psychotherapy with the use of medication much more often than the more effective therapists. Additionally, more effective therapists, compared with moderately and less effective therapists, expect therapy with depressed patients to require more treatment sessions before patients begin to manifest therapeutic change. Also, more effective therapists had significantly ($p < .023$) less variability in the therapeutic outcome among the patients they treated in the TDCRP than did moderately and less effective therapists. The greater variability in therapeutic outcome among the patients of less effective therapists suggests that the less effective therapists are able to work effectively with some, but not all, of their patients, whereas more effective therapists are able to work effectively with almost all their patients. It is important to stress that these differences among different levels of effective therapists are particularly impressive because they occurred in a relatively homogeneous group of well-trained and experienced therapists who participated in three well-specified, manual-

ized treatment conditions in three independent research sites. Relatively few significant differences were found, however, among the three groups of therapists on their attitudes about the etiology of depression or about the techniques they considered essential for the treatment of depression.

The overall results in the comparison of more, moderately, and less effective therapists in the TDCRP indicate that qualities of the therapist are also important dimensions that appear to influence therapeutic outcome. Overall, the results of our analyses of data from the TDCRP are consistent with prior findings (Burns & Nolen-Hoeksema, 1992; Horvath & Symonds, 1991; Krupnick et al., 1996) that therapeutic outcome is significantly influenced by the interpersonal dimensions of the treatment process—by personal qualities of patients and therapists and their ability to establish an effective therapeutic relationship—rather than by the techniques and tactics described in treatment manuals.

Related Research

In addition to the above analyses of the TDCRP data, several recent studies of brief cognitive and pharmacological treatment of depression provide further support for the influence of patients' personality styles on therapeutic outcome. Peselow, Robins, Sanfilipo, Block, and Fieve (1992), investigating the responses to pharmacotherapy among 217 depressed outpatients, found that patients with a high autonomous–low sociotropic profile on the SAS responded better to antidepressants than patients who had a high sociotropic–low autonomous profile. According to Peselow and colleagues (1992), these findings support Beck's (1983) contention that the autonomous form of depression includes endogenomorphic characteristics. However, in another study, Rector, Bagby, Segal, Joffe, and Levitt (2000), investigating depressed outpatients treated with either cognitive therapy ($N = 51$) or pharmacotherapy ($N = 58$), found that DEQ self-criticism did not have an effect on pharmacotherapeutic response, which stands in contrast to Beck's (1983) hypothesis (see also Blatt & Maroudas, 1992, p. 161). Consistent with the TDCRP analyses summarized earlier, Rector and colleagues found that pretreatment self-criticism predicted poorer response to cognitive therapy. Moreover, self-criticism change scores before and after treatment predicted therapeutic response such that the degree to which self-criticism was reduced predicted therapeutic outcome.

Studies by Zettle and colleagues (Zettle, Haflich, & Reynolds, 1992; Zettle & Herring, 1995) lend further support to the importance of the patient's personality style in brief treatment of depression. Zettle and colleagues compared the responses of sociotropic and autonomous depressed outpatients to individual and group cognitive therapy for depression. Following Beck's (1983) hypothesis that sociotropic patients should benefit more from an approach that emphasizes the supportive/helping nature of the therapeutic relation, while autonomous patients should benefit more from an approach that emphasizes problem solving, the authors predicted that sociotropic patients would demonstrate greater therapeutic response in cognitive group therapy, while autonomous patients would demonstrate greater therapeutic response to individual cognitive therapy. Results were largely consistent with the hypothesis: Patients who were matched to their "preferred" mode responded better to therapy, as assessed by depressive symptoms (Zettle et al., 1992) or "remission" indicated by a lower score on the Beck Depression Inventory (Zettle & Herring, 1995). In summary, these various studies demonstrate the importance of patient characteristics in determining therapeutic response to particular forms of brief treatment.

LIMITATIONS AND IMPLICATIONS OF RESEARCH

One of the unfortunate potential consequences of the search for ESTs is that its emphasis on therapeutic technique and tactics can lead to the neglect of exploring differences among patients, differences that can have an impact on interpersonal relationships in the therapeutic process. The predominant emphasis on RCTs and comparative treatment trials by the major sources of research funding (such as NIMH, National Institute of Drug Abuse [NIDA], and pharmaceutical companies) discourages attempts to explore systematically the subtle interpersonal processes that research indicates are involved in psychotherapy, as well as how patient dimensions affect treatment outcome. Psychotherapy research needs to include systematic, empirical, evidence-based attempts to understand more fully the factors that contribute to therapeutic outcome in ways that inform clinical practice and facilitate clinical training and research.

Findings from our further analyses of data from the NIMH-TDCRP indicate that differences among treatments are not readily apparent in reduction of symptoms. Active treatments seem to be equally effective in symptom reduction. But significant differences among treatments were found in follow-up assessment of the degree to which patients developed adaptive capacity to cope with stressful life events. Thus, it is essential to look at the impact of treatment beyond the reduction of manifest symptoms and to include a reduction in vulnerability to life stresses as a major indicator of therapeutic gain. Patients usually seek treatment not only to reduce their troublesome and disruptive symptoms, but also to find more effective ways of coping with life's problems.

Findings from our further analyses of the data from the TDCRP also indicate that differences among patients are critical for understanding the nature of the therapeutic process and the factors that contribute to therapeutic outcome. Pretreatment characteristics of patients, predominantly their level of pretreatment perfectionism, had a major role in determining therapeutic outcome primarily through their impact on interpersonal processes—on the therapeutic alliance and on the social network patients establish and maintain outside of treatment (Shahar et al., 2001; Zuroff et al., 2001). Differences in outcome at termination and follow-up are related to the qualities of the interpersonal process established between patient and therapist rather than differences in therapeutic technique.

The differentiation between anaclitic and introjective personality configurations, between patients preoccupied with either issues of relatedness or issues of self-definition, enabled us to demonstrate that this clinical differentiation affects the nature and extent of therapeutic change in various forms of treatment including psychoanalysis, supportive-expressive psychotherapy, and several manualized therapies for the brief treatment of depression, including pharmacotherapy. Anaclitic patients, those with greater investment in interpersonal relatedness, showed greater improvement in long-term supportive-expressive psychotherapy, while introjective patients, those with greater investment in cognitive functioning, showed greater improvement in psychoanalysis. The fact that more ideational patients did better in psychoanalysis in the MPRP and, as reported by Sotsky and colleagues (1991), in CBT in the TDCRP suggests that both short-term CBT and long-term psychoanalysis emphasize change in cognitive structures, in contrast to the interpersonal emphasis of supportive-expressive psychotherapy in the MPRP and short-term IPT in the TDCRP (Sotsky et al., 1991), which were more effective with more interpersonally oriented patients. These research findings indicate that therapeutic change can be understood primarily by differentiating among patients and appreciating differences in the needs, concerns, motives, resources, and vulnerabilities of different types of patients, and how patient characteristics affect the treatment process.

It is important to note, however, that even our research on the impact of anaclitic and introjective dimensions in the therapeutic process, which goes beyond the limitations of RCTs of manualized treatments, is itself limited on several accounts. One of the primary limitations of these studies is the assessment of the anaclitic and introjective dimensions. While the dichotomous classification of anaclitic and introjective patients had ample reliability and validity (for the Riggs-Yale Project and the Menninger Psychotherapy Research Project, see Blatt, 1992; Blatt & Ford, 1994), this classification does not take into account patients who have both predominant anaclitic and introjective features. These patients, who were not able to consolidate into a relatively stable, albeit vulnerable, personality organization, may be even more vulnerable than "pure anaclitic" and "pure introjective" patients. The "double" vulnerability, as well as the therapeutic responses of these patients, should be investigated. Self-report measures of the anaclitic and introjec-

tive dimensions, primarily the DEQ, but also the SAS, PSI and DAS, are also limited. Psychometric studies focusing on these instruments revealed only a modest convergence between anaclitic and introjective dimensions assessed in each instrument (Blaney & Kutcher, 1991), suggesting that each instrument taps slightly different elements of these personality dimensions. This limitation was most apparent in our reanalyses of data from the NIMH-TDCRP. While our analyses using the DAS Perfectionism subscale, which taps introjective characteristics, were very productive, analyses using the DAS Need for Approval subscale yielded much weaker results. It is difficult to know whether the relatively weaker results obtained with the Need for Approval subscale in the TDCRP are attributable to the scale or to the construct which it intends to measure (that is, the anaclitic dimension of personality). Recent analyses, for example, demonstrate that DAS Need for Approval taps both introjective and anaclitic characteristics (Shahar, 1999; Shahar & Priel, 2001).

Design-related limitations should be pointed out as well. The findings obtained from the Riggs-Yale Project and from the Menninger Psychotherapy Research Projects were based on retrospective analyses of the data. Both projects represent labor-intensive attempts to examine the effects of long-term psychotherapy, the Riggs-Yale Project in a naturalistic setting and the Menninger Psychotherapy Research Project in a quasi-experimental design. Moreover, both projects relied on extensive and high-quality data sets, derived from careful and detailed case reports that were transformed into quantitative data by judges, using reliable and valid rating scales, as well as from comprehensive psychological test protocols. Similar studies today would strive to increase sample size and would probably rely on recent measures of psychological change, including changes in mental representations of self and significant others (Blatt & Auerbach, 2001). In addition, current studies might conduct several, instead of two, waves of measurement, although it would be important to remember, as argued above, that a multiwave design may interact differentially with the anaclitic and introjective personality dimensions, thereby changing the object of our observations.

THERAPEUTIC PRACTICES

Given the limitations of manualized treatments, which have been pointed out in this and other chapters in this volume, the most obvious, straightforward recommendation arising from our analyses of data from the TDCRP is to stress the importance of a warm, accepting, essentially optimistic attitude of therapists toward their patients in establishing and maintaining a constructive therapeutic alliance, regardless of the therapeutic modality. Though the therapist's contribution to the establishment of the therapeutic alliance is a necessary, but not sufficient condition, patients' characteristics can have an enormous impact, both positive and negative, on this alliance.

As is evidenced from our analyses of data from the TDCRP, patients' pretreatment perfectionism had a major impact on the quality of the therapeutic alliance in brief, manualized treatment of depression, which in turn greatly restricted perfectionistic patients' ability to benefit from treatment. While we do not have direct access to the struggles of perfectionist patients that may have served as obstacles for their ability to contribute to and maintain the therapeutic alliance, other studies of self-critical perfectionism (for example, Blatt, Wein, Chevron, & Quinlan, 1979; Mongrain, 1998; see review in Blatt, 1995c) suggest that perfectionistic individuals have malevolent, harsh, and punitive representations of significant others. These malevolent representations interfere with self-critical perfectionist individuals' interpersonal relations with significant others in general, and with their therapists in particular. In the course of therapy, perfectionist patients are likely to project aspects of these negative internal representations to the therapist, thus actively disrupting the therapeutic alliance. The demanding evaluative experimental design, which may cause perfectionist patients to feel that they are being tested, or worse yet, that they are on trial (R. Sills-Shahar, June 2001, personal communication), the brevity of treatment (which may activate the ambivalence of perfectionistic patients toward close and nurturing relations), and the limitations posed on the types of issues that are discussed and worked through in the course of manualized treatment (which may restrict perfectionistic patients' feeling of being understood), are all features of RCTs that can be detrimental for perfectionist patients.

The recommendation for therapists is again straightforward: Be aware of the ways in which (perfectionistic and other) patients perceive you in early stages of the course of treatment, of how such perceptions are tied to patients' internal representations of self and others, and how these representations actively limit the capacity of these patients to participate in therapeutic alliance. Therapists need time, patience, openness, and an acute sensitivity to interpersonal processes, both within patients and within the therapists themselves, in order to address these obstacles. Though highly perfectionistic patients are seriously limited in the benefit they might gain from brief treatment for depression, data (Blatt, Zuroff, et al., 1996) suggest that patients at moderate levels of perfectionism are able to gain from brief treatment for depression if they feel initially in the treatment process that the therapist is empathic, open, and available.

In addition to attending carefully to the therapeutic alliance throughout the treatment process, therapists should be alert to the ways in which patients actively generate a negative social environment outside of treatment. Earlier in this chapter we drew from the emerging theoretical perspective of "Action Theory" (Brandstater, 1998; Lerner, 1983) to understand the ways in which anaclitic and introjective patients create detrimental social conditions, such as life stress and lack of social support (Priel & Shahar, 2000; Shahar & Priel, 2001). Perfectionism not only interferes with the therapeutic alliance, but it also interferes with these patients establishing satisfying social relations. This interference with the therapeutic alliance and with social relations greatly limits patients' ability to benefit from treatment (Shahar et al., 2001). This generation of a risk-related context by perfectionist patients derives from their negative internal representations of self and/or significant others, including their therapist. This generation of a risk-related context should be identified by the therapist as early as possible in the course of treatment, because it is subsequently implicated in patients' difficulties in maintaining a constructive therapeutic alliance and achieving therapeutic gain.

A final point arising from our review of research on the anaclitic and introjective dimensions is that anaclitic and introjective individuals experience the world very differently (Blatt & Zuroff, 1992). Hence, they are likely to respond very differently to treatment-related events, such as symptomatic changes and therapeutic interventions (such as directive suggestions, clarifications, reflections, interpretations, and reframing). The identification of patients' personality organization (that is, whether they are predominantly anaclitic or introjective) can enhance therapists' understanding of their patients' responses to the treatment process and to stressful events that occur in their lives. Optimally, this sensitivity to aspects of patients' personality organization may help therapists to be more attentive to patients' particular needs (Blatt & Felsen, 1993). Specifically, perfectionistic patients need to feel early on that the therapeutic environment is supportive and accepting—that it is a therapeutic environment that will help them perceive themselves and others in less critical ways. This will facilitate their capacity to enter actively into the therapeutic process and thereby come to understand more fully how their negative anticipation of self and others impairs their capacity to establish productive and satisfying interpersonal relationships.

REFERENCES

American Psychiatric Association Commission on Psychotherapies. (1982). *Psychotherapy research: Methodological and efficacy issues*. Washington, DC: American Psychiatric Association.

Angyal, A. (1951). *Neurosis and treatment: A holistic theory*. Edited by E. Hanfmann & R. M. Jones. New York: Wiley.

Arieti, S., & Bemporad, J. R. (1978). *Severe and mild depression: The therapeutic approach*. New York: Basic.

Arieti, S., & Bemporad, J. R. (1980). The psychological organization of depression. *American Journal of Psychiatry, 137*, 1360–1365.

Bakan, D. (1966). *The duality of human existence: An essay on psychology and religion*. Chicago: Rand McNally.

Barrett-Lennard, G. T. (1962). Dimensions of therapist responses as causal factors in therapeutic change. *Psychological Monographs, 76* (Whole no. 562).

Barrett-Lennard, G. T. (1985). The Relationship Inventory now: Issues and advances in theory, method, and use. In L. S. Greenberg & W. M. Pinsof (Eds.), *The psychoanalytic process: A research handbook* (pp. 439–476). New York: Guilford.

Beck, A. T. (1983). Cognitive therapy of depression: New perspectives. In P. J. Clayton & J. E. Barrett (Eds.), *Treatment of depression: Old controversies and new approaches* (pp. 265–290). New York: Raven.

Beck, A. T., Epstein, N., Harrison, R. P., & Emery, G. (1983). *Development of the Sociotropy-Autonomy Scale: A measure of personality factors in psychopathology*. Unpublished manuscript, University of Pennsylvania, Philadelphia.

Benjamin, J. (1995). *Like subjects, love objects: Essays on recognition and sexual differences*. New Haven: Yale University Press.

Benjamin, L. S. (1974). Structural analysis of social behavior. *Journal of Psychological Review, 81*, 392–345.

Beutler, L. E. (1991). Have all won and must all have prizes? Revisiting Luborsky et al.'s verdict. *Journal of Consulting and Clinical Psychology, 59*, 226–232.

Blaney, P. H., & Kutcher, G. S. (1991). Measures of depressive dimensions: Are they interchangeable? *Journal of Personality Assessment, 56*, 502–512.

Blatt, S. J. (1974). Levels of object representation in anaclitic and introjective depression. *Psychoanalytic Study of the Child, 29*, 107–157.

Blatt, S. J. (1990). Interpersonal relatedness and self-definition: Two personality configurations and their implications for psychopathology and psychotherapy. In J. L. Singer (Ed.), *Repression and dissociation: Implications for personality theory, psychopathology & health* (pp. 299–335). Chicago: University of Chicago Press.

Blatt, S. J. (1991). A cognitive morphology of psychopathology. *Journal of Nervous and Mental Disease, 179*, 449–458.

Blatt, S. J. (1992). The differential effect of psychotherapy and psychoanalysis on anaclitic and introjective patients: The Menninger Psychotherapy Research Project revisited. *Journal of the American Psychoanalytic Association, 40*, 691–724.

Blatt, S. J. (1995a). Why the gap between psychotherapy research and clinical practice: A response to Barry Wolfe. *Journal of Psychotherapy Integration, 5*, 72–76.

Blatt, S. J. (1995b). Representational structures in

psychopathology. In D. Cicchetti & S. Toth (Eds.), *Rochester symposium on developmental psychopathology: Vol. 6. Emotion, cognition, and representation* (pp. 1–33). Rochester, NY: University of Rochester Press.

Blatt, S. J. (1995c). The destructiveness of perfectionism: Implications for the treatment of depression. *American Psychologist, 50,* 1003–1020.

Blatt, S. J. (1998). Contributions of psychoanalysis to the understanding and treatment of depression. *Journal of the American Psychoanalytic Association, 46,* 723–752.

Blatt, S. J., & Auerbach, J. S. (2001). Mental representation, severe psychopathology, and the therapeutic process: Affect and self-reflexivity in borderline and schizophrenic patients. *Journal of the American Psychoanalytic Association, 49,* 113–159.

Blatt, S. J., & Berman, W. (1984). A methodology for the use of the Rorschach in clinical research. *Journal of Personality Assessment, 48,* 226–239.

Blatt, S. J., & Blass, R. B. (1990). Attachment and separateness: A dialectic model of the products and processes of psychological development. *Psychoanalytic Study of the Child, 45,* 107–127.

Blatt, S. J., & Blass, R. B. (1996). Relatedness and self definition: A dialectic model of personality development. In G. G. Noam & K. W. Fischer (Eds.), *Development and vulnerabilities in close relationships* (pp. 309–338). Hillsdale, NJ: Erlbaum.

Blatt, S. J., D'Afflitti, J. P., & Quinlan, D. M. (1976). Experiences of depression in normal young adults. *Journal of Abnormal Psychology, 85,* 383–389.

Blatt, S. J., & Felsen, I. (1993). "Different kinds of folks may need different kinds of strokes": The effect of patients' characteristics on therapeutic process and outcome. *Psychotherapy Research 3,* 245–259.

Blatt, S. J., & Ford, R. (1994). *Therapeutic change: An object relations perspective.* New York: Plenum.

Blatt, S. J., Ford, R. Q., Berman, W., Cook, B., & Meyer, R. (1988). The assessment of change during the intensive treatment of borderline and schizophrenic young adults. *Psychoanalytic Psychology, 5,* 127–158.

Blatt, S. J., & Maroudas, C. (1992). Convergence of psychoanalytic and cognitive behavioral theories of depression. *Psychoanalytic Psychology, 9,* 157–190.

Blatt, S. J., Quinlan, D. M., Chevron, E. S., McDonald, C., & Zuroff, D. (1982). Dependency and self-criticism: Psychological dimensions of depression. *Journal of Consulting and Clinical Psychology, 50,* 113–124.

Blatt, S. J., Quinlan, D. M., Pilkonis, P. A., & Shea, T. (1995). Impact of perfectionism and need for approval on the brief treatment of depression: The National Institute of Mental Health Treatment of Depression Collaborative Research Program revisited. *Journal of Consulting and Clinical Psychology, 63,* 125–132.

Blatt, S. J., Sanislow, C. A., Zuroff, D. C., & Pilkonis, P. A. (1996). Characteristics of effective therapists: Further analyses of data from the NIMH TDCRP. *Journal of Consulting and Clinical Psychology, 64,* 1276–1284.

Blatt, S. J., & Shichman, S. (1983). Two primary configurations of psychopathology. *Psychoanalysis and Contemporary Thought, 6,* 187–254.

Blatt, S. J., Wein, S. J., Chevron, E. S., & Quinlan, D. M. (1979). Parental representations and depression in normal young adults. *Journal of Abnormal Psychology, 88,* 388–397.

Blatt, S. J., & Zuroff, D. C. (1992). Interpersonal relatedness and self-definition: Two prototypes for depression. *Clinical Psychology Review, 12,* 527–562.

Blatt, S. J., Zuroff, D. C., Bondi, C. M., & Sanislow, C. A. (2000). Short and long-term effects of medication and psychotherapy in the brief treatment of depression: Further analyses of data from the NIMH TDCRP. *Psychotherapy Research, 10,* 215–234.

Blatt, S. J., Zuroff, D. C., Bondi, C. M., Sanislow, C., & Pilkonis, P. (1998). When and how perfectionism impedes the brief treatment of depression: Further analyses of the NIMH TDCRP. *Journal of Consulting and Clinical Psychology, 66,* 423–428.

Blatt, S. J., Zuroff, D. C., Quinlan, D. M., & Pilkonis, P. A. (1996). Interpersonal factors in brief treatment of depression: Further analyses of the National Institute of Mental Health Treatment of Depression Collaborative Research Program. *Journal of Consulting and Clinical Psychology, 64,* 162–171.

Bowlby, J. (1980). *Attachment and loss: Vol. 3. Loss: Sadness and depression.* New York: Basic.

Brandstater, J. (1998). Action perspectives on human development. In W. Damon & R. M. Lerner (Eds.), *Handbook of child psychology* (pp. 807–863). New York: Wiley.

Brown, G. W., & Harris, T. (1978). *Social origins of depression: A study of psychiatric disorders in women*. London: Tavistock.

Burns, D. D., & Nolen-Hoeksema, S. (1992). Therapeutic empathy and recovery from depression in cognitive-behavioral therapy: A structural equation model. *Journal of Consulting and Clinical Psychology, 60*, 441–449.

Buss, D. M. (1987). Selection, evocation, and manipulation. *Journal of Personality and Social Psychology, 53*, 1214–1221.

Butler, S. F., & Strupp, H. H. (1986). Specific and nonspecific factors in psychotherapy: A problematic paradigm for psychotherapy research. *Psychotherapy, 23*, 30–40.

Cane, D. B., Olinger, L. J., Gotlib, I. H., & Kuiper, N. A. (1986). Factor structure of the Dysfunctional Attitude Scale in a student population. *Journal of Clinical Psychology, 42*, 307–309.

Cohen, S., & Wills, T. A. (1985). Stress, social support, and the buffering hypothesis. *Psychological Bulletin, 98*, 310–357.

Coyne, J. C. (1976). Toward an interactional description of depression. *Psychiatry, 39*, 28–40.

Coyne, J. C. (1994). Self-report distress: Analog or ersatz depression? *Psychological Bulletin, 116*, 29–45.

Coyne, J. C., & Whiffen, V. E. (1995). Issues in personality as diathesis for depression: The case of sociotropy-dependency and autonomy self-criticism. *Psychological Bulletin, 118*, 358–378.

Cronbach, L. J. (1953). Correlation between persons as a research tool. In O. H. Mowrer (Ed.), *Psychotherapy: Theory and research* (pp. 376–389). New York: Ronald.

Cronbach, L. J. (1957). The two disciplines of scientific psychology. *American Psychologist, 12*, 671–684.

Cronbach, L. J. (1975). Beyond the two disciplines of scientific psychology. *American Psychologist, 30*, 116–127.

Cronbach L. J., & Gleser, G. G. (1953). Assessing similarity between profiles. *Psychological Bulletin, 50*, 456–474.

Dance, K. A., & Neufeld, R. W. J. (1988). Aptitude-treatment interaction research in the clinical setting: A review of attempts to dispel the "patient uniformity" myth. *Psychological Bulletin, 104*, 192–213.

Edwards, A. L., & Cronbach, L. J. (1952). Experimental design for research in psychotherapy. *Journal of Clinical Psychology, 8*, 51–59.

Elkin, I. (1994). The NIMH Treatment of Depression Collaborative Research Program: Where we began and where we are now. In A. E. Bergin & S. L. Garfield (Eds.), *Handbook of psychotherapy and behavior change* (4th ed., pp. 114–135). New York: Wiley.

Elkin, I., Parloff, M. B., Hadley, S. W., & Autry, J. H. (1985). NIMH Treatment of Depression Collaborative Research Program: Background and research plan. *Archives of General Psychiatry, 42*, 305–316.

Elkin, I., Shea, M. T., Watkins, J. T., Imber, S. D., Sotsky, S. M., Collins, J. F., Glass, D. R., Pilkonis, P. A., Leber, W. R., Dockerty, J. P., Fiester, S. J., & Parloff, M. B. (1989). NIMH Treatment of Depression Collaborative Research Program: General effectiveness of treatments. *Archives of General Psychiatry, 46*, 971–983.

Frank, J. D. (1979). The present status of outcome studies. *Journal of Consulting and Clinical Psychology, 47*, 310–316.

Frank, J. D. (1982). Therapeutic components shared by all psychotherapies. In J. H. Harvey & M. M. Parks (Eds.), *Psychotherapy research and behavior change* (Vol. 1, pp. 5–37). Washington, DC: American Psychological Association.

Freud, S. (1957). Civilization and its discontents. In J. Strachey (Ed.), *The standard edition of the complete psychological works of Sigmund Freud* (Vol. 21). London: Hogarth. (Original work published 1930)

Hammen, C. (1991). Generation of stress in the course of unipolar depression. *Journal of Abnormal Psychology, 100*, 555–561.

Hartley, D. E., & Strupp, H. H. (1983). The therapeutic alliance: Its relationship to outcome in brief psychotherapy. In J. Masling (Ed.), *Empirical studies of psychoanalytic theories, 1*, 1–27. Hillsdale, NJ: Erlbaum.

Hollon, S. D., DeRubeis, R. J., & Evans, M. D. (1996). Cognitive therapy in the treatment and prevention of depression. In P. M. Salkovskis et al. (Eds.), *Frontiers of cognitive therapy* (pp. 293–317). New York: Guilford.

Horvarth, A. O., & Symonds, B. D. (1991). Relation between working alliance and outcome in psychotherapy: A meta-analysis. *Journal of Counseling Psychology, 38*, 139–149.

Imber, S. D., Pilkonis, P. A., Sotsky, S. M., Elkin, I., Watkins, J. T., Collins, J. F., Shea, M. T., Leber, W. R., & Glass, D. R. (1990). Mode-specific effects among three treatments for depression. *Journal of Consulting and Clinical Psychology, 58*, 352–359.

Kazdin, A. E. (1986). Comparative outcome studies of psychotherapy: Methodological issues and strategies. *Journal of Consulting and Clinical Psychology, 54*, 95–105.

Krupnick, J. L., Sotsky, S. M., Simmens, S., Moyer, J., Elkin, I., Watkins, J., & Pilkonis, P. A. (1996). The role of the therapeutic alliance in psychotherapy and pharmacotherapy outcome: Findings in the NIMH Treatment of Depression Collaborative Research Program. *Journal of Consulting and Clinical Psychology, 64*, 532–539.

Lambert, M., Shapiro, D. A., & Bergin, A. E. (1986). The effectiveness of psychotherapy. In S. L. Garfield & A. E. Bergin (Eds.), *Handbook of psychotherapy and behavior change* (3rd ed.). New York: Wiley.

Lerner, R. M. (1983). Children and adolescents as producers of their own development. *Developmental Review, 2*, 342–370.

Loewald, H. W. (1962). Internalization, separation, mourning, and the superego. *Psychoanalytic Quarterly, 31*, 483–504.

Luborsky, L. (1975). Clinicians' judgements of mental health: Specimen case descriptions and forms for the Health Sickness Rating Scale. *Bulletin of the Menninger Clinic, 39*(5), 448–480.

Luborsky, L., Diguer, L. A., McLellan, A. T., & Woody, G. (1995, July). *The psychotherapist as a neglected variable: New studies of each therapist's benefits to their patients.* Paper presented at the 1995 meeting of the Society for Psychotherapy Research, Vancouver, British Columbia, Canada.

Luborsky, L., Diguer, L. A., Seligman, D. A., Rosenthal, R., Krause, E. D., Johnson, S., Halperin, G., Bishop, M., Berman, J. S., & Schweizer, E. (1999). The researcher's own therapy allegiances: A "wildcard" in comparisons of treatment efficacy. *Clinical Psychology: Science and Practice, 6*, 95–106.

McAdams, D. P. (1985). *Power, intimacy, and the life story: Personalogical inquiries into identity.* Homewood, IL: Dorsey.

McClelland, D. C. (1986). Some reflections on the two psychologies of love. *Journal of Personality, 54*, 334–353.

Mongrain, M. (1998). Parental representations and support-seeking behaviors related to dependency and self-criticism. *Journal of Personality, 66*, 151–173.

Mongrain, M., Vettese, L. C., Shuster, B., & Kendal, N. (1998). Perceptual biases, affect, and behavior in the relationships of dependents

and self-critics. *Journal of Personality and Social Psychology, 75*, 230–241.

Mongrain, M., & Zuroff, D. C. (1994). Ambivalence over emotional expression and negative life events: Mediators of depression in dependent and self-critical individuals. *Personality and Individual Differences, 16*, 447–458.

Monroe, S. M., & Simons, A. D. (1991). Diathesis stress theories in the context of life stress research: Implications for the depressive disorders. *Psychological Bulletin, 110*, 406–425.

Pennebaker, J. W. (1997). *Opening up: The healing power of expressing emotions.* New York: Guilford.

Peselow, E. C., Robins, C. J., Sanfilipo, M. P., Block, P., & Fieve, R. R. (1992). Sociotropy and autonomy: Relationship to antidepressant drug treatment response and endogenous-nonendogenous dichotomy. *Journal of Abnormal Psychology, 101*, 479–486.

Potthoff, J. G., Holahan, C. J., & Joiner, T. E., Jr. (1995). Reassurance seeking, stress generation and depressive symptoms: An integrative model. *Journal of Personality and Social Psychology, 68*, 664–670.

Priel, B., & Besser, A. (2001). Dependency and self-criticism among first-time mothers: The roles of global and specific support. *Journal of Social and Clinical Psychology, 19*, 437–450.

Priel, B., & Shahar, G. (2000). Dependency, self-criticism, social context and distress: Comparing moderating and mediating models. *Personality and Individual Differences, 28*, 515–525.

Rector, N., A., Bagby, R. M., Segal, Z. V., Joffe, R. T., & Levitt, A. (2000). Self-criticism and dependency in depressed patients treated with cognitive therapy or pharmacotherapy. *Cognitive Therapy and Research, 24*, 571–584.

Robins, C. J. (1995). Personality-event interaction models of depression. *European Journal of Personality, 9*, 367–378.

Robins, C. J., Ladd, J., Welkowitz, J., Blaney, P. H., Diaz, R., & Kutcher, G. (1994). The Personality Style Inventory: Preliminary validation studies of a new measure of sociotropy and autonomy. *Journal of Psychopathology and Behavioral Assessment, 16*, 277–300.

Robins, C. J., & Luten, A. G. (1991). Sociotropy and autonomy: Differential patterns of clinical presentation in unipolar depression. *Journal of Abnormal Psychology, 100*, 74–77.

Rogers, C. R. (1957). The necessary and sufficient conditions of therapeutic personality change. *Journal of Consulting Psychology, 21*, 95–103.

Rude, S. S., & Burnham, B. L. (1995). Connectedness and neediness: Factors of the DEQ and SAS dependency scales. *Cognitive Therapy and Research, 19,* 323–340.

Segal, Z. V., Shaw, B. F., & Vella, D. B. (1987, August). *Life stress and depression: A test of the congruence hypothesis for life event content and depressive subtypes.* Paper presented at the meeting of the American Psychological Association.

Shahar, G. (1999). *Interrelations between various measures of personality vulnerability to depression.* Unpublished manuscript, Ben-Gurion University of the Negev, Israel.

Shahar, G., Blatt, S. J., Zuroff, D. C., Krupnick, J. L., & Sotsky, S. M. (2001). *Disruptive effects of perfectionism on interpersonal relations in brief treatment for depression.* Manuscript submitted for publication.

Shahar, G., & Priel, B. (2001). *Self-criticism predicts a distress-related social context; Dependency predicts a mixed context: Further support of an action model of vulnerability.* Manuscript submitted for publication.

Shapiro, D. A., & Shapiro, D. (1982). Meta-analysis of comparative therapy outcome studies: A replication and refinement. *Psychological Bulletin, 92,* 581–604.

Shoham-Salomon, V., & Hannah, M. T. (1991). Client-treatment interactions in the study of differential change processes. *Journal of Consulting and Clinical Psychology, 59,* 217–225.

Shor, J., & Sanville, J. (1978). *Illusions in loving: A psychoanalytic approach to intimacy and autonomy.* Los Angeles: Double Helix.

Smith, B., & Sechrest, L. (1991). The treatment of Aptitude X Treatment interactions. *Journal of Consulting and Clinical Psychology, 59,* 233–244.

Smith, M. L., Glass, G. V., & Miller, T. I. (1980). *The benefits of psychotherapy.* Baltimore, MD: Johns Hopkins University Press.

Snow, R. E. (1991). Aptitude-treatment interactions as a framework for research on individual differences in psychotherapy. *Journal of Consulting and Clinical Psychology, 59,* 205–216.

Sotsky, S. M., Glass, D. R., Shea, M. T., Pilkonis, P. A., Collins, J. F., Elkin, I., Watkins, J. T., Imber, S. D., Leber, W. R., Moyer, J., & Ovilveri, M. E. (1991). Patient predictors of response to psychotherapy and pharmacotherapy: Findings in the NIMH Treatment of Depression Collaborative Research Program. *American Journal of Psychiatry, 148,* 997–1008.

Stiles, W. B., Shapiro, D. A., & Elliott, R. (1986). Are all psychotherapies equivalent? *American Psychologist, 41,* 161–180.

Strupp, H. H., & Binder, J. L. (1984). *Psychotherapy in a new key: A guide to time limited dynamic psychotherapy.* New York: Basic.

Urist, J. (1973). *The Rorschach test as a multi-dimensional measure of object relations.* Unpublished doctoral dissertation, University of Michigan.

Urist, J. (1980). Object relations. In R. H. Woody (Ed.), *Encyclopedia of clinical assessment* (Vol. 1, pp. 821–833). San Francisco: Jossey-Bass.

VandenBos, G. R., & Pino, C. D. (1980). Research on the outcome of psychotherapy. In G. R. VandenBos (Ed.), *Psychotherapy: Practice, research, policy* (pp. 23–69). Beverly Hills, CA: Sage.

Wallerstein, R. S. (1986). *Forty-two lives in treatment: A study of psychoanalysis and psychotherapy.* New York: Guilford.

Wampold, B. E., Mondin, G. W., Moody, M., Stich, F., Benson, K., & Ahn, H. (1997). A meta-analysis of outcome studies comparing bona fide psychotherapies: Empirically, "all must have prizes." *Psychological Bulletin, 122,* 203–215.

Weissman, A. N., & Beck, A. T. (1978, August-September). *Development and validation of the Dysfunctional Attitudes Scale: A preliminary investigation.* Paper presented at the 86th annual convention of the American Psychological Association, Toronto.

Wiggins, J. S. (1991). Agency and communion as conceptual coordinates for the understanding and measurement of interpersonal behavior. In W. W. Grove & D. Cicchetti (Eds.), *Thinking clearly about psychology: Vol. 2, Personality and psychotherapy* (pp. 89–113). Minneapolis: University of Minnesota Press.

Wortman, P. M. (1983). Meta-analysis: A validity perspective. *Annual Review of Psychology, 34,* 223–260.

Zettle, R. D., Haflich, J. L., & Reynolds, R. A. (1992). Responses to cognitive therapy as a function of treatment format and client personality dimensions. *Journal of Clinical Psychology, 48,* 787–797.

Zettle, R. D., & Herring, L. (1995). Treatment utility of the sociotropy/autonomy distinction: Implication for cognitive therapy. *Journal of Clinical Psychology, 51,* 281–289.

Zubin, J., & Spring, B. (1977). Vulnerability: A new view of schizophrenia. *Journal of Abnormal Psychology, 86,* 103–126.

Zuroff, D. C. (1992). New directions for cognitive models of depression. *Psychological Inquiry, 3,* 274–277.

Zuroff, D. C., Blatt, S. J., Krupnick, J. L., & Sotsky, S. M. (2001). *Vicissitudes of life after short-term treatment of depression: Stress reactivity and its moderators.* Manuscript submitted for publication.

Zuroff, D. C., Blatt, S. J., Sotsky, S. M., Krupnick, J. L., Martin, D. J., Sanislow, C. A., & Simmens, S. (2000). Relation of therapeutic alliance and perfectionism to outcome in brief outpatient treatment of depression. *Journal of Consulting and Clinical Psychology, 68,* 114–124.

Zuroff, D. C., & de Lorimer, S. (1989). Ideal and actual romantic partners of women varying in dependency and self-criticism. *Journal of Personality, 57,* 825–846.

Zuroff, D. C., & Duncan, N. (1999). Self-criticism and conflict resolution in romantic couples. *Canadian Journal of Behavioral Science, 31,* 137–149.

Zuroff, D. C., & Fitzpatrick, D. (1995). Depressive personality styles: Implications for adult attachment. *Personality and Individual Differences, 18,* 253–265.

Zuroff, D. C., Quinlan, D. M., & Blatt, S. J. (1990). Psychometric properties of the Depressive Experiences Questionnaire in a college population. *Journal of Personality Assessment, 55,* 65–72.

18

Expectations and Preferences

Diane B. Arnkoff
Carol R. Glass
Stephanie J. Shapiro

In order for psychotherapy to be effective, the client must engage actively in the process. It is incumbent on researchers to address the factors that benefit or impede the client from participating in therapy. "Rather than argue over whether or not 'therapy works,' we could address ourselves to the question of whether or not 'the client works'!" (Bergin & Garfield, 1994, p. 825).

To that end, this chapter reviews the empirical evidence on attributes of clients prior to psychotherapy, specifically, their expectations and preferences about therapy. Client expectations and preferences have been thought by many authors to influence the client's willingness to engage in and be influenced by the therapist and the process of therapy. Publications on this topic originated in the 1950s, and the topic continues to be discussed to the present day. Client expectations can be either about the outcome of therapy or about the roles clients or their therapists will play in the process. Preferences can be for specific roles, for a certain type of psychotherapy, or for a therapist with specific demographic characteristics. The research linking expectations and preferences with outcome of therapy will be reviewed, and implications for practice will be discussed.

The studies reviewed here were all conducted on actual psychotherapy, although some examined expectations or their disconfirmation after only one session. Excluded from this review are studies that were analogues of therapy, that is, studies using introductory psychology students that involved hypothetical descriptions of therapy, because of questionable ecological validity. Also excluded are studies in which expectations were manipulated or roles were experimentally induced.

DEFINITIONS

Outcome Expectations

The general term *client expectancy* has been used to refer to client expectancy for therapeutic gain as well as to expectations clients may have about psychotherapy procedures, the therapist's role, and the length of therapy (Garfield, 1994). Client expectations for psychotherapy outcome, which Goldstein (1962) calls "patient prognostic expectancies," are the expectations that therapy will lead to change. These expectations for receiving help have also been referred to as "expectancy traits," which should be distinguished from "expectancy states" in which participants are randomly assigned to groups receiving experimental instructions or treatment rationales intended to instill either high or low expectations of change (Garfield, 1994).

The focus of this research is thus on positive outcome expectancies for the efficacy of the *therapy*, not on the therapeutic effectiveness or helpfulness of the *therapist*. It is also important to note that clients' beliefs concerning the helpfulness of therapy are not the same as their "motivation for treatment," which might include their desire to change, as well as their willingness to cooperate, keep appointments, and work between sessions. Although these constructs could be highly related, it is conceivable that clients could be distressed and highly motivated to receive help, yet have low expectations or faith that psychotherapy could help them (Rosenthal & Frank, 1956).

Mobilization of hope, as J. D. Frank (1973) argues, plays an important role in many forms of healing. Outcome expectations are thus one of the key nonspecific or common treatment factors that are thought to be basic processes operating in all approaches to psychotherapy, perhaps accounting for findings showing many different approaches to be equally effective (J. D. Frank, Gliedman, Imber, Stone, & Nash, 1959; Garfield, 1981) and for change observed as a result of attention placebos (Kazdin & Wilcoxon, 1976; Rosenthal & Frank, 1956).

The importance of outcome expectations has been a topic of interest to therapists from a range of theoretical orientations. For example, J. D. Frank (1973) quotes Freud (1953, p. 289) as saying that "expectation colored by hope and faith is an effective force with which we have to reckon . . . in *all* our attempts at treatment and cure." One of the first studies to find a relationship between anticipation of outcome and therapy change was conducted by a student of Carl Rogers with outpatients receiving client-centered therapy (Lipkin, 1954). In the 1970s, behavior therapists focused on the role of expectations of help as a psychological placebo effect. They urged that the effectiveness of specific techniques such as systematic desensitization be evaluated in comparison to control groups of equal credibility in order to evaluate the extent to which therapeutic effects are due to a specific therapy ingredient above and beyond nonspecific treatment effects based on expectations alone (Kazdin & Wilcoxon, 1976).

Role Expectations

Role expectations are defined as patterns of behavior viewed as appropriate or expected of a person who occupies a particular position. In the case of psychotherapy, clients have role expectations both of themselves and of the therapist (Berzins, 1977; Goldstein, 1962; Richert, 1983).

Goldstein (1962) indicates that clients expect their therapists to play a number of different roles, including parent, temporary respite, ideal companion, and authority figure. He also notes that mutual interdependence and reciprocity are important concepts in role expectations. Apfelbaum (1958) conducted a cluster analysis of expected therapist roles and found three clusters: nurturant (guide, giving, protecting), model (diplomatic, permissive listener but not protective), and critic (analytical, demanding responsibility). Rickers-Ovsiankina, Geller, Berzins, and Rogers (1971) conceptualized Apfelbaum's types on a developmental continuum, from more dependent (nurturant) to less dependent (model). They added a fourth dimension, cooperative, which comes about only toward the end of treatment. Another typology of expected roles is that of Heine and Trosman (1960), who described the guidance model and the collaboration model. Tinsley, Workman, and Kass's (1980) Expectations about Counseling measure has four empirically derived factors: personal commitment (the client role); facilitative conditions (genuineness, trustworthiness, and acceptance on the counselor's part); counselor expertise (the counselor as directive, empathic, and expert); and nurturance from the counselor.

The question arises as to how role expectations are thought to make a difference in outcome. Orlinsky, Grawe, and Parks (1994) state that the effect of the therapist's interventions depends critically on the client's receptiveness to them. Goldstein (1962) hypothesizes that discrepancies between client and therapist on expected roles will hurt the therapeutic relationship, and that in successful therapy, expectations will converge over time. Although many studies have simply assessed expectations rather than confirmation or disconfirmation of expectations, it is the clash or congruence of expectations between client and therapist, leading to compatible or incompatible therapy behavior, that is thought to be the key (Garfield, 1971).

Tracey and Dundon (1988) postulate several types of incongruence of expectations, which are usually not distinguished: client expectations of the therapist compared with actual therapist behavior (a type frequently assessed in the literature); client expectations compared with therapist expectations for therapist behavior (another common focus in the literature); client expectations compared with therapist expectations for client behavior; client expectations compared with the client's actual behavior (the topic of their study); and therapist expectations of client behavior compared with actual client behavior. It has been assumed that any of these types of incongruence leads to poor outcome.

The hypothesized relationship between disconfirmations of expectations and outcome has also varied in the literature (Tracey & Dundon, 1988). A typical assumption is that there is a linear relationship between disconfirmation and outcome, that is, the less clients and therapists act in accord with clients' expectations, the worse the outcome. A second type of possible relationship is curvilinear, that is, that there is an optimum concordance, and discrepancy either in the direction of disconfirmation or of a greater concordance than the client expects is associated with a poorer outcome. The final type of relationship of disconfirmation and outcome was described by Duckro, Beal, and George (1979) as bidirectional: a bad outcome is predicted if the lack of congruence is in the undesired direction, but a better outcome is predicted if the lack of congruence is in the preferred direction.

Preferences

The definition of client preferences is similar to that of expectations, except that the behavior or attribute of the therapist or therapy is valued or desired, as opposed to expected (Berzins, 1977; Richert, 1983). Van Audenhove and Vertommen (2000) define a mismatch between a client's preferences and what is possible in therapy as a *discrepancy* (e.g., a misconception about what goes on in a particular type of treatment). Alterna-

tively, they use the term *incongruence* to refer to a mismatch between what the client wants or prefers and what the therapist thinks is preferable.

Far less attention has been paid in the literature to preferences than to expectations. At least three types of preferences, however, have been identified: role preferences, preferences for type of psychotherapy (psychotherapy vs. medication, or for one type of psychotherapy over another), and preferences for demographic features of the therapist (e.g., gender, race, ethnicity, age, or sexual orientation). Several studies have found that role preferences differ from expectations (Hoffman, 1982; Rawlings, 1986; Tracey & Dundon, 1988). For example, Tracey and Dundon found that clients anticipated receiving less advice than they preferred to get. Both Hoffman and Rawlings found that expectations and preferences did become more congruent over time.

CLINICAL EXAMPLES

Outcome Expectations

The construct of expectancy for therapeutic gain can be positive (clients' faith that therapy will be of help or predicting satisfaction with results of treatment), ambivalent (conflicting feelings as to how therapy will turn out or uncertain as to whether or not they will be satisfied with the end results), or negative (lack of confidence or anticipating displeasure with results of experience in treatment) (Lipkin, 1954).

A number of studies before 1975 asked clients prior to therapy to complete symptom questionnaires twice, once as they presently felt and again as they expected to feel after therapy, where expectancy was measured by the difference between these ratings. More recently, clients have been directly asked to rate their faith in or optimism about the treatment, expectation of improvement, or anticipated helpfulness of psychotherapy on Likert-type scales, with items such as: "I expect to get: a lot worse . . . completely better" (Rizvi, Reynolds, Comtois, & Linehan, 2000); "I think I'll feel better as a result of my group: very false . . . very true" (Lightsey, 1997); and

"The treatment . . . is likely to: help me a great deal . . . make no difference . . . make me worse" (Lax, Basoglu, & Marks, 1992). In one case, how well clients expected to do was assessed by multiplying the number of pounds they expected to lose by a confidence rating associated with that expectation (Bradley, Poser, & Johnson, 1980).

Borkovec and Nau (1972) pioneered the use of a brief questionnaire to assess whether the rationales of placebo therapies generated equivalent ratings of credibility and expectancy for improvement (on 10-point Likert scales) as did two behavioral interventions for public-speaking anxiety. They asked undergraduates, "How confident would you be that this treatment would be successful in eliminating fear of speaking before a group?" (p. 258), along with three questions more related to perceived credibility of treatment. Until recently, researchers using this and similar questionnaires have been more interested in establishing treatment equivalency than in examining the relationship between expectations and therapy outcome. If credibility and expectancy items are summed to yield a total score, which is then related to treatment outcome, it should be noted that the measure no longer provides a "pure" assessment of expectancy for therapeutic gain. Holt and Heimberg's (1990) Reaction to Treatment Questionnaire (RTQ) has been used in several recent studies. This measure consists of the four Borkovec and Nau questions (yielding a treatment "credibility" score) and nine items assessing clients' confidence that the treatment would eliminate anxiety in specific social situations (a situationally based "confidence" or outcome expectancy score).

Role Expectations

In an early study, Garfield and Wolpin (1963) gave a questionnaire to clinic clients and found that 27% thought that most of the time would be taken up with the patient's early life, and 47% with their life just before therapy. Half thought that the most important thing the therapist does is to help the patient understand him or herself better, but 33% thought that advice was most important. Most preferred advice to understanding themselves. Forty percent thought the therapist could read their mind at least moderately. "Patients appear to be seeking a sincere, understanding, sympathetic, interested and competent person who would be unlikely to engage in criticism, anger or ridicule. They also want someone who will not be pessimistic about them, nor turn them away, but who will at the same time not deny that the patient has difficulties" (p. 360). Tinsley, Bowman, and Barich (1993, p. 50) surveyed counseling psychologists about unrealistic client expectations, and reported that many clients were seen as having a "naive, wishful, or magical view of counseling."

In another early study, Kamin and Caughlan (1963) interviewed former Veterans Administration clinic clients about their experiences in therapy. Negative quotes from patients included: "There were long periods when we didn't talk at all. I didn't know what he was aiming at, he didn't ever explain." "If I go to an expert, I expect him to tell me what he knows. This business of saying 'hm' is strictly out." "I thought they'd give me tests, talk to me a while, arrive at a diagnosis, and then write the prescription." "He'd just sit and stare at me and I'd wonder what he was thinking" (p. 665). Positive quotes from the former clients included: "She did not keep the aura of superiority around her—seemed to listen with more personal interest." "I could talk to him and he could understand me." "He was a real nice man. It was comfortable to talk to him" (p. 665). Kamin and Caughlan concluded that "almost 75% entered therapy with no clear concepts of its modus operandi. They understood neither their own role, nor that of the therapist . . . repeatedly commented that therapists were too passive, disinterested, cold, incomprehensible, enigmatic, even though polite, patient, and probably well meaning. . . . The therapists are analytically oriented, but the patients are not" (p. 666).

In a more recent publication that takes theoretical orientation into account, Walborn (1996) gives examples of incongruent expectations: "Some believe that the therapist is going to tell them what is wrong with them and will fix them, as in the physician/patient relationship that they are used to. Some clients seeing a cognitive therapist may expect to lay on a couch and to talk of childhood memories. Some clients going to see a psychodynamic or experiential therapist may be distraught at the lack of input from the therapist" (p. 122).

Studies addressing role expectations have used interviews or a large variety of questionnaires. Two frequently used measures with adequate psychometric properties are Berzins's (1971) Psychotherapy Expectancy Inventory—Revised, which was devised on clients, and Tinsley and colleagues' (1980) Expectations about Counseling questionnaire, which was devised on students. Disconfirmation of expectations has been assessed in a variety of ways: client expectations assessed before therapy compared with perceptions after a variable number of sessions; comparison of expectations with what is assumed to be offered; comparison of expectations with what therapists say they do; and post-therapy interviews on what clients remember expecting and what they remember getting. The last strategy is likely to be particularly suspect.

Preferences

Researchers have examined preferences for type of therapy by comparing the outcome of clients who received their preferred method with the outcome of clients who received a treatment other than the one they preferred. Preferences are typically measured in three ways: through factor-based questionnaires, pretherapy ratings of descriptions of various treatments, and ratings of treatment following participation in an actual session.

While most researchers developed their own questionnaires to measure client preferences, Hardy, Barkham, Shapiro, Reynolds, and Rees (1995) used a scale from a pre-existing instrument to assess treatment principle credibility, which they define as beliefs about the treatment of psychological problems and attitudes toward different treatment methods. The Opinions about Psychological Problems Questionnaire (Pistrang & Barker, 1992) asks clients to rate their agreement (ranging from "disagree strongly" to "agree strongly") with statements determined to correspond to factors representing either cognitive-behavioral or psychodynamic-interpersonal therapy methods. Examples of these items include: "A good way to help me with my problems would be learning to understand the childhood origins of the problem" and "A good way to help me with my problems would be learning to replace negative thoughts with positive ones." Elkin and colleagues (1999) asked clients to rate, on a Likert scale, how helpful each of 11 aspects of treatment would be in treating their depression. The 11 items, including "learning more realistic attitudes about myself and the world" and "learning how to resolve family conflicts," corresponded to a priori scales for cognitive-behavioral therapy, interpersonal therapy, or medication.

Three studies presented descriptions of various theoretical orientations and asked clients to rate their preferences. Clients in Devine and Fernald's (1973) study watched videotaped demonstrations of therapeutic techniques and rated how well they liked each of them. Van Dyck and Spinhoven (1997) gave participants a written description of in vivo exposure therapy with and without hypnosis and had them rate the strength of their preferences. Rather than describing specific treatment modalities, Atkinson, Worthington, Dana, and Good (1991) presented written descriptions of thinking-, feeling-, and action-oriented therapies, and asked clients to rank their preferences from highest to lowest. In contrast, one study assessed preferences after actual sessions. Addis and Jacobson (1996) asked participants at the end of each session how closely the session matched what they believed to be helpful about therapy.

RESEARCH REVIEW

Outcome Expectations

The beginnings of research on client outcome expectations can be traced in part to a pivotal article by Rosenthal and Frank (1956), in which they reviewed research on drug placebo effects and its implications for psychotherapy evaluation. These authors concluded that "patients entering psychotherapy have various degrees of belief in its efficacy, and this may be an important factor in the results of therapy, but this has not been studied, to our knowledge" (p. 296).

Our review of the subsequent research on the relationship between client expectations of change and therapy outcome is organized around the type of outcome measures used. As shown in table 18.1, a total of 24 studies were categorized as

Table 18.1. Relationships Between Outcome Expectations and Psychotherapy Outcome

Outcome Measure	Significant Relationship	Mixed Findings	No Relationship
Continuation in psychotherapy		Gunzberger et al. (1985)	Goldstein (1960b); Safren et al. (1997)
Client self-report	Friedman (1963); Goldstein & Shipman (1961); Heine (1962); Lipkin (1954); Maki et al. (2000); Martin et al. (1977); Safren et al. (1997); Tollinton (1973); Uhlenhuth & Duncan (1968)	Chambless et al. (1997); Hardy et al. (1995); Keijsers et al. (1994); Kim et al. (2000); Lax et al. (1992); Morrison & Shapiro (1987)	Goldstein (1960b); Heine & Trosman (1960); Lightsey (1997); Piper & Wogan (1970)
Behavior	Bradley et al. (1980)		Chambless et al. (1997)
Therapist report			Brady et al. (1960)
Independent clinician rating	Martin et al. (1977); Safren et al. (1997)		
Therapeutic alliance	Rizvi et al. (2000)		
Composite	Mathews et al. (1976)		
Total number of studies	$N = 12$	$N = 7$	$N = 7$

Note: A study is counted only once in a column.

finding either a significant relationship between expectations and outcome (12 studies), mixed findings (7 studies), or no relationship (7 studies). (The subtotals sum to greater than the number of studies reviewed because there were two studies in which findings varied across types of assessment.) Most of the studies with mixed findings reflect the more recent trend toward multiple self-report measures of outcome, so that it was possible to find a relationship with one outcome variable but not another.

An interesting historical trend was noted. Seven of the studies were published between 1956 and 1963, only eight in the 25 years from 1965 to 1989, and nine since that time (1990 to 2000). Thus, Garfield's (1994, p. 216) observation that "research interest in expectancies has peaked and investigations of this type have diminished" may have been accurate when he reviewed the literature in the early 1990s, but is no longer true.

Continuance in psychotherapy. Few studies have assessed the relationship between client expectations and premature termination or duration of psychotherapy. Of those that have, the box score shows that support is lacking. Although Gunzberger, Henggeler, and Watson (1985) found expectation ratings made at the end of the first session predicted duration of treatment, pretherapy ratings did not. Two other studies failed to find a significant relationship.

Client self-report. Fairly strong support has been obtained in nine studies for the significant relationship between expectations and self-report measures of outcome, although it should be noted that a nearly equal number of studies have yielded mixed ($n = 6$) or no relationships ($n = 4$).

Behavior. It is unfortunate that so few studies have used outcome measures of clients' behavior change. We can draw no firm conclusions from those that have, since one found a highly significant relationship between outcome expectations and actual weight loss, while another found no relationship between credibility/expectancy ratings and change on observer ratings of anxiety and skill.

Therapist report. The one study that used therapist reports of outcome did not find a significant relationship between expectations and outcome.

However, it should be noted that expectations were assessed using projective measures of unknown validity.

Clinician rating. The most consistent support for the relationship between expectations and outcome comes from two studies that found significant correlations between expected improvement and change on independent clinicians' ratings of adjustment or severity.

Therapeutic alliance. Only one recent study has touched on the relationship between expectancies and the therapeutic alliance, but results are promising. Client expectancies were the best predictor of alliance after the first session, over and above therapist variables, client adjustment, and symptoms.

Composite. One study, which used a composite treatment outcome score comprised of seven outcome measures representing self-report, behavioral, therapist ratings, and assessor's ratings, found that expectancy was a significant predictor of outcome.

Indirect support. Indirect evidence for the importance of outcome expectations often is cited from studies and meta-analyses that examine change in nontreated controls. For example, significant relationships between expected and perceived improvement were found in control group patients awaiting therapy (who had received only an intake interview and testing). Controls also improved to the same extent as patients undergoing group and individual psychotherapy, leading to the conclusion that symptomatic change could be produced by expectancies and nonspecific professional contact (Goldstein, 1960a).

Placebo treatments can be seen as producing their effects by a combination of factors including client expectancy, suggestion, and therapist attention (Bootzin & Lick, 1979). Kirsch (1990) thus concluded that findings from meta-analyses of studies with actual clients (analogue studies excluded) show that expectancy can account for at least half of the effectiveness of psychotherapy. For example, Andrews and Harvey (1981) found that the effect size for placebo therapies was .55 (less than psychodynamic and behavioral and cognitive-behavioral therapy, but greater than client-centered therapy and counseling), whereas D. A. Shapiro and Shapiro (1982) found a placebo treatment effect size of .71 (greater than psychodynamic and humanistic approaches, but less than behavioral or cognitive therapies).

Role Expectations

In general, studies of this nature have addressed either expectations directly related to an outcome measure or expectation disconfirmation, although a few have investigated both. Table 18.2 shows the citations and box score results for expectation-to-outcome analyses and disconfirmation-to-outcome analyses combined; the box score for each separately was quite similar. A total of 37 studies were identified: 21 with significant positive relationships, 12 with mixed support, and 8 showing no relationship to outcome. In the following, we discuss the adequacy of measurement of expectations. Poor measurement as defined here includes anecdotal report or interview with no quantification or consensus analysis of the qualitative data. Measurements with unknown psychometric qualities generally include studies in which a measure of expectations was created for the study, but no psychometric data were reported. Studies with adequate measurement generally used either Berzins's (1971) Psychotherapy Expectancy Inventory—Revised or Tinsley and colleagues' (1980) Expectations about Counseling questionnaire.

Continuation. Most studies, particularly the older ones, have used continuation in therapy vs. premature termination as the outcome measure. The findings appear to be positive for the relationship between expectations (or disconfirmation) and psychotherapy outcome, although 10 with positive results were classified as using poor measurement, and 1 that used poor measurement had mixed results. Of the studies that had measures with either unknown or adequate psychometrics, six found positive results, two had mixed results, and five showed no relationship. It tended to be the older studies that reported significant findings but had poor measurement. Further, many of the earlier studies dealt with unrealistic expectations of lower-class clients leading to dropout from psychodynamic therapy (for example, Baum & Felzer, 1964). A. Frank, Eisenthal, and Lazare (1978) argue that this literature is

Table 18.2. Relationships Between Role Expectations and Psychotherapy Outcome

Outcome Measure	Significant Relationship	Mixed Findings	No Relationship
Continuation in psychotherapy	Baum & Felzer (1964); Borghi (1968); Clemes & D'Andrea (1965); Day & Reznikoff (1980); Fiester (1977); Freedman et al. (1958); Hankoff et al. (1960); Heine & Trosman (1960); Kamin & Caughlan (1963); Overall & Aronson (1963); Rabin et al. (1985); Rawlings (1986); Richardson & Cohen (1968); Rogers (1960); Yalom (1966)	Atlas (1993); Farley et al. (1975); Horenstein & Houston (1976)	Brennan (1990); Hardin et al. (1988); Heppner & Heesacker (1983); Hoffman (1982); Silverberg (1982)
Client self-report	Heine (1962); Isard & Sherwood (1964); Jacobs et al. (1972); Kamin & Caughlan (1963); Schonfield et al. (1969)	Brennan (1990); Gaston et al. (1989); Heppner & Heesacker (1983); Martin et al. (1976); Severinsen (1966); Silverberg (1982)	Rosen & Wish (1980); Volsky et al. (1965)
Therapist report	Jacobs et al. (1972); Kamin & Caughlan (1963); Schonfield et al. (1969)		Silverberg (1982)
Independent clinician rating	Jacobs et al. (1972); Kamin & Caughlan (1963)	Gaston et al. (1989)	Otto & Moos (1974); Silverberg (1982)
Therapeutic alliance		Al-Darmaki & Kivlighan (1993); Pattison (1992); Tokar et al. (1996)	Brennan (1990)
Total number of studies	$N = 19$	$N = 12$	$N = 8$

Note: A study is counted only once in a column.

problematic because it confounded class and chronicity, because there may be fewer class differences in readiness for psychotherapy than in the past (also see Lorion, 1978), and because different, more flexible approaches to therapy make the previous literature less applicable.

Client self-report. The table shows five studies significantly relating client self-report of symptoms or satisfaction with either expectations or disconfirmation of expectations, six with mixed results, and two finding no relationship. Two of the significant-relationship studies had poor measurement, making conclusions equivocal.

Therapist report and clinician ratings. Few studies had outcome measures completed by therapists; three (one with poor measurement) found significant results, and one found no relationship. Similarly, few studies incorporated independent clinician ratings. Two (one with poor measurement) found significant results linking expectations or disconfirmation of expectations with outcome, one had mixed results, and two found no relationship.

Therapeutic alliance. Alliance as an outcome measure is relatively recent in this literature, and all studies used measures of role expectations with known psychometric properties. Three had mixed results, and one found no relationship.

Most of the studies on role expectations examined a linear relationship between expectations and outcome. Two (Horenstein & Houston, 1976; Severinsen, 1966) found that those who continued in therapy were in the middle on confirmation of expectations, in support of the curvilinear model (Duckro et al., 1979). To a limited extent, Tracey and Dundon (1988) found support for the bidirectional model, namely, that only disconfirmation in the nonpreferred direction is a negative predictor for outcome.

Two studies have examined expectations for the duration of therapy. Hochberg (1986) found

that expectations for duration were unrelated to actual duration. However, Pekarik and Wierzbicki (1986) found that the correlation between the client's expected number of sessions and the actual number was significant, but not strongly so.

Preferences

Preferences for role. Table 18.3 shows findings for the relationship between role preferences and psychotherapy outcome. Only four studies have been conducted, and three do *not* support the hypothesis that preferences are significantly related to outcome.

Table 18.3. Preferences Related to Psychotherapy Outcome

Outcome Measure	Significant Relationship	Mixed Relationship	No Relationship
Role Preferences			
Client self-report			Gladstein (1969); Goin et al. (1965); Pohlman (1964)
Therapist report			Pohlman (1964)
Independent clinician rating			Pohlman (1964)
Composite	Tracey & Dundon (1988)		
Total number of studies	$N = 1$		$N = 3$
Preferences for Type of Therapy			
Continuation in psychotherapy	Elkin et al. (1999)		Bakker et al. (2000); Carlson (1981)
Self-report	Chilvers et al. (2001)	Addis & Jacobson (1996); Hardy et al. (1995)	Atkinson et al. (1991); Bakker et al. (2000); Carlson (1981); Elkin et al. (1999); van Dyck & Spinhoven (1997); Wallach (1988)
Behavior		Devine & Fernald (1973)	van Dyck & Spinhoven (1997); Wallach (1988)
Therapist report			Bakker et al. (2000)
Independent clinician rating			Chilvers et al. (2001); van Dyck & Spinhoven (1997)
Therapeutic alliance		Elkin et al. (1999)	
Total number of studies	$N = 2$	$N = 4$	$N = 7$

Note: A study is counted only once in a column.

Preferences for type of therapy. The bottom of table 18.3 summarizes the results of 10 studies linking type of therapy preferences with therapy outcome. Of the three studies that examined continuation in therapy, two found no relationship and one found a significant relationship between preference and continuation. In the one significant finding, Elkin and colleagues (1999) investigated the match between clients' preference for medication or psychotherapy (grouping together cognitive-behavior therapy and interpersonal therapy) and found that fewer clients who were matched to their preferred treatment dropped out.

Among studies investigating the relationship between preference for treatment and client self-reported outcome, one recent study (Chilvers et al., 2001) found that depressed clients assigned to therapy after expressing a preference for it had a better self-reported outcome than did those who were randomized to receive therapy. Six studies, however, found no significant relationship, while two found mixed results. Similarly, two of three studies in which behavior change was a measure of outcome found no relationship between match to preferred treatment and outcome, and one found mixed results.

Only one study used therapist report as an outcome measure. It found no relationship with match to preferred treatment. The same was true for the two studies that employed independent clinician ratings to assess outcome. Finally, Elkin and colleagues (1999) assessed the relationship between match to preferred treatment and the therapeutic alliance. Alliance ratings were significantly higher for clients who received their preference of psychotherapy or medication. However, for the participants who preferred one of the psychotherapy conditions and were matched or mismatched with their specific choice of type of psychotherapy, the match was not related to client-rated alliance scores.

Preference for therapist demographic variables. A number of studies have examined preferences of clients from different cultural backgrounds for the racial/ethnic characteristics of their therapists (for reviews, see Atkinson, 1983, 1987; Harrison, 1975; Sue & Lam, 2002). There is also a body of literature that examines the relationship between race/ethnicity and counseling outcome, without

consideration of client preferences (for a review, see Atkinson, 1983). Surprisingly, however, we could find no studies that examined whether the confirmation or disconfirmation of clients' preferences for race/ethnicity of the therapist was related to psychotherapy outcome.

Many studies have examined male and female clients' preferences for the gender of their therapist (e.g., Fuller, 1964; Pikus & Heavey, 1996). Likewise, there is a body of literature that has studied client-therapist gender matching versus mismatching, and its relationship to outcome (for example, Jones & Zoppel, 1982; Orlinsky & Howard, 1980; Sue & Lam, 2002). However, we identified only one study that actually examined the relationship between preference for therapist gender and psychotherapy outcome. Zlotnick, Elkin, and Shea (1998) asked male and female depressed clients whether they believed a male or female therapist would be most helpful to them. The results indicated that clients matched with a therapist of their preferred gender did not significantly differ from those mismatched in either dropout rates or outcome. Moreover, there were no differences on a client-rated measure of counselor empathy between the matched and mismatched groups.

MEDIATORS AND MODERATORS

Outcome Expectations

Client expectations themselves are often considered to be a mediating variable through which psychotherapy leads to change, but in this section we will consider mediators and moderators of the expectation-outcome relationship. Based on research demonstrating a relationship between expectations and psychotherapy outcome, many reviews and studies reach conclusions that expectancy of therapeutic gain plays a role in influencing the outcome of psychotherapy. Kirsch (1990, p. 104), for example, concludes that "believing that one will feel better is enough to make one feel better." Although clinically appealing, this conclusion is premature in that such causal relationships *cannot* be demonstrated on the basis of correlational research. As Wilkins (1973) points out, you may "expect" it will rain when you see lightning and dark clouds, and yet such an expectation is nothing more than a meteorological prediction, with no causal effect on the weather. Although low expectancies could cause clients to improve less, they might also represent an accurate prediction that this treatment would not work for them, or it could be the case that both low expectancy and poor outcome are caused by some unknown third variable (Chambless, Tran, & Glass, 1997). Self-reported expectancies and outcomes may both even be affected by demand characteristics (Wilkins, 1978). Thus, we agree with Wilkins (1979, p. 843) that "whether client expectancies of gain cause any client gain remains a philosophical and empirical question."

If such a causal link does exist, the mechanisms by which expectations could mediate change are still largely unknown (Lick & Bootzin, 1975). Certainly clients need a sense of hope that the therapy or therapist can help in order to decide to seek therapy to begin with, as well as to remain in treatment (J. D. Frank, 1974). Thurer and Hursh (1981) conclude that client expectations of change may be more associated with the decision to initially get involved in therapy and have less direct influence on therapeutic outcome.

Additionally, positive expectations may decrease feelings of hopelessness and increase confidence, relief, and hope, which could have an immediate effect on client improvement (Kirsch, 1990; Murray & Jacobson, 1978). As J. D. Frank (1973, p. 136) noted, "favorable expectations generate feelings of optimism, energy, and well-being and may actually promote healing." With regard to behavior change, expectation of therapeutic benefit may produce change by motivating anxious clients to pay more attention to and comply with treatment procedures, and thus expose themselves more extensively to phobic stimuli in the natural environment (Bootzin & Lick, 1979; Lick & Bootzin, 1975).

Along with the effect of expectations held by clients prior to the first session, the rationales for treatment given by the therapist early in therapy may be reassuring, lead clients to feel that their problem is not unique and that there is a credible and effective treatment available (Garfield, 1981), and instill confidence that some change will be experienced. Further, a therapist who conveys the impression in the first few sessions that therapy will lead to improvement may increase clients' expectations that they will get better (Kirsch, 1990). At least 70% of successful clients rate their therapist's confidence that they would improve as either very or extremely important, along with their encouragement and reassurance (Garfield, 1981).

The relationship between initial expectations and outcome may be moderated by "personality difficulties" (Tollinton, 1973). Tollinton found that expectations of improvement were not as predictive of actual improvement after neuroticism scores were taken into account. Generalized self-efficacy (willingness to initiate and stick with a task in the face of adversity) is another variable found to moderate the relationship between expectations and outcome (Lightsey, 1997).

J. D. Frank (1974) has proposed that if patient and therapist expectations affect the duration and outcome of treatment, outcomes should be improved if expectations are congruent. In fact, Lennard and Bernstein (1960) report that two clients receiving psychoanalytically oriented therapy who expected to make some progress within the first few weeks of therapy, but whose therapists did not expect progress until after the fourth month, dropped out after the third and seventh sessions. However, two clients who expected progress to take place later than thought by their therapists remained in treatment for over a year and a half. This would suggest that, in addition to outcome expectation congruence, mutual expectations for when progress will take place may be important. In an early study, although no relationship was found between duration of therapy and patient expectation of improvement, the combined patient and therapist expectations of improvement were related to treatment duration (Goldstein, 1960b). Thus, therapist expectancies may need to be considered in order to fully explain the relationship between outcome and client expectations.

Role Expectations

Walborn (1996) hypothesizes that socializing the client operates as a mediating variable. The behavior of the therapist may blunt the impact of expectations and preferences that were held when the client entered therapy. The converse of this argument comes from Jacobs, Muller, Anderson, and Skinner (1972), who speculate that clients' unrealistic expectations lead to behavior to which therapists react negatively.

Little research has been conducted on the moderating effect of the client receiving therapy from different schools of psychotherapy. Gaston, Marmar, Gallagher, and Thompson (1989) did one of the few studies, dealing with three psychotherapies for depression in the elderly. They found that results depended on the type of therapy. For brief dynamic therapy, they did not find that expectations of insight and support were related to outcome. They argue that perhaps the therapists were able to address unrealistic expectations, or that clients experienced what was offered and accepted it. They suggest investigating therapist behavior that addresses expectations during therapy. For cognitive therapy, however, expectations of behavioral and cognitive changes were related to outcome. There was a positive relationship between medication and environmental expectations and interpersonal functioning for behavior therapy, but expectations of this type negatively related to interpersonal outcome for dynamic therapy. They note that these findings are consistent with the content of these treatments.

The majority of this literature begins with the assumption that expectations and preferences exert an important influence and that the therapist offers a static treatment that does not take these into account. Schonfield, Stone, Hoehn-Saric, Imber, and Pande (1969) were among the few to investigate whether both client and therapist adjust to each other. They found that it was not simply that clients moved in their expectations toward what the therapist expected; in fact, there was no difference between clients and therapists in their contribution to convergence. Thus, improvement related to an agreement on methods, and the conclusion was that therapists adjust to clients as well as vice versa (that is, therapists choose what to do based on the client). Gaston and colleagues (1989) note that expectations may not be very stable in light of therapeutic experience, so that any research that treats expectations as a static construct may not adequately capture the phenomenon.

Preferences

A number of mediating factors in the relationship between preferences and outcome have been proposed. It has been suggested that clients who receive a treatment they believe in and prefer may be more likely to engage in the early stages of therapy (Elkin et al., 1999), work harder (Devine & Fernald, 1973), and comply with and continue in treatment longer (Hardy et al., 1995), leading to better outcome.

It is likely that the same mediators operate in the relationship between outcome and the preference for demographic characteristics of the therapist, such as gender and race/ethnicity. In addition, being matched with a therapist with preferred characteristics may have an effect on the therapeutic alliance.

In reviewing the literature on whether client preferences for type of therapy relate to therapy outcome, it seems that the existence of such a relationship depends on the type of therapy in question. For example, Hardy and colleagues (1995) asked clients to rate their preferences for the treatment principles of cognitive-behavior therapy (CBT) and psychodynamic-interpersonal (PI) therapy. They found that clients' ratings of principles of both treatments were positively correlated with many outcome measures for those receiving PI, but not for those receiving CBT.

Devine and Fernald's (1973) study also found mixed results, depending on the type of therapy clients received. Clients were asked to rate their preferences for systematic desensitization (SD), encounter approach (EA), rational-emotive therapy (RET), and modeling and behavioral rehearsal (MBR). Those who received EA or RET as their preferred therapy had significantly greater reductions in fear when compared to those who were either randomly assigned to therapy or received a nonpreferred therapy. However, those who received SD or MBR as their preferred treatment did not show any differences in outcome compared to those whose preferences were not matched or who were randomly assigned. Devine and Fernald suggest that MBR and SD may be robust enough treatments that preferences actually play less of a role. Thus, the results of these studies suggest that the type of treatment may moderate the relationship between preferences and outcome.

In addition, two studies suggested that a moderating factor influencing the success of treatment may be whether clients' explanations for the causes of their psychological troubles match the explanatory model underlying their preferred treatment (Addis & Jacobson, 1996; Atkinson et al., 1991). For example, clients who believe that their problems stem from childhood issues may not do well in cognitive-behavioral treatment, even if they state that they prefer that treatment. Thus, for the preferred treatment to be more effective, its conceptualization of the etiology of psychopathology should match that of the client.

LIMITATIONS OF THE RESEARCH

Outcome Expectations

The way in which expectations have been assessed may have an important effect on study findings. Early research was marked by a tendency to assess outcome expectancy as the discrepancy between Q-sorts or symptom questionnaires completed with "present self" and "expected self" instructions, with outcome defined by change in ratings of present self from pre- to post-therapy on the same measure (for example, Friedman, 1963; Goldstein, 1960b; Goldstein & Shipman, 1961; Tollinton, 1973). The results of these studies could be highly influenced by client desires to be consistent or to make a good impression by reporting a reduction in symptoms similar to the one they had recently said they expected (Friedman, 1963).

Later studies have relied on total scores from measures with a combination of credibility or motivational items added to those that assess faith in treatment or expectations of success. Thus, some of the significant relationships (Maki, Hecker, Fowler, & Roberson-Nay, 2000; Safren, Heimberg, & Juster, 1997), mixed findings (Chambless et al., 1997; Hardy et al., 1995; Keijsers, Hoogduin, & Schaap, 1994; Morrison & Shapiro, 1987), and lack of relationships obtained between expectation and outcome (Chambless et al., 1997) cannot be interpreted purely as an indication of

the relationship between expectation and outcome. However, expectations of benefit may develop partly from perceived treatment credibility (Hardy et al., 1995).

As Garfield (1994) points out, it may be problematic that self-reports of both expectations and outcome have been relied upon in most studies, and that expectancies are sometimes inferred rather than actually assessed. In part due to the fact that research supporting the effect of outcome expectancy on psychotherapy gain was based only on self-reports (and not on objective measures of symptom reduction), Wilkins (1973) concluded that data necessary to establish the role of client expectancy of therapeutic gain as a construct accounting for psychotherapeutic improvement did not yet exist. Fortunately, later research in support of the relationship between expectations and outcome has included measures of behavior (Bradley et al., 1980) and ratings by independent clinicians (Martin, Friedmeyer, Moore, & Claveaux, 1977; Safren et al., 1997).

Additionally, *when* expectations are assessed may play a role in the results. Most studies have assessed initial expectancies prior to therapy, although some have used measures at the end of the first session after presentation of the therapy rationale. One study that assessed expectations both before and after the first session found that clients who terminated prematurely on or before the fourth session and those who continued in counseling did not differ significantly on pretreatment expectations, but that terminators were significantly less likely than continuers to report following the first session that the session had fulfilled their expectations and consider that counseling would be helpful (Gunzberger et al., 1985).

The relationship to therapy outcome of clients' appraisals during therapy of the likelihood of its success may also be important to examine (Hardy et al., 1995). For example, Holt and Heimberg (1990) report that treatments were rated as less credible and expectations for improvement were lower when the RTQ was completed at the end of session 4 compared to the end of session 1 of cognitive-behavioral group therapy. These authors thus conclude that "credibility and outcome expectancy erode when exposed to treatment reality" (p. 214), perhaps as clients become more cynical early in therapy before they have made much progress. The way in which clients' pretherapy expectations change as result of their experience in therapy is an important area for future research.

Role Expectations

As in the outcome expectancies literature, measurement is a serious concern in studies on role expectations (Duckro et al., 1979; Tracey & Dundon, 1988). As noted earlier, the measurement of role expectations has been variable and frequently poor. Outcome variables also have been measured in a wide variety of ways, not all of high quality. Dropout or continuation in therapy has often been ascertained simply through an arbitrary figure of a certain number of sessions attended (Pekarik, 1985). Tracey and Dundon (1988) used a better measure of premature termination: they categorized it as having occurred if a client came for fewer than four sessions and did not return for scheduled sessions, and if the final outcome evaluations were below the sample mean. Further, the type and duration of therapy is often not reported in these studies, particularly the early ones. Quite a few studies determine an outcome after only one session.

Most studies in the literature are on individual adult outpatient therapy. Yalom (1966) reported on reasons for dropout from group therapy, and Otto and Moos (1974) studied inpatient treatment and a day hospital. Only three studies dealing with child psychotherapy and parent counseling were located (Day & Reznikoff, 1980; Farley, Peterson, & Spanos, 1975; Richardson & Cohen, 1968).

Preferences

The major limitation of the research reviewed is how little there is. Most of the literature that does exist has been quite recently published, indicating that this may be a growing area of inquiry. In the literature on preferences for therapy type, there is wide variation in the method of presenting the orientation choices to the client. A number of the studies included participants who varied in diagnoses and severity of symptoms, which may have confounded detection of a relationship,

because certain disorders may respond better to certain types of therapy. Finally, we could locate only one study relating preferences for demographic characteristics of the therapist to outcome, suggesting that this is a topic that would be important to address in the future.

THERAPEUTIC PRACTICES

Outcome Expectations

Client outcome expectancies are indeed related to the results of psychotherapy in most studies (as summarized in table 18.1). However, the widely held belief that clients' expectancies of therapeutic gain have direct effects on psychotherapy outcome cannot be supported by the empirical literature. Correlational research cannot lead to causal conclusions that client expectancies *influence* the outcome of psychotherapy, or that the effectiveness of placebos is due to their *producing* positive expectations. It is certainly possible, if not probable, however, that a causal relationship does exist. More studies have shown positive or mixed findings than negative ones, suggesting that outcome expectations are an important topic for therapists to address with their clients.

Clients' initial expectations can be supported or disconfirmed by their actual experiences in therapy. Kirsch (1990) suggests that not too great an initial change should be promised so that even small changes can be interpreted as a sign of improvement, and clients' experience of therapy as effective is likely to lead to greater change in the future. It is important for therapists to promote positive expectations about treatment outcome that are realistic rather than overly optimistic, so that there is a greater likelihood they will be confirmed.

Many of those who have written on outcome expectations propose that expectations be explicitly assessed and discussed (for example, Kirsch, 1990; Safren et al., 1997). It is certainly the case that a client's overt skepticism should be addressed. However, it may be unwise to ask a client to state outcome expectations if the therapist suspects these are negative. In that case, a change toward hope of a good outcome would require the client to admit that he or she was wrong. Further, a therapist is likely to be less convincing in overtly arguing that therapy can help than through demonstrating it through empathy, conveying expertise in areas the client is facing, and displaying sincere enthusiasm. We agree with Garfield (1981) that these actions can raise the client's hope of change and thus improve morale. In fact, the therapist's ability to convey concern and competence may be the most potent feature that raises clients' positive expectations about outcome (J. D. Frank, 1968).

The arousal of positive expectations and the activation of the client's belief that he or she is being helped may be especially important in producing early relief of discomfort, while symptomatic changes due to relearning may appear later in therapy (J. D. Frank et al., 1959; Howard, Lueger, Maling, & Martinovich, 1993). Wilkins (1971) attributes a large part of therapy effectiveness to the skill of the therapist in developing an "expectancy of therapeutic gain" as well as providing praise for improvement. Similarly, Chambless and colleagues (1997) suggest that cognitive-behavioral therapists need to develop methods for enhancing clients' expectancy for benefit from treatment, taking time to build a rationale for treatment and its credibility before beginning a behavior change program.

In practical terms, then, the therapist should display his or her knowledge of the problems the client is facing and the means for addressing those problems in therapy. The therapist can use statements such as "It's really good that you sought help for this" and "What you're concerned about is exactly the kind of thing therapy can help with." Additionally, indications of specific research findings (in nontechnical terms) can be extremely important, both with regard to the problem and its treatment. For example, the therapist could say something like, "It's been found that what you're doing by avoiding the situations in which you've had panic attacks is what almost everyone does to try to make sure they don't have another panic attack. So it's the panic attacks that come first, and we need to be sure to address those as well as the avoidance that comes after. There's a specific treatment approach for panic attacks that's been shown to be quite effective, and let me tell you how it works."

This type of approach, raising the client's outcome expectations by demonstrating that the therapist can help, may be more useful than explicitly asking the client if he or she thinks therapy can help. However, if the client is clearly showing signs of being skeptical about treatment, it is important to be empathic about the client's uncertainty, and to normalize it. If the client seems to be doubting the value of entering therapy, the therapist can ask how the client is feeling about trying it and then can make statements such as, "It's quite common not to be enthusiastic at first, until you've tried it out, but let me suggest you keep an open mind. As I say, the type of problem you're experiencing has been shown to be quite successfully dealt with by the type of therapy I offer."

Role Expectations

As in the outcome expectations literature, many who have written about role expectations assume that they have a major influence on outcome. However, our review of the literature on role expectations leads to a similar conclusion to that of Duckro and colleagues (1979), that the findings are equivocal even for a correlational relationship, much less a causal one, between role expectations and outcome. Particularly when the quality of measurement of expectations is taken into account, there is no outcome measure for which the significant findings outweigh the mixed and negative findings. However, clinicians need to assess expectations and correct them when they are inaccurate (Lorion, 1978). Some expectations may be based on inexperience with therapy and could be relatively easily modified once the client engages in therapy and discovers the nature of it through experience (Van Audenhove & Vertommen, 2000).

In the earlier literature, it was assumed that therapy was of a given (psychodynamic) type, and that clients needed to fit into it. Overall and Aronson (1963) note that some researchers have undertaken role expectations research to figure out who should be turned away from therapy, whereas they are more in favor of adapting to the client. Similarly, A. Frank and colleagues (1978) argue that therapists should assess what a client wants and start from there. Another clinical perspective is provided by Strupp (1978), who points out that unrealistic expectations do not just come from ignorance, but reflect the client's dynamics. In this perspective, the therapist's task is to deal with the issues that lead the client to expect something that cannot take place.

Van Audenhove and Vertommen (2000) advocate a negotiation approach, which involves the therapist investigating the client's perspective, informing the client of the therapist's own perspective, negotiating between the therapist and client, and letting the client choose. In this view, therapy should be made explicit so discrepancies can be corrected, for example, in type of method, therapist characteristics, roles in therapy, setting, and duration.

Specific procedures to correct clients' role expectations have also been advocated and studied. For example, Yalom (1966) states that in group therapy clients need to be oriented to the process that will take place, and to be told that they need to stay for at least a dozen meetings. Role preparation interviews and other informational methods have been shown to be beneficial to psychotherapy outcome (see Hoehn-Saric et al., 1964). One important avenue for role preparation has been in services to ethnic minority clients, who may not be knowledgeable about psychotherapy (Sue, Zane, & Young, 1994).

However, as with outcome expectations, it may not be necessary or possible to accomplish persuasion toward new role expectations entirely through explicit discussion or information giving. Therapists can infer the type of role the client wants the therapist to take through assessing the client's activity level, deference toward the therapist, information the client presents or omits in discussing the presenting problem, and responses to interventions calling for self-understanding and access to feelings (Richert, 1983). Much discussion probably goes on implicitly rather than explicitly and is part of the therapist's interpersonal influence. Unrealistic expectations seem to be common, and yet many clients stay in therapy. It is clearly possible to accommodate and persuade the client that the setting, the therapist, and the work will be beneficial. Thus, the negotiations that lead the client to new expectations so that he or she can stay and benefit can be subtle.

These negotiations can include trying to draw out a passive client or giving a ballpark figure of the length of therapy to a new client who wants to know how long it will take. The answer a therapist will give the client seeking advice will, of course, depend on the theoretical orientation of the therapist. He or she can reflect that the client feels strongly about making a decision, and then can model problem solving by clarifying the client's goals and brainstorming with the client an initial method of approaching the problem. The therapist can suggest that the client read a trade book on a problem or method, such as F. Shapiro and Forrest's book (1997) on eye movement desensitization and reprocessing (EMDR), and can be thorough in presenting the rationale for an uncomfortable procedure such as EMDR or exposure and response prevention.

Preferences

The literature on the relationship of various types of client preferences to outcome is sparse, and those few studies primarily show negative or mixed results. If this lack of research is representative of therapists' emphasis also, then therapists should pay more attention to their clients' preferences and to accommodating them insofar as possible or clinically useful. Addis and Jacobson (1996) and Devine and Fernald (1973) both emphasize the benefit of educating clients about therapeutic techniques and treatment rationales. In this way, the therapy consumer can make more informed choices, and client-therapist matches can be facilitated.

Elkin and colleagues (1999) suggest that therapists should be aware that their clients may come to therapy with preferences, should assess these preferences at the beginning of therapy, and should be responsive to them. This way, if the therapist's orientation differs somewhat from the client's preferences, the therapist may want to refer the client elsewhere, or postpone interventions that would be more difficult for the client to accept until the client is more comfortable and engaged in the process. However, ultimate success comes from eventually helping the client conceptualize problems in different ways and adopt new ways to deal with them (Arnkoff, Glass, Shea, McKain, & Sydnor-Greenberg, 1987).

Therapists can explicitly ask their clients, "What do you want to see happen here?" It may be important to let the client know that therapy can, in fact, address at least some of the client's preferences (Arnkoff et al., 1987; Glass & Arnkoff, 1982). It can also be beneficial to ask a client what he or she does *not* want to see happen in therapy. For example, often clients report that they do not want a silent therapist, or a therapist who dwells exclusively on childhood. A therapist whose style is different from the client's previous therapy can explain how he or she works. On the other hand, a therapist whose style may be perceived by the client as similar to a previous unsatisfactory therapist can either take the opportunity to provide a rationale for this approach or can refer the client elsewhere before therapy gets under way.

CONCLUSION

The research reviewed here does not yield enough information for practicing therapists because of methodological weaknesses or a lack of studies, although it appears particularly wise to raise the client's outcome expectations early in therapy. Expectations and preferences are a topic on which clinicians could collaborate with researchers to study the early phase of therapy as it is typically practiced. The negotiations that take place about the client's hopes and desires are subtle, and clinicians could help researchers design studies that would better capture clinical reality.

REFERENCES

Addis, M. E., & Jacobson, N. S. (1996). Reasons for depression and the process and outcome of cognitive-behavioral psychotherapies. *Journal of Consulting and Clinical Psychology, 64,* 1417–1424.

Al-Darmaki, F., & Kivlighan, D. M., Jr. (1993). Congruence in client-counselor expectations for relationship and the working alliance. *Journal of Counseling Psychology, 40,* 379–384.

Andrews, G., & Harvey, R. (1981). Does psychotherapy benefit neurotic patients? A reanalysis of the Smith, Glass, and Miller data. *Archives of General Psychiatry, 36,* 1203–1208.

Apfelbaum, B. (1958). *Dimensions of transference in psychotherapy.* Berkeley: University of California Press.

Arnkoff, D. B., Glass, C. R., Shea, C. A., McKain, T. L., & Sydnor-Greenberg, J. M. (1987). Client predispositions toward cognitive and social skills treatments for shyness. *Journal of Integrative and Eclectic Psychotherapy, 6,* 154–164.

Atkinson, D. R. (1983). Ethnic similarity in counseling psychology: A review of research. *The Counseling Psychologist, 11*(3), 79–92.

Atkinson, D. R. (1987). Research on cross-cultural counseling and psychotherapy: A review and update of reviews. In P. Pedersen (Ed.), *Handbook of cross-cultural counseling and therapy* (pp. 191–197). New York: Praeger.

Atkinson, D. R., Worthington, R. L., Dana, D. M., & Good, G. E. (1991). Etiology beliefs, preferences for counseling orientations, and counseling effectiveness. *Journal of Counseling Psychology, 38,* 258–264.

Atlas, B. D. (1993). Premature termination in psychotherapy: The role of patient expectations and the intake interview. *Dissertation Abstracts International, 54*(4), 2186B.

Bakker, A., Spinhoven, P., van Balkom, A. J. L. M., Vleugel, L., & van Dyck, R. (2000). Cognitive therapy by allocation versus cognitive therapy by preference in the treatment of panic disorder. *Psychotherapy and Psychosomatics, 69,* 240–243.

Baum, O. E., & Felzer, S. B. (1964). Activity in initial interviews with lower-class patients. *Archives of General Psychiatry, 10,* 345–353.

Bergin, A. E., & Garfield, S. L. (1994). Overview, trends, and future issues. In A. E. Bergin & S. L. Garfield (Eds.), *Handbook of psychotherapy and behavior change* (4th ed., pp. 821–830). New York: Wiley.

Berzins, J. I. (1971). *Revision of Psychotherapy Expectancy Inventory.* Unpublished manuscript, University of Kentucky, Lexington.

Berzins, J. I. (1977). Therapist-patient matching. In A. S. Gurman & A. M. Razin (Eds.), *Effective psychotherapy: A handbook of research* (pp. 222–251). Elmsford, NY: Pergamon.

Bootzin, R. R., & Lick, J. R. (1979). Expectancies in therapy research: Interpretive artifact or mediating mechanism? *Journal of Consulting and Clinical Psychology, 47,* 852–855.

Borghi, J. H. (1968). Premature termination of psychotherapy and patient-therapist expectations. *American Journal of Psychotherapy, 22*, 460–473.

Borkovec, T. D., & Nau, S. D. (1972). Credibility of analogue therapy rationales. *Journal of Behavior Therapy and Experimental Psychiatry, 3*, 257–260.

Bradley, I., Poser, E. G., & Johnson, J. A. (1980). Outcome expectation ratings as predictors of success in weight reduction. *Journal of Clinical Psychology, 36*, 500–502.

Brady, J. P., Reznikoff, M., & Zeller, W. W. (1960). The relationship of expectation of improvement to actual improvement of hospitalized psychiatric patients. *Journal of Nervous and Mental Disease, 130*, 41–44.

Brennan, M. J. (1990). Client-counselor role expectations and outcomes of counseling. *Dissertation Abstracts International, 50*(11), 5307B.

Carlson, M. S. (1981). The effect of similarity of therapist and client preferences for therapy approach on premature termination and satisfaction with psychotherapy. *Dissertation Abstracts International, 41*(10), 4335A.

Chambless, D. L., Tran, G. Q., & Glass, C. R. (1997). Predictors of response to cognitive-behavioral group therapy for social phobia. *Journal of Anxiety Disorders, 11*, 221–240.

Chilvers, C., Dewey, M., Fielding, K., Gretton, V., Miller, P., Palmer, B., Weller, D., Churchill, R., Williams, I., Bedi, N., Duggan, C., Lee, A., & Harrison, G. (2001). Antidepressant drugs and generic counselling for treatment of major depression in primary care: Randomised trial with patient preference arms. *British Medical Journal, 322*, 772.

Clemes, S. R., & D'Andrea, V. J. (1965). Patients' anxiety as a function of expectations and degree of initial interview ambiguity. *Journal of Consulting Psychology, 29*, 397–404.

Day, L., & Reznikoff, M. (1980). Social class, the treatment process, and parents' and children's expectations about child psychotherapy. *Journal of Clinical Child Psychology, 9*, 195–198.

Devine, D. A., & Fernald, P. S. (1973). Outcome effects of receiving a preferred, randomly assigned, or non-preferred therapy. *Journal of Consulting and Clinical Psychology, 41*, 104–107.

Duckro, P., Beal, D., & George, C. (1979). Research on the effects of disconfirmed client role expectations in psychotherapy: A critical review. *Psychological Bulletin, 86*, 260–275.

Elkin, I., Yamaguchi, J. L., Arnkoff, D. B., Glass, C. R., Sotsky, S. M., & Krupnick, J. L. (1999). "Patient-treatment fit" and early engagement in therapy. *Psychotherapy Research, 9*, 437–451.

Farley, O. W., Peterson, K. D., & Spanos, G. (1975). Self-termination from a child guidance center. *Community Mental Health Journal, 11*, 325–334.

Fiester, A. R. (1977). Clients' perceptions of therapists with high attrition rates. *Journal of Consulting and Clinical Psychology, 45*, 954–955.

Frank, A., Eisenthal, S., & Lazare, A. (1978). Are there social class differences in patients' treatment conceptions? *Archives of General Psychiatry, 35*, 61–69.

Frank, J. D. (1968). The influence of patients' and therapists' expectations on the outcome of psychotherapy. *British Journal of Medical Psychology, 41*, 349–356.

Frank, J. D. (1973). *Persuasion and healing: A comparative study of psychotherapy* (Rev. ed.). Baltimore, MD: Johns Hopkins University Press.

Frank, J. D. (1974). Therapeutic components of psychotherapy: A 25-year progress report of research. *Journal of Nervous and Mental Disease, 159*, 325–342.

Frank, J. D., Gliedman, L. H., Imber, S. D., Stone, A. R., & Nash, E. H. (1959). Patients' expectancies and relearning as factors determining improvement in psychotherapy. *American Journal of Psychiatry, 115*, 961–968.

Freedman, N., Engelhardt, D. M., Hankoff, L. D., Glick, B. S., Kaye, H., Buchwald, J., & Stark, P. (1958). Drop-out from outpatient psychiatric treatment. *Archives of Neurology and Psychiatry, 80*, 657–666.

Freud, S. (1953). Psychical (or mental) treatment. In J. Strachey (Ed.), *The complete psychological works of Sigmund Freud* (Vol. 7). London: Hogarth. (Original work published 1905)

Friedman, H. J. (1963). Patient-expectancy and symptom reduction. *Archives of General Psychiatry, 8*, 61–67.

Fuller, F. F. (1964). Preference for male and female counselors. *Personnel and Guidance Journal, 42*, 463–467.

Garfield, S. L. (1971). Research on client variables in psychotherapy. In A. E. Bergin & S. L. Garfield (Eds.), *Handbook of psychotherapy and behavior change* (pp. 271–298). New York: Wiley.

Garfield, S. L. (1981). Critical issues in the effectiveness of psychotherapy. In C. E. Walker (Ed.), *Clinical practice of psychology* (pp. 161–188). Elmsford, NY: Pergamon.

Garfield, S. L. (1994). Research on client variables in psychotherapy. In A. E. Bergin & S. L. Garfield (Eds.), *Handbook of psychotherapy and behavior change* (4th ed., pp. 190–228). New York: Wiley.

Garfield, S. L., & Wolpin, M. (1963). Expectations regarding psychotherapy. *Journal of Nervous and Mental Disease, 137*, 353–362.

Gaston, L., Marmar, C. R., Gallagher, D., & Thompson, L. W. (1989). Impact of confirming patient expectations of change processes in behavioral, cognitive, and brief dynamic psychotherapy. *Psychotherapy, 26*, 296–302.

Gladstein, G. A. (1969). Client expectations, counseling experience, and satisfaction. *Journal of Counseling Psychology, 16*, 476–481.

Glass, C. R., & Arnkoff, D. B. (1982). Think cognitively: Selected issues in cognitive assessment and therapy. In P. C. Kendall (Ed.), *Advances in cognitive behavioral research and therapy* (Vol. 1, pp. 35–71). New York: Academic.

Goin, M. K., Yamamoto, J., & Silverman, J. (1965). Therapy congruent with class-linked expectations. *Archives of General Psychiatry, 13*, 133–137.

Goldstein, A. P. (1960a). Patient's expectancies and non-specific therapy as a basis for (un)-spontaneous remission. *Journal of Clinical Psychology, 16*, 399–403.

Goldstein, A. P. (1960b). Therapist and client expectation of personality change in psychotherapy. *Journal of Counseling Psychology, 3*, 180–184.

Goldstein, A. P. (1962). *Therapist-patient expectancies in psychotherapy*. Oxford, UK: Pergamon.

Goldstein, A. P., & Shipman, W. G. (1961). Patient expectancies, symptom reduction and aspects of the initial psychotherapeutic interview. *Journal of Clinical Psychology, 17*, 129–133.

Gunzburger, D. W., Henggeler, S. W., & Watson, S. M. (1985). Factors related to premature termination of counseling relationships. *Journal of College Student Personnel, 26*, 456–460.

Hankoff, L. D., Englehardt, D. M., & Freeman, N. (1960). Placebo response in schizophrenic outpatients. *Archives of General Psychiatry, 2*, 33–42.

Hardin, S. I., Subich, L. M., & Holvey, J. M. (1988). Expectancies for counseling in relation to premature termination. *Journal of Counseling Psychology, 35*, 37–40.

Hardy, G. E., Barkham, M., Shapiro, D. A., Reynolds, S., & Rees, A. (1995). Credibility and outcome of cognitive-behavioural and psychodynamic-interpersonal psychotherapy. *British Journal of Clinical Psychology, 34*, 555–569.

Harrison, D. K. (1975). Race as a counselor-client variable in counseling and psychotherapy: A review of the research. *The Counseling Psychologist, 5*, 124–133.

Heine, R. W. (Ed.). (1962). *The student physician as psychotherapist*. Chicago: University of Chicago Press.

Heine, R. W., & Trosman, H. (1960). Initial expectations of the doctor-patient interaction as a factor in continuance in psychotherapy. *Psychiatry, 23*, 275–278.

Heppner, P. P., & Heesacker, M. (1983). Perceived counselor characteristics, client expectations, and client satisfaction with counseling. *Journal of Counseling Psychology, 30*, 31–39.

Hochberg, M. G. (1986). Client-therapist role expectations and psychotherapy duration. *Dissertation Abstracts International, 46*(10), 3595–3596B.

Hoehn-Saric, R., Frank, J., Imber, S., Nash, E., Stone, A., & Battle, C. (1964). Systematic preparation of patients for psychotherapy: I. Effects of therapy behavior and outcome. *Journal of Psychiatric Research, 2*, 267–281.

Hoffman, S. S. (1982). An investigation of patient and therapist role expectations and preferences related to premature termination in short-term psychotherapy. *Dissertation Abstracts International, 43*(1), 251B.

Holt, C. S., & Heimberg, R. G. (1990). The Reaction to Treatment Questionnaire: Measuring treatment credibility and outcome expectancies. *The Behavior Therapist, 13*, 213–214, 222.

Horenstein, D., & Houston, B. K. (1976). The expectation-reality discrepancy and premature termination from psychotherapy. *Journal of Clinical Psychology, 32*, 373–378.

Howard, K. I., Lueger, R. J., Maling, M. S., & Martinovich, Z. (1993). A phase model of psychotherapy outcome: Causal mediation of change. *Journal of Consulting and Clinical Psychology, 61*, 678–685.

Isard, E. S., & Sherwood, E. J. (1964). Counselor behavior and counselee expectations as related to satisfactions with counseling interview. *Personnel and Guidance Journal, 42*, 920–921.

Jacobs, M. A., Muller, J. J., Anderson, J., & Skinner, J. C. (1972). Therapeutic expectations, premorbid adjustment, and manifest distress level as predictors of improvement in hospitalized patients. *Journal of Consulting and Clinical Psychology, 39,* 455–461.

Jones, E. E., & Zoppel, C. L. (1982). Impact of client and therapist gender on psychotherapy process and outcome. *Journal of Consulting and Clinical Psychology, 50,* 259–272.

Kamin, I., & Caughlan, J. (1963). Subjective experiences of outpatient psychotherapy. *American Journal of Psychotherapy, 17,* 660–668.

Kazdin, A. E., & Wilcoxon, L. A. (1976). Systematic desensitization and nonspecific treatment effects: A methodological evaluation. *Psychological Bulletin, 83,* 729–758.

Keijsers, G. P. J., Hoogduin, C. A. L., & Schaap, C. P. D. R. (1994). Predictors of treatment outcome in the behavioural treatment of obsessive-compulsive disorder. *British Journal of Psychiatry, 165,* 781–786.

Kim, H. J., Grisham, J. R., & Hofmann, S. G. (2000, November). *Treatment expectancy: Further evidence for its role as a moderator in the treatment of social phobia.* Paper presented at the Association for Advancement of Behavior Therapy, New Orleans.

Kirsch, I. (1990). *Changing expectations: A key to effective psychotherapy.* Pacific Grove, CA: Brooks/Cole.

Lax, T., Basoglu, M., & Marks, I. M. (1992). Expectancy and compliance as predictors of outcome in obsessive-compulsive disorder. *Behavioural Psychotherapy, 20,* 257–266.

Lennard, H. L., & Bernstein, A. (1960). *The anatomy of psychotherapy: Systems of communication and expectation.* New York: Columbia University Press.

Lick, J., & Bootzin, R. (1975). Expectancy factors in the treatment of fear: Methodological and theoretical issues. *Psychological Bulletin, 82,* 917–931.

Lightsey, O. R. (1997). Generalized self-efficacy expectancies and optimism as predictors of growth group outcomes. *Journal for Specialists in Group Work, 22,* 189–202.

Lipkin, S. (1954). Clients' feelings and attitudes in relation to the outcome of client-centered therapy. *Psychological Monographs, 68*(1, No. 372), 1–30.

Lorion, R. P. (1978). Research on psychotherapy and behavior change with the disadvantaged: Past, present, and future directions. In S. L. Garfield & A. E. Bergin (Eds.), *Handbook of psychotherapy and behavior change* (2nd ed., pp. 903–938). New York: Wiley.

Maki, K. M., Hecker, J. E., Fowler, E., & Roberson-

Nay, R. (2000, November). *Predicting response to self-directed treatment for social phobia.* Paper presented at the Association for Advancement of Behavior Therapy, New Orleans.

Martin, P. J., Friedmeyer, M. H., Moore, J. E., & Claveaux, R. A. (1977). Patients' expectancies and improvement in treatment: The shape of the link. *Journal of Clinical Psychology, 33,* 827–833.

Martin, P. J., Sterne, A. L., & Hunter, M. L. (1976). Share and share alike: Mutuality of expectations and satisfaction with therapy. *Journal of Clinical Psychology, 32,* 677–683.

Mathews, A. M., Johnston, D. W., Lancashire, M., Munby, M., Shaw, P. M., & Gelder, M. G. (1976). Imaginal flooding and exposure to real phobic situations: Treatment outcome with agoraphobic patients. *British Journal of Psychiatry, 129,* 362–371.

Morrison, L. A., & Shapiro, D. A. (1987). Expectancy and outcome in prescriptive vs. exploratory psychotherapy. *British Journal of Clinical Psychology, 26,* 59–60.

Murray, E. J., & Jacobson, L. I. (1978). Cognition and learning in traditional and behavioral psychotherapy. In S. L. Garfield & A. E. Bergin (Eds.), *Handbook of psychotherapy and behavior change* (2nd ed., pp. 661–687). New York: Wiley.

Orlinsky, D. E., Grawe, K., & Parks, B. K. (1994). Process and outcome in psychotherapy—Noch einmal. In A. E. Bergin & S. L. Garfield (Eds.), *Handbook of psychotherapy and behavior change* (4th ed., pp. 270–376). New York: Wiley.

Orlinsky, D. E., & Howard, K. I. (1980). Gender and psychotherapeutic outcome. In A. M. Brodsky & R. T. Hare-Mustin (Eds.), *Women and psychotherapy: An assessment of research and practice* (pp. 3–34). New York: Guilford.

Otto, J., & Moos, R. (1974). Patient expectations and attendance in community treatment programs. *Community Mental Health Journal, 10,* 9–15.

Overall, B., & Aronson, H. (1963). Expectations of psychotherapy in patients of lower socioeconomic class. *American Journal of Orthopsychiatry, 33,* 421–430.

Pattison, L. A. (1992). An exploratory study of the relationship between client expectations, session evaluation, and working alliance across the first four sessions of therapy. *Dissertation Abstracts International, 53*(4), 2072B.

Pekarik, G. (1985). Coping with dropouts. *Profes-*

sional Psychology: Research and Practice, 16, 114–123.

Pekarik, G., & Wierzbicki, M. (1986). The relationship between clients' expected and actual treatment duration. Psychotherapy, 23, 532–534.

Pikus, C. F., & Heavey, C. L. (1996). Client preferences for therapist gender. Journal of College Student Psychotherapy, 10, 35–43.

Piper, W. E., & Wogan, M. (1970). Placebo effect in psychotherapy: An extension of earlier findings. Journal of Consulting and Clinical Psychology, 34, 447.

Pistrang, N., & Barker, C. (1992). Clients' beliefs about psychological problems. Counselling Psychology Quarterly, 5, 325–335.

Pohlman, E. (1964). Should clients tell counselors what to do? Personnel and Guidance Journal, 42, 456–458.

Rabin, A. S., Kaslow, N. J., & Rehm, L. P. (1985). Factors influencing continuation in a behavioral therapy. Behaviour Research and Therapy, 23, 695–698.

Rawlings, W. J. (1986). Relationship between congruence of client and therapist: Expectations and preferences and continuation in psychotherapy. Dissertation Abstracts International, 47(6), 2028A.

Richardson, C. H., & Cohen, R. L. (1968). A follow-up study of a sample of child psychiatry clinic dropouts. Mental Hygiene, 52, 535–541.

Richert, A. (1983). Differential prescription for psychotherapy on the basis of client role preferences. Psychotherapy: Theory, Research and Practice, 20, 321–329.

Rickers-Ovsiankina, M. A., Geller, J. D., Berzins, J. I., & Rogers, G. W. (1971). Patient's role expectancies in psychotherapy: A theoretical and measurement approach. Psychotherapy: Theory, Research and Practice, 8, 124–126.

Rizvi, S. L., Reynolds, S. K., Comtois, K. A., & Linehan, M. M. (2000, November). Therapeutic alliance in the treatment of borderline personality disorder. Paper presented at the Association for Advancement of Behavior Therapy, New Orleans.

Rogers, L. S. (1960). Drop-out rates and results of psychotherapy in government aided mental hygiene clinics. Journal of Clinical Psychology, 16, 89–92.

Rosen, A., & Wish, E. (1980). Therapist content relevance and patient affect in treatment. Journal of Clinical Psychology, 36, 242–246.

Rosenthal, D., & Frank, J. D. (1956). Psychotherapy and the placebo effect. Psychological Bulletin, 53, 294–302.

Safren, S. A., Heimberg, R. G., & Juster, H. R. (1997). Clients' expectancies and their relationship to pretreatment symptomatology and outcome of cognitive-behavioral group treatment for social phobia. Journal of Consulting and Clinical Psychology, 65, 694–698.

Schonfield, J., Stone, A. R., Hoehn-Saric, R., Imber, S. D., & Pande, S. K. (1969). Patient-therapist convergence and measures of improvement in short-term psychotherapy. Psychotherapy: Theory, Research and Practice, 6, 267–272.

Severinsen, J. (1966). Client expectation and perception of the counselor's role and their relationship to client satisfaction. Journal of Counseling Psychology, 13, 109–112.

Shapiro, D. A., & Shapiro, D. (1982). Meta-analysis of comparative therapy outcome studies: A replication and refinement. Psychological Bulletin, 92, 581–604.

Shapiro, F., & Forrest, M. S. (1997). EMDR: The breakthrough therapy for overcoming anxiety, stress, and trauma. New York: Basic.

Silverberg, R. T. (1982). Effects of confirmation or disconfirmation of client role expectations on client satisfaction, length of therapy, and outcome ratings of psychotherapy. Dissertation Abstracts International, 42(8), 3442B.

Strupp, H. H. (1978). Psychotherapy research and practice: An overview. In S. L. Garfield & A. E. Bergin (Eds.), Handbook of psychotherapy and behavior change (2nd ed., pp. 3–22). New York: Wiley.

Sue, S., & Lam, A. (2002). Cultural and demographic diversity. In J. C. Norcross (Ed.), Psychotherapy relationships that work. New York: Oxford University Press.

Sue, S., Zane, N., & Young, K. (1994). Research on psychotherapy with culturally diverse populations. In A. E. Bergin & S. L. Garfield (Eds.), Handbook of psychotherapy and behavior change (4th ed., pp. 783–817). New York: Wiley.

Thurer, S., & Hursh, N. (1981). Characteristics of the therapeutic relationship. In C. E. Walker (Ed.), Clinical practice of psychology (pp. 62–82). Elmsford, NY: Pergamon.

Tinsley, H. E. A, Bowman, S. L., & Barich, A.W. (1993). Counseling psychologists' perceptions of the occurrence and effects of unrealistic expectations about counseling and psychotherapy among their clients. Journal of Counseling Psychology, 40, 46–52.

Tinsley, H. E. A., Workman, K. R., & Kass, R. A. (1980). Factor analysis of the domain of client expectancies about counseling. *Journal of Counseling Psychology, 27,* 561–570.

Tokar, D. M., Hardin, S. I., Adams, E. M., & Brandel, I. W. (1996). Clients' expectations about counseling and perceptions of the working alliance. *Journal of College Student Psychotherapy, 11,* 9–26.

Tollinton, H. J. (1973). Initial expectations and outcome. *British Journal of Medical Psychology, 46,* 251–257.

Tracey, T. J., & Dundon, M. (1988). Role anticipations and preferences over the course of counseling. *Journal of Counseling Psychology, 35,* 3–14.

Uhlenhuth, E. H., & Duncan, D. B. (1968). Subjective change with medical student therapists: II. Some determinants of change in psychoneurotic outpatients. *Archives of General Psychiatry, 18,* 532–540.

Van Audenhove, C., & Vertommen, H. (2000). A negotiation approach to intake and treatment choice. *Journal of Psychotherapy Integration, 10,* 287–299.

Van Dyck, R., & Spinhoven, P. (1997). Does preference for type of treatment matter? *Behavior Modification, 21,* 172–186.

Volsky, T., Jr., Magoon, T. M., Norman, W. T., & Hoyt, D. P. (1965). *The outcomes of counseling and psychotherapy: Theory and research.* Minneapolis: University of Minnesota Press.

Walborn, F. S. (1996). *Process variables: Four common elements of counseling and psychotherapy.* Pacific Grove, CA: Brooks/Cole.

Wallach, H. S. (1988). Clients' expectations and results of psychological therapy for dysmenorrhea. *Dissertation Abstracts International, 49*(5), 1961B.

Wilkins, W. (1971). Desensitization: Social and cognitive factors underlying the effectiveness of Wolpe's procedure. *Psychological Bulletin, 76,* 311–317.

Wilkins, W. (1973). Expectancy of therapeutic gain: An empirical and conceptual critique. *Journal of Consulting and Clinical Psychology, 40,* 69–77.

Wilkins, W. (1978). Expectancy effect versus demand characteristics: An empirically unresolvable issue. *Behavior Therapy, 9,* 363–367.

Wilkins, W. (1979). Expectancies in therapy research: Discriminating among heterogeneous nonspecifics. *Journal of Consulting and Clinical Psychology, 47,* 837–845.

Yalom, I. D. (1966). A study of group therapy dropouts. *Archives of General Psychiatry, 14,* 393–414.

Zlotnick, C., Elkin, I., & Shea, M. T. (1998). Does the gender of a patient or the gender of a therapist affect the treatment of patients with major depression? *Journal of Consulting and Clinical Psychology, 66,* 655–659.

19

Assimilation of Problematic Experiences

William B. Stiles

The assimilation model (Stiles et al., 1990) offers an approach to customizing the therapeutic relationship through responsiveness to the degree of assimilation of clients' problems. Briefly, the therapist discerns a problem, assesses its assimilation level, and works with the client, using the chosen therapeutic approach, to move the problem from one level to the next.

DEFINITIONS

The assimilation model conceptualizes psychotherapy outcome as change in relation to particular *problematic experiences*—memories, wishes, feelings, attitudes, or behaviors that are threatening or painful, destructive relationships, or traumatic incidents—rather than as change in the person as a whole. It suggests that, in successful psychotherapy, clients follow a regular developmental sequence of recognizing, reformulating, understanding, and eventually resolving the problematic experiences that brought them into treatment. The sequence is summarized in the eight stages or levels of the Assimilation of Problematic Experiences Scale (APES), used in table 19.1, which are numbered 0 to 7: (0) Warded off/dissociated; (1) Unwanted thoughts/active avoidance; (2) Vague awareness/emergence; (3) Problem statement/clarification; (4) Understanding/insight; (5) Application/working through; (6) Resourcefulness/problem solution; and (7) Integration/mas-

tery. The APES uses both cognitive and affective features to characterize each level, which represent anchor points along a continuum, rather than discrete states. Clients may enter treatment at any point along the APES continuum, and any movement along the continuum might be considered as therapeutic progress.

In assimilation research, we identify problematic experiences, extract multiple passages dealing with them from tapes or transcripts of completed therapies, and study how the expressions of each problem change across sessions. We observe that the problematic experiences change from being feared or unwanted in early sessions to being understood and integrated by the end of successful treatments. As one way to formulate this, following Piaget (1970), we can say the problematic experience is assimilated into a *schema*—a way of thinking and acting that is developed or modified within the therapeutic relationship (accommodation) in order to assimilate the problematic experience (Stiles et al., 1990).

The process of assimilation can also be described using the metaphor of voice (Honos-Webb & Stiles, 1998; Stiles, 1997, 1999a, 1999b, 1999c). This metaphor expresses the theoretical tenet that the traces of past experiences are active agents within people and are capable of communication. The traces can act and speak. Dissociated (unassimilated) voices tend to be problems, whereas assimilated voices can be resources—available to be called upon when circumstances

Table 19.1. Assimilation of Problematic Experiences Scale (APES)

0. Warded off/dissociated. Client is unaware of the problem; the problematic voice is silent or dissociated. Affect may be minimal, reflecting successful avoidance.

1. Unwanted thoughts/active avoidance. Client prefers not to think about the experience. Problematic voices emerge in response to therapist interventions or external circumstances and are suppressed or avoided. Affect is intensely negative but episodic and unfocused; the connection with the content may be unclear.

2. Vague awareness/emergence. Client is aware of a problematic experience but cannot formulate the problem clearly. Problematic voice emerges into sustained awareness. Affect includes acute psychological pain or panic associated with the problematic material.

3. Problem statement/clarification. Content includes a clear statement of a problem—something that can be worked on. Opposing voices are differentiated and can talk about each other. Affect is negative but manageable, not panicky.

4. Understanding/insight. The problematic experience is formulated and understood in some way. Voices reach an understanding with each other (a meaning bridge). Affect may be mixed, with some unpleasant recognition but also some pleasant surprise.

5. Application/working through. The understanding is used to work on a problem. Voices work together to address problems of living. Affective tone is positive, optimistic.

6. Resourcefulness/problem solution. The formerly problematic experience has become a resource, used for solving problems. Voices can be used flexibly. Affect is positive, satisfied.

7. Integration/mastery. Client automatically generalizes solutions; voices are fully integrated, serving as resources in new situations. Affect is positive or neutral (that is, this is no longer something to get excited about).

Note: Assimilation is considered as a continuum, and intermediate levels are allowed; for example, 2.5 represents a level of assimilation halfway between vague awareness/emergence (2.0) and problem statement/clarification (3.0).

would benefit from their capacities and talents. The interlinked traces of experiences that have been assimilated previously can be considered as a community of voices within the person. In successful therapy, a problematic, unwanted voice establishes contact with the community, negotiates an understanding, and is assimilated into the community. For example, in one successful treatment (Stiles, 1999b), Debbie's sudden, uncontrolled, angry outbursts (a problem) were gradually assimilated and transformed into a capacity for appropriate assertiveness (a resource). The process of contact between the problematic voice and the community can be described as building a meaning bridge. A meaning bridge is any sign (word, image, gesture, etc.) or system of signs that means the same thing to both the author and addressee of a communication (for example, the problematic voice and the community). In Debbie's case, an element of the meaning bridge was the concept of a "rejecting" aspect of herself—a complement or shadow to Debbie's predominant experience of being "rejected." This concept was introduced by the therapist as a way of naming the angry outbursts (that is, the problematic voice). Debbie used the name "rejecting" for talking about and to this problematic aspect of herself as she assimilated it.

CLINICAL EXAMPLE: THE CASE OF JOHN JONES

As a clinical example, I review part of a previously published assimilation analysis of the case of John Jones, who was a 25-year-old married teacher and counselor at a small college (Stiles, Meshot, Anderson, & Sloan, 1992). Our data were the published transcripts of his 20-session psychodynamic treatment (Snyder, 1963). The treatment was considered successful from the perspective of client, therapist, and assessment instruments.

We read the transcripts and constructed a catalog of the topics discussed, listing the attitudes expressed along with the objects of those attitudes. Then we identified three insight events, that is, moments of new understanding (APES level 4; see table 19.1) that John achieved during the therapy. We then searched forward and backward through our catalog to construct lists of passages on topics related to each insight.

The first such insight concerned John's acknowledgment of his homosexual desires. During the early sessions, John denied or rejected these feelings. He stressed his ability to accept homosexuality in others, but he found the idea of having such desires himself to be repugnant. During therapy, however, he made accommodations in his "ability to accept," which allowed him to acknowledge, accept, and express his own homosexual feelings toward his therapist. We identified the following passage from session 6 as marking this insight (APES level 4). We could say that the voice of John's homosexual feelings could speak without being suppressed or contradicted.

I'd probably reject actually going through the act. But the idea isn't that repugnant to me. I'd probably enjoy it. As far as you're concerned, I'd probably enjoy it. Now, why couldn't I say that before?

Searching back through our catalog, we found the first passage that dealt with homosexuality in session 2:

I would be very upset if I discovered this [homosexuality] were true of me. But in trying to check this sort of thing against my reactions to these people, consciously, they don't cause me too much anxiety. There is this much; when instances were reported of a homosexual, in the hospital, I like to think my attitude toward them has been more accepting and more understanding than that of other staff people. Maybe I'm defending some of the feelings I have myself.

Although John denied awareness of homosexual impulses, his (intellectualized) hypothesis that he was defending against such feelings suggests that they were not completely warded off (that is, they fell between APES levels 0 and 1). By session 3, John was able to acknowledge his homosexual feelings briefly:

Sure, I have some homosexual urges; so what? I'm making fairly adequate heterosexual adjustment, and I'm not upset by people who are overtly homosexual. I keep having a feeling that we're wasting time on this. Let's move on!

This active, explicit avoidance (interruption by the dominant community) indicates that these were unwanted thoughts (APES level 1), although the initial acknowledgment suggests the beginnings of vague awareness.

John's growing awareness was signaled in session 4 by his briefly raising the issue of homosexuality, which he had previously described as wasting time, "because it is a threatening thing to me." Then, during session 5, John became obsessed with the thought that his therapist was looking at his penis. This was very upsetting (strong negative affect is characteristic of vague awareness, APES level 2). He did not reveal this feeling at the time, but he began session 6 by describing it. This led to a clear problem statement (APES level 3): "I guess what you're getting at, and I'm avoiding, is that I'm a homosexual." John then discussed his repugnance at being a homosexual, explicated the problem statement, and worked toward the insight (APES level 4) that occurred later in session 6 (quoted earlier). He remained focused on the problematic experience despite powerful feelings of anxiety.

In later sessions, John continued to work through and apply his newly achieved understanding (APES level 5) and may have reached the beginnings of a solution to his problem. With the problematic experience understood (though not completely mastered), its importance receded and it was less upsetting, as illustrated in this passage from session 12:

It's one thing to make the intellectual admission that there are some homosexual ways in which I behave, but to face this kind of thing seriously is still threatening. . . . You know, the idea of sodomy has a certain amount of appeal to me, whereas before I think I'd have given you the reaction that this was pretty repugnant. I don't know whether this is progress of a sort or not.

Assimilation does not imply homogenization. After they have been assimilated, the experiences remain distinctive—able to express themselves when circumstances trigger them. What changes is their availability (assimilated experiences—or voices—emerge smoothly when called upon) and the associated emotion. Whereas encountering unassimilated material is distressing, encountering assimilated material is pleasant or neutral.

COMPARISON WITH THE TRANSTHEORETICAL MODEL

Both the assimilation model and the transtheoretical model (Prochaska & Norcross, chapter 16 in this volume) are meant to describe psychological changes that occur in successful psychotherapy of any type. Both models are designed to bridge the gap between psychotherapy process and outcome by focusing on incremental changes in particular problems. They describe small-scale progress that global outcome measures might overlook. For example, a problem's progress from warded off (APES level 0) to emergence (APES level 2) or, in the transtheoretical model, from precontemplation to contemplation, might be accompanied by a seemingly paradoxical increase in subjective distress, as clients confront (rather than avoid) the problem. Without the models to offer an explanation, such an increase might be incorrectly interpreted as deterioration, whereas these models indicate that this could be a case of getting worse on the path to getting better.

The transtheoretical model has been most intensively studied with respect to quitting smoking. The assimilation model has been most intensively studied with respect to time-limited (8–20 session) psychotherapy of depression. These origins have helped to shape the ways the models describe change. Whereas the transtheoretical model is cast as a model of readiness to change (that is, focused on identified problematic behaviors), the assimilation model is cast as a description of the sequence of psychological change itself. Insofar as readiness can be considered as part of the change sequence, the two models can be considered as alternative perspectives on the same underlying psychological change process. For example, a problem at the unwanted thoughts/active avoidance stage (APES level 1) might also be described as being at the "precontemplation" level with respect to readiness to change.

RESEARCH REVIEW

The assimilation model's description of change has been derived mainly from a series of intensive case studies, in which problematic experiences have been tracked across sessions in tapes or transcripts of completed psychotherapies. The therapies have been conducted using a variety of approaches, including psychodynamic, interpersonal, cognitive, process-experiential, and client-centered. These studies have used assimilation analysis, a systematic, theoretically based, qualitative approach to case study (Stiles & Angus, 2001; Stiles, Meshot, et al., 1992) illustrated briefly in the foregoing review of the case of John Jones. The studies have yielded a provisional description of the assimilation sequence, summarized in the APES (table 19.1).

Interpretive research (qualitative, theoretically based case studies) can be confirmatory as well as exploratory. Interpretive and hypothesis-testing research are alternative strategies for scientific quality control on theory (Stiles, 1993). In hypothesis-testing research, scientists extract or derive one statement (or a few statements) from a theory and compare this statement with observations. If the observations match the statement (that is, if the scientists' experience of the observed events resembles their experience of the statement; see Stiles, 1981), then people's confidence in the statement is substantially increased, and this, in turn, yields a small increment of confidence in the theory as a whole. In interpretive research, scientists compare their observations with many statements at once. A case study, for example, may compare a large number of observations based on a particular individual with a correspondingly large number of theoretical statements. Such studies ask, in effect, how well the theory describes the details of a particular case. The increment or decrement in confidence in any one statement may be very small. Nevertheless, because many statements are examined, the increment (or decrement) in people's confidence in the whole theory may be comparable to that stemming from a statistical hypothesis-testing study. A few systematically analyzed therapy cases that match a clinical theory in precise or unexpected detail may strongly support a theory, even though each component assertion may remain tentative when considered separately.

Interpretive Studies

Assimilation analyses of cases have yielded a variety of examples of problematic experiences that have been assimilated, to a greater or lesser degree, following the pattern described in the model and the APES. Each case was different and has, in varied proportions, drawn upon, confirmed, modified, and elaborated aspects of the model. There has also been much overlap, and the aggregate offers a substantial basis for confidence in the model. The cases (pseudonyms) and problematic experiences have included the following: (1) John made partial progress in assimilating an angry resentment of people that led to a sense of anxiety or panic in social situations (Stiles et al., 1991). (2) Joan assimilated a feeling of emptiness that seemed to stem from a deep-seated feeling of personal inadequacy (Stiles et al., 1991). (3) John Jones assimilated his homosexual feelings by accommodating his acceptance-of-others schema to include himself (Stiles, Meshot, et al., 1992). (4) Mrs. M. assimilated a wish to develop her own personal space, which at times meant putting her own needs before those of her children (Shapiro, Barkham, Reynolds, Hardy, & Stiles, 1992). (5) June assimilated a sense of personal vulnerability, which was expressed in anxiety over talking about her feelings (Stiles, Shapiro, & Harper, 1994). (6) Marie assimilated a guilt-producing wish to let go of her mother (Field, Barkham, Shapiro, & Stiles, 1994). (7) Jane Davis assimilated the problematic expression of risky feelings, the avoidance of which had led to use of third-person constructions and other objectifying language in describing her own feelings (Stiles, Shapiro, Harper, & Morrison, 1995). (8) Lisa assimilated her resentment at her husband's gambling (Honos-Webb, Stiles, Greenberg, & Goldman, 1998) and a sense of personal responsibility for others' hurtful behaviors (Honos-Webb, Stiles, Greenberg, & Goldman, in press).

(9) George made steps toward assimilating an urge to avoid his wife and run away, though progress stalled, and assimilation was not far advanced by the time treatment ended (Honos-Webb et al., 1998). (10) Jan assimilated problematic voices of neediness and weakness and of rebellion (Honos-Webb, Surko, Stiles, & Greenberg, 1999). (11) Fatima made progress in assimilating the trauma of her infant daughter's death (Varvin & Stiles, 1999). (12) Debbie assimilated her verbal outbursts, which became a resource of appropriate assertiveness (Stiles, 1999b). (13) Vicky assimilated expressions of her sexuality in ways that were related to but somewhat augmented problems in her relationship with her mother (Knobloch, Endres, Stiles, & Silberschatz, 2001). The cited studies include examples of dialogue illustrating each of the APES levels.

Hypothesis-Testing Studies

There have also been a few hypothesis-testing studies bearing on the assimilation model. Two of these have been based on the consideration that clients' *aptitude* for responding to one treatment or another may depend on the APES level of their presenting problems more than their diagnosis or stable aspects of their personality. Theoretically, problems at low APES levels are poorly formulated or dissociated, so that psychodynamic, experiential, or interpersonal approaches, which emphasize exploration, might be most appropriate. On the other hand, problems at intermediate APES levels are relatively well formulated and might be more efficiently addressed by cognitive or behavioral approaches, which emphasize more prescriptive techniques. The studies were based on the first and second Sheffield Psychotherapy Projects (SPP1 and SPP2; see Shapiro et al., 1994; Shapiro & Firth, 1987), which compared a cognitive-behavioral (CB) treatment with a psychodynamic-interpersonal (PI) treatment.

Treatment Order and Thematic Continuity

The crossover design of SPP1 (eight sessions of one treatment followed by eight sessions of the other) permitted an examination of the suggestion that the PI and CB approaches tend to focus on problems at different levels of assimilation. The hypothesis was that progress *on particular problems* would be relatively smooth and steady for clients who received treatment in the PI-CB order (thematic continuity: first becoming aware of unassimilated experiences and formulating a problem in PI sessions, then pursuing rational solutions in practical situations in CB sessions) whereas progress would tend to follow a discontinuous course for clients in the CB-PI order (thematic discontinuity: first solving problems sufficiently assimilated to be stated clearly, then changing focus at mid-treatment to explore less formulated problems). This was tested by examining plots of the severity of each of 10 individualized target problems, rated three times a week across the course of their treatment. Discontinuities would appear as relatively curved plots, indicating that progress on a problem occurred at different rates in the two segments of treatment. Consistent with the hypothesis, 41.5% of the CB-PI clients' plots were classified as curved, whereas only 15.8% of the PI-CB clients' plots were classified as curved (Stiles, Barkham, Shapiro, & Firth-Cozens, 1992).

Aptitude-Treatment Interaction

Customizing at the level of treatment choice could involve using APES levels in assigning clients to alternative treatments. A study drawing on SPP2 (in which clients received either CB or PI treatment but not both) found that clients whose problems were rated in the problem statement/clarification region (roughly, APES level 2.5 or higher; see table 19.1), as assessed from the first 20 minutes of their first session, improved significantly more when assigned to CB treatment than when assigned to PI treatment. Among clients in this study whose presenting problems were rated as vague awareness/emergence or lower (roughly, APES level 2.0 or lower), the improvement was equivalent in the two treatments. This aptitude-treatment interaction was large enough to account for essentially all of the difference in outcomes between the two treatments (Stiles, Shankland, Wright, & Field, 1997). If intake interviewers could assess the APES level of the presenting problems, they might assign clients to treatments more appropriately.

LIMITATIONS OF THE RESEARCH REVIEWED

The assimilation model has been used as a way to understand the process and outcome of therapy, not as an approach to conducting therapy. The reviewed research has examined the strength of the assimilation model, rather than the value of any particular technique. Thus, the results point to a way of thinking about the relationship rather than prescribing particular therapist behaviors.

On the other hand, interpretive research, such as assimilation analysis, can help overcome the *responsiveness problem*, which bedevils much research on the effectiveness of psychotherapy processes and relationships. Responsiveness refers to behavior that is affected by emerging context and occurs on many levels, including choice of an overall treatment approach, case formulation and planning, strategic use of particular techniques, and moment-by-moment adjustments within interventions (Stiles, Honos-Webb, & Surko, 1998). Successful responsiveness defeats attempts to find naturalistically observed linear relations between outcome and any aspects of technique that can be volitionally controlled (for example, interpretations, self-disclosures, advice, providing feedback). So long as clients tend to receive as much as they require, highly effective ingredients may have null or even negative correlations with outcome variables. Even if interpretation is an effective technique, for example, giving huge numbers of additional interpretations will not speed clients' progress (see Stiles, 1988; and Stiles & Shapiro, 1994, for further explanation and examples). Because of such problems, naturalistically observed linear relations between process or relationship variables and outcome variables, whether positive, negative, or null, are not to be trusted.

Evaluative aspects of the process or of the relationship, such as empathy and the alliance, take responsiveness into account but by the same token involve different behaviors across clients and occasions (for example, maintaining a strong alliance involves using many behaviors responsively rather than performing a consistent profile of behaviors with all clients on all occasions). Interpretive research, such as assimilation analysis, takes responsiveness into account and offers clinical specificity in the form of particular instances of interventions that appeared effective (or ineffective) in context (Stiles, 1993; Stiles et al., 1998). Generality is provided via the theory or model that was assessed in the research (that is, support for the theory encourages more general application).

THERAPEUTIC PRACTICES

The assimilation model suggests not only a generic treatment goal—to facilitate the client's progress along the assimilation continuum—but also a series of specific subgoals, corresponding to the APES levels. This guidance is not a mechanical prescription, however, but involves appropriate responsiveness to client requirements as they emerge during treatment. As the client changes, the therapeutic relationship changes (or should change) responsively, reflecting the evolving goals, feelings, and behaviors that represent therapeutic progress.

Markers

Markers of assimilation levels are recognizable types of events in psychotherapy discourse that are empirically and theoretically linked to those levels. Research on finding and describing reliably recognizable markers has yielded more than two dozen candidates (Honos-Webb, Surko, et al., 1999). For example, in the *fear of losing control marker*, the client expresses a fear that discussing or exploring a topic will be disruptive to daily life or to long-held beliefs, leading to panic or dangerous or embarrassing outbursts. This marker signals APES level 1, the emergence of unwanted thoughts (Honos-Webb, Lani, & Stiles, 1999). Markers of a problem's current level of assimilation, expressed in terms of the APES, could guide therapists in facilitating the problem's movement to the next level (Stiles et al., 1995). For example, within any theoretical approach, the way of responding to a client who is trying to suppress unwanted thoughts (APES level 1) would differ from the way of responding to a client who has already formulated an explicit problem to work on (APES level 3). Markers of assimilation levels detected at intake could be used in selecting appropriate treatments or treatment strategies.

Zone of Proximal Development

When an interacting client and therapist are considered jointly, they may reach higher levels on the APES than when the client is considered alone (Leiman & Stiles, in press). For example, the dyad jointly may be able to formulate a problem (APES level 3) while the client alone would be avoiding the topic (APES level 1). This difference may be understood using a concept drawn from developmental psychology, the zone of proximal development (ZPD; see Stetsenko, 1999). It has been defined as "the distance between the actual developmental level as determined by independent problem solving and the level of potential development as determined through problem solving under adult guidance or in collaboration with more capable peers" (Vygotsky, 1978, p. 86). Applied to the psychotherapeutic relationship, the ZPD can be understood as the segment of the APES continuum within which a problematic voice can proceed from one level to the next with the therapist's assistance (Leiman & Stiles, in press). Interventions aimed outside of the client's ZPD, regardless of the therapist's theoretical approach, are likely to be ineffective. For example, explanations or interpretations aimed at fostering understanding (APES level 4) may be useless or counterproductive for a client with a narrow ZPD whose problem is in the process of painfully emerging (APES level 2).

Relationship Differences Across Approaches

Therapists using different theoretical approaches appear to use the ZPD differently to facilitate movement through the APES levels. In one pair of assimilation analyses, a client-centered therapist's interventions followed the APES level of client's own descriptions, while the client took the initiative to advance to higher levels (Glick, Stiles, & Greenberg, 2000). In contrast, a cognitive-behavioral therapist tended to lead the client in APES terms, in effect challenging her and pulling her along (Osatuke, Stiles, Shapiro, & Barkham, 2000). Graphically, the client-centered case made smooth but gradual progress along the APES continuum, whereas the cognitive-behavioral case followed a sawtooth pattern—movement toward greater assimilation through repeated sequences of a rapid advance followed by a falling back to an earlier level. Each "tooth" seemed to represent a different narrow topic or domain, reflecting the therapist's strategy of focusing on issues one by one, actively leading the client to the cutting edge of each issue.

ACKNOWLEDGMENT   I thank Meredith J. Glick, Michael Gray, Carol L. Humphreys, James A. Lani, Katerine Osatuke, and D'Arcy Reynolds for helpful comments on drafts of this chapter

REFERENCES

Field, S. D., Barkham, M., Shapiro, D. A., & Stiles, W. B. (1994). Assessment of assimilation in psychotherapy: A quantitative case study of problematic experiences with a significant other. *Journal of Counseling Psychology, 41*, 397–406.

Glick, M. J., Stiles, W. B., & Greenberg, L. S. (2000, June). Assimilation patterns in a case of client-centered psychotherapy. In W. B. Stiles (Moderator), *Assimilation analysis of client-centered and cognitive-behavioral therapy and methodological developments*. Panel presentation at the Society for Psychotherapy Research meeting, Chicago, IL.

Honos-Webb, L., Lani, J. A., & Stiles, W. B. (1999). Discovering markers of assimilation stages: The fear of losing control marker. *Journal of Clinical Psychology, 55*, 1441–1452.

Honos-Webb, L., & Stiles, W. B. (1998). Reformulation of assimilation analysis in terms of voices. *Psychotherapy, 35*, 23–33.

Honos-Webb, L., Stiles, W. B., Greenberg, L. S., & Goldman, R. (1998). Assimilation analysis of process-experiential psychotherapy: A comparison of two cases. *Psychotherapy Research, 8*, 264–286.

Honos-Webb, L., Stiles, W. B., Greenberg, L. S., & Goldman, R. (in press). Responsibility for "being there": An assimilation analysis. In C. T. Fischer (Ed.), *Qualitative research methods for psychology: Vol. 1. Human science case demonstrations*. San Diego, CA: Academic.

Honos-Webb, L., Surko, M., Stiles, W. B., & Greenberg, L. S. (1999). Assimilation of voices in psychotherapy: The case of Jan. *Journal of Counseling Psychology, 46*, 448–460.

Knobloch, L. M., Endres, L. M., Stiles, W. B., & Silberschatz, G. (2001). Convergence and divergence of themes in successful psychotherapy: An assimilation analysis. *Psychotherapy, 38*, 31–39.

Leiman, M., & Stiles, W. B. (2001). Dialogical sequence analysis and the zone of proximal development as conceptual enhancements to the assimilation model: The case of Jan revisited. *Psychotherapy Research, 11*, 311–330.

Osatuke, K., Stiles, W. B., Shapiro, D. A., & Barkham, M. (2000, June). Assimilation patterns in a cognitive-behavioral therapy case. In W. B. Stiles (Moderator), *Assimilation analysis of client-centered and cognitive-behavioral therapy and methodological developments*. Panel presentation at the Society for Psychotherapy Research meeting, Chicago, IL.

Piaget, J. (1970). Piaget's theory (G. Gellerier, & J. Langer, Trans.). In P. H. Mussen (Ed.), *Carmichael's manual of child psychology* (3rd ed., Vol. 1, pp. 703–732). New York: Wiley.

Shapiro, D. A., Barkham, M., Rees, A., Hardy, G. E., Reynolds, S., & Startup, M. (1994). Effects of treatment duration and severity of depression on the effectiveness of cognitive-behavioral and psychodynamic-interpersonal psychotherapy. *Journal of Consulting and Clinical Psychology, 62*, 522–534.

Shapiro, D. A., Barkham, M., Reynolds, S., Hardy, G., & Stiles, W. B. (1992). Prescriptive and exploratory psychotherapies: Toward an integration based on the assimilation model. *Journal of Psychotherapy Integration, 2*, 253–272.

Shapiro, D. A., & Firth, J. A. (1987) Prescriptive vs. exploratory psychotherapy: Outcomes of the Sheffield Psychotherapy Project. *British Journal of Psychiatry, 151*, 790–799.

Snyder, W. U. (1963). *Dependency in psychotherapy: A casebook*. New York: Macmillan.

Stetsenko, A. P. (1999). Social interaction, cultural tools, and the zone of proximal development: In search of a synthesis. In S. Chaiklin, M. Hedegaard, & U. J. Jensen (Eds.), *Activity theory and social practice: Cultural-historical approaches* (pp. 235–252). Aarhus, Denmark: Aarhus University Press.

Stiles, W. B. (1981). Science, experience, and truth: A conversation with myself. *Teaching of Psychology, 8*, 227–230.

Stiles, W. B. (1988). Psychotherapy process-outcome correlations may be misleading. *Psychotherapy, 25*, 27–35.

Stiles, W. B. (1993). Quality control in qualitative research. *Clinical Psychology Review, 13*, 593–618.

Stiles, W. B. (1997). Signs and voices: Joining a conversation in progress. *British Journal of Medical Psychology, 70,* 169–176.

Stiles, W. B. (1999a). Signs and voices in psychotherapy. *Psychotherapy Research, 9,* 1–21.

Stiles, W. B. (1999b). *Signs, voices, meaning bridges, and shared experience: How talking helps.* Visiting Scholar Series No. 10 (ISSN 1173–9940). Palmerston North, New Zealand: School of Psychology, Massey University.

Stiles, W. B. (1999c). Suppression of CBA voices: A theoretical note on the psychology and psychotherapy of depression. *Psychotherapy, 36,* 268–273.

Stiles, W. B., & Angus, L. (2001). Qualitative research on clients' assimilation of problematic experiences in psychotherapy. In J. Frommer & D. L. Rennie (Eds.), *Qualitative psychotherapy research: Methods and methodology* (pp. 111–126). Lengerich, Germany: Pabst.

Stiles, W. B., Barkham, M., Shapiro, D. A., & Firth-Cozens, J. (1992). Treatment order and thematic continuity between contrasting psychotherapies: Exploring an implication of the assimilation model. *Psychotherapy Research, 2,* 112–124.

Stiles, W. B., Elliott, R., Llewelyn, S. P., Firth-Cozens, J. A., Margison, F. R., Shapiro, D. A., & Hardy, G. (1990). Assimilation of problematic experiences by clients in psychotherapy. *Psychotherapy, 27,* 411–420.

Stiles, W. B., Honos-Webb, L., & Surko, M. (1998). Responsiveness in psychotherapy. *Clinical Psychology: Science and Practice, 5,* 439–458.

Stiles, W. B., Meshot, C. M., Anderson, T. M., & Sloan, W. W., Jr. (1992). Assimilation of problematic experiences: The case of John Jones. *Psychotherapy Research, 2,* 81–101.

Stiles, W. B., Morrison, L. A., Haw, S. K., Harper, H., Shapiro, D. A., & Firth-Cozens, J. (1991). Longitudinal study of assimilation in exploratory psychotherapy. *Psychotherapy, 28,* 195–206.

Stiles, W. B., Shankland, M. C., Wright, J., & Field, S. D. (1997). Aptitude-treatment interactions based on clients' assimilation of their presenting problems. *Journal of Consulting and Clinical Psychology, 65,* 889–893.

Stiles, W. B., & Shapiro, D. A. (1994). Disabuse of the drug metaphor: Psychotherapy process-outcome correlations. *Journal of Consulting and Clinical Psychology, 62,* 942–948.

Stiles, W. B., Shapiro, D. A., & Harper, H. (1994). Finding the way from process to outcome: Blind alleys and unmarked trails. In R. L. Russell (Ed.), *Reassessing psychotherapy research* (pp. 36–64). New York: Guilford.

Stiles, W. B., Shapiro, D. A., Harper, H., & Morrison, L. A. (1995). Therapist contributions to psychotherapeutic assimilation: An alternative to the drug metaphor. *British Journal of Medical Psychology, 68,* 1–13.

Varvin, S., & Stiles, W. B. (1999). Emergence of severe traumatic experiences: An assimilation analysis of psychoanalytic therapy with a political refugee. *Psychotherapy Research, 9,* 381–404.

Vygotsky, L. (1978). *Mind in society: The development of higher psychological processes* (M. Cole, V. John-Steiner, S. Scribner, & E. Souberman, Eds.). Cambridge, MA: Harvard University Press.

20

Attachment Style

Björn Meyer
Paul A. Pilkonis

Since the publication of John Bowlby's seminal works more than 30 years ago (for example, Bowlby, 1969), attachment theory has inspired an impressive amount of research and theoretical speculation on the function and structure of close relationships. Whereas early studies focused primarily on attachment during childhood (for example, Ainsworth, Blehar, Waters, & Wall, 1978), recent years have witnessed a proliferation of research on adult attachment, especially in the area of romantic relationships (for example, Hazan & Shaver, 1987, 1994; Simpson & Rholes, 1998). Psychotherapy researchers have also become active in exploring attachment theory's implications (see Mace & Margison, 1997; Strauss, 2000).

In this chapter, we review the key ideas defining attachment theory, describe research linking attachment styles to adult psychotherapy, review research linking attachment style to treatment outcome, and propose evidence-supported guidelines for psychotherapists working with adult patients. More extensive expositions can be found in Bowlby (1969, 1988), Cassidy and Shaver (1999), Hazan and Shaver (1987, 1994), Holmes (1996), and Simpson and Rholes (1998), among others.

DEFINITIONS AND MEASUREMENT

Adult attachment styles describe people's comfort and confidence in close relationships, their fear of rejection and yearning for intimacy, and their preference for self-sufficiency or interper-

sonal distance (for more technical definitions, see Cassidy & Shaver, 1999). Attachment styles are formed in response to real-life experiences with caregivers and other people, and they reflect mental representations of others, of oneself in relation to others, and of relationships in general.

Theory

One assumption of attachment theory is that infants are inherently motivated to form close emotional bonds with caregivers because natural selection promoted the evolution of such motivation (Chisholm, 1996; Simpson, 1999). Thus, infants will seek to stay within close proximity to caregivers, which ensures their protection and maximizes the probability of survival. When infants perceive threat in the environment, the attachment system is activated, triggering feelings of anxiety and behavioral expressions of distress (such as crying, pleading). These signals prompt the attachment figure to respond by increasing proximity and providing physical and emotional support. Feelings of security in the infant are thus reestablished.

The experience that distress can be managed, that personal action reliably triggers the supportive activation of the social environment, has profound implications for children's development. Based on such experiences, children form "internal working models"—mental representations of caregivers' sensitivity and responsiveness. These mental models are thought to influence how people perceive, interpret, and act in relationships across their life span. If caregivers respond sensitively and consistently to children's needs and distress, positive working models are formed, such that the child comes to think of others as trustworthy, and of him or herself as worthy of others' responsiveness.

Attachment theory also contains the idea that emotional and behavioral disturbances result from caregivers' failure to respond adequately to children's needs and distress. If caregivers respond inconsistently, others will tend to be viewed as unpredictable, and relationships as uncertain and in need of constant monitoring. Children who experience caregivers' consistent lack of responsiveness, in turn, may learn that others cannot generally be relied upon, and their internal working models will come to reflect the notion that distance and self-sufficiency are preferable. Thus, attachment theory posits that early experiences with caregivers carry over into adulthood, influencing perceptions, expectations, and behaviors in relationships across the life span.

Not all adult relationships qualify as attachment relationships, however. Only those involving four definitional features can be said to be attachment relationships: (1) seeking and maintaining physical proximity (*proximity maintenance*); (2) seeking comfort or aid when needed (*safe haven*); (3) experiencing distress on unexpected or prolonged separations (*separation distress*); and (4) relying on the attachment figure as a base of security from which to engage in exploratory and other nonattachment activities (*secure base*) (see Hazan, 2000).

Evidence

Many of the hypotheses defining attachment theory have received empirical support (see Cassidy & Shaver, 1999; Simpson & Rholes, 1998). For example, evidence supports the idea that humans are inherently motivated to form lasting affectional bonds (see Baumeister & Leary, 1995). Evidence also indicates that children's attachment styles can be distinguished reliably, even across cultures (van Ijzendoorn & Kroonenberg, 1988; van Ijzendoorn & Sagi, 1999; but see Rothbaum, Weisz, Pott, Miyake, & Morelli, 2000).

The strange-situation paradigm (Ainsworth, Blehar, Waters, & Wall, 1978), in which children's responses to maternal separation and reunion are analyzed, has served as a catalyst for empirical progress in this area. Using this methodology, a variety of infant attachment types can be identified reliably, including the secure, anxious-ambivalent, and avoidant patterns. Following maternal separation, securely attached infants are comforted by the mother's return and resume play and exploration. Anxious-ambivalent children, in contrast, are not easily soothed and remain preoccupied with vigilantly monitoring their mothers' whereabouts, seemingly to ensure her uncertain presence. Avoidant infants, in turn, remain aloof and disinterested upon the mother's return, consistent with the hypothesis that they have learned to prefer distance and autonomy. A fourth pattern—disorganized/disoriented attachment—describes infants who have not developed a consistent strategy for coping with the stress involved in the strange situation.

As predicted by the theory, caregivers' sensitivity and responsiveness have been found to contribute to the formation of attachment styles, even though child temperament also plays a role (Belsky, 1999; DeWolff & van Ijzendoorn, 1997; Goldsmith & Alansky, 1987). As one would expect, inconsistent maternal responsiveness tends to lead to anxious-ambivalent attachment, whereas consistent unresponsiveness begets the avoidant style. Once formed, these attachment styles show considerable stability across development (Hamilton, 2000; Waters, Merrick, Treboux, Crowell, & Albersheim, 2000). For example, among 60 infants whose attachment style was classified at 12 months of age, 72% retained their initial secure-insecure classification 20 years later, and changes in attachment could usually be explained by the occurrence of negative life events (Waters et al., 2000). Evidence suggests that negative interpersonal experiences, such as parents' depression or divorce, can cause enduring shifts in attachment (Beckwith, Cohen, & Hamilton, 1999). Conversely, some data suggest that greater security in attachment can be "earned" or "acquired" during the course of development (for example, Beckwith et al., 1999; Phelps, Belsky, & Crnic, 1998).

Adults form mental representations of their capacity to form close emotional bonds, of others' trustworthiness, and of relationships in general (Bartholomew & Horowitz, 1991; Bretherton & Munholland, 1999; Griffin & Bartholomew, 1994). These mental representations—internal working models—influence thinking about and behaving in the context of close relationships, allowing for the classification of distinguishable adult attachment styles (Brennan, Clark, & Shaver, 1998; Solomon & George, 1999). As with children, adult attachment is often classified as secure, anxious-ambivalent (or preoccupied), and avoidant. Secure attachment reflects people's sense of comfort and confidence about relatedness, preoccupied attachment is marked by fear of rejection and yearning for intimacy, and avoidant attachment indicates discomfort with closeness and defensive self-sufficiency.

Measurement

There are at least two approaches to the measurement of attachment in adults. The first approach is based on the idea that the manner in which adults speak about past and present relationships provides clues about their internal working models. This "narrative approach" has culminated in the assessment of adult attachment via the analysis of semistructured interviews, for example, the Adult Attachment Interview (AAI; see George, Kaplan, & Main, 1985; Solomon & George, 1999). In this procedure, spoken narratives about attachment experiences are transcribed and analyzed, yielding classifications of attachment "states of mind." For example, adults with "autonomous" or secure attachment are able to communicate with coherence, balance, and emotional genuineness, even about difficult childhood experiences. Those with "dismissing" or avoidant attachment, by contrast, tend to idealize early experiences and describe events in a detached or contradictory manner. Finally, those with preoccupied attachment often seem overwhelmed with early relationship experiences, unable to elaborate coherently without being flooded by emotions. The AAI was developed for the purpose of identifying parental correlates of children's attachment, and, as hypothesized, AAI dimensions are linked with children's attachment styles (for example, Benoit & Parker, 1994).

A second approach to the measurement of adult attachment is the use of self-report instruments (Brennan, Clark, & Shaver, 1998; Shaver, Belsky, & Brennan, 2000). These questionnaires are often based on Hazan and Shaver's work (Hazan & Shaver, 1987, 1994), who, in turn, based their dimensions on Ainsworth's classification of secure, ambivalent, and avoidant attachment (Ainsworth et al., 1978). Self-reports of adult attachment converge to a substantial degree, and it is now possible to use brief (36 to 40 items) questionnaires containing items culled from many measures (Fraley, Waller, & Brennan, 2000). Evidence suggests that self-reported romantic attachment styles can be captured by two continuous dimensions—anxiety and avoidance—which emerge from factor analyses of attachment-related item sets (Brennan, Clark, & Shaver, 1998). The anxious dimension is thought to reflect people's mental model of the self; the avoidant dimension, people's model of others (see Brennan, Clark, & Shaver, 1998). Combinations of these dimensions yield four adult attachment styles (see Bartholomew & Horowitz, 1991): Secure (positive self and other models), preoccupied (negative self and positive other), fearful-avoidant (negative self and negative other), and dismissing-avoidant (positive self and negative other). Self-reports of romantic attachment converge only moderately with the AAI-derived attachment "states of mind" (Shaver, Belsky, & Brennan, 2000), suggesting that these instruments capture somewhat different facets of attachment.

In addition to attachment-related narratives and self-report instruments, questionnaires measuring attachment in the context of psychotherapy have been developed (Hoger, 1999; Mallinckrodt, Gantt, & Coble, 1995). Therapy contains many of the features that characterize the child-caregiver relationship, including, for example, the therapist's comforting presence, the potential for emotion regulation, and the provision of a "secure base" that allows for the safe exploration of difficult psychological territory (Bowlby, 1988). In a way that is similar to how children attach to caregivers and how adults attach to romantic partners, patients can be said to attach to their therapist. Patients' internal working models, then, may influence perceptions, interpretations, expectations, and actions in response to the therapy situation.

Adult attachment styles have been shown to be associated with a host of theoretically predicted variables. For example, self-reports of romantic attachment have predicted the success of forming intimate relationships (Hazan & Shaver, 1994; Klohnen & Bera, 1998). In general, securely attached people form healthy, committed, and lasting relationships; those with preoccupied attachment form tumultuous, intense relationships; and those with avoidant attachment form uncommitted, brief relationships (cf. Feeney, 1999; Hazan & Shaver, 1994; Klohnen & Bera, 1998). Compared to those with other attachment styles, securely attached people tend to trust their partners more easily and cope more constructively when trust has been violated (Mikulincer, 1998). Perceived threats will prompt securely attached persons to seek the support of a partner, whereas avoidantly attached individuals will seek interpersonal distance. These coping differences have been observed when people are faced with laboratory stressors (Simpson, Rholes, & Nelligan, 1992) and even when they confront the threat of war (Mikulincer, Florian, & Weller, 1993).

The links among adult attachment, personality, and psychopathology have also become clearer in recent years (Brennan & Shaver, 1998; Carver, 1997; Dozier, Stovall, & Albus, 1999). For instance, secure attachment shows some overlap with extraversion, avoidant attachment with introversion, and preoccupied attachment with neuroticism (see Carver, 1997). Secure attachment tends to be inversely associated with both Axis I and II pathology, whereas insecure forms of attachment tend to be linked with anxiety, depression, and general maladjustment (Brennan & Shaver, 1998). Certain personality disorders appear to be distinctly associated with attachment styles. For example, preoccupied attachment is highly prevalent among those with dependent personality disorder (Brennan & Shaver, 1998).

CLINICAL EXAMPLE

Jane, a 30-year-old single legal assistant, presented for outpatient psychotherapy one week after discharge from a 10-day stay at the mood disorders unit of a psychiatric hospital. She had become severely depressed after her fiancé had ended their relationship and moved in with another woman. Three days after this breakup, Jane noticed recurrent suicidal thoughts and sought voluntary admission to the hospital. She recovered from suicidal ideation, was started on antidepressant medication, and participated in daily supportive group therapy while on the unit. However, she remained clinically depressed even after discharge.

At the beginning of therapy, Jane scored a 40 on the Beck Depression Inventory (BDI-II; see Beck, Steer, & Brown, 1996). She displayed a broad range of depressive symptoms, with particularly high scores on items measuring sadness, punishment feelings, self-criticalness, crying, loss of energy, and concentration difficulties. In addition to receiving psychotherapy, she continued to be maintained on antidepressant medication.

Jane reported that her current depressive episode was not her first. In fact, she had experienced three prior episodes: one in her late teens after the slow and painful resolution of a long-term relationship, one following the breakup of a relationship in her early twenties, and one after being fired from a sales manager job, prior to entering college at age 23. She received a diagnosis of major depressive disorder, recurrent, severe without psychotic features. No other diagnoses were made on Axis I or II.

Following an initial psychosocial interview, weekly sessions of interpersonal therapy (IPT) were initiated. Given the obvious significance of the recent breakup as a trigger of her depressive episode, the focus within the IPT framework was on role transition and, secondarily, on grieving the lost relationship. Consistent with the IPT protocol, goals included mourning and acceptance of the loss of the old role, helping her regard the new role as more positive, and restoring self-esteem by developing a sense of mastery regarding the demands of new roles (Klerman, Weissman, Rounsaville, & Chevron, 1984).

Jane's depression decreased substantially over the course of treatment, with an initial rapid response (BDI-II decrease from 40 to 26 between sessions 1 and 2) and a subsequent gradual and maintained reduction of symptoms. After 16 IPT sessions, her BDI-II score of 7 reflected only residual symptoms. Follow-up sessions were scheduled at less frequent intervals, but she continued to attend sessions at least once per month for an additional 6 months.

From an attachment perspective, at least three questions were relevant: (1) What was the nature of Jane's internal working models, as reflected in the narrative flow of attachment-relevant experiences? (2) How were her thoughts, beliefs, and attitudes about others and herself (that is, working models) influencing current romantic relationships? (3) What was the quality of her attachment to the therapist? Jane demonstrated remarkable coherence, genuine emotional engagement, and balance in her descriptions of past and current relationships. Further, her attachment to the therapist appeared secure (Mallinckrodt et al., 1995)—the therapeutic alliance was strong and productive (although no formal assessments were performed). The question concerning the relationship between internal working models and

current relationship functioning deserved further clarification, however, and a questionnaire was administered to estimate Jane's attachment in the context of current romantic relationships.

Toward the end of therapy—after session 12—Brennan, Clark, and Shaver's (1998) Experiences in Close Relationships (ECR) questionnaire was given as a measure of Jane's romantic attachment style. This questionnaire yields two scores, one for anxiety (model of the self) and one for avoidance (model of others). Mean scores on both 18-item scales were computed (each of which can range from 1 to 7), and the intersection of these two scores was plotted (see figure 20.1). By dividing each scale at its midpoint (neutral response), four quadrants of attachment were derived. For example, a combination of high anxiety and low avoidance corresponds to the quadrant of preoccupied attachment. This method yielded

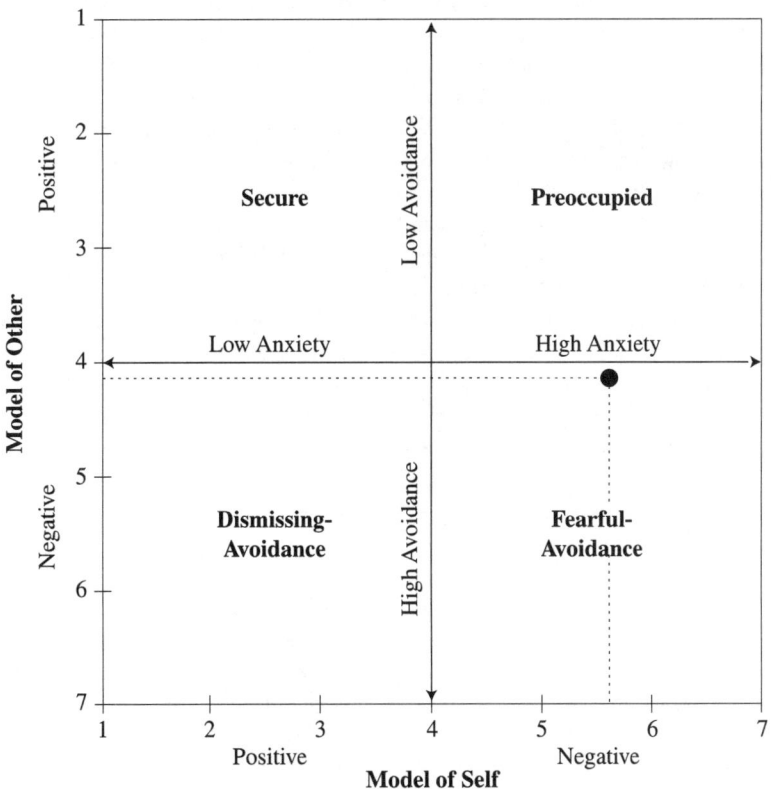

Figure 20.1. Jane's Romantic Attachment Style: Results from the Experiences in Close Relationships (ECR) Questionnaire (Brennan, Clark, & Shaver, 1998)

a quick estimate of Jane's predominant romantic attachment style. With scores of 5.7 on the anxiety dimension and 4.2 on avoidance, Jane's responses best fit the pattern of fearful-avoidant attachment, almost into preoccupied attachment.

Despite the low intensity of her depression after the twelfth session (BDI-II = 6), Jane's scores on the ECR revealed a potentially problematic profile, at the borderline of the preoccupied and fearful attachment quadrants (see figure 20.1). A similar conclusion emerged when Brennan, Clark, and Shaver's (1998) algorithm was applied, which references a patient's attachment style to norms derived from 1,082 undergraduates. These analyses suggested that Jane's scores fit best with the fearful, but almost equally well with the preoccupied pattern. Thus, her scores reflected a markedly negative model of the self, combined with an ambivalent model of others. Her responses indicated that she tended to worry a great deal about potential abandonment, that she craved reassurance, but that she also tended to feel uncomfortable with intimacy. This pattern suggested that it might be difficult for her to establish and maintain mutually satisfying intimate relationships and that her negative appraisals of herself and her ambivalent views of others might get in the way of attaining this goal.

Jane's case history and test results suggested that interpersonal relationships had long been troublesome and would likely remain a difficult challenge in the future. The structured information gained from the ECR confirmed and clarified this picture and allowed the therapist to rule out alternative hypotheses. For example, one might have guessed that Jane's relationship difficulties were simply a reflection of her depression, and that problems in this regard would vanish once the depression had lifted. Because she completed the attachment questionnaire at a time when her depression scores had essentially returned to baseline, however, this possibility could be ruled out.

In subsequent sessions, the emphasis of psychotherapy shifted, given this new understanding of Jane's romantic attachment style. Her negative self-model in particular became more of a focus, and the goal became to facilitate more confident self-appraisals in the context of romantic relationships. Once the IPT protocol was completed, re-lapse-prevention work employed a variety of clinical strategies to promote this attachment-related goal. For example, cognitive restructuring and mindfulness training were employed, with the overarching goal of fostering a sense of self-trust and comfort, and reducing anxious preoccupation with the possibility of rejection or abandonment. Specifically, for example, hypothetical scenarios involving abandonment were discussed, and "decatastrophizing" strategies were practiced.

It is too early to say whether the adoption of attachment-related goals or therapeutic strategies was effective in the long term. After about one year, Jane has not experienced relapse and is performing well on the job. She has not entered into a new relationship, but—interestingly—she frequently states that, for the first time since she can remember, she is alone and feels perfectly fine about it. The dramatic urgency of having to find a new partner to fill the void seems to have decreased. Jane continues to be speak in a genuine and balanced manner about her past and present relationships, and her alliance with the therapist remains strong. Her case illustrates how attachment-related considerations can influence case conceptualization, treatment planning, and psychotherapy outcome.

RESEARCH REVIEW

Recent studies have begun to examine the multifaceted relationships between attachment styles and psychotherapy. Our review focuses on links between (1) patient attachment and treatment outcome, (2) patient attachment and the therapeutic alliance, and (3) therapist attachment and treatment process and outcome.

Patient Attachment and Outcome

The question of whether patients' attachment styles influence psychotherapy outcome was addressed in three recent studies. In their longitudinal study at the Cassel Hospital in London, Fonagy and colleagues (1996) administered the AAI to 82 inpatients, most of whom were diagnosed with mood disorders and severe personality disorders. All patients received individual and group psychoanalytic therapy, with an average duration of more than 9 months. Although securely attached patients tended to function more optimally than others at both admission and discharge, those classified as dismissive exhibited the greatest amount of relative improvement over the course of treatment. This finding might be interpreted as "regression to the mean"—the tendency of extreme scores to shift toward more moderate levels when assessed at a second time-point (Fonagy et al., 1996). On the other hand, one might conclude that inpatients with dismissive attachment really do benefit more than others from long-term psychoanalytic therapy. As suggested by Fonagy and colleagues (1996, p. 29), "It is perhaps easier to draw someone's attention to past relationships as determinants of current difficulties when they have previously avoided concerning themselves with such issues."

Attachment styles were also examined as potential predictors of treatment response in a study by Pilkonis and colleagues (Meyer, Pilkonis, Proietti, Heape, & Egan, 2001). Among 149 patients (80% outpatients) at a psychiatric hospital in Pittsburgh, attachment dimensions were assessed with the use of a semi-structured psychosocial interview, followed by consensus ratings of several attachment prototypes (see Pilkonis, 1988). In contrast to the AAI's focus on the *form* of patients' narrative, Pilkonis's rating system relies more directly on reported *content*. For example, a patient who reports a high level of comfort in relationships and few difficulties in recovering from interpersonal rejection would receive a high score on secure attachment, with less emphasis on the coherence of the verbal report. Over the course of six months, secure attachment predicted relative improvement, as measured by a global rating of psychosocial functioning, whereas other attachment dimensions were unrelated to outcome (Meyer et al., 2001).

In a third study on the link between attachment and treatment outcome, Mosheim and colleagues (2000) used a German version of Pilkonis's (1988) prototype methodology (Strauss, Lobo-Drost, & Pilkonis, 1999) to classify attachment among 65 inpatients diagnosed with eating disorders, mood disorders, or anxiety disorders. Secure attachment emerged as a significant predictor of therapy-goal attainment over an average treatment duration of seven weeks. Patients who

were rated as comfortable and confident in past and present relationships (that is, securely attached patients) tended to benefit more than others from treatment.

Differences in measurement, in treatment type, and in patient functioning make it difficult to directly compare the results from these three studies. Nonetheless, in all three studies, securely attached patients were functioning best at the end of treatment. Under some conditions, securely attached patients may benefit more than others from treatment (Mosheim et al., 2000), but under other conditions—when patients are more severely impaired and receiving longer-term intensive treatment—those with dismissive attachment may show the best relative trajectory (Fonagy et al., 1996). Securely attached patients might tend to engage productively in most therapy settings, whereas those with dismissing attachment may require more concentrated or targeted interventions, helping them overcome their characteristic detachment. Once they do connect emotionally with a therapist, however, improvement might be all the more dramatic.

It may be difficult to disentangle the effects of patient attachment on treatment outcome, in part, because therapists respond flexibly to patient styles, changing interventions on a moment-to-moment basis to accommodate emerging clinical needs (see Stiles, Honos-Webb, & Surko, 1998). Patients with dismissive attachment may require—and perhaps elicit—more active interventions that facilitate emotional expression and connection. Those with preoccupied attachment may require more supportive interventions that help contain overwhelming emotions. Patients with secure attachment, in turn, may be judged as able to work productively without "customizing" interventions.

The notion that patients' attachment styles elicit different therapeutic responses was explored in a recent study conducted at the University of Leeds (Hardy et al., 1999). In this study, 16 patients in psychodynamic-interpersonal therapy were asked to identify significant events that had occurred in selected sessions. For example, one patient described as significant the therapeutic discussion about "exploring my relationships with my father and grandfather" (p. 40). Using a classification system often applied to the AAI, Hardy and colleagues analyzed transcripts of 10 session segments. Segments that appeared coherent and collaborative were classified as secure, whereas others were classified as dismissing or preoccupied. Consistent with predictions, "Therapists responded to preoccupied styles with reflection, and to dismissing styles with interpretation" (Hardy et al., 1999, p. 51). Thus, as hypothesized, therapists appeared to adjust their interventions in response to patient characteristics, facilitating affective engagement when patients appeared to be emotionally removed (dismissing attachment), and using supportive, containing strategies when patients were emotionally overwhelmed (preoccupied attachment).

In summary, studies using narrative-analysis as well as interview-based approaches suggest that attachment matters in several ways. Individual differences in patients' attachment styles appear to predict traditional measures of outcome and, on a more microscopic level, they predict how therapists respond to patients' verbalizations.

Patient Attachment and Alliance

Additional research has demonstrated that patients' attachment styles also relate to therapy process on an intermediate level of analysis, between the extremes of overall outcome and in-session verbal exchange. This research has focused on linkages between attachment styles and the therapeutic alliance, which, in itself, is a potent predictor of outcome (see Orlinsky, Grawe, & Parks, 1994).

In a study conducted in London, Eames and Roth (2000) investigated the relationships between patients' self-reported attachment styles and the quality of the alliance. Among 30 adult outpatients, the majority of whom received cognitive-behavioral therapy, patient self-reports of attachment correlated with the quality of the therapeutic alliance and with ruptures in the alliance. These relations were prospective in nature; attachment styles were measured at the beginning of therapy, and alliance and rupture ratings were made in sessions 2 to 5. Whereas securely attached patients tended to form effective alliances, fearful (anxious-avoidant) patients tended to experience problems. Interestingly, some evidence also suggested that both the preoccupied

and dismissing attachment dimensions were associated with positive alliance ratings. Patients who yearn for intimacy and fear abandonment might strive with particular persistence to establish a close alliance, given their concern over potential rejection. In contrast, patients with dismissing styles might defensively deny problems in the alliance or establish only a superficial relationship while remaining reluctant to connect and self-disclose on a more genuine, personal level (Eames & Roth, 2000).

Associations between attachment and the therapeutic alliance were also examined in a study by Finnish psychotherapy researchers Kanninen, Salo, and Punamäki (2000). Among 36 Palestinian political ex-prisoners, attachment was measured with a newly devised paper-and-pencil instrument. All patients were asked to describe, in writing, their childhood experiences, their relationship with their parents, and how they thought their upbringing had affected their adult personality. Content and coherence of these responses were rated, and, based on these ratings, patients were classified as secure, preoccupied, or dismissing. All patients participated in individual or group therapy focusing on trauma-related issues, and all completed working alliance questionnaires at early, middle, and late stages of therapy. Although attachment styles did not affect outcome per se, group differences were observed in the formation of the therapeutic alliance. Whereas securely attached patients formed relatively stable alliances throughout treatment, those with preoccupied attachment reported a poor alliance in the middle but very strong alliance in the later stages of therapy. By contrast, patients with dismissing attachment reported deteriorating alliances toward the end of therapy.

Kanninen and colleagues (2000) concluded that internal working models appeared to influence patients' responses to therapists. Those with preoccupied attachment—always aiming to preempt the threat of rejection—responded particularly sensitively to changing interventions over the course of therapy. In the middle stages of treatment, when therapists challenge and confront problematic patterns, such patients tended to infer rejection and, accordingly, notice problems in the therapeutic relationship (Kanninen et al.,

2000). Toward the end of therapy, however, as gains are consolidated and the tone becomes more supportive, they came to view the alliance in unrealistically positive terms. In contrast, patients with dismissing attachment may superficially rate the alliance as strong in early and middle phases of therapy. By the end, however, as they remain detached and fail to establish a genuine emotional connection, dismissing patients may become aware of problems in the alliance.

Another study that examined how patient attachment style contributes to the therapeutic alliance was conducted by Mallinckrodt and colleagues (1995), who developed the Client Attachment to Therapist Scale (CATS) and examined its correlations with a self-report of therapeutic alliance. The CATS is a 36-item questionnaire measuring three facets of patients' attachment to their therapist: patients' perception of their therapist as emotionally supportive or responsive (secure), patients' appraisal of their therapist as disapproving or rejecting (avoidant), and patients' wish be closer or have a more intimate relationship with their therapist (preoccupied/merger). A German questionnaire of patients' attachment to therapists has also been developed (Hoger, 1999); however, this instrument has not yet appeared in English translation.

Among 129 outpatients from the Pacific Northwest, both the secure and fearful-avoidant CATS scales correlated with various aspects of the alliance (Mallinckrodt et al., 1995). For example, securely attached patients, who perceive their therapist as responsive, accepting, and caring, were more likely to endorse a strong alliance. In fact, the magnitude of correlations (around .80) suggested that some CATS scales share a common conceptual core with the working alliance (see Robbins, 1995). Interestingly, there was no relationship between preoccupied attachment and a total alliance scale. Thus, yearning "to be at one" (Mallinckrodt et al., 1995, p. 311) with the therapist is no guarantee for successful therapy. Indeed, in their frantic efforts to avoid rejection, patients with preoccupied attachment may try to submissively please and appease their therapist without engaging in the more risky task of identifying and openly discussing difficult personal problems (that is, agreeing on therapeutic tasks and goals).

Although the CATS may provide an efficient estimate of patients' perceptions and attitudes regarding their therapist, the constructs it assesses appear to be distinct from those measured by romantic attachment scales. CATS subscale scores related only weakly or not at all to self-reports of romantic attachment (Mallinckrodt et al., 1995), suggesting that people's mental representations of their therapist are separable from those they hold of romantic partners. Consistent with theoretical predictions, however, some of CATS's dimensions relate to early experiences with caregivers. Specifically, patients who exhibit avoidant-fearful attachment to their therapist tend to recall more negative family experiences (Mallinckrodt, King, & Coble, 1998). Conceivably, when people experience repeated family conflict, their mental models of others will come to reflect this aspect of relationships, and others—including therapists—will be viewed as potentially hostile or rejecting.

In summary, evidence is converging to suggest that patients' attachment styles influence important parameters of the therapeutic alliance. Patients' mental representations of the self and others in relationships may predict how their therapists respond to them within sessions (Hardy et al., 1999) and how effective they are at establishing a therapeutic alliance (Kanninen et al., 2000; Mallinckrodt et al., 1995).

Therapist Attachment

Although patients' working models are important factors in psychotherapy, it may be equally important to consider therapists' attachment styles. For example, clinicians with secure attachment may handle ruptures in the relationship with patients more easily, whereas those with anxious or preoccupied attachment—given their characteristic fear of rejection—may have difficulties in this regard.

In Rubino, Barker, Roth, and Fearon's (2000) study, this hypothesis was tested and partially supported. Seventy-seven trainee-therapists from England viewed videotaped vignettes of simulated ruptures in the therapeutic alliance and were asked to respond as if they were interacting with actual patients. Each vignette depicted a patient with either a secure, dismissing, fearful, or preoccupied attachment, and therapists were asked to complete self-reports of attachment in close relationships. Independent raters judged the therapists' empathy and depth of interpretation in response to the vignettes. Although results were complex, and some hypotheses were not supported, findings suggested that therapists scoring higher on an anxious-attachment dimension tended to respond less empathically. This was especially true in response to patients with secure and dismissing attachment. Consistent with attachment theory, then, therapists' attachment style—their characteristic level of comfort, anxiety, or avoidance in the context of relationships—may influence the way they practice therapy. Based on the results of their study, Rubino and colleagues (2000, p. 416) concluded that "more anxious therapists might interpret ruptures as an indication of their patients' intention to leave therapy, and their own sensitivity toward abandonment might diminish their ability to be empathic."

Therapists' attachment was also considered in a study by Tyrrell, Dozier, Teague, and Fallot (1999). Adult attachment interviews were administered to a sample of 54 patients with severe mental disorders and to their 21 case managers. Whereas most patients were classified as insecurely attached, most case managers received the secure classification. This study revealed interactions between patients' and case managers' attachment styles in the prediction of the quality of the working alliance, global life satisfaction, and global psychosocial functioning. In each case, the interactions involved a preoccupied vs. dismissing attachment dimension. Findings suggested that complementary combinations between case managers' and patients' attachment worked best: Preoccupied patients fared best when they worked with dismissing case managers, and—vice versa— dismissing patients fared best when they worked with preoccupied case managers.

Consistent with previous research on client-clinician matches (for example, Beutler et al., 1991), dissimilarities between patients' and therapists' interpersonal style appeared advantageous, supporting the view that patients benefit from interventions that counteract their problematic style of relating to others. Overly emotional patients may require emotion-containing interventions, whereas emotionally detached patients may

need interventions that facilitate affective expression and connection (see Hardy et al., 1999; Stiles et al., 1998). To the degree that patients and therapists happen to be matched in such complementary constellations, therapy may have a natural advantage. Tyrrell and colleagues (1999) noted appropriately that caution is warranted in interpreting their findings and that studies with different patient and therapist populations, alternative measurement approaches, and longitudinal designs are needed to establish the replicability and generalizability of such interactive effects.

Summary

In summary, a growing literature suggests that both patients' and therapists' attachment styles influence important aspects of process and outcome in individual adult psychotherapy. People's mental representations of themselves and of attachment figures—whether they are reflected in manner of speech or in self-reports—make a difference in terms of how therapists respond to patients and in terms of treatment response. Not surprisingly, much of the evidence points to the benefits of a secure attachment style. Patients who feel comfortable in relationships and are not overly concerned about rejection tend to form stable and effective alliances (Kanninen et al., 2000; Eames & Roth, 2000) and may thus benefit more from treatment (Mosheim et al., 2000). At the same time, greater relative improvements may sometimes occur among patients with insecure forms of attachment. This is illustrated by Fonagy and colleagues' (1996) findings that dismissing patients improved more than others in psychoanalytic treatment.

Research is also beginning to demonstrate that therapists' attachment influences treatment. Therapists who tend to worry about rejection may be prone to respond less empathically to some patients (Rubino et al., 2000), at least in analogue research, and complementary matches between therapists' and patients' attachment may affect the quality of the alliance (Tyrrell et al., 1999).

Although attachment styles are important in the prediction of therapy process and outcome, they should not be viewed in isolation. Weinberger's (1995) model captures how attachment processes along with other factors may influence patients' response to treatment. According to his view, patients can learn to face their problems and gain mastery (and eventually improve) to the degree that their therapeutic relationship provides a secure base. Positive expectancies of therapist availability and responsiveness may then give rise to adaptive, problem-focused coping. Given mastery experiences that follow from effective coping, patients may then be more likely to develop further expectations of success, continue to act on these expectations, and eventually attribute therapeutic success to their own efforts. Secure attachment between therapist and patient thus sets into motion a beneficial, self-sustaining cycle that leads eventually to improved functioning. Emerging evidence appears to support such a model. For example, patients who are more securely attached to their therapist form better working alliances and view themselves as more socially efficacious (Mallinckrodt et al., 1995).

LIMITATIONS OF THE RESEARCH

Despite the encouraging findings linking attachment and psychotherapy response, several limitations ought to be noted as well. First, considering the weak convergence among the narrative-analysis approach, self-reports of romantic attachment, and self-reports of patients' attachment to therapists, it will be important to delineate more clearly the conceptual and empirical boundaries of these constructs. Although equivalent labels are sometimes used for the various attachment measures, the lack of convergence suggests that this practice may be misleading. A second problem concerns the heterogeneity of therapies and samples being studied. It is difficult to draw conclusions on how attachment influences the course of treatment when treatments themselves vary dramatically. A third and obvious problem concerns the low number of studies. Fourth, the extant research is largely correlational and indirect. Additional direct evidence from prospective studies is needed. The challenge for research in this area will be to further articulate how therapists can be optimally responsive to patients with different attachment styles, and to test how such responsiveness impacts therapeutic effectiveness.

MODERATORS AND MEDIATORS

What factors determine the strength and direction of the relationships among attachment styles and therapy outcome? What mediators explain how attachment styles influence alliance, outcome, and similar indicators of therapeutic success or failure? The multifaceted nature of attachment and psychotherapy makes it difficult to agree on cross-cutting moderators and mediators. Nevertheless, some of the constructs that have the potential to moderate and mediate the relations between attachment and therapy are discussed in this section.

Moderators

Patients' cultural background may moderate the relations among attachment styles and therapy processes. Attachment theory postulates the existence of universal principles and mechanisms underlying human relatedness. However, this universality assumption has recently been questioned. Rothbaum and colleagues (2000) criticized attachment theorists' tendency to exalt Western virtues of autonomy and independence while "pathologizing" Eastern virtues, such as nurturance and dependency. This bias underscores the need to study how culture and ethnicity influence the relations between attachment and therapy. Conceivably, patients from Western cultures benefit when therapists facilitate exploration and individuation, whereas patients from cultures that value passive accommodation may benefit more from gentle, nurturing interventions (Rothbaum et al., 2000). Culture and ethnicity, then, may moderate associations between attachment styles and therapy process and outcome, but much more research is needed to illuminate such processes.

Mediators

It is also challenging to delineate factors mediating the various linkages between attachment styles and therapy process and outcome. Social-cognitive models that explain how stable individual differences account for situation-specific behaviors (for example, Mischel & Shoda, 1995) may be useful in guiding searches for potential mediators in this area. Such models seem applicable because attachment styles describe temporally stable but nevertheless situation-specific individual differences. For example, when a patient with avoidant attachment perceives that he or she is trapped by excessive intimacy, he or she may withdraw and seek greater distance. When a preoccupied patient perceives the threat of rejection, he or she may cling even more persistently. Attachment styles, then, describe stable yet context-dependent patterns of behaviors, thoughts, and feelings. The social, cognitive, and affective factors that mediate such processes have been examined by Mischel and Shoda (1995).

Mischel and Shoda (1995) argued that context-dependent but yet temporally stable patterns of behavior can be explained by specific constellations in certain "cognitive-affective units." These units include, for instance, differences in people's encoding of information, differences in expectancies, beliefs, and emotional reactions, and differences in goals, values, competencies, and plans. Specific aspects of situations (such as the degree of interpersonal threat inherent in a situation) are thought to activate cognitive-affective units, which then activate or inhibit related units. Although the units themselves remain stable over time (for example, people often hold the same goals and values over time), behavioral output varies depending on contextual input and activation or inhibition of cognitive-affective units. Thus, the model explains how invariant features of personality give rise to situation-specific patterns of behavior.

THERAPEUTIC PRACTICES

1. Assess patients' attachment styles. Several reliable and valid measures of adult attachment have been developed in recent years, and many of these instruments can be used efficiently in clinical practice. These instruments include Brennan, Clark, and Shaver's (1998) Experiences in Close Relationships questionnaire and Mallinckrodt and colleagues' (1995) Client Attachment to Therapist Scale. These questionnaires permit clinicians to obtain quantitative estimates of patients' attachment styles in romantic relationships and in the context of therapy. Unfortunately, no

similar measure is currently available to estimate attachment as it is reflected in patients' speech.

Patient attachment styles suggest specific constellations of internal working models; for example, preoccupied attachment suggests a negative model of the self combined with a positive model of others. Given the assumption that positive self and other models are most desirable, therapists who identify problematic working models gain information about specific treatment goals. For instance, in working with a patient showing signs of dismissing avoidant attachment (positive self and negative other model), the goal would be to increase the positivity of the "other" model.

Given the importance of cultural differences (see Rothbaum et al., 2000), however, therapists should consider that it is not always advisable to facilitate autonomy and individuation. Family and cultural context needs to be evaluated, and attachment-related therapy goals must be adjusted accordingly. For example, in cultures where communal integration is valued, dependency-related traits may not be maladaptive or needing to be changed (Rothbaum et al., 2000).

2. Address patients' attachment style as it relates to therapeutic alliance. Patients present to therapy with different interpersonal or attachment styles, which then pull for different interventions (Hardy, Stiles, Barkham, & Startup, 1998; Hardy et al., 1999). Being adequately responsive to these styles means "giving in" to these pulls but also countering them by complementary therapeutic action. Preoccupied patients pull for emotional-experiential interventions, but they may benefit as well from cognitive-behavioral strategies that help modulate overwhelming feelings. Similarly, avoidant patients pull for rational-cognitive interventions but may benefit also from strategies that facilitate emotional engagement (Hardy et al., 1999). Therapists ought to recognize the potential influence of patients' attachment styles on the quality of the therapeutic alliance. Building a strong alliance may require an individualized balancing of patient attachment style with congruent and complementary therapeutic action.

3. Consider modification of attachment style as a treatment goal. Because there are no empirical data on this question, therapists would be well advised to exploit their existing repertoire of in-

terventions in the pursuit of attachment-related treatment goals. For instance, if a therapist assesses a patient's attachment style, identifies a preoccupied pattern, and sets the goal of bolstering the inadequate self-model, it would seem advisable to employ any interventions serving this goal. Behavioral therapists might reinforce desirable in-session behavior (such as moments of mature, autonomous action) by differentially responding to such events (see Kohlenberg & Tsai, 1991). Cognitively oriented therapists might aim to challenge or refute negative attachment-related thoughts. Regardless of the specific strategies, the therapeutic goal could be derived from attachment considerations, and the effectiveness of intervention strategies would be judged in reference to progress toward those goals.

4. Assess supervisees' attachment styles. Clinical supervision might be enhanced by including assessments of clinicians' attachment styles. This information could then be used to match therapists with patients. The benefits of such matching have not been demonstrated empirically, however, and it would be premature to adopt this in routine clinical practice. But supervisors should recognize that therapists' attachment can influence interventions on a microscopic level. For example, therapists with anxious forms of attachment might tend to respond less empathically than others (Rubino et al., 2000). It would seem advisable, then, to measure and monitor therapists' as well as clients' attachment over the course of therapy and to suggest adjustments in interventions accordingly. These adjustments might involve establishing optimal complementarity between patients' and therapists' interpersonal styles, such that preoccupied patients' overwhelming emotions are contained, and dismissive patients' emotional disengagement is effectively challenged.

REFERENCES

Ainsworth, M. D. S., Blehar, M. C., Waters, E., & Wall, S. (1978). *Patterns of attachment: A psychological study of the strange situation.* Hillsdale, NJ: Erlbaum.

Bartholomew, K., & Horowitz, L. M. (1991). Attachment styles among young adults: A test of a four-category model. *Journal of Personality and Social Psychology, 61,* 226–244.

Baumeister, R. F., & Leary, M. R. (1995). The need to belong: Desire for interpersonal attachments as a fundamental human motivation. *Psychological Bulletin, 117,* 497–529.

Beck, A. T., Steer, R. A., & Brown, G. K. (1996). *Manual for the Beck Depression Inventory* (2nd ed.). San Antonio, TX: Psychological Corporation.

Beckwith, L., Cohen, S. E., & Hamilton, C. E. (1999). Maternal sensitivity during infancy and subsequent life events relate to attachment representation at early adulthood. *Developmental Psychology, 35,* 693–700.

Belsky, J. (1999). Modern evolutionary theory and patterns of attachment. In J. Cassidy & P. R. Shaver (Eds.), *Handbook of attachment: Theory, research, and clinical applications* (pp. 141–161). New York: Guilford.

Benoit, D., & Parker, K. C. H. (1994). Stability and transmission of attachment across three generations. *Child Development, 65,* 1444–1456.

Beutler, L. E., Engle, D., Mohr, D., Daldrup, R. J., Bergan, J., Meredith, K., & Merry, W. (1991). Predictors of differential response to cognitive, experiential, and self-directed psychotherapeutic procedures. *Journal of Consulting and Clinical Psychology, 59,* 333–340.

Birtchnell, J. (1997). Attachment in an interpersonal context. *British Journal of Medical Psychology, 70,* 265–279.

Bowlby, J. (1969). *Attachment and loss.* New York: Basic.

Bowlby, J. (1988). *A secure base: Parent-child attachment and healthy human development.* New York: Basic.

Brennan, K. A., Clark, C. L., & Shaver, P. R. (1998). Self-report measurement of adult attachment: An integrative overview. In J. A. Simpson & W. S. Rholes (Eds.), *Attachment theory and close relationships* (pp. 46–76). New York: Guilford.

Brennan, K. A., & Shaver, P. R. (1998). Attachment style and personality disorders: Their connections to each other and to parental divorce, parental death, and perceptions of parental caregiving. *Journal of Personality, 66,* 835–878.

Bretherton, I., & Munholland, K. A. (1999). Internal working models in attachment relationships. In J. Cassidy & P. R. Shaver (Eds.), *Handbook of attachment: Theory, research, and clinical applications* (pp. 89–111). New York: Guilford.

Carver, C. S. (1997). Adult attachment and personality: Converging evidence and a new measure. *Personality and Social Psychology Bulletin, 23*, 865–883.

Cassidy, J., & Shaver, P. R. (1999). *Handbook of attachment: Theory, research, and clinical applications*. New York: Guilford.

Chisholm, J. S. (1996). The evolutionary ecology of attachment organization. *Human Nature, 7*, 1–38.

DeWolff, M., & van Ijzendoorn, M. (1997). Sensitivity and attachment: A meta-analysis on parental antecedents of infant attachment. *Child Development, 68*, 571–591.

Dozier, M., Stovall, K. C., & Albus, K. E. (1999). Attachment and psychopathology in adulthood. In J. Cassidy & P. R. Shaver (Eds.), *Handbook of attachment: Theory, research, and clinical implications* (pp. 497–519). New York: Guilford.

Eames, V., & Roth, A. (2000). Patient attachment orientation and the early working alliance: A study of patient and therapist reports of alliance quality and ruptures. *Psychotherapy Research, 10*, 421–434.

Feeney, J. A. (1999). Adult romantic attachment and couple relationships. In J. Cassidy & P. R. Shaver (Eds.), *Handbook of attachment: Theory, research, and clinical applications* (pp. 355–377). New York: Guilford.

Fonagy, P., Leigh, T., Steele, M., Steele, H., Kennedy, R., Mattoon, G., Target, M., & Gerber, A. (1996). The relation of attachment status, psychiatric classification, and response to psychotherapy. *Journal of Consulting and Clinical Psychology, 64*, 22–31.

Fraley, R. C., Waller, N. G., & Brennan, K. G. (2000). An item response theory analysis of self-report measures of adult attachment. *Journal of Personality and Social Psychology, 78*, 350–365.

George, C., Kaplan, N., & Main, M. (1985). *Adult attachment interview*. Unpublished manuscript, University of California, Berkeley.

Goldsmith, H. H., & Alansky, J. A. (1987). Maternal and infant temperamental predictors of attachment: A meta-analytic review. *Journal of Consulting and Clinical Psychology, 55*, 805–816.

Griffin, D., & Bartholomew, K. (1994). Models of the self and other: Fundamental dimensions underlying measures of adult attachment. *Journal of Personality and Social Psychology, 67*, 430–445.

Hamilton, C. E. (2000). Continuity and discontinuity of attachment from infancy through adolescence. *Child Development, 71*, 690–694.

Hardy, G. E., Aldridge, J., Davidson, C., Rowe, C., Reilly, S., & Shapiro, D. A. (1999). Therapist responsiveness to patient attachment styles and issues observed in patient-identified significant events in psychodynamic-interpersonal psychotherapy. *Psychotherapy Research, 9*, 36–53.

Hardy, G. E., Stiles, W. B., Barkham, M., & Startup, M. (1998). Therapist responsiveness to client interpersonal styles during time-limited treatments for depression. *Journal of Consulting and Clinical Psychology, 66*, 304–312.

Hazan, C. (2000). The place of attachment in human mating. *Review of General Psychology, 4*, 186–204.

Hazan, C., & Shaver, P. R. (1987). Romantic love conceptualized as an attachment process. *Journal of Personality and Social Psychology, 52*, 511–524.

Hazan, C., & Shaver, P. R. (1994). Attachment as an organizational framework for research on close relationships. *Psychological Inquiry, 5*, 1–22.

Hoger, D. (1999). Der Bielefelder Fragebogen zu Klientenerwartungen (BFKE): Ein Verfahren zur Erfassung von Bindungsstilen bei Psychotherapiepatienten. [The Bielefeld Questionnaire on Client Expectations: A method for assessing attachment styles among psychotherapy patients]. *Psychotherapeut, 44*, 159–166.

Holmes, J. (1996). *Attachment, intimacy, autonomy: Using attachment theory in adult psychotherapy*. Northvale, NJ: Aronson.

Kanninen, K., Salo, J., & Punamäki, R. L. (2000). Attachment patterns and working alliance in trauma therapy for victims of political violence. *Psychotherapy Research, 10*, 435–449.

Klerman, G. L., Weissman, M. M., Rounsaville, B. J., & Chevron, E. S. (1984). *Interpersonal therapy of depression*. New York: Basic.

Klohnen, E. C., & Bera, S. (1998). Behavioral and experiential patterns of avoidantly and securely attached women across adulthood: A 31-year longitudinal perspective. *Journal of Personality and Social Psychology, 74*, 211–223.

Kohlenberg, R. J., & Tsai, M. (1991). *Functional analytical psychotherapy: Creating intense and curative therapeutic relationships*. New York: Plenum.

Mace, C., & Margison, F. (1997). Attachment and psychotherapy: An overview. *British Journal of Medical Psychology, 70*, 209–215.

Mallinckrodt, B., Gantt, D. L., & Coble, H. M. (1995). Attachment patterns in the psychotherapy relationship: Development of the Patient Attachment to Therapist Scale. *Journal of Counseling Psychology*, 42, 307–317.

Mallinckrodt, B., King, J. L., & Coble, H. M. (1998). Family dysfunction, alexithymia, and client attachment to therapist. *Journal of Counseling Psychology*, 45, 497–504.

Meyer, B., Pilkonis, P. A., Proietti, J. M., Heape, C. L., & Egan, M. (2001). Attachment styles, personality disorders, and response to treatment. *Journal of Personality Disorders*, 15, 371–389.

Mikulincer, M. (1998). Attachment working models and the sense of trust: An exploration of interaction goals and affect regulation. *Journal of Personality and Social Psychology*, 74, 1209–1224.

Mikulincer, M., Florian, V., & Weller, A. (1993). Attachment styles, coping strategies, and posttraumatic psychological distress: The impact of the Gulf War in Israel. *Journal of Personality and Social Psychology*, 64, 817–826.

Mischel, W., & Shoda, Y. (1995). A cognitive-affective system theory of personality: Reconceptualizing situations, dispositions, dynamics, and invariance in personality structure. *Psychological Review*, 102, 248–268.

Mosheim, R., Zachhuber, U., Scharf, L., Hofmann, A., Kemmler, G., Danzl, C., Kinze, J., Biebl, W., & Richter, R. (2000). Bindung und psychotherapie: Bindungsqualität und interpersonale probleme von patienten als mögliche einfluss faktoren auf das ergebnus stationärer psychotherapie. [Quality of attachment and interpersonal problems as possible predictors of inpatient therapy outcome.] *Psychotherapeut*, 45, 223–229.

Orlinsky, D. E., Grawe, K., & Parks, B. K. (1994). Process and outcome in psychotherapy—Noch einmal. In A. E. Bergin & S. L. Garfield (Eds.), *Handbook of psychotherapy and behavior change* (4th ed., pp. 270–376). New York: Wiley.

Phelps, J. L., Belsky, J., & Crnic, K. (1998). Earned security, daily stress, and parenting: A comparison of five alternative models. *Development and Psychopathology*, 10, 21–38.

Pilkonis, P. A. (1988). Personality prototypes among depressives: Themes of dependency and autonomy. *Journal of Personality Disorders*, 2, 144–152.

Robbins, S. B. (1995). Attachment perspectives on the counseling relationship: Comment on Mallinckrodt, Gantt, and Coble (1995). *Journal of Counseling Psychology*, 42, 318–319.

Rothbaum, F., Weisz, J., Pott, M., Miyake, K., & Morelli, G. (2000). Attachment and culture: Security in the United States and Japan. *American Psychologist*, 55, 1093–1104.

Rubino, G., Barker, C., Roth, T., & Fearon, P. (2000). Therapist empathy and depth of interpretation in response to potential alliance ruptures: The role of therapist and patient attachment styles. *Psychotherapy Research*, 10, 408–420.

Shaver, P. R., Belsky, J., & Brennan, K. A. (2000). The adult attachment interview and self-reports of romantic attachment: Associations across domains and methods. *Personal Relationships*, 7, 25–43.

Simpson, J. A. (1999). Attachment theory in modern evolutionary perspective. In J. Cassidy & P. R. Shaver (Eds.), *Handbook of attachment: Theory, research, and clinical applications* (pp. 115–161). New York: Guilford.

Simpson, J. A., & Rholes, W. S. (1998). *Attachment theory and close relationships*. New York: Guilford.

Simpson, J. A., Rholes, W. S., & Nelligan, J. S. (1992). Support seeking and support giving within couples in an anxiety-provoking situation: The role of attachment styles. *Journal of Personality and Social Psychology*, 62, 434–446.

Solomon, J., & George, C. (1999). The measurement of attachment security in infancy and childhood. In J. Cassidy & P. R. Shaver (Eds.), *Handbook of attachment: Theory, research, and clinical applications* (pp. 287–316). New York: Guilford.

Stiles, W. B., Honos-Webb, L., & Surko, M. (1998). Responsiveness in psychotherapy. *Clinical Psychology: Science and Practice*, 5, 439–458.

Strauss, B. M. (2000). Attachment theory and psychotherapy research: Editor's introduction to a special section. *Psychotherapy Research*, 10, 381–389.

Strauss, B. M., Lobo-Drost, A. J., & Pilkonis, P. A. (1999). Einschätzung von Bindungsstilen bei Erwachsenen: Erste Erfahrungen mit der deutschen Version einer Prototypenbeurteilung. [Evaluation of attachment styles in adults: First results with the German version of a prototype evaluation.] *Zeitschrift für Klinische Psychologie, Psychiatrie und Psychotherapie*, 47, 347–364.

Tyrrell, C. L., Dozier, M., Teague, G. B., & Fallot, R. D. (1999). Effective treatment relationships for persons with serious psychiatric disorders: The importance of attachment states of mind. *Journal of Consulting and Clinical Psychology*, 67, 725–733.

Van Ijzendoorn, M. H., & Kroonenberg, P. M. (1988). Cross-cultural patterns of attachment: A meta-analysis of the strange situation. *Child Development*, 59, 147–156.

Van Ijzendoorn, M. H., & Sagi, A. (1999). Cross-cultural patterns of attachment. In J. Cassidy & P. R. Shaver (Eds.), *Handbook of attachment: Theory, research, and clinical applications* (pp. 713–734). New York: Guilford.

Waters, E., Merrick, S., Treboux, D., Crowell, J., & Albersheim, L. (2000). Attachment security in infancy and early adulthood: A twenty-year longitudinal study. *Child Development*, 71, 684–689.

Weinberger, J. (1995). Common factors aren't so common: The common factors dilemma. *Clinical Psychology: Science and Practice*, 2, 45–69.

21

Religion and Spirituality

Everett L. Worthington, Jr.
Steven J. Sandage

Imagine the following clinical scenario in which a therapist is wrapping up an intake session with a new client.

Therapist: Do you have any spiritual or religious commitments I should know about?

Client: Yes, I am a Christian, and I came to see you because my pastor told me he heard you speak at a conference and found out you are a Christian, also. I would like it if you would start future sessions in prayer because I believe that there is no real healing apart from God's presence.

At one level, this interaction calls for a specific therapeutic decision about the appropriateness and the effectiveness of including a spiritual or religious practice (that is, prayer) in psychotherapy. At another level, the relationship between the therapist and client is already being negotiated in the specific area of religion. The therapist could decide to grant or decline the client's request for prayer in session, or the therapist could propose some other alternatives (for example, include prayer as part of relaxation homework interventions).

Perhaps even more important than the outcome of the client's request is the way in which spirituality and religiosity influence the client-therapist relationship. What if the therapist responds defensively out of religious ambivalence and refuses to pray? What if the therapist agrees to the request but prays in a manner that is spirit-ually unacceptable to the client? What if by taking the lead in prayer the therapist reinforces emotional dependence or over-spiritualization on the part of the client? What if opening the first few sessions in prayer relaxes and builds rapport with an anxious client who feels culturally ashamed for seeking professional help? Or what if the therapist initiates a deeper dialogue with the client about religion and spirituality prior to responding directly to the client's request? This complicated set of possibilities makes responding a definite challenge; no alternative eliminates risks to the therapeutic relationship and treatment outcome.

The interface of spirituality and religion in psychotherapy evident in the foregoing scenario is just one example out of hundreds we have experienced in clinical practice. The U.S. population is highly religious, with approximately 92% of the population being affiliated with a religion and 96% professing a belief in God or a universal spirit (Gallup, 1995; Shafranske, 1996b). Recent surveys also indicate that roughly 90% of Americans pray; 71% are members of a church or synagogue; 42% attend religious worship services weekly or almost weekly (Hoge, 1996); 57% report praying at least once a day; and 88% consider religion either very important or fairly important in their lives (Hill et al., 2000). Therefore, many clients will engage their spiritual and religious beliefs when they try to cope with life stressors and emotional struggles (Pargament, 1997).

Yet research suggests that while psychologists and therapists are generally favorable toward spirituality and religion (E. W. Kelly, 1995), they also tend to be substantially less conventionally religious and less religiously affiliated than the general public in the United States (Bergin & Jensen, 1990; Shafranske, 1996b; Shafranske & Malony, 1990). Psychologists and therapists tend to be more positive about spirituality than religion, and a smaller percentage embed their spirituality within a religious tradition than is the case in the general public (Shafranske, 1996b). Since quality clinical training in religious and spiritual issues in therapy appears to be rare (Richards & Bergin, 2000; see Shafranske, 1996a), the religious differences between therapists and the general public could be problematic, particularly in the case of highly religious clients (E. L. Johnson & Sandage, 1999).

Over the past two decades the volume and quality of the literature on religion and spirituality in psychotherapy have increased exponentially. The growing awareness in the 1970s and 1980s that psychotherapy is inherently value-laden resulted in revised ethical guidelines in psychology (APA, 1992) that called for attention to the religious diversity of clients (Richards & Bergin, 2000). Worthington, Kurusu, McCullough, and Sandage (1996) published a 10-year review of empirical research on religion in psychotherapeutic processes and outcomes to update a previous 10-year review (Worthington, 1986). They noted a tremendous increase in the volume and quality of scientific research on religion and psychotherapy.

In this chapter, we review the empirical research on the influence of religion and spirituality in psychotherapy processes and outcomes. We will also outline some empirically supported clinical implications for working with religious and spiritual issues and the associated relational dynamics in psychotherapy.

DEFINITIONS OF RELIGION AND SPIRITUALITY

There are important distinctions between the terms "religion" and "spirituality." The word "religion" comes from the Latin root *religio*, which refers to "a bond between humanity and some greater-than-human-power" (Hill et al., 2000). Wulff

(1997) argues that the term "religion" has historically been understood as including both the personal, dynamic quality of religious experience and the social and organizational aspects of religion. Religion (or religiosity) is best understood as a multidimensional construct that serves to integrate an ultimate concern, the "web of significance" provided by social and communal identity, and specific moral and spiritual practices (Marty & Appleby, 1991). Contemporary views seem increasingly to emphasize the differences between religion and spirituality with "religion" being limited to formal institutional structures and "spirituality" referring to the more experiential dynamics of personal meaning and transcendence (Hill et al., 2000; Wulff, 1997).

An important distinction in research on the psychology of religion is between intrinsic and extrinsic religiosity (Donahue, 1985). People who are intrinsically religious have a personalized religious commitment and view their faith as an end in itself, while people who are extrinsically religious view their faith as a means to other ends (for example, social affiliation). Intrinsics are more likely than the extrinsics and the "indiscriminantly proreligious" (those high in both intrinsic and extrinsic religiosity) to be mentally healthy (Batson, Schoenrade, & Ventis, 1991; Gartner, 1996). A third major orientation, "quest" religiosity, has been developed as an alternative to intrinsic and extrinsic orientations and investigated in numerous studies (Batson et al., 1991). Those who score high on the quest scale view their faith as an inclusive, open-ended search and strongly value religious doubt.

The word "spirituality" comes from the Latin root *spiritus*, which signifies breath or life (Hill et al., 2000). Spirituality can be defined in relation to consciousness (Helminiak, 1996) or in relation to transcendence (Miller & Thoresen, 1999). For individuals of many cultures and faiths, religion and spirituality will be intimately connected. Such individuals will tend to interpret personal spiritual experience and meaning through the worldview lens shaped by their religious community and tradition. However, some sociologists of religion speculate that increasing numbers of individuals in the West do not view spirituality as embedded within religion (Roof, Carroll, & Roozen, 2000). Spilka (1993) suggested three general categories of contemporary views of spirituality: (1) *God-oriented spirituality*, which connects spiritual experience to a personal God; (2) *world-oriented spirituality*, which connects spiritual experience to ecology or nature; and (3) *humanistic-oriented spirituality*, which connects spiritual experience to human potential and self-actualization. These categories are not mutually exclusive but they do highlight differing spiritual orientations.

Hill and colleagues (2000) propose helpful criteria for defining religion and spirituality. They suggest that both religion and spirituality involve "feelings, thoughts, experiences, and behaviors that arise from a search for the sacred" (p. 23). They use the term "sacred" to refer not just to things a person values (for example, self-esteem or relational authenticity). Rather, "sacred" refers to a "divine being, divine object, Ultimate reality, or Ultimate Truth" (p. 23). In addition, religion differs from spirituality in that religion can also involve nonsacred goals. For example, a client once related that he was attending singles groups at a number of area churches not out of a "search for the sacred" but out of a search for a date. This is an expression of extrinsic religiosity where religious behavior is a means to other "nonsacred" ends. Hill and colleagues also suggest that religion involves means and methods of searching for the sacred that are validated and supported by an identifiable tradition or group of people, whereas many contemporary forms of spirituality specifically resist the necessity of group validation.

Therapists often embrace the idea of spirituality-apart-from-religion or spirituality as more important than religion (Shafranske, 1996b). Most clients, to the contrary, probably see spirituality within their religion. Therapists might underestimate the clinical impact of differing from clients in the degree to which they embed spirituality within religion. Some highly religious clients might become anxious if a therapist talks about "spirituality" without engaging more traditional religious language. Conversely, other clients might have an aversion to references to religion but identify strongly with certain language about spirituality (Rose, Westefeld, & Ansley, 2001). This requires therapists to assess clients' religious and spiritual values and practices, as well as reflect on the kinds of religious and spiritual language used in therapy (Doherty, 1999).

CLINICAL EXAMPLES

Religiosity and spirituality of clients and therapists enter into therapy at various points and in different ways—often strongly affected by the setting. For example, some clients request explicitly religious therapy. The therapy might be performed by a member of the clergy within a religious setting. The therapy might occur within a pastoral counseling setting. Therapy might be conducted within a practice in which the therapist explicitly labels himself or herself as a "Jewish therapist" or "Christian therapist" or the like. Therapy might also occur in a secular facility by a therapist who is either religious or not, spiritual or not. Regardless of the setting, religious and spiritual dynamics can influence the formation of the therapeutic relationship in diverse and complicated ways. We will describe four clinical examples of such influence.

Clinical Example 1: The Aggressively Religious Client

It is not uncommon for highly religious clients to try to clarify the role that religion will play from the outset of therapy. This is likely to occur when the therapist is labeled as explicitly religious or if a religious gatekeeper (for example, a member of the clergy) recommended a therapist because he or she is known to be of similar religion as the client. Highly religious clients frequently administer a "theology test" to their therapists.

For example, Larry (age 33) was a Christian Anglo male who challenged his therapist with a series of questions during an intake for couples therapy—"What do you consider God's role in healing? How do you see God guiding people's lives? What is your view on the biblical roles for husbands and wives?" To the therapist who is not familiar with dealing with highly religious clients, such straightforward questioning can be perceived as aggressive, defensive, and anxious. Alternatively, such direct questioning might be a result of clients holding religion as their most central value and not wishing to expose themselves to the threat of therapists who hold contrasting worldviews. Some highly religious clients will be satisfied simply to know that a therapist can be identified as a member of their religious community (for example, Christian or Muslim) who could be expected to be supportive of religious values. Other clients like Larry will not be satisfied with general information about the therapist's religious identification or attitude toward religious values and will want a thicker description of the therapist's religious beliefs and values. In Larry's case, his questions might be due to content he wants to engage in therapy (in this case, gender roles in marriage), to his interpersonal style (suspicious, mistrustful, analytical), or to an interaction of both.

Clinical Example 2: The Nonreligious Client with a Religious Therapist

Other clients might be personally opposed to religious influence. They might aggressively insist that religious content be excluded from therapy. This could be challenging for some religious therapists or if members of the client's family system expect religion to be included in therapy.

For example, Laura (age 16) was a nonreligious depressed, Italian-American adolescent brought to a session with a Christian therapist by her father. The daughter walks into the intake session obviously perturbed and explains to the therapist, "I told my dad I didn't want to see a *Christian* therapist again. Then he tells me on the way over here that you are a *Christian* therapist but that their priest thinks I'll like you. Incredible! I don't believe their [her parents'] God crap anymore, but he just doesn't get it."

This could potentially create a dilemma for the explicitly religious therapist. Therapists who value religion and spirituality obviously differ in how they incorporate them in therapy (Tan, 1997). Some therapists prefer an *implicit* approach that involves personal awareness of the ways in which religion and spirituality influence his or her own therapeutic values and theoretical assumptions. Other therapists prefer a more *explicit* approach that goes beyond awareness of implicit values and assumptions and involves using religious and spiritual practices in therapy. Practicing within the ethical guidelines of the mental health professions would require that therapists be willing to at least suspend the explicit use of religious and spiritual practices if that is the preference of a particular client.

Even if a therapist is willing to take a more implicit approach to religion and spirituality in therapy, disagreement between clients and therapists on fundamental beliefs might impair the therapists' willingness and ability to help. Some forms of client religiosity or spirituality (for example, Satanism or White Supremacy religions) might be troublesome even for highly tolerant therapists. If plentiful referral sources are available, this is not a problem. But if the practice is in a rural area or small town with few choices among therapists, an accommodation might need to be reached. In the case of Laura, the therapist will become triangulated with the father and daughter unless there is an initial honest negotiation with both the father and the daughter about how religious issues will be handled in therapy. The therapist might want to explore Laura's feelings about her parents' Catholicism and her own changing beliefs, but early questions without establishing adequate rapport could be perceived by Laura as an attempt to side with her parents and persuade her that her religious doubts are wrong.

Clinical Example 3: Religion Interacting with Acculturation

Religion and spirituality are aspects of culture and, as such, may well interact with issues of acculturation. For example, Trinh (age 20), a Vietnamese-American college student, came to the counseling center at his university reporting stress related to family conflicts. Trinh had recently converted to Christianity through a campus ministry and was planning on getting baptized. His parents had immigrated to the United States with their own parents as teens and were Buddhist. They were confused and upset by Trinh's religious conversion, and Trinh was equally confused as to how to handle the conflict. This case illustrates the intersection of religion and acculturation. This family was dealing with generational differences in acculturation and corresponding religious loyalties. From an individualistic or culturally uninformed perspective, a therapist might naively encourage Trinh to simply "do what feels right." A more culturally sensitive approach could help Trinh to better understand and negotiate the acculturation dilemmas he and his family are facing. Trinh might be able to arrive at an understanding of his parents' concerns and find ways to express cultural loyalty while still seeking to develop his own cultural and religious identity.

Clinical Example 4: Spiritual or Religious Imbalances in Relational Systems

Clients are always part of relational systems, even when they present for therapy alone. Relational imbalance can be expressed through spiritual or religious issues, such as when one spouse is perceived to be the more "spiritual" or "religious" one. For example, Ellen (age 38) and Andre (age 33) were an African-American couple who sought therapy for marital conflicts. Ellen had a much stronger sense of her spiritual and religious identity and grew tired of trying to get Andre involved in church and spiritual discussions. She desired to experience spiritual growth and intimacy with Andre, whereas Andre did not know where he was in his own spiritual journey. He referred to Ellen pejoratively as the "religious one" and "the preacher." Ellen hoped the therapist would help her get Andre to church, and Andre hoped the therapist would get Ellen to back off.

A couple like Andre and Ellen can represent: (1) differences in values about religion and spirituality; (2) differences in individual faith development; (3) a system that is imbalanced in power or functioning; or (4) a combination of these factors. A therapist could easily become triangulated through religious or spiritual issues in a case like this by siding exclusively with Ellen or Andre. A first step is to assess whether the couple is simply struggling with value differences or whether the religious or spiritual differences symbolize more significant systemic patterns in the relationship.

These four clinical examples highlight some key religious and spiritual issues that can emerge in psychotherapy. We will now provide a review of the outcome research on religion and spirituality in psychotherapy.

RESEARCH REVIEW

The empirical research relevant to the impact of religion and spirituality on psychotherapy has progressed in the past 15 years (McCullough, 1999; Worthington et al., 1996) but is still quite limited. The vast majority of studies has been conducted with largely Christian samples, and much more research is needed with more participants from other religious traditions and spiritual orientations. We have grouped our summary review of the available research into two general categories: religious and spiritual values in psychotherapy, and religion-accommodative psychotherapy outcome studies.

Religious and Spiritual Values in Psychotherapy

Several studies have investigated the role of religious and spiritual values in psychotherapy (for a more detailed review, see Worthington et al., 1996). Only a few studies have focused specifically on the influence of therapists' religious and spiritual values or the convergence and matching of clients' and therapists' religious values. Most of the research in this area is analogue and examines the influence of the religious values of potential clients on perceptions of therapists described as having differing kinds of religious value orientations. Unfortunately, these studies offer only limited connections to therapy outcome. However, this research does suggest some potential implications for relational processes in therapy.

Therapist Values

There has been a surprising lack of research investigating ways in which therapists' own religious and spiritual values impact their work as therapists. Even less relates these values to treatment outcome. In general, therapists appear to value spirituality in both therapy and in their own personal lives. In a national survey of members of the American Counseling Association, E. W. Kelly (1995) found that 85% of the respondents endorsed the statement that "seeking a spiritual understanding of the universe" was important to them personally. Other studies (see Sorenson, 1994, 1997) provide insights regarding therapists' religious values and spiritual experiences, but they do not link to outcome data.

Client Values

A greater number of studies has investigated the influence of clients' religious and spiritual values.

Worthington (1988) developed a model for understanding the values of highly religious clients, which started with the premise that highly committed religious people (those who score in the top 10 to 15% on measures of religious commitment) tend to view the world differently than do less religiously committed people. In Worthington's model, the worldview schemas used by highly religious clients to evaluate others (including therapists) are comprised of three primary value dimensions—authority accorded to religious leaders, Scripture, or sacred doctrine and identification with one's religious group. He hypothesized that people have differing "zones of toleration" for accepting different values held by others. For example, a highly committed Orthodox Jewish client might strongly prefer a therapist who is also an Orthodox Jew, is recommended by the client's rabbi, and utilizes the Hebrew Bible in session. That client might have trouble accepting a therapist who differs markedly on these value domains. Another Orthodox Jewish client might have similar preferences but a broader zone of toleration for therapist differences. Limited evidence supports this model, most notably the power of high religious commitment as predicting (1) preference for value-similar therapists; (2) pretherapy expectations of therapy; (3) reactions to challenges to behavior, beliefs, and values; (4) estimation of client continuation in therapy after a challenge; and (5) perception of counselors. For instance, highly religious clients have been found to prefer religiously similar therapists. This has been true for samples of Orthodox Jews (Wikler, 1989) and Protestant Christians (Keating & Fretz, 1990) for individual therapy. It has also been found to be true for Protestant Christians' preferences for marital therapy (Ripley, Worthington, & Berry, 2001)

Religious beliefs seem to be less predictive of people's perceptions of individual therapy than do religious values, at least in analogue research. Morrow, Worthington, and McCullough (1993) had students watch a videotape of counselors supporting, challenging, or ignoring a client's religious values. Religious beliefs did not predict whether participants thought the client would improve more by seeing the counselor who supported her values rather than the counselor who challenged her values. Participants, regardless of beliefs, indicated they would be less likely to return to see the counselor who challenged the client's religious values than the supportive or ignoring counselors. Interestingly, the counselor who ignored the client's religious values was rated as more persuasive than either of the other two counselors (supportive or challenging). The authors refer to a previous finding by Pecnik and Epperson (1985) that counselors labeled "Christian" were rated as less expert by both Christians and non-Christians, suggesting that religiously supportive counselors might be at risk for seeming less professional.

Using the same stimulus videotapes but measuring religious values in addition to religious beliefs, McCullough and Worthington (1995) replicated their earlier finding that, regardless of religious beliefs, students preferred the counselors who did not directly challenge the client's religious values. However, they found that religious *values* predicted differential preferences for and expectations of counseling with therapists who either challenged or supported religious beliefs. Participants with high religious values reacted more strongly to differences in the therapist behavior (for example, supportive versus challenging of clients' religious beliefs) than did moderately or low religious observers. This interaction was again observed due to differences in religious values. That is, participants who highly valued their religion said they were more likely to refer a Christian friend to the supportive counselor than to the challenging counselor, while there was no such difference for those whose religious values were less salient. Participants with high toleration for different religious groups were more attracted to the counselor who supported clients' religiosity than to the counselor who challenged clients' religiosity. McCullough, Worthington, Maxey, and Rachal (1997) replicated McCullough and Worthington's (1995) findings for numerous combinations of client and therapist gender in the videotaped interactions. Female counselors were perceived as more religious and more effective than the male counselors. All three of these analogue studies are limited by using observer's (nonclient) perceptions of videotaped, circumscribed counseling episodes.

Another major area of analogue research on client perceptions of religious values is related to the effects of pretherapy information regarding counselors' religious values. A typical design of studies in this area is to present students or actual clients with brief written informed consent descriptions of the religious values of counselors and then ask for ratings of preferences and expectations about counseling. Several important findings have emerged from this body of work (Worthington et al., 1996):

1. Highly religious Jews, Mormons, Protestants, and Roman Catholics tend to prefer religiously similar counselors (Worthington et al., 1996). However, counselors who are described as religious might be rated as less expert (Pecnik & Epperson, 1985) unless other information about counseling experience is added.

2. Highly religious Christians may anticipate negative experiences in counseling with secular or nonreligious counselors (Worthington & Scott, 1983; Ripley, Worthington, & Berry, 2001) even if those counselors indicate an openness to "spirituality" (Keating & Fretz, 1990). Spirituality not connected to more traditional forms of religiosity might be suspect for these clients, while other clients seem to prefer forms of spirituality that are disembedded from traditional religion (Ganje-Fling, Veach, Kuang, & Houg, 2000).

3. Information about a counselor's religious values might affect the nature of client disclosure (Wyatt & Johnson, 1990). Highly religious clients may tend to be more disclosing with religiously similar counselors. Conversely, less religiously committed clients tend to be more disclosing when a counselor is not perceived as explicitly religious.

4. Highly religious evangelical Christians tend to expect more explicit integration of religious interventions into counseling when counselors are identified as Christian (Worthington & Gascoyne, 1985).

5. Highly religious clients tend to see religious issues as central to counseling, while most other clients do not expect counseling to focus primarily on religious issues (Wyatt & Johnson, 1990).

6. The amount and type of pretherapy information about a counselor's religious values tend to make a difference in client expectations about counseling outcomes, with more information about the values of Christian counselors being related to more positive expectations (Lewis & Epperson, 1991).

7. Highly religious couples often treat marriage as sacred (Mahoney et al. 1999). For this population, both religious values and religious beliefs have been found to affect perceptions of marital therapy, with highly religious Christians preferring and expecting better outcomes with a Christian than a non-Christian marital therapist (Ripley, Worthington, & Berry, 2001).

To summarize, disclosure by therapists of religious values might be problematic from the perspective of highly religious clients if: (1) clients' religious values differ substantially from those of the therapist; (2) clients start to censor their own disclosures in response to the therapist's religious values; (3) clients have strong negative stereotypes about religious people; (4) sessions become too focused on religion and not on other therapeutic sources of gain; and (5) the therapist offers interpretations that assume a greater similarity of spiritual and religious values than is actually the case.

To date, nearly all the research has been analogue research and not directly connected to outcome data. We do not know, for example, how preferences that derive from religious similarities and differences are related to outcomes of therapy.

Client spirituality has received comparably less attention in research than client religiosity. In a rare clinical study, Ganje-Fling and colleagues (2000) compared the spiritual well-being of two groups of clients receiving psychotherapy at an urban nonreligiously affiliated mental health clinic. One group ($n = 43$) was receiving therapy for childhood sexual abuse, and the comparison group ($n = 34$) was receiving therapy for other reasons. The two groups reported similar levels of spiritual well-being. However, both groups of clients scored lower in spiritual well-being than did samples of medical outpatients and hospice workers. Ganje-Fling and colleagues also found that both groups of clients in their sample were quite comfortable engaging spiritual issues in therapy and considered spirituality as important for problem resolution. It is noteworthy that according to the clients, they were much more likely to raise spiritual issues in therapy than were their therapists. The authors acknowledged the limitation presented by their use of a Christian-oriented measure of spiritual well-being. The modest response rates in this study also raise the question of self-selection and whether those clients who chose to participate were more interested in spiritual and religious issues than those who did not participate.

Rose and colleagues (2001) also found clients ($n = 74$) at six mental health centers to generally have a preference for discussing spiritual and religious issues in counseling. Therapists at participating mental health centers were asked to invite their clients to participate in this study of preferences concerning spirituality and religion in counseling. The authors were unable to determine participation rates across sites and possible selection bias among therapists. The vast majority of participants were White (92%) and women (87%). Interestingly, nearly 40% of the participants reported no current religious affiliation. More than half (55%) of the clients indicated a desire to discuss spiritual or religious concerns in counseling, 22% said that their desire to discuss spiritual and religious concerns in counseling depended on other factors (for example, relevance to problems), and only 18% indicated they preferred not to discuss spiritual or religious issues. Six clients (8%) described being willing to discuss spiritual but not religious issues in response to a final open-ended question asking participants to explain the reasons for their quantitative responses. Previous spiritual experiences strongly predicted client preferences for discussing spiritual and religious issues in counseling. Clients who reported higher levels of prior spiritual experiences had a strong tendency to prefer to discuss spiritual and religious issues.

Therapist-Client Religious Convergence

Considerable literature has been published on whether therapy produces a convergence of values between therapists and clients (for a review, see Beutler, Machado, & Neufeldt, 1994). In general, clients in most forms of therapy (not specifically religious therapy) tend to move toward therapists' values in successful psychotherapy, though not always. T. A. Kelly and Strupp (1992) examined 36 therapist-client dyads in the Vanderbilt Interpersonal Psychodynamic Therapy Study and found clients did not change during the course of therapy in the degree to which they valued "salvation" or "wisdom" (p. 36) on the Rokeach Value Survey (Rokeach, 1973).

Does matching therapists and clients according to religious or spiritual values affect treatment outcomes? Only three clinical studies have actually tested this question. Kelly and Strupp (1992), in the outcome study mentioned earlier, found that clients and therapists differed significantly in the value they placed on salvation, with therapists generally placing it quite low in their value rankings. Client-therapist similarity in valuing salvation was positively correlated with independent clinicians' ratings of improvement, suggesting this particular religious value might function as an important matching variable.

But there is also some evidence that matching the religiosity of therapists and clients is not crucial for successful outcomes. Martinez (1991) assessed the religious values of and followed 30 clients who completed at least five sessions of therapy at a university counseling center. Unfortunately, the Martinez study used an unvalidated measure of client improvement. Therapist-client religious value convergence was correlated with therapists' but not clients' ratings of improvement, which is consistent with other research on value convergence in therapy (see Beutler et al., 1994). Initial dissimilarity of religious values positively correlated with ratings of improvement. Clients rated their improvement as higher when their religious values were initially more liberal than their therapists' religious values. Therapists' ratings of client improvement correlated with initial dissimilarity when the clients' pretherapy religious values were more liberal than the therapists' values.

The finding that both therapist and client ratings of improvement were higher when the client was initially more religiously liberal than the therapist is challenging to interpret. Martinez (1991) suggests that clients who are more religiously conservative than their therapists might be less likely to benefit from therapy in a secular setting than more religiously liberal clients. Perhaps it was uncomfortable for some religiously conservative clients in his study to seek help in a secular university setting, or some may have had trouble discussing their values with more religiously liberal therapists. Related to this, it seems possible that religiously conservative individuals who chose to seek help at a secular counseling center could potentially differ in some important ways from religiously conservative individuals who chose to seek help with their own religious community (for example, through pastoral counseling).

Another study also suggests that therapist-client matching of religious values may not contribute to improved treatment outcomes. In a study that we review more thoroughly in the next section, Propst, Ostrom, Watkins, Dean, and Mashburn (1992) found that nonreligious therapists could effectively deliver a religiously accommodative approach to cognitive therapy for depression with highly religious clients. These two studies are not definitive. Propst and colleagues (1992) recruited people for participation in an experiment. Their commitment to remain in the study might conceivably differ from the commitment of actual clients to actual therapy, especially in a market economy in which other therapists are readily available. The small sample and measurement problems in the Martinez (1991) study also are significant limitations. Consequently, questions of the outcome effects of matching or mismatching therapists and clients on religious values are very much open questions.

Religion-Accommodative Psychotherapy Outcome Studies

A small group of outcome studies has been conducted on religion-accommodative psychotherapy. These studies have tested therapy approaches that "accommodate" standard therapies to the values of highly religious clients or compare the efficacy of standard and religion-accommodative treatments. Unfortunately, these studies have tended to ignore relational or therapeutic alliance variables, and Christianity and Islam are the only religious traditions that have been accommodated in outcome research thus far. The studies we review are grouped as Christian-accommodative individual psychotherapy, Muslim-accommodative individual psychotherapy, and Christian-accommodative group interventions.

Christian-Accommodative Individual Psychotherapy

Five studies have compared standard and Christian-accommodative versions of individual psychotherapy. All five studies have employed cognitive or cognitive-behavioral therapies (CBT), using either Beck's cognitive therapy or Ellis's (1962) rational-emotive therapy (RET) in the treatment of depression, which led to a recent meta-analysis of this group of studies (McCullough, 1999). We will group the studies based on specific theoretical orientation (Beck or RET) and then report the results of the meta-analysis.

In a study utilizing Beckian cognitive therapy, Pecheur and Edwards (1984) conducted one of the earliest outcome studies comparing Christian-accommodative and "secular" versions of cognitive therapy. Clients were student volunteers from a Christian college who scored in the depressed range on the Beck Depression Inventory (BDI), the Hamilton Rating Scale for Depression (HRSD), and a single-item visual analogue observer rating scale. Clients ($n = 21$) were matched on depression severity and randomly assigned to either secular CBT, religious CBT, or a wait-list control (WLC) condition. Both treatments involved eight 50-minute sessions of manualized individual psychotherapy based on Beck's approach (Beck, Rush, Shaw, & Emery, 1979). However, religious CBT integrated clients' religious beliefs into the therapeutic strategies (for example, training clients to use self-statements such as "God loves, accepts, and values us just as we are"). The two treatments did not differ from each other in outcomes but outperformed the WLC condition in reducing client depression at post-treatment and one-month follow-up.

Propst (1980; Propst et al., 1992) conducted two controlled outcome studies comparing Christian-accommodative versions of Beckian CBT for depression with a standard "secular" version of CBT. Propst (1980) randomly assigned student volunteers who scored in the mild to moderate range on the BDI and in the moderate range or higher on a religiosity measure to either a religious CBT condition ($n = 9$), a religious placebo condition (group discussion of religious issues), a nonreligious CBT condition ($n = 11$), or a WLC condition. Treatment involved eight sessions of individual therapy delivered by nonreligious therapists following manualized interventions. The main difference between the two treatments was that in the Christian-accommodative therapy clients were instructed to replace negative cognitions with religious imagery ("I can visualize Christ going with me into that difficult situation in the future as I try to cope"). In contrast to the findings of Pecheur and Edwards (1984), participants in both the religious CBT and the religious placebo conditions showed more positive change on the dependent measures of depression than did participants in either the nonreligious CBT or WLC conditions. Religious CBT was the only treatment that generated changes on the behavioral dependent measure of group assertiveness.

Propst et al. (1992) again compared the efficacy of Beckian CBT with a manualized, religion-accommodative version of CBT that employed Christian religious imagery (Propst, 1988). Clients were recruited from the community and scored in the clinical range for depression on the HRSD and in the moderate range on measures of religious commitment. Clients were randomly assigned to 18 individual sessions of nonreligious CBT ($n = 19$), religious CBT ($n = 19$), pastoral counseling treatment (PCT; $n = 10$), or WLC ($n = 11$). All clients in both CBT conditions completed the entire course of treatment. Therapists for CBT were ten graduate students, with five self-identifying as religious and five not. The religiosity of the therapists and the two CBT treatments were crossed, creating four combinations: (1) religious CBT–religious therapist; (2) religious CBT–nonreligious therapist; (3) nonreligious CBT–religious therapist; and (4) nonreligious CBT–nonreligious therapist. All PCT therapists were religious and were instructed to spend 75% of sessions using nondirective listening and 25% discussing Bible verses or religious themes of interest to the clients. Dependent measures, collected at post-treatment, 3-month, and 2-year follow-up, included the BDI, a modified form of the HRSD, and a clinician rating of general social adjustment.

Clients in both religious CBT and PCT reported significantly lower post-treatment depression and better social adjustment than did clients in either the nonreligious CBT or WLC conditions. Surprisingly, these differences were due largely to the superior performance of nonreligious therapists in the religious CBT condition. Significant interactions between therapist religiosity and type of CBT on the BDI and the Social Adjustment Rating Scale showed that nonreligious therapists actually secured better outcomes in the religious CBT condition than in the nonreligious CBT condition. While clients in all the treatments decreased in depression, the least effective condition was the nonreligious therapists doing standard CBT. Client ratings of therapist skills did not differ across groups. Clients in all therapy conditions remained significantly less depressed at three months and two-year follow-up. It is also noteworthy that the PCT condition outperformed standard versions of cognitive-behavioral therapy on measures of depression at post-treatment.

Two outcome studies have compared Christian-accommodative and standard versions of RET. W. B. Johnson and Ridley (1992) compared the efficacy of manualized versions of standard RET and Christian RET, which the authors developed. Clients were volunteers who scored in the mildly depressed range or higher on the BDI and scored in the "intrinsic" range on a measure of religious motivation. Clients were blocked on gender randomly assigned to either the standard ($n = 5$) or Christian-accommodative ($n = 5$) treatments. Both treatments consisted of six 50-minute sessions over a 3-week period with the same counselor (the first author of the study). The CRET treatment complemented standard RET by using Christian beliefs to dispute irrational beliefs, encouraged the use of Christian imagery homework, and utilized brief prayer in sessions. At post-treatment, both treatments had reduced clients' depression and automatic negative thoughts, while the Christian RET was also effective in reducing clients' irrational beliefs (but standard RET was not). There were no differences between treatments in client ratings of the counselor's expertise, trustworthiness, and attractiveness.

W. B. Johnson, Devries, Ridley, Pettorini, and Peterson (1994) conducted a more sophisticated and larger version of the Johnson and Ridley (1992) study. Client volunteers were recruited from a theological seminary and area churches. Clients met inclusion criteria similar to the previous study. Clients were randomly assigned to either the standard RET ($n = 16$) or Christian RET ($n = 16$) treatments. Therapists for the study were two second-year Christian doctoral students in clinical psychology who were trained specifically in the treatment protocol for the study, and each therapist treated eight RET and eight Christian RET clients. Treatment consisted of eight individual therapy sessions delivered over 8 weeks. Therapy was monitored to ensure adherence to the manualized treatment protocol. The only dropouts were three Christian RET clients. Both treatments significantly reduced depression, irrational thinking, automatic negative thoughts, and general pathology, though the treatments again showed no differential effects in outcome measures nor in clinical significance indices.

McCullough (1999) conducted a meta-analysis of the five outcome studies reviewed in this section. All five studies compared standard and Christian religion-accommodative therapies for depression. The mean effect size for the difference between the religion-accommodative and standard treatments at the one-week follow-up assessment was $d = 0.18$, which was not reliably different from zero. This suggests that the religion-accommodative approaches were no more and no less efficacious than the standard approaches to the treatment of depression. McCullough (1999) pointed out the limitations of a meta-analysis of such a small number of studies with relatively small samples and short follow-up periods. He also called for research exploring the differential effects of religion-accommodative and standard treatments for a wider variety of mental health problems (such as anxiety, anger, or marital conflict). Religion-accommodative versions of other therapeutic schools of thought (such as solution-focused or narrative therapy) should also be investigated.

In summary, the small body of outcome research to date on Christian-accommodative approaches to individual psychotherapy for depres-sion suggests that such approaches are as effective as standard approaches. While two studies (Propst, 1980; Propst et al., 1992) found religion-accommodative approaches to outperform standard approaches, the general body of research suggests they are no more efficacious than standard treatments. Therefore, McCullough (1999) suggests that client preference might be an important criterion for decisions about employing standard or religion-accommodative treatments for depression. Highly religious clients may prefer a religion-accommodative therapy, while most others may be satisfied with or even prefer standard approaches to therapy.

Muslim-Accommodative Individual Psychotherapy

Three individual psychotherapy outcome studies have compared a Muslim-accommodative approach to treatment with a standard approach. All three studies were conducted in Malaysia by the same lead author.

Azhar, Varma, and Dharap (1994) randomly assigned highly committed Muslim patients meeting the American Psychiatric Association's *Diagnostic and Statistical Manual of Mental Disorders* (1987) criteria for generalized anxiety disorder to a standard treatment comprised of weekly supportive psychotherapy plus anxiolytic medication ($n = 31$) or a treatment that supplemented the supportive psychotherapy plus medication with weekly sessions of religious psychotherapy ($n = 31$). So, patients in the religious psychotherapy condition received more treatment than those in the standard condition. The approach to supportive psychotherapy employed in the study was not clarified, nor was the total amount of supportive psychotherapy received by patients (it seems to have ranged from 12 to 16 sessions). Religious psychotherapy included discussion of religious issues pertinent to the patient, reading verses from the Qu'ran, and encouraging prayers of relaxation. Therapist variables were not assessed. The types, amount, and protocol for therapist training were also not described. The dependent measure was psychiatrists' rating of patients using the Hamilton Anxiety Rating Scale. At 3-month follow-up, patients in the standard-plus-religious psychotherapy condition were rated as significantly lower in anxiety than were those in the standard condition. However, there was no difference between the groups at 6-month follow-up. It is impossible to draw conclusions about the specific role of religiosity in the treatment because variables were often imprecisely specified and no process measures were taken.

Azhar and Varma (1995b) conducted a similar study with Muslim patients meeting criteria for dysthymic disorder. Patients were randomly assigned to the standard treatment consisting of weekly supportive psychotherapy and antidepressant medication ($n = 32$) or the same treatment supplemented again by weekly sessions of religious psychotherapy (described in a similar fashion as Azhar et al., 1994). Like the previous study that treated patients with anxiety, patients in the group receiving standard-plus-religious psychotherapy were rated lower in depression (HRSD) than were patients in the standard treatment group at one-month and three-month follow-up but not at six months.

Azhar and Varma (1995a) also treated 30 Muslim patients meeting criteria for major depression who were grieving the loss of a loved one. Patients ($n = 15$) were randomly assigned to a standard treatment condition involving supportive psychotherapy plus antidepressant medication or to a condition involving the standard treatment plus weekly sessions of religious psychotherapy. As in the earlier studies, the authors do not clarify the exact number of sessions of psychotherapy but describe a range of 12–16 sessions per patient. While Azhar and Varma describe the religious psychotherapy as including similar elements as the earlier study, they identify the religious psychotherapy in this study as consistent with Beck's CBT for depression (Beck et al., 1979). Patients in the group receiving the supplemental religious psychotherapy were again rated lower in depression than were patients in the standard treatment group at 1-month and 3-month follow-up periods, but this time the differences also held up at 6 months. However, the fact that the religious psychotherapy was based on an empirically validated cognitive-behavioral approach to treating depression, which patients in the standard treatment group did not receive, makes it impossible to assess the contribution of the religion accommodation.

The strength of the three studies investigating Muslim-accommodative therapies is their application to actual patients suffering from anxiety, dysthymic, and major depressive disorders. The weakness is the lack of specificity, which makes it impossible to determine whether the positive and at least moderately lasting effects are due to the therapy elements, the religious elements, or both.

Christian-Accommodative Group Interventions

Three studies have tested Christian-accommodative group interventions. Richards, Owen, and Stein (1993) adapted Propst's (1980) religious imagery treatment into a group intervention for perfectionistic Mormon clients. The eight-session weekly group treatment utilized a synthesis of Mormon spiritual and religious teachings with CBT techniques. The Spiritual Well-Being Scale (Ellison, 1983) was used in addition to measures related to depression. Clients were undergraduates at Brigham Young University and formed two groups co-led by the same two pre-masters students. Six of the original 21 clients dropped out, resulting in 15 clients at post-test. At post-test, clients scored lower on depression and perfectionism and higher on self-esteem, existential well-being, and religious well-being than at pre-test. Important limitations of this study include the lack of a control or comparison group, high attrition, and the confounding factor that some clients were also receiving individual therapy at the time of the study.

Hawkins, Tan, and Turk (1999) compared the efficacy of a Christian CBT program with a standard CBT program for inpatient treatment of clinical depression of Christian adults. Like Richards and colleagues (1993), they included the Spiritual Well-Being Scale as an outcome measure. Treatments involved both group and individual therapy. Patients voluntarily entered an inpatient hospital, met diagnostic criteria for major depression, and as part of their inpatient regimen, chose either the Christian CBT ($n = 18$) or Beckian CBT ($n = 11$) program. Both programs involved basic CBT interventions. The intervention was not manualized. Christian CBT treatment involved the use of prayer and biblical perspectives within the interventions. Attendance was required at daily group sessions. The average length of inpatient treatment was 7.5 days for the Christian CBT group and 5.4 days for the Beckian CBT group. The authors do not describe the amount of time patients spent in group and individual sessions, so equivalence of the two treatment conditions cannot be established. Therapists all had at least 4 years of clinical experience with CBT. A supervising psychiatrist discharged patients from the programs.

Both groups demonstrated significantly reduced depression and increased spiritual well-being (both religious and existential well-being). Reduced depression was significantly correlated with improvement in spiritual well-being. Post-treatment patient satisfaction scores were equivalent for both groups. Patients in the Christian CBT showed greater improvement in spiritual well-being than did patients in the standard CBT group. This finding must be interpreted cautiously, however. Patients selected treatment conditions, which leaves open the possibility that those who chose the Christian CBT program were more oriented toward spiritual growth. The relationship between depression and spiritual well-being in this study offers a unique contribution to the outcome research on religion-accommodative therapies.

Rye and Pargament (in press) compared two different 6-week forgiveness group therapies for college women who had been hurt in a romantic relationship. This study did not require that participants meet certain clinical inclusion criteria, but several clinically relevant variables were measured along with forgiveness at post-test and 6-week follow-up (for example, anxiety, depression, and anger). Volunteer clients were randomly assigned to a secular forgiveness group, a religiously integrated forgiveness group, or a no-treatment control group. Clients in both treatment conditions improved significantly more than did the no-treatment control group on measures of forgiveness, hope, and religious and existential well-being. Participants in the secular forgiveness condition also showed significant treatment effects on measures of depression, anger, hurt, and the avoidance of hope. There was no differential efficacy between the two treatment groups in forgiving. Process data suggested that participants used religiously based forgiveness strategies in both treatment conditions.

LIMITATIONS OF THE RESEARCH REVIEWED

The current literature explores a few areas of religion and spirituality in psychotherapy, primarily the role of clients' religious values in therapy, the effects of therapist-client matching on religious values, and efficacy of religiously accommodative CBT. Research on religion and spirituality in psychotherapy needs to be broadened and deepened, but even more, the field needs to widen its boundaries.

The roles of client values and therapist-client matching have been explored in analogue research. Research with actual clients and therapists is sorely needed.

CBT has been accommodated to both Christian and Muslim clients—mostly those who are depressed (with one study of anxious patients). The focus on CBT that is religiously accommodative includes nine outcome studies from five different laboratories or clinics. In all cases, religious CBT has been as effective as CBT for religious clients; in several cases, it has been better. This might be considered about 75% along the road to being an empirically supported intervention. To reach that status, randomized multisite clinical trials are needed. Further, standardization and specification of the intervention is required.

To broaden the scope of inquiry, investigators need to develop other religiously and spiritually accommodative therapies. Worthington, Berry, and Parrott (2001) have classified religions as mostly conscientiousness-based religious (emphasizing norms, laws, and adherence to prescribed religious and moral behavior) and warmth-based religions (emphasizing emotional experience and expression of worship, devotion and love). In general, some religions tend to be more conscientiousness-based (Judaism, Islam) and others more warmth-based (Christianity, Buddhism, and Hinduism). More specifically, there are no religiously accommodative therapies that integrate Hinduism, Buddhism, or Judaism that have been empirically investigated, although some have been articulated. For example, Dialectical Behavior

Therapy (DBT) does incorporate some principles and practices drawn from Zen Buddhism (Linehan, 1993), but religion has not been part of research on DBT.

In addition, some additional specification is needed within Christianity and other religious traditions. Within Christian traditions, approaches might be tailored to Roman Catholics, clientele that use inner healing, prayer, and other spiritual practices, and ethnically diverse traditions (e.g., Asian-American, African-American, Native American, or Latin American religious traditions). There is also a need to move beyond religiously accommodative individual and group therapies toward research on such therapies for couples and families.

All research studies to date have been efficacy studies with more or less experimental control of variables. Effectiveness studies are sorely needed. Given that there may be more than 50,000 professional therapists who explicitly label themselves as "Christian counselors" or "Christian therapists" (Wylie, 2000), a strong need exists to determine what actually is going on in "Christian therapy," with whom, and whether it is effective at improving mental health, religiosity, and spirituality.

Typically, religious accommodative counseling has been compared to secular counseling of the same ilk. In the three studies of Muslim-accommodative therapy, the therapy was treated as an adjunct to supportive treatment plus medication. Many indigenous interventions promoting mental health may exist within religious congregations. For example, lay counseling (Toh & Tan, 1997), pastoral counseling (Propst et al., 1992), marriage enrichment interventions, and 12-step approaches (Thoresen et al., 1998) might already exist within a client's religious community and the client might or might not be availing himself or herself of those resources. Clients from some cultures will also consult traditional healers and shamans as an adjunct to therapy. Effectiveness studies of religious-accommodative therapies alone and in conjunction with each of the adjuncts are needed.

The examination of outcome variables has also been undifferentiated. Most studies have relied on relief of symptoms. A few have examined spiritual well-being. Future studies need to examine changes in personality qualities that are valued by religious traditions. These might include altruism, love, compassion, forbearance, wisdom, gratitude, and forgiveness. Perhaps religious therapies ought to be expected to affect prayer (meditative, confession, gratitude, healing, or intercession), contemplation, acceptance, worship, commitment to social justice, and moral conscience. In addition, both religious spirituality and nonreligious spirituality need to be better explicated and measured. Obviously, researchers interested in religion, spirituality, and psychotherapy have many opportunities for breaking new ground.

THERAPEUTIC PRACTICES

The research we have reviewed on religion and spirituality generate several implications for clinical practice.

1. Clinicians should include religion and spirituality as a standard dimension of clinical assessment (for helpful guidelines, see Richards & Bergin, 1997). General religious descriptors (such as religious group or denomination) can be informative, but religious values and spiritual experiences are more relevant to therapy. Clients who highly value their religious commitments and clients who report high levels of spiritual experience can be expected to have the strongest feelings about the ways religious and spiritual issues are handled in therapy. Therapists should be aware that these clients often want to discuss religious and spiritual issues and may respond negatively if their religious values are directly challenged. Marital therapists should pay particular attention to the religious beliefs and values of highly committed Christian clients.

2. Religion-accommodative therapies (Christian and Muslim) are available and effective, primarily for the treatment of depression. To date, these therapeutic approaches appear to be most relevant for working with highly religious clients who prefer interventions that are consistent with their religious worldviews.

3. The limited empirical research on matching therapist-client religiosity has yielded mixed results, so we only offer tentative clinical guidelines. It is not clear that therapists and clients must be matched on religion in order for therapy to be effective. This is particularly true when cli-

ents are more religiously liberal than their therapists (Martinez, 1991) and the interventions match the religiosity of the client (Propst et al., 1992). Religious matching appears to be more important when clients strongly value salvation and therapy does not involve the use of religiously accommodative interventions (T. A. Kelly & Strupp, 1992).

REFERENCES

American Psychiatric Association. (1987). *Diagnostic and statistical manual of mental disorders* (3rd ed., rev.). Washington, DC: Author.

American Psychological Association. (1992). Ethical principles for psychologists and code of conduct. *American Psychologist, 47*, 1597–1611.

Azhar, M. Z., & Varma, S. L. (1995a). Religious psychotherapy as management of bereavement. *Acta Psychiatrica Scandinavia, 91*, 223–235.

Azhar, M. Z., & Varma, S. L. (1995b). Religious psychotherapy in depressive patients. *Psychotherapy and Psychosomatics, 63*, 165–173.

Azhar, M. Z., Varma, S. L., & Dharap, A. S. (1994). Religious psychotherapy in anxiety disorder patients. *Acta Psychiatrica Scandinavia, 90*, 1–3.

Batson, C. D., Schoenrade, P. A., & Ventis, W. L. (1991). *Religion and the individual: A social-psychological perspective.* New York: Oxford University Press.

Beck, A., Rush, J., Shaw, B., & Emery, G. (1979). *Cognitive therapy of depression.* New York: Guilford.

Bergin, A. E., & Jensen, J. P. (1990). Religiosity of psychotherapists: A national survey. *Psychotherapy, 27*, 3–7.

Beutler, L. E., Machado, P. P. P., & Neufeldt, S. A. (1994). Therapist variables. In A. E. Bergin & S. L. Garfield (Eds.), *Handbook of psychotherapy and behavior change* (4th ed., pp. 229–269). New York: Wiley.

Doherty, W. J. (1999). Morality and spirituality in therapy. In F. Walsh (Ed.), *Spiritual resources in family therapy* (pp. 179–192). New York: Guilford.

Donahue, M. J. (1985). Intrinsic and extrinsic religiousness: Review and meta-analysis. *Journal of Personality and Social Psychology, 48*, 400–419.

Ellis, A. (1962). *Reason and emotion in psychotherapy.* New York: Stuart.

Ellison, C. W. (1983). Spiritual well-being: Conceptualization and measurement. *Journal of Psychology and Theology, 11*, 330–340.

Gallup, G., Jr. (1995). *The Gallup poll: Public opinion in 1995.* Wilmington, DE: Scholarly Resources.

Ganje-Fling, M., Veach, P. M., Kuang, H., & Houg, B. (2000). Effects of childhood sexual abuse on client spiritual well-being. *Counseling and Values, 44*, 84–91.

Gartner, J. (1996). Religious commitment, mental health, and prosocial behavior: A review of the empirical literature. In E. P. Shafranske (Ed.), *Religion and the clinical practice of psychology* (pp. 187–214). Washington, DC: American Psychological Association.

Hawkins, R. S., Tan, S. Y., & Turk, A. A. (1999). Secular versus Christian inpatient cognitive-behavioral therapy programs: Impact on depression and spiritual well-being. *Journal of Psychology and Theology, 27*, 309–318.

Helminiak, D. A. (1996). A scientific spirituality: The interface of psychology and theology. *International Journal for the Psychology of Religion, 6*, 1–19.

Hill, P. C., Pargament, K. I., Hood, R. W., Jr., McCullough, M. E., Swyers, J. P., Larson, D. B., & Zinnbauer, B. J. (2000). Conceptualizing religion and spirituality: Points of commonality, points of departure. *Journal for the Theory of Social Behaviour, 30*, 51–77.

Hoge, D. R. (1996). Religion in America: The demographics of belief and affiliation. In E. P. Shafranske (Ed.), *Religion and the clinical practice of psychology* (pp. 21–42). Washington, DC: American Psychological Association.

Johnson, E. L., & Sandage, S. J. (1999). A postmodern reconstruction of psychotherapy: Orienteering, religion, and the healing of the soul. *Psychotherapy, 36*, 1–15.

Johnson, W. B., DeVries, R., Ridley, C. R., Pettorini, D., & Peterson, D. R. (1994). The comparative efficacy of Christian and secular rational-emotive therapy with Christian clients. *Journal of Psychology and Theology, 22*, 130–140.

Johnson, W. B., & Ridley, C. R. (1992). Brief Christian and non-Christian rational-emotive therapy with depressed Christian clients: An exploratory study. *Counseling and Values, 36*, 220–229.

Keating, A. M., & Fretz, B. R. (1990). Christians' anticipations about counselors in response to counselor descriptions. *Journal of Counseling Psychology, 37*, 293–296.

Kelly, E. W., Jr. (1995). *Spirituality and religion in counseling and psychotherapy.* Alexandria, VA: American Counseling Association.

Kelly, T. A., & Strupp, H. H. (1992). Patient and therapist values in psychotherapy: Perceived changes, assimilation, similarity, and outcome. *Journal of Consulting and Clinical Psychology*, 60, 34–40.

Lewis, K. N., & Epperson, D. L. (1991). Values, pretherapy information, and informed consent in Christian counseling. *Journal of Psychology and Christianity*, 10, 113–131.

Linehan, M. M. (1993). *Cognitive-behavioral treatment for borderline personality disorder*. New York: Guilford.

Mahoney, A., Pargament, K. I., Jewell, T., Swank, A. B., Scott, E., Emery, E., & Rye, M. (1999). Marriage and the spiritual realm: The role of proximal and distal religious constructs in marital functioning. *Journal of Family Psychology*, 13, 321–338.

Martinez, F. I. (1991). Therapist-client convergence and similarity of religious values: Their effect on client improvement. *Journal of Psychology and Christianity*, 10, 137–143.

Marty, M. E., & Appleby, R. S. (Eds.). (1991). *Fundamentalisms observed*. Chicago: University of Chicago Press.

McCullough, M. E. (1999). Research on religion-accommodative counseling: Review and meta-analysis. *Journal of Counseling Psychology*, 46, 92–98.

McCullough, M. E., & Worthington, E. L., Jr. (1995). College students' perceptions of a psychotherapist's treatment of a religious issue: Partial replication and extension. *Journal of Counseling and Development*, 73, 626–634.

McCullough, M. E., Worthington, E. L., Jr., Maxey, J., & Rachal, K. C. (1997). Gender in the context of supportive and challenging religious counseling interventions. *Journal of Counseling Psychology*, 44, 80–88.

Miller, W. R., & Thoresen, C. E. (1999). Spirituality and health. In W. R. Miller (Ed.), *Integrating spirituality into treatment: Resources for practitioners* (pp. 3–18). Washington, DC: American Psychological Association.

Morrow, D., Worthington, E. L., Jr., & McCullough, M. E. (1993). Observers' perceptions of a counselor's treatment of a religious issue. *Journal of Counseling and Development*, 71, 452–456.

Pargament, K. I. (1997). *The psychology of religion and coping: Theory, research, practice*. New York: Guilford.

Pecheur, D. R., & Edwards, K. J. (1984). A comparison of secular and religious versions of cognitive therapy with depressed Christian college students. *Journal of Psychology and Theology*, 12, 45–54.

Pecnik, J. A., & Epperson, D. L. (1985). Analogue study of expectations for Christian and traditional counseling. *Journal of Counseling Psychology*, 32, 127–130.

Propst, L. R. (1980). The comparative efficacy of religious and nonreligious imagery for the treatment of mild depression in religious individuals. *Cognitive Therapy and Research*, 4, 167–178.

Propst, L. R. (1988). *Psychotherapy in a religious framework: Spirituality in the emotional healing process*. New York: Human Sciences.

Propst, L. R., Ostrom, R., Watkins, P., Dean, T., & Mashburn, D. (1992). Comparative efficacy of religious and nonreligious cognitive-behavioral therapy for the treatment of clinical depression in religious individuals. *Journal of Consulting and Clinical Psychology*, 60, 94–103.

Richards, P. S., & Bergin, A. E. (1997). *A spiritual strategy for counseling and psychotherapy*. Washington, DC: American Psychological Association.

Richards, P. S., & Bergin, A. E. (Eds.). (2000). *Handbook of psychotherapy and religious diversity*. Washington, DC: American Psychological Association.

Richards, P. S., Owen, L., & Stein, S. (1993). A religiously oriented group counseling intervention for self-defeating perfectionism: A pilot study. *Counseling and Values*, 37, 96–104.

Ripley, J. S., Worthington, E. L., Jr., & Berry, J. W. (2001). The effects of religiosity on preferences and expectations for marital therapy among married Christians. *American Journal of Family Therapy*, 29, 39–58.

Rokeach, M. (1973). *The nature of human values*. New York: Free Press.

Roof, W. C., Carroll, J. W., & Roozen, D. A. (2000). *The post-war generation and establishment religion: Cross-cultural perspectives*. Boulder, CO: Westview.

Rose, E. M., Westefeld, J. S., & Ansley, T. N. (2001). Spiritual issues in counseling: Clients' beliefs and preferences. *Journal of Counseling Psychology*, 48, 61–71.

Rye, M. S., & Pargament, K. I. (in press). Evaluation of a secular and religiously integrated forgiveness group therapy program for college students who have been wronged by a romantic partner. *Journal of Clinical Psychology*.

Shafranske, E. P. (Ed.). (1996a). *Religion and the*

clinical practice of psychology. Washington, DC: American Psychological Association.

Shafranske, E. P. (1996b). Religious beliefs, affiliations, and practices of clinical psychologists. In E. P. Shafranske (Ed.), *Religion and the clinical practice of psychology* (pp. 149–164). Washington, DC: American Psychological Association.

Shafranske, E. P., & Malony, H. N. (1990). Clinical psychologists' religious and spiritual orientations and their practice of psychotherapy. *Psychotherapy, 27*, 72–78.

Sorenson, R. L. (1994). Therapists' (and their therapists') God representations in clinical practice. *Journal of Psychology and Theology, 22*, 325–344.

Sorenson, R. L. (1997). Transcendence and intersubjectivity: The patient's experience of the analyst's spirituality. In C. Spezzano & G. J. Gargiulo (Eds.), *Soul on the couch: Spirituality, religion, and morality in contemporary psychoanalysis* (pp. 163–199). Hillsdale, NJ: Analytic.

Spilka, B. (1993, August). *Spirituality: Problems and directions in operationalizing a fuzzy concept*. Paper presented at the annual meeting of the American Psychological Association, Toronto, Canada.

Tan, S. Y. (1997). The role of the psychologist in paraprofessional helping. *Professional Psychology: Research and Practice, 28*, 368–372.

Thoresen, C. E., Worthington, E. L., Jr., Swyers, J. P., Larson, D. B., McCullough, M. E., & Miller, W. R. (1998). Religious/spiritual interventions. In D. B. Larson, J. P. Swyers, & M. E. McCullough (Eds.), *Scientific research on spirituality and health* (pp. 104–128). Washington, DC: National Institute for Healthcare Research.

Toh, Y. M., & Tan, S. Y. (1997). The effectiveness of church-based lay counselors: A controlled outcome study. *Journal of Psychology and Christianity, 16*, 260–267.

Wikler, M. (1989). The religion of the therapist: Its meaning to Orthodox Jewish clients. *Hillside Journal of Clinical Psychiatry, 11*, 131–146.

Worthington, E. L., Jr. (1986). Religious counseling: A review of published empirical research. *Journal of Counseling and Development, 64*, 421–431.

Worthington, E. L., Jr. (1988). Understanding the values of religious clients: A model and its application to counseling. *Journal of Counseling Psychology, 35*, 166–174.

Worthington, E. L., Jr., Berry, J. W., & Parrott, L., III. (2001). Unforgiveness, forgiveness, religion, and health. In T. G. Plante & A. Sherman (Eds.), *Faith and health: Psychological perspectives* (pp. 107–138). New York: Guilford.

Worthington, E. L., Jr., & Gascoyne, S. R. (1985). Preferences of Christians and non-Christians for five Christian counselors' treatment plans: A partial replication and extension. *Journal of Psychology and Theology, 13*, 29–41.

Worthington, E. L., Jr., Kurusu, T. A., McCullough, M. E., & Sandage, S. J. (1996). Empirical research on religion and counseling: A ten-year update and prospectus. *Psychological Bulletin, 119*, 448–487.

Worthington, E. L., Jr., & Scott, G. G. (1983). Goal selection for counseling with potentially religious clients by professional and student counselors in explicitly Christian or secular settings. *Journal of Psychology and Theology, 11*, 318–329.

Wulff, D. M. (1997). *Psychology of religion: Classic and contemporary* (2nd ed.). New York: Wiley.

Wyatt, S. C., & Johnson, R. W. (1990). The influence of counselors' religious values on clients' perceptions of the counselor. *Journal of Psychology and Theology, 18*, 158–165.

Wylie, M. S. (2000, January/February). Soul therapy. *Family Therapy Networker, 24*, 26–37, 60–61.

22

Cultural and
Demographic Diversity

Stanley Sue
Amy G. Lam

The purpose of this chapter is to examine the empirical support for customizing the therapeutic relationship for women, ethnic minorities, gay/lesbian/bisexuals, and individuals from lower social classes. At first glance, the grouping of such diverse populations may seem inappropriate and even insulting, a veritable wastepaper basket of diverse groups. However, these groups share several important elements in common. Specifically, they are considered oppressed groups in society, have been subjected to detrimental stereotypes, have not been targeted for much psychological research, and are often underserved or inappropriately served in the mental health system. In the end, the meaningfulness of best practices for these various groups is an empirical question that is best answered from research findings.

In trying to accomplish our goal, we reviewed treatment outcomes research for the groups and used the research to help us develop empirically supported practices. We also examined whether generalities in the principles of effective treatment exist for the different groups. In doing so, three considerations are important to keep in mind. First, care must be taken not to infer that the groups are too similar. Second, there are significant within-group differences that must be acknowledged. Third, individuals have multiple group memberships and identities (for example, being ethnic, a woman, and a lesbian), and it is

presently difficult to address the effects of these identities simultaneously. From the very outset, it should be noted that the breadth and depth of research on treatment processes and outcomes for women, ethnic minority groups, gay/lesbian/ bisexual individuals, and members of lower social classes are woefully inadequate. Moreover, investigators will not find a high degree of scientific rigor in the available research. Given that probably all practitioners encounter members of these demographically diverse groups, it is important to formulate best practices, despite the relative lack of definitive research. There is an increasing urgency to provide effective treatment to these groups, as reflected in the "cultural competency" movement, which tries to identify the cultural knowledge, skills, and awareness that permit one to effectively work with clients from diverse populations (S. Sue, 1998).

The American Psychological Association (APA) has developed psychotherapy guidelines for working with women (Task Force on Sex Bias and Sex Role Stereotyping in Psychotherapeutic Practice, 1978), ethnic minorities (APA Office of Ethnic Minority Affairs, 1993), and lesbian, gay, and bisexual individuals (Division 44/Committee on Lesbian, Gay, and Bisexual Concerns, 2000). Many of the guidelines are admonishments against inappropriate treatment. For example, in working with women, they warn against sexist practices, responding to women as sex objects, fostering traditional sex roles, and biases/stereotypes. Similarly, guidelines for ethnic minority clients stress the importance of knowledge of the culture and background of clients, recognition of biases and prejudices on the part of the therapist, necessity of communicating in the language of the client, and awareness of the sociopolitical context of the client. They are similar in that appeals are made to engage in moral, ethical practices when dealing with traditionally oppressed groups. Most of the guidelines are hortatory in encouraging appropriate behaviors and practices. However, the guidelines do not clearly delineate psychotherapeutic processes to follow and are for the most part not based on empirical studies.

Our research review addresses several different questions for each population: First, is there evidence that these diverse populations fare less well in treatment than mainstream populations? The contrasts we try to make are women versus men; ethnic minority versus majority clients (primarily European Americans); lesbians, gays, and bisexuals (LGBs) versus (largely) heterosexuals; and lower-class individuals versus middle- and upper-class individuals. Obviously, in making such comparisons, it is possible for one group to show poorer outcomes than another group but for psychotherapy to be valuable for both groups. Second, does matching of therapists with clients in terms of gender, ethnicity, sexual orientation, and socioeconomic class improve outcomes? Third, are treatment outcomes better when population-specific strategies are used—feminist therapies, ethnic-specific strategies, and so on—with members of the population? By population-specific interventions, we are referring to therapies or strategies that have been created especially for a particular population. These questions are important to address because they probably underlie most of the existing guidelines. If treatment outcomes are not different between populations, if therapist-client matches have no effect, and if specific treatment strategies are not differentially beneficial, then there is no need to formulate special treatment guidelines for these populations. In our analysis, we review the research for the four groups and then offer suggestions for therapeutic practices.

GENDER

Effectiveness of Therapy with Women

Empirical research suggests that women fare similarly or better in psychotherapy outcomes compared to men. Several research reviews indicate that gender is not a significant main effect in psychotherapy outcome studies (Beutler, Crago, & Arizmendi, 1986; Brodsky & Hare-Mustin, 1980; Garfield, 1994; Orlinsky & Howard, 1980). That is, psychotherapy seems to be just as effective for women as for men. Garfield (1994) conducted a major review of client gender effects in psychotherapy. He found that most empirical studies have yielded no significant differences between men and women with regards to premature termination (Affleck & Garfield, 1961; Berrigan & Garfield, 1981; Craig & Huffine, 1976; Frank, Gliedman, Imber, Nash, & Stone, 1957; Heisler, Beck, Fraps, & McReynolds, 1982; Koss, 1980; Roldolfa, Rapaport, & Lee, 1983) and treatment outcomes (Gaylin, 1966; Hamburg et al., 1967; Knapp, Levin, McCarter, Wermer, & Zetzel, 1960; Luborsky, Mintz, & Christoph, 1979; Siegel, Rootes, & Traub, 1977; Sloane, Staples, Cristol, Yorkston, & Whipple, 1975).

Most recently, Thase and colleagues (1994) examined how depressed men and women respond to cognitive-behavioral therapy. They compared 40 men and 44 women on the Beck Depression Inventory (BDI), Hamilton Depression Rating Scale, and Global Assessment Scale (GAS) after 16 weeks of cognitive-behavioral therapy. Results indicated that neither gender nor the interaction between gender and length of treatment were significantly related to these outcome measures. Two earlier but well-known studies, the Penn Psychotherapy Project (Luborsky et al., 1979) and the Temple University Study (Sloane et al., 1975), also found that the effectiveness of treatments was independent of the gender of the clients.

However, a few empirical studies have found gender effects in therapy favoring women. In a Duke University Counseling Center study conducted by Talley and colleagues (Talley, Butcher, Maguire, & Pinkerton, 1992), significant gender effects were found. Specifically, females were found to show a greater percentage of symptom reduction in brief psychotherapy compared to males (Talley et al., 1992). Additionally, three older empirical studies found that women did better than men in psychotherapeutic outcomes (Kirshner, Genack, & Hauser, 1978; Mintz, Luborsky, & Auerbach, 1971; Seeman, 1954). However, two of the studies had small sample sizes. Thus, the reliability of the results is questionable (see Garfield, 1994, for review).

In sum, the majority of studies comparing women and men in psychotherapy have found that improvement in therapy is independent of client gender. The few studies that do find a significant gender effect reveal that women do better than men in treatment.

Client and Therapist Match

The research on the relationship between gender match for clients and therapists indicates that match may be related to client satisfaction ratings, therapist ratings of client improvement, and indirect outcomes (such as length of treatment and dropout). We found three studies examining the relationship between client-therapist gender match and treatment outcomes (Jones, Krupnick, & Kerig, 1987; Jones & Zoppel, 1982; Zlotnick, Elkin, & Shea, 1998). Zlotnick and colleagues (1998) examined whether same-gender match and mixed-gender match were related to psychotherapy processes and outcomes. Using the data set from the National Institute of Mental Health Treatment of Depression Collaborative Research Program, they found that the type of therapist seen (same gender or opposite gender) was not related to attrition rates, depression ratings after treatment, or the client's perception of therapist empathy. Furthermore, clients' beliefs about who would be more helpful (that is, a male or female therapist) and their match or mismatch with this expectation were not related to outcome. These findings are in contrast to other studies conducted by Jones and his colleagues (Jones et al., 1987; Jones & Zoppel, 1982), which suggest that gender match is related to improved symptom outcome and more satisfaction with therapy.

Jones and colleagues (1987) utilized a data set from the Center for the Study of Neuroses at the University of California, San Francisco. Sixty fe-

male clients with either male or female therapists were evaluated. Results indicated that clients were more satisfied when treated by female therapists, as opposed to male therapists. Additionally, independent clinical evaluators found that women with female therapists showed significantly less intrusive symptomatology at follow-up than women with male therapists. Regression analyses comparing the relative influence of therapist gender, client age, and pretreatment symptom levels on post-treatment symptomatology indicated that therapist gender had a significant influence on outcomes but was not the most important contributor of outcomes. Specifically, pretreatment symptom levels accounted for the most variance in outcomes (.22), with client age (.13) and therapist gender (.08) accounting for less variance. This study was limited in that it only examined female clients' experiences with therapists and did not examine male clients' experiences.

In the first of a two-part study, Jones and Zoppel (1982) compared therapy processes and outcomes across four groups of client-therapist dyads (that is, female-female, female-male, male-male, and male-female). This study measured client outcomes in terms of therapist ratings. Results indicated that while male and female clients were rated equally in terms of improvement in therapy, female therapists were more likely than male therapists to rate female clients as showing more improvement. In general, female therapists were more likely to rate their clients as having more success in therapy and reported better therapeutic alliances with their clients than male therapists.

In the second study, Jones and Zoppel (1982) conducted interviews of clients' assessment of the psychotherapy experience. They found that clients did not report significant gender matching effects on therapy outcomes. However, gender match was found to be significantly related to length of treatment, with same-gender dyads reporting significantly longer lengths of treatment than mixed-gender dyads. Finally, an early study by Persons, Persons, and Newmark (1974) found that while all clients improved in psychotherapy, clients in same-gender dyads were more satisfied with therapy and felt their therapist was more helpful than clients in opposite-gender dyads.

Empirical research on gender and therapy outcomes has found interaction effects between gender and other client characteristics such as age, ethnicity, martial status, and diagnosis, as well as therapist experience. For example, in a sample of female clients, Orlinsky and Howard (1976) found that the degree of sensitivity to the sex of one's therapist was related to various client characteristics. Compared to other groups (single women over 29, young married women, divorced women, and older married women), single unmarried women between the ages of 23 and 28 reported significantly higher ratings of satisfaction with female therapists. Additionally, in contrast to clients with personality disorders, depressed clients reacted more strongly to therapist gender. Depressed clients who had women therapists reported receiving more encouragement and mastery insight.

Fujino, Okazaki, and Young (1994) found an interaction effect with ethnicity and gender match on therapy outcomes in a sample of clients from outpatient services in Los Angeles County mental health facilities. For Asian American female clients, being jointly matched on ethnicity and gender significantly decreased the likelihood of premature termination and increased the number of sessions. Being matched solely on gender was also associated with lower dropout rates for Asian American females. For Asian American men, being matched on ethnicity predicted more sessions and a higher final GAS score. Being jointly matched on ethnicity and gender was also related to higher final GAS scores. For White American women, being jointly matched was related to lower dropout rates as well as more sessions. For White American men, neither ethnic or gender match was related to treatment outcomes (Fujino et al., 1994).

Hill (1975) examined how therapist experience level and gender interacted in terms of client ratings of satisfaction in therapy. Results indicated that experienced female therapists were rated as more empathic and facilitative than their inexperienced counterparts. In contrast, inexperienced male therapists were more empathic than their experienced counterparts. In general, it was also found that clients of female therapists reported more satisfaction with therapy than those with male therapists.

The limited number of studies on gender match seems to indicate that gender match may be related to client satisfaction and indirect outcomes. While two studies also found match to be related to higher therapist ratings of improvement, other direct outcomes were not related to match. Therefore, more rigorous studies need to be conducted to examine if gender match is an important variable in direct psychotherapy outcomes; they should be targeted toward uncovering the possible interaction of other variables with gender.

Feminist Therapies

Feminism is defined as the principle that women should have political, economic, and social rights equal to those of men (Gilbert & Scher, 1999). Although there are various approaches to feminist therapy, three common elements are: the importance of the sociocultural context, an egalitarian relationship between therapist and client, and a woman-valuing and self-validating process (Gilbert & Scher, 1999; Worell & Remer, 1992). In therapy, clients learn to be aware of sociocultural sources of problems and acknowledge the impact of discrimination and oppression in the lives of women, rather than focusing solely on intrapsychic causes of personal difficulties. An egalitarian relationship between therapist and client is also promoted. Therapy is a collaborative process in which both the therapist and the client are seen as experts (Gilbert & Scher, 1999; Worrell & Remer, 1992). Finally, a woman-valuing and self-validating process seeks to validate the female experience, while identifying and embracing a client's strengths (Gilbert & Scher, 1999; Worell & Remer, 1992).

Few research studies have explicitly examined treatment outcomes on feminist therapies (Brodsky & Hare-Mustin, 1980; Gilbert & Scher, 1999). We were able to locate only two studies assessing the effectiveness of gender awareness therapy. In one study involving psychiatric patients in a day treatment program (Sirkin, Maxey, Ryan, French, & Clements, 1988), results showed that both women and men saw the importance of how gender influenced their illness and perceived difficulty in society. Alyn and Becker (1984) conducted another study examining the effect of a women's awareness group with women with chronic and severe mental disorders. Results indicated that women participating in the women's awareness groups improved in their self-esteem and sexual knowledge. There were no differences in attitudes toward women. However, both these gender awareness therapy studies had relatively small sample sizes, and one study did not have a control group.

Consciousness-raising groups have been advocated as an alternative therapy to traditional psychotherapies. In these groups, women share their personal experiences in order to gain an awareness of society's influence on their problems (Nassi & Abramowitz, 1978). Weitz (1982) conducted a study to examine the effectiveness of consciousness-raising as a therapy in decreasing depression. Follow-up interviews and assessment measures on 73 women found that participants attributed psychological benefits to the consciousness-raising group. For example, 48% of the participants stated that the group participation helped them to be more socially interactive, while another 26% stated that the group provided emotional support. Moreover, 45% of the women in this group began to see their problems more as a function of societal issues rather than personal problems. Test scores also suggested that levels of self-esteem increased significantly after participation in the groups. Finally, it was found that the mean level of depressive symptoms (as measured through the Center for Epidemiologic Study–Depression Scale) was significantly reduced after group participation. It should be noted that the study did not include a control group to examine whether this therapy was better than traditional therapies.

We found one study that examined the impact of feminist therapy on battered women. Rinfret-Raynor and Cantin (1997) compared feminist group therapy, feminist individual therapy, and a comparison group of standard individual treatment among 181 battered women. It was hypothesized that the feminist group therapy would be superior to the feminist individual therapy and that both feminist therapies would be superior to the standard treatment. Effectiveness was measured through levels of violence experienced, self-esteem, assertiveness, social adjustment, and marital adjustment. Results indicated that while therapy in general was helpful, there were no dif-

ferences among the therapies. One limitation to this study was that participants were not randomly assigned to the three different treatment groups, but were rather assigned to a group as they came to seek treatment. Another potential limitation to the study was that the comparison standard treatment may have been similar to the feminist treatments in terms of actual approaches to therapy and therefore did not produce significantly different treatment effects than the feminist therapies.

In summary, the results of the four empirical studies on feminist therapies have not provided definitive results on the superiority of feminist therapies to traditional therapies. While the studies have indicated the potential usefulness of feminist therapies, two of these studies did not have comparison or control groups. Additionally, one comparative study did not find differences between feminist and standard therapy.

Conclusions

Extant studies indicate that women benefit from therapy and that match is related to client satisfaction and indirect outcomes. However, there is no strong empirical evidence for the superiority of client-therapist gender match over nonmatched dyads for direct outcomes and feminist therapy over traditional forms of therapy. The lack of strong evidence may reflect the absence of many rigorous studies or the real lack of effects. Another possibility is that best practices are strongly influenced by individual differences among women and men. That is, matching or feminist therapy may be more appropriate for some clients or situations (for example, women with feminist issues or women who experience domestic violence or abuse). The future task is to determine the appropriateness of these conditions for clients.

ETHNIC MINORITIES

In this section, we review research on the effectiveness of therapy with ethnic minority groups. Specifically, we evaluate research on client-therapist ethnic match and ethnic-specific therapies tailored for minority clients. In our review, we focus on African Americans, American Indians,

Asian Americans, Latino Americans, and (non-Hispanic) White Americans. The term "ethnic minority" will refer to the four non-White groups. As mentioned earlier, members of various ethnic minority groups show a great deal of heterogeneity, especially in terms of ethnic identity, ethnic language proficiency, acculturation levels, social class, and spiritual faith.

Effectiveness of Therapy with African Americans

African Americans have been found to exhibit either similar or worse outcomes than Whites in psychotherapy. That is, while three studies have found no ethnic differences (Jones, 1978, 1982; Lerner, 1972), three other studies have found that African Americans do worse in therapy (Brown, Joe, & Thompson, 1985; Markowitz, Spielman, Sullivan, & Fishman, 2000; S. Sue, Fujino, Hu, Takeuchi, & Zane, 1991). Lerner (1972) conducted one of the first treatment outcome studies with African Americans and found that across the sample of African American and White clients, all clients tended to improve after treatment. Similarly, Jones (1978, 1982) found that client outcomes were not related to race of the client and that African American and White clients improved after therapy.

Three studies, however, have indicated that African Americans do not improve as much as other populations. Specifically, Brown and colleagues (1985) found that ethnic clients (that is, African Americans and Mexican Americans) had more unfavorable outcomes upon discharge from drug treatment programs when compared to White American clients. In another study of ethnic minority clients within the Los Angeles County Mental Health System, S. Sue and colleagues (1991) found the post-treatment GAS scores of African Americans to be lower than that of other ethnic groups (that is, Asian, Mexican, and White Americans), even after controlling for pretreatment scores. Most recently, a randomized control study by Markowitz and colleagues (2000) found that African American HIV-positive clients in a cognitive-behavioral treatment for depression fared worse than either Latino or White American clients, after controlling for pretreatment depression scores. African American partic-ipants in the cognitive-behavioral treatment also had worse outcomes than African Americans who received other treatments (such as interpersonal therapy, supportive therapy, supportive therapy with imipramine).

In sum, while no studies have found African Americans to have more favorable outcomes than Whites, some studies have found no differences, while others have found African Americans to benefit less from therapy than other ethnic groups.

Client and Therapist Match

Studies on ethnic match for African Americans have indicated that match does not affect direct outcomes (such as symptom reduction, functioning, or subjective well-being), but may affect indirect outcomes (such as length of treatment and dropout rates). Three studies have shown that race of client and therapist had no effect on outcomes (Jones, 1978, 1982; Lerner, 1972). In Lerner's (1972) study, both African American and White American clients were paired with White therapists, and no differences between African American and White American clients were found in terms of outcomes. Additionally, Jones's (1978, 1982) studies found that the race of the therapist and client had no effect on outcomes.

Studies have demonstrated that while ethnic match may not be directly related to outcomes, it may be indirectly related to outcomes through length of treatment and dropout rates. Furthermore, treatment duration has been found to be positively related to treatment outcomes (Orlinsky, Grawe, & Parks, 1994). For example, S. Sue and colleagues' (1991) study found that ethnic match was related to greater number of therapy sessions but unrelated to GAS scores for African Americans within the Los Angeles County Mental Health System. Rosenheck, Fontana, and Cottrol (1995) found that African American veterans who were matched with White therapists, as opposed to African American therapists, had higher rates of early termination and fewer treatment sessions.

In contrast to these studies, Gamst and colleagues (Gamst, Dana, Der-Karabetian, & Kramer, 2000) found that among African Americans at one mental health center, being matched was associated with fewer treatment sessions and lower

Global Assessment of Functioning (GAF) scores than being unmatched, even after controlling for covariates. These findings differ from other studies in terms of match effects. It is unclear if the findings from Gamst and colleagues (2000) are confined to one institution or have greater generalizability.

Ethnic-Specific Therapies

Literature discussing culturally specific forms of therapy for African Americans is quite extensive. However, we could not locate any empirical studies that have tested the therapeutic outcomes of psychotherapy advocated in this theoretical literature.

Effectiveness of Therapy with American Indians

Compared to other ethnic minority groups (such as African Americans, Asian Americans, and Latino Americans), there have been even fewer empirical examinations on treatment effectiveness with the American Indian population (Manson, Walker, & Kivlahan, 1987; Neligh, 1988). Manson and colleagues' (1987) review found anecdotal and clinical reports of the effectiveness of different therapies with this population, but did not report any empirical studies of treatment effectiveness. We found only one empirical study on treatment effectiveness. Query (1985) compared the outcomes of White Americans and American Indians in a substance abuse treatment program and found that American Indians did not benefit from treatment as much as White Americans. Because of the relative dearth of empirical studies examining the effectiveness of treatments, no statements can be made concerning how effective treatments are for this population.

Client and Therapist Match

Empirical research on client-therapist ethnic match is sparse. These studies tend to focus on client satisfaction and preference variables, as opposed to more direct assessments of client outcomes in therapy. Two preference studies have indicated ethnic match may not be as important as other therapist characteristics. Dauphinais, LaFrom-

boise, and Rowe (1980) found trustworthiness to be more important than the ethnicity of a person. In an analogue study where high school students rated one of four counseling conditions, interviewer ethnicity was not found to interact with the trustworthiness of the counseling model (LaFromboise & Dixon, 1981). Other studies have suggested that ethnicity of the counselor is important for client-perceived counselor effectiveness and client preferences (Bennett & BigFoot-Sipes, 1991; Dauphinais, Dauphinais, & Rowe 1981; Havilland, Horswill, O'Connell, & Dynneson, 1983). However, these studies are limited in that they do not assess direct psychotherapy outcomes. Finally, ethnic matching among American Indians may be a moot issue because of the scarcity of American Indian therapists.

Ethnic-Specific Therapies

It has been proposed that family-network therapy may be culturally consistent with American Indian values favoring an extended family social group (Manson et al., 1987). However, there have been no empirical studies testing the effectiveness of family-network therapy.

Traditional methods of healing including sweat lodges and talking circles are increasingly being incorporated into mental health treatments (Gutierres, Russo, & Urbanski, 1994; Gutierres & Todd, 1997; Manson et al., 1987). Gutierres and colleagues (Gutierres et al., 1994; Gutierres & Todd, 1997) have found that compared to control groups, a culturally enhanced substance abuse program has been related to increased treatment completion as well as lowered levels of depression for American Indians. However, no reports were made concerning how the program worked to decrease substance abuse. Therefore, while some preliminary evidence indicates that culturally specific therapies may be related to outcomes, more studies examining how these therapies affect direct outcomes are needed.

Effectiveness of Therapy with Asian Americans

A limited number of effectiveness studies have been conducted with Asian Americans. While there have been no differences in outcomes between Asians and Whites on psychological functioning (S. Sue et al., 1991; Zane & Hatanaka, 1988), ethnic differences may exist on client satisfaction variables. Specifically, two studies found that Asians reported less satisfaction with their treatment and progress in therapy than Whites (W. M. L. Lee & Mixson, 1995; Zane, 1983).

Client and Therapist Match

The extant studies examining client-therapist ethnic match seem to indicate that match may be related to indirect outcomes for Asian American clients. A series of analyses of the Los Angeles County Mental Health System (Flaskerud & Hu, 1994; Fujino et al., 1994; Lau & Zane, 2000; Sue et al., 1991; Takeuchi, Sue, & Yeh, 1995) revealed that ethnic match was associated with less likelihood of dropout and increased length of therapy. More specifically, it appears that ethnic and language match may be especially important for treatment outcomes with limited–English-speaking clients (Sue et al., 1991). Gamst, Dana, Der-Karabetian, and Kramer (2001) also found that match was associated with more treatment sessions.

Ethnic-Specific Therapies

It has been hypothesized that Western treatments should be modified to better treat Asian Americans (see Chin, 1998; Chung & Okazaki, 1991; E. Lee, 1997; D. Sue & Sue, 1991). Despite these arguments, however, there have been no empirical studies comparing the effectiveness of Western models of therapy with culturally specific treatments or empirical studies on the effectiveness of culturally modified treatments for Asian Americans. Most research on "culturally sensitive services" for Asian Americans have focused on ethnic and language match (Sue, Zane, & Young, 1994).

Additionally, some studies have examined counseling styles (for example, directive vs. nondirective) and Asian American clients' preferences for these counseling styles. Empirical studies suggest that a directive, problem-solving approach to therapy is seen as more credible and is preferred and expected by Asian American clients (Atkinson, Maruyama, & Matsui, 1978; Tan, 1967;

Yuen & Tinsley, 1981). While one study did not find a relationship between directive style and therapist credibility for Chinese or White American students, the authors suggested that this may be related to elements of confrontation in their directive style condition, which were absent in the directive approaches used in other studies (Akutsu, Lin, & Zane, 1990).

Effectiveness of Therapy with Latino Americans

Rosenthal (2000) recently reviewed outcomes research for Latino American clients. Rosenthal's (2000) review suggests that while there is still a paucity of empirical research in the area, existing research does indicate that Latino Americans improve after psychotherapy treatments. However, existing research has mostly examined how Latino Americans fare with different types of therapies, rather than comparing Latino American clients with mainstream White American clients. Interestingly, one study of the Los Angeles County Mental Health System indicated that compared to Whites, African Americans, and Asian Americans, Mexican Americans were the most likely to improve after treatment (S. Sue et al., 1991). Moreover, while many have suggested that culturally specific therapies are superior to traditional therapies for Latino Americans, there is still a need for more empirical research to test this hypothesis.

Client and Therapist Match

Four studies have examined the relationship between ethnic match and variables such as outcomes, premature treatment, or treatment duration for Latino American clients. S. Sue and colleagues (1991) found that match is associated with better treatment outcomes, decreased premature termination, and increased length of treatment. Furthermore, when these clients were divided into two groups based on primary language, ethnic match was significantly related to a decrease in premature dropout and positive treatment outcomes for those whose primary language was Spanish. Subsequent analyses with this data set also find similar results (Takeuchi et al., 1995). Flaskerud's study (1986) revealed that language and ethnic match were significantly related to lower dropout. In a study by Gamst and colleagues (2000), findings indicated that ethnic match was associated with higher GAF scores. Collectively, the four studies offer some evidence of the importance of ethnic match, especially for unacculturated Latino Americans.

Ethnic-Specific Therapies

Psychotherapy research with Latino Americans has recently focused on the development of culturally sensitive treatments. Two therapies that seem to be consistent with Latino cultural values are *cuento* therapy (Costantino, Malgady, & Rogler, 1986, 1994; Malgady, Rogler, & Costantino, 1990a, 1990b) and family therapy (Padilla & Salgado de Snyder, 1987; Szapocznik et al., 1989). These treatments tend to integrate the value of *respeto*, as well as the importance of the family, which may play a role in the effectiveness of these treatments.

Cuento therapy was created by three researchers to provide a culturally sensitive method of modeling adaptive behavior for Puerto Rican children through folktales. Costantino and colleagues (1986) compared the effectiveness of *cuento* therapy, art/play therapy, and a no-intervention control group for Puerto Rican children in kindergarten through third grade. They found a treatment by grade level effect. After 20 weeks of treatment, first-graders who received *cuento* therapy had less anxiety than children in the no-intervention control group but did not differ significantly from children in the art/play therapy. Subsequent studies have also supported the effectiveness of *cuento* therapy for Puerto Rican children with anxiety and aggression issues (Malgady et al., 1990a, 1990b). Recently, Costantino and colleagues (1994) examined the effectiveness of *cuento* therapy with other Latino groups. They found that *cuento* therapy was effective in reducing anxiety and phobic symptoms compared to a control group for Dominican and Central American children. These studies qualify *cuento* therapy as a probably efficacious therapy for Puerto Rican children. If another controlled outcome study conducted by another group of investigators could demonstrate the effectiveness of *cuento* therapy

over another treatment, *cuento* therapy would qualify as a well-established treatment.

Family therapy has also been shown to be potentially useful with Latino clients. Szapocznik and colleagues (1989) compared structural family therapy, individual psychodynamic child therapy, and a control condition for Latino boys with behavioral and emotional problems. They found both therapy conditions to be more effective than the control condition with regard to treatment duration and premature dropout. However, no differences between the treatment conditions were found with regard to decreases in symptomatology. At follow-up, however, it was found that while boys in the individual therapy declined in family functioning, boys in the family therapy condition continued to improve in family functioning. Thus, preliminary evidence suggests that this form of family therapy may be useful for Latino clients.

Conclusions

In general, the limited studies examining effectiveness of therapy with ethnic minorities indicate that minorities tend to exhibit either similar or worse outcomes than Whites in psychotherapy. Moreover, ethnic match may be important for indirect treatment outcomes, especially for less acculturated ethnic minority clients. Finally, empirical studies on ethnic-specific treatments are sparse for African Americans and Asian Americans. There is some empirical support for ethnic-specific treatments for Latino American clients, as well as preliminary support for ethnic-specific treatments for American Indian clients. Given the increasing need to provide culturally competent services, future studies should focus on comparing the usefulness of ethnic-specific treatments over traditional mainstream treatments.

SEXUAL ORIENTATION

Effectiveness of Therapy with Lesbian, Gay, and Bisexual Individuals

Knowledge of the effectiveness of different therapies for LGB individuals is scant (Dunkle, 1994).

Only recently has the shift of therapy for LGB persons moved away from treating their homosexuality toward treating their presenting concerns. Dunkle (1994) conducted one of the few reviews of treatment outcome studies with gay male clients. Only six studies were found from the period of 1975 to 1993. Of the six studies, four were nonexperimental in nature. Moreover, all therapies were group or couples interventions and mostly cognitive-behavioral in orientation. Treatment outcomes were measured through self-report satisfaction indices in three of the studies, while two studies examined behavioral changes in clients. One study examined both self-report satisfaction and behavioral changes. The three studies solely examining satisfaction indices reported that treatment was effective. Both studies measuring behavioral indices of change found significant changes in behavior after therapy. The study that examined both the self-report and behavioral change measures found that only the self-report measures showed significant improvement after therapy. Because of the nonexperimental nature of the majority of these studies, Dunkle (1994) concluded that definitive statements regarding the effectiveness of certain therapies for gay male clients could not be made.

Since Dunkle's 1994 review, three studies on the effectiveness of HIV risk-reduction programs for gay men (Choi et al., 1996; Peterson et al., 1996; Roffman et al., 1997), one study on a bereavement support group for gay men (Goodkin et al., 1999), and two studies examining treatment for depression for gay clients (M. R. Lee, Cohen, Hadley, & Goodwin, 1999; Markowitz et al., 1998) have been conducted.

The three studies examining the effectiveness of HIV risk-reduction interventions seem to indicate that these programs are effective for gay men. Choi and colleagues (1996) examined the efficacy of brief group counseling in reducing HIV risk in Asian American and Pacific Islander men who have sex with men. Participants were randomly assigned to the intervention and control groups. The treatment consisted of a 3-hour group counseling session focused on HIV risk reduction. At the 3-month follow-up, the treatment group reported significantly fewer partners than the control group. However, there were no differ-

ences between the groups on unprotected anal intercourse. Therefore, while the intervention seemed to be effective in reducing one risk behavior (number of sexual partners), it was not effective in reducing another risk behavior (unprotected sexual intercourse).

Peterson and colleagues (1996) evaluated an HIV risk-reduction intervention on a group of African American homosexual and bisexual men. Three hundred eighteen participants were randomized into a single-session group, a triple-session group, or a wait-list control group. Regression analyses indicated that there was a significant treatment effect on unprotected anal intercourse. Those in the triple-session intervention group were less likely to engage in unprotected sex than those in the single-session group. Interestingly, the study did not find the triple-session group to be better than the control group. This may be related to the fact that the control group had lower pre-intervention levels of risky behavior. Distinctions between gay and bisexual men were also not made.

Roffman and colleagues (1997) also conducted a study examining the effectiveness of a 17-session cognitive-behavioral group therapy to reduce HIV transmission among 129 gay and bisexual men. Findings indicated that participants in the counseling intervention had approximately 2.3 times the odds of success in reducing HIV risk than those in the control condition. However, because of the small sample size, the authors stated the odds ratio was not found to be significant at the .05 level. Additionally, counseling had significantly different effects on gay and bisexual men. Exclusively gay men who were in the treatment group were almost four and a half times more likely to be successful in reducing HIV risk than gay men in the control condition. For bisexual men, there were no significant differences on risk reduction between the treatment and control groups.

One randomized control study on a bereavement support group for gay men has been conducted (Goodkin et al., 1999). A total of 166 participants were assigned to either 10-session bereavement therapy groups or control groups. Results indicated that the intervention was effective for both HIV-1-seropositive and -seronegative participants in reducing the composite grief and distress index when controlling for other confounds. There were no intervention effects for depression and anxiety for both HIV-1-seropositive and -seronegative participants.

Two studies have examined the effectiveness of treatment for depression in HIV-positive individuals. M. R. Lee and colleagues (1999) examined a group cognitive-behavioral therapy for the treatment of depression among 15 gay men with AIDS or symptomatic HIV infection. Modifications were made to the therapy procedures, extending treatment to 20 weekly 2-hour sessions, as well as giving clients permission to continue any other therapy (including pharmacotherapy) they were receiving. Results indicated that the cognitive-behavioral therapy had a high retention rate, with 13 of the 15 clients remaining in therapy. Outcome measures indicated significant reductions in depressive symptomatology. The results must be tempered, as the limitations of the study included a small sample size, lack of control group, and the use of other therapies in addition to the cognitive-behavioral therapy.

A more rigorous study on the effectiveness of therapy with HIV-positive clients with depression was conducted by Markowitz and colleagues (1998). A total of 101 participants were randomly assigned to 16 weeks of treatment with interpersonal psychotherapy, cognitive-behavioral therapy, supportive therapy, or imipramine plus supportive therapy. While the sample included individuals of both genders and different sexual orientations, most clients were male and gay. Overall results indicated that depressive symptomatology decreased across groups over time. However, there were differential benefits among the different treatment groups. HIV-positive clients in the interpersonal psychotherapy and supportive psychotherapy with imipramine groups had significantly greater improvements on depression measures than those in the cognitive-behavioral or supportive therapy groups.

These findings provide evidence that psychotherapy interventions are effective for gay men. Moreover, treatments focused on gay men may not be as effective with bisexual men. Therefore, it is critical for researchers to distinguish between gay men and bisexual men in treatment outcome studies.

Client and Therapist Match

Although it has been frequently suggested that LGB clients should be treated by LGB therapists to increase treatment effectiveness (Cabaj, 1996; Gartrell, 1984; Riddle & Sang, 1978; Rochlin, 1982), current empirical research on client-therapist match on sexual orientation is limited. To date, there are only three published empirical studies on the effects of client-therapist match on sexual orientation, and they provide only partial support for the importance of match.

Liljestrand, Gerling, and Saliba (1978) examined how client-therapist match on sexual orientation was related to treatment outcomes. Treatment outcomes included examining the sex roles of the client; comfort with sexual orientation; general outcomes of self-knowledge, self-acceptance, and self-actualization; and an overall outcome measure of the three specific dimensions mentioned above. Results indicated that client-therapist match on sexual orientation was related to better outcomes in dealing with sexual orientation. Gender match was not found to be related to any of the outcomes. An interaction effect between sexual orientation and gender match was not tested. This study suggests that sexual orientation match may be especially important when dealing with issues of sexual orientation.

Brooks (1981) and Liddle (1996) conducted surveys examining gay and lesbian clients' ratings of helpfulness of therapy and therapists. Brooks (1981) found that there was a significant difference in lesbian client perceptions of helpfulness of heterosexual male therapists and all other therapists (that is, heterosexual female, lesbian, gay therapists). Specifically, 66% of those indicating that therapy was helpful had female therapists, either heterosexual or lesbian. In contrast, 74% of those indicating that therapy was damaging had heterosexual male therapists.

Liddle (1996) found that lesbian and gay clients did not rate gay, lesbian, bisexual, and heterosexual female therapists differently on perceived helpfulness. However, all were perceived as more helpful than both heterosexual male therapists and female therapists whose sexual orientation was unknown. The finding that heterosexual female therapists were no less helpful than gay, lesbian, and bisexual therapists suggests that heterosexual therapists can be effective with the lesbian and gay population (Liddle, 1996). Taken together, these studies point to the possibility that match may be important for LGB clients, especially when dealing with issues regarding sexual orientation. Moreover, sexual orientation match is partially supported, as females of both orientations have not been shown to produce differential effects on clients, whereas heterosexual males are thought to have a negative influence on lesbian and gay clients. It should be noted, however, that the outcome measures were limited to client perceptions of helpfulness and not direct outcome measures.

Gay Affirmative Therapies

Gay affirmative therapy is defined as a therapy that celebrates and advocates the authenticity and integrity of LGB persons and their relationships, rather than viewing LGB individuals as marginal and measured with a heterosexual norm (Bieschke, McClanahan, Tozer, Grzegorek, & Park, 2000; Garnets, Hancock, Cochran, Goodchilds, & Peplau, 1991; Morrow, 2000). Affirmative therapies are thought to counteract the effects of a homophobic society and promote a positive regard for the client (Lebolt, 1999). We could locate no empirical research on the effectiveness of gay affirmative therapies in treating LGB individuals.

Conclusions

Although psychotherapy seems to be effective with gay men, existing empirical studies do not allow us to determine whether gay men fare better, worse, or similarly to heterosexual clients. Unfortunately, there is little empirical research on the effectiveness of treatments for lesbians and bisexuals, as well as the effectiveness of gay affirmative therapies. Client-therapist match on sexual orientation may be especially important for clients facing issues related to their sexual orientation. Future research should focus attention on conducting treatment outcomes studies on relatively unexamined lesbian and bisexual individuals, as well as examining the empirical effectiveness of gay affirmative therapies.

SOCIAL CLASS

Socioeconomic status (SES) is an important client variable that is often ignored in psychotherapy. SES is an indicator of individuals' social position in society that helps determine their access to power, privilege, resources, and rewards in the community where they live (Williams & Rucker, 1996). Unlike other diversities discussed so far (gender, race/ethnicity, and sexual orientation), SES is more difficult to study. In fact, SES is a complex construct that has many operational definitions. Furthermore, race and ethnicity have been found to correlate with SES, and many studies confound race and SES effects (Acosta, 1980; Vail, 1978). The heterogeneity of operational definitions and confounding race effects have made the generalization of research in this area more difficult (Lorion & Felner, 1986).

With respect to psychotherapy studies, researchers have mainly focused on the effectiveness of psychotherapy with economically disadvantaged clients (Lorion & Felner, 1986). While several studies have examined the relative effectiveness of specific therapies (such as psychodynamic or behavioral) for low-income clients, most of the literature on social class and therapy has been focused on how social class correlates with acceptance for, and duration of, treatment (Garfield, 1994). In fact, when compared with the other diverse populations discussed in this chapter, social class as a variable has been the least studied in conjunction with treatment outcomes research. For example, in the 1996 Division 12 review of empirically validated psychological treatments, no mention of low-income clients was made (Chambless et al., 1996). Additionally, in Lorion and Felner's 1986 review, only 138 empirical articles were found that focused on low-SES clients and treatment outcomes, with fewer than 10 studies that could be classified as rigorous (that is, including control group, pre- and postmeasures, and follow-up). Garfield's 1994 review of social class and treatment outcomes also found few, if any, empirical studies on this topic. In both these reviews, most of the studies found were conducted during the 1960s and 1970s, with few, if any, studies conducted recently. Because the empirical studies are dated and few in number, our review is limited.

Effectiveness of Therapy for Individuals with Low Socioeconomic Status

Several reviews of the relationship between social class and direct therapy outcomes have found no relationship between these variables. Luborsky, Chandler, Auerbach, Cohen, and Bachrach (1971) reviewed five studies and found no SES effect in therapy. Lorion's 1973 review concluded that social class was related to treatment assignment and duration, but not to direct outcomes.

Despite the dearth of research on social class and outcomes research, several studies have suggested that social class is related to psychotherapy dropout. Several review articles have pointed to the greater likelihood of premature termination for clients of lower SES (Baekeland & Lundwall, 1975; Garfield, 1986, 1994; Reis & Brown, 1999; Wierzbicki & Pekarik, 1993). Baekeland and Lundwall (1975) provided one of the first reviews of psychotherapy dropout. Their review of 74 psychotherapy dropout studies indicated that client SES was one of the major variables strongly associated with dropout. Garfield (1986) reviewed 86 dropout studies and also concluded that dropout was most strongly related to client social class. Wierzbicki and Pekarik (1993) conducted a meta-analysis on 125 dropout studies. The mean dropout rate was 47%. Significant effect sizes were found for two social class variables—education and SES. Clients who had lower levels of education and were of lower SES were at increased risk of premature termination. Finally, the most recent review of psychotherapy dropouts indicated that SES is still a consistent predictor of dropout (Reis & Brown, 1999). As mentioned previously, length of treatment is significantly associated with direct outcomes (Orlinsky et al., 1994).

It has been hypothesized that differences in client expectations regarding therapy are an underlying reason for premature termination (Garfield, 1986). Two studies have found the relationship between SES and premature termination to disappear when client expectations of treatment duration are accounted for (Pekarik, 1991; Pekarik & Wierzbicki, 1986). Two older studies also support this finding, showing that clients whose expectations of therapy were not congruent with actual therapy were less likely to return for treatment (Jacobs, Charles, Jacobs, Weinstein, & Mann, 1972; Overall & Aronson, 1963). Therefore, client expectations seem to play a critical role in the duration of therapy.

Client and Therapist Match

One way of reducing premature termination may be to match clients with therapists in terms of social class (Mitchell & Namenek, 1970). Unfortunately, we could not find any systematic research on the relationship of SES matching with treatment outcomes. We did find two studies that examined the effect of SES match to client expectations and self-exploration in therapy (Carkhuff & Pierce, 1967; Foon, 1986). However, these variables are not measures of direct outcomes.

Population-Specific Therapies

Unlike feminist or gay affirmative therapies, specific alternative forms of therapy have not been identified for clients of low-SES backgrounds. However, several studies have examined social class effects with regard to different existing therapies (Lorion & Felner, 1986). In particular, a long-standing belief by some psychologists is that low-SES clients are less likely to benefit from insight-oriented therapies and more likely to benefit from directive and time-limited therapies that focus on symptom relief and an active role for the therapist (Garfield, 1986; Lorion, 1974; Siassi & Messer, 1976).

We located two studies that have examined the benefits of time-limited therapy (Koegler & Brill, 1967; Stone & Crowthers, 1972). Stone and Crowthers (1972) provided crisis and short-term therapy to blue-collar workers. Results of their program indicated that of the 393 clients served, fewer than 3% dropped out. A more rigorous study conducted by Koegler and Brill (1967) compared brief contact therapy with medication to traditional insight-oriented therapy among low-SES clients. They found no significant differences in symptom reduction between the brief and insight-oriented treatments. Taken together, these limited studies do not wholly support the benefits of time-limited therapy over insight-oriented therapy.

Three empirical studies provide preliminary evidence for the use of active, directive therapy for low-SES clients (Goin, Yamamoto, & Silverman, 1965; Organista, Munoz, & Gonzalez, 1994; Satterfield, 1998). Organista and colleagues (1994) conducted a study on the effectiveness of group and individual cognitive-behavioral therapy on 175 low-income and minority clients suffering from depression. Results indicated that BDI scores significantly decreased from pretreatment to posttreatment. The dropout rate for the sample was 58%. This rate is considerably higher than other rates reported for cognitive-behavioral therapy with non–low-income clients. However, this finding is consistent with literature suggesting high dropout rates for low-SES clients.

Satterfield (1998) also conducted a study examining the benefits of a 16-week cognitive-behavioral group therapy for a group of 23 depressed, low-SES clients. Results indicated a dropout rate of 25%. The author stated that this percentage was lower in comparison to the dropout rate from Organista and colleagues (1994) (58%). Satisfaction surveys indicated a high percentage of client satisfaction. Modest changes were also found in BDI scores. After a 3-month follow-up, clients still reported a 30% reduction in BDI scores. This study was limited by its small sample size. Moreover, both Organista and colleagues' (1994) and Satterfield's (1998) studies did not compare cognitive-behavioral therapy to a control group or another therapy.

Goin and colleagues (1965) compared active, directive therapy to insight-oriented therapy. They recruited clients who were seeking therapy that focused on active advice giving. Forty clients were selected and randomly assigned to a congruent condition (advice therapy) or an incongruent condition (insight-oriented therapy). Results indicated that while there was a trend indicating that clients in the advice group were more satisfied with therapy, because of the small sample size, there was no statistical difference in the percent-

age of satisfaction between the two groups. No significant differences between the groups were found in terms of length of treatment.

In conclusion, there is preliminary evidence suggesting that directive therapies may be beneficial for low-SES clients, while there is less clear evidence for the benefit of time-limited therapy. However, in the absence of more rigorous studies, definitive statements cannot be made about the effectiveness of these therapies for low-SES clients.

Conclusions

Despite the important influence of socioeconomic status on an individual's life, this variable has been widely ignored by psychotherapy researchers. Although research has found that low-income clients are less likely to stay in treatment and more likely to drop out prematurely compared to higher-income clients, little is known on how to effectively work with these clients. Moreover, it seems that there are still biases and stereotypes that psychologists have with regard to this population. A major task is to increase attention toward the psychotherapeutic needs of individuals from lower socioeconomic backgrounds.

LIMITATIONS OF THE RESEARCH

From our review, we identify several limitations in terms of the quantity and quality of psychotherapy research on women, members of ethnic minority groups, LGBs, and members of lower social classes. First, there is a disappointing paucity of research on treatment outcomes, especially for ethnic minority groups, LGBs, and members of lower social classes. In the case of women, more research findings are available. Psychotherapy appears to be effective, but findings also suggest that outcomes are sometimes not as positive for some of these groups (for example, ethnic minorities) than for mainstream groups (for example, European Americans). Second, much of the available research has methodological limitations, such as the lack of comparison groups, random assignment of clients to treatments, and adequate sample sizes. Third, most studies involving ethnic minorities and individuals from a lower social class deal with effectiveness rather than efficacy. Indeed, hardly any of the studies used as the basis for empirically supported treatments have included ethnicity or class as variables of interest. In the case of lesbian, gay, and bisexual individuals, most studies of treatment outcomes have failed to ascertain the sexual orientation of clients, so this variable is not routinely examined. Fourth, widely argued conditions for improving treatment outcomes—such as matching of therapists and clients and population-specific treatments—are mostly based on theoretical orientation, clinical observations, and social-political-ethical considerations rather than research. This is not to imply that these conditions are ineffective or irrelevant. Indeed, there are good reasons to use them. However, many of these strategies have not been subjected to rigorous research tests. Perhaps one of the highest priorities in mental health efforts should be to conduct systematic research on these groups.

THERAPEUTIC PRACTICES

Given the above limitations, in the concluding section we present therapeutic practices concerning the match of therapist and client, population-specific strategies, and avoidance of mistakes. The first two sets of practices reflect empirical evidence. The last set of practices reflects current practice and is offered in the absence of empirical research.

Match of Therapist and Client under Appropriate Conditions

The question of whether clients should be paired with therapists who match their gender, ethnicity, sexual orientation, and social class is complex. Advocates from diverse groups have argued that similarity is important, presumably because of the greater likelihood that therapists and clients share cultural elements and experiences. Clients may feel more comfortable and understood and be more self-disclosing.

Several conclusions are justified. The existing empirical evidence for the benefits of match is mostly found in client satisfaction variables and

indirect outcomes. There are several reasons why there may not be a significant relationship between direct outcomes and match. First, it has been suggested that direct outcome measures such as the GAS may not be reliable and sensitive measures (Sue et al., 1994). Second, match may be related to interpersonal attraction, which results in longer treatment sessions, but is unrelated to direct outcomes (Sue et al., 1994). Third, match may be unrelated to direct outcomes as therapist match on gender, ethnicity, sexual orientation, or social class is only one of many characteristics that may be matched. Fourth, matches in demographic characteristics may be moderator variables because beneficial effects may be dependent on the interaction of match and client characteristics. Fifth, matches involving ethnicity, gender, sexual orientation, or social class may not result in cultural matches. For example, a highly acculturated, non–Chinese-speaking Chinese-American therapist may have tremendous difficulties working with a recent Chinese immigrant with limited English proficiency. Thus, we suggest that match may be important in certain, but not all, conditions. As mentioned previously, S. Sue and colleagues (1991) found that ethnic match was particularly important for unacculturated ethnic minority clients. Another issue to consider is freedom of choice. Some clients do have preferences for these therapist characteristics and these preferences should be honored in almost all situations. However, given therapist shortages or accessibility problems, many clients are unable to find matches.

Population-Specific Strategies of Therapy

A number of suggestions have been made concerning therapeutic strategies to use when working with women, ethnic minority, lesbian/gay/bisexual, and lower socioeconomic class clients. Engaging in feminist therapy and ethnic-specific tactics appears to be valuable. When examining the empirical evidence, it is important to acknowledge that few studies have examined the relative benefits of population-specific therapies in comparison to mainstream therapies. With that said, existing research findings on the use of group-specific tactics are mixed, with some studies showing the tactics to be effective and other studies not demonstrating their superiority. The value of population-specific treatments appears to be well supported in the case of Latino American clients. Again, it is highly likely that such strategies are better suited for some, but not all, members of the group. For example, feminist therapy may be more beneficial with women who are dealing with issues of oppression, status differences, and domestic violence; ethnic minorities who are relatively unacculturated may respond better to ethnic culture-specific forms of intervention than those who are highly Americanized. As in the case of therapist and client match, the effectiveness of population-specific strategies may largely depend on the type of client.

Avoidance of Mistakes

One common complaint among experts working with diverse groups is that many therapists make mistakes. They engage in stereotypes, inappropriate language, or biases. It is vital for therapists to be aware of inappropriate conduct and to use appropriate behaviors in treatment. Behaving appropriately is not a matter of being "politically correct." Political correctness implies that one conforms because of social desirability rather than the intrinsic appropriateness of the behavior. Calling an African American man a boy is inappropriate, and not just a matter of political correctness. Many mistakes, of course, are subtle, but they have the potential of reducing credibility of, and rapport with, the therapist. While research has not been directed to this issue, there is an abundance of experts who have discussed the problem. Avoidance of these mistakes is mentioned in the APA guidelines for psychotherapy with women, ethnic minorities, and lesbians, gays, and bisexuals. Being sensitive to possible mistakes implies that one is aware of one's own values and attitudes as well as knowledge of the client's culture and group.

In summary, the current state of the field suggests that there is a dearth of research on treatment outcomes with diverse populations. As such, the empirically supported therapeutic practices that we have provided are not definitive and should not be seen as opposed to current guidelines. Rather, our review underscores the need for more rigorous research regarding psychotherapy outcomes with diverse clients, in order to inform guidelines for these populations.

ACKNOWLEDGMENT This study was supported in part by the National Research Center on Asian American Mental Health (National Institute of Mental Health Grant MH59616). The authors gratefully acknowledge the assistance of Yuko Onodera and Melinda Tran.

REFERENCES

Acosta, F. X. (1980). Self-described reasons for premature termination of psychotherapy by Mexican American, Black American, and Anglo-American patients. *Psychological Reports, 47*, 435–443.

Affleck, D. C., & Garfield, S. L. (1961). Predictive judgments of therapists and duration of stay in psychotherapy. *Journal of Clinical Psychology, 17*, 134–137.

Akutsu, P. D., Lin, C. H., & Zane, N. W. S. (1990). Predictors of utilization intent of counseling among Chinese and White students: A test of the proximal-distal model. *Journal of Counseling Psychology, 37*, 445–452.

Alyn, J. H., & Becker, L. A. (1984). Feminist therapy with chronically and profoundly disturbed women. *Journal of Counseling Psychology, 31*, 202–208.

APA Office of Ethnic Minority Affairs (1993). Guidelines for providers of psychological services to ethnic, linguistic, and culturally diverse populations. *American Psychologist, 48*, 45–48.

Atkinson, D. R., Maruyama, M., & Matsui, S. (1978). Effects of counselor race and counseling approach on Asian Americans' perceptions of counselor credibility and utility. *Journal of Counseling Psychology, 25*, 76–85.

Baekeland, F., & Lundwall, L. (1975). Dropping out of treatment: A critical review. *Psychological Bulletin, 82*, 738–783.

Bennett, S. K., & BigFoot-Sipes, D. S. (1991). American Indian and White college student preferences for counselor characteristics. *Journal of Counseling Psychology, 38*, 440–445.

Berrigan, L. P., & Garfield, S. L. (1981). Relationship of missed psychotherapy appointments to premature termination and social class. *British Journal of Clinical Psychology, 20*, 239–242.

Beutler, L. E., Crago, M., & Arizmendi, T. G. (1986). Therapist variables in psychotherapy process and outcome. In S. L. Garfield & A. E. Bergin (Eds.), *Handbook of psychotherapy and behavior change* (3rd ed., pp. 257–310). New York: Wiley.

Bieschke, K. J., McClanahan, M., Tozer, E., Grzegorek, J. L., & Park, J. (2000). Programmatic research on the treatment of lesbian, gay, and bisexual clients: The past, the present, and the course for the future. In R. M. Perez, K. A. DeBord, & K. J. Bieschke (Eds.), *Handbook of counseling and psychotherapy with lesbian, gay, and bisexual clients* (pp. 309–335). Washington, DC: American Psychological Association.

Brodsky, A. M., & Hare-Mustin, R. T. (1980). Psychotherapy and women: Priorities for research. In A. M. Brodsky & R. T. Hare-Mustin (Eds.), *Women and psychotherapy: An assessment of research and practice* (pp. 385–409). New York: Guilford.

Brooks, V. R. (1981). Sex and sexual orientation as variables in therapists' biases and therapy outcomes. *Clinical Social Work Journal, 9*, 198–210.

Brown, B. S., Joe, G. W., & Thompson, P. (1985). Minority group status and treatment retention. *International Journal of the Addictions, 20*, 319–335.

Cabaj, R. P. (1996). Sexual orientation of the therapist. In R. P. Cabaj & T. S. Stein (Eds.), *Textbook of homosexuality and mental health* (pp. 513–524). Washington, DC: American Psychiatric Press.

Carkhuff, R. R., & Pierce, R. (1967). Differential effects of therapist race and social class upon patient depth of self-exploration in the initial clinical interview. *Journal of Consulting Psychology, 31*, 632–634.

Chambless, D. L., Sanderson, W. C., Shoham, V., Johnson, S. B., Pope, K. S., Crits-Christoph, P., Baker, M., Johnson, B., Woody, S. R., Sue, S., Beutler, L., Williams, D. A., & McCurry, S. (1996). An update on empirically validated therapies. *The Clinical Psychologist, 49*, 5–18.

Chin, J. L. (1998). Mental health services and treatment. In L. C. Lee & N. W. S. Zane (Eds.), *Handbook of Asian American psychology* (pp. 485–504). Thousand Oaks, CA: Sage.

Choi, K. H., Lew, S., Vittinghoff, E., Catania, J. A., Barrett, D. C., & Coates, T. J. (1996). The efficacy of brief group counseling in HIV risk reduction among homosexual Asian and Pacific Islander men. *AIDS, 10*, 81–87.

Chung, R. C. Y., & Okazaki, S. (1991). Counseling Americans of Southeast Asian descent: The impact of the refugee experience. In E. E. Lee & B. L. Richardson (Eds.), *Multicultural issues in counseling: New approaches to diversity* (pp. 107–126). Alexandria, VA: American Association for Counseling and Development.

Cortese, M. (1979). Intervention research with Hispanic Americans: A review. *Hispanic Journal of Behavioral Sciences, 1*, 4–20.

Costantino, G., Malgady, R. G., & Rogler, L. H. (1986). Cuento therapy: A culturally sensitive modality for Puerto Rican children. *Journal of Counseling and Clinical Psychology, 54*, 639–645.

Costantino, G., Malgady, R. G., & Rogler, L. H. (1994). Storytelling through pictures: Culturally sensitive psychotherapy for Hispanic children and adolescents. *Journal of Clinical Child Psychology, 23*, 13–20.

Craig, T. J., & Huffine, C. L. (1976). Correlates of patient attendance in an inner city mental health clinic. *American Journal of Psychiatry, 133*, 61–65.

Dauphinais, P., Dauphinais, L., & Rowe, W. (1981). Effects of race and communication style on Indian perceptions of counselor effectiveness. *Counselor Education and Supervision, 21*, 72–80.

Dauphinais, P., LaFromboise, T., & Rowe, W. (1980). Perceived problems and sources of help for American Indian students. *Counselor Education and Supervision, 20*, 37–46.

Division 44/Committee on Lesbian, Gay, and Bisexual Concerns Joint Task Force on Guidelines for Psychotherapy with Lesbian, Gay, and Bisexual Clients. (2000). Guidelines for psychotherapy with lesbian, gay, and bisexual clients. *American Psychologist, 55*, 1440–1451.

Dunkle, J. H. (1994). Counseling gay male clients: A review of treatment efficacy research: 1975-present. *Journal of Gay and Lesbian Psychotherapy, 2*, 1–19.

Flaskerud, J. H. (1986). The effects of culture-compatible intervention on the utilization of mental health services by minority clients. *Community Mental Health Journal, 22*, 127–141.

Flaskerud, J. H., & Hu, L. (1994). Participation in and outcome of treatment for major depression among low income Asian-Americans. *Psychiatry Research, 53*, 289–300.

Foon, A. E. (1986). Effect of locus of control on counseling expectations of clients. *Journal of Counseling Psychology, 33*, 462–464.

Frank, J. D., Gliedman, L. H., Imber, S. D., Nash, E. H., Jr., & Stone, A. R. (1957). Why patients leave psychotherapy. *Archives of Neurology and Psychiatry, 77,* 283–299.

Fujino, D. C., Okazaki, S., & Young, K. (1994). Asian-American women in the mental health system: An examination of ethnic and gender match between therapist and client. *Journal of Community Psychology, 22,* 164–176.

Gamst, G., Dana, R. H., Der-Karabetian, A., & Kramer, T. (2000). Ethnic match and client ethnicity effects on global assessment and visitation. *Journal of Community Psychology, 28,* 547–564.

Gamst, G., Dana, R. H., Der-Karabetian, A., & Kramer, T. (2001). Asian American mental health clients: Effects of ethnic match and age on global assessment and visitation. *Journal of Mental Health Counseling, 23,* 57–71.

Garfield, S. L. (1986). Research on client variables in psychotherapy. In S. L. Garfield & A. E. Bergin (Eds.), *Handbook of psychotherapy and behavior change* (3rd ed., pp. 213–256). New York: Wiley.

Garfield, S. L. (1994). Research on client variables in psychotherapy. In A. E. Bergin & S. L. Garfield (Eds.), *Handbook of psychotherapy and behavior change* (4th ed., pp. 193–228). New York: Wiley.

Garnets, L., Hancock, K. A., Cochran, S. D., Goodchilds, J., & Peplau, L. A. (1991). Issues in psychotherapy with lesbians and gay men: A survey of psychologists. *American Psychologist, 46,* 964–972.

Gartrell, N. (1984). *Issues in psychotherapy with lesbian women.* Wellesley, MA: Stone Center for Developmental Services and Studies.

Gaylin, N. L. (1966). Psychotherapy and psychological health: A Rorschach function and structure analysis. *Journal of Consulting Psychology, 30,* 494–500.

Gilbert, L. A., & Scher, M. (1999). *Gender and sex in counseling and psychotherapy.* Boston: Allyn and Bacon.

Goin, M. K., Yamamoto, J., & Silverman, J. (1965). Therapy congruent with class-linked expectations. *Archives of General Psychiatry, 13,* 133–137.

Goodkin, K., Blaney, N. T., Feaster, D. J., Baldewicz, T., Burkhalter, J. E., & Leeds, B. (1999). A randomized controlled clinical trial of a bereavement support group intervention in human immunodeficiency virus type 1-seropositive and -seronegative homosexual men. *Archives of General Psychiatry, 56,* 52–59.

Gutierres, S. E., Russo, N. F., & Urbanski, L. (1994). Sociocultural and psychological factors in American Indian drug use: Implications for treatment. *International Journal of the Addictions, 29,* 1761–1786.

Gutierres, S. E., & Todd, M. (1997). The impact of childhood abuse on treatment outcomes of substance users. *Professional Psychology: Research and Practice, 28,* 348–354.

Hamburg, D. A., Bibring, G. L., Fisher, C., Stanton, A. H., Wallerstein, R. S., Weinstock, H. I., & Haggard, E. (1967). Report of Ad Hoc Committee on central fact gathering data of the American Psychoanalytic Association. *Journal of the American Psychoanalytic Association, 15,* 841–861.

Havilland, M. G., Horswill, R. K., O'Connell, J. J., & Dynneson, V. V. (1983). Native American college students' preference for counselor race and sex and the likelihood of their use of a counseling center. *Journal of Counseling Psychology, 30,* 267–270.

Heisler, G. H., Beck, N. C., Fraps, C. L., & McReynolds, W. T. (1982). Therapist ratings as predictors of therapy attendance. *Journal of Clinical Psychology, 38,* 754–758.

Hill, C. E. (1975). Sex of client and sex and experience level of counselor. *Journal of Counseling Psychology, 22,* 6–11.

Jacobs, D., Charles, E., Jacobs, T., Weinstein, H., & Mann, D. (1972). Preparation for treatment of the disadvantaged patient: Effects on disposition and outcome. *American Journal of Orthopsychiatry, 42,* 666–674.

Jones, E. E. (1978). Effects of race on psychotherapy process and outcome: An exploratory investigation. *Psychotherapy: Theory, Research, and Practice, 15,* 226–236.

Jones, E. E. (1982). Psychotherapists' impressions of treatment outcome as a function of race. *Journal of Clinical Psychology, 38,* 722–731.

Jones, E. E., Krupnick, J. L., & Kerig, P. K. (1987). Some gender effects in a brief psychotherapy. *Psychotherapy, 24,* 336–352.

Jones, E. E., & Zoppel, C. L. (1982). Impact of client and therapist gender on psychotherapy process and outcome. *Journal of Consulting and Clinical Psychology, 50,* 259–272.

Kirshner, L. A., Genack, A., & Hauser, S. T. (1978). Effects of gender on short term psychotherapy. *Psychotherapy: Theory, Research, and Practice, 15,* 158–167.

Knapp, P. H., Levin, S., McCarter, R. H., Wermer, H., & Zetzel, E. (1960). Suitability for psychoanalysis: A review of 100 supervised analytic cases. *Psychoanalytic Quarterly, 29*, 459–477.

Koegler, R. R., & Brill, N. Q. (1967). *Treatment of psychiatric outpatients.* Norwalk, CT: Appleton-Century-Crofts.

Koss, M. P. (1980). Descriptive characteristics and length of psychotherapy of child and adult clients seen in private psychological practice. *Psychotherapy: Theory, Research, and Practice, 17*, 268–271.

LaFromboise, T. D., & Dixon, D. N. (1981). American Indian perception of trustworthiness in a counseling interview. *Journal of Counseling Psychology, 28*, 135–139.

Lau, A., & Zane, N. W. S. (2000). Examining the effects of ethnic-specific services: An analysis of cost-utilization and treatment outcome for Asian American clients. *Journal of Community Psychology, 28*, 63–77.

Lebolt, J. (1999). Gay affirmative psychotherapy: A phenomenological study. *Clinical Social Work Journal, 27*, 355–370.

Lee, E. (1997). *Working with Asian Americans: A guide for clinicians.* New York: Guilford.

Lee, M. R., Cohen, L., Hadley, S. W., & Goodwin, F. K. (1999). Cognitive behavioral group therapy with medication for depressed gay men with AIDS or symptomatic HIV infection. *Psychiatric Services, 50*, 948–952.

Lee, W. M. L., & Mixson, R. J. (1995). Asian and Caucasian client perceptions of the effectiveness of counseling. *Journal of Multicultural Counseling and Development, 23*, 48–56.

Lerner, B. (1972). *Therapy in the ghetto: Political impotence and personal disintegration.* Baltimore, MD: Johns Hopkins University Press.

Liddle, B. J. (1996). Therapist sexual orientation, gender, and counseling practices as they relate to ratings on helpfulness by gay and lesbian clients. *Journal of Counseling Psychology, 43*, 394–401.

Liljestrand, P., Gerling, E., & Saliba, P. A. (1978). The effects of social sex-role stereotypes and sexual orientation on psychotherapeutic outcomes. *Journal of Homosexuality, 3*, 361–372.

Lorion, R. P. (1973). Socioeconomic status and traditional treatment approaches reconsidered. *Psychological Bulletin, 79*, 263–270.

Lorion, R. P. (1974). Patient and therapist variables in the treatment of low-income patients. *Psychological Bulletin, 81*, 344–354.

Lorion, R. P., & Felner, R. D. (1986). Research on psychotherapy with the disadvantaged. In S. L. Garfield & A. E. Bergin (Eds.), *Handbook of*

psychotherapy and behavior change (3rd ed., pp. 739–776). New York: Wiley.

Luborsky, L., Chandler, M., Auerbach, A. H., Cohen, J., & Bachrach, J. M. (1971). Factors influencing the outcome of psychotherapy: A review of quantitative research. *Psychological Bulletin, 75*, 145–185.

Luborsky, L., Mintz, J., & Christoph, P. (1979). Are psychotherapeutic changes predictable? Comparison of a Chicago counseling center project with a Penn psychotherapy project. *Journal of Consulting and Clinical Psychology, 47*, 469–473.

Malgady, R. G., Rogler, L. H., & Costantino, G. (1990a). Hero/heroine modeling for Puerto Rican adolescents: A preventive mental health intervention. *Journal of Counseling and Clinical Psychology, 58*, 469–474.

Malgady, R. G., Rogler, L. H., & Costantino, G. (1990b). Culturally sensitive psychotherapy for Puerto Rican children and adolescents: A program of treatment outcome research. *Journal of Counseling and Clinical Psychology, 58*, 704–712.

Manson, S. M., Walker, R. D., & Kivlahan, D. R. (1987). Psychiatric assessment and treatment of American Indians and Alaska Natives. *Hospital and Community Psychiatry, 38*, 165–173.

Markowitz, J. C., Kocsis, J. H., Fishman, B., Spielman, L. A., Jacobsberg, L. B., Frances, A. J., Klerman, G. L., & Perry, S. W. (1998). Treatment of depressive symptoms in Human Immunodeficiency Virus–positive patients. *Archives of General Psychiatry, 55*, 452–457.

Markowitz, J. C., Spielman, L. A., Sullivan, M., & Fishman, B. (2000). An exploratory study of ethnicity and psychotherapy outcome among HIV-positive patients with depressive symptoms. *Journal of Psychotherapy Practice and Research, 9*, 226–231.

Mintz, J., Luborsky, L., & Auerbach, A. H. (1971). Dimensions of psychotherapy: A factor-analytic study of ratings of psychotherapy sessions. *Journal of Consulting and Clinical Psychology, 36*, 106–120.

Mitchell, K. M., & Namenek, T. M. (1970). A comparison of therapist and client social class. *Professional Psychology: Research and Practice, 1*, 225–230.

Morrow, S. L. (2000). First do no harm: Therapist issues in psychotherapy with lesbian, gay, and bisexual clients. In R. M. Perez, K. A. DeBord, & K. J. Bieschke (Eds.), *Handbook of counseling and psychotherapy with lesbian, gay, and bisexual clients* (pp. 137–156). Washington, DC: American Psychological Association.

Nassi, A. J., & Abramowitz, S. I. (1978). Raising consciousness about women's groups: Process and outcome research. *Psychology of Women Quarterly, 3,* 139–156.

Navarro, A. M. (1993). Efectividad de las psicoterapias con Latinos en los Estados Unidos: Una revision meta-analitica. *Revista Interamericana de Psicologia, 27,* 131–146.

Neligh, G. (1988). Major mental disorders and behavior among American Indians and Alaska Natives. *American Indian and Alaska Native Mental Health Research, 1,* 116–150.

Organista, K. C., Munoz, R. F., & Gonzalez, G. (1994). Cognitive behavioral therapy for depression in low-income and minority medical outpatients: Description of a program and exploratory analyses. *Cognitive Therapy and Research, 18,* 241–259.

Orlinsky, D. E., Grawe, K., & Parks, B. K. (1994). Process and outcome in psychotherapy—Noch einmal. In A. E. Bergin & S. L. Garfield (Eds.), *Handbook of psychotherapy and behavior change* (4th ed., pp. 270–378). New York: Wiley.

Orlinsky, D. E., & Howard, K. I. (1976). The effects of sex of therapist on the therapeutic experiences of women. *Psychotherapy: Theory, Research, and Practice, 13,* 82–88.

Orlinsky, D. E., & Howard, K. I. (1980). Gender and psychotherapeutic outcome. In A. M. Brodsky & R. T. Hare-Mustin (Eds.), *Women and psychotherapy: An assessment of research and practice* (pp. 3–34). New York: Guilford.

Overall, B., & Aronson, H. (1963). Expectations of psychotherapy in patients of lower socioeconomic class. *American Journal of Orthopsychiatry, 33,* 421–430.

Padilla, A. M., & Salgado de Snyder, N. (1987). Counseling Hispanics: Strategies for effective intervention. In P. Pedersen (Ed.), *Handbook of cross-cultural counseling and therapy* (pp. 157–164). Westport, CT: Greenwood.

Pekarik, G. (1991). Relationship of expected and actual treatment duration for adult and child clients. *Journal of Clinical Child Psychology, 20,* 121–125.

Pekarik, G., & Wierzbicki, M. (1986). The relationship between clients' expected and actual treatment duration. *Psychotherapy, 23,* 532–534.

Persons, R. W., Persons, M. K., & Newmark, I. (1974). Perceived helpful therapists' characteristics, client improvements, and sex of therapist and client. *Psychotherapy: Theory, Research, and Practice, 11,* 63–65.

Peterson, J. L., Coates, T. J., Catania, J., Hauck,

W. W., Acree, M., Daigle, D., Hillard, B., Middleton, L., & Hearst, N. (1996). Evaluation of an HIV risk reduction intervention among African-American homosexual and bisexual men. *AIDS, 10,* 319–325.

Query, J. N. (1985). Comparative admission and follow-up study of American Indians and Whites in a youth chemical dependency unit on the North Central Plains. *International Journal of the Addictions, 20,* 489–502.

Reis, B. F., & Brown, L. G. (1999). Reducing psychotherapy dropouts: Maximizing perspective convergence in the psychotherapy dyad. *Psychotherapy, 36,* 123–136.

Riddle, D. I., & Sang, B. (1978). Psychotherapy with lesbians. *Journal of Social Issues, 34,* 84–100.

Rinfret-Raynor, M., & Cantin, S. (1997). Feminist therapy for battered women: An assessment. In G. K. Kantor, & J. L. Jasinski (Eds.), *Out of darkness: Contemporary perspectives on family violence* (pp. 219–234). Thousand Oaks, CA: Sage.

Rochlin, M. (1982). Sexual orientation of the therapist and therapeutic effectiveness with gay clients. *Journal of Homosexuality, 7,* 21–29.

Rodolfa, E. R., Rapaport, R., & Lee, V. E. (1983). Variables related to premature terminations in a university counseling service. *Journal of Counseling Psychology, 30,* 87–90.

Roffman, R. A., Downey, L., Beadnell, B., Gordon, J. R., Craver, J. N., & Stephens, R. S. (1997). Cognitive-behavioral group counseling to prevent HIV transmission in gay and bisexual men: Factors contributing to successful risk reduction. *Research on Social Work Practice, 7,* 165–186.

Rosenheck, R., Fontana, A., & Cottrol, C. (1995). Effect of clinician-veteran racial pairing in the treatment of post-traumatic stress disorder. *American Journal of Psychiatry, 152,* 555–563.

Rosenthal, C. (2000). Latino practice outcome research: A review of the literature. *Smith College Studies in Social Work, 70,* 217–238.

Satterfield, J. M. (1998). Cognitive behavioral group therapy for depressed, low-income minority clients: Retention and treatment enhancement. *Cognitive and Behavioral Practice, 25,* 65–80.

Seeman, J. (1954). Counselor judgments of therapeutic process and outcome. In C. Rogers & R. F. Dymond (Eds.), *Psychotherapy and personality change* (pp. 99–108). Chicago: University of Chicago Press.

Siassi, I., & Messer, S. B. (1976). Psychotherapy with

patients from lower socioeconomic groups. *American Journal of Psychotherapy, 30*, 29–40.

Siegel, S. M., Rootes, M. D., & Traub, A. (1977). Symptom change and prognosis in clinic psychotherapy. *Archives of General Psychiatry, 34*, 321–331.

Sirkin, M., Maxey, J., Ryan, M., French, C., & Clements, O. (1988). Gender awareness group therapy: Exploring gender-related issues in a day-treatment population. *International Journal of Partial Hospitalization, 5*, 263–272.

Sloane, R. B., Staples, F. R., Cristol, A. H., Yorkston, N. J., & Whipple, K. (1975). *Psychotherapy versus behavior therapy.* Cambridge, MA: Harvard University Press.

Stone, J. L., & Crowthers, V. (1972). Innovations in program and funding of mental health services for blue-collar families. *American Journal of Psychiatry, 128*, 1375–1380.

Sue, D., & Sue, D. W. (1991). Counseling strategies for Chinese Americans. In C. C. Lee & B. L. Richardson (Eds.), *Multicultural issues in counseling: New approaches to diversity* (pp. 79–90). Alexandria, VA: American Association for Counseling and Development.

Sue, S. (1998). In search of cultural competence in psychotherapy and counseling. *American Psychologist, 53*, 440–448.

Sue, S., Fujino, D. C., Hu, L. T., Takeuchi, D. T., & Zane, N. W. S. (1991). Community mental health services for ethnic minority groups: A test of the cultural responsiveness hypothesis. *Journal of Consulting and Clinical Psychology, 59*, 533–540.

Sue, S., Zane, N. W. S., & Young, K. (1994). Research on psychotherapy with culturally diverse populations. In A. E. Bergin & S. L. Garfield (Eds.), *Handbook of psychotherapy and behavior change* (4th ed., pp. 783–817). New York: Wiley.

Szapocznik, J., Rio, A., Murray, E., Cohen, R., Scopetta, M., Rivas-Vazquez, A., Hervis, O., Posada, V., & Kurtines, W. (1989). Structural family versus psychodynamic child therapy for problematic Hispanic boys. *Journal of Counseling and Clinical Psychology, 57*, 571–578.

Takeuchi, D. T., Sue, S., & Yeh, M. (1995). Return rates and outcomes from ethnicity-specific mental health programs in Los Angeles. *American Journal of Public Health, 85*, 638–643.

Talley, J. E., Butcher, T., Maguire, M. A., & Pinkerton, R. S. (1992). The effects of very brief psychotherapy on symptoms of dysphoria. In J. E. Talley (Ed.), *The predictors of successful very brief psychotherapy: A study of differences by gender, age, and treatment variables* (pp. 12–45). Springfield, IL: Thomas.

Tan, H. (1967). Intercultural study of counseling expectancies. *Journal of Counseling Psychology, 41*, 122–130.

Task Force on Sex Bias and Sex Role Stereotyping in Psychotherapeutic Practice. (1978). Guidelines for therapy with women. *American Psychologist, 33*, 1122–1123.

Thase, M. E., Reynolds, C. F., Frank, E., Simons, A. D., McGeary, J., Fasiczka, A. L., Garamoni, G. G., Jennings, R., & Kupfer, D. J. (1994). Do depressed men and women respond similarly to cognitive behavior therapy? *American Journal of Psychiatry, 151*, 500–505.

Vail, A. (1978). Factors influencing lower-class Black patients remaining in treatment. *Journal of Consulting and Clinical Psychology, 46*, 341.

Weitz, R. (1982). Feminist consciousness raising, self-concept, and depression. *Sex Roles, 8*, 231–241.

Wierzbicki, M., & Pekarik, G. (1993). A meta-analysis of psychotherapy dropout. *Professional Psychology: Research and Practice, 24*, 190–195.

Williams, D. R., & Rucker, T. (1996). Socioeconomic status and the health of racial minority populations. In P. M. Kato & T. Mann (Eds.), *Handbook of diversity issues in health psychology* (pp. 407–423). New York: Plenum.

Worell, J., & Remer, P. (1992). *Feminist perspectives in therapy: An empowerment model for women.* New York: Wiley.

Yuen, R. K. W., & Tinsley, H. E. (1981). International and American students' expectations about counseling. *Journal of Counseling Psychology, 28*, 66–69.

Zane, N. (1983, August). *Evaluation of outpatient psychotherapy for Asian and non-Asian American clients.* Paper presented at the American Psychological Association Conference, Anaheim, CA.

Zane, N., & Hatanaka, H. (1988, October). *Utilization and evaluation of a parallel service delivery model for ethnic minority clients.* Paper presented at the conference on Recent Trends and New Approaches to the Treatment of Mental Illness and Substance Abuse, Oklahoma Mental Health Research Institute, OK.

Zlotnick, C., Elkin, I., & Shea, M. T. (1998). Does the gender of a patient or the gender of a therapist affect the treatment of patients with major depression? *Journal of Consulting and Clinical Psychology, 66*, 655–659.

23

Personality Disorders

Lorna Smith Benjamin
Christie P. Karpiak

Personality disorder is defined by the American Psychiatric Association's *Diagnostic and Statistical Manual of Mental Disorders* (4th ed., p. 629) as "an enduring pattern of inner experience and behavior that deviates markedly from the expectations of the individual's culture, is pervasive and inflexible, has an onset in adolescence or early adulthood, is stable over time, and leads to distress or impairment." There are 10 frequently observed patterns defined by the *DSM-IV*. These are subdivided into three groups or clusters. Cluster A includes Paranoid, Schizoid, and Schizotypal personality disorders. Cluster B includes Antisocial, Borderline, Histrionic, and Narcissistic personality disorders. Cluster C describes Avoidant, Dependent, and Obsessive-Compulsive personality disorders. Individuals who do not meet criteria for one or more of these categories but who have enduring patterns of inner experience and behavior that are associated with distress or impairment can be classified as Personality Disorder not otherwise specified (NOS).

By definition, personality disorders are enduring. Merikangas and Weissman (1986, p. 274) note, "Personality disorders constitute one of the most important sources of long-term impairment in both treated and untreated populations. Nearly one in every 10 adults in the general population, and over one-half of those in treated populations, may be expected to suffer from one of the personality disorders." The presence of personality disorder is associated with greater utilization of treatment resources (Bender et al., 2001). Com-plicating matters, specific personality disorders show associations with specific Axis I syndromes. For example, "Significantly elevated odds ratios were found for co-occurrence of current mood disorders with avoidant and dependent personality disorders; anxiety disorders with borderline, avoidant, and dependent personality disorders; psychotic disorders with schizotypal, borderline, and dependent personality disorders" (Oldham et al., 1995, p. 571). If an Axis I disorder is comorbid with personality disorder, the response of the Axis I disorder to treatment is diminished (Shea, 1993; Perry, Banon, & Ianni, 1999; Hardy, Barkham, Shapiro, Stiles, Rees & Reynolds, 1995; Johnson, Rabkin, Williams, Reiman, & Gorman, 2000). Whatever the determinants of efficacy, they appear to be weaker when treating personality disorder.

Personality disorders have long been seen as unresponsive to usual and customary treatment methods. However, effective methods have been documented in the past decade and continue to be developed and refined.

Following a brief summary of studies of efficacy in treating personality disorder, this chapter will focus on theory and empirical data on the role of the therapy relationship in effective treatments of personality disorder. The therapy relationship is defined as the pattern of inner experience and behavior that emerges between the patient and therapist during psychotherapy. Three aspects are considered later in this chapter in separate sections: the therapist, the patient, and their interaction. Assessment should include perspectives of the patient, the therapist, and objective observers.

CLINICAL EXAMPLES

Our clinical examples come from two treatment approaches that have been empirically supported as effective with personality disorder.

Linehan's Dialectical Behavioral Therapy

The first example of a demonstrably effective approach is Linehan's (1993a, 1993b) dialectical behavior therapy (DBT) for the treatment of borderline personality disorder (BPD). Linehan (1993a) proposes that the cause of BDP is dysfunction of emotional regulation, and that this deficiency has a biological base. If a child is regularly invalidated, he or she will have difficulty maintaining emotional equilibrium. Dysregulation is more salient if caregivers fail to teach how to label affect and to give lessons in how to regulate arousal and tolerate distress. Hence, DBT treatment requires that the therapist consistently validate patients, and the therapy centers on teaching skills in emotion regulation, distress tolerance, core mindfulness, and interpersonal effectiveness. The teaching usually is done in individual and group therapy sessions. DBT is not a simple approach, and we do not presume to characterize it fully here. However, for purposes of this review, we shall attempt to select some of the central tenets of DBT theory and practice so that we can proceed with a discussion of elements of the therapy relationship that are associated with the effectiveness of DBT.

A central feature of DBT is that the therapist must strike a balance between acceptance and change. The therapist accepts the patient as is, but also expects and facilitates change. Linehan recognizes the paradox of this position and explains why it is necessary. "Unfortunately, a therapeutic approach based on unconditional acceptance and validation of the patient's behaviors proves equally problematic and, paradoxically, can also be invalidating. If the therapist urges the patient to accept and validate herself, it can appear that the therapist does not regard the patient's problems seriously" (1993a, p. 222).

While recognizing that validation cannot be unconditional, Linehan nonetheless places substantial emphasis on it. There are three steps in validating: (1) active observations of direct communication and public acts as well as intuiting the patient's unstated emotions, thoughts, values, and beliefs; (2) reflection of the patient's feelings, thoughts, assumptions, and behaviors; and (3) direct validation in which "the therapist looks for and reflects the wisdom or validity of the patient's response, and communicates that the response is understandable . . . the patients' feelings, thoughts and actions make perfect sense in the context of the person's current experience and life to date" (Linehan, 1993a, p. 224)

For skills training in DBT, there also are rather specific instructions. These include "strategies" that help the therapist accomplish the teaching goals of the approach. One example of a skills training strategy is cheerleading. "The idea is to talk to yourself as you would talk to someone you care about who is in a crisis. Or talk to yourself as you would like someone else to talk to you" (Linehan, 1993b, p. 100). Linehan clearly expects patients to activate and/or acquire skills they need to function well.

Patients are expected to receive the therapy offered and to refrain from behaviors that interfere with other patients' therapy as well as patient behaviors that burn out the therapist (Linehan, 1993a, p. 131). Therapy rules are designed to reduce these so-called therapy-interfering behaviors. For example, "Clients who drop out of therapy are out of therapy" (Linehan, 1993b, p. 23).

In sum, illustrative elements of the therapy relationship inherent in DBT include validation, cheerleading, the balance between acceptance and change, and injunctions against therapy-interfering behaviors.

Piper, Rosie, Joyce, and Azim's Day Treatment Program

Piper and colleagues create a therapeutic community by implementing principles of milieu therapy as described originally by Main (Piper, Rosie, Joyce, & Azim, 1996). They have explored a variety of milieu treatments. We shall focus on their day treatment program (DTP), which has six features: (1) encouraging responsibility in the patients; (2) fostering mutual respect between staff members and patients; (3) expecting participation of patients in the treatment of their peers; (4) collaborating with higher-order systems; (5) avoiding abdicating authority, on the one hand, and abuse of power, on the other, by the designated staff members—in other words, the judicious use of authority; and (6) operating multiple groups at multiple levels throughout the system (p. 168).

In extracting therapy relationship factors inherent in these principles, we conclude that the first three mainly describe mutual affirmation (validation) between patients and staff and within patient and staff groups. These principles require that participants have a sense of self that is clearly defined but also connected to others, and a willingness to disclose and discuss—the ability to listen and to acknowledge the perspectives of others. These same relationship patterns are extended to a system level for principles 4 and 6. Principle 5 is similar to Linehan's dialectic between acceptance and change. Within the accepting, respectful context, limits are set. Examples of forbidden behaviors include missing sessions, having social contact with group members outside the therapy context, failing to attend AA and work the program, leaving the site for lunch, and so on. In DTP, as in DBT, the ultimate limit is to deny continued participation in the treatment if the patients do not exhibit adequate compliance with it.

A therapy transcript that illustrates relationship factors inherent in principles 1, 2, and 3 follows. The excerpt shows how patients are allowed free expression in a safe context where they are encouraged to learn about the impact of their behaviors on others. They receive direct feedback on the consequences of their behavior. Other group members are a part of the therapy relationship. The general idea is to encourage people (patients in groups; staff in systems) to engage in discussion and develop insight about patterns and their meanings. The therapist facilitates articulation of views and feelings and helps consolidate the learning, which in this example is about the purposes and impact of anger. Patterns

are considered both in the context of the group itself and in important relationships outside of the group (Piper et al., 1996, p. 198).

Therapist H: So, Faye, what's been happening for you recently?

Faye: I've been dealing with my anger passive aggressively.

Dr. Rosie: In the hopes of what?

Faye: I tried to be direct with my anger last week, but it didn't help.

Dr. Rosie: What didn't it help?

Faye: I don't feel different.

Kay: The results weren't what you wanted? You got angry and nothing changed?

Dr. Rosie: What didn't happen?

Faye: The group didn't change.

Dr. Rosie: So you are angry because the group didn't change. You were hoping that if the group would change, then you would change.

Faye: I don't know.

Kay: Faye, I want to give you some feedback. I see you thinking things through a lot. I hope you stay in the program. I'd like to encourage you to keep talking.

Group members then talked about how the group had or had not been helpful to them. The conversation eventually honed in on the pattern of trying to "control one's life through controlling others" (Piper et al., 1996, p. 200). After complaining about Dr. Rosie, Faye tells Kay about a problem she has in her current love relationship. She has just finished describing an accusatory fight between the two of them (p. 201).

Dr. Rosie: It sounds like what we were talking about earlier. You are both trying to change each other.

Faye: That's right.

Kay: It sounds like he should be in the DTP. You are getting a mixed message.

Faye: I don't think I could change enough to make the relationship work.

Kay: I think Dr. Rosie is pointing out that we may both be trying to change our partners. . . . I feel somehow that if I'm better then the relationship will be better. But that's not true. I can only do my part of it.

It is important to note that this kind of discussion has the potential to enhance personal responsibility taking and to reduce externalization, two items that typically are high on the list of needed skills for personality disordered individuals.

Relationship Factors Common to the Two Illustrative Approaches

The core relationship factors shared by these two approaches begin with acceptance of and respect for the patient or client. These features of therapist behavior also typically are emphasized in client-centered and psychodynamic psychotherapies. They are frequently modeled within cognitive-behavioral therapies as well. A more unusual relationship factor in these two illustrative approaches to personality disorder is the explicit emphasis on what Linehan calls the dialectic between acceptance and change. Both note that, while relationship factors like tolerance and acceptance are basic to the approach, certain behaviors are clearly forbidden and actively blocked. There is no "noncontingent acceptance." In fact, contingencies for violations of therapy rules are clearly in place.

Despite these key similarities, DBT and DTP are not identical. There are differences between them such as rationale and particular rules. The interpersonal differences in the therapy relationship appear to be that in the DTP there is relatively more emphasis on affirmation, while in the DBT, there is more structure and more teaching. Such differences in base rate between cognitive behavioral and psychodynamic therapies have been recorded formally in other contexts (for example, Jones & Pulos, 1993, p. 306). Therapist behaviors in both approaches are described as warm, but the psychodynamic group gives more autonomy, while the cognitive-behavioral group exerts more influence.

RESEARCH REVIEW

Research That Establishes Efficacy of Treatment of Personality Disorder

Before focusing on research studies of therapy relationship and outcome, it is important to es-

tablish that there are effective treatments for personality disorder. We begin with the evidence in support of the two illustrative approaches, DBT and DTP, and then examine promising treatment models that have not yet been subjected to formal efficacy studies.

Evidence in Support of the Two Illustrative Approaches

A recent summary of studies of effectiveness of DBT is offered by Koerner and Linehan (2000). Compared to TAU (treatment as usual), patients in DBT showed reduced parasuicidal behavior, better treatment retention, and fewer days of inpatient psychiatric hospitalization. Various other findings almost always demonstrated that DBT is effective in controlling parasuicidal behavior, although studies differed in which additional variables (including comorbid Axis I symptoms) did or did not reflect better performance for DBT. There are a number of carefully designed randomized control studies under way in various parts of the world, and DBT is also being tested for its ability to target substance abuse and binge-eating behaviors. Commenting on the Koerner and Linehan review, Scheel (2000) agreed that findings to date are promising but called for continued research to test the generality of results. In accord with that request, Low and colleagues (2001) have shown that DBT was effective in controlling deliberate self-harm behavior in a population of British inpatients.

Piper and colleagues have conducted an impressive series of studies that consistently show DTP (and related variants of milieu treatment) is effective in treating a variety of personality disorders (for example, McCallum, Piper, & O'Kelly, 1997; McCallum & Piper, 1999). In their 1996 book, Piper and colleagues reported: "Treated patients showed significantly better outcome than control patients for seven of the 17 outcome variables: social dysfunction, family dysfunction, interpersonal behavior, mood level, life satisfaction, self-esteem, and severity of disturbance associated with individual goals of treatment as rated by an independent assessor. The findings could not be accounted for by diagnosis or use of medication. Benefits were maintained over the follow-up period. The average treatment-versus-control effect size for all 17 variables was .71" (Piper, Rosie, Joyce, & Azim, 1996, p. 757).

Evidence from a Wide Variety of Other Approaches

Starting in the 1990s, there have been several reviews of studies that have established efficacy in the treatment of personality disorder. These include the reviews of Shea (1993), Crits-Christoph (1998), Perry et al. (1999), Bateman and Fonagy (2000), and Piper and Joyce (2001). Perry and colleagues (1999) provided formal estimates of effect sizes. Their meta-analysis drew from the literature from 1974 to 1998 and considered only studies that used systematic methods to diagnose personality disorder, validated outcome assessments, and reported data to permit within condition effect sizes or permitted determination of recovery from personality disorder. There were 15 studies that met these criteria. The authors concluded, "Psychotherapy is an effective treatment for personality disorders and may be associated with up to a sevenfold faster rate of recovery in comparison with the natural history of disorders" (p. 1312). The mean pre/post effect sizes within treatments were large: 1.11 for self-report measures and 1.29 for observational measures. They estimated that 25.8% of personality disorder patients recovered per year of therapy.

Fully aware of the limitations of the studies in their review, they nonetheless concluded that if treatment is allowed to continue quite a bit longer than the 6 or 12 or 18 weeks so characteristic of the efficacy literature, personality disorders can improve. They remarked, "Studies should include longer durations of treatment. Most patients with personality disorders do not recover rapidly. Some who do recover rapidly may in fact represent false positive cases. Treatments of less than 1 year's duration may better be characterized as treating crises, a series of crises, symptoms of distress, or a concurrent Axis I disorder rather than core personality disorder psychopathology" (Piper et al., 1999, p. 1320).

Our own review of the evidence, which included on-line searches of the domains of psychology, psychiatry, and medicine, confirmed conclusions of earlier reviewers. We would add an emphasis on studies from a variety of sites in Europe consistent with the findings reported by Piper and colleagues (1999). The European studies clearly show that long-term group and milieu treatments not only are effective, but yield results that are stable on long-term follow-up (for example, Wilberg et al., 1999; Dolan, Warren, & Norton, 1997; Bateman & Fonagy, 2001). The effectiveness of groups within a structured milieu is convincingly underscored by Piper and Joyce (2001) in their very recent review. We also note that there is impressive diversity in the types of approaches that are proving effective, provided they can be offered for at least a year. These therapies include cognitive behavioral (Linehan, 2000), psychodynamic (Junkert-Tress, Schnierda, Hartkamp, Schmitz, & Tress, 2001; Høglend, 1993; Winston et al., 1994), self psychology (Monsen, Odland, Faugli, Daae, & Eilertsen, 1995; Stevenson & Meares, 1992; Muran, in press), brief adaptive therapy and short-term dynamic therapy (Muran, in press), supportive therapy (Rosenthal, Muran, Pinsker, Hellerstein, & Winston, 1997; Hellerstein et al., 1997), and other group and partial hospitalization approaches (Piper et al., 1996; Budman, Demby, Soldz, & Merry, 1996; Bateman & Fonagy, 1999; Wilberg et al., 1999).

Worth highlighting is the psychotherapy based on self psychology (Stevenson & Meares, 1999) that significantly reduced inpatient costs in a population of borderline personality disorder for the year following treatment compared to the year preceding treatment. Going right to the bottom line, Stevenson and Meares summarized, "These figures represent an average decrease in costs per patient of $21,431. By using the schedule fee as the basis, the estimated cost of therapy per patient was approximately $13,000, representing a saving/patient of $8,431 or approximately $250,000 over the total cohort in the first year after treatment" (p. 473).

Promising Models Not Yet Validated in Formal Protocols

Studies on the effectiveness of treatments for personality disorder are relatively recent and have been appearing with escalating frequency. In addition to the approaches already mentioned, there are theoretically coherent, well-operationalized treatments that have not yet been tested by formal clinical trials. All are supported by case studies, and some by small pilot studies. A few are accompanied by formal studies of variables that characterize patients who responded more to treatment but that lack statistical tests of overall effectiveness of the approach relative to a contrast condition. Many, like DBT, focus particularly on treatment of borderline personality disorder. These include cognitive analytic therapy (CAT; see Ryle & Golynkina, 2000), transference focused psychotherapy (Clarkin, Yeomans, & Kernberg, 1999), and other variants of cognitive-behavioral therapy (Layden, Newman, Freeman, & Morse, 1993; Davidson & Tyrer, 1996). Some newer approaches claim to apply to several, if not all, of the personality disorders described in the *DSM-IV*. Examples include cognitive therapy (Beck, 1999) and interpersonal reconstructive therapy (IRT; see Benjamin, in press).

A Pilot Study of Interpersonal Reconstructive Therapy

Interpersonal Reconstructive Therapy (IRT) will be used later to help interpret the empirical findings from formal clinical trials. IRT (Benjamin, 1996b, in press) draws on attachment, social learning, and object relations theories and invokes only principles that are well supported in the empirical literature (Benjamin & Pugh, 2001). IRT seeks to be effective when treating individuals who have failed to respond to more than one previous treatment, usually including medications as well as psychotherapies. This, of course, includes a large number of individuals with personality disorder.

Pilot data in support of IRT's effectiveness are available on a sample of eight individuals. All had failed at previous multiyear treatments under more than one treatment approach. Six of the eight had previously made multiple suicide attempts and been hospitalized, most of them more than once. Many began treatment while taking antidepressants and/or anxiolytics. Two also were initially on antipsychotics, and one of these was on lithium as well. Patients came from Benjamin's private practice (five) and from graduate student therapists (three) who had at least two years of training in IRT. Students started with their cases as inpatients and followed them as outpatients. Three of the eight patients ended treatment naturally, while the others terminated because of disruptions due to moving. All patients from these two sources were included only if (1) they completed the Retrospective Assessment of the Therapy Experience (RATE) form (Strupp, Fox, & Lessler, 1978); (2) they initially rated themselves as 1 or 2 on the 5-point severity of disturbance scale in the RATE; (3) they participated in IRT for at least one year; and (4) they provided pre- and post-data on at least one of two measures of symptoms, either the the Wisconsin Personality Disorders Inventory (WISPI; see Klein et al., 1993) or the Symptom Checklist (SCL-90-R; see Derogatis, 1977).

Outcome was tested by a nonparametric test (Wilcoxon Signed Ranks) of differences in WISPI and SCL-90-R scores before and after treatment. There was significant improvement ($p < .01$) for SCL-90-R GSI (General Symptom Index) and PDL (Positive Distress Level) summary scales. Significant individual scale changes were established for somatization, interpersonal sensitivity, anxiety, and phobic anxiety. Significant improvement also was observed on WISPI scales Narcissism, Borderline, Avoidant, and Dependent. All eight cases ended IRT treatment off medications by choice. Although five had been essentially nonfunctional (had lost their jobs) at the beginning of treatment, all patients were functioning satisfactorily in jobs at termination. The fact that participants began treatment with severe disturbance and long-term records of intractability suggests that IRT made a difference. No matter how promising this small sample and the many supervisory cases that clearly improved when transferring to IRT, formal protocols are required before IRT has formally documented efficacy.

Therapy Relationship and Outcome in Personality Disorders

The Therapy Alliance as a "Basic Condition"

There is a vast literature that suggests a good therapy alliance is associated with better outcome regardless of approach or population. A recent illustrative meta-analysis was prepared by Martin, Garski, and Davis (2000). Because the alliance is so critical to outcome, Safran and colleagues (for example, Safran & Muran, 1996) have created and tested a model for repairing ruptures in the therapy alliance. Details appear in Safran, Muran, Samstag, and Stevens (chap. 12, this volume). At Beth Israel Hospital, there have been a number of informative studies of different effective personality disorder treatments (Muran, in press). Many of these include a focus on the role of the therapy relationship and on variables inherent in repairing the therapy alliance. Scales designed to assess the perspective of the therapist and the patient and their interaction have been developed and are presently being applied to document how to repair the alliance when treating personality disorder.

The Therapy Relationship as a Vehicle for Change

While most psychotherapies presume a good alliance is a necessary condition for treatment, many approaches add that the therapy relationship itself is a vehicle for change. A prominent example is Kernberg's (2001) transference focused psychotherapy (TFP) for borderline personality disorder. The central theme of TFP is that a particular internalized object relationship is played out in the therapy relationship. With the help of "clarification, confrontation and interpretation" (p. 201) of the distortions manifest in the therapy relationship, the patient becomes able to develop a more integrated sense of self and of significant others. Similarly, Layden, Newman, Freeman, and Morse (1993) state, "Cognitive therapy for BPD is modified so as to treat the therapeutic relationship as one of the central issues of therapy" (p. 119), and "There are 3 main goals in establishing therapeutic relationships with BPD patients: (1) to connect, (2) to develop mutual trust and positive regard, and (3) to learn about the patient's major modes of operation in life as a function of how he or she deals with the therapist" (p. 58). In IRT, the therapy relationship likewise is seen as an opportunity for learning about patterns and their early roots. According to IRT, the therapy relationship also provides a "secure base" from which patterns with important others can be explored and renegotiated. It also encourages and assists improvement in relationships with current

loved ones and provides a model for better self-care.

Therapist Contributions and Outcome

Therapist Adherence to Relationship Elements

Correlations between outcome and measures of therapist behavior that directly reflect the therapy model, including relevant aspects of the therapy relationship, are not easy to find. We identified only one such study: If the therapist used Linehan's dialectic between acceptance and change (Shearin & Linehan, 1992), fewer parasuicidal episodes followed in the next week. However, an attempt to replicate that finding failed (H. Schmidt, personal communication, May 2001). Other theorists and investigators currently are gathering data that focus specifically on what the therapist does (relationship; technique) that is associated with outcome (C. Muran, personal communication, April 2001; J. Monson, personal communication, April 2001).

Therapist Behaviors That Keep the Patient in Therapy and on Task

It is not unusual for an individual with personality disorder to ask for treatment and then to miss appointments or drop out altogether. Staying in therapy might be seen a primitive version of a therapy alliance. A therapist's ability to help a personality disordered patient remain in treatment has long been considered vital to good outcome. Yeomans, Selzer, and Clarkin (1993) explained how to do this using a therapy contract when treating borderline personality disorder. This contract includes the usual agreements regarding fees, missed sessions, rules for phone contact, and so on. In addition, after an individualized assessment, there needs to be a shared understanding that behaviors that undermine therapy, like not paying, coming intoxicated, or suicide attempts, must cease so that therapy can begin. They are not the target of treatment, but the prerequisites for treatment—the process of learning about problem habits as they unfold in the therapy relationship (Yeomans, Selzer, & Clarkin, 1993, pp. 256–257). This group found that therapists' contributions to the therapy contract and to the alliance in a sample of 36 women with borderline personality disorder correlated with length of treatment. It would be irresponsible to view staying in therapy per se as an index of good treatment. Since securing the therapy has been shown to be associated with outcome, continuing in treatment makes sense only when the patient and therapist are engaged in the therapy task.

Therapist Limit Setting and Confrontation

As mentioned previously, in both DBT and DTP, clear limits are set. Yeomans and Clarkin (1992) comment on why this is difficult for many dynamically oriented psychotherapists: "Most therapists are trained to take a very nondirective approach with patients, based on the understanding that they will deal with problems as they come up, rather than put them on the agenda in advance. In our experience, this traditional approach leads to difficulties in the treatment of borderline patients" (p. 2). They also state, "Therapists, believing they were being harsh and dictatorial, felt guilty about making any 'demands' of their patients and often failed to appreciate the fundamental link between establishing the contract and psychodynamic principles" (p. 1).

Cognitive behavioral therapists working with personality disorder, likewise, recognize the need to set clear, direct limits and guidelines, rather than engage in treatment as usual. In CBT, that often means engaging in highlighting of problematic, automatic beliefs. Confrontation, a more complex form of limit setting, also has been tested with personality disorders (Hellerstein et al., 1997), and is characteristic of short-term dynamic therapy (STDP). In that study, the contrast condition was brief supportive therapy, and each approach did equally well. Therapy alliance within each sample was again significantly related to outcome.

The research literature relating limit setting or confrontation per se to outcome is not very rich. An informative overview was offered by Pam (1994) but was not specific to treatment of personality disorder. Pam concluded, "When done properly, setting limits makes working with acting-out patients viable, enabling them both to master devastating early experiences and to replace restraint by others with self-control. Techniques are addressed which lead to the responsible and effective use of power, but at the same time observing the social and practical limits inherent in the approach" (p. 432). A recent study of caseworkers working with severely disordered mentally ill individuals (Neale & Rosenheck, 2000) tallied examples of limit setting by case managers working in community programs. They set limits in the form of verbal guidance, mechanisms for money management, contingent withholding of services or support, enforced hospitalization, and invocation of external authorities.

Transference Interpretations

Transference interpretations of the therapy relationship are considered central to many psychodynamic approaches. There is no universal definition of transference interpretation, but there may be consensus that transference interpretation at least means that there is a discussion of the therapy relationship as it is shaped by the patient's mental structure. Transference interpretation, then, applies the technique or rationale of the approach to the therapy relationship (also see Crits-Christoph & Connolly, chap. 15, this volume).

Ogrodniczuk and Piper (2001) reviewed recent studies of transference within psychodynamic treatments of personality disordered individuals. They concluded: "First, a strong therapeutic alliance is imperative for successful exploration of the transference. Second, transference-focused work should be balanced with supportive interventions. Third, the patient's quality of object relations and his or her ability to work within the transference should be considered" (p. 297). Piper and colleagues (1993) found that a better alliance in patients with high quality of object relations showed better outcome when transference interpretations were more concentrated (constituted a higher proportion of the interventions) and were congruent with a case formulation. Working with a sample of five personality disordered individuals, Bond, Banon, and Grenier (1998, p. 301) reported, "Transference interpretations were followed by a deterioration in the therapeutic alliance when the alliance was weak, but by enhanced work when the alliance was solid. In patients with both strong and weak alliances, defense interpretations and supportive interventions enhanced therapeutic work without increasing defensiveness. Supportive interventions seemed to prepare the way for exploration and to repair ruptured alliances." Therapy alliance, repair of rupture, and increased therapy work are usually associated with better outcome.

In conclusion, the effects of transference interpretation depend on interactions with many patient and therapy variables. On the basis of limited available studies, it appears that transference interpretation may be most effective when relevant to case formulation, when given in a supportive context, when there is a good alliance, and when the person is psychologically minded.

Patient Contribution

Ability to Form an Alliance

Horvath and Luborsky (1993) reported that therapy alliances are more likely to be weak in patients who have difficulty maintaining social relationships, poor family relationships, little hope for success, poor object relations, and who are defensive. Such problems are more likely to be found among personality disordered individuals. It follows that forming a therapy alliance is a primary challenge when treating personality disordered individuals.

Specific Personality Disorder Diagnoses

Despite the difficulties, it is possible to develop an alliance with some personality disordered individuals, and the association with outcome is positive. For example, when working with drug abusers, Gerstley and colleagues (1989) reported that good alliances emerged even with some antisocial personality disordered persons. When alliance was better, outcome was better.

Different personality disorders present different challenges and it is difficult, and perhaps inappropriate, to say that one disorder is more difficult to treat than another. Diagnosis and outcome likely interact with treatment approach. Support for this expectation is offered by Ogrodniczuk, Piper, Joyce, and McCallum (2001), who compared interpretive and supportive individual psychotherapies and found that specific disorders reacted differently to different approaches. For example, patients with schizotypal personality disorder had less favorable outcome (anxiety, depression, and general symptoms) in interpretive therapy compared to other personality disordered patients in the study, but a more favorable outcome in supportive therapy.

Some investigators have reported that number of criteria met or total number of personality disorders for which the patient qualifies is an effective predictor of outcome. These investigators also found that a greater number of personality disorders was associated with less favorable outcome across the two forms of therapy in their study. Ryle and Golynkina (2000) divided 27 subjects into good and poor outcome groups and found that poor outcome was associated with greater severity of borderline features and a history of self-cutting, alcohol abuse, and unemployment.

Identity Disturbance

Over 25 weeks, Hull, Clarkin, and Kakuma (1993) traced the weekly SCL-90-R ratings of 40 hospitalized females with borderline personality disorder. They found that level of identity and interpersonal problems as defined by their interpretation of Kernberg for these individuals were powerful predictors of symptom course. Poorer self-definition in relation to others was associated with poorer outcome.

Quality of Object Relations and Psychological Mindedness

As indicated previously, Piper and his colleagues have found that personality disordered individuals with higher quality of object relations (QOR) scores and greater psychological mindedness are more likely to respond well to treatment (Ogrodniczuk & Piper, 2001). This effect varies depending on interactions between treatment approach and patient characteristics. For example, Piper, Joyce, McCallum, and Azim (1998) noted that QOR facilitated outcome in interpretive but not in supportive therapy. More recently, this research group has assessed interactions between psychological mindedness, QOR, and specific personality disorders (McCallum & Piper, 1999). Again, psychological mindedness facilitated outcome, but more in some personality disordered groups (such as dependent) than in others (such as borderline or paranoid).

THERAPY RELATIONSHIP: MEDIATORS AND MODERATORS

In interpreting the research findings on connections between the therapy relationship and outcome in the treatment of personality disorders, it makes sense to consider whether identified effects would be causal or catalytic. We identified one brief report that attempted to make this distinction. Westerman, Foote, and Winston (1995) treated 42 personality disordered individuals randomly assigned to short-term dynamic psychotherapy (STDP) or brief adaptive psychotherapy (BAP).

STDP is based on Davanloo principles, and BAP is based on ego-psychological principles with a strong emphasis on interpretive technique. Therapy alliance was measured in terms of a "co-ordination construct" between patient and therapist. Outcome was measured by patient ratings on a social adjustment scale and on target complaints. Correlations between alliance and outcome were computed for each of four phases in treatment. Both groups showed an overall positive association between this measure of alliance and outcome. However, for STDP, there was a progressive increase in the magnitude of that association. For BAP, there was a progressive decrease. There was a significant linear trend within each group, but the signs were opposite. The authors reasoned that if coordination within the therapy relationship itself increases with treatment and if that characterizes the most successful cases, the relationship events must include the effective agents. In the BAP group, the alliance effect diminished over time.

Westerman and colleagues (1995) observed that the therapy relationship is not central in BAP, and other investigators have likewise noted that associations between alliance and outcome are strongest early in therapy. One might speculate that a good alliance is necessary to begin the

therapy procedure but that in some approaches, like BAP, other effects become more important later on. Therapies that concentrate on the therapy relationship as the central arena (STDP and TFP, for example), by contrast, would be required to show that the nature of that relationship is increasingly associated with outcome as treatment continues. The Westerman and colleagues (1995) study makes the competing models for the role of the therapy relationship clear. It also makes use of the fundamental truth, first posited by David Hume in the eighteenth century, that causal arguments must be supported by sequential observations (Hume, 1748/1947).

In determining whether the therapy relationship is a mediator or a moderator it obviously will be important to have a series of well-designed studies that contrast treatment approaches that differentially emphasize the role of the therapy relationship in change. Researchers should assess adherence to treatment models, with specific measures of any theoretical role for the therapy relationship. Finally, it will be helpful if comparable measures of outcome are agreed upon by all. If Structural Equation Modeling is to be used to address these questions, sample sizes will need to be much larger than in most of the studies to date.

LIMITATIONS OF THE RESEARCH REVIEWED

Work Is Just Beginning

While there is rapidly accumulating evidence that treatment of personality disorder can be effective, there are few studies that directly assess therapist behavior in the therapy relationship in relation to outcome. Available literature suggests that effectiveness is associated with a good therapy alliance and a willingness to set limits, usually via therapy rules or contracts. The alliance may function differently depending on the treatment approach and attributes of the patient. It is essential to continue exploration of exactly what it is in the alliance that "does the work" and how. Given the likely importance of limit setting in the treatment of personality disorder, it will be important in future studies more systematically to define and assess limit setting and relate it to outcome. Similarly, varying definitions of confrontation and their specific relation to outcome need better articulation.

As newer studies accumulate, it will be important that they consistently invoke the usual standards for clinical trials. Some desired attributes would include randomized assignment of patients to contrasting treatments and adequate sample sizes. Assessments from the perspectives of participants and observers should provide reliable and valid measures of patient and therapist characteristics and behaviors in therapy, reliable and valid measures of the therapy relationship, reliable and valid measures of adherence to the therapy model, and consensual domains of outcome. For example, studies reviewed often report changes in comorbid Axis I symptoms, but do not always assess changes in personality disorder itself.

The Essential Need to Report on Noncompleters

Psychotherapy studies are very difficult to bring into line with standard clinical trials protocol because they are expensive, difficult to implement under controlled conditions, and usually take a long time—especially when treating personality disorder. This population is difficult to hold in treatment, frequently disrupts the treatment system (including research protocols), and quite often presents life-and-death challenges in ways not so predictably faced in therapy studies of individuals with mild or moderate levels of Axis I disturbance.

A few of the studies in our review reported whether or not their cases committed suicide, but this was not the norm. We would call for routine reporting on noncompleters. The concern would be with the number of cases that dropped out and what happened to them. There should be a report of the number of cases that committed suicide, that were sent to prison, that had to be removed from protocol because of escalating pathology, or that were engaged in any other personality disordered actions (such as murder, child abuse) that ended their participation in the study. Since these "artifacts" are essentially "facts" for this group of patients, it is especially important to consider them when evaluating the success of a treatment. If a number of people who

get worse or kill themselves don't "count" in the outcome measures, we are less impressed with results. We would note this problem is not unique to the study of personality disorder. It also should be addressed when reporting on efficacy any approach with any disorder, including the treatment of Axis I disorders such as depression or schizophrenia.

THERAPEUTIC PRACTICES

There are effective psychotherapy treatments for personality disorder, and they come from a variety of theoretical and practical perspectives. No single approach has been proven to be superior to any other, but all those empirically examined to date have been proven to be superior to no treatment. A better therapy alliance is associated with a better outcome. However, with personality disorders, it often is difficult to develop a good therapy alliance, generally defined as collaborative work on the therapy task. When an alliance can be developed, the mechanisms of action and the results may vary depending on the approach (BAP versus STDP), technique (response to transference interpretations), and patient qualities (diagnosis or psychological mindedness). Limit setting within a good alliance also is characteristic of successful therapies with personality disorders.

It makes sense to try to go beyond these conclusions and identify by inspection the common features shared by successful treatments of personality disorder. These are empirically inspired and informed principles, but not yet empirically validated. On the basis of their review of the literature, Bateman and Fonagy (2000) suggested that effective treatments for personality disorder tend "(a) to be well structured; (b) to devote considerable effort to enhancing compliance; (c) to have a clear focus, whether that focus is a problem type of behavior such as self-harm or an aspect of interpersonal relationship patterns; (d) to be theoretically highly coherent to both therapist and patient; (e) to be relatively long term; (f) to encourage a powerful attachment relationship between therapist and patient, enabling the therapist to adopt a relatively active rather than a passive stance; and (g) to be well integrated with other services available to the patient" (Bateman & Fonagy, 2000, p. 9 of PDF on-line version).

On the basis of his review, Livesley (2001) compiled a list of features of successful therapies for personality disorder. For the patient, effective therapies will encourage problem recognition, self-exploration, acquisition of new behaviors, and consolidation and generalization of new learning. Effective therapists will use strategies that build and maintain collaboration (repair ruptures in the therapy alliance), validate, and enhance motivation for change.

We add an interpretation of the research findings in terms of IRT (Benjamin, 1996b; in press). Our analysis attempts specifically to address the questions of why and how the therapy alliance functions when treating this population, why and how limit setting is important, and why the group/milieu treatments appear to be so effective.

IRT begins with a specific method of case formulation that allows the clinician and the patient to relate presenting problems directly to habits, rules, principles, and loyalties developed in relation to early loved ones. The definitions of problem patterns and their links to key figures are operationalized by structural analysis of social behavior (SASB; see Benjamin, 1996a). The approach is organized by the belief that a successful therapy must consistently address the underlying motivations that organize the patterns of the disorder. This general idea is illustrated by a chronically suicidal patient who believes certain loved ones hate her and want her out of the way. She reacts to her internalized working models (Bowlby, 1977) of those loved ones and does them a favor by deleting her existence. IRT would require that her therapy consistently focus on helping her give up the wish to get the approval of that internalization by providing him or her with what he or she apparently wants. Benjamin (1993) explains, "Every psychopathology is a gift of love" (p. 1).

The task of giving up underlying wishes (differentiation) is accomplished by requiring therapy interventions to conform to a "core algorithm," which, among other things, includes empathy plus adherence to one of five therapy steps. These are (1) enhance collaboration, (2) learn about problem patterns and the reasons for them, (3) block problem patterns, (4) enhance the will to change, and (5) learn new, more adaptive patterns. The disordered patterns to be given up are attributed to the Regressive Loyalist, or the Red parts of the patient. The Red is opposed by the Growth Collaborator, or Green parts of the patient. Green is the healthy part of the person that wants to grow and change, to "have a life."

Most personality disordered individuals begin therapy in a very Red condition. The first task therefore is to strengthen Green. In other words, the first task is, as the research literature shows, to construct and maintain a good therapy alliance. At the same time, Red patterns must be contained, and here the literature on limit setting and contracts is helpful. Patients quickly and easily understand the Red/Green metaphor. The alliance in IRT requires that the Green will work with the therapist to contain, bargain with, and transform the Red. With this contract in place, patients willingly agree to and sometimes laugh about therapist behaviors that invoke control, paradoxical injunction, or irony that trumps or deflects Red. Therapists are freed up from the idea that infinite love and tolerance will do the job. With the Red/Green metaphor, patients also can accept the idea that the therapist will not be as totally loving and accepting as they might wish. It is important to underscore that the IRT therapist does not simply stomp out the Red. That is unwise and impossible. There are times to "cozy up" to the Red or it will destroy the therapy altogether. Rather than try to exorcise or kill the Red, the IRT therapist bargains with, negotiates with, and attempts to address and reframe "its" needs in better ways. This parallels the DBT dialectic between acceptance and change.

An alliance to contain the Red and grow the Green is a necessary but not sufficient condition for effective treatment. Engaging and maintaining the will to change mark the ultimate crossroad. According to IRT, therapist activities here are most critical. For example, collaboration with the therapist and/or the group can nudge the patient in the direction of change by the simple mechanism of receiving approval and avoiding disapproval. A patient contemplating self-mutilation may hate the idea of having to tell the group that he turned Red last night. If he resists the urge, he will receive the approval of the group for being

Green. If he does not, he has to detail the episode in a milieu that is not admiring. If the patient cares enough about the group (that is, has a meaningful attachment), the self-mutilating act is appreciated only by old internalizations, and not by viable current relationships.

As the treatment continues, patients internalize the therapy relationship and its norms, and they begin to match the old internalizations in strength. In other words, they begins to engage in the Green self-talk learned in the therapy rather than the old Red that originally was internalized from an early loved one. To generate internalizations that can match the old ones, the therapy relationship must be warm, influential, palpable, and real. It is a mediator of change. In IRT, this is accomplished by providing a safe base from which to explore new ways of relating, by supporting the development and internalization of better relationships in the patient's current life, and by providing a more benign and helpful orientation toward the self. Well-run, well-focused, well-modulated, and constructive group or milieu therapies likely have a tremendous advantage over simple one-on-one therapy dialogue when it comes to internalizing new norms, rules, and loyalties. That may be why so many different group approaches are reporting stable success in the treatment of personality disorders.

In closing, it is vital to add that a group (or individual therapist) that allows pathological ways of relating, like scapegoating, chronic blaming, or sulky withdrawal will activate and enable the personality disorder. In fact, groups that review self-destructive or other destructive episodes in a covertly appreciative way may well encourage contagion. The Red/Green analysis from IRT would caution that when treating personality disorders, only well-structured models like those offered by Piper and colleagues and by Linehan would be effective.

ACKNOWLEDGMENT We would like to thank our colleagues and friends Marjorie Klein, Aaron Pincus, Tracey Smith, Jennifer Skeem, Kevin Smith, Allan Zuckoff, and Robert Coufal, who made helpful comments on earlier versions of this chapter.

REFERENCES

American Psychiatric Association. (1994). *Diagnostic and statistical manual of mental disorders* (4th ed.).Washington, DC: Author.

Bateman, A., & Fonagy, P. (1999). Effectiveness of partial hospitalization in the treatment of borderline personality disorder: A randomized controlled trial. *American Journal of Psychiatry, 156,* 1563–1569.

Bateman, A. W., & Fonagy, P. (2000). Effectiveness of psychotherapeutic treatment of personality disorder. *British Journal of Psychiatry, 177,* 138–143.

Bateman, A., & Fonagy, P. (2001). Treatment of borderline personality disorder with psychoanalytically oriented partial hospitalization: An 18-month follow-up. *American Journal of Psychiatry, 158,* 36–42.

Beck, A. T. (1999). Cognitive aspects of personality disorders and their relation to syndromal disorders: A psychoevolutionary approach. In C. R. Cloninger (Ed.), *Personality and psychopathology* (pp. 411–430). Washington, DC: American Psychiatric Press.

Bender, D. S., Dolan, R. T., Skodol, A. E., Sanislow, C. A., Dyck, I. R., McGlashan, T. H., Shea, M. T., Zanarini, M. C., Oldham, J. M., & Gunderson, J. G. (2001). Treatment utilization by patients with personality disorders. *American Journal of Psychiatry, 158,* 295–302.

Benjamin, L. S. (1993). Every psychopathology is a gift of love. *Psychotherapy Research, 3,* 1–24.

Benjamin, L. S. (1996a). *Interpersonal diagnosis and treatment of personality disorders* (2nd ed.). New York: Guilford.

Benjamin, L. S. (1996b) An interpersonal theory of personality disorders. In J. F. Clarkin (Ed.), *Major theories of personality disorder* (pp. 141–220). New York: Guilford.

Benjamin, L. S. (in press). *Interpersonal reconstructive therapy.* New York: Guilford.

Benjamin, L. S., & Pugh, C. (2001). Using interpersonal theory to select effective treatment interventions for personality disorder. In J. Livesley (Ed.), *Handbook of treatments for personality disorder* (pp. 414–436). New York: Guilford.

Bond, M., Banon, E., & Grenien, M. (1998). Differential effects of interventions on the therapeutic alliance with patients with personality disorders. *Journal of Psychotherapy Practice and Research, 7,* 301–318.

Bowlby, J. (1977). The making and breaking of affectional bonds. *British Journal of Psychiatry*, *130*, 201–210.

Budman, S. H., Demby, A., Soldz, S., & Merry, J. (1996). Time-limited group psychotherapy for patients with personality disorders: Outcomes and dropouts. *International Journal of Group Psychotherapy*, *46*, 357–377.

Clarkin, J. F., Yeomans, F. E., & Kernberg, O. F. (1999). *Psychotherapy for borderline personality*. New York: Wiley.

Crits-Christoph, P. (1998). Psychosocial treatments for personality disorders. In P. E. Nathan & J. M. Gorman (Eds.), *A guide to treatments that work* (pp. 544–553). New York: Oxford University Press.

Davidson, K. M., & Tyrer, P. (1996). Cognitive therapy for antisocial and borderline personality disorders: Single case study series. *British Journal of Clinical Psychology*, *35*, 413–429.

Derogatis, L. R. (1977). *SCL-90 Administration, scoring and procedures manuals for the Revised Version-R*. Baltimore, MD: Johns Hopkins University School of Medicine Clinical Psychometrics Research Unit.

Dolan, B., Warren, F., & Norton, K. (1997). Change in borderline symptoms one year after therapeutic community treatment for severe personality disorder. *British Journal of Psychiatry*, *171*, 274–279.

Gerstley, L., McLellan, A., Alterman, A., Woody, G., Luborsky, L., & Proat, M. (1989). Ability to form an alliance with the therapist: A possible marker of prognosis for patients with antisocial personality disorder. *American Journal of Psychiatry*, *146*, 508–512.

Hardy, G. E., Barkham, M., Shapiro, D. A., Stiles, W. B., Rees, A., & Reynolds, S. (1995). Impact of Cluster C personality disorders on outcomes of contrasting brief psychotherapies for depression. *Journal of Consulting and Clinical Psychology*, *63*, 997–1004.

Hellerstein, D. J., Rosenthal, R. N., Pinsker, H., Samstag, L. W., Muran, J. C., & Winston, A. (1997). A randomized prospective study comparing supportive and dynamic therapies: Outcome and alliance. *Journal of Psychotherapy Practice and Research*, *7*, 261–271.

Høglend, P. (1993). Personality disorders and long-term outcome after brief dynamic psychotherapy. *Journal of Personality Disorders*, *7*, 168–181.

Horvath, A. O., & Luborsky, L. (1993). The role of therapeutic alliance in psychotherapy. *Journal of Consulting and Clinical Psychology*, *61*, 561–573.

Hull J. W., Clarkin, J. F., & Kakuma, T. (1993). Treatment response of borderline inpatients. A growth curve analysis. *Journal of Nervous and Mental Disease*, *181*, 503–508.

Hume, D. (1748/1947). An enquiry concerning human understanding (Section IV). Reprinted in D. J. Bronstein, Y. H. Krikorian, & P. P. Wiener (Eds.), *Basic problems of philosophy* (pp. 373–390). New York: Prentice-Hall.

Johnson, J. G., Rabkin, J. G., Williams, J. B. W., Reiman, R. H., & Gorman, J. M. (2000). Difficulties in interpersonal relationships associated with personality disorder and Axis I disorders: A longitudinal community-based investigation. *Journal of Personality Disorders*, *14*, 42–56.

Jones, E. E., & Pulos, S. M. (1993). Comparing the process in psychodynamic and cognitive-behavioral therapies. *Journal of Consulting and Clinical Psychology*, *61*, 306–316.

Junkert-Tress, B., Schnierda, U., Hartkamp, N., Schmitz, N., & Tress, W. (2001). Effects of short-term dynamic psychotherapy for neurotic, somatoform, and personality disorders: A prospective 1-year follow-up study. *Psychotherapy Research*, *11*, 187–220.

Kernberg, O. F. (2001). The suicidal risk in severe personality disorders: Differential diagnosis and treatment. *Journal of Personality Disorders*, *15*, 195–208.

Klein, M. H., Benjamin, L. S., Rosenfeld, R., Treece, C., Husted, J., & Greist, J. H. (1993). The Wisconsin Personality Disorders Inventory: I. Development, reliability, and validity. *Journal of Personality Disorders*, *7*, 285–303.

Koerner, K., & Linehan, M. M. (2000). Research on dialectical behavior therapy for patients with borderline personality disorder. *Psychiatric Clinics of North America*, *23*, 151–167.

Layden, M. A., Newman, C. F., Freeman, A., & Morse, S. B. (1993). *Cognitive therapy of borderline personality disorder*. Boston, MA: Allyn & Bacon.

Linehan, M. M. (1993a). *Cognitive-behavioral treatment of borderline personality disorder*. New York: Guilford.

Linehan, M. M. (1993b). *Skills training manual for treating borderline personality disorder*. New York: Guilford.

Linehan, M. M. (2000). The empirical basis of dialectical behavior therapy: Development of new treatments versus evaluation of existing treatments. *Clinical Psychology: Science and Practice, 7,* 113–119.

Livesley, W. J. (2001). A framework for an integrated approach to treatment. In W. J. Livesley (Ed.), *Handbook of personality disorders: Theory, research and treatment* (pp. 359–376). New York: Guilford.

Low, G., Jones, D., Duggan, C., Power, M., & MacLeod, A. (2001). The treatment of deliberate self-harm in borderline personality disorder using dialectical behavior therapy: A pilot study in a high security hospital. *Behavioral and Cognitive Psychotherapy, 29,* 85–92.

Martin, D. J., Garske, J. P., & Davis, M. K. (2000). Relation of the therapeutic alliance with outcome and other variables: A meta-analytic review. *Journal of Consulting and Clinical Psychology, 68,* 438–450.

McCallum, M., & Piper, W. E. (1999). Personality disorders and response to group-oriented evening treatment. *Group Dynamics: Theory, Research, and Practice, 3,* 3–14.

McCallum, M., Piper, W. E., & O'Kelly, J. (1997). Predicting patient benefit from a group-oriented, evening treatment program. *International Journal of Group Psychotherapy, 47,* 291–314.

Merikangas, K. R., & Weissman, M. M. (1986). Epidemiology of DSM-III Axis II personality disorders. In A. J. Frances & R. E. Hales (Eds.), *American Psychiatric Association Annual Review* (Vol. 5, pp. 258–278). Washington, DC: American Psychiatric Association.

Monsen, J., Odland, T., Faugli, A., Daae, E., & Eilertsen, D. E. (1995). Personality disorders and psychosocial changes after intensive psychotherapy: A prospective follow-up study. *Scandinavian Journal of Psychology, 36,* 256–268.

Muran, J. C. (in press). A relational approach to understanding change: Multiplicity and contextualism in a psychotherapy research program. *Psychotherapy Research.*

Neale, M. S., & Rosenheck, R. A. (2000). Therapeutic limit setting in an assertive community treatment program. *Psychiatric Services, 5,* 499–505.

Ogrodniczuk, J. S., Piper, W. E., Joyce, A. S., & McCallum, M. (2001). Using DSM Axis II information to predict outcome in short-term individual psychotherapy. *Journal of Personality Disorders, 15,* 110–122.

Ogrodniczuk, J. S., & Piper, W. E. (2001). Day treatment for personality disorders: A review

of research findings. *Harvard Review of Psychiatry, 9,* 105–117.

Oldham, J. M., Skodol, A. E., Kellman, H. D., Hyler, S. E., Doidge, N., Rosnick, L., & Gallaher, P. E. (1995). Comorbidity of Axis I and Axis II disorders. *American Journal of Psychiatry, 152,* 571–578.

Pam, A. (1994). Limit setting theory, techniques, and risks. *American Journal of Psychotherapy, 48,* 432–440.

Perry, J. C., Banon, E., & Ianni, F. (1999). Effectiveness of psychotherapy for personality disorders. *American Journal of Psychiatry, 156,* 1312–1321.

Piper, W. E., & Joyce, A. S. (2001). Psychosocial treatment outcome. In W. J. Livesley (Ed.), *Handbook of personality disorders.* New York: Guilford.

Piper, W. E., Joyce, A. S., McCallum, M., & Azim, H. F. (1998). Interpretive and supportive forms of psychotherapy and patient personality variables. *Journal of Consulting and Clinical Psychology, 66,* 558–567.

Piper W. E., Rosie, J. S., Azim, H. F., & Joyce, A. S. (1993). A randomized trial of psychiatric day treatment for patients with affective and personality disorders. *Hospital and Community Psychiatry, 44,* 757–763.

Piper, W. E., Rosie, J. S., Joyce, A. S., & Azim, H. F. A. (1996). *Time-limited day treatment for personality disorders: Integration of research and practice in a group program.* Washington, DC: American Psychological Association.

Rosenthal, R. N., Muran, J. C., Pinsker, H., Hellerstein, D., & Winston, A. (1997). Interpersonal change in brief supportive psychotherapy. *Journal of Psychotherapy Practice and Research, 8,* 55–63.

Ryle, A., & Golynkina, K. (2000). Effectiveness of time-limited cognitive analytic therapy of borderline personality disorder: Factors associated with outcome. *British Journal of Medical Psychology, 73,* 197–210.

Safran, J. D., & Muran, J. C. (1996). The resolution of ruptures in the therapeutic alliance. *Journal of Consulting and Clinical Psychology, 64,* 447–458.

Scheel, K. R. (2000). The empirical basis of dialectical behavioral therapy: Summary, critique, and implications. *Clinical Psychology: Science and Practice, 1,* 68–86.

Shea, M. T. (1993, Spring). Psychosocial treatment of personality disorders. *Journal of Personality Disorders,* Supplement, 167–180.

Shearin, E., & Linehan, M. M. (1992). Patient therapist ratings and relationship to progress in Dialectical Behavior Therapy for borderline personality disorder. *Behavior Therapy, 23,* 730–741.

Stevenson J., & Meares, R. (1992). An outcome study of psychotherapy for patients with borderline personality disorder. *American Journal of Psychiatry, 149,* 358–362.

Strupp, H. H., Fox, R. E., & Lessler, K. (1978). *Patients view their psychotherapy.* Baltimore, MD: Johns Hopkins University Press.

Westerman, M. A., Foote, J. P., & Winston, A. (1995). Change in coordination across phases of psychotherapy and outcome. *Journal of Consulting and Clinical Psychology, 63,* 672–675.

Wilberg, T., Urnes, O., Friis, S., Irion, T., Pedersen, G., & Karterud, S. (1999). One-year follow-up of day treatment for poorly functioning patients with personality disorders. *Psychiatric Services, 50,* 1326–1330.

Winston, A., Laikin, M., Pollack, J., Samstag, L. W., McCullough, L., & Muran, J. C. (1994). Short-term psychotherapy of personality disorders. *American Journal of Psychiatry, 151,* 190–194.

Yeomans, F. E., Selzer, M. A., & Clarkin, J. F. (1992). *Treating the borderline patient: A contract-based approach.* New York: Basic.

Yeomans, F. E., Selzer, M., & Clarkin, J. F. (1993). Studying the treatment contract in intensive psychotherapy with borderline patients. *Psychiatry: Interpersonal and Biological Processes, 56,* 254–263.

Part IV

CONCLUSIONS AND GUIDELINES

24

Empirically Supported Therapy Relationships: Conclusions and Recommendations of the Division 29 Task Force

Steering Committee

CONCLUSIONS OF THE TASK FORCE

- The therapy relationship (as defined in chapter 1) makes substantial and consistent contributions to psychotherapy outcome independent of the specific type of treatment.
- Practice and treatment guidelines should explicitly address therapist behaviors and qualities that promote a facilitative therapy relationship.
- Efforts to promulgate practice guidelines or evidence-based lists of effective psychotherapy without including the therapy relationship are seriously incomplete and potentially misleading on both clinical and empirical grounds.
- The therapy relationship acts in concert with discrete interventions, patient characteristics, and clinician qualities in determining treatment effectiveness. A comprehensive understanding of effective (and ineffective) psychotherapy will consider all of these determinants and their optimal combinations.
- Adapting or tailoring the therapy relationship to specific patient needs and characteristics (in addition to diagnosis) enhances the effectiveness of treatment.

- The following list embodies the Task Force conclusions regarding the empirical evidence on *general elements of the therapy relationship* primarily provided by the psychotherapist. Definitions and examples of each element are provided in the respective chapters.

    Demonstrably Effective
    Therapeutic alliance
    Cohesion in group therapy
    Empathy
    Goal consensus and collaboration

    Promising and Probably Effective
    Positive regard
    Congruence/genuineness
    Feedback
    Repair of alliance ruptures
    Self-disclosure
    Management of countertransference
    Quality of relational interpretations

- The following list embodies the Task Force conclusions regarding the empirical evidence on *customizing the therapy relationship to individual patients* on the basis of patient behaviors or qualities. For example, clients presenting with high resistance have been found to respond better to self-control methods and minimal therapist directiveness, whereas patients with low resistance experience improved outcomes with therapist directiveness and explicit guidance. Definitions and examples of the following patient characteristics are provided in the respective chapters.

Demonstrably Effective as a Means of Customizing Therapy
Resistance
Functional impairment

Promising and Probably Effective as a Means of Customizing Therapy
Coping style
Stages of change
Anaclitic/sociotropic and introjective/ autonomous styles
Expectations
Assimilation of problematic experiences

- Current research on the following patient characteristics is insufficient for a clear judgment to be made on whether customizing the therapy relationship to these characteristics improves treatment outcomes. Definitions and examples of the following patient characteristics are provided in the respective chapters.

Attachment style
Gender
Ethnicity
Religion and spirituality
Preferences
Personality disorders

- The preceding conclusions do *not* by themselves constitute a set of practice standards but represent current scientific knowledge to be understood and applied in the context of all the clinical data available in each case.

RECOMMENDATIONS OF THE TASK FORCE

General Recommendations

1. We recommend that the findings and conclusions of this Task Force be widely disseminated in order to enhance aware-

ness and use of what "works" in the therapy relationship.
2. At the same time, readers are encouraged to interpret these findings in the context of the limitations of the Task Force's work, as explicated in the opening chapter of this report.
3. These findings and conclusions represent initial steps in aggregating and codifying available research. We recommend that future Task Forces be established periodically to review these findings, include new elements of the relationship, incorporate the results of non-English publications (where practical), and update the conclusions.

Practice Recommendations

4. Practitioners are encouraged to make the creation and cultivation of a therapy relationship characterized by the elements found to be demonstrably and probably effective in this report a primary aim in the treatment of patients.
5. Practitioners are encouraged to adapt the therapy relationship to specific patient characteristics in the ways shown in this report to enhance therapeutic outcome.
6. Practitioners are encouraged to routinely monitor patients' responses to the therapy relationship and ongoing treatment. Such monitoring leads to increased opportunities to repair alliance ruptures, to improve the relationship, to modify technical strategies, and to avoid premature termination.
7. Concurrent use of empirically supported relationships *and* empirically supported treatments tailored to the patient's disorder and characteristics is likely to generate the best outcomes.

Training Recommendations

8. Training programs in psychotherapy are encouraged to provide explicit and competency-based training in the effective elements of the therapy relationship.
9. Accreditation and certification bodies for mental health training programs are encouraged to develop criteria for assessing the adequacy of training in empirically sup-

ported therapy relationships in their evaluation process.

10. Both graduate training and continuing education programs are encouraged to offer modules on empirically supported therapy relationships and on systematically adapting the therapy relationship to the individual patient.

Research Recommendations

11. Researchers are encouraged to examine the specific mediators and moderators of the links between demonstrably effective relationship elements and treatment outcome.

12. Researchers are encouraged to progress beyond experimental designs that correlate frequency of relationship behaviors and outcome measures to methodologies capable of examining the complex associations among patient qualities, clinician behaviors, and therapy outcome.

13. Researchers are encouraged to avoid a "therapist-centric" view of the therapy relationship and to study both patients' and therapists' contributions to the relationship and the ways in which those contributions combine to impact treatment outcome.

14. Although the cumulative research convincingly shows that the therapy relationship is crucial to outcome, relatively little is known about how to create and sustain the relationship and about why the relationship works. These are vital questions for future research.

15. Observational perspective (i.e., therapist, patient, or external rater) is a fundamental consideration that ought to be addressed in future studies and reviews of "what works" in the therapy relationship. Agreement among observational perspectives provides a solid sense of established fact; divergence among perspectives holds important implications for clinical practice.

16. Since many of the important variables reviewed in this report are not subject to randomization and experimental control, we recommend that standard research paradigms include the use of rigorous qualitative methods and statistically controlled correlational designs.

Policy Recommendations

17. The APA Division of Psychotherapy is encouraged to educate its members and leaders in the benefits of empirically supported therapy relationships.

18. Mental health organizations as a whole are encouraged to educate their members about the improved outcomes associated with using empirically supported relationships along with evidence-based treatments.

19. Finally, we recommend that the APA Division of Psychotherapy and mental health organizations advocate for the research-substantiated benefits of a facilitative and individually responsive human relationship in psychotherapy.

Appendix: Evaluation of Research Studies

After reading the respective chapters, three raters rendered numerical ratings on the empirical support for the particular relationship element being related to favorable psychotherapy outcome. The ratings pertained solely to empirical studies linking the relationship element to psychotherapy outcome, broadly defined. The three raters were, in each case, an independent reviewer, the book editor, and the chapter author(s). The rating dimensions and response format follow.

Dimensions	Low		Medium		High
Number of supportive empirical studies	1	2	3	4	5
Consistency of empirical results	1	2	3	4	5
Independence of supportive empirical studies, e.g., different investigators, different measures	1	2	3	4	5
Magnitude of positive relationship between the relationship element and outcome, e.g., strength of relationship, effect size	1	2	3	4	5
Evidence for direct causal link between relationship element and outcome, e.g., unconfounded lagged correlations, path analysis, prospective studies	1	2	3	4	5
Ecological or external validity of the research	1	2	3	4	5

The mean ratings for the individual relationship element or patient quality follow. The sole exception is personality disorders; we could not locate a sufficient number of empirical studies on the therapy relationship with patients suffering from personality disorders to generate ratings.

Elements of the Therapy Relationship	Number of Studies	Consistency of Results	Independence of Studies	Magnitude of Relationship	Causal Evidence	External Validity
Therapeutic alliance	5.0	4.0	4.7	3.0	1.7	4.3
Cohesion in group therapy	4.3	3.7	4.0	3.3	3.0	3.5
Empathy	4.0	3.3	4.0	3.0	2.0	4.5
Goal consensus & collaboration	3.7	4.0	3.3	3.7	2.0	4.0
Positive regard	4.0	3.3	3.3	2.3	2.0	3.7
Congruence/genuineness	3.0	2.7	2.3	2.3	1.3	4.3

Elements of the Therapy Relationship	Number of Studies	Consistency of Results	Independence of Studies	Magnitude of Relationship	Causal Evidence	External Validity
Feedback	2.7	3.7	3.3	2.7	1.5	3.5
Repair of alliance ruptures	2.0	2.3	2.3	2.0	1.3	2.7
Self-disclosure	2.0	3.3	3.0	2.3	1.0	2.5
Countertransference management	2.0	4.0	3.0	3.3	2.7	3.3
Relational interpretations	2.0	2.7	3.3	2.3	1.3	2.7

Elements of Customizing Therapy Relationship	Number of Studies	Consistency of Results	Independence of Studies	Magnitude of Relationship	Causal Evidence	External Validity
Resistance	3.7	4.7	3.7	3.0	3.0	3.5
Functional impairment	3.7	3.7	4.0	3.3	2.3	3.5
Coping style	3.0	3.7	3.0	3.0	2.7	4.0
Stages of change	3.3	3.7	2.7	2.7	3.0	4.0
Anaclitic vs. introjective dimensions	2.3	4.0	3.0	3.3	2.7	3.7
Expectations	3.0	3.0	4.0	2.3	1.3	3.5
Assimilation of problematic experiences	2.7	4.3	2.3	3.0	2.0	4.7
Attachment style	2.0	2.7	3.0	3.0	1.7	3.3
Religion and spirituality	2.0	2.7	2.3	1.7	1.7	3.0
Ethnicity matching	2.0	2.0	2.0	1.7	1.0	3.3
Gender matching	1.7	1.3	2.7	1.3	1.0	2.7

Index